No More Cold Calls

The Complete Guide To Generating — And Closing — *All* The Prospects You Need To Become A Multi-Millionaire By Selling Your Service

Dr. Jeffrey Lant

Published by JLA Publications
A Division of Jeffrey Lant Associates, Inc.
50 Follen St., Suite 507
Cambridge, MA 02138
(617) 547-6372

No More Cold Calls

The Complete Guide To Generating
— And Closing — *All* The Prospects
You Need To Become A Multi-Millionaire
By Selling Your Service

Dr. Jeffrey Lant

Dedication:

I dedicate this book to two of my partners in the companies I have spun off from Jeffrey Lant Associates, Inc., the service company I founded in 1979. Specifically I want to pay tribute to Bill Reece and Dan McComas. Bill has helped make a success of my Sales & Marketing Success Dek and electronic moving message display company; Dan, as director, is doing the same with my National Copywriting Center. Not only are they top professionals in their fields, constantly exhibiting vision and competence, but what's equally important they are fine human beings, men of integrity, daily exhibiting their client-centered ideals. It is my pleasure to have my life blessed by them and my coffers increased by them. As they know only too well, I push them hard... but I recognize they are the best in the business. Thank you, Bill & Dan!

Contents

Introduction

Why I Wrote This Book, What's In It And How to Use It

If you are selling a service in America and are not yet a millionaire it had better be 1) because you have only been in business a short time, or 2) you expect a maiden aunt to leave you a bundle. There is no other reason not to be rich, really rich, from selling services.

And this book proves it.

Here in the next 16 chapters, you get precisely what you need to create the *process* that provides *all* the prospects you need to become a millionaire selling your service . . . and how to work with these prospects so your millionaire status is *assured*.

This is no idle claim on my part, either. For the last fourteen years, I have helped literally millions of people launch, develop and maintain businesses that have delivered their financial objectives. These people have found helpful information in my Sure-Fire Business Success columns that now reach over 1.5 million monthly in over 200 publications in many countries; through my Sales and Marketing Success Card Deck, reaching 100,000 different people every 90 days, through the hundreds of thousands of people who get my quarterly Sure-Fire Business Success Catalog regularly, in my many workshops and talk programs, through the audio and video cassettes I produce, in my dozens of Special Reports and in my "Get Ahead" entrepreneurial books of which this is the 9th.

In the pages ahead, I shall spare no effort to give you just what you need to fulfill the promise of this book's title. If you've read one of my books before, you know precisely what I mean. It is my life's aim to upgrade the quality of "how-to" information so that it really does deliver what the author promises. I continue to achieve this objective here.

What's more, if having finished this book you're unhappy, perplexed or need additional information, I do what other so-called authorities do not: I provide you with my direct-dial phone number . . . (617) 547-6372. Unlike any other author in the entire world, this way of contacting me is printed in all my books, articles and Special Reports. You'll find it on my audio cassettes. It runs in my Sure-Fire Business Success Catalog and on the millions of post cards mailed through my Sales & Marketing SuccessDek. No other authority anywhere is as accessible as I am, and while this is a burden that is always threatening to overwhelm my ability to handle it, I still remain able to do so. Thus this unique guarantee: if you don't think I've handled a subject in sufficient detail; if you are perplexed about it . . . if you need further information, call me.

If the information you need is in any of my other books or materials, I'll direct you to it . . . and, rest assured, suggest you buy it. If I can give you a referral elsewhere, I will. If I have new information on the matter, I'll provide it — free — if immediately available. And if you need consulting assistance, I'll tell you how much it'll cost to do what you want. Fair enough? But if the information you need is in this book and you've been too slothful to find and study it, don't expect me to be particularly gracious as I put a flea in your ear and frog-march you back to your studies. You must do your part, and I have no problem reminding you of that.

Why do I offer this guarantee? This book — like all my books — deals with a subject that keeps changing. For the remainder of our lives . . . for the remainder of this planet's life . . . some people will be selling services because other people will be wanting and needing services. But the means the service sellers will use to sell their benefits to those wanting them will necessarily change. The utilitarian, sensible and timely means suggested in this volume will over time change and need to be rethought and further developed. I, for one, intend to stay current about what works and why. And you must, too, if you are to achieve your objectives expeditiously. Thus, this book must change . . . as it will in all further editions, just like all my books.

But what must not change is the compact between us. In the pages of this book, I stand forth as your consultant. I shall be urging you, prodding you, even occasionally angering and infuriating you to become the consummate — and most successful — service seller possible. Like many people who read my material, you may find the necessary tasks exhausting . . . but like many more, you will probably thank me for my candor, hard-hitting honesty and, I am glad to report, my integrity. I do not offer some magical road to success (like many less scrupulous "how-to" practitioners) . . . but I do offer a road that will take you to where you want to go . . . if you are willing to stay on it.

The relationship we begin in these pages need not — indeed should not — end with the conclusion of this book. I have met thousands of my readers over the years . . . and have become good friends with many; two, indeed, are my business partners. I invite you into this band, too. If you got this book from me directly, I shall be in touch with you regularly through my Sure-Fire Business Success Catalog — until such time as you stop buying these good-for-you products/ services and so get unceremoniously zapped from my list (a subject I discuss in the following pages).

If you received this resource from any one of the thousands of other outlets which carry it — bookstores, libraries, catalogs, independent vendors — you must take the responsibility on yourself to contact me. When you do, I'll happily send you free profit-making information for at least a year, information that will substantially benefit you further. Frankly, if you cannot make a phone call to me to achieve such results, I shall profoundly despair of your chances for success . . . but not for too long since I have many others to assist who are making progress.

Why I Wrote This Book

I wrote this book for three main reasons, to:

1. damn the prevailing mediocrity of information on the selling of services;
2. help you become a multi-millionaire through the selling of your services, and
3. swell the ample coffers of my own considerable fortune.

A few words about each of these reasons is definitely in order.

Damning The Mediocrity of The Existing Information On The Selling Of Services

As I write I am looking at a new book entitled *Marketing Services: Competing Through Quality*. Its authors, Leonard Berry and A. Parasuraman, are two full professors of marketing at Texas A & M University. I want you to know right away that these two men should be ashamed of themselves for producing a work of so little value and usefulness.

The problems begin right from the title of Part I of their book: "An Integrative Framework for Marketing Services." Now I ask you: WHAT THE HELL DOES THIS MEAN? Where is the benefit for the service seller earnestly and hopefully seeking advice from these exalted mandarins? I, for one, don't want an "integrative framework"; I want to know — right this minute — what I have to do to sell more of my services and make more money. This is the only reason why anyone should write a book about selling services . . . and the only reason why anyone should study one.

To be sure, the professors' book is built on the unarguable premise that "the essence of services marketing is service." True enough. But 212 pages later, we poor readers still have no idea *specifically* how to leverage good service through a *detailed* process that helps us achieve our own financial objectives. The good professors, apparently lulled by their tenured positions, leave out *everything* — and I do mean everything — that could possibly assist service sellers like you and me achieve any semblance of financial success. Yet they have the breath-taking audacity to begin their "Acknowledgements" section with these words:

"In this book, we bring together our combined 30-plus years of studying and writing about services marketing. . . ."

Now look at the words "studying and writing about services marketing." Note they don't say something like "making money selling services." And this, I submit, is at the root of the problem.

Well-meaning but technically inadequate authorities like Berry and Parasuraman *study and write* about marketing services . . . but they are not now out in the trenches, have not been out before, *actually marketing services* . . . much less making a substantial fortune marketing services. Their findings, therefore, delivered in the usual impenetrable fog that passes for respectable academic prose these days, are laughably inadequate for real people who must spend their limited time and limited resources selling services in order to reach their own objectives. Yet because these two gentlemen have standing at a reputable university and have, so they say, devoted their lives to this topic, a major publisher (in this case MacMillan's Free Press) brings forth their work . . . and sets it out as a royal road to marketing services.

Now I want to tell you something: I utterly reject this book and the entire genre of unhelpful literature that it represents. I scorn the authors who wrote it for their naivete and selfishness. I defy them to show me specifically how their findings help service sellers like you and me run and develop service businesses that have to make money against increasing competition. And I denounce the editors at MacMillan's Free Press for publishing a work that is so pompous, ill-conceived and unhelpful.

Sadly, however, I must tell you that this jejune work is entirely representative of the kind of literature which we service sellers have had to assist us.

Until now.

Now you have at your side a man who has made a fortune selling services by developing and implementing a sensible process . . . the very process you will find in these pages. You do not need unusual intelligence to make a success of this process; certainly the high-blown academic "intelligence" of Professors Berry and Parasuraman would be a positive draw-back. You do not need a vast fortune to implement its methods, though you need to be conscious about money and where it makes sense to invest it. You do, however, need will and desire, an unrelenting focus on the wants of the (hopefully growing) markets you wish to serve, daily work to motivate prospects within these markets to contact you — and a sense of your own responsibility for your own success. These are crucial.

Helping You Become A Millionaire By Selling Your Services

I had to laugh at one of the blurbs on the back of that service selling travesty *Marketing Services*. It comes from Jeffrey Heilbrunn, president of the American Marketing Association, no less, and reads: "Buy this book . . . before someone from Japan buys your company." This quote is a joke, of course. Heilbrunn should be ashamed of himself for uttering it and Messrs. Berry and Parasuraman should hang their heads low for believing and publishing such rubbish.

First, think about the range of service sellers. It encompasses anyone doing something to make someone else's life better — be that professional or personal. Think! That's a tailor, massage therapist, engineer, lawyer, accountant, home-maker home health care worker, plumber, pet groomer, photographer, baby-sitter, financial planner . . . yea, even unto copy writers and marketing consultants and specialists in writing how-to books and promoting them. We are all — all of us in our millions and millions — service sellers. And not one of us works for or runs a business that some over-rich tycoon in Japan is about to snap up at a bargain price.

Second, I detest the Japan-bashing in this sentiment. The major reason the Japanese are walloping us is because they were smart enough to institute an offensive trade policy that discriminated against our goods while our government failed to study and implement means of breaking this policy and aggressively promoting our own. I do not like the results of what the Japanese have done in our nation, but I realize that it is our own criminally negligent trade policies and sophomoric government response which have landed us in the soup. That the Japanese want to maximize their advantage is understandable; that we do so little to maximize ours is ludicrous. But I have news for Mr. Heilbrunn: the offensive Japanese trade practices do not include taking over your service business — or mine.

What we need instead of this tendency to blame someone for our problems is a recognition that *each* of us selling services has the means to become rich — yes even very rich — if we get smarter — a lot smarter — about using our service businesses as a wealth-producing tool.

I firmly believe that there isn't a service being offered in this nation that doesn't offer the possibility of making you a millionaire. By this I most decidedly do not mean that you can continue to offer your service the way you do now and get rich. No, I certainly don't mean that! What I do mean is that whether your service is catering corporate affairs or being a dentist, each business offers a means of becoming rich — if you know how money can be made with your business, if you create an aggressive marketing program, and if you keep implementing and developing this program day in, day out.

This book is going to challenge not merely your thinking . . . but your entire way of doing business and perhaps even your entire lifestyle and thought process. I shall be pushing you over and over again to investigate just what you are doing . . . and to determine if you need to make changes to reach your financial objectives, indeed whether you can afford the luxury of maintaining your current operations without making changes. But by the end of this book, you are going to know what to do . . . and how to do it . . . so you can generate all the prospects you need to become a multi-millionaire. If you don't become rich as a result, it's your own fault!

This resource is a hammer calculated at once to destroy practices that just don't make sense for you . . . and to build new practices that ensure you of becoming wealthy faster.

Towards these ends, nothing in this book is theoretical. I know. I have lived its suggestions for many years now. And I am perfectly happy to tell you precisely what works — and why . . . and what doesn't work.

This is a cook-book for successfully marketing services . . . and like all other cook-books needs to be carefully followed until such time as you have become a master chef able to use your own experience and imagination to make creative changes. At that point, I ask you to be in immediate touch with me. I need such masters in my life, and I welcome them with open arms in the true spirit of profit-making comradeship!

Swelling My Own Ample Coffers

I am a wealthy man; indeed, I am a millionaire. But things did not begin that way. My parents didn't bankroll me . . . I had no wealthy patron to cover my mistakes with soothing bank drafts. I have never had a business course in my life and have never been taught the established, the "right" way of doing things. No, indeed!

In 1979, not so long after I finished my 4th (and gratefully final) college degree, I took $100 of my very limited funds and invested in my consulting business, that is to say in myself. I have never had to put another dime into my business . . . but have taken out hundreds of thousands thanks to the success of my many projects, consulting, books and information materials, workshops, card deck, catalog, column and various other products. An aggressive — and profitable — investment program has helped me build a significant capital base and an annual income of tens of thousands more, an amount that now expands yearly without much help from me.

I want to make it clear why I am telling you this. It is not some prideful boast; that is *infra dig*. Rather, I abhor the "authorities" who write get-rich books (whether quick or otherwise) who are themselves not rich.

No one should write a "how-to" book or other information product who has not lived every syllable and achieved the promise of the product's title. To do otherwise, as so many writers do to my certain knowledge, is to propagate a lie. You have a right to know whether my methods work, whether I stand 100% behind them, and whether they have brought me success. Let me answer you plainly: They do! I do! They have!

Unfortunately, the information business is populated by people who do not know their subjects; people who have not achieved themselves what they say others can achieve with their products; people who would never let you contact them outside the controlled circumstances of their expensive seminars for fear that their own ignorance would be unmasked. I know many of these people . . . and perhaps I shall tell everything I know about them someday in the first great exposé of America's hoax-ridden information industry. But not today . . . Today I am concerned only that you know you are dealing with a man who has risen thanks to the help he has provided millions of others, others who have overwhelmingly been happy to trade part of their limited resources for some of the tools I have fashioned to assist them. For make no mistake about it, I am not a "self-made" man. No one who achieves success is ever that.

I have risen thanks to the deliberate decisions of tens of thousands of men and women around the world who have picked up the phone, sent in an order form, enrolled in a workshop program . . . or otherwise taken some conscious action that involved sending me money in return for one of the many means I have to help them. *I have, you see, been made by others . . . just as you will be.* And the more you are able to offer others not just the promise, but the substantial reality of vital assistance, the more you will advance towards your own exalted objectives. Never, never, never forget this! Here is the true theme of this book and the germ of your own enhanced prosperity.

What You'll Find In These Pages

This book is divided into 16 chapters and, briefly, I'd like to introduce them to you.

I begin the book in Chapter 1 with "Thirty Reasons Why You're Currently Sabotaging Your Chances Of Becoming A Multi-Millionaire Selling Services." If you solve these thirty problems, you will become a millionaire selling your service. That's why if you find yourself failing to reach this objective, you should return to this chapter again and again until you have solved every single one of these problems.

In Chapter 2, you'll learn how to create the Multi-Million Dollar Plan. Here you start breaking away from the service sellers whose businesses run them to become the future millionaire who uses your business to make money. You know about having to plan your work and work your plan . . . here are the details you need so you can successfully do so.

Once you've got the plan, you need to gather — and store — client-centered cash copy. That's what you'll learn to do in Chapter 3. This is the process you must go through *before* you write any marketing communications. Most service sellers don't plan these communications . . . and don't do what's necessary to get the proper information they need to motivate people. They just write. Result? They don't make their investment back, much less any profit.

Once you've got the right material — the skeleton — for your marketing communications, then and only then should you produce them. In Chapter 4, you'll master the components of marketing communications that get your prospects to respond . . . and learn how to create all the communications themselves. Thereafter you'll never be at a loss for how to create the right marketing communication . . . the communication that gets the person you're addressing to do what you want him to do!

Before you start using these powerful marketing communications, however, you've got some more work to do in your office. In Chapter 5, you'll find out how to turn your personal computer into the most client-centered marketing department imaginable. You'll find out what to put in it and how to organize all your data so that you are prepared to deal effectively with both prospects and clients . . . so you get more business faster!

Beginning in Chapter 6, we take up the issue of how to generate all the leads you need in many different ways. This chapter deals specifically with how you'll use the free media — that's print and electronic — to get your prospects to contact you and tell you they want the benefits you can provide through your service business.

In Chapter 7, you'll learn how to get leads from talk programs, including speeches, lectures, workshops, continuing education courses, *etc.* You may be giving such programs already, but after you read this chapter you'll know how to use them effectively to get client prospects . . . and to make them want to hire you promptly.

Chapter 8 takes up the question of how to use direct response marketing to get leads. You'll find out how to use direct mail to get prospects to call you . . . by learning what to send them, when to send it, and how to effectively follow up when they do contact you.

You'll learn how to get still more leads in Chapter 9, where we discuss the effective use of classified and small space ads. Most ads for most service sellers do not work; they don't keep a steady stream of leads coming and they don't make money. To make sure this doesn't happen to you, pay real close attention to the tips in this chapter so you keep your leads coming and turn these prospects quickly into new customers.

You'll swell your lead streams still further by paying attention to what's in Chapter 10, where you'll learn about the effective use of card decks, electronic moving message display units, package stuffer programs and other specialized lead-generating programs. The purpose of this book is to ban demeaning, dehumanizing, and frustrating cold calling from your life. This chapter provides still more ways you can use right now to achieve this objective.

Once you've got these leads coming in steadily, you must close them just as steadily. That's where Chapter 11 comes in. Here you'll learn what to do with your leads so you get more customers faster. What you'll learn in this chapter is crucial to your success. Pay close attention to it!

Chapter 11 deals with closing prospects who have not previously bought your services. Chapter 12 takes up the question of how to get more business from people who have already bought from you . . . been happy with what you provided . . . but are not buying as much as you'd like . . . or they need. Getting more business from your existing client base is one of the things you must succeed in doing to become a millionaire faster; this chapter tells you how.

In Chapter 13, the discussion on customers continues. Specially, this chapter takes up the question of how to keep deriving income from your customer base longer. Your customer base is one of your capital assets; this chapter shows you how to derive maximum benefit from it.

Chapter 14 takes up the question of how to handle the excess number of leads you've generated. When you follow the guidelines in this book, you won't just have the number of leads you need to become rich; you'll have more. Here you'll learn how to derive maximum benefit from all the leads you generate . . . including developing profitable relationships with independent contractors.

If you're really committed to becoming really rich, Chapter 15 is made for you. It tells you how to create a Mobile Mini-Conglomerate and takes up the question of the many ways available for you to make maximum income from the technical and problem-solving information at your disposal. You'll learn how to go beyond delivering the service yourself and even having your part- and full-time employees and independent contractors do so. You'll find out how to make money from problem-solving products like special reports, audio cassettes, booklets and books, from the products and services of other providers, from talk programs, and from catalogs.

Finally, in Chapter 16 you'll find out how to take the money from all the successful divisions of your company and create a profitable investment program. No really rich person earns all his money every year . . . and neither will you. You'll find out how to turn your income into capital and your capital into further income, deriving a greater and greater percentage of your income from the greater and greater agglomerations of capital, the regularly expanding foundation of your wealth.

A Final Hint About How To Approach This Resource

This is not a book you can either read or entirely grasp in one sitting. It demands time, indeed prolonged study and consideration. Nor are you going to like everything you read in these pages. I am a forceful man of decided opinions; and it is beyond even my sanguine nature to think I can secure the agreement of everyone to all that I propose. Moreover, the human animal is often a slothful animal; we don't enjoy the thought that we may have previously wasted much of our time and energies and may have to rethink our course and work harder along entirely new and different lines. I understand this.

Many people reading this book will decide the game is not worth the candle, that it's going to take too much time, too much energy, too much thought to achieve the desired objective. They will swell the great ranks of the also-rans while offering up reasons a-plenty why they failed. I have no time for such people and rigorously flush them out of my life, just as I advise you to do. Nor do I take their criticisms seriously; I do not expect those who have failed to achieve success to appreciate those of us who have and all that we are now enjoying. Why should they?

While the road to success may be open to vast numbers of people, those who achieve success necessarily constitute an elite. Those who do not make it into this elite will cavil, criticize and censure those who do; I see this daily and experience my share. Believe me, that comes with the territory, and you must learn to ignore it. You must also learn to congregate with those in the elite who have achieved success, especially those whose success currently is greater than your own. These are your true peers, and you should hark unto them.

I am one of these people, and I offer you the hand of fellowship and my association in this great quest of human development. As you start implementing the many suggestions in the hundreds of pages that follow, understand that I am working right along with you to help you achieve the furthest dreams of your wildest imagination. I am a fellow worker in the vineyard, one who understands precisely what you must do and precisely how frustrating, enervating and uncertain this work can sometimes be. No one's success is effortless; no one's is a straight line without deviation. And it won't be that way for you either, whatever my lesser colleagues of the "how-to" genre tell you.

Thus, on days when you are weary, depressed or even despairing, return to these pages. They are filled with practical ideas to help you transform a blighted situation into one of promise and achievement. And if by chance sustained study here doesn't help spur you ahead, call me. Sometimes just knowing there is a friend only a few digits away, a friend who really does understand what it takes to implement all that follows and all you must do to achieve success, will be just what you need to start moving forward again.

Now it's truly time to begin to transform your life and your service business . . . to add new profit-making activities and delete unprofitable ones . . . to do everything, in short, to achieve the promise of this book's title: GENERATING — AND CLOSING — ALL THE PROSPECTS YOU NEED TO BECOME A MULTI-MILLIONAIRE BY SELLING YOUR SERVICE. I am pleased and honored that you have chosen me as your guide for reaching so important an objective in your life.

Cambridge, Massachusetts

November, 1992

Jeffrey

1

Thirty Reasons Why You're Currently Sabotaging Your Chances of Becoming A Multi-Millionaire Selling Services . . . Solve These Problems and Your Millionaire Status Is Assured

There is nothing magical about becoming a service seller millionaire. Indeed, achieving this status is inevitable . . . if you follow a series of sensible steps and make sure that you solve the leading problems that cause people to fail. In this chapter I've listed and briefly discussed these problems. Solve them and you will get rich.

What's unique about this chapter is that each of these reasons concludes with a box where you can pledge yourself to doing what's necessary to avoid making this mistake . . . and commits you to doing what's necessary in the future to make sure it doesn't hobble your development. While checking this box may seem like kids' stuff, let me assure you it isn't.

Most "how-to" writers simply provide you with information; sometimes this information is useful, sometimes it isn't. But the format in which they work and present information is virtually always the same: author tells you; you either take in the information and act on it or not. My approach is different.

I am not behaving and do not wish to be perceived as the standard "author." Instead, I want to establish a client-consultant relationship. Yes, I'll be providing useful information . . . but I don't just want you

1

to consider it. I want you to take responsibility for implementing it. That's where the boxes come in.

I want you to understand that there are mistakes which will keep you from succeeding; indeed, if upon studying this book, you make some (much less most) of the mistakes in this chapter, there's no hope for your success. And I want you to understand that *you* have to assume responsibility for not making these mistakes once . . . or ever again. This responsibility begins by making a pledge to yourself. That's why at the end of each separate error, I ask you to make a pledge to yourself to do what's necessary to avoid this mistake. Taken collectively, all the mini-pledges add up to a major commitment on your part to do what's necessary to succeed . . . and to understand that your success rests entirely on yourself and on no one else.

In this sense, then, this chapter, the chapter that offers the least "how-to" information in the book, may actually be the most important. That's because without assuming this kind of responsibility you cannot succeed. Further, it provides an overview of the killing mistakes you can make (probably are making now) that prevent success. Thus, if you find yourself failing to succeed sufficiently quickly. . . . or worse, find that you're not succeeding at all . . . you must return to this chapter and read it again and again and again, each time committing yourself to doing what's necessary to avoid the mistakes that follow.

I guarantee you that if you understand the problems that can defeat you . . . and have pledged . . . and repledged . . . yourself to solving and avoiding them, you will not only be far ahead of other service sellers who neither understand the errors they're making nor have pledged to avoid them . . . but you stand poised to reach your financial objectives.

To give yourself the greatest possible boost towards achieving this book's objective, read this chapter with pen in hand. Read and truly understand each problem. And when it comes time to pledge yourself to doing what's necessary to solve this problem, don't make the commitment mindlessly but with full deliberation. I want this commitment seared into your consciousness and actualized in each day's activities. Then and only then will this chapter truly work for you.

Avoidable Error #1
You Do Not Really Desire To Become
A Millionaire Selling Services

In my work, I meet lots of people, thousands and thousands of people, who all tell me they want to succeed. It's a kind of American mantra and virtually all my countrymen give frequent lip-service to the concept of desiring success.

At the same time, I witness one self-defeating behavior after another from these people . . . people who tell you on the one hand that, of course, they want to succeed . . . while on the other cannot be induced to return a phone call in a timely fashion; get you the data you need for a joint venture proposal; or process an order, much less upgrade it.

In just the last few days alone, I can tick off the following all-too-common problems:

- the Connecticut list broker who, despite being asked several times, fails to get the necessary paperwork to a list owner who wants him to represent his names. As a result the names the list owner has available for rental and which will provide commission income for the broker are not on the market and benefit no one.

- the Massachusetts mortgage re-financing company where it takes six calls before basic paperwork is sent;

- the Virginia copy writer who gets so many responses to a card-deck advertisement promoting his services that he gets overwhelmed . . . and answers none of them.

- the Alabama advertising executive who is owed 100,000 cards by an organization he made a swap with. That organization asks the executive over and over again to send his art-work but not only does the executive fail to do so, he never even bothers to take a call on the subject, despite the fact that the cards he is owed will bring him substantial business.

Are these people just disorganized . . . are they irredeemably stupid . . . or is something else going on here?

Years ago I believed that people would always act in their own self-interest and that if this interest were spelled out to them in sufficient detail they would act accordingly. I no longer believe this.

After many years in business, I now believe that most people are in business for social reasons, *e.g.* that it gives them something to do, someplace to go, and provides them with ready-made friends and associates and a daily structure. Making money, much less achieving success in the terms of this book, is neither their first priority nor indeed of any importance whatsoever . . . whatever they may say to the contrary.

As this realization dawned on me, a lot I had previously witnessed became substantially easier to understand . . . if no easier to accept.

Now I start from the proposition that until he proves otherwise, the business person I'm dealing with is not interested in making money but rather in merely getting by. That he will do only as little as possible to bring in the amount of money he needs to maintain his current situation, not all that is called for to improve it and to ensure his own success.

What's missing in these millions and millions of business people — so many of them selling services — is the desire to succeed and to improve. And without this desire nothing else is possible.

Desire is the *sine qua non* of success. My dictionary defines it like this: "to wish or long for; covet; crave." I think, however, one of these words is out of place. That is the word "wish." That is too weak a word. Desire is not about "wishing" for something; it is about aggressively wanting it . . . thereby mentally conditioning oneself for doing what's necessary to make sure it actually happens.

Desire, you see, is a gnawing feeling deep in one's being that one is necessarily incomplete until one achieves the object of the desire. This object is longed for . . . coveted . . . craved . . . and regularly and assiduously worked for until achieved.

The entire concept of desire, however, is at odds with the prevailing "I'm okay; you're okay" insipidity of our culture. A person consumed with desire is not "okay" within himself . . . until he has achieved the objective. He is necessarily incomplete . . . and knows it. What's more, this sense of "incompleteness" is a good thing, for without it there would be no developmental action or initiative whatsoever.

Sentimentalist pop-philosophers won't like my writing this. They offer the preposterous notion that simply being alive . . . simply being here and taking up space makes one an entirely valuable person. That one can be valuable and complete and even admirable by doing nothing more than being. I reject this notion absolutely. Being, unless it follows a substantial process of becoming, can never be regarded as somehow valuable, much less complete and satisfactory.

The truth is that despite many pronouncements to the contrary, ours is not a culture that feels comfortable with people who are striving for success. Success seekers after all are necessarily energetic, thrusting, active, imaginative, creative, often unconventional and frequently bumptious and irreverent. It has always been thus. One way and another from our earliest days all sorts of influences are brought to bear on us to shear away these traits.

We are told to take it easy; don't work too hard; slow down and smell the flowers and, one of the most irritating, have a nice day. We are told in short, to stop being active, imaginative and adventuresome and instead become torpid, slow-moving, passive and acquiescent.

Well-meaning but fundamentally misdirected parents, teachers, friends and associates, continually work to wear away the passion and desire that every one of us brought so amply into the world. For each of us came into the world, as all babies do, resonating unceasing desire and abundant passion.

Look at a baby. He is a bundle of unrepressed and constantly expressed desires. He wants. Then he wants more. He is unafraid to announce these wants in often blood-curdling ways . . . indeed, until taught, he has no concept that these wants are not entirely acceptable and must be curtailed. Yet soon the insidious process of diminishment begins. He learns that to achieve acceptance (and the prospect of "peace" that others claim accompanies it) he must lower his wants and accept a growing number of constraints. Thus social acceptance is built upon self-diminishment and the containment of desire.

Most people, and of course most service sellers, never get beyond this stultifying situation. They have been so successfully socialized by our purportedly success-focused but actually success-denying culture that it is inconceivable any of them could truly achieve meaningful success. Thus they become victims of the "take it easy" culture . . . and are doomed.

At this point, you may be arching your back a bit, may well be thinking, "But this is America . . ." where the nation's religion is success. True, the nation's religion may be success, but we are far from doing what is necessary to inform people what it really takes to achieve success.

Success in 20th century America is like a goddess in Ancient Rome. All may know about this goddess . . . all may talk of her . . . all may indeed worship her. But few, very few, know what really needs to be done to achieve salvation.

How can I be so sure?

Walk into any school room in America today, and I defy you to show me that there is a Success Curriculum in place. Our students learn to fit in. They don't learn even the rudiments of what it takes to be a success in this country. Now as in the days you and I went to school, the best and brightest can go through the entire process of "education" without learning even the most elementary aspects of what it takes to make, maintain and develop wealth. Yet making, maintaining, and developing wealth is what business is all about... and without business success our American life-style is necessarily doomed to fail.

The question then becomes: if desire is crucial to achieving success as a service seller . . . and if we have spent a lifetime within the confines of a culture that works in ways both explicit and insidious to diminish desire (and hence ourselves) . . . what must we do to rekindle and develop desire?

To begin we must commit ourselves to rekindling, nurturing and fostering desire.

This is, of course, easy to say and less easy to achieve. But let me give you some suggestions for doing this:

- commit yourself to rediscovering desire;

- understand that desire directed to positive ends is a positive good and that without it you cannot succeed;

- avoid mediocre people who are content with an undesirable lot. These people cannot possibly help you achieve success;

- congregate with people who are nurturing desire . . . that is, people who are consumed with the passion for success. You'll know such people immediately: they radiate a positive "can do" attitude which manifests itself in everything they do;

- look for signs within yourself that you are giving way to an acceptance of situations that are not conducive to your success;

- ask yourself over and over again whether you are pursuing
things that you desire (or are dropping things that you
desire to stop) . . . or are doing merely what others want
you to do. If you are following the dictates of others and
abandoning what you yourself desire, how can you expect
to be a success?

I can tell you this right away: when you begin desiring success and
begin manifesting this desire in your manner, behavior, attire, attitude
and entire consciousness, you probably won't get any support from
the people around you, unless you move in an extraordinarily uplifting
circle. Instead, you'll be greeted with some variation of the "who does
he think he is?" theme that dooms so many. Expect this lack of support
. . . and inwardly resolve to escape from this environment as soon
as possible.

Note I say "inwardly resolve". Make the decision . . . live the decision
. . . but do not share the decision with anyone who is not prepared
to fully endorse what you're doing. Your job is not to convince the
rest of the world that what you're doing is correct. It is simply to do
what's necessary to ensure your success. As Henry Ford II once said,
"Never complain. Never explain." Here is where those words are
particularly applicable.

We all know the saying that "misery loves company." Those who are
unsuccessful — and are never going to be successful — love each
other's company, too. And when you come from an environment
where these people predominate — and the odds are that you do —
you have two choices: 1) you can accommodate yourself to these
people and find yourself ground down to their level, or 2) you can
resolve to escape from them and either move to or create an environment where success can result.

I'll tell you this: if you remain in an unnurturing environment, no
matter how much you *say* you want to achieve success. . . no matter
how much lip-service you give to the success rhetoric in which our
country abounds, you are doomed to failure. Because your remaining
in such an environment proves that you are without the necessary
desire that you need to succeed.

Desire, you see, abhors passive acceptance. Desire is a fuel; by its very
nature it involves movement, action, activity. It is a transformational
idea . . . not a static concept. And if you say it without living it,
everything in this book will come to naught in your life.

Now commit!

☐ From this moment on, I *desire* to achieve success by becoming a multi-millionaire selling my service. I understand that others, perhaps members of my family and closest friends, will not sympathize with what I am doing and may, indeed, do everything possible to inhibit me and ensure my failure. But I do not intend to let them lower me to their level. I know that right now I may not truly understand the concept of desire and how to harness it to my success chariot. I understand I am probably making too many concessions now and probably talk more about desire than manifesting in my behavior a real desire to succeed. However I intend to do everything I can to nurture the innate desire to have more that is within me, whatever others may say. Henceforward I commit myself to manifesting my desire in ways that will build my business . . . instead of merely talking about it. Desire, I now understand, is not a word; it is an action . . . and it is an action I intend to take daily from now on!

Avoidable Error #2
You're Working For The Sake Of Work,
Not To Achieve The Goal Of Financial Independence

Look around you. Everywhere you go you see people working. Most of these people work hard over the course of many years. Still, at the end of the day only the tiniest percentage of them will achieve financial independence, the only reason why work really makes sense.

Why is this? Certainly, if all workers were asked if they wanted financial independence, the ability that is to comfortably exist by living off the income from their capital, they would resoundingly and in overwhelming numbers answer yes. Why, then, does survey after survey show how few Americans ever achieve this state? Why do so many after a lifetime of toil live in cramped circumstances?

Is it because most of our fellow countrymen are stupid? Ill-informed? Lazy? Short-sighted?

I am thinking right now of just one of the many people I know who is in this sad situation. He is now in his late thirties. He works hard in a local hospital running an important department. He is single and has no dependents and a salary in the mid forty thousand range.

Despite these benefits, his financial situation, like that of so many Americans, is deplorable. He has no nest egg whatsoever. The sum total of his assets is a pension plan that now has about $3,500 in it. A few years ago he binged out on credit cards and is now paying the price for over indulgence. Even with the recent decreases in interest payments, he's still finding it hard to make a dent in the amounts he owes and maintain any kind of decent lifestyle.

When he thinks about his situation, this fellow gets depressed . . . as who wouldn't? And therefore, he's decided, like the proverbial ostrich, that he won't think about it. Indeed, getting him to confront the reality of his situation is difficult. Like Aesop's deluded grasshopper who'd rather play, this guy would rather go to the movies, the quintessential American escape. I feel sorry for him. . . but by avoiding focusing on his situation, this man has determined his own fate. And it is not a pretty one as will become increasingly clear over the next years.

Don't let this be you.

If you are going to become a multi-millionaire selling services, you cannot afford the luxury of failing to concentrate on your present situation and on the realities of your life. Perhaps the major reality of your life is just how little time you have available to achieve financial independence. Here's what I mean . . .

If you live to achieve the biblical three-score and ten, you will have 25,550 days or 662,040 hours. Of this, 17,240 days fall between the ages of 25-65, the years when you combine the best health and professional focus. However, roughly 1/3 of this time you'll spend sleeping, leaving approximately 11,480 days. Of these, 2,080 will be Sundays and hence necessarily less productive. Another 320 will be holidays. That leaves about 9,080 working days. There will also be days when you're traveling (for business or pleasure), days when you're not feeling well . . . or days when you're just plain worn out and can't bear the thought of doing anything else. Let's say, then, that you've got about 8,500 good days to ensure your success.

But let's say you're already 35 years old. One quarter of this time is already gone. Or say you're 45, my present age. Half's been used up by then . . . and the clock continues to tick . . . against you.

This much, however, is clear: whether you do anything or not, you're going to run out of time. The real question is: during the time you have left, will you be sufficiently structured, directed and organized to trade the time remaining for the achievement of things which are meaningful to you and those who are important to you? Or will you simply let the time run through your hands?

People like my ostrich-like acquaintance are letting their time slip through their fingers without understanding that it is finite and unrecoverable. Future millionaires like you cannot afford to make this mistake. You must take as your goal turning the time you have remaining into enough financial capital to ensure yourself the lifestyle you want to achieve. This means exactly and realistically determining how much work time you have left . . . and how much capital you'll need for financial independence.

Once you have determined these numbers (you get further information in Chapter 16), write down your goal of financial independence in a precise way like this:

> By age 55, I will have income-producing capital investments of $2,500,000. These investments will provide me with financial independence since the lifestyle needs of myself and my family can be fully covered by this sum.

Now you have what is absolutely essential to the millionaire service seller and which most Americans decidedly lack: a goal. With this goal, and an acute understanding of the time limitations which affect all of us, you can begin the process of Mind Channeling.

What? *Mind Channeling.* That is, you can begin the process of focusing the mind only on what is important and of assistance in achieving the goal . . . and weeding out all the other activities in life which obstruct or delay this achievement.

Goals by their very nature focus the mind. And focus by definition is both inclusive (you include only things which are helpful) and exclusive (you exclude everything that isn't).

Sometimes these things are in the business domain. Will making this next phone call help me achieve my objective faster . . . or won't it? Will traveling across town during rush-hour to see a man who's expressed only the most limited interest in my service? Does maintaining nothing more than my current service (which produces no more than $45,000 a year in profit) make sense when I know that if I only do this I cannot have financial independence?

Sometimes these things are personal. Will spending an hour at the grocery store this evening when there are still calls to be made on the West Coast help me reach my financial objective? Does rearranging my furniture make sense when I haven't sent out the last of the media releases about the new service we're developing? How about that temper of mine? Isn't the time and energy that takes up better used elsewhere?

See? When you realize — *really* realize — that time is absolutely finite and when you've posited a goal that is absolutely vital to you . . . you have a means for deciding what's important and what isn't; what should be done today . . . and what can safely be left undone . . . or done (even perhaps less well) by others.

With a goal, you are well and truly on your way to success.

Now commit!

☐ I promise to work towards an understanding both of the finite amount of time at my disposal and to setting as my goal the achievement of financial independence at a definite time. I shall no longer regard all things professional and personal as of equal weight and equally demanding of my time. I shall do only those things that maximize the return on my finite amount of time and help me reach my goal. I realize that in the achievement of this goal, I may well falter. But I promise to do all that I can both to keep before me how limited my time is . . . and to reaffirm to myself the importance of my goal and to work towards achieving it.

Avoidable Error #3
You Don't Really Want To Help People

As I write this section, I am thinking of a nurse specializing in maternal child health. She was hired by a local visiting nursing agency I know to establish and develop a new division within the organization with this specialty.

For months I urged, pleaded, wheedled, scolded and hectored the executive director of this agency to get the nurse out and into local hospitals from whence most of the business would come. But the executive director took no action, instead merely assuring me that the nurse was an expert clinician and that this was the most important thing. Not surprisingly, the program languished and in an age of acute recession and turmoil in the medical community tens of thousands of dollars of very scarce resources were absolutely wasted.

And the reason? Our nurse professional thought the necessary marketing of this program was "beneath" her!

Now think what this idiot was saying in effect: we have a good program. Even a superb program. If people need it, they'll do what's necessary to find it. I won't lift a finger because I'm a "professional" ... and it is beneath me to do anything that will make their lives easier and bring them to me — where they can get the quality services I say I have available — any earlier and any easier.

Well, this woman may have been a qualified clinician, but she was a deplorable human being.

If you want your service business to be a success, if you want to achieve millionaire status as a service seller, you must want to help people ... and you must pledge yourself to doing *everything* that's necessary both to make people aware of what you've got for them ... and ensure they can avail themselves of it easily and conveniently. This is not merely the mark of a superb marketer ... but of a truly caring human being.

Since the inception of my practice, I've come in personal contact with literally thousands of service sellers. Most make a living wage; very, very few are millionaires. Without exception, however, the millionaires are totally dedicated to helping other people. They are truly caring, thoughtful, empathetic and concerned.

What's more, they show these qualities in everything they do.

How different, for instance, from a former insurance agent of mine. I dropped him because over time I came to see that he was shallow, self-seeking, pompous and condescending, traits which were reinforced in my mind when he called me during the writing of this chapter. He just wanted to "touch base." "Do you need anything?", he barked. I was in the middle of my writing period for the day and wasn't eager to talk or be disturbed. He didn't care. He was on the line ... and what possible value could my time be compared to his?

Did he ask if it was convenient for me to talk?

Did he offer me any reason for the call? Any benefits he might have for me that might make me want to listen?

No, no indeed. He'd probably read in some book, or heard in some course, that it was a good idea to "touch base" with past customers. But he had no idea how that was done ... and clearly hadn't thought it through. He merely blundered on, increasing my contempt for the man. "How's business, Jeff?" he said, causing me to wince. "Jeff"? For after representing me for two or three years, he *still* had no conception (despite being frequently corrected) that I detest the abbreviated version of my name. Yes, after all that time, he still had no idea what to call me . . . despite my attempts to tell him. People who truly care, listen . . . and take notes for future reference. The inferior do whatever they wish, unknowing, uncaring, thoroughly obnoxious withal.

In a couple of very uncomfortable minutes, the boor had run through his canned questions and was through, ready to go on to the next victim, certain that if he called enough of them one would present him with the opportunity he needed to meet the day's quota. On my part, I hung up the phone irritated; irritated that I had taken the call, irritated that the man was such a fool that he didn't even know how foolish he was; irritated that I was irritated and hence wasting time and energy on a person who was obviously beyond hope.

Of course Jack Baker will never learn. But does Prudential Financial Services care? I doubt it. He can be as obnoxious and insufferable as he likes . . . so long as he meets his quota. If he doesn't, of course . . . off with his head!

But one thing is clear: here's a man who doesn't care a whit about people. Who sees them only as unfortunately necessary counters on his road to success. "Marketing," he is fond of saying, "is just a numbers game." Of course, in a certain way of looking at things, he's right. But the millionaire service seller realizes each number is a person. Each of these people has hopes, dreams, aspirations . . . each is looking, not merely for good service, but for human contact and understanding. Remembering this, of course, isn't just crucial for one's own self-esteem . . . it also makes good business sense.

Long ago I discovered that the American consumer isn't as stupid as he's frequently pictured. Most people are quite capable of knowing when they're being abused or condescended to and, if mostly quietly, they vote with their feet, taking future business elsewhere and damning the service seller by not contributing to the flow of the referral business which is so necessary for the economic health of all of us who aspire to riches.

Jack Baker may know this; he may have heard it at a workshop . . . or read it in a book. But he doesn't really get it. That's why when he calls me (and very likely lots of other people) he comes across as entirely self-seeking, arrogant, condescending and boorish. Really, would you buy insurance . . . or anything else . . . from such a man? If I mentioned any of this, chances are he'd get defensive. And instead of asking me why I felt this way, he'd react in the classic fashion of the turkey cock through the ages. He'd puff out his chest and spew out a cascade of mindless comments. Why, how could I possibly be right when he'd just received a company citation for excellence; when his mail-box is filled with the testimonials of ecstatic people; when his monthly sales totals, even in a recession, are something to write home about? In short, when everything was just as good as it could be?

Well, maybe everything he'd tell me might be true. After all, you can fool lots of the people lots of the time. But I know one thing: the situation at his end is not as good as it could be . . . because I'd taken myself . . . and my money . . . elsewhere. Moreover, I'd deprived him of a steady stream of referrals, referrals that are a crucial part of any profitable service business.

Maybe Jack Baker will end up a multi-millionaire selling his service. He's told me often enough that he will. But it's going to take him just a little bit longer to get there, since "Jeff" isn't helping . . .

To succeed as a service seller, to achieve millionaire status, means constant participation in a balancing act. You must never forget yourself, of course; it does not do to compromise your own goals and principles. But you must be equally aware of the only person who can make you rich: your prospect and your customer. He has just expectations, too. And you must be aware of them and cater to them.

Note I use two verbs: awareness and catering.

Awareness takes into account an understanding of the situation of the prospect.

- He may not be available during your regular business hours;
- He may have financial conditions to take into account;
- Your standard operating procedures may not apply in his situation.

In short, your prospect and his situation may not be a perfect fit with you and your current operating procedures. But it is always your task, never the prospect's, to accommodate the prospect's situation and negotiate the means of getting to a mutually beneficial agreement.

This necessarily involves catering, which means being flexible.

- Do you really need to set strict times when the prospect can get in touch with you?

- Instead of telling the prospect that you can't accommodate him, why not tell him under what circumstances you can . . . and let him make the choice about whether he accepts your proposition?

- If you cannot handle the prospect's business right now, instead of merely disappointing him, couldn't you make a definite referral to someone who can help?

You see, the essence of running a service business is being helpful. Not slavish. Not subservient. Not obsequious. But helpful. And caring. The successful service seller understands that he is helping to create a compact between two people . . . between the person who needs his assistance and can rightly be asked to follow certain reasonable procedures about getting it . . . and between the service seller who has available the means of assistance and is offering to provide it in every reasonable way . . . and, perhaps, for special consideration, even in unreasonable ways as well.

To succeed as a service seller means regularly asking yourself if you have provided all reasonable means of accommodating prospects and clients. For instance, do you have ways of

- responding promptly to requests for information and further details;

- making sure all phone calls get dealt with in a timely fashion;

- providing your service when you said you were going to . . . and explaining delays (rather than simply forcing the customer to suffer through them without explanations);

- taking care of customer complaints?

And all the other things that crop up in service businesses?

Sadly, the vast majority of service businesses do not have these means in place. Of these, you could merely say that they were disorganized, and leave it at that. Such disorganization, however, is the sign of a much more fundamental problem. These businesses operate with a fundamental contempt for the prospect and customer. They value their own time and procedures more than they value the prospect's and customer's. Their own needs are always paramount to the customer's; the customer is always a burden, never an opportunity.

Over the years I have collected hundreds of personal incidents with service businesses that sadly prove what I've written. True, many of these incidents involve employees rather than owners; but the conduct of an employee is the responsibility of the owner. Therefore no employer should ever say, as the owner of a local Gnomon Copy said to me one day after a particularly infuriating incident involving one of his employees, "Well, you know how hard it is to get good help these days," thus saying, so he thought, all there was to be said about the matter.

With ever more people in the world, with the level of callousness towards these people daily higher and more socially acceptable, successful service sellers must make a conscious effort to stand apart from this invidious trend of our times.

When you do, of course, you will face the possibility that some people will try to exploit you. There will always be people who see in reasonable conduct and humane practices weakness and fertile ground for exploitation. As soon as you sense this, shun these people. Reasonable behavior is owing to reasonable people only. The rest deserve the shortest of shrifts.

But with reasonable people, stretch to serve them. Think how you can better accommodate them. Then do accommodate them.

As I can personally attest, when you do, these reasonable people will first be astonished . . . and then deeply grateful . . . and will do what they can to assist you. My own business has grown in large measure because I have overcome the hateful notion that "marketing is nothing more than a numbers game" and realized that it is a people process. Each person, properly handled and treated, has the possibility of helping to make me richer and build my business; conversely, each has within him the means of limiting both. What I do to him — not just for him — is the crucial variable in each case. Help, you see, is not a word; it is an action . . . and to the service businessperson it is an action which must be the foundation of his business. For truly helpful action indicates, beyond any amount of words, that you truly do have the welfare of your prospects and customers at heart.

Now commit!

☐ I pledge myself to helping improve the condition of my prospects and clients. I understand that as I ameliorate their circumstances, they will necessarily improve mine, not just through current business but through future business and through the many referrals that will inevitably result. For reasonable people, I shall think hard and long about how to accommodate them. In their satisfaction shall be the seeds of my prosperity, now and forever. Equally, I shall jettison all the unreasonable people, the grasping, rapacious, and exploitative, for I understand that reasonable conduct is owing only to the reasonable. But for these I shall do all in my power, because I understand that help is not merely a word . . . it is the operating philosophy of the successful service seller . . . me!

Avoidable Error #4
You Have No Annual Dollar Objectives

You know you must have a goal . . . and must operate a truly helpful, client-centered service business. Very well. *Now* you must focus on achieving specific dollar objectives, for by using client-centered behavior to achieve these regular objectives you will certainly succeed in reaching your goal, no matter how exalted.

As I write, I am thinking about the cleaners across the street. It is, of course, a service business and, like so many of these, it is run by a family. I use it because it's handy and because they do reasonably good work, but if another establishment ever opens which can do as much, I'll change my allegiance in a minute. Why? Because the owner is unkempt and surly; because the place is shabby and disagreeable; because the help can still not spell "Follen" street, despite the fact that it's 100 yards away (I kid you not); because, in short, it's a parody of what a service business in the 'nineties should be.

Now I ask you, do you think that each November or December, the owner sits down to review his goal, calibrate how he is advancing towards it and consider his operating practices? To set reasonable (that is reachable but challenging) financial objectives for the next year, and to plot out (and set down) a series of marketing steps which, when implemented, will bring about the desired objectives? GET REAL! Why, not one of the five (mostly grossly overweight) employees in the shop even knows my name or can even spell it, despite the fact that I've given it to them maybe a hundred times over the last several years. And this, of course, is only one of the hundreds of reasons why the owner will never be a multi-millionaire through the sale of his service.

Don't let this happen to you.

If you are going to become a millionaire selling services, you are going to do so through two means, because you

1. regularly reach precise financial objectives, and
2. invest a portion of this income in capital which will, soon or in the longer-term, produce additional income.

I want to consider #1 here.

If you want to reach a precise goal, you need precise objectives. Properly understood, objectives are subsets of the goal and the goal can only be achieved on schedule by the timely achievement of the objectives.

Thus, say that you wish to have $2,500,000 in capital by age 55. Say your current age is 40 and that you presently have 10% of the desired amount in capital (not including your residence). You therefore have $2,250,000 more to raise. This doesn't count income from your capital, of course . . . but for now I'd like to defer discussing that. Here I'd like simply to focus on how much you need to raise yearly from the sale of units of your service. $2,250,000 divided by 15 years equals $150,000 yearly (again, remember, this is exclusive of interest earned from investments, interest which, if reinvested, diminishes the number of dollars you must raise from the sale of your service.)

Sitting where you are today, this may seem like an impossibility, but I assure you, it isn't. The solution begins in understanding the problem, understanding what needs to be accomplished and how much time you have to accomplish it in . . . then considering just what you can (and must do) to achieve this objective.

If you are going to become a millionaire selling your service, you need to break down your goal into annual, then semi-annual, then quarterly, then monthly, then weekly, then daily . . . and even hourly . . . allotments. Thus, if you need to *net* $150,000 yearly, each work day (of which each year has about 293) must produce about $512 . . . every single one. Each hour (counting 8 to a day) must generate about $64.

What we're doing here is very, very important. For one thing, it focuses your mind on precisely what you need to do to accomplish your objective. Virtually everyone I know says he wants to be a millionaire, but I've never met a person yet who can tell me precisely how much he needs to make in an hour . . . or day . . . or week to achieve that objective by the time he says he wants to achieve it. Thus, they are off to a bad start.

Further, once you see the daily or weekly objectives in print, they lose a good deal of their frightfulness. While $2.25 million may be difficult for any of us to consider (I, for one, have never seen this much money in cash), we can all relate to $64, or just a little more than $1 a minute.

Further, once we have considered what we need to raise to reach our objective (always remembering that interest on our capital will also help us), we will start arranging our business life accordingly.

Take my slovenly cleaning shop owner across the street. If I asked him if he wanted to be a multi-millionaire selling his service, I'd lay odds he'd say yes. If I asked him when he wanted to be a multi-millionaire, he'd say now (that's why he plays the lottery, after all). The fact that his answer is fatuous demonstrates right away why he has so little likelihood of achieving the objective. But if I asked him how his current operating procedures, the services he offers, how he offers them, *etc.* connect with achieving his objective, he'd no doubt scratch his head in complete bewilderment. In other words, he doesn't have the slightest idea how and even if what he does now could make him a millionaire . . . even if he did everything right! That's why he's doomed to be a worker the rest of his life . . . and not a multi-millionaire.

But this won't happen to you!

Once you've determined your goal, do the math and come up with the annual (then semi-annual, quarterly, monthly, *etc.*) objectives you must reach to achieve this goal. Now ask yourself if you can possibly reach this objective doing business the way you're currently doing it. Odds are you cannot. Thus, once you've solved one problem by setting the objective you want, you'll need to start thinking about how to solve the other problem, arranging your professional life so that you can achieve it. But, for right now, it's enough to pledge yourself to setting that objective.

Now commit!

☐ I realize that merely wanting to be a multi-millionaire selling services will never be enough. I must set — and work for the achievement of — precise dollar objectives in a precise period of time. I promise that I shall set such objectives, write them down, arrange my life to do what's necessary to achieve them, post them where I can see them daily, and carry them with me wherever I go. I understand that to achieve this objective, I must live it, and I therefore promise to make whatever changes in my business are necessary to maximize achievement of my objective on time.

Avoidable Error #5
You Don't Have Financial Objectives
For Each Service You Offer

You now know how many dollars you must make in each period of time. Generating this many dollars is a direct function of selling a precise number of units of your service. When you succeed in selling this precise number of units, you reach your financial objectives. It's as simple as that.

Selling these precise numbers of your service units means several things:

1. analyzing your operation to discover just what services you are currently selling;

2. determining how many dollars each service generates;

3. deducing whether you can reasonably expect these services to generate more dollars in the next reporting period (or are you just *hoping* they will?);

4. setting precise dollar objectives for each service;

5. creating the marketing plan — and implementing it — which will realize these dollar objectives.

Let's begin by analyzing your operation.

Take a friend of mine from New Jersey who operates a counseling/consulting service. Here is what he offers:

• direct one-on-one counseling with clients in his office;

• one-on-one telephone counseling with clients nationwide;

• workshops in which he teaches his techniques;

• articles he writes outlining his techniques;

• audio cassettes he produces detailing his techniques;

• a book he has written and self-published offering his techniques.

You will notice that not all of these are classic "services" per se. However, I want to make something very clear: I reckon as a service a "how-to" product in which the producer acts as a service provider. This applies here.

What this fellow needs to know is whether doing what he's doing now, augmented by any interest he may reinvest from his capital investments, will enable him to become a multi-millionaire. In other words, is what he's doing now sufficient . . . or must it be augmented . . . or significantly changed to enable him to meet his objectives?

Let's say he needs to net $150,000 a year, $64 an hour. To see if this is possible with each of his activities, he must know what each of these activities currently nets, that is what is left after he deducts the cost of doing business from gross income.

Once he knows what each nets, he must evaluate how much time/trouble went into the generation of this money . . . in order to determine if raising the dollar objective for the category makes sense. Can he reasonably expect to make more money, or is that an impossibility given all that would have to be done?

Only after performing this evaluation will our service-seller know whether 1) he can afford the luxury of continuing his current operations unaltered, or 2) he can afford to maintain the current kinds of activities but must raise the dollar objectives for some or all, or 3) he needs to make significant adjustments both in *what* he does and *how much* he must do of it — the likeliest outcome.

If you can reach your financial objectives with your current activities, fine. Commit your objective to paper.

If you've made the informed decision that you can reach your objectives by increasing the financial return on some or all of your professional activities, write down the subtotals for each category.

The real problem comes if neither your current activities nor reasonably enhanced outcomes for them will provide what you need to reach your overall financial objective. You have two options: scaling back your financial objective . . . or rethinking what you're doing.

For the moment, I advise you to do the second of these. Your current activities — and enhancements of them — will produce a percentage of the money you need. For now, keep your overall financial objective the same and put the remaining dollars you need to raise in a new service category marked "to be determined." By the time you've finished this book, you should be able to fill this in. Otherwise, you're going to have to wait longer to achieve your goal.

Either way you now have the objectives you need . . . if you take the pledge.

Now commit!

☐ I realize that becoming a multi-millionaire selling my service will be determined by my mounting a series of steps. I know I must net a certain number of dollars yearly, and I know that each of my service activities must contribute a specified amount. I promise to do what's necessary to find out just how much each of my activities must net . . . and to rearrange my life and services (by reasonably increasing outcomes and by adding profitable new services) so that I can reach my objective. I know that only by the continual achievement of precise objectives can my overall goal be reached!

Avoidable Error #6
You're Offering Your Clients/Buyers Too Little Choice

As I said above, the most likely outcome of your analysis of your current activities will be to show that you can't reach your financial objectives either by doing what you're doing now . . . or by merely increasing the dollar totals for each category. The probability is, you're going to have to rethink your offerings. This means thinking about your clients/buyers and what they want. Remember, you will get rich . . . and richer faster . . . by catering to them rather than merely considering your own comfort. This is where the concept of choice comes in; the service professional who fails to ponder this concept significantly retards his progress.

While each service business will necessarily approach the business of choice differently, each should consider the following questions:

- Can you offer some or all of what you do at the premises of the client?

The client should be offered the option of coming to you . . . or having you come to him.

- Can you offer what you do in different locations?

Does the client have to come to a single place?

- Can you offer a way for the client to work along with you directly, thereby saving money?

The client should be offered the possibility of working along with you, of doing some of the work himself and having you do varying amounts of the rest. Some clients, of course, will want you to do everything

. . . others, because of financial limitations or personal preference, will want to do some themselves.

- Can you offer your service at expanded times?

Not everyone can do everything between 9 a.m. – 5 p.m. in your time zone.

- Can you offer what you do in different formats?

Many service sellers seem to think they must always be personally present to provide their benefits. That's one format, to be sure. But what about newsletters, booklets, books, audio and video cassettes? These are also viable formats for offering many service-related benefits to clients.

- Can you offer your service at a group, not just individual, rate?

Can you fashion some aspect of your service so that more than one person could benefit from it at the same time?

- Can you offer your service so that the client can benefit from it wherever he is?

If a person wants your benefit, can you accommodate him?

- Can you offer your service so that the person can pay for it on an installment plan?

Not everybody (especially these days!) has all the money they need for everything they want. It's a good idea to see if you can provide credit — including payment with credit cards — for what you offer.

- Can you offer your service so that people can get all they want but work towards it in installments?

Sure, your clients may want to have the best of what you offer, but it's your responsibility to think about how they can get it from you one piece at a time.

- Can you offer your service at a lower cost than other people?

It's up to you to study the cost basis for what you're offering *vis à vis* what your competitors have available. Properly marketing a cost benefit should give you a market advantage.

- Can you offer a regular maintenance or oversight program that will preserve or enhance client benefits and give you regular entré into their lives?

Once your clients have benefits, it makes sense to stay in regular touch with them to maintain them.

- Can you offer an introductory rate for your benefit?

People who haven't used your service are probably skeptical about you and what you can do for them. Make it easy for them to take action to get in touch and make an agreement with you.

- Can you offer 100% client satisfaction?

If the client isn't happy, will you keep working until he is?

- Can you offer your service in other countries?

Aren't there people abroad who can benefit from what you've got?

- Can you offer your service in such a way that each person who uses it will always have your name, address and phone number along with it?

This way he can always get in touch with you . . . or can easily refer you to others when he talks about or recommends what you've done for him.

- Can you train others to offer your service so you can deal with still more people?

Must you do everything yourself?

I could go on, but I think you get the idea.

Don't just rush over these questions, either. Read them again. In these questions — and the others that will occur to you as you constantly review the operations of other service businesses — you'll get the inspiration you need to use choice as a means of assisting you to become a millionaire.

Note what I say about reviewing the operations of other service businesses. Don't be so daft as to contemplate the question of choice by yourself. Start looking at the ways other service businesses deliver their benefits. Obviously, you'll pay closest attention to competitors. But don't overlook the rest.

All service business sellers confront one crucial problem: how to generate maximum customer dollars in the shortest period of time for the least amount of work and aggravation. Millions and millions of service sellers confront this problem daily. Thus, it's inevitable that some should come up with means that will be useful to you.

Sadly, most service sellers have created businesses that are designed for their own comfort and life style, not their clients'. This is absurd. Until you have made the amount of money you want, you are necessarily at the beck and call of your customers. Their choices are everything . . . your own are frankly insignificant. That's why you must work hard and long . . . must study other service sellers . . . and must continually contemplate the issue of choice.

Now commit!

☐ I understand that providing my clients and prospects with maximum choice about how they can get my benefits is to my interest. I promise to study what both my competitors and other service businesses generally are doing to accommodate their customers, and so get more business. Until such time as I have realized my financial objectives — when I can afford to do things my own way and no other — I shall stay focused on customer choice and accommodation.

Avoidable Error #7
You Are Technically Ill-Equipped By Not Understanding Your Business And How Money Can Be Made From It

Ever go into a store and ask an employee if they have a certain thing or know where it is? More often than not they cast a lackadaisical eye at you and tell you they don't know; nothing in their body language or attitude indicates they'll bother to find out, either. Infuriating isn't it? "Why don't they know their business?", we wail.

Many well-meaning service sellers have a related problem that is hurting them even more, however. They don't understand how money is made from their business.

At this point I must remind you of something you must never forget: the point of working is *not* to work . . . but to make sufficient money to gain financial independence. No other objective makes sense, and any one who offers any other is terminally stupid. Certainly, you should like what you do . . . equally you should have fun at it . . . but you should never forget that the purpose of work . . . until such time as you have achieved financial independence . . . is and can only be the achievement of financial independence. This means studying the structure of your business and understanding how money can be made from it.

Years ago, promising young men (and much more rarely women) were apprenticed into a business in order to learn it. During that period they were expected to follow orders and, if they were smart, keep their eyes and ears open taking in useful information. Bit by bit they were given assignments of increasing responsibility in order to test them for greater responsibilities still. The bright and successful were advanced . . . the also-rans were left behind. Through this system, people came to know a business . . . and to understand where money was made in it.

Sadly, almost no service seller . . . and certainly none I've ever met . . . has ever gone through anything remotely like this. Indeed, many service sellers (particularly after the entrepreneurial explosion of the late 'seventies and 'eighties) came to their businesses with almost no business or financial savvy whatsoever. Most knew how to render their service (in which they'd had experience) but few knew how money was to be made in offering it. Incredible!

Each business in the world offers a means to get rich, often very rich indeed. Take a peek at any business, and you will find at its zenith a number of people who may be both personally wealthy and have command of significant amounts of capital. Under them are more people who are regularly using their businesses to generate significant amounts of money and are on their way to securing wealth, often indeed more wealth than people currently at the top of the profession. Further down there are the people who are merely getting by . . . or those who are failing to get by and are on the verge of dropping out. Often these numbers are very large, indeed.

If you are determined to end up among the wealthy, make your business the constant object of your study asking yourself one insistent question: how did the rich people in my service area get to be that way . . . and what can I learn to do like them to become rich myself? Here are steps you can follow:

- Join relevant trade associations. If for instance you want to know how financial planners get rich, you've got to consort with financial planners.

- Ask tough questions at meetings and lectures. It has astonished me for many years just how sophomoric most questions at meetings are. The questions you ask should all be
  of the "Where's the money in that activity?" variety.

- Introduce yourself to and befriend the purportedly richest
  people in your service specialty. All rich people know how
  they got to be rich; the unrich can only guess. Associate
  with people who have answers . . . and pay attention.

- Study each aspect of your business to see how others make
  money with it;

- If you can't see how money is to be made in an activity . . .
  or are failing to comprehend some important aspect of it
  . . . don't ponder the question secretly. Seek out those in
  your industry who may know the answers.

- Become an assiduous reader — and critic — of trade publications. Tell the editor what kinds of articles you want . . .
  and contact people who provide information you need and
  urge them to do more. Urge everyone to be as specific as
  possible about providing "how-to" details. It's amazing just
  how much pabulum most business publications dispense
  and just how tolerant of it the readers are. Don't accept
  this!

- Don't expect successful people to spill their guts out to you
  merely because you're a nice person. Really rich people are
  circumspect and often become increasingly quiet, private
  people as they get richer. Why not? They already have a
  system that works . . . and they have no obligation to share
  it. This means you've got to persist . . . and cannot take no
  for an answer. Remember, you need to know what worked
  for them . . . in case it will work for you!

- Get skeptical. When the subject is money, most people are
  liars.

It should go without saying — but probably doesn't — that you need
to subject *each* means used by others in your business to make money
to scrutiny. You might consider each a university-level subject needing
intense analysis and consideration. That is why the study of how to
make money is a life-time's work . . . not something you can do over
a glass of sherry in the evening. Will you do this . . . or will you be
like most service sellers who keep working but have no understanding
how the work connects to the vital question of making money? They

focus on *work* . . . you must focus on *money* and on the *process* in your business that produces it.

Now commit!

☐ I understand that the richest people offering my kind of service wouldn't be offering it unless they were making money from it. I promise to do everything that's necessary to truly understand how people in my business make money and how they use their businesses to get rich. I understand that this is not a subject that can be investigated in a day, a month, even a year . . . but needs my continual focus throughout the time I'm in business. I shall never rest until I know how each aspect of my business produces money.

Avoidable Error #8
You Are Technically Ill-Equipped Because You Lack Necessary Marketing Skills And Attributes

As you're beginning to discover, there's lots of work to becoming a multi-millionaire selling services. You can do this work a lot better, however, if you've got certain technical skills and attributes that'll assist you in your marketing. The skills include:

- researching
- planning
- focused listening
- client-centered speaking
- client-centered writing
- organization and follow up.

The attributes include:

- persistence
- having a thick skin
- cheerfulness and good humor.

Here are some words about each.

— Researching

Service sellers succeed because they become masters of finding and using pertinent information. You can never know everything you need to make a success of your business . . . but you can always know where to find just what you need.

Resource

Use *Finding Facts Fast* by Alden Todd (Ten Speed Press). I've recommended this handy little resource in many of my books. It remains the best short work on finding information when you need it. (Like many of my recommendations, this one is available through The Sure-Fire Business Success Catalog that ends this book.)

— Planning

Millionaire status doesn't just happen. It's planned for and achieved by conscious effort. All service selling millionaires are necessarily superb planners. Each recognizes he has limited resources — including time and money — and wants to make the best of them. This is where planning comes in.

Resource

For my money, the best business-planning guide on the market is still *The Business Planning Guide: Creating A Plan For Success In Your Own Business* by David H. (Andy) Bangs, Jr. 143 pages, you can get your copy from Upstart Publishing, 12 Portland Ave. , Dover, NH 03820 (603) 749-5071.

— Focused Listening

Face it: you're not getting any smarter when you're talking. For that you need to master the art of listening. Because listening is something we have all been doing since we were born, we tend to undervalue it, to think we're already experts at it. Nothing could be further from the truth.

I've been playing a game for years now with people I've just met. About 10 minutes after I meet them . . . after they've had a chance to tell me a little bit about themselves, I ask if they'd like to hear 10 significant things I've learned about them. I then reel off 10 insightful comments about who they are, where they've come from, what their expectations are in life, problems they face, even how they feel about themselves right now. People are absolutely astonished and constantly sputter, "How do you know so much about me? " Some even conjure the devil to explain my ability to "read" them so well.

The truth is, I merely listen to what they say . . . and make certain intelligent deductions, à la Mr. Sherlock Holmes, based on their clothes, word choice, *etc.* It's an art to be sure . . . but one easily learned because it's so helpful in establishing you as client-centered. Unfortunately, most people don't have the skills to master it, which is why when I ask them to tell me 10 things about myself, most people say perhaps one or two and then say "But we've just met . . . . how do you expect me to know anything?" How, indeed, when they've not mastered the arts of concentration . . . and focused listening.

Is this so very difficult? Not at all. Your prospects and clients will be telling you, right from the first moment they contact you, exactly what they want to achieve. Moreover, they'll be throwing off plenty of clues about how they want you to help them and about their own situations. All you have to do is pay attention. Moreover, each client has what I call "The Major Message" . . . this is the thing of most importance that the client wishes to achieve and which constitutes his major reason for approaching you at this time.

By listening to the prospect . . . by considering his word choice, way of presenting the information, even his general manner of delivery, you'll get a significant look into what kind of person he is and what he wants from you. Just listen! Silence, you see, really is golden.

Resource

Just because you "listen" all the time, doesn't mean you're good at it. That's why you should get "High Performance Listening" by Dr. Rick Bommelje. This set of audio cassettes comes with a helpful manual of tips that will make you a better listener. Contact him at Organizational Training Specialists, 8889 Butternut Blvd., Orlando, FL 32817 (407) 679-7280.

— Client-Centered Speaking

I have a friend who sells a very useful computer service, and I'm thinking of him as I write this section. He's a man who came from poor antecedents; his education probably stopped at high school, and while he's technically adept and helpful, he's never made any attempt to raise his speaking skills. Accordingly, he speaks far too rapidly . . . and laces his language with the kind of locker-room smut that one gratefully left behind in the 12th grade. The immutably middle-class people to whom I've referred him have all found him hard to tolerate thanks to this problem. What a pity!

Speech immediately defines us. It tells others — beyond the power of the words themselves — of our education, social class, and professional achievements. Rightly or wrongly, as Professor Higgins once tried to explain to Colonel Pickering, we are defined by our speech. It also tells people whether you are focused on who they need you to be. Locker room smut may be acceptable in, well, locker rooms, but it definitely doesn't work with professionals who are hiring a computer specialist to solve their technical problems.

The success of your service business rests in part on your ability to master the essentials of clear, precise communication, including the necessary ability to inform people precisely what you can do to improve their situations and precisely how you'll be doing it.

Listen to most service sellers. They don't have the ability to:

- marshal information

- arrange it in order of interest to the listener

- present it succinctly and precisely

- rearrange the information based on what the prospect says.

One of my friends, who sells a particular service, exemplifies this problem. We have many dealings and often these involve costly projects with intricate specifications and tight deadlines. Not surprisingly, as the man paying the bill for these projects, I want to be kept informed about precisely what's happening with them and, where there are problems, exactly how matters stand and what is being done to rectify the situation. I am the client, so you'd think my wishes might prevail.

Think again.

Each time my colleague calls, he begins by asking how I am, then launches into what can only be described as an historical monologue about everything that has taken place in relation to the project since we last talked, leading up step by step to what's happening now. In due course, as I wait impatiently, he arrives at the information I want to know.

This is terrible communication, principally because it forces the client to wait to hear what's important. I have to listen to a heap of garbage of no earthly interest until such time as I either 1) get so frustrated I have to cut in and ask for the real message (thereby making me seem rude), or 2) sit back and wait impatiently for the man to get to the point.

If I didn't get many other benefits from this person, I tell you in all seriousness I'd kill him. But if he were a more resolutely client-centered individual, he'd do what was necessary to switch over from "and then . . . and then" communication . . . to "here's what you want to hear" communication. In short, he'd become more client-centered with how he uses speech.

Resource

There are many resources on speaking better. Of these, I still like two books by Joan Detz. While neither deals precisely with how to speak to clients, both have helpful information that can easily be applied in this kind of situation. They are *How To Write And Give A Speech* and *Can You Say A Few Words?* (Both are published by St. Martin's Press.) Claudyne Wilder's book *The Presentations Kit: 10 Steps For Selling Your Ideas* will also assist you. (John Wiley & Sons is the publisher.)

—Client-Centered Writing

The same is true, of course, with writing. Your progression to millionaire status will be faster if you learn to write clear, immediately understandable prose — the kind of prose most seller sellers can only currently imagine.

Writing this kind of prose is not, after all, so very difficult, if you consider the person you are writing to. What does he want from you? Once you know, you should ask yourself to what extent you can provide it.

- If you are giving him everything he wants, begin the communication by saying so.

- If you are only able to provide part of what he wants, begin the communication by saying what you can provide . . . only then following with what you cannot . . . and why not. If under certain circumstances (which do not currently prevail) you could provide what he wants, say what those are.

- If you are not able to provide what the person wants, again say why and again say what could get you to change. Indicate that you want to work together and express regret that circumstances prevent you from doing so now. End in a friendly fashion and again express your hope that you can work something out.

Consider how different these suggestions are from a letter I've just received from a sales representative from a competing card deck. I've previously had some problems with this company failing to live up to its agreements, and I let them know in no uncertain terms I didn't appreciate it. But I also said that I was willing to work things out (under certain conditions) and keep working together for our mutual benefit; in short, despite problems, I kept the door open.

For months I heard nothing. Then one day their sales rep, obviously needing some cards in her next issue, called to apologize and say she hoped we could work together. I offered conditions which were mutually beneficial and asked her to think it over and get back to me. She did . . . in a crisp, cold letter that simply said she talked the possibilities over with the publisher who had rejected everything. And that was that.

However, as I pointed out in my response, that wasn't that. Even though the publisher had rejected things for now . . . I realized that "now" wasn't "always" and that things would change — and the publisher's mind along with it. I asked the sales rep to call me back when this had occurred — in other words, I *still* kept the door open instead of needlessly closing it.

Writing is a marvelous thing. Unlike speech (except for all but the very best) writing offers the possibility of total control over what you offer. Even when you're enraged, you can present yourself, thanks to the marvel of editing, as calm, rational, entirely in control, and still *client-centered*.

— Organization And Follow-Up

When was the last time this happened to you: you want to purchase some service and call for further information. The person at the other end is busy and says she'll call you back. And that's the last you hear of it. How do you feel about that company? What can you deduce about their level of organization and client-centeredness?

I think, for instance, of a fellow called George Van Valkenburg in San Diego. Every time I call him, he swears he'll call me back "in ten minutes." Yet to this day, he's never returned a single phone call of mine despite the fact that it is in our mutual interest.

Finally, I wrote to the man and told him in all candor what I thought of his juvenile habits. Predictably, he didn't respond . . .

We all know people like this . . . and the sad thing is many of them run service businesses.

As I'll discuss later, with the cost effective computerization of even the smallest home-based office, there is absolutely no reason for any service business to be disorganized or fail to operate with strict follow-up procedures.

Every business should have a computer file for:

- prospects
- customers
- lapsed customers.

And a means of accessing current information about each group.

I, for instance, have a file with the name of each person who's inquired about using my services as a workshop leader or lecturer, the date he inquired, the information that was sent, the person (along with address and phone number) who may have referred me, and a listing of all subsequent contacts. Do you have as much on the prospects inquiring about your services? I wonder.

The other day I was listening to Medical Editor Dr. Timothy Johnson on the "Good Morning, America" program. He was discussing the issue of breast implants and how there is no national register of those who had the surgery and what happened to them. Thus women who are considering whether to have the surgery or not are forced to make a crucial decision on the basis of inadequate information. Who's to blame for this situation? I'd like to nominate the supposedly client-centered physicians who perform the surgery (and like the fees), but who can't be bothered to keep the necessary records. You be different!

Being organized and following up efficiently make sense either when you can provide the client with what he wants . . . or when you can not. While your clients want what you've got for them as quickly as you can provide it . . . they'll be impressed (and not hold grudges) when you inform them about why you can't meet a deadline. Face it: everybody's failed to meet a deadline in his life. You're no different. What needs to be different is how you handle the situation.

Attributes

— *Persistence*

We all know that "quitters never prosper" but what nobody ever explained was how enervating, if necessary, persistence is to success.

At the first function I attended at Harvard, the Chairman of the History Department, the eminent (if rather ludicrous) scholar H. Stuart Hughes told us that we were the "best and the brightest." It was the first time I'd heard the phrase, and I was, in the classic Harvard tradition, entirely prepared to believe him. Essentially this man of privilege and precious little experience told us that the kingdoms of the world would not only be available to us . . . but would beg us on bended knee to take them over. It was, to put it mildly, a wildly inaccurate assessment of events . . . and as such I was wildly unprepared to face reality . . . much less the reality of transforming oneself from the mind-set of a crown prince to that of a service seller with no idea whatsoever how to become a millionaire.

Persistence — and the ability to turn every situation (no matter how unpromising) to profit — was what made the difference.

Although still well on the sunny side of fifty, I am now reckoned the Grand Old Man of my profession; it sometimes amuses me the amount of deference I get as a result. But I reckon this deference is the coin the less successful pay to my persistence, for if I have achieved any eminence whatsoever it's entirely because I have refused to accept anything other than the eminence which they now say I have.

You be the same way.

It is fatuous to think you know everything you need to know now . . .

It is fatuous to think you will not make mistakes along the way . . .

It is fatuous to think that you will turn every opportunity into profit . . .

It is fatuous to think that you will never make a mistake, much less a costly one . . .

It is fatuous to think that you will get the highest rate of return from all your activities . . . and from every dollar you invest . . .

But I'll tell you something: YOU CAN MAKE EVERY SINGLE ONE OF THESE MISTAKES AND STILL BECOME A MULTI-MILLIONAIRE. And I'm here to confirm it.

. . . So long as you persist and refuse to accept anything less than the goal you crave.

— Having A Thick Skin

I have something of the utmost seriousness to tell those of you who believe the world is a rational place in control of a benevolent intelligence: GET OVER IT.

In embarking on the journey to millionaire status as a service seller, you have begun a task of unending challenge. Towards this end you will necessarily encounter many people. Most of these people have no particular reason to believe you, certainly not to help you. And they will act accordingly.

You will encounter people of gross manners, vulgarity, limited education, laughable ideas; people who specialize in condescension and power plays, physical, verbal, and even sexual abuse; people of the laxest morals, and those with no morals at all; people whose good intentions cause astonishing problems, and those who cause astonishing problems from the complete lack of good intentions. You will encounter thieves, hypocrites, liars, perverts, religious zealots, bigots, the infuriatingly stupid, and the merely bumbling. Through this maze you must pilot your enterprise with diligence, craft, shrewdness, vitality, efficiency, intelligence and, yes, with grace.

For the achievement of this almost god-like objective, it will help if you cultivate several new layers of protection . . . developing the thickest of skins.

I, for one, was born with only one layer of epidermal protection . . . and it has taken years to build up several more. It is with special pleading, therefore, that I urge you to ask yourself at all times whether, in confronting one of the innumerable variety of oafs and inadequates whom you will come across, whether they have really affected your vital interests . . . or just your pride. For the former, there are lawyers. For the latter, you merely need thicker skin.

As I get older, I despair at just how much time people spend in defense of their pride. Don't you be one of them. Resolve to do business with the devil himself, if you can thereby advance your interests. I am neither asking you to become the devil, nor his disciple; I am simply saying stay focused on the achievement of your objective and keep doing whatever is necessary to thicken your skin until such time as even the most callous of remarks and circumstances can occur without causing you to wince, much less waver. Then you are truly the master of your fate.

— *Cheerfulness And Good Humor*

No section on the necessary technical skills and attributes for achieving success as a service seller could possibly be complete without a reference to these two attributes. They are crucial . . . and eminently related to the point above.

Personally, I have always taken things far too seriously. Believing in the perfectibility of man, I have been constantly exercised by evidence of his present corruption, particularly when evidence has been pointed at me. I have therefore made it my particular study to be of good cheer.

This is easy to do, of course, when things are going well. When funds are plentiful and clients happy, keeping your good humor's no trick. And that's why I'll say nothing about this situation. However, when things are bleaker, or altogether grim, that's another matter.

For such an eventuality, I suggest you put away right now something to cheer you up. The last Tsar of all the Russias kept in his desk drawer slips with favorite boyhood jokes he had shared with a long-dead brother. These lightened the tensest moments. Norman Cousins, when he thought he was dying, found relief in The Marx Brothers. Personally, I keep a case of champagne on hand and a shelf of well-thumbed books. Moet Chandon and *War And Peace* induce calmness and the possibility, at least, of optimism.

You must find your own talismans. And you must use them.

Good humor, you see, is a prop. It can get you through a bad situation; it can help pull you out of a worse one. It is therefore a necessary instrument in your millionaire's tool-kit.

A few months ago I was giving a lecture in Chicago to the National Nurses in Business Association. The audience was full of hundreds of bright-eyed and bushy-tailed nurses, mostly women, who were building an exciting variety of entrepreneurial ventures. I was very glad to be there . . . and the day was exhilarating for all of us . . . all of us that is but one sour-faced Michigan woman who came in a severe black outfit that did nothing to soften a visage of bitterness and misanthropy. A sixty-ish massage therapist, she found her practice dying from lack of repeat business. The most cursory look at her told why: she had lost the gift of cheer and humor.

She seethed through my presentation and the joy of the others made her even angrier. At last she got up to ask an absurd question about why the prices on the back of my books were not the same as the prices in the catalog in the books. She accused me of trying to rip people off. I explained that the price on the back was the price bookstores used and that the price inside included shipping, but she was unsatisfied.

Her anger, of course, had nothing whatever to do with book prices . . . and everything to do with a twisted life gone astray. I pitied this woman from the depths of my soul . . . and at the next break I specifically sought her out to give her some additional assistance. However, she told me she didn't want to talk to me (though she stayed the rest of the day) and wouldn't shake hands. Later she wrote a message to the organizers of the meeting telling them she didn't want me to get her address and that she didn't want to get anything from me beyond the book she was just ordering!

With that book I sent her a note containing a few home truths. I told her to:

- get a hair-style that was friendlier, less austere;
- never wear black again unless she wore a sparkling diamond with it;
- smile occasionally;
- never refuse to shake hands with someone who means her well, and
- buy herself a good joke book and read it until the tears rolled down her cheeks . . . at which time she should call a few client prospects and invite them to stop by for something that would do them some good, too.

Needless to say this poor woman never responded to my letter. She undoubtedly found it cheeky and impertinent, though I was in deadly (if witty) earnest. A person without a smile in his repertoire, without a cheerful word at the ready, is a person who cannot possibly make a success of a service business, despite all the technical dexterity in the world.

If you meet my dour massage therapist from Michigan remind her of this. And never forget it yourself.

Now Commit!

☐ I realize that if I don't possess certain technical skills and attributes, I will make the achievement of my aspiration more difficult, perhaps even impossible. Therefore, I promise to take the time to develop the necessary technical skills of researching, planning, focused listening, client-centered speaking, client-centered writing, and organization and follow up. I also promise to cultivate the attributes of persistence, having a thick skin, and cheerfulness and good humor.

Avoidable Error #9
You Haven't Gathered A Complete Understanding Of Your Market(s)

Would you set out on an important journey without knowing where you were going? Well, running a service business without knowing whether there are sufficient numbers of people to support it and without knowing the means of connecting with them is just as stupid. Yet it happens all the time.

I was recently asked to review a marketing letter from a fellow in Los Angeles who has a consultation service helping would-be boppers get recording contracts. Sensible? You be the judge. To determine if such a business makes sense you'd need answers to questions like:

- How many such people are there?
- Where are they located?
- Is this number growing or not?
- Do prospects have the means to pay for such consultation?
- Can he sell them other products/services?
- And, importantly, how can this fellow connect with them on a cost-efficient basis so that, at the end of the day, he has a profit?

Sadly, instead of answering these and related questions, the service seller in question had given way to enthusiasm, had decided there were so many prospects in the land that research about them was superfluous and had rushed to draft a marketing letter — at which time he called me in to advise him on its content.

Predictably, I was appalled by his judgment and activities. Market research, you see, must *always* precede copy content. Yet how often it does not . . . how often, as in this case, there is no market research at all!

I want to be very blunt with you: untempered enthusiasm has killed any number of businesses, and it could kill yours, too. What you need, instead, is hard-headed factual analysis.

This analysis has two major subsets:

1. who else is approaching these prospects (competitors), what are they doing and how are they making (or not making) money, and

2. what is the current state of the designated market(s) and what is their state projected to be in one year? Five years?

#1 I shall be addressing shortly. I want to address #2 now.

The best way to consider a market is to think of it as a body of people who can, properly approached and handled, provide you with your multi-million dollar fortune. The only reason you have selected this body of people — as opposed to another — is you've decided, after detailed research and analysis, that by offering them your benefits you are assured not merely of a living wage but of the continual superfluity from whence you develop capital. That is, you are not approaching them merely because you have benefits to offer . . . but because you have benefits *and* your prospects exist in sufficient numbers with sufficient resources that, given a competent marketing program, your success is assured. To determine if this is the case, you must research your market(s) along the lines suggested by the questions the consultant above did not ask. The key things you need to know are:

- Is the number of my prospects constant or growing? How do I know?

- Can I get easy and sustained access to my prospects? How do I know?

- Will the cost of this access destroy the prospect of profit? How do I know?

- Can my prospects afford the cost of what I'm offering them? How do I know?

- Can I derive extra income from my prospects by offering

additional, complementary services/products? How do I know?

- Can I derive extra income by renting my mailing list? How do I know?

- Can I cut my marketing costs by using free media to attract my buyers? How do I know?

You probably wonder why I end each question with the additional query "How do I know?" Some of my critics get irked with this kind of Lantian repetitiveness. However, I understand how easy it is to be taken with the prospect of riches and to lose sight of just how hard-headed one must be before committing a penny. I don't want you to rush ahead too quickly without really thinking through why you suppose your service will make money. Although figures differ, the fact remains that the vast majority of all new businesses — including all service businesses — still fail to make money. More concentration on research and analysis at this early stage of development would substantially cut this number, thereby increasing the number of business people making money.

Now commit!

☐ I understand that research and analysis of my projected market(s) is a necessary precondition of profit. Even though I may not like this stage of development much, I pledge to gather the necessary information about my markets until I am *absolutely* sure there are enough prospects, properly disposed, easily reached on a continuing basis, to ensure my profitability.

Avoidable Error #10
You Haven't Studied Your Competitors

Many people dislike their competitors as a matter of principle. I'm not one of them. Properly understood, your competitors are best understood as people who are working to provide you with crucial information about your market. Your job, therefore, is to study them and their operations, to find out what works and what doesn't, and, after analyzing this information, to move to out position them.

Let's take my Sales & Marketing Success Card Deck, for instance. Before launching this deck, I hired a researcher to gather crucial information about my putative competitors and about the card-deck industry in general. I wanted to know:

- how many different competitors there were in my target market;

- what they charged advertisers for card space;

- how many cards there were on average in each competitor's deck;

- what actual production costs were to print and distribute the cards (including lay-out, printing and postage);

- how my competitors handled prospect identification and closing.

Only by scrutinizing this kind of information could I deduce the following:

- were my competitors vulnerable in any way, or had they cornered the market;

- where could price savings be effected that might make my deck more profitable;

- how could I position my deck so that it was an obviously superior value to my competitors and hence likely, in the face of a recession in the advertising industry, to prosper?

In this case, research clearly demonstrated that:

- advertiser prices in the industry were significantly inflated and hence my competitors were vulnerable;

- actual costs (including the two major variables of list rental and printing) could be significantly lowered by the implementation of certain tactics, and

- therefore prices could be significantly lowered, thereby providing my nascent deck with a major competitive advantage.

Net result? Despite a major recession and a war, my Sales & Marketing Success Deck within 18 months became the nation's second largest deck in size, not merely competing with but generally beating in size and quality "major" competitors with many more years of experience. Yes, I am a believer in competitor market research . . . and you should be, too.

Now commit!

☐ I shall not let my enthusiasm about my service offering get the better of me! Instead of getting carried away by all the money I'm sure to make . . . I promise to spend the necessary time, even if burdensome, in getting all the information I need about my competitors . . . so I can out position them and ensure that my service is better value than theirs and hence easier to market.

Avoidable Error #11
Approaching Your Market(s) Before You Really Understand What Prospects Want

There are only two crucial parts to marketing: preparation and execution. Of these preparation is arguably the more important . . . and it is the aspect that far too many exuberant service sellers skip in their haste to make contact with the prospects, the people they are SURE are going to make them RICH!

Whoa!!!

If you're going to succeed as a service seller, you must first understand, really understand your market(s). You must know what they want to achieve . . . and what they are frightened of or anxious about. Successful marketing, you see, is built on your mastering and using one or both of these necessary client-centered props: hope for gain . . . or fear of loss. Of these, fear of loss, as marketing studies have confirmed often enough, is by far the stronger. However, you need to consider both.

Thus, before you even THINK of approaching any of your prospects, you need to open up two files. Let's call them HOPE and FEAR. Both are about your prospects. Into each file, which you can keep both in hard copy and on computer, you should enter *everything* that pertains to your prospects. And, believe me, everything about your prospects can easily be sorted into one or both of these files.

While you may initially simply append the data, at some point you've got to go back and arrange the data so that they're more useful for marketing purposes. Each entry should begin either "You hope. . . ." or "You fear . . .", the "you", of course, being the prospect.

Let me explain very clearly what's happening here.

In today's *Boston Globe* (January 10, 1992) there is an article about the failing presidential candidacy of Nebraska Senator Bob Kerrey, a candidacy which began with so much promise. Says commentator Steven Stark, "The biggest disappointment in the field so far, the occasionally charismatic Kerrey has had a hard time talking about anything but himself. This campaign, like John Glenn's in '84, is all resumé: *his* hospital stay, *his* Vietnam experience, *his* businesses. Kerrey doesn't seem to understand that elections aren't about candidates; they're about the country." Remember, I am writing this section *before* the New Hampshire primary . . . yet I think Stark's analysis about the unlikeliness of a Kerrey nomination is accurate.

What Stark is talking about, of course, is that Kerrey doesn't understand that presidential campaigns (which are just a specialized marketing activity) are about people (unfortunately Stark uses the rather weaker word "country"). And that this means concentrating on *their* hopes and fears. Kerrey, like all unsuccessful marketers, merely says ME, ME, ME. . . . which may be okay for opera singers . . . but is certain death for would-be millionaires (and presidential candidates.)

Don't make this mistake.

Note: As events turned out, the Kerrey candidacy never did get off the ground. Right until the end he never got a client-centered message . . . indeed, couldn't even figure out that one was necessary. That and his irritatingly dour countenance killed a candidacy which started with so much promise. Learn, reader, learn!

Understand that there are only two people in each marketing equation . . . there is li'l ol' you . . . and there is the all-important prospect, *who is everything*. Yes, *everything*, for the prospect isn't just important; *he is all important*.

I said this recently in a speech to a group of several hundred well-heeled commercial realtors who practice through Oncor International. "Only the prospect matters. You don't." Having said this, I saw consternation . . . disgust . . . anger . . . even hatred . . . on their all too often over-fed and smugly self-satisfied faces.

Why this eruption of rage?

Because I was telling these panjandrums of real estate that they were *never* going to be as important as their prospects; that their prospects would *always* be more important than they . . . because it was only through satisfying the prospect that they could achieve their own desires. Sounds obvious, no?

Yet these spoiled darlings, the tassel loafered residue of the 'eighties, were deeply affronted by this client-centered message. "Not important," they sputtered . . . Why if that were true, why are we so rich?" Easy.

Woody Allen once said that just showing up is 9/10's of success. The people in the opulent lecture theater in San Diego merely showed up to the 'eighties, the biggest feeding frenzy of the century. Credit was easy; commercial real estate boomed; even a trained sea l could have lazed into prosperity in that trough. Yet some dared call their prosperity a matter of intellect . . . or even moral superiority! Absurb!

The 'nineties, I warned, would be different. Now client-centered marketing . . . marketing that focused on prospect wants . . . and prospect fears . . . would be crucial. Not marketing based on the pretensions of a bunch of egotistical, aging wunderkinds. No, they didn't like hearing this one bit.

In an age of scarce resources, so well exemplified by these days, the egotists who don't understand "you want . . ." and "you fear . . .", who do not research their markets and cater to them are as obsolete as dinosaurs . . . and much less interesting.

Now commit!

☐ Research — and proper logging and arrangement of the information — about prospect wants and fears must precede any contact with these prospects. I shall not rush ahead to try to attempt to motivate people to buy what I'm selling until such time as I can say, without fear of contradiction, that I understand, truly understand, just what they want . . . and just what they fear. Only then will I proceed
. . because only then will I know that I'm going in the right direction.

Avoidable Error #12
You Don't Know The Difference Between Features And Benefits . . . And Wrongly Focus On The Features!

Every marketing book in existence talks about features and benefits and recommends focusing on the benefits. But most service sellers still don't know the difference and almost always end up focusing on the wrong thing, the features. Consider this example from the 1992 "Best of America" conference brochure which was sent to over 300,000 trainers whom they wanted to attend their annual convention:

"Embedding Customer Service Into Your Organizational Culture" by Dana Robinson, President, Partners in Change, Inc.

Determine whether your organization is ready for real customer service. Discuss what is usually done to institute customer service and why it doesn't work. Learn a proven process for mapping a service cycle so it can be improved to meet customer needs . . . Ms. Robinson is recognized for her diagnostic skills and ability to design and implement front-end assessments for organizations that want to enhance human performance . . ."

Need I say this is terrible feature-ridden prose, the errors compounded by the me-centered information about "Ms. Robinson"? Let's take a look . . .

To begin with, you've got to understand the difference between features and benefits. An easy way of differentiating them is to remember that there are always only two parties to any marketing transaction: the person with the benefit and the person wanting the benefit.

Features are best understood as aspects of what is being offered, aspects which focus on the person *with* the benefit. Thus: "Ms. Robinson is recognized for her diagnostic skills. . . ." This is about the marketer . . . not the all-important prospect.

Benefits, on the other hand, always focus on — and are of value to — the person *wanting* what is being offered. All good marketing documents always present their content so that it's exclusively focused on this person.

Another way of understanding features and benefits is to remember that *all* features can be rendered with the words "I have . . ." and *all* corresponding benefits with the words "You get. . . ."

Now, from the perspective of the all-important prospect/client, what do you think he's more interested in: what *you* have . . . or what *he* gets? Put this way it's obvious, isn't it? He cares — and will always care — about what he gets; never about what you have. That's why benefits will always be more important than features.

Now let's return to our execrable — and all too typical — example.

Take the headline/title of the workshop (and, remember, a workshop *is* a service offering). Does it offer a feature . . . or a benefit? If you're thinking feature, you're right. *Customer service*, you see, is a *feature*. It's what an organization offers (has) . . . not what a customer wants (gets). Thus the title of this workshop is wrong, because it offers no benefit to those attending.

The reason why Ms. Robinson probably made this mistake in her title is because she didn't consider who was coming (or should come) to her workshop and what *they* wanted.

Face it: instituting a customer-service program is work. People, and especially contemporary American professionals, don't like work much. What Ms. Robinson is therefore asking her prospects to do is come to a session that's going to tell them how to work harder. But she's offering no carrot if they complete that work satisfactorily. Now she may know (but certainly doesn't say) that the carrot of customer service is organizational profit. Customers are more likely to buy again from an organization that handles them properly than one that doesn't. Hence the organization profits (or should . . . or there's no point to this exercise). But where does Ms. Robinson link the compelling concept of profit with the uncompelling notion of work? The answer is, she doesn't!

Even her word choices are infelicitous and in fact condescending. The word "embedding" in the title is remarkably poor diction. It's not a client-centered word and conjures up the notion of very difficult work indeed. A poor choice. And the words "why it doesn't work" are condescending to the audience. These, however, are minor problems compared to the fact that:

1. the service marketer has forgotten who her audience is and what they want;

2. doesn't tantalize and excite them with the possibilities of what they can get but only de-motivates them with all they have to do (and for what?), and

3. fails to understand that marketing is always about prospects . . . never about marketers.

All in all, Ms. Robinson (whose self-designation, by the way, makes her appear aloof and unfriendly) comes across as selfish, pedantic and pompous, without a benefit in her brief case. Now would *you* buy a "front end assessment" from such a person???

To further your understanding of the concept of benefits, consider the squirrels who live in the oak trees on the Cambridge Common across the street from where I'm writing you. I have enlisted these intelligent beasties as members of my Marketing Research Department. Their fee is fairly reasonable, consisting as it does of Jeffrey's favorite snack foods a little off their prime. Squirrels know the difference between features and benefits and will show you, too, for the price of a handful of potato chips.

Go to the foot of any oak tree on the Common and shout, "Squirrels, I have something in my pocket for you . . . something really good . . . something you're going to like a lot," and see what happens. To curtail the suspense, I'll tell you: nothing happens. Not one squirrel comes out, no matter how hungry it is. *Telling* them you have something appetizing for them just doesn't cut it . . . because telling them is a feature, not a benefit.

Then take the bag out of your pocket and shake it loudly. In a minute, a few fury heads pop out of the tree trunks. Spread a few crumbs on the ground, and they start moving cautiously down the limbs. Scatter a few big chips on the ground; they scurry to greet you.

Hold more in your hand and soon enough you're going to have a squirrel right beside you and a regular party surrounding you. You see, squirrels are a lot smarter than you think: they know that benefits motivate, not features and that the more tangible and believable these benefits are the faster they motivate. When are you going to be as smart as these "dumb" animals?

Now commit!

☐ I know that only other people can make me rich, and I know that these people can be better motivated by my transforming everything I do into a benefit, not merely presenting it as a feature and hoping for the best. I therefore promise to turn everything I do into a line beginning with "you get . . ." and to do everything I can to make these lines specific and believable. Once I truly know what my prospects can get if they take action, I need never worry about coming on too strong in offering it to them, for I'll KNOW they'll be better off with the benefits I have available than without them.

Avoidable Error #13
You Have Not Mastered The Necessary Elements Of Client-Centered Cash Copy

In my experience, service sellers constantly try to write their marketing communications (brochures, ads, letters, *etc.*) without being remotely ready to do so. It's the old "cart before the horse" thing. As a result, what they produce is usually lamentably inaccurate and only wastes their time and money. This, however, is entirely avoidable.

I've written an entire book about what I'm going to say here, and I advise you to study **CASH COPY** if you're really sincere about producing and distributing rigorously client-centered marketing materials that get people to act NOW . . . which is the *only* kind of marketing materials you should ever produce.

Cash-copy marketing communications are composed of certain indispensable building blocks. Before you begin to create the communications themselves, you've got to know what these crucial components are and how to fashion them. These blocks consist of:

- the benefits (in priority order) that constitute just what the prospect will get when he uses your service. To make life easier, each of these should begin with the words "you get . . ." (or equivalent).

- a timed offer that induces immediate action. If your benefits seem to be available forever, then there is no reason for prompt action by the prospect . . . and he will therefore turn his attention (and funds) to more pressing matters;

- a clear indication of what will happen to the prospect if he doesn't act now. Not only will benefits be lost . . . but adverse consequences will occur.

Complementary blocks consist of:

- testimonials. You should be accumulating the evidence of people — people like the prospects (*not* celebrities, unless these are prospects) who have profited from your service and are willing to say so — and how much;

- post scripts and envelope teasers. These both offer and reinforce the leading benefits you have available.

- biographical details. These details show the benefits you've been able to bring to other clients. They are about demonstrated results you've helped others achieve . . . not about where you've been. In other words, this is *not* a resumé; it's a list of client-centered successes you've been instrumental in helping others achieve.

Chances are you don't have any of these building blocks now. But you will . . . you will. Or you'll produce selfish marketing documents like one I just received from Virginia-based marketer Jeff Davidson. Davidson is the author of many marketing books and really ought to know better. As this marketing package shows he's become fixated on who he is and what he has available rather than on the prospect (in this case me) who can help him achieve his objectives.

The (form) letter I'm looking at is dated January 5, 1992 and begins with four sections: the first three (in the upper right hand corner) consist of 1) bibliographical details about his new book *Breathing Space*; 2) a list of book-jacket endorsers, and 3) media in which Davidson has recently been featured. These three sections are followed, on the left-hand margin, by Davidson's name, address and phone in large type. Indeed, these constitute the largest type on the page; (tells you something, doesn't it: "I'm Jeff Davidson. Here's where I live!!!").

The letter begins in this way: "It's no illusion, Mr. Lant . . .

> The pace of society has sped up. New buildings are erected in a month. Wars can be completed in weeks. Movies are deemed smash hits or duds after one week-end. Prescription glasses are ready in 60 minutes. Fax machines transmit pages in seconds."

By this time, I'm severely bored. "What," I wonder, "in the sam hill does all this palaver have to do with me?"

The truth is, I don't find out until the very last line: "Appreciating how busy you must be and respecting the environment, I've limited this package to concise information you can use to determine if *Breathing Space* will sell in your catalog." Oh, so at last we know what Davidson wants . . . *in the very last line.*

I'm going to tell you several things that I can deduce from this fourth-rate piece of work:

- Davidson is fixated on Davidson. He leads with himself, in gory detail; indeed, the first 1/3 of the page is entirely about him. This tells you something about the guy and his focus.

- He doesn't understand anything about catalog merchandise managers. We *are* busy people . . . we *do* get heaps of things to select from. But what makes us sit up and take notice is something we think we can make money from. We want the service seller's professional judgment about how well we can do and why he thinks this way. But, tellingly, Davidson never once mentions the word "money" or "profit" in his cover letter. What does this tell you about his degree of client-centeredness?

- He lays sanctimonious claim to "respecting the environment" . . . but wastes his printed page with stuff we all know ("the pace of society has sped-up") that connects to nothing. Some people might believe he's an enviro-zealot; I'm not one of them. I'd say he's just trying to hitch his wagon to the prevailing star.

Further Davidson, who ought to be ashamed of himself for producing this kind of garbage, makes every single one of the cash-copy errors I've enumerated above:

- there are no benefits to the prospect (people who run catalogs and want to make money from them);

- there's no timed offer to induce immediate action (indeed, after reading Davidson's windy, undirected prose, I have no idea what I'm supposed to do) and what I'll get if I do it right away;

- there's no indication what I'll lose if I don't take immediate action.

Further, there are neither envelope teasers nor client-centered post-scripts, and the biographical details are all resumé-oriented, that is about Davidson and not about what Davidson has done in the past to make real people achieve substantial and meaningful results. But, Glory Hallelujah!, we know he's been "featured in 'Your Personal Best'. . . ." Now isn't that just jim dandy!

I'm using Davidson as an example for two reasons: 1) to show you that even purported "marketing experts" (as he very much claims to be) can make the most elementary mistakes and 2) to give you a good illustration of what to *avoid*. And if, by chance, it induces Jeff to become client-centered, why that's just fine with me, too. It's about time this "marketing expert" started understanding the basics of marketing.

Now commit!

☐ I promise never to send another "me centered" marketing document so long as I live! I pledge to study the elements of cash-copy marketing and only to produce documents that rigidly focus on my *prospects*, never on myself! If any section, even a *line* in a document focuses on me, I'll know at once it is wrong and must be changed to be about my prospect and what he *wants* and *fears*. That's the only kind of marketing document I'll ever produce.

Avoidable Error #14
Your Marketing Communications Are Too Complicated; There Is Too Much Of The Wrong Thing

This point is related to the one above . . . only this one focuses on the marketing communications that service sellers create . . . and why so many of them are over-done and, hence, unsuccessful.

Recently I gave a program for service sellers in the Jacksonville, Florida area. As usual, I encouraged members of the audience to bring all their current marketing communications, including ads, cover letters, brochures, *etc.* And, as usual, my heart sank when I reviewed them, since these people were spending thousands and thousands of dollars creating marketing communications that generally missed the point.

Too many service sellers think the solution to their underpopulated client base is to be found in four-color printing, expensive inks and papers, and more, not fewer, pages of "stuff" they can rain down upon their hapless prospects.

If this is you, get over it!!!

First, let me share a little about my own operation with you. Around here, we err on the side of parsimony. I realize I can *always* spend money; that's not difficult. The trick is *not* spending money — and yet motivating the prospects and getting the clients anyway. I am therefore constantly working to see how *little*, rather than how much, I can put into the hands of prospects to get them to take action. I suggest you dedicate yourself to this philosophy, too.

One of the men in my Jacksonville audience thought differently. He sells a specialized service to physicians and carries to each a package consisting of *at least* 20 different brochures and medical studies. Just looking at it suggests lots and lots of work. Unfortunately, two critical aspects were missing from this package:

- the benefits the doctors/prospects get by using the service, and

- the immediate action the doctors should take to get these benefits.

Stupidly, the service seller makes doctors deduce these things for themselves. This is ridiculous!

When you begin to contemplate the question of what *form* your client-centered communications should take, remember that the content is always more important than that form and that whatever you do must highlight the benefits to the prospect . . . and clearly indicate the action you want him to take. These two aspects must be present *in whatever you do.*

The communications for all service businesses should be very, very simple and may include:

- the standard three-fold 8 1/2" x 11" brochure;

- an 8 1/2" x 11" fact sheet composed of the most frequently asked questions and your most client-centered answers;

- a cover letter to new prospects;

- a letter to prospects who haven't responded yet or whom you have not yet been able to contact;

- a letter to prospects who have recently bought one of your services, with inducements for buying something else;

- a letter to lapsed customers with reasons (that is, benefits) why they should return.

For most service businesses, this is quite enough to get started.

As I write this, I realize how angry my Jacksonville service seller would be with my recommendations. "But the physicians want all the medical studies I have," he'd mutter. "I just can't leave them out." Very well. But instead of simply dumping all this material on your audience, digest it for them. Either include significant findings in your brochure or tell people (either in your main three-fold brochure or Q & A brochure) that specific medical studies are available *upon request.* Contrary to what this fellow thinks, more is not necessarily better; all physicians do not want this material (at least until they are really seriously considering adding the service). Moreover, it's very expensive to provide it to prospects who are not serious.

Personally, while I did produce a brochure the first year I was in business, I quickly came to see that you could accomplish most everything in a cover letter that you could do in a brochure and that a cover letter could be more easily tailored to the prospect's situation. Thus, for over 10 years I did without several of those marketing communications that other service sellers regard as mandatory, namely business cards, printed stationery, yellow pages advertising and brochures. Yet things went swimmingly notwithstanding. . . It wasn't until I established my card-deck, where there are more prospects than can conveniently be dealt with simply and quickly by letter, that I felt we needed a formal brochure. These days I have three: one each for the card-deck and electronic moving message display divisions of my company and for my workshop lead-generating program.

Now commit!

☐ I realize I can spend lots and lots of money creating marketing communications for and about my service. However, I also realize that the punch of these communications is in their content, not necessarily their form, and that "more" doesn't necessarily mean better. I therefore pledge, first, to spend time making the content of my communications rigorously client-centered and, second, to produce the simplest and fewest marketing communications.

Avoidable Error #15
You Don't Understand All The Marketing Alternatives Available To You . . . And Don't Attempt To Use The Least Expensive First

Barely a day goes by around here but some service seller contacts me for information about how I can create a direct mail campaign for him . . . only "money's tight, you know, Jeffrey." Hmmm. When are these people going to learn . . .

When you're new to business . . . or find yourself in the middle of a pronounced business downturn . . . money is always tight. That's when you've got to think long and hard about how to achieve your objectives by using as little of your money as possible.

Now, most service sellers have spent years getting an education in what they do . . . and more years working for others perfecting their skills before starting out on their own. By comparison, they may have spent only a few hours studying the subject of marketing, the crucial variable that can make them rich, or doom them to lives of frustration and sparseness. This just doesn't make any sense to me. Thus, the First Rule of Success as a service marketer is this: you've got to know as much as, if not more, about marketing than you do about providing your service. And the Second Rule: you should always explore (and profit from) the inexpensive alternatives before committing money to the expensive ones. Let's look at each of these.

Just as there are many ways to skin a cat, there are many ways to reach your prospects. These ways include, but are certainly not limited to:

- paid advertising (both print and electronic)
- paid direct mail
- free publicity
- no-cost-to-prospect workshops and seminars
- workshops and seminars prospects pay to attend
- package stuffer/insert programs
- lead generator programs
- networking.

The first thing you've got to do is commit yourself to knowing and understanding *all* these means of connecting with your prospects. Each is a perfectly valid marketing activity. The real question is: once you've created the most focused client-centered benefits (a necessary precondition for success), which alternative(s) constitutes the best vehicle for delivering these benefits (along with the motivational offer)? That is, which will produce the greatest number of qualified leads at the lowest possible cost?

The answer to these questions is not blowin' in the wind; it can be produced by rational analysis and experimentation. But first you must study.

What is staggering to me (though after all these years I should perhaps be inured to such stupidity) is just how little service marketers know about the marketing alternatives available to them. Instead, most seem stuck in a rut; they know about direct marketing, of course, and always tend to request assistance in this area first. Some have done workshops (mostly with poor results for reasons which will become apparent later) . . . and many episodically network.

Let me be very plain with you: all the while you are in business it is your task to master *all* the variables of marketing, to know what they are and to know how they work. You can know your service inside and out and still fail in business, because you fail to understand marketing alternatives and to determine the best ones for what you're offering . . . that is to say the least expensive that produce the desired results.

Once you know all the marketing alternatives that exist, it is your responsibility to see whether the least expensive of them will produce the desired results. The Lant rule is and always has been: explore the least expensive alternatives first; *only spend your money when absolutely necessary . . . and as little of it as possible!*

By following this rule and making sure all your marketing communications have the utmost in client-centered benefits, you will gain a considerable competitive advantage, particularly if you work at home and keep your expenses to the barest minimum, as I do.

Thus, ask yourself at every opportunity: can I reach the body of people I wish to reach for less money but with the same client-centered message?

Asking this question, which of these alternatives makes sense:

- swapping an article (with Resource Box including your address and phone number) in a professional newsletter for a targeted mailing list of prospects, or renting a mailing list from a list fulfillment service and creating and mailing a direct mail piece;

- going on a radio show to discuss means the audience (your client prospects) can use to achieve what they want (and providing them with your phone number so they can get in touch right away) . . . or buying a paid commercial on the same station to announce what you have available;

- making a deal with an organization that has your client prospects among its members and promoting a program through their newsletter . . . or putting on a free workshop for your client prospects and buying paid advertising in local newspapers to promote it;

- swapping 1000 of your flyers to be inserted into the outgoing packages/mail of an organization reaching similar prospects to yours in return for inserting 1000 of their flyers into your outgoing packages/mail . . . or buying an ad in a specialized newsletter or publication;

- inserting a letter full of client-centered benefits into all your outgoing mail . . . or paying for and sending a special letter to all your prospects with these benefits?

See where this is going?

Many, many service sellers think that being in business means spending money on expensive marketing alternatives. Perhaps they want to be big shots; some, I know, are insecure and need the ego-gratification of seeing their names on expensive marketing communications. I recall, for instance, a friend of mine with a computer consulting practice who went to a Boston bank and borrowed about $10,000. She sunk virtually all of this into one brochure that she sent to about 1000 client prospects. Each brochure, a mini work of art, cost about $8. Net result? She didn't get a single nibble . . . and within 6 months she was out of business, bankrupt. She was warned about doing this, but she's the kind of person who never listens to anyone . . . and the final result, if sad, was predictable. (By comparison, for $10,000 I can produce about 100,000 32-page newsprint catalogs packed with all kinds of client-centered messages. And, no, I don't think newsprint is "beneath" me, although people ask me about that all the time . . .)

There are only four things that matter in business, and they are inextricably related:

- getting your client-centered message to the people who want to hear about it;

- delivering client-centered benefits to the people who want them;

- cutting the cost of delivering this message to the barest minimum while producing the number of leads you need, and

- continually making a profit (and reinvesting a portion of it for the development of your long-term capital base).

Everything else is a mere technicality.

Now commit!

☐ I have spent years perfecting my ability to deliver my service . . . and now I realize I must spend as much time perfecting my ability to market it. Indeed, I promise to study marketing so long as I'm in business! Thus, I pledge to learn about all the means that exist to connect with my prospects and how they work. Further, I shall endeavor to learn everything I can about how to generate the number of prospects I need without spending all my money; indeed, I shall set as one of my objectives spending the least amount of money possible, using the least expensive marketing alternatives instead of more expensive ones, so long as I produce the number of leads and clients I need to meet my financial objectives.

Avoidable Error #16
You Have Not Developed A Detailed, Written Marketing Plan (Using Inexpensive Marketing Expedients Whenever Possible) For Generating The Number Of Prospects And Clients You Need

Over the last many years, I've been conducting an informal study of the service sellers taking my workshops and lecture programs, people requesting my marketing consulting assistance, and many of those buying my marketing books. "Do you," I want to know, "have a *written* marketing plan for generating the prospects and clients you need to meet your financial objectives?" Alarmingly, not even 1% of those queried has such a thing.

What are they thinking of?

How can service sellers, or any marketers for that matter, expect to achieve their objectives if they have not scrutinized the alternatives, selected the most apt, and written down a precise series of steps for achieving their objectives? All these people *say* they want to be a success. So why don't they take this sensible step which will help them achieve this result?

There are, I think, any number of reasons. Service sellers are:

- lazy. It takes time to think through what you're going to do to market (that is, build) your business; time and sustained thoughtfulness;

- procrastinators. There's always another fire to put out . . . and it's all too easy to put off necessary planning because of something that seems "urgent" today;

- averse to planning. Many service selling entrepreneurs are
  — or like to consider themselves — free spirits; planning
  seems to constrict them and as such holds no appeal;

- sure they have the plan in their head. It's amazing how
  many people seem to think that a few vague thoughts about
  marketing constitutes a marketing plan. The only plan that
  counts is the plan that's written.

- afraid a plan will reveal their inadequacies when they fail to
  achieve the written objectives. This is a really silly "reason."
  The first time you create a plan, you are very likely not to
  achieve the objectives. The first plan, no matter how well
  considered, is of necessity an experiment. You don't know
  precisely how well you're going to do; precisely how well
  things will turn out. How could you? But plans can be
  edited and the fact that yours certainly will be is no reason
  to abandon the benefits of the marketing planning process.

Thus if you insist on reaching your financial objectives, I foresee a
written marketing plan in your future.

Now let me say something about this written plan:

- It need not be elaborate.

Many people don't do a plan because they feel it has to be produced
on vellum with gold-tipped edges and presented in a royal presentation folder. This is nonsense.

Your plan can be produced on a personal computer and as such can
easily be written, produced, and, as necessary, edited. Moreover, it
can be quite short; two or three pages should be all you need for a
year's marketing plan.

- It needs to have precise financial objectives to be achieved.

These objectives are the reason you're working, and when you achieve
these objectives, remember, you achieve your overall goal.

- It must state the precise marketing vehicles you'll be using,
  when you'll be using them (dates and frequencies); the cost
  of using them and how many sales you need from each one
  to break even.

Remember, this means taking into account not merely the cost of the
activity but also the cost of responding to the prospects, including
materials and, where applicable, personnel.

Note: once you've written the various marketing alternatives you'll be using, look at them again: are you *sure* you can't find a less expensive option that'll produce the number of leads/sales you need?

- It needs to have a section where you can log responses from each activity and so determine what worked and what didn't.

This will force you to code all your marketing activities to determine what's working and/or inquire of prospects which alternative they've responded to. There's no way you can possibly remember all this information, and you absolutely must have it to determine what gets repeated, and what doesn't.

As you evaluate these results, don't hesitate to rework your plan accordingly. A plan is a necessary tool for your success; you need one, to be sure, but you need not be slavish to what doesn't work, or abandon the tool itself because some aspect of it isn't working well. Revise! Here's where a computer is invaluable.

Now commit!

☐ For whatever reason, I've failed to produce a marketing plan and now I know that that was pretty damn stupid. Henceforward, I shall end each year by scrutinizing the final marketing plan of the year before and using this as the basis for the marketing year to come. I shall make this plan concise and focused on which marketing activities work best for achieving my objectives, and I shall keep it in a state that's easy for me to get at, update and revise as necessary. Moreover, wherever possible I shall make sure that the marketing activities I use are the least expensive available; after all, my objective is to put money in my pocket, not money into my marketing budget!

Avoidable Error #17
You Don't Live By The Rule Of Seven

How many advertisements do you see in a single day, a week? Considering the ads on television and radio, in newspapers and magazines, the ones that come via the mail . . . and, these days, the ones that even pop up on your fax machine, you may be assailed by up to 7000 ads every single week. Most, of course, are not applicable to your situation; many are contradictory. Still, how many . . . even of those that interest you . . . do you get around the concentrating on? Responding to? A pretty paltry number, right?

Why then, do you think your prospects are any different? They spend their time ignoring ads . . . just like you do!!!

. . . which is why the Rule of Seven was born.

The Rule of Seven starts from the undeniable premise that the vast majority of people ignore the advertisements they see, even if these contain information, products and services that they want; that the only way for the advertiser to motivate prospects to action is for him to hammer home his client-centered benefits over and over again, at least 7 times in eighteen months, until even the dimmest prospect knows what he's got available.

There are several crucial parts to this formulation:

- the Rule of Seven implies that motivating people is not the result of a single act but the result of a conscious client-centered process carefully prepared and orchestrated;

- the advertiser must hone his client-centered benefits before attempting to motivate his prospects. It is the conjunction of client-centered benefits, with the right market(s) and a hammering home of these benefits that produces the results;

- the benefits must be brought to the attention of the *same* prospects at least 7 times in a defined amount of time before that prospect can reasonably be expected to know about them;

- the 7 "hits" must take place in a period of time not longer than 18 months;

- each "hit" must be accompanied by a limited offer which provides special reason for the prospect to act NOW.

Should any part of this sequence not be followed, the benefits of the Rule of Seven will be considerably diminished . . . and you'll be wasting some or all of your time and money.

This, however, is precisely what most service sellers do. Over the years I've noticed a curious phenomenon about service sellers. They seem to act as if their prospects were prisoners in a room without windows and doors, prisoners who were given nothing to do all day; who saw nothing and were starved of all information of any kind. For such people the service seller's message would not only be important, it would be the highlight of the prospect's day, perhaps his entire life. Of course he'd read it . . . study it . . . and respond to it, immediately.

Now, if our prospects were in such a situation, the receipt of our messages, no matter how self-centered, how badly written, how bereft of benefits and unfocused, would produce the desired result: the prospect would indeed read everything and would take immediate steps to establish contact, thereby enabling the service seller to make the sale.

But, of course, our prospects are most assuredly NOT in this isolated and neglected condition. Think of their lives. They are inundated with marketing messages . . . indeed, these messages arrive so frequently that most are screened out, or else there would be time for nothing else but considering marketing messages.

Of course, you ought to know this . . . for you are in the same situation. And because you are in the same situation, knowing how hard you work to screen out the distractions presented by other peoples' marketing messages, you should realize just how hard you're going to have to work to snag a neuron in the brains of your prospects.

. . . For this is precisely what you must do.

Right now, close your eyes and visualize the inner brain of your prospect. Note that there are a few empty neurons there. Now visualize your information . . . replete with motivational client-centered benefits . . . being stored inside those neurons so securely that the information will remain with the prospect forever.

Your job, you see, is not merely to bring your client-centered message to the prospect's attention . . . not even simply to get him to consider it and take action upon it. No, what you *really* want is to get into the prospect's brain with your message and have that message remain there, actively working, forever.

This is what the Rule of Seven can do for you.

Now commit!

☐ I've been guilty of episodic marketing. I've been sending my marketing communications without benefit of a plan and have been failing to target my designated prospect groups and to bring my client-centered message to their attention again and again and again, at least 7 times in 18 months, until I'm absolutely sure they know not only that I exist but know precisely what they can get from my service. Never again! From now on, I promise never to launch a marketing sequence unless I can and will continue it the right number of times; for only by continuing it the right number of times can I be certain my targeted prospects will understand how I can help them.

Avoidable Error #18
You Don't Keep Good Records Of The Results Your Marketing Produces . . . So You Don't Know What To Do Again (Because It Worked) . . . And What To Avoid (Because It Didn't)

I have alluded to this point before, but because of its importance I wanted to call your particular attention to it.

Once you start marketing, start record keeping. Why? Because if you don't, you're going to waste your money in unproductive ways. It's as simple as that. To make this work as easy as possible, do this:

- Set up a text file in your computer where *each* individual marketing activity is listed;

- List the kind of action that took place (*e.g.* "classified ad in local newspaper") and the date it took place;

- Make sure to keep a hard copy of any marketing communications that are involved in the activity (like a copy of the classified ad);

- Code each marketing document. A code could be something like "Department SG" or "Ask for Nancy." ("Nancy" being the code name for this particular activity.)

- If responses are being mailed in, be sure to count and log each day's responses as they arrive. (Keeping records this way will enable you to pinpoint peak days of response and plan accordingly in the future);

- If responses are being phoned in, make sure to brief anyone answering the phone to ask for the code. Asking for the code must become a regular part of answering the phone.

I'm sure that you, as the service seller, understand how important establishing this system is. It will clearly show you what works . . . and what doesn't. Unfortunately, people you have working for you may not be as quick on the uptake. Indeed, with one organization I was working for, the people who answered the phone found asking for the code information so bothersome that they simply stopped requesting it, until I got the owner to say that she'd dock their pay for each time they "forgot." That worked. Just how important this information was to the owner quickly became apparent.

Like so many service providers she had been brainwashed to believe that a yellow pages ad was absolutely necessary. Did these ads work? Did they make her any money? She hadn't the slightest idea, although she was spending over $40,000 a year on such ads!

I insisted that her business identify the source of every call. And after we overcame the aversion of her very lazy staff . . . we started seeing an astonishing trend develop. The vast majority of leads came from existing business contacts and referrals; not even 1% came through people getting information from the yellow pages and following it up. Thus, the business was able to save over $30,000 a year by reducing their yellow pages advertising to the absolute minimum. So you see, tracking pays off!

Now commit!

☐ I know I've been pretty remiss about keeping track of how my various marketing activities perform; I have hunches about them, to be sure, but precious little hard data. Not any more! I promise to keep track of exactly how many leads (and, in due course, how many clients and dollars) each activity generates so I know whether it makes sense to repeat (or expand) it . . . or cut it back or drop it altogether. Of course this makes sense. And now I'll be doing it!

Avoidable Error #19
You Haven't Fully Integrated Your Computer Into Your Marketing

Many people think I work alone . . . but that simply isn't true. My computer and I are taking over the known world, and I assure you this objective wouldn't be a serious possibility without The Machine. It's sad that most service sellers aren't as well organized.

The computer, you see, is arguably the most important business tool ever developed for service sellers. It gives us two things we must have to succeed, the ability to:

- store, organize and call up in precise order and at will vast amounts of prospect and customer data, and

- create, edit, and store documents and marketing communications.

When you maximize both these advantages, you step appreciably closer to becoming a multi-millionaire selling services.

Let's consider both of them.

— *Storing, organizing and calling up prospect and customer data*

To succeed as a service seller, you're going to come in contact with a truly staggering amount of data. You need to know:

- the names, addresses and phone numbers of your prospects;

- ditto of your buyers;

- what the buyers bought and when;

- the names, addresses, phone numbers and service interests of past buyers, whom you may be able to retrieve.

Frankly, even with the smallest micro-business, I don't see how you're going to be able to maintain (much less use) all these data efficiently without a computer, and I hope you won't try.

— *Creating, editing and storing documents and marketing communications*

You're also going to be composing, editing and storing (for review and future use) any number of business and marketing documents. The computer makes it easy for you to handle these tasks efficiently.

If this is true, however, why are so many service businesses either 1) computer-less or 2) under-computerized? That is, either they don't have any computer at all . . . or aren't using the computer they have effectively. There are, I think, several "reasons" which bear considering:

- "Computers are too expensive";

- "They're complicated to use";

- "My business is too small to warrant buying one";

- "I've gotten along without one all this time; I can get along without one even longer";

- "Sure we've got a computer, and we keep our mailing list on it. What else could we possibly use it for?"

Let me say as strongly as possible: these "reasons" are all absurd ... They do, however, tell you a lot about the people who utter them, and the service businesses they're running. Either without a computer or without a computer fully integrated into their businesses, these benighted folk are telling us that they are:

- small and plan on staying that way;

- not interested in maximizing either their efficiency or their ability to respond to prospects and customers;

- without a clue about how their own time could be better spent, and

- not really serious about becoming millionaires.

Consider the case, for instance, of one service seller I know who runs a business assisting consultants launch their practices. He offers a newsletter and one-on-one business development assistance. Now this fellow was on the consulting scene many years before I came into it; indeed, he was ideally situated to take advantage of the boom in the subject that took place in the late '70's and '80' s. However, he missed it.

I'm sure one of the reasons he missed the boat was that he failed to computerize. Indeed, when I was in the process of setting up my own computer system, he was the *only* person who advised me not to do so since, he said, computers weren't necessary; *he* wasn't going to waste his money on one. It was a breathtakingly stupid judgment from a man who was trying to make an income by providing up-to-date business advice!

Not long afterward, the Computer God took his revenge on this poor creature. During a flood, the man's basement (where he kept all his hard-copy records of subscribers, *etc.*) was inundated and all the data were lost. It literally took him years to recover . . . and, of course, many subscribers dumped him because he was so disorganized. It goes without saying that this fellow, who was once so ideally situated to become not merely one of the nation's leading authorities on consulting but one of the richest, too, is today a mere also-ran with trifling influence. I'd say his views on computers helped produce this disappointing result.

What will help you avoid this result is both reviewing what you do and where the computer can assist you. As you've already seen, a computer is crucial in keeping prospect and customer data. It's also invaluable with marketing communications.

The marketing (hence profit) success of your service business, like all such businesses, is based on your ability to handle promptly and efficiently a series of situations that recur daily. These situations include:

- responding knowledgeably and appropriately to prospects who call your business in response to your various marketing activities;

- sending these prospects the appropriate client-centered communication based on what they want;

- following up these prospects by telephone promptly;

- following up these prospects by letter if you cannot connect with them by phone;

- offering existing customers more benefits both by letter and by phone;

- following them up promptly;

- recontacting both by letter and by phone lapsed customers who haven't bought from you in a while.

All these activities can and will occur in marketing your service business. With each the computer is important because on your computer you'll have available all the necessary client-centered benefits and cash copy modules, phone scripts and marketing communications you'll need. *Warning:* if you don't have these available now on computer, you are severely hampering your ability to become a multi-millionaire.

Now commit!

☐ Whether I don't have a computer at all or am not currently fully integrating my computer into my marketing no longer matters. I promise to reform! I know that a personal computer is crucial in both organizing my prospect and client data and helping me create a truly power house marketing department, and I'm not going to be fool enough to try to do my marketing without it. Indeed, I pledge to review every aspect of both my data storage and prospect and customer contact and see how I can integrate the computer more efficiently into what I do. I realize this will be of the utmost assistance in advancing me to millionaire status.

Avoidable Error #20
It Takes You Too Long To Respond To Your Prospects And Customers

This point is related to the one above, but it needs to be reviewed separately because of its importance.

Consider this situation. You have worked hard to do your service development, your market research and to create client-centered marketing communications. You've researched the different marketing vehicles available to you and have sunk your money in a wise selection. As a result, the leads begin pouring in. What do you do? It's obvious isn't it? Well, ISN'T IT?

Apparently not.

In one of the first issues of my new card-deck, I ran a very client-centered card for a New Jersey copy writer. About 10 days after the deck mailed, he began to get leads . . . hundreds of them. As each day's crop came in, he fell deeper into despair until finally he simply sat in his basement office surrounded by so many leads he was totally incapacitated. In the end, he actually lost money on the ad because he couldn't handle the necessary follow-up.

I used to think this story simply represented one man's tragedy. Since then, however, I've seen this scenario repeated over and over again, and I've decided it's a real (if to me baffling) problem.

Before you undertake any marketing activity, you must be prepared to respond to the leads IMMEDIATELY. Not in a week or two . . . not in a month . . . but TODAY! Nor is this difficult.

Before even one person responds to your marketing gambit, you already know he'll fall into one of these categories:

- He'll either buy today or he won't;

- If he buys today, you need to be able to accommodate him immediately;

- If he doesn't buy today, he'll need follow-up. This follow-up (either by letter or phone or in person) will induce him to buy tomorrow . . . or it won't. So he'll buy tomorrow, you must send him today that which will produce the desired result. If he doesn't buy tomorrow, you must do what it takes to get him to buy the day after tomorrow.

See where this is going? Once you have begun any marketing activity, any marketing activity whatsoever, you have begun an unrelenting process, a process which must consist of your ability to deal with the prospect or client *at whatever stage he falls.*

All marketing activities, you see, fall at some point along a spectrum of possible buyer interest. At one end of the spectrum is "Mom," the person who'll buy anything you do; all you have to do is ask. At the other end is the "Devil," the person who wouldn't buy what you have available if you were God Himself. In between, the rest of the prospects fall out between those who are fairly easy to motivate to those needing constant romancing. Except for the Devil (whom you must be able immediately to identify but who is pointless to beguile), you need to be prepared *in advance* to work with all of them.

Let me say again what I've been stressing: marketing consists of just two parts, planning and execution. This point is a planning point. You must think through *every* kind of response you'll get to your marketing activity and prepare yourself to meet it. This includes creating the relevant marketing communication and having it available on computer. Then when the prospect responds, you'll be ready to take IMMEDIATE ACTION.

And I do mean IMMEDIATE . . .

- Phone calls should ALWAYS be returned the day they are made, within the hour if at all possible. Just abiding by this single recommendation will increase your credibility and revenues considerably. Think how often you've made a phone call to a service seller and failed to have that call returned at all, much less the same day. Indeed, it's an article of faith around here that you can judge the bank balance (and client-centered operation) of a service business by the speed at which he returns calls. Personally, I NEVER wrap up my day until EVERY SINGLE call made to me has been answered either with a return phone call or letter.

- Information requested should be sent THE SAME DAY it's asked for;

- These requests should be followed up one week later, where applicable. It's your responsibility to follow up the prospect's request immediately; it is equally your responsibility not to give the prospect too much time with the material. Five business days is a sufficient amount of time for you to wait after mailing before you follow up, much less if you fax;

- When the prospect tells you he hasn't reviewed the material yet, ask him when he's going to do so and SCHEDULE A FOLLOW-UP DATE TO DISCUSS IT. Don't leave the initiative in the hands of the prospect.

- When a prospect tells you he can't go ahead with your service just now, ask why. Ask when he'll be ready to go ahead. Follow up accordingly.

I hope you've noticed something about this approach: the initiative, and the responsibility for action, are *always* on you . . . *never* on the prospect. It is *your* responsibility to prepare yourself for dealing with a prospect at any point in the sales sequence. It is *your* responsibility to follow up promptly. It is *your* responsibility to keep the prospect focused on next steps . . . and to make sure that these next steps are achieved by you in an organized and focused fashion.

Some foolish service sellers won't use this kind of concentrated approach. Why?

- Some think it's beneath them. "My service is so superior, you should crawl on your belly to get it, and even then I might not condescend to offer it to you."

- Others think that this kind of focused approach will offend prospects. Let me tell you something: it only offends those who aren't really prospects in the first place, just window shoppers.

- Still others are squeamish about being so "aggressive."

Let me tell you something else: prospects, particularly those who are unfamiliar with your business and how it works, will appreciate this kind of professional focus and control. They'll be grateful you know both what they want and what you're doing and have created a system that gives them what they want in a timely, efficient way. As a result, don't you think they'll prefer you to those who are merely technically competent in your field? After all, those people can only do the job. You can do that — and orchestrate a process in which the prospect — and ultimately the customer — feels secure and comfortable at all times. Which is so much better.

Now commit!

☐ In the past I realize I may have been ill-prepared to follow up my marketing activities in the most prompt, efficient and client-centered manner. But no more! From now on, I shall be ready to respond to a prospect, whatever his level of interest, even before this prospect presents himself. I shall think through *everything* that needs to be done and create the necessary means of doing it before even a single prospect appears. I shall therefore be able to follow up promptly and thoroughly whatever happens.

Avoidable Error #21
You Spend Too Much Time With People Who Can't — Or Won't — Buy Your Service *Now*

There are only two types of people in the service seller's universe: people who can (and will) buy his service now . . . and the rest. Of these two categories, THE FIRST IS ALWAYS MORE IMPORTANT.

Reread the preceding paragraph.

Sadly, too many service sellers don't organize their businesses accordingly. Say they run an ad and receive a number of responses. The democratically minded service seller treats all these leads identically. After all, they reason, each is a lead. Each has the possibility of becoming a prospect; therefore each must be treated similarly.

Of course this is rot.

The only leads worth spending serious time and resources on are the leads that promise, first, immediate business and, second, business in the near or intermediate term. All others are necessarily of lesser importance and must be treated accordingly.

Thus, what you've got to do is discover the seriousness of intent of each prospect. That will determine how you handle this prospect. You can discover this seriousness of intent in several ways:

- When a prospect calls, you can ask necessary probing questions on the phone;

- When a prospect writes, you can insist on a telephone number for response and follow up in order to ask the necessary questions;

- When you don't have the prospect's telephone number, you can develop and send him a Client Survey Questionnaire which, when completed, provides the data you need to make an assessment.

Do you do this now? Allow me to doubt it.

I have a friend in Maine who's a superb computer technician offering a series of services. Recently, he's started running ads in national publications and is getting many responses, many by phone. This should enable him to qualify his leads, right? But does he *do* it? Why, just the other day he told me that 1) he often forgets to ask for his prospects' phone numbers, and 2) instead of asking them probing questions about their level of need for what he sells, simply sends them packets of information. Since each packet costs him $4-5 to mail out, this is a very expensive commitment on his part. Stupid, too, since he doesn't have a clue how serious they are . . . and whether they deserve his attention — or the circular file.

I reiterate the obvious point that so often ceases to be considered at all: the objective of business is to make money. It is not to supply prospects (some of whom may be nothing more than freebie seekers) with "information." Your object is to send client-centered information *only* to those who have the means of acting and are reasonably ready to act now or in the near future.

Consider the difference between my Mainer friend's approach . . . and mine. The other day (while I was at breakfast, of course), the phone rang and a fellow from Ohio asked me for a catalog. I was, at that point, perfectly prepared to send it to him. Then he uttered the fateful phrase, "I never order from catalogs. I just look at 'em and throw 'em away." Thereupon I told him that I wouldn't be sending him my catalog, thanked him for calling and hung up.

Moments later he was on the phone again. He said he was going to report me to the "president of your company." I told him his request was duly noted . . . but I still wouldn't send him the catalog. With the noise from his grinding teeth in the background, I politely rang off again . . . without giving him what he wanted.

Let me make one thing perfectly plain to you: you are not in the business of satisfying the freebie seekers, the merely curious, the people who don't have money, *etc., etc., etc.* You are under no obligation to accommodate them.

The curious notion has taken root in this nation that a business is a social institution; that our job is to make happy all and sundry who contact us. THIS IS RIDICULOUS. Service sellers only have an obligation to 1) offer the best possible service; 2) bring this service to the attention of those who want it and have the means of paying for it, and 3) ignore the rest.

Thus your job is to do what I call "cut to the chase" as quickly as possible. Consider what I do with my card deck. The deck is an expensive enterprise to produce and though my prices are only about 1/3 of my competitors', advertising in it still involves the serious financial commitment of at least $1200. I generate the bulk of my leads for this service in three ways, through:

- my Sure-Fire Business Success Catalog;

- articles run in my Sure-Fire Business Success Column, and

- a lead generator card that runs in each issue of the deck itself.

In this fashion, I generate hundreds of leads from people who are thereby indicating a preliminary interest in advertising; in fact, the response is many times more than the number of spaces I have available at any time.

A large percentage of these prospects call me. That is, of course, the way I like it, because I can qualify them immediately by asking a series of questions about:

- the product/service they have available;

- when they are thinking of running a card (in time for my next issue? The issue after that? Or not until hell freezes over?)

- whether they have any experience with card decks? Do they have a card available?

- whether they've shopped around and compared prices? (Always an advantage to me.)

- whether they have the funds available to purchase a card?

The answers to these questions determine what I do to them next.

If they are only looking and have no plans or funds to commit, I tell them I'll keep them on the mailing list and make sure they get the next issue of the deck . . . or maybe the next two. I advise them to contact me when they're ready . . . since I know that they'll be getting my catalog and deck anyway (remember The Rule of Seven). Too, I enter them into a data base of delayed contacts with a date when they think they might be ready. Future contact is thereby ensured . . . but not present contact. *That* is reserved for prospects who give different answers . . . answers that establish them as worthy of my limited time and attention now.

I advise these people of two important things: 1) any offers that are available, and 2) how much space is remaining. Both are important. For instance, in order to stimulate prompter payment (always a benefit and particularly one in the kind of recession during which I started this service), I tell them they can have a guaranteed position among the top 20 cards if they pay 60 days before publication. I let them know how many spaces are remaining in the top twenty . . . and indeed in the deck itself. With both these facts I remind them that there are advantages to be gained if they act today . . . not tomorrow. Thus, in every issue there are those who (to their advantage and mine) move to take these benefits.

You must do the same.

First, take your oath that you will work to differentiate good prospects from the not-so-good. Then deal as severely as you must (but always with courtesy, mind) with those who cannot produce income now or in the near term. That includes sending them a polite little note telling them when and under what circumstances you're prepared to be of assistance. As Winston Churchill once said, when you're going to hang a man you can afford the white gloves. Now is the time to remember this.

Then focus *exclusively* on those who want your service and are ready to take action. These are your bridal candidates and must be treated accordingly.

Furthermore, remember this: if at any time you can't tell whether a prospect belongs in one camp or another, ask him this: "What will it take for us to do business today?" If the answer is vague or windy, do what's necessary — albeit politely — to get rid of him. Once you're in business, after all, you're no longer a democrat; you can't afford to be. If you think otherwise, I suggest you become an underpaid social worker.

Now commit!

☐ I know I'm too nice. I know I've spent too much time in my business with the wrong sort of people . . . people who can't or won't buy my service now. Believe me, I'm sorry. I promise not to let this happen anymore. I pledge to institute a qualifying system which will enable me, in the most courteous possible way, to discover if my prospect *really* is a prospect, or just a time waster. I shall not feel guilty about doing what's necessary to discover this information, not least because if I am wasting my time with people who don't want or can't afford what I've got available I'm not only hurting myself and my millionaire prospects but also keeping what I've got from people with whom I ought to be connecting.

Avoidable Error #22
You Are Not Working To Get
A Steady Stream Of Referrals

Pity the poor Jeffrey! Not so long ago he decided to take some of his business gains and invest them in creating a more suitable (read comfortable) environment for himself. And so he decided to remodel. He asked his remodeled friends for leads and, at last, took one . . . to his ultimate chagrin. Why? Because the man whose company he selected for the job didn't understand that you can only succeed in running a service business when you arrange matters so that you get a steady stream of lucrative referrals from satisfied customers.

Oh, don't get me wrong. The fellow *wanted* referrals and pestered me for them over and over again. He just didn't know how to arrange his business so that he'd get them.

The process of getting referrals starts from *before* you have any work at all. First, you've got to understand the importance of referrals to your business; second, you must arrange the provision of your service so that you get them, and third you must request them. My remodeler had no problems with #1 and #3 . . . where he fell down flat was #2.

You must understand that one of the things you get from a job well done is referrals. All service sellers know how important these referrals are. Few, however, have established a *system* that produces these referrals in a predictable, rather than in an episodic, way. You're probably one of these sad souls. But no longer!

Here's the system that'll help you:

- Set a referral objective for each job. This objective should be a *minimum* of one referral for each successfully completed assignment;

- After focusing the new client on what you'll be doing for him and how much better off he'll be as a result, tell him

that you'd like at least one referral at the end of the job if
he's entirely happy with the work. At this point the client
has nothing to lose and will probably agree;

- Make sure you inform the client what you're going to do
  and when you're going to do it. This kind of client-centered
  communication helps build the necessary relationship that
  produces, in the end, the referrals you need;

- If problems crop up, don't wait for the client to bring them
  to your attention. Alert the client about what's happening
  . . . or is likely to happen. Make sure you've thought
  through what can be done about these problems before
  upsetting the client unnecessarily;

- Have regular meetings with the client. Take notes at these
  meetings. Keep records of what you've promised to do,
  what you've done and what still needs to be accomplished.
  Start off each of these meetings by telling the client what
  you've accomplished since the last meeting;

- At the end of your assignment, show the client that you
  accomplished what you promised you would;

- Then ask for a referral, including name, address, and telephone number. Ask if the (now satisfied) client would be
  good enough to send a note or call the new prospect directly on your behalf. At this point, there's no reason why
  this shouldn't happen.

- Then ask for another referral. After all, you've done good
  work. Don't you deserve it?

- After contacting the referral, let the referrer know what
  happened. If things get bogged down, ask for his assistance;
  if things go well, thank the referrer lavishly . . . and perhaps even send a small token of your regard.

Most service sellers don't do this. They leave referrals (which after
all represent future income with minimal marketing expense) to
chance. But you won't, will you?

Now commit!

☐ Okay, so I haven't been getting full value from all the good work
I've done. I provide my service . . . and move on. Maybe I get a referral
. . . maybe I don't. But that's history. From now on I'm going to arrange
my business not only so that the client gets the good result he's entitled
to, but so that I get the best possible referrals . . . and lots of 'em.

Avoidable Error #23
You Fail To Upgrade Clients Immediately

Whom do you think represents the best chance for your next sale? A prospect who has never heard of you . . . or a person who has used your service and is happy with the results? Put this way it's obvious, isn't it? Why, then, do so many service providers think so much more about those who've never bought from them . . . than about those who have?

Think of my dentist, for instance. He's one of America's worst marketers. At the end of my visit, if his office assistant is busy (which could mean gossiping with her co-worker), no future visit is scheduled. At some distant point down the road maybe a card is sent about scheduling another visit . . . but maybe it isn't. I've been tracking this marketing ineptitude now for several years. Maybe I schedule a visit . . . maybe I forget and let things go. Does this make sense?

Now, I can understand that office assistants get busy and can't attend to a customer right away. But what I cannot understand is why they don't either 1) call me later the same day or the next (when they do have the time) to schedule an appointment, or 2) why they don't follow up their post card with a phone call, if I don't respond, say, within 72 hours of receipt. The fact that these things don't occur is what makes them inept marketers. And yet dental business is down around the nation . . .

This kind of foolish "marketing" is all too prevalent.

A few months ago I was giving several workshop programs in Omaha, Nebraska. One day I received a scrunched up little note from the masseur at the Omaha YMCA who, as it happened, was an avid (but as it proved not too conscientious) reader of my books. Becoming aware I was going to be in town, he invited me to the "Y" for a complimentary massage. Given the fact that I spend hours a day hunched over a computer keyboard and have developed a few unique pains as a result, I was happy to take him up on his kind offer . . . although spending time in a locker room doesn't generally appeal. Still, I went . . .

Shortly after meeting the friendly masseur, it became obvious why he'd invited me (of course I'd had a premonition): he needed marketing help. He offered a useful service but couldn't attract the right number of people to make the business prosper. Now, there's one thing about giving me anything free: I don't accept presents well and, perhaps due to my pioneer antecedents, like to reciprocate immediately. In any event, stripped down to the buff as I was, I started asking him the necessary questions about his business.

What quickly became apparent was that he:

- didn't have a listing of his clients . . . no, not even a card file;

- had no means of contacting them, and

- never thought of asking them to schedule their next massage when they'd finished their present one. Instead, he waited for his prospects to return for a general work-out and attempted to book them while he was also handing out towels, minding the cash register, *etc.* In short, maybe he'd connect with them . . . maybe he wouldn't.

Needless to say I told him this lunacy had to stop . . . and, despite my state of dishabille, I gave him his marching orders. (One of my suggestions by the way, was to post a message on the ceiling overlooking the massage table: "Don't forget to schedule your next massage before you leave." That way when the customer was flat on his back, the masseur's marketing message could be soaking in. Clever, huh? Next time you're in Omaha, stop by the "Y" and see if he's using it . . . and, yes, his massage is worth it!)

Now what about you?

As is the case with so many other aspects of this book, you need a *process* for handling customer upgrading . . . not just catch-as-catch-can. Here it is:

- Resolve that the first business you get from the customer will not be your last;

- Resolve that your next business will follow the first as soon as possible. Indeed, make this a game. See how quickly you can get the customer to commit to more business, always making sure he's paid for the last!

- While you're working on the customer's project, ask leading questions designed to elicit his want for other things you provide. Once you've entered into a working relationship with your customer, eliciting this information is quite easy. Indeed, depending on the nature of what you do, you'll know certain things the customer needs before he does.

(When the remodeler was working on my house, for instance, he knew before I did that the wiring needed to be replaced; it didn't take me long to agree to this addition to his original assignment which significantly increased the value of the job to the service provider.)

- Once you know what the customer wants or needs, compile the benefits to him of immediate action;

- Look for an appropriate opening (usually towards the end of your first assignment or at a time the customer is particularly happy with you . . . or with the world) to suggest going on to another assignment;

- Schedule the work as soon as possible.

If the prospect cannot go forward to the next project now (perhaps because of limited funds), at least get him to tell you that this project is something he wants . . . or needs. Find out what may be holding him back from going ahead. If you can finesse the difficulty and make a constructive proposal, do. If you cannot do so, at least log the prospect's desire and the date you intend to revive the matter. Keep such information available in the computer and browse through it regularly, recontacting the client appropriately. NEVER GIVE UP. The satisfied customer who needs/wants more will always be your readiest source of future business.

Now commit!

☐ I know! I know! I haven't been mining my satisfied customers for new business quickly enough. I'm like that marketing inept dentist of yours. But that's all about to change. I'm going to inquire into their situations earlier and look for wants and needs. I will not leave the initiative to the prospect about getting back in touch with me. I know it's always my responsibility to suggest new things the client should do . . . and to do what's necessary to nail down the specifics AS SOON AS POSSIBLE. Moreover, if the client isn't ready to go ahead with a new purchase/project very soon after the ending of the previous one, I know it's my responsibility to stay in touch and keep the contact warm. And now I will!

Avoidable Error #24
You Don't Take Care Of Unhappy Customers Promptly Enough . . . Or Graciously Enough

To provide a service in twentieth century America is to be open to constant complaints from those who don't feel you've done your job well enough. Grousing isn't new, of course; it's part of the human condition and as long as there are people, there will be those who'll complain. Still, the rooting of the "entitlement mentality" has lead to a proliferation of complaints . . . at the same time that the level of service has fallen, thus providing a basis for many of them. It's a vicious circle, one you'll be touched by as well. So, get ready.

In the service seller's world there are two types of complainers:

- those who have a basis in fact for their complaint;
- those who do not.

Here's how to deal with each.

— *Those who have a basis for their complaint*

I am going to start from the (perhaps unwarranted) assumption that you want to do good work and that you're not a lazy pig trying to rip off an unsuspecting public. If this is, indeed, the case you're going to want to do everything possible to accommodate your clients when they have reasonable grounds for complaint.

In writing this section, I am thinking of a printing company I use. They produce a high quality product at a reasonable price. Their customer service, however, leaves a good deal to be desired. Although they give lip service to the proposition that they are human, in fact that tell you in ways grand and subtle that "We never make a mistake." This is, of course, their first mistake, and many of their troubles follow as a direct result. Just as they do with a Florida-based company I know which produces a variety of motivational and self-help products and services. Neither is willing to own up to the fact that (imagine!) they do make mistakes.

Don't be the same way.

If you want to keep your rational and fair-minded (if momentarily aggrieved) customers, you're going to have to take responsibility for your actions . . . and proceed accordingly. This means owning up to mistakes directly . . . instead of arrogantly denying you're capable of doing anything wrong.

Next, put yourself in the listening mode. Ask the customer to detail precisely what the problem is . . . and, whenever possible, precisely what he'd like you to do about it. While the customer is talking, force yourself (if you must) to listen patiently to what he's saying. Don't interrupt and, by all means, don't defend your work. *Listen.* You can't formulate the proper response until you know just what's bugging the customer.

As the customer is talking, ask yourself whether it would help solve the problem if you had a list of the problems (and possible solutions) in writing from the customer. Note I say "problems and possible solutions" rather than a sheet of blue language from an outraged customer. Whenever possible these discussions should be free of personalities and fiery language. Instead, the focus should always be on what's wrong and what can be done to correct it . . . process issues. When a customer is outraged, you need to diminish the anger by saying, "Believe me. We're going to solve your problem. So, please, let's just focus on what the problem is and what can be done about solving it." It's your job to return the customer to the discussion at hand each time he veers off into rage and bad language. These help no one.

If you need the customer's points in writing, either 1) ask the customer to mail or fax a memo with the pertinent information, or 2) volunteer to write the points down for consideration.

Writing things down is a very good idea for at least two reasons: 1) it gives both parties control, and 2) gives them the chance to consider their response. While a person may well blow off a lot of colorful steam in person or over the phone, he's much less likely to write the same language down. Thus, the mere act of writing helps defuse the situation.

Once the points are written, inform the client just how long you'll need to consider them, how you'll be considering them (are you going to have to discuss the points with others?), and when you'll be getting back to the client. This last point is particularly important . . . and usually handled ineptly.

When you're confronted by an angry customer, the obvious tendency is to get away from the person by either 1) hiding or 2) overpromising or 3) both. But this is wrong.

At this point, you need to re-establish your control of the situation . . . and the customer's confidence in you. This means promising a realistic time for responding to the customer's anger . . . and meeting this obligation religiously. If you don't, you're only compounding the problem.

I just went through a situation like this with the printer mentioned above. Due to the fact that the company had just moved a portion of their operation to a new plant, they were experiencing many production delays with an important job of mine. However, instead of adequately assessing just how much time they'd need and their ability to deliver the goods, they promised action after action they were incapable of delivering. In the final analysis, my job did go out on time and in good order . . . but we were left with a distinct (and reasonable) feeling that the company was composed of bumblers who had no idea how to do their job . . . or how to handle a justly concerned customer.

Once you've promised action to the aggrieved customer, follow through. Report regularly to the customer . . . even if you can only report that you are still looking into the situation. In short, don't abandon the customer to doubt. This can only work against you.

In the meantime, work assiduously to provide the customer with as much as can reasonably be done. If you cannot provide the customer with everything he wants, put the best face on things: tell the customer all you're giving him, not all you're failing to provide. Provide the best possible reasons for not giving the customer the rest. In short, be client-centered.

At some point, even the most onerous assignment will be completed. But before it can be considered over, you must write a generous "end-of-project" note to the customer telling him how sorry you are that there were problems, reminding him of what you did to accommodate him, and, whenever possible, sending a small present. In short, doing the handsome thing. This is not the moment, of course, to ask for another assignment; you both need a cooling off period. However, it is the moment to say that you hope you will work together again. Chances are you will!

How different this is from the standard approach of most service sellers who:

- deny there's any problem at all;

- deny they have any responsibility for it;

- leave the customer feeling humiliated and angry at the lack of intelligent responsiveness;

- fail to listen to what the customer has to say;
- fail to respond in a timely and intelligent manner;
- fail to propose reasonable and problem-solving actions;
- fail to live up to their commitments (even the commitment of when they'll respond);
- don't end the project with civility or even an expression of sadness that there were problems, and
- in sum, are perfectly willing to lose the customer rather than confront the problem in a thorough and constructive fashion.

Don't make these errors. Satisfied customers will carry your message to other prospects and get you business; dissatisfied customers will trumpet their experiences . . . and deny you that business. Sure you'd rather there weren't any problems; the customer feels the same way. Problem, however, will arise from time to time, and if you don't handle them satisfactorily, you'll lose not only the customer's current business but any prospect of referral business from the people he talks to.

— *Those who have no basis for their complaint*

To be sure, sometimes the service seller is not at fault; sometimes a customer is just plain difficult. What should you do then?

Again, the first question to be asked is: do you want to do business with this person again, or not? Many service sellers act as if they've taken an oath to God to deal with everyone in the world. This is not true.

One of the delights of running a profitable service business, and of developing capital (along lines I'll suggest shortly) is that, after a while, you're going to have the luxury of selecting your clientele. Note I say "after a while." That moment occurs, by the way, when you fully implement the tactics of this book, which is all the more reason to get crackin'!

You should do everything possible to reach this point as soon as possible.

If you are not yet at that point and need the money, I suggest you follow the steps above and treat the unreasonable and complaining customer as if he were reasonable. He'll still complain, of course, but this exercise in saintliness should motivate you to generate more prospects faster and as such is useful.

However, say that the customer is unreasonable, and you either don't particularly need the business — or want to endure the grief. What then?

- Once you've decided you don't want to work with this person again (and don't mind losing any future referral business), resolve in your own mind how far you'll go to accommodate him;

- Write a client-centered letter offering all that you're going to do and how much this is in the interest of the client. Do not tell him all he's not going to get . . . and never, ever give vent to your (probably unprintable) feelings about this person. Just tell him what you're going to do . . . what he's going to get. Ask for an immediate response;

- If the client doesn't get back to you in, say, 72 hours after receipt of your proposal, call him. Don't look weak. Stay in charge . . . even if dealing with this person is personally unpleasant;

- If the client accepts some or most of your proposal, the relationship can be salvaged. At that point, send the client a personal letter saying you're glad you've been able to work things out and saying you'll work hard to give the client what he wants. Again, behave handsomely;

- If on the other hand, the client is adamant about the inadequacy of your proposal, ask him to WRITE precisely what he wants — and why. It's now time to put the responsibility on the client;

- It may be that the client's proposal will contain suggestions you can accept. If so, do. If it's possible to salvage this relationship, you should.

If the client's proposal has no room for negotiation, what then? This is obviously tougher. In this case:

- Write back and tell the prospect it doesn't look as if there are any grounds for compromise. Express your regret that this is so. Say you've tried to compromise, have offered solutions and want a solution, but that, for reasons previously given (and here reprised) you cannot do more. This letter must breath rationality and compromise, not least because you may be forced to show it in court. In this letter say that you must regretfully stop work on any current projects. Also present your bill for any work already done. Indicate that this bill is payable within 30 days, or whatever constitutes standard terms in your industry or under your contract with the client. Conclude this letter by telling the client you are sorry all this has happened, that you want to complete the assignment and work together and that you hope the client will think things over and come up with more suggestions for repairing the relationship and enabling things to go forward.

- Now wait. You have done what you can do, and it's up to the client to do some thinking and, one hopes, takes constructive action. Or at least to show you that he's serious about wanting to end the relationship, too.

- If you are owed no more money, this relationship is finished. If you are and if you are not paid in a timely manner, contact the customer the day the money is owed. Simply request the money. If the customer doesn't indicate payment will be immediately forthcoming, say nothing more. But that day send a certified letter (the kind that must be signed for) indicating that if payment is not received within 7 days you will take legal action. Do not indulge in any attacks on the customer or his integrity. Just state the facts and what you'll do. If the customer pays, fine. Send a letter of thanks and regret that all this has happened. If the customer doesn't pay, sue.

- On the day you file papers with the court, tell the customer you've sued him and again say in your blandest manner that you hope he'll pay to avoid more unpleasantness. Again, engage in no recriminations. Remember, this correspondence may end up in court.

Using this method the chances are good the client will pay you before going to court, especially if you've got a signed contract (you do, don't you?). After all, he doesn't want to be embarrassed by all the evidence of your many attempts to solve the problem in a reasonable way. Moreover, if you do go to court, the chances are very good you'll win. Whatever happens, however, write the client a letter expressing your regret and disappointment and wishing him well. Two or three lines will do nicely. Why do this? For two reasons, really: 1) because it's the civil thing to do and establishes you as a genuinely genteel person, and 2) because it closes the issue and enables you to move on to other projects feeling good about yourself and how you've handled the matter. This is most worthwhile, indeed.

Now commit!

☐ With the best will in the world, I know some of my clients will become irritated, aggrieved, angry. This is a normal part of bus iness. But I promise to do what's necessary so that their unhappiness doesn't destroy the possibility of future business. I promise to take a pro-active approach to customer service, one that demonstrates my client-centeredness and control of the situation. I promise to do this even with the difficult, demanding people I'll inevitably encounter, working hard to be rea-sonable and solution-oriented even with people I don't want to work with in future. However, once these people have shown themselves to be irretrievably obstinate and impossible to work with, I'll do what's necessary to terminate the engagement as soon as possible but with all civility . . . and to take prompt, effective legal action. I'm a pro-fessional, after all, not a patsy.

Avoidable Error #25
You Don't Use Your Success With A Particular Kind Of Client To Get Immediate Business From Others Who Are Similar

Many years ago when I was the newest and greenest consultant on the block I secured a fund raising contract with a community health organization. By implementing a series of procedures which I've outlined in my book **DEVELOPMENT TODAY: A FUND RAISING GUIDE FOR NONPROFIT ORGANIZATIONS**, I helped this orga-nization raise more money in a year than it had ever raised before. We were all happy . . . not least myself, because I knew that I could leverage this success with this kind of organization to get similar organizations to hire me. And so it will be with you.

If you want to turn yourself into a millionaire selling services, you must:

- help someone achieve success with your methods;
- identify others who want to achieve the same success;
- sell these others the prospect of success (rather than your-self);

- then work to achieve success with these new clients, ultimately leveraging this to gain still more clients.

Consider what this sequence really means:

- You must, first, have methods that work. You will never
  become a multi-millionaire selling services until such time
  as you've perfected a series of sensible steps that produce
  for your designated clients the results they want to have.

- You must do *everything possible* to put yourself in a situation
  with a client where you get the chance to show what you
  can produce. When you're newly in business this may mean
  keeping your fee below your competitors (or even volun-
  teering to do the work), working longer and harder hours,
  and providing extra service. The important thing, however,
  is that you put yourself in a position to demonstrate results
  . . . results that other people in the same situation will want
  to duplicate.

- You must, while working with the first client, set about
  identifying others who will want similar results. Indeed, if
  you're smart, you will never undertake to work with a
  client until such time as you have discovered whether you
  can get easy access to others who will want you to duplicate the same results once you show you can deliver them.
  In other words, you won't deal with Client 1 until you are
  sure you can use what you produce to get Client 2, *etc.* This
  includes getting the names of people who make purchasing
  decisions, their titles, mailing addresses and phone numbers.
  While you're working getting results with Client 1, you
  should be gearing up to bring these results to other prospects.

My recommendations here focus on two things: 1) achieving substantial results as soon as possible, and 2) getting yourself organized to
bring these results to the attention of others who want to replicate
them. Let's take an example of how this might work in practice.

Take my fund raising consultation service. My first assignment, many
years ago, was with a community health organization. There are
dozens of such organizations around Massachusetts, and more still
around New England. The key is finding out just where they are and
the names of the people who could retain my services.

By quizzing the executive director I was working with, I discovered
there was a statewide organization of her peers, people running similar

organizations. Its membership list, however, was proprietary. But I needed this list!

Here's where you've got to stay focused on your objective. Yes, it may be difficult to get the list, but the list is crucial. Not getting it means you're either going to have to 1) do a lot of extra work locating the organizations, calling them, logging the data, *etc.*, or 2) give up altogether and go on to an entirely different kind of organization. Neither makes sense. Instead, consider:

- who has the list;

- what do I have to do to get it?

In point of fact, many people have this list:

- the statewide organization;

- members of the organization;

- your client.

Your job is to get it, and you can do so many ways:

- by joining the statewide organization;

- offering to do an assignment for that organization that would pay you, in part, with the list;

- networking among people you know in the organization to see who could give you the list;

- asking your client for it.

In the event, not being a community health executive director, they didn't want me in their organization; getting the list that way was, therefore, an impossibility. But the other options were all possibilities. Ultimately, I simply waited for a moment when my client was particularly well disposed towards me and asked, very casually, if I could borrow the list for a couple of days. Thank goodness for photo-copying machines . . .

What I'm saying here is that there may be many ways for you to reach your objective. The important thing is to know what you need, consider your options, and do what's necessary to get the information you need.

But once you've got it, SELL CLIENT SUCCESS, NOT YOUR SERVICE.

Is this difficult to grasp? I hope not. What do you think a community health organization would rather get: a fund raising consultant, or the money they need to run their programs? It's obvious it is the *money*, the substantial results you've achieved with your service, which can, in this instance, be used to motivate prospects to see you and sign up for your service.

When should you start leveraging this success? THE MINUTE YOU HAVE IT. As you see, I've been stressing preparation for leveraging. You don't go out and get the names and addresses of prospects *after* you've achieved success; you do it *before*. You presume there will be success, and you prepare accordingly. Thus, once there is demonstrated success, you move out in an organized and focused fashion IMMEDIATELY. You do not need to take advantage of the results you've produced in an assignment until the end of that assignment; you start as soon as the results do.

Some service sellers resist this kind of focus; they reason that by concentrating on a particular group they are losing money from others who should also be using their service. This is, of course, nonsense. The objective here is not to work. It's to make money — which you'll do in two ways: by profiting from your assignments and cutting your expenses. Instead of roaming around looking for business, it's very much to your advantage to focus squarely on those people who want the benefits you've delivered to others. By using a thorough-going, concentrated marketing process relying on The Rule of Seven, you'll get many clients among the designated group. . . all at reasonable cost.

While this profitable process is going on, you should be identifying related bodies of prospects who'd like to achieve comparable results. A community health organization, for instance, is a social welfare institution. What other related social welfare institutions might want to achieve comparable results? Now it's time to focus on getting *these* organizations as clients . . . and producing success for them, too.

Only in this way can you produce maximum profit at minimum expense . . . not least because prospects won't be tempted to waste your time in endless selection proceedings and picayune questions when you are so admirably positioned as the deliverer of the successful results they desire.

Now commit!

☐ I'm not going to waste my time in the future getting just one client in just one area . . . and another in another. I'm going to focus on particular groups of clients and work hard to deliver success to them. Once I have this success, I'm, first, going to market this success to others within the group who want it . . . and then to related groups who also want it. In short, I shall stop marketing myself as a mere service provider . . . and start marketing myself as a person who delivers demonstrated success to those who'll do what's necessary to get it — which means first hiring me!

Avoidable Error #26
You Believe You Can Only Make Money From What You Know By Providing The Service Directly . . . Instead Of Mastering The Means Of Producing And Distributing Products That Contain Your Problem-Solving Methods

The objective of this book, remember, is to assist you in becoming a multi-millionaire as quickly as possible. To do this, you need to reconsider the entire notice of service as well as the notion of how you currently provide this service and how you might do so more profitably. This means considering how to deliver your service in new ways, including in *products*.

Most service sellers suffer from the absurd notion that they, or an employee, must physically deliver their service in order for their business to make money. Nothing could be further from the truth.

Let me give you an example of what I mean. Several months ago I had a pointed conversation with a Maryland copy writing consultant I know. When I first met him he was piddling along making, it seemed, just enough money for his family and himself to survive. The first problem he had to overcome was that he didn't have a lead generating system that would provide him with the number of qualified prospects he needed. The lack of such a system meant he was always scrambling for leads. This unproductive activity meant he couldn't focus on his money-making work.

The first thing I did was get him into my card deck and so solve the problem of qualified leads. Now he had them . . . in spades. Then he looked, to my horror, to be settling into *another* kind of rut: being satisfied with being a worker bee.

Now the great thing about worker bees, but only from the queen's perspective, is that these insects don't know they are the *workers*. They are happy to cater to others. If they ever do get a sense of how limited their lives are, the entire bee world will be turned upside down.

My service providing friend was in this position. He was better off than before; he was experiencing comparative affluence, but he still didn't have in place the system that would make him *rich*. I told him in no uncertain terms that what he was doing wasn't very smart . . . *if* getting rich was his objective. I told him he needed two-fold diversification: 1) to find others to offer his service and 2) to create service-centered products that brought his methods to others who could profit from them. So far he's only done the first. However, the additional money he's made has convinced him (and me) that he'll soon be doing the second. This advice, then, is particularly for him — and those like him who have had the dawning awareness that you're not going to get really rich until such time as you develop products which can be used by others to achieve the results which hitherto you've just been delivering in person.

These products include:

- *problem-solving* articles

- *problem-solving* special reports

- *problem-solving* booklets

- *problem-solving* books

- *problem-solving* audio cassettes

- *problem-solving* video cassettes.

I trust you did not overlook the key words "problem-solving"?

When a person hires your service he does so because he has a problem that needs a solution. You are the engine which, through your problem-solving process, produces a desired result for the prospect.

Hitherto, you've probably only delivered this problem-solving benefit yourself, or through employees and independent contractors. Now I ask you to take a different view — to think how you can *package* your problem-solving information in one of the above formats and so bring it, through any one of many different distribution channels, to people who either 1) can't afford to work with you one-on-one, or 2) are not geographically convenient *but who nonetheless have the problem you can solve and will pay for your solution.*

To make this system work, you must:

- understand that you have readily available profit-making information that others will pay for . . . if it helps them achieve their objectives;

- conceive of your market as more than just the people you or your employees can serve personally;

- brainstorm all the services you provide and determine the most lucrative and exportable;

- brainstorm the most likely problem-solving products based on probable profit and ease of marketing;

- consider the different formats available to you;

- identify distribution alternatives.

Let's look at each of these.

— Understand that you have readily available problem-solving information that others will pay for . . . if it helps them achieve their objectives

One of the things you get from being in business — if you have half a brain and use it — is a wide variety of "insider" information. This information includes (but is certainly not limited to):

- how to solve problems quicker and better;

- where to get supplies and equipment from reliable and inexpensive sources;

- tricks for finding, working with and motivating employees to produce more profit for the enterprise;

- marketing gambits that have worked for you . . . and those which haven't, *etc.*

The insider information you have comes in two varieties:

- problem-solving information that is of interest to *customers,* and

- problem-solving information that is of interest to *people who want to establish businesses like yours.*

Sadly, very, very few service business owners make wider use of this information beyond 1) helping the customers in their own business, and 2) perhaps providing some mentoring advice and assistance to one or two people launching similar businesses.

This is ridiculous.

The information you've acquired in building your service business constitutes a form of capital, indeed one of your major sources of capital. The more perceptive and intelligent you've been about establishing your business, the more success you've had developing it, the more worthwhile this information is; the more reason you've got to exploit it for profit and the more stupid you are for not doing so.

Yet the sad fact is most service sellers make no organized attempt to sell what they know beyond the terms of their regular business.

— *Conceive of your market as more than just the people you or your employees can serve personally*

Take the man running the cleaning establishment across the street. I doubt he thinks of the information he knows as being worth anything beyond the 10-15 square blocks that constitute his marketing territory. In other words, he's decided that the information he has about the cleaning and preservation of clothing and the setting up and maintenance of a profitable cleaning business is useful only within one tiny area. Yet just by stating this problem, you see how ridiculously this fellow has handled his knowledge capital. Of course these *two* distinct kinds of problem-solving information are valuable elsewhere — if he'll expand his idea of what constitutes his markets and how he can assist them.

Most service sellers think small; no, not even small — microscopically. Their world is limited by the number of people they (or their employees) can see in a day, a week, a month. Thus they end up serving only those within the tiniest of ranges. As a result their influence and their incomes are woefully reduced.

But it shouldn't be this way!

You must consider that your move to millionaire status means ascending a series of plateaux:

- *first* you must master a body of problem-solving information;

- *then* you must begin to profit by utilizing this information within a defined area where you can apply it to obtaining solutions for a designated body of customers;

- *then* you can diversify by offering your customers additional problem-solving techniques;

- *then* you can recruit others to offer your problem-solving techniques in other, expanded areas;

- *then* you can offer your problem-solving techniques through products both to those who either cannot afford your direct one-on-one service or are not conveniently located for doing so or who wish to replicate your successful business techniques.

The sad fact is only an insignificant number of service business owners ever fully implement this series of profit-making steps. At best, most implement the first four . . . and those incompletely. They are thus left in the ridiculous situation of knowing much that others can profit from . . . but not packaging and marketing it to their own — and their expanded markets' — advantage.

— Brainstorm all the services you provide and determine the most lucrative and exportable

Each service business is based on a series of services. Some of these are more lucrative than others. The important thing is to:

- list all the services you provide;
- prioritize them in order of the most lucrative first.

Back in my early days as a fund raising consultant for non-profit organizations, I offered many services including:

- advising boards of directors on the elements of successful fund raising;
- writing development proposals;
- researching corporations and foundations that might give an organization money;
- meeting weekly with executive directors and providing on-going oversight for their development activities, *etc.*

These activities were not all equally remunerative.

What I as a service seller had to do before diversifying into problem-solving products is the same thing you've got to do . . . examine the services you offer, determine which is the most lucrative, and also which can more easily be exported to broader markets.

One of the things I knew and profited from, for instance, was a detailed knowledge of the Boston corporate and foundation funding scene; I knew which places were more likely to give money to which kinds of *local* causes. But while this knowledge was most useful and salable hereabouts, it was of very limited value when exported to other areas;

after all the number of organizations outside Greater Boston being able to avail themselves of this information is decidedly limited.

Thus, you must always keep in mind just what you know that's most universally applicable — and only use this in your products. Don't forget: you must consider not only the information you know that's of value to the customer . . . but also to those who want to establish businesses like yours. Thus, in my case I ended up doing a book that contained techniques for nonprofit organizations wanting to raise money . . . and a series of books for the large number of people who wanted to establish successful consulting practices, in fund raising and *all* other areas.

>   — *Brainstorm the most likely problem-solving products based on probable profit and ease of marketing*

Here is where many service sellers who do want to take advantage of their information to expand their markets broadly go seriously wrong. The vast number of that relatively small number who understand that they have valuable information available both on their techniques and on how to profit from them by establishing a comparable business make a serious mistake at this point. Even if they wish to go ahead and package what they know . . . they make an error about how to market it.

Go into any reasonably good book store, for instance, and you will find any number of books by service sellers; indeed the famous How-to-do-it Bookstore in Philadelphia contains books by almost no one else. These people, however, have all determined that they can turn what they know and can do into profit better by having their problem-solving information packaged and distributed by others. I do not necessarily agree and think that making this decision without all the facts is a serious mistake. You will hardly find this a surprising deduction from a man who wrote **HOW TO MAKE A WHOLE LOT MORE THAN $1,000,000 WRITING, COMMISSIONING, PUBLISHING AND SELLING "HOW-TO" INFORMATION.**

Moreover, I do not think it necessarily makes sense to jump immediately to the book level . . . much less a book distributed by a mainline publisher. Why? Because books are not always the most profitable format for the information you have . . . much less books distributed by others where you get only a small royalty on the sale.

Here is where you have to understand all the different formats available to you . . . how each works, how much each costs to develop and how each is marketed. The complete answer to these questions lies outside this book and, besides, has already been exhaustively dealt with by me in the title mentioned above, which I recommend to you here.

Before continuing the discussion turn briefly to the catalog in the back of this book and leaf through the "R" numbers. These are five-page computer generated special reports which I currently sell for $6 each, three for $14. To put things in perspective, I make as much for *one* of these reports as you would make on two $30 books with a 10% royalty. That is, I make as much from five single pages of client-centered prose as you would make on the sale of two 250-400 page books. It takes me about 2-3 hours to produce such a report which I can update and sell for a lifetime. It would probably take you a couple of years to produce the book . . . and if it has the lifespan of most books will be out of print within two years. Moreover, you must wait 6 months for your royalties if you publish with a main-line publisher; I sell my reports direct and get the money direct . . . and daily.

Now, I am not advocating not writing problem-solving books. I am not even necessarily advocating not publishing with a main-line commercial publisher. But I *am* advocating understanding the power and profitability of shorter formats such as special reports, booklets — and audio cassettes. These do not entail massive production costs and, if properly marketed, can become significant profit centers. The key is understanding how you will market them.

— Identify Distribution Alternatives

There are many reasons why service sellers fail to look into the profit-making potential of products. Sometimes, of course, they're just lazy; sometimes they are so busy putting out fires in their businesses that they are just too tired and distracted to be able to consider anything else. Often they don't take the time to study the different formats available to them — and the necessary means of marketing each of the formats. Even if they want to go ahead, therefore, they see their options in too limited a fashion. The result is that they may drift to the wrong format with the wrong manufacturer, simply because they haven't done their homework.

When you decide to expand your income by developing new problem-solving products for your expanded markets, you must give thought to two matters: production and marketing. Of these marketing is by far the more important. And marketing necessarily means distribution.

Since the advent of the desktop publishing revolution, the means for producing problem-solving products have risen exponentially. Indeed, never in the history of the planet has it been so easy to *produce* such a product. Unfortunately, however, the means of distribution have not developed to this extent. The key, therefore, is understanding and taking advantage of all the means available to you to connect with your prospects and get them to buy at the lowest possible cost to you. Here are some distribution means to be aware of:

- free publicity
- direct mail
- package stuffer programs
- workshops and talk programs
- other people's catalogs
- your own catalog
- an independent dealer network
- bookstores
- libraries.

I am not here going to explore each of these; that information, too, you'll find in **HOW TO MAKE A WHOLE LOT MORE THAN $1,000,000**. . . . What's important to understand is that only through a complete understanding and proper use of these — and all — distribution channels will you realize the profit on your information that you ought.

Now commit!

☐ During the time I've been in my service business, I've amassed a substantial body of information both about solution methods of my service . . . and the means of running a business like mine. It's true I am not now making systematic, profitable use of this information. But no longer! I realize I don't have to make money simply by offering my service on a one-to-one basis or through my employees. I can produce problem-solving products and sell them to people across the nation . . . or around the world. The important thing is that I understand all the formats that are available to me and the various distribution channels. Once I know *how* money can be made with each, then I can make the right decision about how to produce and distribute the valuable information I have available.

Avoidable Error #27
Mastering Time Management Techniques: Doing The Most Important Things First

These days scarcely a day goes by but some curious creature doesn't ask me how I get everything done. Some ask me about how many hours of sleep I need; others have asked (I kid you not!) if they could come by and just watch me work for a day or two to get a handle on how it's all done. The trick, however, is that there is no trick: to do all that I have to do I've had to become a master of time management . . . and so will you.

I've already run the numbers for you about how much time each of us gets. It's really a pretty paltry amount. However, the solution to doing what you need to do begins with a recognition of just how little time you really get . . . and just how precious it is. This being the case it behooves those of us striving to be multi-millionaires to make the best possible use of what we've got, hence time management.

Each day is made up of two kinds of activities, those that make money and those that do not. If making money is your priority, you must give the priority to those activities that help you achieve this objective.

One of the great myths that emerged from the first wave of the women's movement was "Super Mom." You remember her. She's almost a comic character now, but not so long ago many otherwise intelligent women were working like the dickens to become like this paragon. Super Mom worked a full time, high-stress job; was always well groomed; kept a perfect house; spent lots of "quality time" with her kids; was never anything other than a perfect, passionate lover for her spouse; undertook a host of community activities and, of course, was always available for friends and family who needed her.

Personally, I never met a person like this . . . although I've met women who were in the pits of despair because, with all their skills and desire to succeed, they were constantly failing — and couldn't figure out why. But I'll tell you why: Super Mom is a mythological creature. And so is Super Dad. And, much more important for our purposes, so is SUPER SERVICE SELLER.

These are all impossible role models and must be discarded before we can even begin to make any real progress with the all-important question: how can I achieve maximum results with the small amount of time I've got available?

The truth is, it takes time to master each of the necessary steps you must surmount to become a millionaire. While you are focusing on mastering the essentials for each step, you are going to have very limited time to do other things. I admit that this sometimes bothers me. I am, for instance, writing this section on a national holiday. Much of the rest of the nation isn't working; one of my friends took off for Florida for a long week-end and asked me to go with him. Sure, I *could* have knocked off today; sure, I *could* have gone to Florida. But I've got a deadline for this book. Who set this deadline? I did. I made the decision that I'd be better off in the long-run by reaching this deadline than by sloughing off like most other people.

Until you achieve the financial status that you want, you're going to have to make a lot of these sacrifices, too. What's more, you can't worry about them . . . or let other people's more indulgent habits deflect you from what you need to do. That, however, is just what the myths of Super Mom, Super Dad and Super Service Seller do . . . they deflect you. They make you *think* that other people are rather effortlessly achieving goals that you ought to be able to achieve, too — if only you were smart enough, organized enough, efficient enough, well rounded enough. FORGET IT!

Focus instead on *objective management.*

This means arranging your time to achieve what you must achieve *today* so that you keep on track for the achievement of your larger objectives and overall goal.

Say your objective is making $250 each day, that only by achieving this amount each day could you achieve your overall objective. If you are not married or otherwise involved in a relationship (I'm not . . . right now), it is, I admit, relatively easier to focus on achieving this objective. After all, I don't have either to ask any one else's permission to do what needs to be done to achieve this objective . . . or to negotiate for the necessary time to do it. If you're married, however, you may well have to do so, which is why you need to be as explicit as possible with your Significant Others (spouse and children) about precisely what needs to be done to achieve your objective. They cannot be expected to be either understanding or of assistance if they don't know what's happening or why you're making the choices you are.

Successful time management begins, therefore, by reconciling the people around you to the choices you want to make and making sure they will help you achieve them. If they understand and will help, it will make your task easier; if they will not, you know where you stand and can take appropriate action. Either way, you've got to know. You see, it just doesn't make sense to pretend that you can successfully meet everyone's (often conflicting) expectations at the same time that you are moving towards becoming a service selling millionaire. Trying can easily leave you feeling frustrated, angry, and exhausted . . . all of which deplete the energy and focus you need to make necessary progress towards achieving your objective.

I don't know a single service selling millionaire who was able to achieve this level of success and *while working on achieving it* still:

- be the perfect "Father Knows Best" parent;
- be available at will to all his friends and extended family;
- keep a perfect house (unless he had help);
- devote heaps of time to community projects and volunteer activities, *etc.*

These people had to focus . . . just as you'll have to focus.

Later, of course, after some of these people have achieved an enviable level of success they bemoan the sacrifices they made, overcome by a sort of "Is that all there is?" ennui. But this isn't fair . . . or healthy. One should never look back on one's life and want to do it differently. That's ridiculously self-punishing.

Instead, one should realize that the achievement of substantial success in terms of this volume takes the kind of sustained effort and focus that most people simply won't make. You can't achieve success any other way, and you shouldn't think you can. You shouldn't rue the sacrifices you must make; that's self-defeating. And you shouldn't rue having made them, especially if by having made them you've achieved the objective.

Let me tell you something else while I'm at it: you must not feel sorry for yourself along the way because you cannot do what others are doing. The grasshopper will always play while the ant's at work . . . but remember the grasshopper's fate.

To that end I'm reminding myself today as the snow falls outside and as my friend basks in sunny Florida that he lives in a small apartment without amenities, has an infinitesimal net worth, an annual income less than 1/5 as much as mine, no pension fund, *etc., etc., etc.* Yes, it's unfortunate that I cannot play today . . . but it's necessary . . . and as such must be done without any regret. Just as you must do it, too.

Thus:

- Note the dollar objective you must make each day;

- List all the tasks that must be accomplished during the day, dividing them into two categories, "the ones you must accomplish to reach the dollar objective" and "the rest";

- Do the tasks on the first list in order of those that promise the largest return and will enable you to meet your daily quota. These calls get returned first. These letters get written first. Then and only then do lesser priority tasks . . . or avoid doing them at all.

What is important to keep in mind about time management is that it cannot succeed unless you are clear about what objective you must reach during the day . . . the week . . . the month. That must be crystal-clear and explicit. It also cannot succeed if you value all activities the same. You must prioritize them according to whether they help you achieve your objective, or not. If they don't help you achieve the objective, you can and should ignore them — without guilt and regret, now or later.

Guilt and regret, you see, have no place in your life now. Make the choices that need to be made; carry out the work that needs to be done. Deliberation now precludes regret later.

Now commit!

☐ I vow to give up the myth of being a Super Person. I can't afford it. I have only so much time to achieve my objective, and there are many things I must give up to do so. I cannot regret this; I must simply face the fact that this is a reality of the human condition and proceed accordingly. Thus, I recognize the very finite quality of the time I have available and the need in this time to perform certain necessary tasks that are essential to my becoming a service-selling millionaire. These tasks now have priority in my life, and I shall so arrange matters that they get done. Others may not understand these priorities. Where necessary, I shall explain to them why I've decided upon this course and work for their understanding and assistance. But the fact remains, if I am to achieve my objective, I must do certain things and must arrange my life accordingly. And I will!

Avoidable Error #28
Not Developing An Investment Program

Time and compound interest are going to help you become a multi-millionaire . . . but only if you have a regular investment program.

Do you?

Every survey shows that by the time most Americans get to retirement age they have to accept a lowered standard of living; indeed millions after working hard all their lives are actually impoverished. Frankly, this appalls me, and I here intend to do everything I can to make sure you don't suffer from this horrifying fate.

This means developing capital . . . and the investment program that produces it.

Say you are today 45 years old and invest $1000. At an annual return of 10%, in 25 years your investment will be worth nearly $11,000, or a little over $1000 a year — for life. To be sure, this doesn't take into consideration years when the return might be lower (in some years, of course, it may also be higher) or the taxes you'll have to pay (unless you use a tax-deferred program, as you ought). But the fact remains, you're going to be a lot better off if you invest . . . than if you don't.

This kind of investment is crucial for two major reasons:

1. You're going to get older and frailer and progressively less able to do the work you're able to do so well today. This is a human inevitability. What is equally predictable is that you won't like living less well as you age;

2. The work you do now must be regarded as the basis for capital development as well as current income, otherwise there will, in future, be no capital . . . and hence no later income.

This being the case, why don't more service sellers have a certain investment program? There are, I think, several reasons:

• Some have no self-control. We all know people who'd rather have something new today than take the money they would have spent and invest it for a better lifestyle tomorrow. Moreover, marketing trends accentuate this problem. Many ads are of the "you deserve it" variety which provide people with a good "reason" for acting against their best longer term interests;

- Others already seem to live so sparsely that there seems no possible way to squeeze even a penny for any investment;
- Still others give no thought whatsoever to the future. As long as their present is comfortable, that's all they care about. "The future," they suggest by their lifestyle, "will take care of itself."

With "reasons" like these, a pinched future is absolutely assured.

But not for you!

The first day you are in business is the first day you begin your business-generated investment program. This means:

- understanding and contributing the maximum amount to such tax-deferred investments as IRAs, Keoghs, 401-Ks, *etc.* No money grows faster than tax-deferred money, and you must take advantage of these options to the maximum extent, even if this does mean making sacrifices in your current lifestyle;
- familiarizing yourself with basic investment strategies. There are three basic areas in which you must specialize when you're running a service business: service development; service marketing; and capital development and maintenance (which includes both income development and investment). Each of these is crucial for developing long-term capital, and none must be neglected;
- making investments at regular intervals, especially at times when this seems most difficult.

When you're a millionaire you're going to have money to invest. Believe me. It's neither particularly difficult nor particularly praiseworthy to run an investment program when you're rich. Any fool can do that. Where it is difficult and praiseworthy is when you're less well off, even poor . . . when you have a host of other expenses and demands on your limited income. BUT THIS IS THE EXACT MOMENT WHEN YOU MUST LAUNCH AND MAINTAIN YOUR REGULAR, INVIOLATE INVESTMENT PROGRAM.

To do this means:

- setting a daily, weekly and monthly investment objective;
- working to make sure you achieve these objectives, either by selling more of your services . . . or cutting more of your expenses;

- reviewing both your business and personal expenses to see where you can cut-back, and

- investing first, not last.

Here's a trick I use. I invest at least weekly, often daily. I get ready to make the next investment by writing a check and dating it for the day I intend to make the investment. I leave that check on my deck where I can see it . . . and I do what's necessary to make sure I *can* fulfill that commitment to myself on the desired day. When you do this you'll find you're benefiting from the power of Mind Channeling which works so well here, as elsewhere.

Before I leave this section, I would like to add just a few more words. One of the many deplorable things about the second-rate American educational system is how we hide the reality of their future lives from students. Most of them are going to end up worse off than their parents. This is a fact. What is equally a fact is that not even 1% of them are going to leave high school or even college knowing what they need to know to avoid this fate . . . and this includes an understanding of how to generate more money than they need to maintain a decent lifestyle and how to use that money as the basis for creating capital, the true basis of wealth. Not even 1%. This is a scandal.

You came out of this kind of educational system, as I did, and as a result we have to overcome this lack of information and use our businesses not merely to work ourselves into an early grave but to leverage them for the achievement of capital. Thus, you must commit yourself not merely to developing a business but to using that business to build wealth. This means understanding the means of developing capital available to you . . . and doing what is necessary to take advantage of them . . . especially when this is most difficult for you.

Now commit!

☐ I admit I've concentrated on knowing how to provide my service rather than on all three of the necessary aspects of running a service business: developing services, marketing services, and investing the profit in ways that produce capital. But not any more! We live in a capitalist nation, and I want to get the benefits of being a capitalist. I shall therefore learn which investment alternatives (both tax-deferred and taxable) are available to me and arrange my business and personal affairs (even at moments of difficulty) so that I am continually augmenting my investment accounts. This is the way to the wealth I desire!

Avoidable Error #29
You Don't Lead The Life Of
The Service-Selling Impresario

When you determine to use your service business to attain substantial wealth, you become a player in a great game. It's a game with glittering prizes . . . and one that many who play lose. The ones who fail are those who don't understand the rules of this game, or understanding these rules, refuse to play to their fullest capacity. They won't:

- work after 5 p.m.;

- develop client-centered marketing documents;

- diversify their service line;

- expand their marketing territories;

- launch and sustain a demanding investment program . . .

. . . or do any of the myriad other things that it takes to build a profitable service business. Yet they have the audacity to say they want to be a success . . . while bitterly berating others who have done what it takes to succeed.

I have no time for these people — and neither should you.

The service selling impresario is *always* client centered . . . even when the client calls in the middle of your favorite television show (as three people did last evening while I was watching "Masterpiece Theater.")

The service selling impresario is *always* ready to listen to the person who proposes ways for you to be more efficient and client-centered.

The service selling impresario is *always* prepared to go just the little bit extra to accommodate the client, the little bit extra being just what his less client-centered clients will not do.

You see, establishing and running a profitable service business is not just about business . . . it's about how you view your relationship to the world. Those people who are destined to be millionaires selling services see themselves as having a unique relationship with the people on this planet. They have pledged themselves to providing the utmost in client-centered solutions and cannot rest until they are comfortable that what they are offering is as good as it can be. They do this not just because this level of quality is valuable to the client . . . but because it is good for their own souls, too.

Such people find their own fulfillment in part by putting themselves on the line for their clients. They do not hide behind company names that mean nothing . . . behind secretaries and others who screen them from the world. They have no need for this kind of bogus protection. Such people are proud of what they offer . . . proud of all the work that has gone into it . . . confident that what is being offered is to the benefit of the prospect and are glad to tell them so . . . person to person.

The future service selling millionaire is a person justifiably confident in what he offers. While he is right not to suffer fools gladly (for they waste time and resources better spent elsewhere), he is happy to do EVERYTHING POSSIBLE to connect with people who want a better life, the better life the service seller knows he can deliver. Indeed, his mind is always open to those who offer constructive ideas about how this connecting process can be expedited. As for the rest, he need never apologize for ignoring them and casting them out of his life.

For this developing millionaire, life is never some quixotic adventure; it is rather a carefully calculated march to a certain objective. Each deliberate step along the way is a cause for celebration: the desired end is just that much closer to fulfillment.

For such a person — for you! — life doesn't just happen. It is made to happen. As such your success is predictable . . . the inevitable outcome of all that has gone before, all you have worked for and orchestrated.

Now commit!

☐ I admit it. I *say* I want success, but all too often I haven't *lived* to achieve it. I've imposed artificial barriers on the growth and development of my service business. But no longer. I realize I am not just developing a business but developing myself as well and that I was not put on this earth to express as little of myself as possible . . . but as much. I shall do this . . . and do everything, too, to bring this enterprise with all its capacity for good into the lives of those who need it.

Avoidable Error #30
You Don't Regularly Take Time To Think About Your Operations And What Could Be Improved

The service business you're running today can be improved today . . . and tomorrow . . . and the day after tomorrow. Moreover, it must be if you expect to attract all the clients you need to become a millionaire. The business you're running today *cannot* be the business you run tomorrow.

We all know that the pace of change is dramatic. Yet the human beast is a sluggish animal who dislikes change and generally does all he can to avoid it . . . rather than to accommodate and turn it to his advantage. BUT THIS CANNOT BE YOU!

Each day you must ask yourself one little question: "What can I do to make things better in my business right now?"

Initially this question may overwhelm or depress your: there will be so many beneficial changes you can make.

Fortunately, you do not need to make them all today. Just focus on the single one which today will help you reach your financial obj ective quicker . . . help you get to more prospects . . . help improve your efficiency and degree of client-centered operations. *Just do that single thing.* Postpone the rest for another day. But each day do that one thing that will help boost your efforts.

We all talk about change. We read about it. The concept of change is with us always. But how few of us integrate the concept of change into the successful operation of our service businesses. Change for most service sellers is the enemy . . . not a necessary precondition of our success.

Yet you will succeed faster and to a greater extent through your ability to:
- identify necessary changes in your business;
- evaluate the alternatives before you, and
- integrate each beneficial change as smoothly as possible.

Of these points the first is the most important because it is the one that is most easy to evade.

I have never met a successful service seller yet who wasn't committed to dumping the old for the new whenever he was thoroughly convinced that the new would assist him make more money and develop his business faster than holding tight to the "tried and true." Such people, you see, hold tight only to their commitment to assist the greatest number of people with their problem-solving service. That is inviolate; everything else is open to constant scrutiny and immediate change as warranted.

It takes time, of course, to identify necessary changes, evaluate alternatives and integrate each beneficial change. The successful service seller spends it willingly, even at times when other matters seem to call for more immediate attention. All he needs is reasonable assurance that the contemplated change is one that will better help his clients get what they want . . . and himself reach his own financial objectives.

Once you have this reasonable assurance, make the change. And move closer to your status as a multi-millionaire.

Now commit!

☐ All too often I'm so involved in "running my business" that I do not take the time to identify both the changes that need to be made so I can reach my financial objective faster . . . and to scrutinize the available means of assisting me. As a result, I often get the feeling that change is passing me by. No longer! I not only realize that change is unavoidable but indeed desirable . . . if it helps me serve more people better and makes me richer. Towards this end I promise to keep reviewing my business operations to see where changes can and should be made and the necessary alternatives which will enable me to achieve my objectives.

The End Of The Beginning

You have now completed the longest chapter in this book. What's more important you have just completed a contract with yourself to understand the 30 greatest errors you can make, perhaps have been making, in running your service business . . . and to solving them.

One final word: return to this chapter often. Review the avoidable errors and make sure you're not making any of them. Becoming a multi-millionaire selling services is not a pipe-dream. It involves a simple, easy-to-understand process rigorously implemented. If you get bogged down implementing that process, return here first. When you stop making these errors, you are assured of becoming a multi-millionaire. I guarantee it.

2

Crafting the Multi-Million Dollar Plan

As you already know, I'm a big fan of planning. In brief, I believe in:

- deciding what you want;
- creating the plan that'll give it to you, and
- implementing that plan.

Or, in the words of this immortal piece of Lantian doggerel:

> What the mind conceives
> the plan foresees.

Poetaster aside, your plan is crucial for becoming a multi-millionaire selling services. But I'm willing to bet you a dollar, you don't have such a plan. Dumb, huh?

A Few General Words About Planning

Let me be very clear where I'm coming from on the subject of planning. Many books have been written on this subject, and while many have sensible pieces of information, there is a general problem with them. Because they are written by people who specialize in creating business plans and in doing business planning, these people always recommend too much. Their advice is too time consuming. After all, we are interested in creating a handy business document, not a work of art suitable for the National Gallery.

As distinct from these other authorities, I run a service business myself. I'm therefore vividly aware how limited your time is for both considering the subject of planning and writing a formal plan. Of course, I want your planning process to be thorough, but I also want to be realistic about just how much time you have to do a plan, much less implement it. So what I'm proposing is more "rough and ready" than other authorities you can consult. My point, however, is that I'd rather you did *some* planning than none at all; rather you worked from a draft plan subject to constant revision than from a formal document you thought was etched in stone.

What follows, then, is a *realistic* planning process that will produce, if you follow it at all closely, the plan you need to become a multi-millionaire selling services. It's not pretty; certainly not grand. It just works.

The Parts Of Your Plan

One of the ways other writers on the subject of planning go wrong is that they never seem to understand all the parts that really need to be in the plan. In my view successful plans are made up of four distinct parts:

- Part 1: your goal statement;

- Part 2: your profit objective for the next year, the marketing program you need to reach it, and the cost of reaching it;

- Part 3: (to be implemented if Part 2 will not enable you to reach your profit objective) how much additional profit you must make to reach your profit objective, how you must expand your existing marketing program, and what will this cost;

- Part 4: (to be implemented if Parts 2 and 3 will not enable you to reach your profit objective) how much additional profit you must make to reach your profit objective, what new marketing activities you must undertake, and what will this cost.

Let's look at each of these four parts.

Part 1: Your Goal Statement

Every business plan should be headed with your personal goal. This is almost uniformly left out of discussions on creating plans but, arguably, this part is the most important because it both provides and describes your *motivation* for doing all that needs to be done both in planning and implementing your plan.

This part of the plan is short. Indeed, you need only say something like this:

"My goal is to achieve financial independence by age 55. At that time I intend to have annual income from my investments of $100,000 a year. The following plan details how I intend to produce the money I need in the next 12 months to stay on track for achieving my goal at the time I plan to reach it."

This is quite enough. But it is of vital importance. I'd like to draw your attention to a few of the key words and phrases in these three very simple sentences:

1. "My goal" . . . It is vital that you remember at all times that this is *your* personal goal. It is something that *you* have chosen and that *you* have committed yourself to reaching.

2. "financial independence" . . . The entire thrust of this book is to have you amass a sufficiency of capital through the sale of your services. "Financial independence" means being able to generate the totality of your income from your capital investments.

3. "by age" . . . It is vital that you designate a precise moment when you *expect* to reach your goal;

4. "intend" . . . Note I do not say "wish" or "want". I say "intend" because, after all the planning and implementation you'll be doing, you should be certain.

5. "the following plan details how I intend to produce the money" . . . your plan is a precise road map that clearly lays down what you must do, when you must do it, and the results you must have.

6. "next 12 months" . . . plans are best conceived on an annual basis and may then be broken down into smaller units.

7. "at the time I plan to reach it." The plan you're creating now is only a part of a larger, multi-year plan. To achieve your overall goal you must achieve a series of lesser, annual objectives. This is one of them.

Your goals statement is a promise you make to yourself and as such you should sign and date it when your plan is done. You want to be clear about what you've set for yourself . . . and you want to hold yourself accountable . . . *to yourself.*

Part 2: Your Profit Objective For The Next Year, The Marketing Program You Need To Reach It, And The Cost Of Reaching It

The purpose of a plan is to produce that superfluity of money known as profit, because it is only by producing profit that you can reach your income objectives and hence your overall goal.

Towards this end you need to consider three questions:

1. Can I reach my profit objectives for the next year by simply replicating the services I am offering now and the marketing activities I am doing now?

2. If not, can I reach my profit objectives for the next year by offering the same services but increasing my marketing of them?

3. If not, can I reach my profit objectives for the next year by diversifying the services I offer and beginning new modes of marketing?

Just how you develop your plan depends on the answers you give to these three questions. If you can reach your profit objectives for the next year by simply replicating both the services you are offering now and your current marketing activities, your plan is only going to consist of Part 1 (which begins *all* plans) and Part 2. If you can't, then you are going to have to add one or both of the remaining parts. In any case, you must still detail your profit objectives, the marketing activities you'll be using to achieve them, and what it's going to cost you.

Your Profit Objectives

As I've already made quite clear, you will achieve your overall goal by achieving a series of annual profit objectives. Let's say that to reach your goal, you've determined that you must make $100,000 every year *over and above all your business (including marketing) expenses.* This $100,000 — the money you KEEP — is the crucial number, and your plan must be geared to its realistic achievement.

The crucial question here is: is the way you currently do business producing the amount of money you need to meet your profit objective? Not might it ... or could it ... but *is* it?

For some few people reading this book, the answer is that what you are doing now is indeed producing the precise number of dollars you need to meet your financial objectives. If you are not interested in increasing your dollar objective, living standard, *etc.*, then you are on a *maintenance track*; your plan will clearly indicate this. Your task at this point is plain:

- review your last year's marketing activities to see what happened, analyze results and determine costs;

- plot out next year's marketing activities and make conservative response and liberal cost projections for them;

- factor in remaining expenses of running your business.

The result should be a plan that clearly outlines your marketing for the next year, its costs, the return you've projected, and your profit.

Let's see how this works in practice.

Reviewing Your Last Year's Marketing Activities To See What Happened, Analyze Results And Determine Costs

All too often most service business owners are "winging it" through their marketing. Yes, they're marketing, but on a "catch as catch can" basis. There's no plan, no attempt to track responses, and therefore no certain data on which to make tactical decisions through the year. Too many are so busy delivering services and putting out the usual business-related fires, that they allow the scrutiny and research components of marketing to go by the way. This is a big mistake. The result is that too many service business owners never get their marketing running like a predictable machine.

The way to move towards this necessary objective is to review all your marketing activities for the last year. What you're looking for is the following information:

- What did you do?

- When did you do it?

- What did it cost?

- What results did you get in terms of prospect response?

- What results did you get in terms of clients/dollars generated?

Each of these questions has a specific answer you can get . . . if you keep adequate records.

This, however, is the first problem. When you begin to assemble a detailed plan of the kind I'm recommending, you're probably going to find it pretty heavy going, because you've kept lousy records. Thus, my first piece of advice: when you're in the marketing business, you're necessarily in the data generating and hence data collecting business. It is no longer acceptable merely to "do some marketing" and let the chips fall where they may. Those chips are crucial . . . and you've got to know as much about them as possible! Chances are you don't do this now . . . but YOU'RE GOING TO HAVE TO CHANGE!!!

Okay, it's unfortunate that you don't have the data you need now, but this cannot keep you from doing the necessary work. Thus, the first time you begin to assemble a plan like this, JUST DO THE BEST YOU CAN. Let's be realistic with each other: if you don't have the real, hard, specific data you're going to make a number of mistakes and, because you're relying on uncertain memory, at least some of your conclusions may be misleading, even wrong. This is the price you pay for your slack record keeping. Too bad. You've got to start somewhere.

Thus:

- Open up a file in your computer titled "plan/(year)"

- Go through your cash disbursements journal and tabulate your marketing expenses. List expenses for marketing communications, printing, ads, postage, consultants, tele-phone, fax, *etc.* When you're finished you should have a very clear picture of how much money you spent for mar-keting and what you did.

- Now tabulate the number of responses from each activity. Say you ran an advertisement in the yellow pages. It cost $500. How many queries/prospects did you get from this ad between January 1 of the last year and December 31? Okay, so you don't know. Guesstimate. And keep better records this year.

- Now tabulate how many customers/clients you got from this ad and how many dollars they generated. The way to determine this is to go through your cash receivables ledger. Every dollar that's come into your business in the last year has come in for a marketing reason. You need to know why and to distribute the dollars to the appropriate categories. By looking at the source of each dollar, you'll know whether that marketing activity is worth continuing. *Note:* for future reference, you should develop a simple code system and put it next to the deposit amount in your cash receivables journal. Thus "YP" next to the customer name and amount paid means he responded to your yellow pages ad.

A simple chart in your computer will assist you in gathering this information.

Marketing Activity	Date	Cost	Prospects Generated	Dollars Generated

Several things are obvious about this chart:

1. it can easily be kept on your computer;
2. it forces you to code all your marketing activities so you can track response;
3. it forces whoever answers your phone, sorts your mail, *etc.,* to ask for the code and keep track of what happens . . . including, importantly, the dollars generated.

The chances that you're doing this now on a consistent basis are almost non-existent. BUT YOU'RE GOING TO, or you'll keep running your marketing in a helter-skelter fashion.

Reviewing Your Data, Making Deductions And Decisions

This part of the plan, you'll remember, is for people at a mature stage of development for their service businesses; they're making enough money, so they say, to reach their objectives. They don't want more, they just want to let the good times roll. Fair enough. Still, there's no reason for these people to spend an extra dime to reach their objectives. That's just plain stupid.

Now, keep in mind what the single objective of your plan is: to enable you to reach your dollar objective as soon as possible in the year while spending the fewest number of dollars and other resources. Any idiot can spend more dollars than he needs to generate profit; it's the wise and seasoned marketer who understands that the real game is getting maximum return for minimum expense. To achieve this objective, you need to review the chart you've created in the light of the following four categories. *Note:* whatever marketing activity you're doing fits into one of these four categories. You must decide which one so you'll know whether to continue, augment, cut back or delete the marketing activity in question.

- The activity is working at maximum efficiency. You are investing a moderate amount of money in either prospect identification and cultivation or client maintenance in return for the kind of sustained profit you need given the percentage of your annual financial objective this service and activity represent.

- The activity is working at reasonable efficiency. Your investment in both prospect and client development is moderate and your profit return is moderate.

- The activity is working reasonably given the fact that you have not completed a complete cycle of The Rule of Seven. While you have not yet made money (or very little money), there are grounds for believing that this activity will in due course produce profit.

- The activity is not working well. Despite the fact that you have completed a full marketing cycle of The Rule of Seven, the activity is producing little or no money and there are no grounds for thinking this situation will change in the near future.

Now, whatever marketing activity you're doing fits into one of these four categories. You must decide which one so you'll know whether to continue, augment, cut back or delete the marketing activity in question.

Say your chart looks like this:

Marketing Activity	Date	Cost	Prospects Generated	Dollars Generated
yellow pages ad	01/93-12/93	$500	40	$250/1 client
booth at prof. expo	Feb 23	$350	3	$400/2 clients
mailing to past customers	April 1	$600	250	$4,500/8 clients

Before beginning to make any deductions from this information, make sure that your numbers are accurate. While the numbers above may, at first glance, appear complete, upon reflection they're probably not.

- While the yellow pages ad itself was $500, what about the cost of the designer who laid it out for you? Did you count that? Did you also determine the cost of any follow-up mailings you would have done to those prospects? In actual fact, the costs here would be higher than $500 and the loss situation even worse. However, to offset this, is there any reason for thinking that the one client you did get will continue with you longer than his current contract? In other words, is there potential value beyond the present? While you can't count this as definite yet, you can weigh the prospect of future business into your reckoning.

- As for the booth at the professional expo, you've indicated 3 prospects, but in fact what about the mailing list of attendees they made available and which you mailed to? That cost also needs to be factored in and any money generated.

- Regarding the mailing to past customers, did you also figure in the time and expense it took to produce the mailing and any necessary follow-up?

In short, make sure that both your expenses and receipts have been *fully* tabulated.

What Should You Be Doing?

The point of this exercise is to determine what's working for you ... what you should be emphasizing and increasing and what should be cut back. You may be at a mature stage in the development of your service business and the amount of income you want (and work you want to do), but this doesn't mean you can afford to skip over this review process.

While the example I've created is obviously simple and incomplete, even it suggests alternatives for consideration:

- If the yellow pages ad has been written in a client-centered cash-copy style (you'll know after reading the next chapter) and is still not generating enough to pay for itself, either the ad should be cut back to a minimum or dropped altogether. However, the chances are that the ad is written in a "me-centered" not a "you-centered" fashion. If this is the case, it's obvious such a style isn't working and that the ad has to be rewritten. A moderate course of action is: rewrite the ad in a "you-centered" way and keep better track of the responses for one year. Then make a decision accordingly.

- Your present course regarding the booth at the professional expo isn't working very well. Either get yourself hired as a speaker at the expo on a topic that will draw people who can benefit from your service (your booth can be part of your compensation package) and/or launch a more aggressive means of getting people to your booth, presenting the benefits you have available for them and following up faster/better. Without change here, this expenditure is questionable.

- Your mailing to past customers is making money. Why? What are you offering that these people want? Given the cost-benefit ratio here, you need to give consideration to redirecting marketing dollars that aren't working well elsewhere into a second or even a third mailing and probably some telephone follow-up.

A plan forces you to:

- think through the information you'll need;
- set up a system for gathering and categorizing the information;
- analyze the information to see what it means;
- consider various alternative tactics that make sense given the information you've got;
- make appropriate decisions on these various alternatives that influence your future behavior.

Most service businesses aren't following these steps. As a result they make very costly mistakes.

I think of one of my clients, for instance, selling a medical data base service. Each year they were spending about $100,000 on ads in medical journals. They usually took the back inside cover or back page, some of the most expensive space in the publications. The ads were all of the "show the flag" variety, "Hi, mom, we're here." The physician running the program loved them . . . not least because his name appeared in many of them. Nobody, however, knew the answers to the two simple questions I asked when they retained me:

1. How many people respond to these ads?
2. How many dollars worth of service do they buy as a result?

NOBODY KNEW!

As a result, I made them:

1. list all advertising sources that were appropriate for their product (there were about two dozen good print sources);
2. get rate cards for each;
3. design the smallest client-centered ad with changeable code;
4. put in place a mechanism for counting and storing responses;
5. keep track of dollars generated.

These changes saved the client over $60,000 a year . . . and even more important launched a profitable advertising program. (After which the ingrates figured they knew all there was to know about this game and stopped using my services! Of course!)

Plotting Out Next Year's Marketing Activities And Making Conservative Response and Liberal Cost Projections For Them

Once you know what you've done, what's worked (and what hasn't) and, importantly, decided what it makes sense for you to do, it's time to do a chart for the next year. As you create this chart, keep these things in mind:

- Each marketing activity that you plan to do should be indicated on the chart;

- Add the cost of each. Make sure all costs have been factored in, not just the obvious ones;

- Make your response projections conservative. There is always the temptation to think that the rest of the world is as enthusiastic about your service (and your marketing) as you are. They probably aren't, and your projections should mirror their relative disinterest.

Remember: this chart has as its objective showing you precisely what you must do and precisely what results you need to achieve your financial objective for the year. It also forces you to think through exactly what you plan to do to reach these objectives.

Thus, if you have previously run a booth at your professional expo with mediocre results, keeping this item amongst your marketing activities will force you to think through how to achieve better results. If in the past you have gotten just 3 prospects from the show, and if this year you've determined that you need 20 to make money, you're going to have to consider how you can generate the extra 17 people. Will you:

- get yourself hired as a speaker so you can benefit from the pre-expo publicity, get your information into the hands of all those attending your program, get their names, addresses and telephone numbers for prompt follow up, *etc.*;

- create a dazzling offer and incorporate it in some client-centered marketing communications which you'll be far more aggressive about handing out around the expo area;

- retrain the person running your booth to be more client-centered and assertive about meeting people and telling them the benefits your service company has got available?

You get the picture.

To become a millionaire is a matter of unquenchable spirit and sufficient numbers. You've got to dedicate yourself to achieving this objective, and you've got to keep reaching short-term, quantifiable plateaus. This is where your plan comes in. To reach this year's objective with the services you're currently offering, you're going to have to make a number of marketing activities return the right number of prospects, and you're going to have to convert a certain number of these into clients/dollars.

Right now you're suffering because you don't have a precise dollar objective for the year, haven't got a clue about how many marketing activities you've got and how they're working for you (or not working), and what's got to happen in the next year for you to meet your objective. YET YOU HAVE THE AUDACITY TO MOAN ABOUT THE ECONOMY, ABOUT PEOPLE WHO DON'T BUY, ABOUT EVERYTHING UNDER THE SUN. Ridiculous!!! Why, you've got the means of becoming a millionaire. What you've got to do is USE THEM!

Don't Forget Your Overall Expenses

Before your chart is finished, you have one more step to go through: factoring in all the expenses of your business. So far I've advised you to be certain about your *marketing* expenses. Now it's time to factor in all the *other* expenses of your business. After all, you've got to make sure you're generating enough money to cover all these as well as your marketing costs and still have the amount left over you need to reach your financial objective.

The rest of your business expenses will fall into two general categories:

- personnel
- non-personnel office maintenance and administration.

To get the relevant entries under each category, review your cash disbursements journal.

Personnel will consist of items such as:

- salaries
- health care
- pensions
- insurance, *etc.*

Non-personnel office maintenance and administration will include:

- rent
- heat, air conditioning, utilities
- office supplies and equipment
- insurance on premises and office contents, *etc.*

Your completed plan must generate enough money to pay for:

- all your marketing costs
- all your personnel costs
- all your non-personnel costs, and
- this year's contribution to your overall goal.

Now I ask you: can you honestly say that the plan you've now created — a maintenance plan, mind you — actually does this? Or do you just HOPE that it does?

You're not finished with the plan until you KNOW.

If you're uncertain, go back and tinker some more. Let me be clear with you about one thing: there's no disgrace to working and reworking this plan until you're certain. Marketing, you see, is divided into two parts: there is planning and there is execution. During the planning process, you should think . . . and rethink. And rethink, if necessary. During the execution phase, you should *do*, not *plan*.

What is fatal is to spend too little time thinking through a rock-solid marketing plan and to launch the execution phase prematurely, having to zig and zag through it, rethinking your assumptions along the way. Michael Dukakis learned this lesson the hard way during his ill-fated presidential campaign. He didn't bother to think through his marketing strategy before hitting the campaign trail. Thus, when he should have been executing a plan, he was still in the process of conceiving it. This is fatal. I beg you: do not make this mistake!

If Part 2 Doesn't Produce All The Money You Need: Adding Part 3 To Your Plan

If Part 2 provides all the money you need to reach your financial objective, I say more power to you! If it doesn't, don't worry. The truth is, the vast majority of service business owners and the overwhelming majority of people reading this book are not currently running service businesses that can make them multi-millionaires — certainly not in any reasonable period of time. This is only a problem if you say you want to become a multi-millionaire but are not willing to rethink and redirect your business. If you are so willing, there's nothing to worry about. At some point, by following the guidelines of this book, I guarantee you will reach the maintenance stage of your business where it does predictably produce the money you need for your financial objective. I'm at that stage myself . . . but I got to that stage by going through the other stages! And so will you. Thus, let's go on to Part 3.

How Much Additional Profit Must You Make To Reach Your Profit Objective, How Must You Expand Your Existing Marketing Program, and What Will This Cost?

Now that you've completed Part 2 of your plan, you know how much of a short-fall you've got, how much more money you need to meet your annual financial objective. Good. Now that you know the problem, we can begin fashioning the solution. There are two ways to do this: 1) you can immediately rush to the assumption that you're going to have to diversify your service line with all the extra work and costs that that entails, or 2) you can decide an enhanced marketing program for your existing service line will enable you to meet your objectives. Since this is the less expensive alternative, I suggest you try it first. This is what Part 3 of your plan is all about: maximizing dollar return from your current service line by both improving and adding to its profitable marketing.

This part builds on what you've already done in Part 2 and involves considering two questions:

- Can you undertake your existing marketing more efficiently to get the number of dollars you need?

- Must you add additional marketing activities to generate the number of dollars you need?

Now, as you will not be surprised to hear from this frugal man of Scottish descent, before you even consider spending more dollars, you've got to see if you can use your current resources more productively.

In this connection, I'll tell you the story of one of my community health clients. They provide a variety of nursing services. For years they'd spent upwards of $40,000 annually on yellow pages advertising — but without tracking results. The first thing I had them do was keep good records of where their referrals came from. As a result, they discovered that they were overspending on their yellow pages advertising by at least $30,000 annually. Now, this sum was more than adequate to hire a full-time marketing professional who could pay visits to discharge planners of area hospitals. Since this agency received a good percentage of its business from several local hospitals but had never had the time or resources to develop lucrative relationships with others, this course of action made sense. It cut out wasteful marketing and augmented current profitable marketing. In other words it made existing marketing more profitable — without causing the organization to diversify its service line and add new expenses (including new marketing expenses).

Let's see if you can do this.

First, review each of your existing marketing activities. Can you say in all seriousness that you are squeezing full benefit from each of them? I doubt it.

Take the example previously provided:

Marketing Activity	Date	Cost	Prospects Generated	Dollars Generated
mailing to past customers	April 1	$600	250	$4,500/8 clients

First, you must review this in detail.

- Are you merely mailing to past customers once?

- How are you following up? Are you simply using mail? What about phone calls? Or visits, where appropriate?

- Have you scrutinized all your marketing communications to make sure they are rich with benefits and client-centered?

- How quickly are you following up?

- What else are you doing to try to retrieve past customers and get them to buy again?

The sad fact is that most service businesses are lazy businesses. Most exhibit their greatest enthusiasm and energy in their first year or two in business. After that, they fall into routine. And routine, unless it is profitable routine, is the greatest drag on becoming a multi-millionaire I know. Unless what you are doing is *guaranteed* to make you a multi-millionaire in the time you've allocated for the task, what you're doing is killing your ability to get rich.

This is why you've got to review your routine and see what can be salvaged and what needs to be improved — now!

Think, for example, of that New Jersey marketer I previously told you about. He placed a card in my card-deck, and then sat back and waited for his results. They arrived — in heaps. Indeed, there were so many responses that the man (despite being advised this would happen) couldn't handle them all. Instead of thinking through the necessary means of processing them, he let them build up — while he retreated to his basement office in despair and did nothing. Finally, over 500 leads built up — leads that he never answered at all despite the fact that he was selling a service that cost a minimum of $800.

Now, I grant you that this is an extreme case. However, I firmly believe that most service businesses are handling their marketing as ineptly (if not as spectacularly ineptly) as my New Jersey advertiser. This is why you've got to review each of your marketing activities to see if it can be improved and so help sell the number of units of service you need to meet your financial objectives.

Thus, you need to consider the following questions:

— Before The Sale

- Are you prepared to respond to prospect inquiries immediately?

- Are you prepared to follow up quickly?

- Have you developed client-centered marketing communications that "cut to the chase" and hammer home the benefits you've got available — motivating the prospect to make an immediate decision?

- Are you prepared to ask each and every prospect the crucial words, "What will it take for us to do business now?"

- Are you prepared to keep bringing your benefits to the attention of people you've determined are good prospects?

- Are you equally prepared to drop quickly (but civilly) people you've determined are not prospects, instead of wasting more time and other resources on them?

— After The Sale

- Are you prepared to find out what other ways the client can benefit from what you've got and what the client wants to achieve in short order — and in the longer term?

- Are you prepared to address the client directly about these matters — as soon as the client is happy with your work?

- Are you prepared to get the client to provide testimonials and referrals to you — as soon as he's happy with your work?

- Are you prepared to continue to bring client-centered benefits to the attention of this client so long as there is the reasonable certainty he wants to acquire them?

— When A Client Has Lapsed

- Are you prepared to fashion a special offer to lapsed clients to entice them back to the benefits you have available?

- Are you prepared to win them back through letters and through direct telephone conversations?

- Are you prepared to be exceedingly direct with them about the benefits you've got available for them and how much, how very much, you want them back?

In short, are you quite ready to institute a far more assertive and thorough process of handling your present prospects and clients than you are currently using?

If This Assertive Process Isn't Enough

Now, either this new assertive process will produce the number of new clients and new dollars you need — or it won't. That is, by implementing a more assertive policy with the prospects who come in to you now on a regular basis through all your marketing activities and with the clients you've got now and have had in the past, you'll either reach your objective or you won't. One thing, however, is clear to me: when you begin to implement this kind of assertive marketing, you are better off faster. Moreover, if you maintain this kind of assertive marketing, you are better off permanently.

Still, given your current number of prospects, existing clients and past clients, there may not be enough of them — even given your more assertive marketing — to enable you to reach your financial objective. No problem. You need to add more marketing activities . . . and follow up the results with this kind of new assertiveness.

What Kinds Of Marketing Should You Add?

But what should you do? That depends on:

- what has worked for you in the past;
- where your cost per lead is lowest;
- where you can test for the lowest price and with the least risk;
- where you can get the largest number of prospects fastest.

I hasten to add, these things are not always compatible. Perhaps what has worked well for you in the past is doing workshops and talk programs where your prospects are in the audience. Fine. But arranging these programs takes time. There is an opportunity cost here, and if you wait you may not be able to reach your objective this year. Is this acceptable to you? On the other hand, there may be other, faster lead-generating systems, but they are probably going to be more expensive.

What should you do?

1. Don't assume that new is better. Have you really done everything possible to maximize return from your existing prospect flow, current and past clients? Don't take any action *whatsoever* until you're sure you're adequately handling all these sources.

2. Determine how quickly you need additional leads. Say you're going to need 25% more leads to close the number of sales you need. Say that workshops will generate most of these leads but that it takes up to 6 months to arrange them. If you set them up today and start getting additional leads in 6 months, will you have enough time to get the new leads in, convert them to clients, do the work and make the money in order to meet your objective?

3. Have you brain stormed all the various marketing activities available to you and determined which make the most sense? All too often service business owners are not fully conversant with the various means of marketing available

to them, don't know how these means work and cannot, therefore, make an intelligent choice about which option they should be using. The choice they make, therefore, may well be uninformed.

4.   Have you really thought through what needs to happen with the selection(s) you've made so that you derive maximum benefit? For example, had my New Jersey marketing colleague thought through both what would happen with his card-deck advertising and how he would respond to it for maximum advantage, he wouldn't have handled the situation as amateurishly and unprofitably as he did.

In short, before you institute a more aggressive and enhanced marketing program for your existing service line, you need to think through:

- what you need to achieve in terms of service units sold and dollars generated;

- what has worked (and not worked) for you in the past. If you've been making money with an activity, it stands to reason that increasing this activity and making it more organized should make you even more money;

- how any new marketing processes will work and why you think they're suited for your operation;

- how you'll handle the increased flow of leads and business so that the results you get don't overwhelm your ability to handle them.

And remember: you want to do all this while spending the least conceivable amount of money!

Is this possible? YES IT IS!

Take the community health organization I referred to above; it's headed by an executive director who is always demanding a "new idea" from me. One day she told me we should be pitching our service at the lawyers and accountants in the community because they were in a position to refer people to the organization. I balked at this suggestion immediately. "What makes more sense," I said, "creating a new marketing campaign aimed at community lawyers and accountants, or getting our marketing representative to make just one more call every day to a hospital discharge planner who regularly knows about people who need our services and is already in position to refer them to us?"

Put this way, the wayward executive director was (however reluctantly) forced to agree that making additional calls upon discharge planners made infinitely more sense than mounting a new and costly marketing effort to accountants and lawyers.

Take another example. I go to a dentist (a service provider) in Harvard Square. Like most people, I hate going and delay my appointments as long as possible. My dentist told me during my last visit that his business was off and that he had more collection problems these days. Now, given the fact that I'm local, that I pay promptly and am about as good a patient as he's ever likely to have, why is his marketing so inept?

When my appointment is done, his assistant may or may not book the next appointment with me. Sometimes she doesn't do this because she's "busy" chatting with a co-worker; sometimes it's because she's genuinely engaged. In either event, the dentist has missed an excellent marketing opportunity. Now, I can understand that the assistant will sometimes be busy and not be able to book another appointment immediately. But what I cannot understand is why the dentist doesn't ask the assistant to call me later that day or the next to book the appointment. He needs the business and the money . . . yet this never happens.

Moreover, when they do send the inevitable post card after 6 months, they NEVER follow it up with a phone call. Nor even with another card. The sum total of this man's marketing is one rinky-dink postcard.

THIS IS RIDICULOUS . . . and that's why I'll be telling him about this book and particularly why Part 2 of this plan is for him.

This man doesn't so much need a host of new marketing activities as he needs to think through his existing marketing and make it more assertive by:

1. recommending another appointment at the conclusion of the one I'm having;

2. walking me down the aisle to his receptionist and inviting me to book the time;

3. if she's busy right then (this happens), advising me that she'll call today or tomorrow — "What's good for you, Jeffrey?"

4. following up until the next appointment is booked;

5. calling to remind me to have it . . .

. . . and then going through the whole process again once I come in for my appointment. This is a more assertive marketing program, and it cannot but produce more dollars earlier — which is just what it's supposed to do.

And if it doesn't? Why *then* he can explore all the other appropriate marketing possibilities, including (but not limited to):

* mailings to lapsed and tardy patients;

* local card decks (often called val-packs) and paid advertisements;

* free media (tooth care is a perfectly appropriate subject for periodic media);

* speaking engagements in schools, *etc.*;

* cross promotions with other businesses, *etc.*

These, however, should *follow* not *precede* more assertive marketing.

Now, either this more assertive and enhanced marketing of existing services will produce the number of dollars you need, or it won't. If it does, write me and say "Thank you, Jeffrey", because I've saved you a lot of money and aggravation. If it doesn't . . . why, that's what Part 4 of the plan is for.

Part 4: Diversifying And Marketing Your Service Line To Produce The Additional Profit You Need To Reach Your Financial Objective

Both parts 2 and 3 will produce money for you. Problem is, given your business costs and financial objectives, you've determined they cannot produce the money you need to reach your objective. No problem. As above, you know what the problem is, now it's time to come up with the strategy for solving it. Here it is:

* Determine how much money you need to raise in the next year to meet your objective;

* Be certain that your current service line and an enhanced marketing of it will not be able to achieve this objective;

- Once you've determined that diversifying your service line is necessary, brainstorm the various means of diversification that make sense given your current situation (including available resources);

- Gather information on what it takes to create and make money from these additional services;

- Create a short list of possibilities for diversification;

- Be certain you have both the skills, time, money and other resources you need to make a success of these alternatives;

- Gather information on who else is offering the services you are considering, how they are offering them, their prices, *etc.*;

- Draft the kind of service you want, how you want to offer it, benefits you have available, how it will work, its cost, *etc.*;

- Present your draft service to client prospects and gauge their response;

- Make any necessary changes in your service that their responses suggest;

- Brainstorm the means of marketing available to you for launching this service to the appropriate prospect groups;

- Gather all the information you need about each different marketing gambit: who is it targeting, how much does it cost, what kind of approach works best, *etc.*;

- Draft a preliminary marketing plan embodying the marketing means you've selected, when you plan to use them, what you need to make each a success (including proper follow-up procedures), conservative response projections and a conservative guesstimate about how many clients/dollars you may generate *this year.*

Your first impression upon scanning this list is that launching a new service is a lot of work. Well, you're right! It is! In fact, each time you launch a new service, you're really launching a new business, and it must be treated as such. There are a few consolations, however, when the service you're launching is not the first you've started:

- You've already been through this before. While you may not have been as organized the first time as I'm urging you to be now, the fact you've been through this process before will assist you . . . not least because you know what you're getting into and how long it can take to make things profitable. This is all to the good.

- If your new service is a natural outgrowth of services you're already offering, you've already done a lot of the work of getting it off to a good start. Your house mailing list, for instance, of current and past clients will be of the utmost assistance; so will names and addresses of media sources who have covered you in the past and even rate card information for paid advertising.

- You'll be far more realistic in your expectations and your ability to read events. Here's where all your experience, including all the mistakes you've made in the past, begin to pay off.

So, yes, there's a lot of work, but you're going to get through it a lot faster and more efficiently than if you were launching a business for the first time. Let's quickly review each of the steps above to make sure you do.

— Determine how much money you need to raise in the next year to meet your objective

This is crucial. As you know by now, I am insistent that you know precisely how much money you're trying to raise before you get down to the nitty-gritty of raising it.

— Be certain that your current service line and an enhanced marketing of it will not be able to achieve this objective

Because there is a lot of work involved in launching any new service, be absolutely certain you have done everything you can to raise the money you need by more assertive marketing of the services you already have. Do not expand until you're sure.

— Once you've determined that diversifying your service line is necessary, brainstorm the various means of diversification that make sense given your current situation (including available resources)

There is an infinity of ways to diversify a business. All may be appropriate for you someday, but only some are appropriate given your current situation. Thus, while the local dentist may someday want to own a string of dental offices around New England and the nation, what probably makes more sense for him now is to expand the various types of dental services he offers locally. For this, he needs to brainstorm every kind of dental service one could offer . . . and then begin to limit his choices given his current situation and current available resources.

The sad fact is, most service business owners have never taken a moment to understand what additional services make sense given the business they're running and which ones make the most immediate sense given their current situation and resources. This is absurd.

I suggest you keep a file marked "diversification" into which you add your dreams, thoughts, insight, and information about the various kinds of services you could offer. I am insistent about having such a file for each aspect of my business. Thus, for my publishing company, I keep information on future books (that is, how-to service offerings) I both wish to write and publish. I even keep a list of future companies I'd like to start! You see, once you have become master of the process of service diversification, you're going to want to exploit your information and so produce more wealth faster.

— Gather information on what it takes to create and make money from these additional services

One of the things that happened during the decade of the 1980's was that millions of people, seized by the entrepreneurial spirit, went out and launched businesses . . . without first knowing how to make money from those businesses. As a result, many of these people have endured years of unnecessary misery and frustration. Don't let this be you. Do your damnedest to find out how money is actually made from the services you are contemplating adding. This means knowing things like:

- how much it will cost not merely to launch but to maintain this service;
- the price for the service which will ensure utmost competitive advantage with maximum return;
- how expenses can be minimized;
- additional means of deriving profit.

Unfortunately, much of this information is not readily available and much of the rest resides in the brains of competitors who clearly are not interested in letting you have it. What you are looking for, however, is information that will provide you with a competitive advantage and with insight into how to derive maximum profit from the service.

If you approach the necessary information gathering task piecemeal, it is sometimes easier to get the insight you need. Thus, when I launched my card-deck company (a business I knew relatively little about beforehand), I needed information about:

- gathering advertisers;

- saving money on printing;

- reducing my costs for mailing lists, and

- producing cards that would get the maximum response.

Of course, my competitors had the bulk of information on these subjects. However, in this highly competitive field, they were going to share precious little of it. Still, different groups could supply me with what I needed. Thus:

- the advertisers could be weaned from their existing relationships with a significantly lower price. Given my significantly lower overhead, I could provide this. An initial market survey of potential advertisers had clearly indicated that price was a significant consideration for them and that they could be motivated by comparable quality at lower prices. Providing this provided an immediate competitive advantage.

- printing companies were in a position to advise how they could provide lower prices. Prepaying the printing bill produced a discounted price and a good reason for asking advertisers for prepayment (an industry innovation);

- mailing lists are a resource, just like money. While other card-decks were generally competitive, they needed these names, too, and were willing to swap names with me in order to reduce their own list rental charges. They were perfectly prepared to supply information about what they needed in this area and to work with me to get card-deck responsive names without having to pay for them.

- as for producing cards that get maximum response, had I not happened to be an expert in this area myself, I would have had no trouble getting the necessary information either from any number of direct mail specialists or by selecting the cards I liked from other people's decks and calling the advertiser directly to see how he'd done.

In short, while it would have been difficult to secure all the information I needed from one source, by breaking what I needed into bits and approaching a series of individuals it was pretty easy to get what I wanted.

— Create a short list of possibilities for diversification

Over time, you may add any number of new services, both related and unrelated to what you're doing now. Fair enough. But for now you need a short list of possibilities. Three or four should be adequate for your current consideration.

— Be certain you have both the skills, time, money and other resources you need to make a success of these alternatives

The word "diversification" means adding a service and its marketing beyond what you're already doing. You must never forget that you've adopted this course in order to make up for a short-fall from what you're now doing. What you're now doing is taking up time and money and psychic energy. What you don't need is another activity that's going to eat up even more of your resources without producing a disproportionate return on your investment. Never forget this!

That's why, before you make any final determination, you've got to make sure you possess the necessary skills, time, money and other resources you need to launch this new service successfully without threatening the ability of the other services from which you're already deriving income to continue to function profitably. I speak from the heart on this matter given the fact that my current biggest issue is time management, not the ability to conceive, research and launch profitable new ventures.

This means thinking through both what will happen if your new service is popular . . . and what will happen if it isn't, for both, in their individual ways, present challenges that must be met.

If your service is popular and your marketing produces a bumper crop of qualified leads (which should happen as you master this book), will you be able to cope with all the additional demands on your time and the possibility you'll have to commit new resources to managing your success? Be sure. Not so long ago, I ran the following card in my card deck.

Despite the fact that I was charging $3000 a day in the midst of a recession, I was overwhelmed with leads. Because of my other commitments, I didn't have adequate time to follow up these leads, weed out the good prospects from the bad, book appointments, do the consulting, *etc.* In the end, I had to drop this service because I couldn't manage the prosperity coming from it. Ironic, isn't it, that in the midst of a major national recession one would find oneself turning down a plethora of lucrative assignments?

By the same token, what if I'd factored in the need for so many dollars from this new service and found it more difficult to get qualified leads than I'd thought, more difficult to close deals, and that more time had to be committed to ensure results than I'd estimated? Resources (including time, the scarcest of all) would have to be diverted from other projects to salvage this one, thereby possibly threatening the whole.

Thus, you could be threatened equally by an avalanche of prosperity or unplanned for problems. Either way, you must be certain you've got the resources — or can get them — that you need to take care of what develops. This is why launching a new service always entails some risk. Even when you get a bumper crop of qualified leads!

— *Gather information on who else is offering the services you are considering, how they are offering them, their prices, etc.*

What will help is getting as much information from other people in the business as you can about the various alternatives you're contemplating. This is why it's so helpful to maintain a diversification file and pop into it everything about all the additional services you're contemplating and how they're working for others.

Plop in:

- all marketing communications, including cover letters, ads, flyers, brochures, *etc.*;
- price information about what others are charging for the service;
- cost information about personnel, materials, *etc.* that you need to provide the service;
- information on companies that once offered the service . . . but now don't . . . and on those that are offering it in new and expanded ways.

In short, stay alert when you're roaming the neighborhood or when you're traveling. Look in the yellow pages when you're out of town and call service businesses like yours. Ask them to mail you their brochures and marketing communications. If their yellow pages ad looks client-centered, rip it out and take it home.

The important thing is finding out what others in your industry are doing, how they are offering services similar to yours, and whether and how they are making money doing so.

I have for long carried on a relentless war against pointless originality. If you don't need to be original, don't waste your time trying to be. Just figure out what works and, to the greatest extent possible, copy it. This is what the Japanese did with the semi-conductor industry, and they've done it so successfully they took an important U.S. industry and turned it into a multi-billion dollar cash cow for Japan. Enough said.

— Draft the kind of service you want, how you want to offer it, benefits you have available, how it will work, its cost, etc.

Now, having considered your situation and gathered and scrutinized necessary data, it's time for you to sit at your computer and begin to draft an outline of the service you want to offer. Note I say "draft", because the work you're doing now is very much subject to change depending on what happens with the subsequent points.

However, write:

- what the service is going to do;
- how you want to offer it;
- who you're offering it to;
- the specific benefits you have for your prospects;
- precisely how the service is going to work;
- the cost of the service;
- the profit from the service.

Reviewing this information with service business owners, I've frequently been appalled at how unspecific their information is at this point. That is a mistake. Even though this is a draft subject to revision, what you write now needs to be as specific as possible. Vagueness at this point indicates how really little you know about what you're doing and thus how risky what you're doing really is.

Does this look "do-able" to you, especially given your other commitments both personal and professional? Is it sufficiently specific that you can fully describe who you're offering it to, the benefits they get, and what you'll be doing to provide the service?

If not, back to the computer keyboard with you!

— Present your draft service to client prospects and gauge their response

Once you're finished with your draft, you have what amounts to a brochure or précis; the service is now near pre-launch. As such, it's time to test your ideas, as embodied in a preliminary (but well formed) marketing communication, on real people . . . real prospects! What do these all-important people say?

Well, first, you're going to have to round up some of them. Do this:

- Put together a list of about 20 satisfied clients, people who have used your service previously and were happy with their results. Don't use family, friends or anybody else who isn't a real prospect or who won't speak honestly to you.

- Send these people a letter telling them you are putting the fate of a very important idea in their hands. Sound as if you really want their honest opinion and will truly value and take into consideration what they say. Tell them you'll be following up personally.

- If people are local, call 5 days after sending the material and schedule a meeting.

- Either for local people who can't meet or for those out-of-town, schedule a phone meeting. You'll probably need at least 30 minutes with each, maybe an hour.

- Ask if you can tape the meeting. This enables you to pay close attention to what the prospect is saying and not have to worry about taking notes.

- Ask what the prospect likes or doesn't like about what you're proposing, but most important of all, find out if he'd buy what you've got at the price you're proposing. And, if not, why not. After all, these meetings should not only produce valuable information for you but, in due course, highly qualified prospects to buy the new service!

- If the prospect has many criticisms of what you've proposed, or doesn't like it altogether, stay calm. This is what this stage is for. Listen politely. Indeed, listen intently. This is a future prospect, and he's telling you not just what may be wrong with your proposed service but also what would induce him to buy.

- Whatever you've heard, thank the prospect at the end of the meeting and send him a warm note expressing your appreciation. What you've heard is of value, even if it doesn't come with a bouquet of roses. Act accordingly.

— Make any necessary changes in your service that their responses suggest

As a very bright and self-possessed graduate of Harvard University, one of the most difficult things I've learned in my life is to listen. Not just to hear. Not just to acknowledge. But to really *listen* to what other people — particularly people who have something to say — are telling me. Learn, however, I have, often humbly so, and as a result, I've probably made more money than any member of my class. I attribute my success in part to forcing myself to listen to others.

Here is the point where this listening pays off. As a result of the many prospect meetings you've been holding concerning your new service idea, you're heard much. Now it's time to evaluate and, where appropriate, incorporate it into your new service.

Now, let me be plain: I said learn to listen. I didn't say become supine and stupid. Certain things that people, even well informed people, will tell you are going to be flat out wrong and even idiotic. That doesn't mean you shouldn't be grateful for the opportunity to hear them. Equally, it doesn't mean you have to follow their advice.

Just take in the information you've been given, have it readily accessible on tape, consider it thoughtfully, using whatever is sensible — and disregard the rest . . . while thanking the person suggesting it for all his help.

— *Brainstorm the means of marketing available to you for launching this service to the appropriate prospect groups*

Upon completion of the step above, you're going to know whether qualified prospects want what you're proposing. Whether they do or don't, congratulate yourself. If they don't, you've saved yourself a lot of frustration, irritation and expense by not going ahead. True, you haven't yet discovered the diversification of service you need to make your financial objective, but you haven't squandered any more time and money on something that was probably doomed to failure in any event. What's more, you've learned more about what your prospects want and can go back to this series of steps and to the other diversification possibilities more adept at finding what you need. Congratulations!

If your qualified prospects want what you've proposed, congratulations are also due. Stop and savor this moment. You've been told by people who are representative of many other people that they like what you've got. As a result both they and the others like them will soon be putting more money in your pocket. This calls for a celebration, and I hope you give it to yourself!

When this well-deserved event has been properly enjoyed, it's time to get down to the necessary business of brainstorming the various marketing alternatives available to you for launching this new service. Consider means like:

- direct mail and telemarketing to existing and lapsed clients. In selected instances, face-to-face meetings are also advisable. Don't forget going back to the people who provided you with advice. You can show them how they influenced you!
- lead-generating classified and small space ads, val- and card-decks, and direct mail to targeted markets;
- free media;
- workshops and other talk programs, *etc.*

In short, here's the moment where you take under advisement all the various marketing alternatives we'll be discussing throughout this book. Which of these is likely to be the most remunerative given the benefits you now have available?

— *Gather all the information you need about each different marketing gambit: who is it targeting, how much does it cost, what kind of approach works best, etc.*

After you've brain stormed all the marketing possibilities open to you, you know what to do: research your options. Remember, you know how many dollars you're trying to raise through this new service. The objective is to get there as *elegantly* as possible, which means by spending as little money as possible and by generating the largest number of qualified leads as soon as possible.

You may have written as possibilities items like:

- taking an ad in the weekly Rotary club bulletin;
- passing out flyers Saturday morning at the downtown crossing;
- joining a networking club.

Now, after researching all the relevant information about these options, you need to ask yourself which of them really make sense. (By the way, none of the options above does.)

Like all other marketing tasks, you go through this one in hot pursuit of the winning formula you need: where are you going to get the most qualified leads for the lowest possible cost in the shortest possible time? These means are the basis of any successful marketing plan.

— Draft the preliminary marketing plan embodying the marketing means you've selected, when you plan to use them, what you need to make each a success (including proper follow-up procedures), conservative response projections and a conservative guesstimate about how many clients/dollars you may generate this year.

At this point, you should know as well as I what to do: do a first draft on your marketing plan. Write down:

- precisely which marketing means you'll be using;
- how much they cost;
- when you'll be using them;
- your conservative projection for prospects generated;
- your conservative projection for dollars/clients generated . . . THIS YEAR!

Remember, you are launching a new service because you anticipate falling short of your income objective for the year. Thus, this plan must be designed to make up for the short fall so you reach your objective. Does it? And does it do so in a reasonable, reachable way? Is it do-able . . . or is it only dream-able?

Now's the moment to decide . . . before you go out to your targeted audiences eliciting their immediate response.

Once you know, it's time to finalize this plan . . . and execute it. With all that you've done, you have every reasonable assurance you can do so successfully, profitably.

Getting Better Prepared For Next Year

Given the way you currently run your service business, you're probably not going to have all the hard data you need to create the perfect plan the first time you do this. You're certainly not going to have all these kinds of data for any new services you're adding. Not to worry. Yes, your report is not going to be as good as it should be; no, you're not going to be able to make absolutely certain deductions from the data. So what? You're got to do the best you can with what you've got where you are. Teddy Roosevelt was right about that. By the same token, you've got to get better organized for next year.

Thus, at the same time you'ı e working on your first report, create a second computer file named "Report/(next year)." This is where you can store data like:

- expenses

- marketing activities

- prospect response numbers

- client dollars generated, *etc.*

Enter these data when they're immediately available. Creating your next plan will be a comparative breeze . . . and much more complete. As a result, your decision-making powers will necessarily be enhanced, too.

Note: don't just enter hard data, enter your thoughts about why things worked or why they didn't. What should you be doing differently? What are your ideas and observations? You'll find that having both hard data and a preliminary plan will stimulate your creative thinking. Don't lose the benefits of this thinking (which can and will occur just about anytime) by failing to RECORD what's occurred to you.

When To Complete Your Plan

Ideally, you should arrange matters to complete your first plan draft by November 1st of any year. This doesn't mean, of course, that if you're reading this book in April, you shouldn't do a plan for the remainder of the year now. You should. But once you've integrated planning into your business, your regular deadline should be November 1. This gives you 60 days to edit the plan and get ready for the new year.

By the same token, you should do a thorough review of your current year's plan at the same time. Why? Because you still have several weeks to reach your objectives and improve your end-of-the-year results. The mind likes deadlines; deadlines have always stimulated people to action, and the deadline of your plan is no exception. If, upon reviewing your plan on November 1, you find you may well fall short of your results in certain categories, there is still time to improve things. I'll give you one illustration of what I mean.

About a month before I started to write this book, I was informed by my financial planner that one of my mutual funds would not be paying a capital gain for the year, a casualty of the recession. Now, I had counted on a capital gain of about $5,000 from this fund to enable me to meet my financial objective for the year. Learning about this in early December, I was able to rearrange my activities for the month and by doing so I earned the additional $5,000 on schedule. Indeed, I found I even slightly exceeded my objective . . . despite the likelihood of failure only 30 days before. This is the result of having a marketing system that works . . . and of putting Mind Channeling to work focusing your activities to reach your objective.

Conclusion

You may not like planning very much; you may not have done much of it for your business. But promise me you'll start using it now to determine where you should be spending your resources and what makes sense for you to do. You see, if you don't use even the simple kind of planning recommended in this chapter, I frankly don't see how you're going to keep close enough tabs on your activities and expenses and so know what it makes sense to do . . . and what doesn't. Thus, you'll be making it a lot more difficult to achieve your objective. Believe me, this isn't what you want. So kindly follow the suggestions in this chapter closely before you try to *implement* any more unconsidered marketing gambits.

3

How To Prepare The Cash Copy You Need So Your Prospects Contact You

Remember what this book is about: no more cold calls. Cold calls are demeaning. When you make them you have to:

- psych yourself up;

- try cunning ways to get through some guard-like secretary or call screener whose job is to block people like you;

- explain to the prospect (if you're lucky enough to get through) who you are and why you've called.

Most of the time, of course, you don't get through . . . the secretary merely takes a message (if you're lucky) . . . and you have to call back again later, going through the process all over again, on the defensive the entire time.

Believe me, this process is for the birds, and you need to do EVERY-THING you can do avoid it.

That's why you've got to learn how to gather — and store — client-centered cash copy. *And* — as you'll see in the next chapter — how to use it to get people to contact you.

For make no mistake: there are only two kinds of prospect contact. Either prospects contact you . . . or you have to contact them, cold.

I've just gone through the "cold" scenario. Now get motivated by reminding yourself of the "warm" scenario:

- the prospect calls you;

- you ask, quite directly, "how can I help you?";

- the prospect explains;

- graciously you tell him how you can help and how much it's going to cost;

- you also lay out what the prospect has to do next to begin to get the benefits you can offer;

- you provide the prospect's "marching orders," the steps he has to do next to get the process moving.

You do all this in a rat-tat-tat fashion, focused and gracious simultaneously.

At the present time, you may only *imagine* being able to do this but in just the course of the last twenty-four hours I have followed this exact series of steps with *at least* twenty different people who all called me wanting me to do different things for them.

They call me because I've spent years mastering client-centered cash copy . . . copy that's packed with benefits for the prospect if only he'll take the tiny action of picking up the phone NOW . . . or writing NOW . . . to get them.

Getting prospects to contact you doesn't just happen by accident. It's the predictable result of a series of actions that start by considering these three questions:

- *Who* do you want to take action?

- *What* action do you want him to take?

- *When* do you want him to take it?

Before you even think of gathering the necessary cash copy ingredients, you need to answer these questions. Their answers will determine just what material you'll need and, ultimately, how you'll fashion it in your client-centered marketing communications.

— Who do you want to take action?

You cannot gather cash copy material until you know who you are trying to motivate. Sadly, most service sellers act as if all people are the same. But as George Orwell knew, while "all animals are equal, some are more equal than others."

What this means is that you cannot treat current customers the same as lapsed customers . . . or lapsed customers the same as prospects who have never heard from you before. Each of these groups (including all the various kinds of prospects who have never heard of you before) need a different, tailored approach.

This approach has two parts: the *who* and the *action*. It is not enough just to know who you're targeting to buy your service. You've got to remember that getting your message to the attention of these people is only half the battle; the second, arguably more important, half is remembering that you've got to make them ACT. Everything you do is pointless unless the targeted prospect acts. Consider cash copy, therefore, the science and art of using words to induce the greatest number of targeted prospects to take the fastest possible action for the least possible cost to you. It's a game . . . and a game you must master.

— What action do you want the prospect to take?

Oftentimes I ask the business people attending my marketing workshops what action they want their prospects to take upon receiving any of their marketing communications, including ads, letters, brochures, *etc*. Too often they say something silly like "Read it."

Let me tell you something: I don't care whether my prospects read my marketing communications or not. I only care that they *contact* me using one of the ways outlined in the document. They can:

- call
- fax
- write
- stop by, *etc.*

Which of these doesn't so much matter. . . . Thus, while I admit it would be nice if the prospect read the material, his reading it is not the essential thing. *His doing what is necessary to contact me is.*

Therefore, you must ask yourself at all times: what specific action (or actions) do I want the prospect to take when the prospect connects with your marketing message? Further, have you done *everything* possible to make it easy for the prospect to do this thing when the prospect wants to do it . . . not when you want him to do it?

— When do you want the prospect to take action?

Now you know who you want to take action . . . and you know what action you want him to take. The next question is when do you want him to act?

If you read the marketing communications produced by most service sellers (all of whom are purportedly in business to make money) you might deduce that it doesn't matter when the prospect acts. All too often the service seller says in effect, "Here we are. Whenever you get around to contacting me will be fine. Take your time."

This isn't marketing. This is idiocy.

Money *now* is always more important than money *later*. Providing your benefits to the prospect today enriches his life sooner . . . and (not so incidentally) enriches your life sooner, too.

Marketing is the art and science of generating the fastest possible action from designated prospects for the least possible cost. When you want this action is NOW. Cash copy is the art of selecting the right words and fashioning the right message to induce this immediate action.

Setting Yourself Up To Gather The Information You Need

As I trust I've made perfectly clear, there are two stages to marketing: planning and execution. We are still in the planning stage. The objective here is to gather and arrange all the information you need so that you can produce cash copy marketing communications at will. Your computer's going to be a big help to you at this stage.

You're going to need a text file (call it "ingredients") where you list all the different cash copy components you're going to need, including:

- prospect pain information;
- specific benefits the prospect gets from your service;
- offers that get the prospect to act fast;
- testimonials indicating people like the prospect have gotten benefits from your service;
- list of your happy clients with benefits they received from you;
- comparison of your service with those offered by your competitors
- client-centered biography of those offering your service, including yourself.

General Tips About Gathering And Storing Your Information

- As long as you're in business, you're in the business of gathering and storing this kind of client-centered information. It doesn't matter whether you're an old pro or ultra-green rookie, you've got to have this information readily at hand.

- Enter the information as soon as you have it. If you've had a success with a client *today*, enter the information *today*. If someone praises your work today, get the testimonial today and enter it today.

- Date the information when you enter it. While it is true that you'll probably only wish to publish the date of some entries for six months, you'll always want to know when information was entered.

- Whenever possible, add complete details for the source of the information including bibliographic details, names, addresses, phone numbers, *etc.*

Prospect Pain Information

Most service sellers, remember, concentrate on telling the prospect about *themselves.* That is, they provide details about:

- who they are;

- how long they've been in business;

- the features of their service;

- some specifics about their operation, *etc.*

But face it: the prospect isn't interested in you. *He's interested in himself.* Thus, the whole point of client-centered cash copy is to motivate the prospect by using information about himself and of interest to himself to induce him to take immediate action.

Now what do you think is going to induce the fastest action? Telling the prospect something about you . . . or focusing the discussion resolutely on the prospect, his situation, his benefits . . . and on all you have for him that's going to give him what he wants faster?

Obvious, isn't it?

This is where pain comes in.

A prospect either acts to 1) acquire a benefit or 2) to eliminate pain. There is no other reason. Which one of these do you think is more motivational?

If you said "eliminate pain", you're right.

Think about it.

If I said to you 1) schedule an appointment with your dentist now and you can cut down on the likelihood of tooth decay and tooth pain a year from now, or 2) come in now and get rid of your tooth pain now, which one is the more likely to induce *immediate* action?

Eliminating pain is always a stronger motivater than the prospect of acquiring a benefit (or gain). That's why the client-centered marketer becomes a specialist in 1) locating pain points and 2) using them to motivate immediate action.

The question is: where do you get this information?

- Ask your existing clients. You must regard your existing clients as a fountainhead of useful marketing information. You should always be asking them why they're using your service, why they came now instead of later, what pains they're trying to eliminate, problems they're trying to solve, *etc.* People who haven't used their existing clients as an information source will be astonished at just how easy it is to get information from them and just how much they'll tell you.

- Review professional publications, particularly newsletters and monthly periodicals. If these publications are good, they'll be telling you where to make extra money given current conditions . . . and both pending and projected problems.

- Locate government bodies either regulating or researching your industry. These people, too, want to know what's happening with your service and probably produce material of interest to you. You can get in touch with the staffers, get your name on relevant mailing lists, *etc.* In short, let them know what you want and make sure they get it to you.

- Get in touch with experts in your field. Such people regularly produce research findings and publications. Ask to be put on their mailing lists. Buy and study their material.

As this material becomes available to you, remember these four words: "You hurt. I help."

When you're in the service business, you must behave like Mother Theresa. That is, you are in business to help people who hurt. Another way of putting this is: "Problem. Solution." You (prospect) have a problem. I (service marketer/provider) have your solution.

Thus, what you are looking for is evidence of:

- current problems and how much they are hurting your prospects;

- projected problems which if left unsolved will hurt your prospects, and how much.

Open this part of the text file with the words YOU HURT . . .

Now list all the ways your prospects 1) currently hurt, or 2) will hurt in the future if they don't take action today.

Of these two options, the first is stronger, of course, because current pain (even if less hurtful) is more motivational than future pain (even if it's projected to be greater).

It's more motivational, that is, if you talk directly to the prospect about how much he hurts . . . and how you can take away that pain and improve his situation.

Marketing, you see, is always about just two people . . . you, the service provider/marketer, and the prospect. Of these, the prospect is the only one who matters, because it is only the prospect who can make you richer. You cannot make yourself richer. You cannot will yourself the money. You can only *persuade* the prospect to let you have his money in exchange for something he wants.

That is why you must start to arrange all your information in sentences beginning with the word YOU. Thus, "you hurt because . . ."

There is nothing abstract about service marketing. It constitutes an "I-Thou" conversation. No matter how many people you may be serving now . . . or have the potential to serve . . . *all* your marketing has to read and feel as if it involves just two people.

Thus, instead of logging pain information as if it were somehow just data, just unconnected facts, after you've listed it, you must transform it into useful marketing material. You do this by changing each sentence from the disembodied third person to the intense and personal second person.

Say that you're selling a pension service. You discover that 80% of Americans retire to an income significantly lower than the one they had while they were working. There are two ways of using this information. You can regard yourself as an *educator* who tells your prospect this . . . or you can position yourself as a *motivater* who uses this information to get your prospect to act promptly. Who do you think makes the most money? The educator uses the information to inform and doesn't care if it's in the third person. The motivater, however, is only interested in action, resolute and prompt action from the series of individual prospects he's targeted. He must talk to all these people in the second person.

Thus, first list all the painful facts about your prospect's current condition. Then, list all the painful facts that are projected about your prospect's condition. Then, go back and transform each fact into a sentence beginning with the words "you hurt . . ."

If your service eliminates this pain — or this prospect of future pain — then you are already well on your way to creating client-centered cash copy.

Note: obviously this pain information will come to your attention in no particular order. It can also be entered into the computer file in no particular order. However, at some point you'll have to make a qualitative judgment about which items are the most motivational and therefore should be used first in any marketing communications. How do you know? Ask prospects. Ask clients. And try different openings.

Specific Benefits The Prospect Gets By Using Your Service

Several things need to be pointed out about this item:

- Specificity is crucial. The more precise you can be about what the prospect gets, the better.

- The focus must be on benefits, not features. That is, the focus must be on what the prospect *gets* from your service, not the components of that service, how that service works, *etc.*

- Usage needs to be stressed. Merely buying or having your service is insufficient for the prospect to achieve what he wants. He must understand that to achieve the results he wants he needs to engage, participate, use, enjoy, *etc.*

All books on marketing discuss the difference between features and benefits. Yet the sad fact is that most service sellers still don't know how to differentiate them or which to use and how. This makes their lives unnecessarily difficult.

Think of a feature as something *descriptive* of your service. It's about the service. All these, for instance, are features:

- hours of business

- your location

- number of employees

- the way you offer your service

- service prices

- where you offer your service, *etc.*

All these things *describe* some aspect of the service. As such, they are "me-centered" words mainly of interest to you and not of interest to the prospect until he makes a decision to try your service.

On the other hand, benefits are "you-centered". They tell the prospect what he gets rather than what you have. Thus, while each feature is best described through a phrase beginning with the words "I have", each benefit is best described in a phrase beginning with the words "you get."

Now, it's obvious that if you're attempting to motivate a prospect a sentence beginning "you get . . ." is considerably more powerful than one starting "I have . . ." Thus your job is to list:

- all the features of your service, and

- transform each one into a client-centered benefit.

Thus:

Feature ("I Have")	Benefit ("You Get")
a 24-hour order line	Call whenever you want!
1 hour no-charge appointment for prospective clients	free, no obligation opportunity to make sure you're getting what you want!
office a ten-minute walk from the nearest public transportation	here conveniently, inexpensively!
MasterCard/VISA capability	the benefit now and can pay whenever you want!

Get the idea?

Now, the trick to this is that you must:

- list every feature of your service;

- transform every one into a benefit;

- make sure the benefit is as specific and as enticing as possible.

The objective here is plain: it is not merely to tell what you've got . . . it's to motivate a human being to take *immediate* action so you can move to the next stage of the marketing process.

What you're doing is most important. You're fashioning the real reasons why your prospects are going to buy from you. I call this The Case or The Argument. "Look," you're saying, "you get *this* . . . and *this* . . . and *this* . . . and you also get *this!*"

Initially, of course, you can put the features and corresponding benefits in any order. However, after you've listed them all, you've got to prioritize them . . . for *each* prospect group you're going after.

What's the #1 Benefit for the first group you're targeting? The next benefit? And the next? You always lead with the #1 Benefit, instead of leading up to it, because this is the most motivational thing that you've got . . . *for these people.* Please keep in mind that while the service may stay the same, the benefits may change in order depending on whom you're targeting.

Hint: as you develop your Feature-Benefit Chart, show it to existing prospects and clients for their reaction. Have you covered all the features? Have you turned them all into truly motivational benefits? Don't do this work alone. You're doing it to motivate people like your prospects and clients. It makes sense, therefore, to ask them what they think. Do so. Listen. Then alter the wording and the priority of these entries accordingly.

Offers That Get Prospects To Act FAST

We live in a country where prospects with means (while undoubtedly wanting more) suffer from two problems:

1. they have much and may not need to take immediate action;
2. during periods of recession (such as that in which I'm writing), their discretionary income has probably dropped.

Problem #2 will fade with the recession (only to return with the next economic decline). Problem #1 is with us always.

From the marketer's standpoint, therefore, you've got to think up ways that induce faster action either from an overfed, sluggish prospect or from one who's more conscious than ever of just how limited his resources are.

Getting business from these prospects is not, of course, impossible. Even in the midst of the most serious recession, tens of millions of people continue to spend money *every day*, even if they spend less of it. The trick is to fashion offers that induce faster action. In fact, an offer is best understood as a means by which the designated prospect can be induced to take faster action than he would otherwise have taken had the offer/inducement not been provided.

There are many different kinds of offers for selling services. Here are just a few:

- only two openings remain on my client list;
- free one-hour consultation (worth $100) to first five people who call;
- special price (save so much money) if you act by (date);
- more of service if you act by (date);
- special present or gift if you act by (date).

Let's look at what's happening with offers like these.

An offer to be meaningful should:

- give the prospect something of *real value* in return for immediate action, and

- should be *limited*.

Thus, "only two openings remain on my client list." This is a plausible offer if:

- you've just helped deliver substantial success to another client like the prospect, and

- can only work with a limited number of people at any one time delivering this benefit.

Hint: even if you can work with 60 people at one time, it's never a good idea to say that you have more than, say, 4 openings at any one time. Too ready availability breeds procrastination and postpones a buyer's decision.

Or, "free one-hour consultation (worth $100) to first five people who call."

This is an offer that many service sellers misuse. Offering something for free may or may not be persuasive. The fact that it's free to the prospect whereas others must pay $100 for it . . . if the prospect acts now . . . begins to make it truly motivating. Add to this a sense of what benefits the prospect will get during this hour, and you've got something that will get people to call you.

Or, "special price (save so much money) if you act by (date)."

People, especially in a recession, never tire of saving money. So, offer a special price if they take action by a certain time.

Note: the more well-known you become, the less you will use a "special price" offer. This is a fine thing to do when you're starting off . . . especially when you're competing against a more well-known competitor. When you've arrived, however, it's against your professional standing to cut your price. Of course by that time you shouldn't have to, either!

Another Note: the key to price cutting is that you should never actually be giving up anything. You should figure your prices so that you can easily subsidize a few hours of "free" consultations and other prospect-centered giveaways. In other words, existing clients should subsidize these donations. For instance, when you have a retainer client, it's unlikely the client will use all the time he's paid for. Thus, you can use some of the time he's paid for but hasn't used to provide these "free" consultations to others considering buying your service.

Now that you understand that you need an offer . . . and know the crucial components of the most motivational offers, it's time to scrutinize all service businesses to see what kinds of offers they're making. Remember, your job is to not to be original, not to rack your brain trying to think of new ways to motivate people. It's simply to find out from others what works for them . . . and copy them. Thus:

- review all ads, flyers, brochures, letters, *etc.*, produced by service firms to see what kinds of offers they're making and how they're framing these offers. I suggest you divide these into two parts: the very, very good (which you'll copy) and the howlingly inadequate (which you, with all your talents, can surely improve upon and which you should keep around for a good laugh);

- pump service sellers whenever you meet them for ideas about how they motivate prompt prospect action. Americans are a notoriously giving and trusting people. Ask for their assistance . . . you'll get answers. (After a time, of course, you'll know so much about this important subject that you shouldn't be hearing anything new.)

Again, I beg you, as you gather this information, log it. You can, of course, keep a hard copy file for actual documents. And/or simply enter relevant sections into your computer text file. Either way, don't presume to think you'll remember. Human memory's fickle. It's far easier just to copy things that are already in computer memory!

People constantly ask me whether you need to have an offer in *all* your marketing communications. Well, I say, does it matter to you whether the designated prospect responds to your communication fast or not? If not, then don't bother with an offer . . . let the prospect determine when to respond. These days, I must confess, I personally do not put an offer on every marketing communication I use. But then I often receive as many as 500 pieces of mail *a day* and really feel I've greased the process quite enough. When you're at this point and if this is enough money-making mail for you, then you can afford to skip the offer *occasionally*. But if you're not — and want more — why, then, PUT AN OFFER IN EVERY ONE OF YOUR MARKETING COMMUNICATIONS AND STOP ASKING ME SUCH STUPID QUESTIONS.

Testimonials Indicating People Like The Prospect Have Gotten Benefits From Your Service

One of my card-deck colleagues is fond of saying "buyers are liars." Sadly, that's often true. However, I think there's a more profound truth under this observation: buyers have been burnt badly.

As I write, we're in a recession. Buyer confidence, as measured by the Conference Board, is low, albeit improving. Both the president and chairman of the Federal Reserve have expressed helpless bewilderment about why Americans feel this way.

Well, I can tell them: the American consumer is all too often a stupid consumer. Affluence has dulled our sharpness. Our very success has made us prone to making bad decisions. We mistrust our judgment . . . and for good reason. We've made so many bad decisions, we wonder if the next decision we're making is bound to be another mistake. Thus, we become cautious and self-doubting.

As marketers, we've got to be aware of what our prospects are feeling, to be sure, but we've also got to do everything we can to motivate them so that they don't let any negative feelings hold them back from ACTING. This is the point of testimonials, and the good service marketer becomes an expert in both stimulating, fashioning, storing and using them.

Now, the obvious way to stimulate a testimonial is to do work that's worthy of a testament. I'm not going to tell you how to do that; you're supposed to be an expert in your field. Thus, you should be able to do your work so that it provides the gain . . . or release from pain . . . the client wants. If you can't do that, you're never going to be a multi-millionaire.

But if you can, then it's time to get smarter about getting testimonials. Time after time in my workshops I ask participants if any of their clients have said anything good about them in the last 30 days. Lots and lots of hands go up. Their clients have said lots of good things about them! "Okay," says I, "after the client said these good things, how many of how asked for a written testimonial? How many added the testimonial to the stock that can be used for future marketing communications? Indeed, how many may already be using that testimonial to motivate new prospects to take action?" Often no hands go up at all . . .

In other words, your clients are *saying* good things to you all the time . . . but, like most service sellers, you simply let them go in one ear . . . and out the other. You use these testimonials, in short, as a welcome means of building your self esteem and feeling good about yourself . . . instead of to motivate prospects to act. THIS IS RIDICULOUS!

The first job, then, is to understand what a testimonial is for. Its primary job is *not* to make you feel good; it's to stimulate additional business, to leverage a present (or past) success to create a future client. If it also makes you feel good, so much the better, but that must never be its *raison d'être*.

Next, it's to understand the *structure* of the most useful testimonials, so that you get (and stimulate) the right kind. While we are all familiar with testimonials, very few of us have considered what these testimonials should be about. Well, I'll tell you: THE BEST TESTIMONIALS ARE ABOUT BENEFITS PRODUCED BY YOU FOR PEOPLE LIKE THE PROSPECT.

We are all familiar with testimonials that say things like:

- "Great job!"
- "We liked Joe and will use him again!"
- "We had a million laughs with Melissa and think the world of her!"

Who likes these testimonials? Why you do, you the service seller. And no wonder! They're about you . . . they are "me-centered" testimonials.

But does the prospect care? Of course not!!! The prospect wants to know what the person providing the testimonial *got* . . . as a way of confirming that he can get the same results — or better — from you.

Thus, all testimonials should be based on a variation of the "you get benefit now" theme I've been stressing all along: "I got benefits then." And, as above, the benefits should be as substantial as possible. In other words, instead of concentrating on the service provider, the testimonial should state as specifically as possible exactly what benefit(s) the satisfied client got. Instead of "We enjoyed working with Jeffrey," how about "We got an extra $165,000 for our nonprofit organization thanks to Jeffrey Lant's help." Now, I ask you: do you think a prospect cares that you enjoyed "working with Jeffrey", or do you think he'd rather implement a fund raising process that might produce $165,000 — or more? Think hard. I know you know . . .

. . . I also know you know you shouldn't be waiting for people to *offer* testimonials. You should be both asking for them and creating circumstances where testimonials naturally emerge. Here's what I mean:

- In your dealings with customers, ask them what kinds of results they're having. Engage them in conversations about what happened when they used your service. If your service is good, they're going to have good results. And they're going to tell you about them . . . if you ask! When they do, write their words, put them in testimonial form and ask for permission to use them in your marketing materials.

- Ask for testimonials in your marketing communications. I regularly ask people (as I asked you in the beginning of this book) to tell me their success stories, the success stories that have resulted from implementing my methods. You know something? They do . . . in droves. There isn't a day that goes by that I don't receive at least one letter or one telephone call with a success story. I'm a tad blasé about this now. Instead of recording what the caller tells me, I ask him to write it down and mail it to me. The reason? I don't need another good testimonial. Besides, I've learned that people are happy to gratify the guru. This will happen to you, too — if you're good and if your methods work. But until it does, *you* take the initiative to record things and follow up accordingly.

- Don't hesitate to tape testimonials, too. When a person starts saying good things about you (even if you have to prompt him to begin and ask questions to get him to expand and continue), whip out your tape recorder. You can use the tapes as living testimonials . . . or you can excerpt from them for your written marketing communications. *Note:* mark each tape with the name of the person providing the testimonial, his company (if relevant to your service) and date he talked to you.

Once you've got the testimonial, store it properly. I've got a file in my computer marked "testimonial". Since I personally don't use audio testimonials, my testimonials either end up here or, in hard-copy form, in a file folder. The important thing is that you have testimonials for each service you're offering and that each has all the details you need to attribute it properly.

Just what attribution you'll need will depend on who you're targeting for future business. Home-based business people want to know the person providing the testimonial runs a home-based business; this is of no interest at all to people running a non-profit organization who are being helped by a professional working at home. In short, give the prospect what's meaningful for the prospect, and include this information with the testimonial for easy use.

List Of Your Happy Clients With Benefits They Received From You

Related to your testimonial file is a list of your satisfied clients and the benefits they received from you. I call these Success Cases, and every service business needs them.

Here you list the name of the client, your contact person (if the client is a business), name, address, and phone number. Each time you help generate a success for this client, add it here. A handy chart will help you create these Success Cases:

Situation of client when I started   What I did   Results

Let me give you an example based on one of my marketing services.

Situation of client when I started	What I did	Results
had contacts with 10 discharge planners at area hospitals. Generated 540 referrals year previous to hiring me Gross revenues: $214,000.	sent letters made phone calls personal visits	660 referrals $325,000 revenues

This is a very simple chart, but it is based on a profound truth about the service seller's business. You are brought into a client's life in order to transform his situation. He wants you to move him from a place where he is relatively disadvantaged to one where he is comparably better off. To do this, you need to have a clear conception of where he was when you started . . . and where he ends up, thanks to your help. As a result, of course, you establish just how valuable you and your procedures are and as such you not only have a winning Success Case . . . but leverage to attract other comparable clients who want results as good, or better. Moreover, once a client (who can easily lose sight of the forest among the trees) sees what you've done in a table like this, a superb, client-centered testimonial is assured.

Sadly, I scarcely ever meet service sellers who understand this process. They see themselves as service deliverers, as workers. I see myself as a transformational element, bringing crucial skills and technical abilities to a client's situation and thereby enabling him to be better off. The Success Case is a most valuable marketing tool because it clearly indicates that a client is better off . . . and better off thanks to you. Furthermore, if your charts are not showing success, it will force you to think through your operating procedures and consider means of altering them so you will achieve success. This is valuable, too.

I need hardly say that the computer is of the utmost assistance in gathering and storing this information. One of the reasons service sellers don't have this kind of valuable information in their marketing communications is because they don't have an easy way to gather and store it. But with the personal computer this is no excuse.

Make it a point to do a thorough review of a client's situation as soon as you're hired. Enter this information immediately. As you implement your methods and generate successes, enter this information immediately, too. When you've got it, you'll either discover your methods need to be improved to generate more success . . . or you'll have at your finger tips hard data indicating just how valuable your services are. Your desirability — and fees — should rise accordingly.

Comparison Of Your Service
To That Offered By Your Competitors

**See for yourself just how our prices
compare with other companies targeting
business decision makers**

Company	Basic Rate	Second Color	Cost Per 2-Color Card	Add'l For 4-Color
Marketing Bulletin Board (120,000 circ)	$3,550	$150	3.1 cents	$250
Marketing Manager (150,000 circ)	$4,950	$200	3.4 cents	$400
President's Exec Deck (200,000 circ)	$3,995	$200	2.1 cents	$400
Venture Advertising Sales & Marketing (100,000 circ)	$3,000	$300	3.3 cents	$450

...and *all* other decks in the industry
are comparably priced!!!

(source: Standard Rate & Data December, 1991 Edition)

Take a minute and review this chart. What does it tell you? At a glance, you know that if you don't use my services, you're getting screwed . . . which is just the message I want my advertising prospects to have!

Is this message successful? Yes, in two ways:

- Even the dimmest prospect can see that if he goes elsewhere, he's paying too much. This immediately predisposes him in my favor and against my (named) competitors;

- It infuriates my competitors. Even after more than two years of use, they get apoplectic when people point out this chart to them. The day I got an outraged call from one of them calling me "un-American" because of it, I knew I'd fashioned a winner.

The truth is, all service businesses should have a competitor comparison chart and know about how to gather information for it. The real question, however, is whether, once you've got this information, you'll want to use it in your marketing communications. Instead, you may find that it's more useful for internal consumption and planning purposes. Before you make this decision, however, you need to gather the facts. Once you've got them, then you can decide what to do.

You can fashion your competitor chart in many ways, but here's one good one:

Feature	Company A	Company B	Company C, *etc.*

Among features you may like to compare are:

- price
- location
- frequency of service
- personnel skills
- types of materials used
- promptness of delivery
- availability of 800 number for technical support
- credit availability, *etc.*

Just what features are important will vary from service to service. You've got to know what features are important given the service you provide. These are the features you need to compare.

Once you've determined which features you should be researching, you've got to set up the process for gathering the information. In the case of details about the card-deck industry, it's almost ridiculously easy to get much of this information thanks to *Standard Rate & Data;* one trip to the library, and I had a batch of superb information on my competitors against which they've been struggling vainly ever since. You may not be able to get your details so easily. Anyway, once you know what you need, set about getting it:

- Get your hands on all the marketing materials produced by a competitor including ads, letters, brochures, flyers, *etc.* Put a friend on their mailing lists . . . or ask your clients to turn over these materials to you. Once they've hired you, they don't need them, after all, and it's a wise idea to remove materials about competitors to the greater safety of your office instead of leaving them in theirs!

- Call and ask. It's amazing how much information you get if you merely ask for it. I've always believed that if you want to know something, ask the person who knows. Astonishingly often, you get the details you need . . . no questions asked.

- Get your friends to call and ask.

Now, whenever possible, get the information you need in written form. Enter the source of your information along with the data themselves. What makes my card-deck chart so powerful is that all the information is substantiated through a well-known industry source. There's no question that I've invented it. In your case, get the information and enter it along with the source and keep any hard-copy documents in a file marked "competitor." The more damaging this information, the more it undercuts the competitiveness of your competitors, the more it bolsters your own competitive position, the more likely you are to get a complaint from one of your competitors — even if what you're using is absolutely true. Prepare for this. Thus, when the inevitable complaint comes, you need say no more than "We got the information from your spring catalog" and leave it at that.

Note: Not so long ago, I sent a letter to my advertising clients telling them that leading card decks in the industry had gone down in size by up to 1/3 during the current national advertising recession and that only one deck in the industry had grown — mine! I used this as proof that we were doing the right thing by our advertisers and getting them results. I named no names of my competitors. There was no point.

Days after the letter went out, I received a very nasty note from the president of a competing card deck telling me that his deck hadn't gone down in size by 1/3 and that he took offense at what I'd written. In my response I blandly pointed out that while I certainly stuck by what I said about "leading decks" I had to point out I never said his company produced one of them. I signed off wishing him continued success in our very competitive industry. The fool's probably still sputtering about this response which owes much to Henry Ford II's astute comment, "Never complain. Never explain." But, adds Lant, always be able to tersely substantiate when necessary — as when you produce a competitor comparison chart.

The real question, it seems to me, is how you'll use this chart once you've completed it. That depends entirely on what you discover. Say my outraged competitor had put together this chart. His findings would be the same . . . but his use different. Instead of publicizing these findings in an attempt to motivate new business, he would be advised to:

- deduce his strongest competitive advantages and market *these*, and

- reconsider his service and how it's offered in an attempt to make it more competitive, thereafter producing a competitor comparison chart more in his interest.

Client-Centered Biography Of Those Offering Your Service

If you scan the standard marketing communications assembled by most service businesses, you'll find a paragraph or two about the principals of the company or key employees. They go something like this:

"Acclaimed speaker, Sean Joyce has traveled the country, working with supervisors at America's leading organizations including 3M, AT&T, the U.S. Army, W.R. Grace, the Hospital Corporation of America and scores more.

Sean is an expert in team management with a Ph.D. in Industrial Psychology. In addition to lecturing nationwide, he has been personally involved with some of the most winning teams in sports — as an approved players agent for the NFL."

What's wrong with this write-up — and all the others like it? You should know by now: they're about the *seller*, not the *prospect*.

Take the example above. It's the beginning of the biographical write-up in a brochure produced by The Dun & Bradstreet Corporate Foundation for one of their workshops. The marketer wants people to come to a program he's offering on "How supervisors build powerful teams." Sean Joyce is the speaker and as such is crucial to the success of this program. Now I ask you: do you think prospects care about Sean Joyce *per se*, or do you think they're interested in getting the benefits he can deliver . . . and in knowing what kinds of specific benefits he's delivered to other people like them?

Obvious, isn't it?

. . . Unless you're Sean Joyce and Dun & Bradstreet. Instead of telling the prospect about the real, meaningful benefits Joyce has helped his clients achieve, they offer up a series of unsubstantiated "so what?" tid-bits that merely make the guy feel good about himself . . . or are just plain pointless.

- "acclaimed speaker". Who says so? So what?
- "has traveled the country". Obvious. Pointless verbiage.
- "working with supervisors at". Who cares? We're not interested in where he's been. We care about what he's done and the benefits he helped deliver.
- "Sean is an expert". Who says?
- "Ph.D. in Industrial Psychology." Who cares?
- "in addition to lecturing nationwide." More verbiage.
- "personally involved with some of the most winning teams". So what?

There isn't a word here — despite the eminence of the marketer and their "acclaimed speaker" — about what Joyce has helped his clients achieve and which might, therefore, be something the prospect would want to achieve. It's all just unsubstantiated "me-centered" assertion. What a waste!

Let me remind you: in marketing *everything* either works to motivate a prospect to respond immediately — or *it's a complete waste.*

Sun-soaked motivational guru Anthony Robbins makes the same kind of stupid mistakes. Under a paragraph in a marketing communication headed "Anthony Robbins Live" we read:

> "Anthony Robbins has demonstrated his powerful persuasion techniques to tens of thousands of successful people across the United States and Canada.
>
> In fact, his seminars are the most highly attended of their kind in the country. Robbins is the founder of nine companies and the author of *Unlimited Power,* a national best seller, now published in 11 languages."

Do you see what's happening here? The focus is all wrong!!! It's on Joyce . . . or Robbins . . . or, could this be, on you . . . and not on your PROSPECT, the only person who matters.

Occasionally my critics say that I beat a point into the ground. Why, they say, can't I merely say something once and leave it alone? Well, I'll tell you. Me-centered marketing is everywhere . . . and my saying calmly, professionally and once or twice that it's wrong isn't going to change things. It's only by beating the perpetrators of this egotistical nonsense black and blue that change may occur . . . and that I may be able to prevent you from making the same mistakes.

So, I ask you. Is it really relevant to the prospect that Robbins has founded 9 companies? Or has a "national best seller, now published in 11 languages"? OF COURSE NOT. It's only ego gratifying to the marketer himself.

You be different. You focus the discussion on the prospect. You transform your experience from the "I was here" variety to the "here's what happened because I was there" kind.

Your Success Cases will help you . . . just as they'd help Joyce & Robbins, too.

Take the Joyce write-up. He worked at 3M, it says. WHAT DID HE ACHIEVE? What was meaningful about his time there? What did he help them get that others might now want? In other words, just *being* there isn't nearly enough. The prospect needs to know what he ACCOMPLISHED.

Take Robbins. Any idiot could set up 9 companies. We don't know if they're big, small, indifferent, profit-making, or busts. We don't know if lives were changed . . . if transformational products and services were introduced. We know nothing except that a "fact" has been presented which has no intrinsic meaning or value whatsoever.

Marketing of the "Kilroy was here" variety isn't going to help you. What will is creating a chart like this:

I was at (place)	from (date)	I achieved these *specific* results

Again, this is nothing more than a variation of the Success Case, but the emphasis is slightly different. Here the linkage between you, the service seller, and the resulting, impressive success must be explicit. It's not that your company achieved success . . . it's that *you* did. Or whoever the biographical write-up is about. Because, remember, if there is more than one person in your service business, each of those people should be positioned to have success . . . and the successes they've had should be leveraged to generate additional business.

Now look at the Joyce write-up and consider how he could improve it.

I was at AT & T from (date) to (date). I achieved these specific results . . . results which my prospects want to replicate or exceed for the betterment of their lives.

Now you do the same!

The objective of marketing is not to make you feel better. It's to motivate a prospect to take immediate action for the least possible expenditure on the part of the marketer. When you succeed in making this formula work for you, you can do whatever you want with the new resources you're sure to have to make yourself feel better. But don't indulge in mindless ego-gratification here!

Biographical paragraphs in marketing communications, then, are not really about the person being written about. They are simply another variation of the four crucial words in marketing: YOU GET BENEFIT NOW. Only this time, they go "he/she produced benefit then."

Let me tell you something: when you approach prospects and say, "I went to Harvard," they may be impressed with you. However, they don't know how you're going to make their lives better off or why they should invest their money in you. But when you say, "So, you're running a meals on wheels program. I'm just finishing up working with XYZ meals on wheels, and I've helped them raise an additional $65,000," they're listening. They're thinking, implicitly or explicitly, "How did he do it? Can he help me to the same extent . . . or better?" Credibility comes with results, not initialed credentials and not a stupid listing of the places where you've hung your hat.

Unless you're already transforming your experience into "you-centered" marketing, you may not realize how powerful this is. However, over the last 12 years I've been hired by a series of prestigious institutions and corporations for large amounts of money simply on the basis of the demonstrated results I've brought to others like them . . . *without having even the semblance of the paper credentials possessed by others.* Remember, my Ph.D. is in English Victorian (indeed royal) history; I've never had a marketing course in my life. But no one asks me about this. Instead they want to know how I can get them the same or better results that I have helped others achieve. In short, the only credentials that matter are the demonstrated results you have helped others achieve, and it is these demonstrated results that should constitute the heart of your biography — or the biographies of others in your service business — whenever they appear.

Not the egotistical effusions of Anthony Robbins and his ilk.

Last Words

Particularly since I wrote **CASH COPY: HOW TO OFFER YOUR PRODUCTS AND SERVICES SO YOUR PROSPECTS BUY THEM . . . NOW!**, marketers of both products and services have been coming to me in large numbers asking me to review their marketing communications. Most were "me-centered", long on assertions and thin on meaningful, substantial benefits. One of the reasons for this is that the marketers weren't taking time to gather the necessary data on which to base their communications. Instead, they'd wake up one morning, remind themselves they needed a brochure or letter or ad . . . and throw it off without forethought or preparation. The results were predictably disastrous: insubstantial fluff, laced with a heap of self-congratulatory language, could hardly build a million dollar business.

That's why you must gather and store the information recommended by this chapter. I certainly realize that it takes time, patience and perseverance to follow these steps. But I also realize that when you have this information — and have used it in the marketing communications discussed in the next chapter — you no longer have merely to *suggest* what you can do . . . or hint at it . . . or pussy-foot around because you're uncertain. YOU'LL KNOW.

When, for instance, I talk to a card-deck advertiser, I'm not saying I THINK . . . or I SUPPOSE . . . or that COULD BE THE CASE. I hit him with the facts. The knowledge that I possess the facts permeates my voice and gives it a winning quality of confidence that cannot be counterfeited. It permeates my manner . . . and, in sum, it impresses the prospect and gives him confidence in my judgment. With all this client-centered information I don't need to spend time explaining who I am, what I'm about, where I've been or what I can do — it's all at my finger tips, readily available to qualified prospects. Instead, I can move the discussion to where it has to be: on whether the prospect I'm talking to is a real prospect, possessed of the resources he needs to avail himself of my service and ready to take action . . . or whether he's a flat worm, a pitiable human excrescence simply wasting my time whom I can — and should — flush out of my life without a second thought, as quickly as possible.

Because most service sellers don't possess the necessary factual information recommended in this chapter, they spend far, far too much time with people they shouldn't be talking to, perplexed by questions they don't know the answers to, in ways that demonstrate how ill-prepared and uncertain they really are. This isn't what a multi-millionaire does. This person knows he must take time to gather the necessary information that will, considered in its sum total, motivate the largest number of prospects to take immediate action.

Only once he has this crucial data will he fashion the necessary marketing communications that bring his winning information to the attention of the prospects whom he's now certain will be sufficiently motivated by it to move him appreciably closer to his objective of being a richer person.

4

Producing Marketing Communications That Get People To Contact You . . . And The Marketing Communications You'll Use When They Do!

As we begin this important chapter, I would like to remind you what we're doing here: we're trying to get you to create marketing communications — be they ads, flyers, letters, brochures, *etc., etc.* — that GET PEOPLE TO CONTACT YOU instead of putting you in the unbearable and unproductive position of having to contact them. Everything in this chapter is about how you create these communications and what you should be avoiding.

To put you in the mood, I'd like to take a look at a couple of marketing communications I got during the last few days. Exhibit A I picked up at an exhibit booth at a conference I was addressing; Exhibit B was sent in the mail. Before considering these marketing communications I ask you to remember that good, bright, purportedly "client-centered" people just like you and me put these monstrosities together. They poured their time, ideas and money into these documents, and they'd swear they had done everything possible to make them compelling to their prospects. But you and I both know they're wrong, don't we?

Consider Exhibit A, "The Conference Center Concept" produced by the International Association of Conference Centers. Look at their opening panel. Is it "you-" (that is, prospect) centered, or is it about the association?

The first inside panel is even more stupid: it's blank and while I'd like to show this to you, I don't feel like spending my money to show you a blank page. The writer, the marketer thinks that empty space is motivating. Ridiculous!

Then there's that knock-out second inside panel beginning "Toward More Productive Meetings". Look at these words. It's obvious the writer is trying to educate, not motivate. This section reads like a few paragraphs from a multi-volume tome on "The History of Meetings." Where's the motivation? The oomph that's going to rivet a prospect and get him to take action?

Is it in the section headed "Defining Conference Centers"? Now I ask you: does anyone care about "defining conference centers"? I swear, this document must have been written by a refugee from Campus America!

Toward More Productive Meetings

Meetings have long been a fact of business and organizational life. As the burden of continuing education and training falls increasingly on the shoulders of business, meetings have become ever more critical as a communication and training tool worldwide. Meeting planners have appeared on the scene as specialists in producing meetings. Likewise, the hospitality industry has spawned a new breed of facility designed to provide an environment conducive to meeting productivity: conference centers.

If the conference center concept is new to you, it may be because conference centers themselves are relatively new to the meeting scene. While a few such pioneering facilities were established before the 1970s, the majority have been developed only within the past 20 years.

In a conference center setting, meeting planners find everything needed to plan and execute meetings — from specially-designed meeting rooms to specially-trained staff. A conference center, by definition, is a "total meeting environment."

Defining Conference Centers

Conference centers hold a unique slot in the hospitality industry. They exist for one purpose: to provide an environment that will facilitate and support meetings, particularly small-group meetings, averaging 20 to 50 people. As such, they reflect the trend in business toward smaller, regional meetings.

While the name "conference center" has great appeal and has been added to many hospitality facilities, it takes more than a name to become a member of the International Association of Conference Centers (IACC).

This "marketing communication" goes on and on for several more pages, but the thrust never changes. It is nothing more than a pompous collection of egotistical remarks that fail to connect on any level with the prospect and never ask that prospect to take action, must less motivate him to do so now.

You can do better than that. I know it!!!

How about Exhibit B produced by the Brown Learning Community of Brown University? We're looking at the first inside page here.

1

COMPUTER WORKSHOPS

Brown Learning Community members can receive a 50% discount off the tuition of their courses. Corporate Discounts of 10% – 20% (See page 13 for details)

THE PERSONAL COMPUTER

Brown University was one of the first institutions in the country to implement personal computers across the campus, for liberal arts as well as science courses, in academic as well as administrative departments. Brown gained a national reputation for its quick adaptation of PCs for work, as well as research and teaching.

Today, the Thomas J. Watson Sr. Center for Information Technology uses the most advanced technology in the nation, in one of the country's newest computer centers. The IBM training center contains state-of-the-art IBM computers. Macintosh courses are taught on Macintosh II computers with color monitors. All of our computers are networked to each other and to the instructor's computer. All run the latest software. Classes are small and personal. Instruction occurs in a friendly, relaxed environment. Each student learns at his or her own personal computer and at his or her own rate.

UNSURE OF WHERE YOUR INTERESTS LIE?

If you are uncertain about which workshop best suits your needs and experience, call the BLC's computer coordinator, **DON DEMAIO**, at his home (401/245-6748 evenings) to discuss your situation and what might be the best alternative for you. As a non-technical user of computers, Mr. DeMaio is especially sensitive to the needs of the PC user.

TUITION BACK GUARANTEE

If for any reason you feel that your investment in education at the Brown Learning Community did not yield full value, we will refund all or a portion of your tuition, as you choose. To qualify, you must attend at least the first session of the course or notify us of your decision to withdraw at least 48 hours before the beginning of the course.

SOMETHING NEW: ONSITE WORKSHOPS

All classes are taught at our campus computer facility, but we also offer workshops at customer sites. Our instructors are happy to come to your office or place of business and teach. They can focus on actual office situations and/or problems at your own computers.

If you think an on-site class might be better for your business, contact Assistant Dean Joyce Reed at 401/863-3452 for more information.

BROWN LEARNING COMMUNITY

Look at the first column: "Computer Workshops." Boy, aren't those two inert words motivating you? If I came up beside you and seductively whispered "computer workshops" in your ears you'd melt, right?

Or what about the second column with the magic words "Brown University was one of the first institutions in the country to implement personal computers across the campus, for liberal arts as well as science courses, in academic as well as administrative departments"? Doesn't this make you want to rush out and enroll today in every computer course offered by Brown?

This is all "me-" (that is marketer-) centered marketing. Not client-centered. The truth is, there's the nub of a client-centered proposition on the page, but look where this stunted marketer puts the information: on the bottom of the first column on the left (that is the weaker) side. I guess they don't think much of their 50% discount!

Let me tell you something: You can do better than this.

And you will if you remember these three crucial points:

1. The purpose of every marketing communication is to get people to *act;*
2. The purpose of every marketing communication is to get people to *act faster* . . . indeed, to get them to *act NOW;*
3. There is *no other purpose* to any marketing communication.

Thus, *every* word you put into every marketing communication either gets the prospect to act faster . . . or it doesn't. If it doesn't, it doesn't belong in the marketing communication. Got it?

Something else you need to know: all marketing communications are part of the same family. That is, the lowly classified ad in the smallest circulation newspaper is related to the glossiest four-color annual report put out by the biggest corporation. What makes the one successful is what makes the other successful. Unfortunately, exalted "marketers" have forgotten this. They have made a false (indeed fatal) distinction between marketing communications that are supposed to motivate people and those that are supposed to gild the company's image.

Let me tell you something else: I don't believe in gilding a company's image. I do not believe that a marketing communication is the place to support anyone's fragile ego and self-esteem. I do not believe a marketing communication is the place to tell your life story or the life story of your business and services. I do not believe that a marketing communication is the place to indulge in philosophical, social or political ruminations. Yet all these extraneous concerns constantly taint, pollute, disrupt and weaken the large majority of marketing communications.

Instead, I believe that a marketing communication should do one thing and one thing only: compel a targeted prospect to take the fastest possible action and so move you and him closer to the defining moment of marketing, the moment when money or other consideration passes from the prospect to you. UNDERSTAND?

Just how you approach the prospect so that this necessary event occurs will vary. You will use a variety of marketing communications to bring this about. Just what you'll use will depend on where you are in the marketing process. But here are your likeliest communication formats:

When You Want To Generate The First Prospect Response, You'll Be Using:

- Classified ads

- Space ads

- Self-mailer flyers

- Card-decks and other post-card mailings

- Client-centered letters.

After You Receive The Prospect's First Response (And If You Don't Need To Reply In Writing), You'll Be Using:

- Client-centered telephone pointers.

After You Receive The Prospect's First Response (And If You Need To Respond In Writing), You'll Be Using:

- Ad response letter

- Standard three-fold brochure

- Question/Answer brochure

- Capabilities statement

- Client-centered fact sheet

- Client-survey questionnaire

- Success Case(s).

After You Send These Marketing Communications To The Prospect And You Want To Follow Up By Telephone, You'll Be Using:

- Client-centered telephone pointers.

After You've Sent Your Marketing Communications And Attempted (So Far Unsuccessfully) To Connect With The Prospect By Phone, You'll Be Using:

- The Enhanced Urgency letter.

After You've Sold One Of Your Services To Your New Client (But Still Have Additional Services He'll Find Helpful), You'll Be Using:

- An upgrade communication.

Now that I've introduced these different types of marketing communication to you, I'd like to describe them in some detail. As I do so, please keep in mind they are all related and all have a common purpose: they exist solely to get your prospect to take faster action.

Marketing Communications For Generating The First Prospect Response

— *The Classified Ad*

Classified ads are ubiquitous but rarely studied. Yet once you know how to use them, they can provide a useful continuing source of leads for your service business. As with all the prospect-generating forms I'm discussing, the key is understanding their underlying structure and plugging your data into it. Thus, the classified ad must have the following parts:

Target market identifier (who you're talking to) + leading benefit this prospect gets + inducement for immediate action + means of connecting with you via mail or phone + code that indicates where lead came from.

Take a close look at what I've written. Your classified must clearly indicate who the ad is for, what this person gets from you, what will get him to take action now, a means of connecting with you, and a code that clearly indicates where the lead came from.

This is easy enough, right? Well, let's make the game rather more interesting: you should do this in not more than 10 words. I didn't select 10 words at random. This is the number of words most publications running classified ads provide for their basic price. Thus, you are paying an additional word cost for any words over 10. As a good marketer, you want to avoid this whenever possible.

To make sure you can create the right ad in the space you've got available, do the following:

- first, write the ad in complete sentences and then cut back the words until there are no more than what is necessary for the minimum required by the publication;

- reduce your address to the fewest number of words possible. Thus, Jeffrey Lant Associates, Inc., 50 Follen Street, Suite 507, Cambridge, MA 02138 (12 words) becomes JLA, 50 Follen, Cambridge, MA 02138 (6 words . . . or possibly even 5 since some publications count the state and zip code as just one word.)

- blend your code into your address. Thus, the code for your ad in *Entrepreneur* magazine, May, 1993 becomes simply a "/A" attached to the company name: "JLA/A". This code is important, as you know, for tracking responses and enabling you to determine if continuing to advertise in this place at this time makes sense.

Hint: when you're writing classified ads, write at least 6 or 7 at the same time and store them. The key to all marketing communications, including classified ads, is to find an ad that continually generates a profit-making response and then to LEAVE IT ALONE. To find this enviable ad, you need to test a variety of ads in a variety of publications at a variety of times, tracking all responses. Only then are you going to know which are the most generative ads for you and when you should be using them.

— Space Ads

The vast majority of space ads are of the "show the flag", "we're here" variety. Packed with logos and self-laudatory comments, they lavishly and adjectivally extol the unsubstantiated virtues of the advertiser. You already know how I feel about all this.

In fact, space ads are just the big brothers of classified ads; they provide you with a greater expanse to fill with client-centered benefits and the necessary incentives that get people to act now. These ads, of course, come in all sizes. What you should be trying to determine is how *little* space you need to buy to produce the greatest possible response. This is a matter for experimentation and good data keeping. Unfortunately, too many service sellers forget this. While I was writing this chapter I received a telephone call from an MLM representative of White Lion Printing. He'd just taken a full-page ad in a publication in an attempt to build his down-line.

This fellow had NEVER placed an ad before and was sinking all his resources into a single full-page ad in a multi-level marketing magazine. I asked him if he'd bothered to ask the sales rep for the periodical how many responses such ads tended to generate, but he added (without the slightest hint of sheepishness) that he hadn't bothered to do that. I told him he should ask and that he'd probably be better off running four 1/4 page ads (at somewhat more expense) than one one-page ad. However, he rather irritably shrugged off my suggestion. I mean, what do I know? I've only studied the subject for years and written hundreds of profit-making ads! This kind of information can certainly get in the way, though, for a guy who's fueled by blissful ignorance! (*Note:* when I followed up this fellow months later to see what happened, I was hardly surprised to discover he'd lost his shirt.)

Sadly, too many service sellers follow in this ridiculous path. But you won't when you keep these points in mind:

- a profit-making space ad *always* contains a strong reason for immediate action;
- it details not just one but a series of benefits the prospect will get from you when he acts. Thus, "you get this . . . and this . . . and this . . . and also this";
- the ad contains both phone number and mail response possibilities.

Thus, the basic structure of the space ad is: "Act now and get . . ."

In writing the space ad, keep in mind that you want maximum response as fast as possible. Many service marketers get worried when I tell them this saying "But I only want 'qualified' prospects." When they say this *I* get worried! Your job is to motivate the greatest number of prospects to contact you. I get concerned when the service seller is trying to get the prospect to make a premature decision about whether he's right for your service or not. As a marketer, *I* want to make that decision; I don't want the prospect to do so.

Thus, I advise you to craft your ad so that you generate maximum fastest response. You want the greatest number of phone calls and mail responses in the shortest period of time. Then *you* can sort them out according to how many qualified prospects you need in what period of time to reach your objective.

Unsurprisingly, it's usually the most arrogant and inexperienced marketers who are worried about the "quality" of their leads. Recently, for instance, I assisted two separate firms of copywriters create space ads to generate leads for their businesses. The first group frequently voiced their fear that their time would be wasted by having to deal with unqualified leads; the other firm, following my advice, wanted the maximum number of leads in the shortest period of time and resolved that they'd sort out the quality on the telephone and by written follow up.

The first group went out of its way to produce a non-client centered ad laced with qualifiers about who they wanted . . . and implying who they didn't want. The second firm simply stressed client benefits and provided a strong call for immediate action. Hardy surprisingly, the second firm got many more leads than the first; in fact, in the same publication in the same issue their response was at least 5 times the first group's, despite the fact that they were basically offering the same service.

More telling, however, the firm that wrote the client-centered ad made several times the cost of the ad in just 60 days. The first firm made money, too, but not nearly as much.

Your deduction, Dr. Watson?

- Concentrate on client-centered benefits first;
- If you must include qualifiers, put the stress on the client-centered benefit(s), not the client-excluding qualifier(s);
- Stress the immediate call for action even if you have significant qualifiers;
- Resolve that you can better qualify your prospects on the phone or by subsequent mail follow-up than in your ad copy.

And, of course, at all times make sure you follow the basic structure of a profit-making space ad, thus:

your best offer for immediate action here

qualifications on your offer
(like date it ends)

audience qualifier (who you're
speaking to, if necessary)

- biggest specific benefit you, the prospect, get

- next biggest

- next biggest

- next biggest, *etc.* until available space is filled.

Telephone number to use for immediate service. Your company name and address.

— Self-Mailer Flyers

The self-mailer flyer is merely a space ad that you mail directly instead of binding into the pages of a periodical. As such, you should (practically) be able to tell me how it should be written.

The basic problem most service sellers have in writing and using flyers is that they use the space to tell the prospects about themselves . . . instead of motivating immediate action.

The self-mailer flyer, however, provides an easy and inexpensive format for generating a continuing stream of leads which you can first convert to qualified prospects and then into customers. When you're using self-mailer flyers, here are the important points to keep in mind:

- How many must you send to generate the number of leads you need to meet your marketing quota?

- What offers have worked best so you can use them again and, by the same token, which worst, so you can avoid them?

- What benefits are most likely to excite the enthusiasm of the targeted prospects?

What's different about a self-mailer flyer as distinct from a space ad is that with a flyer you'll have more area to fill. Thus, you must keep in mind:

- the prospect-centered message begins where the prospect's eye first alights. That is, you cannot afford to begin your motivating techniques *inside* the flyer; you *begin* on the *outside* and carry on within;

- your marketing message should be stressed on the flyer's mailing panel;

- it should be reinforced in the copy inside the flyer.

Too many service marketers act as if all the motivation and message of a flyer happen *inside*. This isn't true. Flyers have two sides . . . and thus your client-centered message must carry through two sides. Sounds obvious, doesn't it, until you start looking at most service self-mailer flyers which ignore half their space and thus reduce the effectiveness of their message accordingly.

Here, then, is the outline of a self-mailer flyer:

Side 1 — Including mailing panel

stresses major offer
also any limitations (such as
deadline)

Includes your company name, address and telephone number.

Side 2

again stresses major offer & limitations

Opens by clearly pointing to designated prospect saying, in effect, "I'm talking to you!"

List benefits in priority order, thus:

- leading specific benefit ("you get this!")
- next leading benefit ("you get this!")
- next leading, *etc.* ("and you also get this!")

Includes a minimum of two client-centered testimonials or, if testimonials are relatively short, a client-centered testimonial for *each* benefit.

Provides reason why prospect needs to ACT NOW. Does the prospect get a special offer? Avoid further problems? Get benefits faster? This part encourages the prospect to CALL ANYTIME, 24-hours a day, morning, noon or night, holidays, week-ends, whenever. In short, you heap benefits on benefits, further exciting with a limited offer and making it clear to the prospect he can CALL ANYTIME.

— Card-Decks And Other Post-Card Mailings

I feel a real warm spot in my heart for this means of generating prospect response. I've been using card-decks for years and, as you know, now own a card-deck publishing company. During any given month I am mailing at least 200,000 of these cards and oftentimes many more.

In my experience, no better medium exists for generating large numbers of qualified leads than card-deck advertising, so please pay real close attention to what I'm saying here. If you can make card-decks work to generate leads for your business, you'd be crazy not to. Here are the things you've got to keep in mind about them:

- All decks go to a targeted market. If you're not looking for leads in that market, that deck isn't for you.

- A deck card is a space ad in post-card form. Unlike a space ad, however, a deck card is not surrounded by editorial matter. The only thing the prospect sees is a package of ads;

- Prospects read card decks RAPIDLY. I figure that the average prospect goes through his deck next to his waste paper basket, flipping through the cards very rapidly, giving each card about 10-15 seconds at most. What the prospect is looking for is something that screams at him, "HEY, HERE'S SOMETHING FOR YOU!" Thus, if the card doesn't pull the prospect in within 10 seconds, the card failed and ends up in the trash. I estimate that the average prospect replies to about 6 cards in each issue;

- All the prospect is saying in responding is, "I'm sufficiently interested to send in this card. I need you to tell me lots more about the benefits you have available before I'm going to buy anything." Thus, card decks are best used as lead generators rather than sales generators, although I personally know several companies running cards regularly who sell directly from them and do quite well.

- It is important to keep in mind that while you may not be competing with a similar company to yours in any given deck (in my deck, for instance, I try to keep direct competitors out), you *are* competing with other advertisers whose more colorful cards and client-centered messages may actually diminish your response, even though they're not selling the same thing you are.

Another thing to keep in mind: all too often service sellers forget that a deck card has *two* sides, not just one. I see evidence of this all the time. When I ask advertisers to send me a draft of their card copy so I can review it, most send copy for one side only, thus showing that they don't understand that their marketing must take place on *both* sides, not just one. To be sure, the front side (where the color goes) is the most impactful, but the back side is important, too. Don't forget this!

Note: I've pioneered a certain kind of deck card that I'd like to recommend to you. The front side we call the "mini-billboard". Here you provide your major message, offer, *etc.* No space on this side is taken up with a reply or order coupon. Instead, this information is included on Side 2. Side 2 is divided into two parts. As you see from the illustration below, the first half is given over to 1) a confirmation that the prospect wants the benefit you have available and 2) specifics you need so you can provide it to him. The remainder of this side provides your address and a place for a stamp.

❏ Yes, I want to learn how Jeffrey can help me sell more of my products/services faster... FREE!

Print Carefully. We're not mind readers!

Name_____

Title_____

Company_____

Address _____

City _____

State _____ Zip _____

Phone (   )_____

No response without phone number!

For Faster Service,
Call 617-547-6372

Place Stamp Here

Rush to:

Jeffrey Lant's
Free Marketing Info
50 Follen St., Suite 507
Cambridge, MA 02138

Here then is the structure for a successful deck card or individual post card mailing:

Side 1 (color side)

Offer

Major benefit followed by series of additional benefits in priority order.

Reemphasis on offer

Telephone number for immediate prospect follow-up

Side 2 (address side)

— first half

☐ Box confirming benefit you have available and prospect's interest in having it.

Space for prospect's name, company name, address, and, if you need it, phone number.

Note: if you require phone number for action, then use words like this: "No response without phone." You'll get more telephone numbers this way.

— second half

Place for stamp

Your return address

Note: to generate still more responses faster, put this line next to the stamp box: "For faster service call (your phone number) . . . NOW!"

Another Note: while this discussion has concentrated on deck cards the same holds true if you are simply mailing an individual post card to a prospect.

Resource

I need hardly say that if you are selling a service nationwide to the presidents, CEOs and owners of businesses, directors of sales and marketing, entrepreneurs and opportunity seekers, you should be in my Sales & Marketing SuccessDek. It mails quarterly to 100,000 card-deck responsive prospects and offers the lowest prices in the entire card deck industry. Call me for complete details and media kit. I'll be happy to tell you whether your service is suitable for my deck or refer you elsewhere if I'm aware of another one that might assist you. Call me at (617) 547-6372.

— *Client-centered letters*

Most service sellers market through letters at some point. I know, I'm one of them. The question is: do you use the letters wisely, to get the fastest response possible? In thinking about your letter, you need to consider whether something should go with it to increase its impact. Thus, you may have:

- just a letter, or
- a letter plus response card, or
- a letter plus response card plus success case, or
- a letter plus response card plus question-and-answer brochure, or
- a letter plus response card plus standard three-fold brochure.

Because the client-centered letter so often accompanies other marketing communications, you'll need to consider all that I'm telling you about it in the light of the information that follows about the other marketing documents and adapt accordingly. However, let me give you two alternatives: letter alone and letter accompanied by additional client-centered materials.

- Letter Alone

What you're looking for from the client-centered letter that goes alone to a prospect is what you're always looking for: a means of generating the greatest response in the least amount of time for the least amount of money. In this connection, it is my belief that the *fewest* number of words is the best for a *service seller*. Why? Because all a letter can do is generate a prospect response. Ordinarily, you're going to have to talk to the person (either on the phone or in person) to close the sale. For various reasons (including the need to discuss his particular case, available options, and price), the prospect isn't going to buy from a letter alone.

Sadly, many service sellers forget this. They overburden their letter by trying to make it:

- present their case;
- deal with all the prospect's objections;
- give all the information the prospect needs about how the service works, and
- close the sale.

In my opinion, this is too much for a mere letter to do. Instead, I want the letter to do one single thing: get the prospect to act so he gets in touch with me *immediately.* Then I, as service seller, can do what I must to figure out if this is indeed a qualified prospect and take the appropriate actions that result in the sale.

Because I have a very focused objective for my letter, I don't need to create a work of art. All I need to do is pack it with 1) an offer that motivates promptest response and 2) one client-centered benefit heaped on another. One single-sided or back-to-back page is ordinarily quite adequate to meet my objective and get the prospect moving.

Here's what that page should look like:

major offer to prospect . . . limitations on offer

Clear indication of target market as evidenced by salutation (thus: "Dear consultant who's committed to making $100,000 every year.")

Open your letter with pain . . . and lay it on thick.

Or open your letter with the specific benefit the prospect wants. And paint a rhapsodic picture of it.

Tell the prospect he can either avoid pain or get benefit if he takes immediate action. Let this action be the tiniest imaginable thing . . . like calling you right this minute. (Or, as I say, "just dialing 7 /or 10/ little numbers on the phone.")

Heap benefits on the prospect . . . one after another . . . after another. Let the prospect know all these benefits (either gains achieved or pains eliminated) can be his if he contacts you NOW.

Add the testimonial of a satisfied prospect . . . preferably a prospect whose name/position/organization/results would be meaningful to the reader.

Make sure there's a post-script that again reiterates the leading benefit to be achieved . . . the offer you have available . . . the leading pain that will be eliminated . . . if only the prospect ACTS NOW.

• Letter Accompanied By Additional Marketing Materials

Whether your prospect-generating package consists of a single client-centered letter or a package, the purpose is the same: to generate the fastest possible response from the largest number of prospects. In a package, all elements must work towards this objective.

Keeping this in mind, I am often puzzled by the marketing packages I receive from service businesses. They may contain the right components as outlined above but the parts don't work towards the crucial objective. Thus, a service seller may stuff a newspaper article in the packet headed something like "news about us!" (Now, I ask you, does anyone CARE about "news about us"? Remember, they care about themselves and their problems/situations/desires.) Or, they include a stuffy standard three-fold brochure akin to the one misdrawn by The International Association of Conference Centers. How can such a pompous, "me-centered" document help induce action . . . no matter how good the cover letter is? It can't!

Thus, if you decide that your interests are best furthered by putting together a package introduced by a letter, make sure that all the elements work together to produce the desired result. Remember, the only reason for using additional materials is because you've decided that a single letter standing alone will not be as effective as a package of materials. Merely stuffing things in an envelope and mailing them off to the prospect isn't the answer. The objective of all marketing, after all, is not to dump costly stuff on a prospect but to motivate that prospect to action while using the fewest (and hence least expensive) marketing communications. If you're doing things differently, you're simply tossing your money out the window.

Thus, before you assemble a more elaborate packet of materials headed by a letter, you've got to make sure these will all work in tandem to produce the desired result. Hence:

- Begin by reminding yourself of the objective: getting the prospect to respond FAST;

- Ask yourself whether you really need materials beyond a letter. Are you *sure* a letter standing alone won't be able to do the job for you?

- If you've decided that a letter alone won't do, consider your options. The simplest addition to your package is a response card that you can create by following the guidelines for deck cards and post cards;

- If you need additional information, consider which option will work best. If you've just finished producing success for a client like the prospect you're writing to, you'll want to include a Success Case. This says, in effect, "someone like you got substantial results. If you want substantial results, too, call now and let's get started." If you can only work with a certain number of clients at any one time helping them achieve this kind of success, say so. That's a motivater.

- If you need prospects to have answers to certain basic questions about how you work and what it takes to achieve success, include the Question-Answer brochure. This is a qualifying device. It says essentially: "we can help you get the results you want, if you're willing to follow certain steps and adhere to certain practices. Here they are." Before sending this brochure, however, you need to decide whether you want to present this information in person (or on the phone) rather than in this package. Used here it may frighten off prospects who might well be salvageable if they learned the facts from you directly. If you need more clients now rather than fewer, I suggest using this kind of qualifying device sparingly.

- If you want prospects to have standard background information about you, you may want to include your standard three-fold brochure. In fact, it's probable that most service sellers have used a marketing package consisting of cover letter, three-fold brochure and response card. Where they go wrong, however, is failing to make the brochure carry its part of the case to motivate the prospect. You want to make sure your brochure makes it plain that you can either 1) eliminate pain from the prospect's life or 2) achieve gain. Also, this is the place where you heap all the benefits of doing business with you and make sure that each benefit is underscored and supported by an accompanying testimonial offered by a satisfied prospect. What will be left out of this brochure is the offer for immediate action. *That* will be stressed in the cover letter . . . and indeed the real point of including a letter is that only in the letter can you easily test offers and see which ones work best.

Here then is the structure of a package consisting of letter, standard three-fold brochure and response card:

— *Letter*

Opens with offer for immediate action.

Addresses prospect according to pain he's having (which he'd presumably like removed) or gain he wants.

First paragraph of letter stresses either pain or gain.

Follows with benefits to be derived from immediate action.

Provides post-script reinforcing offer.

— Three-fold brochure

Stresses further benefits.

Provides testimonials of satisfied clients.

Provides background information on different services you have available, that is different ways prospect can use to either eliminate pain or achieve gain, always stressing benefits . . . not technique.

Provides client-centered biography about people who provide benefits and how many benefits they have provided to other clients. (Remember: this bio is not a mere listing of where the person has been but what results he delivered.)

— Response card

This card asks the prospect to contact you to start getting the benefit you offer: "Yes, contact me immediately with further details about (benefit you offer)." Provides space for all details you need. Also includes line "For faster service, call . . ." (As always, this line should be repeated next to the box saying "Place stamp here.") Remember: some prospects like to sit back and have you call them. Others want to pick up the phone and get started. You need to be prepared for both.

Note: you can add other items to this packet, like a copy of the article about your service and company. That's fine. Just make sure that you provide a client-centered headline that reinforces in the mind of the prospect the fact that you are not simply providing them with information but motivating them to respond and get the benefit you provide. Thus, you should add a line like this above the headline in any article: "Here's why we can help you get (benefit the prospect wants)." Again, always remember: EVERYTHING in a response generating marketing communication or expanded packet must focus on the prospect and on getting him to take action faster. EVERYTHING!

After You Receive The Prospect's First Response (And If You Don't Need To Reply In Writing)

Believe me, if you:

- focus on your targeted market;

- do the home-work outlined in the previous chapter, and

- fashion all you know into the kinds of prospect-centered marketing communications outlined in this chapter . . .

. . . YOU'RE GOING TO GET LEADS . . . INDEED YOU'LL HAVE A STEADY STREAM OF THESE LEADS. I know. So far my record for leads is about 1000 in a single day — but I'm working to better that. Think what this means: 1000 people from all over the United States (and various foreign countries) contacted me in a SINGLE DAY to say: "Jeffrey, I think you can help me achieve my objectives. Convince me, and I'll do my part to make you a richer guy." Because I'm a lead-generating fanatic, these leads come in every business day of the year (including Saturday). Others come in by phone virtually every day of the year, including most holidays and Sundays.

This will happen to you, too, if you follow these guidelines and produce these kinds of client-centered lead-generating marketing communications.

Don't blow it now. Be prepared to deal with these leads . . . on the phone and in your follow-up marketing communications.

Client-centered Telephone Pointers

When your prospect calls in response to your lead-generator, you're either going to be physically available or you're not. Either way you've got to be ready.

This morning, for instance, I read an article in the *Boston Globe* about a local service provider. A little before 9 a.m. I called to get some more information. There was no answer. And no answering machine. A little after 9, I called again; this time, I got an answering machine telling me that their hours were between noon and 7 p.m. and to call again. There was no way I could leave a message.

Now think about this situation for a minute. The service seller goes to the trouble of getting himself quoted in an article in a major newspaper but hasn't got the brains to set up the system for handling the responses. So far, thanks to the ineptitude of the service seller, I've had to call twice and haven't yet connected. The guy must be an incredible optimist to think that all his inquiries are going to call two or three times to get through to him. But I'll tell you something: I bet he thinks he's as smart as they come . . .

Well, I have something to say about the guy: he's a marketing idiot.

(*Note:* by the way, I find upon rereading this section months later that I never did call this company back. So, indeed, he lost the sale by being unprepared, since I no longer know the name of his organization or any other pertinent information about it.)

Handling The Responses When You're Present

The time to get yourself ready to respond to the leads generated is when you're working on the lead-generating materials themselves. Thus:

- develop your client-centered lead-generating materials;

- develop your client-centered responses to these materials, then

- distribute the lead-generating materials, sit back and get ready for the leads, knowing you can handle the inevitable responses.

So, how should you handle the response? WRITE DOWN WHAT YOU'RE GOING TO SAY!

Most service sellers are trying to do too many things with too few resources. As a result, they're constantly rushed; (I know what I'm talking about!) The way to handle this problem is to think through in advance of any prospect response just what you're going to say.

And what do you want to say? You want to reinforce the major benefit the prospect is calling for. Thus, when a prospect calls to request further details on how you can remodel his bathroom in only one week for the least possible cost, you don't say: "I'll be happy to send you the information." Instead, you say: "Yes, we can remodel your bathroom in only one week for the least possible cost." In other words, you underscore your primary benefit.

This reinforcing is part of the Rule of Seven. The prospect has already seen your benefit at least once. He's responded to it. Now you're reinforcing that benefit for him . . . and trying to discern when he wants it: "When do you want to have your bathroom remodeled?"

As you're well aware, as a service seller, all too often you simply tell the prospect you'll send him information. But I want to tell you something: YOU'RE NOT IN THE INFORMATION SENDING BUSINESS. You're in the business of delivering benefits to qualified prospects and it's your job to:

- reinforce the benefit in the prospect's mind when he contacts you;

- ask him when he wants to have (start enjoying/profiting from) the benefit (thereby indicating the value of the prospect), and

- let him know you'll be back in touch in no more than 5 business days to start talking about getting the benefit.

In other words, the heart of your response to the newly generated prospect is NEVER about sending information. It's always about your ability to give the prospect the benefit and starting to figure out just how badly he wants it, when he wants to get started and his ability to pay for it.

Now let me tell you something: no one was born into this world with the innate ability to provide this kind of client-centered response. You've got to learn this behavior. And learning it starts with you understanding that:

- merely sending out information to the leads that have been generated isn't your business;

- it's always your responsibility to know what your primary benefit is and to reinforce this benefit to the prospect when he contacts you;

- you can't reinforce a benefit that you haven't discerned and understood. Thus, you must spend time thinking through (as outlined in the last chapter) the benefits you have available;

- until such time as this benefit comes trippingly off your tongue, you'd better write it down and read your response off a piece of paper or have it available on a computer screen.

What???

Yes, what I am advocating here is that you:

- craft your client-centered response;

- post it and keep it next to the phone or have it available on computer (if you work at a computer, like I do) and that

- you read it when people call.

If this sounds mechanical to you that's unfortunate. All your life you've been winging your responses when people have called you. As a service seller seeking multi-million dollar status you can't afford that. Thus, write down your response and read it when prospects call . . . until such time as you can deliver an academy-award winning performance without benefit of script.

Note: like all other forms of marketing, you should be testing your telephone prospect responses. Thus, create a half dozen and store them in your computer for future use. Which ones seem the most client-centered? Get the best response? It's your job to keep testing.

Another note: if you're not the one who answers the phone in your service business, it's your responsibility to explain to your receptionist why you're doing this. Very often the most strenuous opposition to client-centered marketing will come from your own employees. In my experience very few of these people understand the connection between the way they handle prospects on the phone and their pay check. Indeed, many seem to regard prospect queries as a rude interruption in their days. Service seller, let me be candid with you: if you permit this kind of selfish, vulgar and stupid behavior among your employees, you don't deserve to be a millionaire. Thus, it's your responsibility to:

- create the benefit responses your employees must use;

- explain why they must use them, and to

- make sure they use them regularly and properly.

This doesn't so much mean listening to them when they answer the phone (your presence will alter the way they usually do), as it means calling in yourself at regular intervals and having people you respect do so and paying close attention to what you hear. Chances are the first few times you do this, you'll be appalled. My advice? When you don't hear the kind of client-centered benefit response you should be hearing, approach the employee immediately and set about changing things. It's always easier to say, "I'll be happy to put the information in the mail for you," than "I'm sending the details today about how you can get the (benefit the prospect wants.") YET THE PROSPECT IS ALWAYS BUYING BENEFITS . . . HE NEVER JUST WANTS INFORMATION.

Should You Really Be Sending Anything At All?

When most service sellers are asked for information . . . they send it. You already know that I disapprove of that. That's why I want to spend a little time advocating that you start the sorting process as soon as the prospect calls. I want you to clearly understand that not all prospects are equal and that you shouldn't be spending the same amount of time and energy on the "tire kickers" as you spend on the reasonable prospects. The trick is knowing which is which. That's why you need a more extensive set of telephone pointers.

I've already pointed out the advantages of reinforcing the prospect-centered benefit that induced the prospect to contact you in the first place. Unfortunately, once you've done this, you might just put your information in an envelope and mail it out thinking you've done your job. Wrong!

One of the reasons I'm such an advocate about instituting an aggressive lead generating program is so that you get the chance to qualify your prospects when they call you. This is particularly important when you start selling services nationwide. In these circumstances, it's a lot easier to handle calls from potential prospects than to do everything it takes to do cold calling. Besides, you keep your phone bill way down!

Thus, tell the prospect, "Before I sent you information about how to get (the benefit the prospect wants), I need to ask you a few questions." The questions you ask should be designed to elicit:

- how quickly the prospect wants the benefit;
- the prospect's familiarity with getting the benefit;
- whether there are situations in the prospect's life right now that preclude him going ahead to get the benefit;
- whether the prospect has shopped for the benefit elsewhere and, if so, with what results;
- whether the prospect is now in a position financially so that he can acquire the benefit, *etc.*

These questions, please note, are not going to occur to you spontaneously. Just like the opening line of your conversation with the prospect, they must be crafted *beforehand,* written, stored for easy accessibility at the moment they're required, and perfected by editing and practice . . . just like with any other marketing communication.

And as with any other marketing communication, doing things in this fashion gives you maximum control over the direction events take.

Sadly, most service sellers don't do this. Even if they work hard to generate maximum response, they devote little or no attention to how respondents are treated (and whether they are motivated to take faster action). They make no attempt to differentiate between respondents, attempting to determine which are the ones they should be concentrating on.

But this is ludicrous! Your job is to generate maximum response, to reinforce the benefit you have available to respondents, and to advance the qualifying process as quickly as possible — with the assistance of a series of necessary sorting questions, all written and easily accessible.

Note: when you ask these kinds of sorting questions, you're going to determine, just as George Orwell determined, that while all animals are equal, some, indeed, are more equal than others. The "more equal" animals get better, prompter, more focused, more complete treatment than the others. Let me make this point very clear for you: marketing is not a democratic event. Marketing recognizes that some people are better than others and must be treated in a different, superior way. It is the essence of marketing that some people have more interest, a greater need, and more money than others. Marketing is not about providing for all people; it is about providing for all those who have the greatest want coupled with the available means for satisfying it. You must work accordingly.

Further, as you ask these questions, the prospects will start falling out along a continuum of possibilities ranging from "Yes, sign me up right this minute!" down to "I'll never, ever, ever do that!" People at the lower end of this continuum should be drastically reduced in priority . . . or dropped altogether. Personally, these days I have no compunction about telling some of the purported "prospects" who call me that they're not ready for what I have available. Because I have regular catalog mailings, I'll add such people to that list so that I keep marketing to them in the hope that they'll upgrade to real prospects. However, if I didn't have this means of regular prospect communication, I'd probably throw the valueless lead away without compunction.

Marketing, after all, is a process, and it is inevitable that the process will throw up people who, while needing your benefits, are not in a position, for whatever reason, to acquire them. When the prospect calls you, if you're smart you want to do everything possible to arrange matters so that you get this necessary information as quickly as possible — and act on it according to what you've discovered. If you "wing it" on the telephone when prospects call you, you cannot effectively achieve this result.

Handling The Responses When You're Not Present

Face it. There are going to be moments when nobody's available to handle your responses. It even happens to me, although I'm the most accessible service seller in the universe. However, you've still got to be ready for these times . . . and you've still got to respond in marketing mode.

Take a minute right now and listen to the outgoing message on your telephone answering machine. Does it go something like this: "Hi, this is Jim at Ajax Service Providers. I'm not available right now. Leave a message after the beep so I can call you back"? Please note: this is *not* a marketing message. This merely turns your phone into an information receptacle. AND IT'S HURTING YOUR BUSINESS. You see, it's your responsibility to direct a benefit-centered message to the prospect WHETHER YOU'RE PHYSICALLY AVAILABLE OR NOT. Thus: "Hi, this is Jim. I want to help you get (benefit the prospect wants), but right now I'm helping someone else get it. Leave your name, address and phone number and please tell me just how fast you want (benefit) so I can prioritize my response to you accordingly."

You've never heard a phone message like this, have you? Instead, you get funny voices and musical crescendos and disparaging comments about answering machines, but never a PROSPECT-CENTERED MESSAGE that reiterates your benefit and asks the prospect to tell you how seriously he wants it. But imagine if you worked this way: you'd be able to reinforce your benefit message and start the necessary sorting process that tells you just how serious the prospect is and enables you to respond accordingly. In short, you'd return not merely to a message — but to a qualified prospect!

After You Receive The Prospect's First Response (And If You Need To Respond In Writing)

Most of your prospects are going to get in touch with you by mail (or fax, a mail equivalent) or telephone. You now know what to do if they telephone you. If they fax, you respond IMMEDIATELY with a series of questions you need answers to so that you can:

- provide the prospect with just the information he wants, and

- determine just how serious the prospect is about going ahead now.

When a person faxes you an inquiry, you should fax back indicating that you're as swift as the prospect . . . and ready to move ahead promptly.

If you are providing your service locally, most of your prospects will call or fax you. When you start providing your service nationally or internationally, your percentage of written queries will increase dramatically. In my case, for instance, at least 80% of my queries are now written and sent by mail. Obviously, you're going to give considerable attention to how you respond. Here's what you should be keeping in mind:

- Your objective is not to send information. It's to qualify the prospect and transform him into a buyer as soon as possible;

- While you certainly want the prospect to call you upon receiving the material, you must be prepared to follow up each response packet with a call.

Let's take a look, first, at the materials you may well send the prospect:

- Detailed response letter
- Standard three-fold brochure
- Question/Answer brochure
- Capabilities statement
- Client-centered fact sheet
- Client-survey questionnaire
- Success cases.

You're not surprised to discover that these are remarkably similar to the materials you may have used in your first mailing to the (as yet unqualified) prospects.

— *Detailed response letter*

Unlike the initial letter you sent, this time your letter is either 1) going to be substantially longer or 2) certainly accompanied by additional marketing communications. Just what you'll provide in this letter depends on who you're trying to motivate, but here are the likely components:

- all the benefits the prospect gets by investing in your service now;

- answers to likely objections;

- what will happen to the prospect if he doesn't act now;

- offer the prospect gets if he acts now . . . and when that offer expires;

- any limitations on the amount of service you can provide now (another motivater to the prospect for immediate action);

- more results-oriented testimonials from those who have already benefited from the service.

As you may imagine, including all this information could easily make this a four-page (two pages, back-to-back) letter. That's acceptable; after all, this is the time to provide the prospect with all that he needs to make a decision. You've sent this information to the prospect because you believed this person could buy your service and was ready to act in a reasonable period of time. Believe me, such people want to know all the necessary details. It is only the unqualified prospects (whom some authorities rightly call "suspects") who find all this information excessive.

Note: make sure you tell the prospect that if you don't hear from him in 5 business days, you'll be calling to get him to do what's necessary so he gets the benefit you have available. Do not write something like, "I'll call to get you to buy my service." Write instead, "I'm be calling you so you can get (benefit the prospect wants.)" No one ever wants to buy your service. But thousands, even millions may crave the benefit you offer.

What goes with this letter depends on what you need the prospect to know so he can make the fastest possible decision about becoming a buyer.

— *Standard three-fold brochure*

You already know what goes in this document, but to refresh your memory check out the brochure below.

How we can offer you the lowest prices in the industry

People want to know what the trick is to offering prices that are easily $^1/_3$ to $^1/_2$ less than anybody else in the industry. *Here's the 'secret':*

■ **Low overhead.** Our overhead is low, and we pass the savings on to you. A large chunk of the additional price you're paying to be in other people's business card decks goes to pay their high overhead requirements. That includes all the fancy packaging you get from them. We put money where it ought to go: into quality printing and quality lists. In a card-deck business these are the only places it makes sense to put money.

■ **Limited credit.** Credit costs money, especially in this economy. So, we ask for payment up-front. This way we can pay the printers up-front which cuts this major cost. We pass these savings on to you. We could give more credit and charge higher prices. But we think it makes more sense to charge you less and have you pay in advance whenever possible.

■ **We participate in the deck, too.** Unlike other card-deck companies which simply publish decks and have to make all their money from selling cards in it, we're different. We make most of our money by selling our own products (mostly books) in the deck. That's just another reason why we're especially finicky about lists. We're just as interested as you are in using the best quality names.

To Get Started Motivating 100,000 Business Decision Makers To Buy Your Offer For The Lowest Prices In The Country (Or To Get A Sample Deck), contact either:

Dr. Jeffrey Lant, Publisher
or Bill Reece, Assistant Publisher

Jeffrey Lant's Sales & Marketing
SuccessDek
50 Follen St., #507
Cambridge, MA 02138

(617) 547-6372
Fax (617) 547-0061

Need help with copywriting for your card or lay-out and design? We can help. Ask for details!!!

Guaranteed

Lowest Published Rates In The Card-Deck Industry!

If you can find someone with lower published prices, we'll match them – promise! (Try to get this pledge from anyone else!)

Now reach 100,000 business decision makers for less than 1.2 cents each!

You can't reach business buyers through card decks for less!!!

 Sales & Marketing **SuccessDek**

Five Reasons Why You Should Advertise In Our Sales & Marketing SuccessDek

1) ***You're paying too much if you advertise anywhere else.*** Why pay 2 to 3 times as much for leads when you can get what you need from us? That's just stupid. (If you can't think of any other way to spend your money except buying overpriced cards in other people's decks, send it our way. We'll know what to do with it!)

2) ***You get high quality deck-responsive names.*** We pay top dollar for our names and the names we use are recent (not older than 120 days), often "hot line" names. We know you want to get access to the best names. We've got 'em. The best names ensure you access to the best leads and most likely buyers. We mail to a minimum of 10 and usually more lists, merged and purged so the same people aren't getting your offer. The final list is zip code corrected to improve list quality even more!

3) ***Free second color.*** You pay extra for color with other decks. You get it free from us. And if you want four-color, you pay virtually cost price. You're paying a premium for four-color processing everywhere else.

4) ***Fewer competitors.*** Ever noticed how in most decks there may be three, four or even 8 competing offers? We know this irritates you. While we can't promise that every offer will be unique, we do our best to cut down the competition in the deck. Our goal is to get you maximum response not just sell cards. We know our success is predicated on your success... and we run our business accordingly.

5) ***Friendly service.*** We really do try harder. Lots of people in the advertising world are difficult, condescending, and rude. We're not perfect either, but we do aim to help you. Frankly, we don't just want your business once. We want you to profit from our lead-generating system for years to come, and we're willing to work hard to make you happy. We don't just want customers. We want friends.

See for yourself just how our prices compare with other companies targeting business decision makers

Company	Basic Rate	Second Color	Cost Per 2-Color Card	Add'l For 4-Color
Marketing Bulletin Board (120,000 circ)	$3,550	$150	3.1 cents	$250
Marketing Manager (150,000 circ)	$4,950	$200	3.4 cents	$400
President's Exec Deck (200,000 circ)	$3,995	$200	2.1 cents	$400
Venture Advertising Sales & Marketing (100,000 circ)	$3,000	$300	3.3 cents	$450

...and *all* other decks in the industry are comparably priced!!!

(source: Standard Rate & Data December, 1991 Edition)

Now look at us:

Jeffrey Lant's
Sales & Marketing SuccessDek
100,000 circulation

Basic Rate	Second Color	Cost Per 2-Color Card	Add'l For 4-Color
$1199	You get 2nd color FREE!	**1.2 cents!**	**$151**

1992 Schedule

Mail Dates	Closing Dates
April 1	March 2
June 30	May 29
October 1	September 2
January 4, 1993	November 23, 1992

Rates

100,000 cards per deck	Cash Price
1 card	$1199
subsequent cards same deck	$1100
Second color	FREE
Four-color process	$151
C/1/S enamel paper stock	upon request
Advertiser-supplied inserts	upon request

Production Requirements

Binding method	Loose deck
Trim size	5 $^1/2$" x 3 $^1/2$"
Maximum copy area	5 $^1/16$" x 3 $^1/8$"
Stock	.007 Hi-bulk

Art Specifications: Screened film negatives, right reading, emulsion side down, 120-line screen. Camera-ready art and veloxes are also acceptable. No bleeds. If camera-ready art is not submitted, we bill you for any charges. These charges are due upon receipt.

The brochure contains details the prospect needs about:

- benefits he gets
- how your service works
- special information on prices, deadlines, *etc.*
- testimonials from those who have received benefits.

The brochure is more informational; the cover letter is more motivational. Or, "the brochure tells; the cover letter sells." This is, however, a relative, not an absolute condition.

— *Question-And-Answer Brochure*

For every business, most prospects have the same questions. The longer you're in business, you know more and more precisely what these questions are. The Q & A brochure enables you to "cut to the chase" with a prospect by providing him with specific answers to predictable questions. This saves you both a lot of time and enables you to focus your attention where it should be: on any specific objection, worry or concern the prospect has which may delay (if not preclude) him taking action.

In creating the question-and-answer brochure, brainstorm the obvious questions prospects keep asking or simply open a computer file called "questions" and list them as you're asked. Here's what people always want to know about my card-deck, for instance:

- Who does the deck go to?
- How many responses will my offer get?
- Is it better to generate leads or go for the direct sale?
- Where do you get the names you mail to?
- What is the real deadline for camera-ready art?
- How can I get a Top 20 position without paying extra for it?
- How long does it take to mail out the decks?
- Do I get a discount if I take a year's contract (four cards)?
- Do I get a discount if I take a second card in the same deck?
- Isn't red the best color to use for spot color??

- If I've never done a card before, can I get copy writing assistance? Graphic arts assistance?

- Why do I need to send in my Insertion Order the day I reserve my space?

- Can I get extra copies of my card made?

- Can I create my own camera-ready art work on my desk-top publishing system?

You get the idea. The important thing when you create a Q & A brochure is that you brainstorm all the questions and then select the most important 10 or 12 that will fit comfortably on an 8 1/2" by 11" flyer. (I like turning these into three-fold brochures, but a back-to-back sheet is fine, too.)

Once you've got the questions, you need to do two things:

1. write client-centered answers, and

2. create a client-centered headline for the whole brochure.

Everything you include in the Q & A brochure must be written from the prospect's stand-point and for the prospect's advantage. Thus, when the client asks who the deck is going to, what he really wants to know is how he should slant his offer to make it of utmost interest to the audience. He doesn't just want facts . . . he wants your guidance about how he can benefit from those facts.

Once you've finished these questions, write the client-centered headline that will put the whole document in perspective. Thus, instead of a headline like "Commonly Asked Questions About ABC Services," write instead "How To Get Thousands Of New Prospects Using ABC Services." In other words, stress the prospect benefit . . . not the "commonly asked questions."

Some service sellers complain that this is hype. I've never understood why. If you can deliver the benefit promised by the headline, it is your job to stress that benefit and use it to motivate faster response from more prospects. A problem only arises if you are technically ill-equipped or unable to deliver that benefit. Then the problem isn't hype; it's lying.

— Capabilities Statement

Some prospects want to know precisely what you've got that enables you to deliver the benefits they want. You tell them in a Capabilities Statement. This statement may use as many as four parts:

- experienced personnel
- necessary machines and equipment
- proven techniques and procedures
- financial resources.

Now, again, I must point out that prospects are not interested in these four categories in the abstract. No, indeed. They simply care about these things because when you have them they get what they want. Thus, as with the Q & A brochure, you need a headline that reinforces the chief benefit that the prospect gets and shows how each of the components you have available is essential in delivering that benefit.

Thus, if you or other key personnel are crucial to getting the prospect what he wants, your headline for this section might read: "Here are the people who get you (benefit the prospect wants.)" Or, "here's the technique (patent/copyright/procedure/process) that gets you (benefit the prospect wants)."

I hope you see why I'm advocating this method. Your prospect will never be as interested in *your* capabilities as in *his* final result. Neither should you force nor expect him to be. Instead, you should clearly show him just how what you have available makes it far more likely (even inevitable) that you'll be able to deliver the benefit he desires . . . whereas that desirable result is oh-so-problematic if he goes elsewhere . . . and completely unattainable if he does nothing at all.

— Client-Centered Fact Sheet

Many service businesses provide fact sheets about their operations. Most, however, focus on the wrong person — the service seller . . . not the service buyer, who is always the most important person in any marketing scenario.

Like the other marketing communications you're developing, this one begins with a brainstorming session. Just what are the facts about your service business? These may include:

- location
- number of employees
- number of clients served
- dimensions of successes provided to clients
- years in business

- service awards and why given
- unique success-delivering techniques and procedures
- hours of business
- whether you deliver service faster than competitors
- whether you deliver service more comprehensively than competitors
- prices
- different service modules available, *etc.*

Now, please note: I am not looking for qualitative evaluations here. Just like Dragnet, all we want is the facts, ma'am, just the facts. Once you have the facts, however, then you can help the prospect evaluate them thanks to a major client-centered headline and minor client-centered sub-headlines. Thus:

Here's why (number of satisfied clients) have selected us to give them (benefit prospect wants)

Now gild the facts with "you get . . ." benefits that precede the facts themselves. Thus:

You get a convenient location. (Follow with factual information about where you are and why it's convenient, if not obvious).

You get personnel who know how to deliver (benefit the prospect wants). (Follow with factual information proving this.)

You get demonstrated success. (Follow with factual information proving this.)

See how this goes. This is a fact sheet, to be sure, but one refocusing the facts on the prospect and through these facts reassuring him and giving him all the reasons he needs for faster action.

— Client-Survey Questionnaire

The client-survey questionnaire is a document the prospect completes and returns to you so you can make your follow-up dealings (which may include contact by phone, a proposal, *etc.*) more client-specific. Thus, this document is composed of a series of carefully constructed questions which tell you:

- how interested the prospect is in going ahead now to secure the benefit you offer;

- whether he has the financial resources he needs to go ahead now;

- what kind of results the client is most interested in achieving;

- whether he's tried to achieve these results recently himself or using another service provider, and

- what is happening to the client because he doesn't have the benefit you provide.

Here are some of the questions I could use for selling my fund raising consultation service to executive directors of social service organizations. Remember, it's the executive director, my prospect, who's providing the data:

1. If you had your way, your organization would raise the following amount of money in the next twelve months:
   ☐ less than $50,000 ☐ $50,000-$75,000 ☐ $75,000-$100,000
   ☐ More than $100,000

2. In the last twelve months you've raised:
   ☐ less than $50,000 ☐ $50,000-$75,000 ☐ $75,000-$100,000
   ☐ More than $100,000

3. Which of the following ways are you currently using to raise money? (Please check all that apply.)
   ☐ Direct mail ☐ Special Events ☐ government proposals
   ☐ proposals to corporations and foundations

4. Which of these ways has been the most profitable for you?
   ☐ Direct mail ☐ Special Events ☐ government proposals
   ☐ proposals to corporations and foundations

5. Which of these ways has been the least profitable?
   ☐ Direct mail ☐ Special Events ☐ government proposals
   ☐ proposals to corporations and foundations

6. Which fund raising alternatives are you interested in exploring to get additional revenues?
   ☐ Direct mail ☐ Special Events ☐ government proposals
   ☐ proposals to corporations and foundations
   ☐ Other (please list)

7. Do you feel that you are doing all that you can right now to raise the money your organization needs?
   ☐ Yes, there's really nothing more we need to do.

☐ No, I'm so busy with so many things, I feel we're missing out on opportunities.

8. Do you feel you have adequate computer equipment and knowledgeable personnel to assist a fund-raising effort?

☐ Yes ☐ No, we could use some help!

9. What is the first thing you'd invest in if you had any new money to spend?

What's great about the Client-Survey Questionnaire is that it is a deft combination of factual details you need ("In the last 12 months you've raised . . .") and prospect wants ("What is the first thing you'd invest in . . .?") As a result, you have at least some of the necessary background information you need and can certainly begin to focus the discussion on what the prospect wants, that is the thing that's going to motivate him to take faster action.

Note that the client-survey questionnaire is not about you in any way. It doesn't suggest what you can do . . . it doesn't promise any results. It simply asks for information. You may wonder whether people will actually take the time to fill out this document. They will, all right, especially if you:

• include a brief preface explaining to the prospect that before you are able to determine if you can assist him and to determine just which means of assisting him make sense, he must provide certain information to you. Explain that you *need* this information to assist the prospect and that you can't go ahead without it. *Note:* the qualified prospect who both wants the benefit and has the means of going ahead to get it now will understand why you want these data. The "window shoppers" won't take the time to give you anything. They'll just want "information" from you. Thus, merely by completing this questionnaire you get a good indication about whether you're dealing with a prospect . . . or a flat worm.

• keep it short. Nobody wants to fill out page after page of questions. Keep your questionnaire to one side of an 8 1/2" x 11" page, if at all possible. If not, keep it to both sides, but that's it.

• ask the prospect to get it back to you as soon as possible. Have him fax it if he can or mail within five days. You can even include a self-addressed (but not stamped) envelope with the questionnaire to expedite mailing. *Note:* if you give workshops with client prospects in attendance, make sure you personally hand a copy of this questionnaire to people when they arrive and ask them to return it when they leave. You'll get up to 90% of those attending to respond, a fantastic response!

Another note: let the prospect know that if you don't hear from him within not more than 5 business days, you'll call him. You've got to let the prospect know both that you can provide the benefit that he wants and that you're enthusiastic and ready to begin doing so. Simply keep a log of all your prospects and the date you sent the client-survey questionnaire to them. Follow up promptly . . . and when you do tell the prospect you're ready to begin providing him with the benefit he's told you he wants . . . not to sell your service!!!

— Success Cases

We end this section with the marketing communication that both completes one part of the marketing cycle and launches the next: the Success Case. Thus, demonstrated success with a client both satisfactorily concludes the first significant cycle of your relationships with him . . . and gives you something meaningful to use to induce additional prospects to become clients. That is why I've always seen the Success Case as the marketing equivalent of Mary Queen of Scots' famous motto, "In my end is my beginning." As you deliver success, so you are admirably positioned both for a later engagement with the client who has already benefited from you . . . and for the prospect who wants you to duplicate for him what you've already shown so well you can deliver to others.

After You Send These Marketing Communications To The Prospect And You Want To Follow Up By Telephone

If you've created client-centered marketing communications that:

- clearly set forth the benefits the prospect gets when he acts, and

- provide a strong offer as incentive for fastest action . . .

you're going to get prospects calling you. If you don't, there's something wrong with the marketing communications you are using; no matter how much time and money you spent creating them, they're not right. You need to go back to the drawing board!

However, even if you've created sharp, benefit-rich, client-centered marketing communications all the people you send your materials to will not respond. Plan on it. They won't respond for one of the following reasons:

- they are interested in getting the benefit you offer and have the necessary resources to acquire it, but they have many others things going on and let the matter slip;

- they are interested in getting the benefit you offer but do not have the necessary resources to acquire it. They make the decision there is no point in contacting you at this time;

- they are not interested in getting the benefit you offer and resolve to do nothing at all with what you've sent beyond throwing it away.

Your job is to figure out AS SOON AS POSSIBLE just which category the prospect is in. This is where the second set of telephone pointers comes in.

As with the previous telephone pointers, these need to be thought through and written. All too often service sellers simply sit down at their telephone and start calling prospects without really thinking through what they're trying to do. The result is evident when the marketer calls:

"Hi, Jeff, this is Dave from ABC Service Providers. Did you get that information I sent you? Have you had a chance to read it yet?"

What's wrong with this opening? EVERYTHING!!! If this call were being made to me:

- the name's wrong. I hate going by Jeff, and I know that the service seller who calls me this either hasn't looked at my name or has decided to shorten it because it sounds friendlier;

- asking me about "information" is wrong. I'm a busy guy. I get "information" from hundreds of people daily. But I don't care about "information." I only care about the benefits I can get;

- asking me if I've "had the chance to read it yet" is wrong. Who can read all the stuff they get these days? I know I can't. Asking me if I've had the chance to read what I've been sent almost always leads me to give a negative response . . . and to get angry at the service seller who makes me look inept and unprepared.

Ladies and gentlemen, let me say again for the millionth time: PUSH BENEFITS. NOT PAPER. And push preparation.

If you've followed the steps I've given you, the prospect has contacted you to get a benefit . . . or series of benefits. When he contacts you he's saying, in effect, "I'm interested in getting the benefit you provide. I'm not sure yet that you're the person who can really deliver this benefit, but I've got an open mind. Persuade me."

When you respond with your client-centered marketing communications, you're saying, in effect, "I know you want the benefit I can deliver. Let me persuade you that I'm the person who can assist you and let me motivate you to do what's necessary so I can get started right away helping you get what you want."

When you follow up this sequence by saying "Did you get the information I sent?", you've blown it . . . because you've gone right back to features, abandoning the only thing the prospect wants: BENEFITS.

This is why you plan what you're going to say. And this is why you write it down.

During the planning phase, brainstorm a series of different responses that properly begin the conversation with the prospect to whom you've already sent your marketing communications. During this planning phase consider the following:

- the prospect has a name he likes to be called. Use this name. Not a name you want to give him. This is so very elementary, but this mistake is made daily by marketers who ought to know better, but don't.

- the prospect may be busy when you call. Even if you have the benefit he wants, he may not be able to consider it just then.

- the prospect may be traveling, out sick, away from his phone, *etc.* He'll need a message. You need to be prepared for this eventuality, too.

— When The Prospect Is Available

"Is this Dave Edwards from ABC? This is Sally Smith from XYZ. You contacted me about getting (benefit you offer and prospect wants). Is now a good time to discuss how you can get it?"

This kind of opening has several advantages. First, you've opened with the name the prospect provided you with; you haven't presumed to call him something he may not like. Second, you've provided him with your name. Third, you've reminded him that he contacted you and that you're following up. Fourth, you've reminded him about the benefit that he wants and which was probably the reason he contacted you in the first place. Fifth, you've asked if this is a convenient time and given him the choice of going ahead now or doing so at a more convenient time later.

Note: on the question of what to call the prospect. Here are some guidelines:

- If the prospect seems about your age or younger and calls you by your first name, use his first name;

- If the prospect is older or has a title such as pastor, doctor or colonel, use the title, at least until the prospect indicates it's acceptable not to;

- If you are uncertain what to call the prospect, ask what he prefers to be called. There's nothing wrong with not knowing what to do; there's everything wrong in making assumptions which may embarrass you and irritate the prospect.

Let me tell you something: these very simple, very client-centered lines will probably not occur to you without planning. Moreover, at least at first, you probably won't be able to remember them exactly without writing them. Be better prepared by preparing for every possible contingency. Thus:

- the prospect is either ready to take your call now, or he's not;

- he either remembers wanting the benefit, or he doesn't;

- he either is serious about wanting to get the benefit now, or he isn't;

- (if he postpones taking action to acquire the benefit) he is either a prospect who is genuinely interested but cannot take action now, or he isn't.

In short, there is much to discover about this prospect so you know precisely what to do with him. You cannot simply "wing it" through this important conversation. Your job is to discover which category this prospect is in and deliver the right client-centered message.

Thus, once you have made your opening and the prospect has indicated that now is a satisfactory time to talk about the benefit, you need to advance the qualifying process. This is done by asking a series of questions. Just what questions you'll fashion will depend on the nature of the service you're selling.

Here are some questions I might use as qualifiers for my copy writing service:

- Have you got a marketing communication you need to complete?

- When do you need it?

- How have you been creating your marketing communications?

- Have you been using another copywriter?

- What kinds of results have you had?

- Have there been any problems?

- What are you trying to accomplish now?

You'll note that these questions have not, so far, dealt with the important matter of cost. Before discussing cost, you need to discern want. What does the prospect want and how quickly does he want it? And what was he thinking he'd do to get the results he wants? Getting information about what the client wants and when he wants it always precedes a discussion of price and procedure.

Let's say, however, the prospect tells you that he has no pressing need right now for the service you offer and that he can pretty much handle what he needs done through an in-house employee or occasional consultant. With this information, the prospect's priority standing necessarily drops. There is no need to discuss your prices, procedures, *etc.* You see, you now know that he doesn't have current need and isn't going to proceed now.

Before ending this conversation, however, you need to find out when he may have need and secure agreement on how and when you'll be able to get back in touch. Thus, "I want to work with you to provide the benefit you want. When do you think you'll want the benefit next?" The prospect will ponder and respond. Then you say, "I'll re-contact you again (at the time prospect said he'd have need). Is that okay with you?" Only at such time as the prospect indicates that he has a real need and wants to set about satisfying it do you discuss prices, techniques, *etc.*, unless all that information is already available in your marketing materials. In this case, of course, the prospect should already have this information, and you should refer him to what you've already sent.

On the other hand, if the prospect has an earlier want and can use the benefit you provide earlier, he'll be much more interested to get into the necessary specifics of procedures and cost. In this case tell him:

- what you can do;

- how you work (your means of delivering the benefit), and

- provide an estimate of what getting that benefit from you and your techniques will cost and what the prospect needs to do next to get the ball rolling.

Note: I am assuming this particular prospect has not completed a client-survey questionnaire, and you do not have enough information to give the prospect detailed answers to these questions. DON'T RUSH YOURSELF IN RESPONDING.

One of the mistakes service sellers make is to rush to provide information to the prospect before they are clear about what the prospect wants and before they think of the various ways they could satisfy this want. Thus, resolve not to discuss the matter of cost and procedure until you are absolutely clear about what the prospect wants. Then ask yourself whether you can provide the cost and procedural information off the top of your head. Or, do you need time to think and structure your response for maximum effect? If the latter, then give yourself this time. Tell the prospect how and when you'll get back in touch. Don't provide incomplete or erroneous information now just because you feel you must "do something". Only do that which will provide the prospect with the details he needs and position you as the individual who can deliver the benefit he wants.

Before leaving this section, I must give you a very important piece of information. As you talk to prospects, you must understand that a two-way interview and assessment process is taking place. The prospect, of course, wants to make sure that you can deliver the benefit you say you can and (particularly if he is a serious prospect) just how you work and how much you cost. In this world, the prospect is absolutely right to subject you to scrutiny and ask the questions that give him the information he needs to feel comfortable about you and your company. Don't begrudge this information. Impart it willingly and candidly.

By the same token, you are scrutinizing and evaluating the prospect. Unfortunately, many service sellers, in their rush to get the business, forget this. Thus, while they are perfectly willing to let the prospect ask them any questions (even outlandish ones), they feel queasy asking the prospect similarly detailed and focused queries. This is wrong. You need to know that:

- the prospect is serious about what he wants;
- he has the ability to follow through and do what's necessary on his part to get the benefit;
- he's not wasting your time.

It is perfectly acceptable and entirely desirable for you to ask the questions that give you the information you need about the prospect so that you feel entirely comfortable about going ahead with him as a client. This includes tackling the financial aspect of affairs directly and without embarrassment.

The only way to be direct and proceed without embarrassment, however, is to make sure that everything you're going to need in this prospect conversation is written; that you have the conversation mapped out whatever direction it takes and that nothing, absolutely nothing, is left to chance and that everything has been arranged so that you find out quickly, easily and civilly all you need to know so you can take the appropriate action.

Thus, plan your response before it is necessary to deliver that response. Then see how that response is received. If you don't feel it went well, tinker with it on the computer and give the altered version, checking that for effectiveness.

People who become multi-millionaires selling services become masters of process. They are wise enough to know that they can't always invent the proper response on the spur of the moment, but they can always plan for that proper response and have it available when they need it.

— When The Prospect Isn't Available

When you're in the business of selling services, you're going to play a lot of telephone tag. Indeed, there have been days when I've called as many as fifty or more people WITHOUT CONNECTING WITH A SINGLE ONE OF THEM. That's why you need to master the art of the Benefit Message.

Many telemarketers have very strong feelings about messages. Some, for instance, actually advocate that in order to maintain control you should never leave a message. I feel this is far too strong. I simply don't have the time to call everyone back as many times as it might take to connect. For me, therefore, it was absolutely crucial to discover what kinds of messages got people to call back. I suspect it's the same for you. That's where the benefit message comes in.

This message is related to the opening of your call when the prospect is available: "This is Sally Smith from XYZ. I'm calling Dave Edwards. You contacted me about getting (benefit you offer and prospect wants). I want to discuss this (benefit) with you. Please call me at (number) so we can get started."

Now, I am not naive enough to believe that this kind of client-centered message will solve all your problems. But this message is better than "Jeffrey Lant called about (service). Please get back to me." The sad truth is most people these days don't return more than a fraction of their calls. However, those people who do call back are solid prospects; with them, you should follow the directions provided above. People who return this message you should be able to close in high numbers. And that is all to the good.

But what about the rest? For these damnable critters, you need a strategy. Here are some suggestions:

- Remember that you are contacting these people to fulfill a quota. Calling people who don't return messages is never fun. Fortunately, you only need to contact them until your quota is filled. This is an activity with limits, and that should help make it bearable. I know that helps me!

- If the prospect is local (not a toll call), follow up your first unreturned call at another time of the day. Thus, if you've called during regular business hours and no one is available and the call has not been returned, try another time: early evening or on the week-end (yes, you can call on Sunday!). Place your call up to three times. Each time you call number your message, thus, "This is Jeffrey Lant calling about (the benefit the prospects wants). This is my third message for you. I want to help you get the (benefit the prospect wants), but I need to hear from you." Don't hesitate to use guilt in your message, thus: "I'm really interested to get started helping you but without hearing from you I can't do anything to be of assistance."

- If the prospect is out of the local area, call twice at different times. Again, use guilt and a numbered message.

Will this system work? Yes. Some people will respond to your client-centered messages and respond. These are your best prospects, and you should close a high percentage of them. Will this system get all these "prospects" to call you? Probably not. Indeed, one of the things I've had to accept is just how many people who respond to an advertisement or other client-centered marketing communication purportedly interested in getting the benefit I'm stressing will fail to respond to either a second marketing communication and as many as three follow-up phone calls. Just what's their problem, anyhow?

Most likely it's that their wants are bigger than their wallets. Sure they want the benefit you've got, but they just don't have the money to get it. Because your marketing communications have been unabashedly client-centered, they've responded. Now, however, there's nothing they can do. However, instead of telling you this, they hide. Frankly, I despise these people. While I can well understand that a person wants to look for benefits even when he doesn't have the money to pay for them, I cannot understand (particularly when the call is local) why he cannot say that. It's probably because it's such a sin in this country not to have the money you need for everything you want; too, most people these days are appallingly ill-bred and hence are likely to lie.

Either way, if you've called two or three times and have failed to get any response, the chances are very high that this was never a real prospect at all. However, before you write the person off as an irredeemable flat worm, you should try one more attempt to generate action.

The Enhanced Urgency Letter

As you'll remember, right from the start I've urged you to position yourself *via à vis* your prospects as having only a limited ability to provide your service. Thus, even though you might be able to take on 100 new clients right now, I've advocated that you tell your prospects you can only take on three or four just now. The limited availability of your service is itself a prime motivater for prospect action. Here's one of the places where you use it.

Say you've just run some kind of prospect-generating marketing communication, like an ad in the local paper. You've received 50 responses and have been able to connect with 25 of them either because they called you, responded to a packet of materials you sent them or were available when you followed up by phone. This still leaves 25 people you need to connect with who have so far been unavailable by phone. It's now time to roll out the Enhanced Urgency Letter.

This hard-hitting letter is composed of the following parts:

- guilt opening
- clearly stated benefits
- limited availability of benefits
- need for immediate action, what prospect needs to do now.

Let's look at each of these parts:

— Guilt opening

The time for anything less than a sledgehammer approach has passed with this prospect. If you're going to salvage him (and the money you've invested in generating him), this is when you need to do it. Thus, open this way:

Dear (prospect by name),

For the last two weeks, I've been trying time after time to get in touch with you. You contacted me (on date) to get (benefit you offer). I WANT TO GET YOU THIS BENEFIT AND I WANT TO START NOW.

Frankly, you're not making my helping you very easy. If you're going to get this benefit, you're going to need to work with me, and this means contacting me today so we can get started.

You've probably never opened a letter like this to a prospect. It may seem over harsh to you. GET OVER IT!!! This person has already responded to a marketing communication, thereby telling you he is at least somewhat interested in the benefit you've got. But thereafter he disappeared. To move him, you need a strong letter, and you can't afford to mince any words.

— Clearly stated benefit

Now remind him of just why it's in his interest to contact you now.

Let me remind you of all you'll be getting when you make the decision to get started:

- Benefit 1
- Benefit 2
- Benefit 3, *etc.*

You were clearly interested enough in securing these benefits to contact me on (date). If you're really serious about having them, pick up the phone RIGHT THIS MINUTE so I can get started giving them to you.

— *Limited availability of benefits*

Make sure you tell the prospect that his ability to get the benefits is limited. Make sure, that is, that he knows that if he doesn't act now, he's going to lose them. Fear of loss is always a stronger motivater than hope for gain. Thus:

> Unfortunately, if you don't act today there's a very good chance you're not going to get these benefits. When you first contacted me, I had (amount of benefit), but today, thanks to the fact that a number of far-sighted people have already taken action to get (benefit you have available), I only have (this amount of benefit left). So, if you want (benefit), you need to act NOW!!!

— *Need for immediate action, what prospect needs to do*

When you are selling a service, you must act like a generalissimo. You need to make it clear what you want people to do . . . and when they need to do it. Don't leave it to them. Don't make the prospect think. Only get him to act and tell him precisely what action he needs to take. Thus:

> To get started getting these benefits, and to make sure you don't lose out, call me now at (number). You'll never get (benefit) if you can't dial these 7 little numbers. So dial them NOW!

A Variation: The "You Missed The Boat" Letter

Whether you're like me and you have only a limited ability to provide a certain service or whether you're simply smart and say you have this limited ability when you don't, you can make good use of the "You Missed The Boat" Letter. This is a variation of the Enhanced Urgency letter, only you send this letter either when you are no longer able to provide the service . . . or say you are not. The point of this letter is to make the prospect feel sorry he's lost the ability to get the benefit and give him the opportunity to tell you he wants to work with you as soon as you can accommodate him. Thus:

Dear (prospect by name),

I've been trying and trying to get in touch with you for the last two weeks. You contacted me on (date) to get (benefit you offer). I've written and called you three times to get started providing this benefit for you.

UNFORTUNATELY FOR YOU, MANY OTHER PEOPLE DID RESPOND PROMPTLY. AND THEREFORE I AM UNABLE TO ACCOMMODATE YOU NOW.

This means that — for the moment — you won't get:

• Benefit #1

• Benefit #2

• Benefit #3, etc.

I wish you'd contacted me . . . because I would have liked to help you!!!

However, if you're still interested in having these benefits, call me now and get on my waiting list. As soon as I'm able to be of assistance, I'll get promptly back in touch with you and we can get started.

Now that you know this service fills up fast, I hope you'll call me today at (number) to let me know you're interested in it. Believe me, I'll start working with you just as soon as I'm able.

Note: believe me, you're going to get responses to this letter. I always do. Often the prospect will say things like, "I never got your letter." Or, "I never got your calls." This is where documentation really helps. "Really?," I say smoothly, "I wrote you on (date) and called you on (dates). I've really made an effort to get in touch with you and get started delivering (benefit you want)." Then start the probing questions which determine just how interested the prospect is in the benefits you have available and when they want to start getting them. Remember: you're almost certain to sign up the prospects who respond to the "You Missed The Boat" Letter. Just keep the discussion focused on what benefits they get . . . and what it takes to work with you to get them.

Another note: Send both the Enhanced Urgency and the "You Missed The Boat" letters promptly. In other words, convey, in the case of the first, real *urgency* ("if you don't act, you really are going to miss out!") and in the second case both regret . . . and yet the need for immediate action. ("It's too bad you didn't act, but if you don't act now, you're going to miss out AGAIN! UNBELIEVABLE!!!")

With apologies to Mao Tsetung, "Marketing is not a dinner party." The only thing that matters is that the prospect takes immediate action to acquire the benefits you've made him want and induced him to take action to acquire . . . and that you sort through the responding prospects as quickly as possible to zero in on those who can and will buy your benefit. *Nothing else matters.*

Many tender plants will find this statement difficult to accept; they try to introduce other, extraneous considerations into the reckoning. This had better not be you. You've told me you want to become a multi-millionaire and if this is really what you want, you'd better understand what marketing is all about . . . and arrange matters accordingly. Including doing everything you can to get the satisfied client to buy again — as fast as possible.

After You've Sold One Of Your Services To Your New Client (But Still Have Additional Services He'll Find Helpful)

To my complete astonishment, many marketing books focus their attention wholly or in large part on getting business merely from people who have never bought from you before. But as all successful service sellers know, the heart of one's profitability is getting people you've served successfully to buy from you again . . . and, say I, as soon as possible. This is where the Upgrade Letter comes in.

As soon as it's obvious the prospect will buy from you, it's your job to start the upgrade process, that is to get him to acquire something else either at the same time as the first service or as soon as possible. Stupid service sellers don't do that. They sell the prospect what the prospects wants and set about providing it. The smart service seller, by comparison, attempts to upgrade the value of the sale by adding on more services.

There are essentially two ways to upgrade a prospect: either in person or by letter. Both are marketing communications and both demand preparation. So that you make the maximum number of upgrade sales, here's what you need to do *before* you connect with any prospect:

- Begin by understanding the value of upgrading. You already know how difficult, vexing and costly it is to get clients. And you already know that to increase the value of a client would help you meet your financial objectives just that much earlier. Act accordingly!

- Understand that your job is not to sell the prospect just one service (unless you only have one service!). It is to sell the prospect *all* the services that will help him achieve his objective and satisfy his wants;

- This means packaging your services in terms of the benefits they offer. Thus, you might have a "basic" service package, an intermediate package, and a deluxe package. Your job is not so much to sell the prospect one of your services . . . but to sell the prospect the service package that is at least one step beyond what he originally wanted to buy. In other words, to show him that he cannot get all he wants by taking only part of what you have available. In short, make what he wants the fuel that gets him to buy the more comprehensive (read "expensive") package you have available.

- Prepare the words you'll use to get the upgrade you seek.

All this planning takes place *before* the prospect buys anything. You are therefore ready to act when he does. Suppose the prospect says he wants to use me to write copy for an ad in my card deck. I need a bridge to upgrade him to the position where he buys not only this copy but also the cover letter and brochure he'll be using to respond to those answering this ad. Thus:

"Of course you want to generate the greatest number of responses to your card. That's natural. But how are you going to ensure that you *close* the greatest number of clients from among those responding?"

Ask the question. Then pause and listen to the client's response. See whether what he is going to do makes sense . . . or whether (as you hope) it can be improved. If what he is proposing will not get him what he wants . . . and you can demonstrate this . . . then you are well on your way to a more lucrative sale. However, you can leave neither the words nor process you need to achieve this more lucrative sale to chance; saying "Is there anything else you'd like?" isn't nearly enough.

All too often the service seller is focused on the sale he's just made rather than what the prospect wants. You are going to become a multimillionaire to the extent that you are able to focus on the wants of your prospects (among whom I include a buyer who has only bought at a beginning level from you) and show them that they can only get what they want by using the maximum amount of your service.

Putting The Whiz, Bang, Zap And Power Into Your Marketing Communications

To my utter astonishment, most service sellers act as if all the words they use in their marketing communications have the same value and thus should be treated the same way.

Take a look at most service seller ads, flyers, brochure, proposals, *etc.* To begin with, don't read the words . . . simply look at a page. If you didn't speak the language that communication was written in would you be able to tell at a glance just what was important? Just what the writer thought was most significant? Most motivational? Most exciting? If the answer is no, then the communication is wrong.

Let me make one thing perfectly clear to you: when you write marketing communications you are not writing a college essay. That is, you are not writing something calm, deliberative, emotionless. Instead you are creating something that's got to motivate an animal . . . a human animal, to be sure . . . but an animal nonetheless. That is why in my marketing class I use the saying, "Ponies. Not people".

When you write a marketing communication, act as if you're trying to motivate a *pony* . . . not a *person*. And remember, you're going to need what fast-track cowboys into mammal management have always needed: spurs, carrots, whips, sugar, reins, boots, the whole bag of tricks.

When you're creating marketing documents, here's the equivalent:

- CAPITAL LETTERS

- exclamation points!!!

- color (you'll have to imagine this as red)

-      indented lines

-   from both margins

- *** asterisks ***

- **bold**

- *italic*

- _____ underlining

- - hyphens -

- — — — dashes

- arrows ➤ ➔ → ⇒ →

- bullets • • • and

- . . . ellipses

The key to using these many emphasizing devices is not to litter a page (or give purists apoplexy) but to make sure the prospect gets the message at a glance. Emphasizing devices are designed to focus the prospect on what's important and drive those things home as fast as possible.

Misguided marketers want the prospect to read everything they've written; they say in effect, "Because I wrote this and because it's important, you're going to have to study this, even if it takes you all day." Most marketers, therefore, are punitive; they hated putting their marketing communications together and they're going to be damned sure everyone suffers as much as they did. This is nonsense.

The crack marketer doesn't care if the prospects reads or listens to anything; he only cares that the prospect responds as soon as possible. He reckons he'll know what to do when that prospect contacts him and can sort real prospects from flakes.

Thus, the consummate marketer spends his time making his message, in whatever form it's carried, as sleek and client-centered as possible. He wants the prospect to know at a glance what's important. He spends his time emphasizing the benefits . . . the offer . . . deadlines . . . and substantial results-oriented testimonials. He knows all words aren't equal, and he carries his major message on words he's worked hard to enhance.

Let's just take one simple letter and enhance it to make it more motivational for the prospect:

Dear (prospect by name),

For the last TWO weeks, I've been trying *time after time* to get in touch with you. *You* contacted me (on date) to get (*benefit you offer*). I WANT TO GET YOU THIS BENEFIT AND I WANT TO START NOW.

Frankly, you're not making my helping you very easy. If you're going to get this benefit, *you're going to need to work with me*, and this means contacting me TODAY so we can get started.

Let me remind you of all you'll be getting when you make the decision to get started:

- *Benefit 1*
- *Benefit 2*
- *Benefit 3, etc.*

You were clearly interested enough in securing these benefits to contact me on (date). If you're really serious about having them, pick up the phone RIGHT THIS MINUTE so I can get started giving them to you.

Unfortunately, if you don't act today *there's a very good chance you're not going to get these benefits.* When you first contacted me, I had (amount of benefit), but today, thanks to the fact that a number of far-sighted people have already taken action to get (benefit you have available), I only have (*this amount of benefit left*). So, if you want (benefit), you need to act NOW!!!

To get started getting these benefits, and to make sure you don't lose out, *call me now at (number).* You'll never get (benefit) if you can't dial these 7 little numbers. So dial them NOW!

Sincerely,

Motivational Marketer

Let me say something about this letter: it's not going into the Metropolitan Museum of Art. Let me tell you something else: IT DOESN'T HAVE TO!!! All it's got to do is make the strongest possible case for the benefits you have available, the offer you're making and what you want the prospect to do — and STRESS THOSE FACTS THROUGH VARIOUS MEANS OF DESIGN AND EMPHASIS. Believe me, if the benefits and other necessary components are there *and* they are stressed, you are going to get responses. Once the prospect calls you, you are well on your well to bagging him.

If . . . if, I say, you can move quickly enough.

The real problem with client-centered marketing communications is how many leads you'll generate. Once you transform your marketing from "me-centered" to "thee-centered", your volume of leads will increase dramatically. Too many service sellers in this situation either fall seriously behind in dealing with all that must be done to qualify and convert the leads (thereby undercutting their standing as client-centered service deliverers) or stop handling the leads altogether, which is so stupid and short-sighted I can hardly believe it — even though many such situations have come to my attention over the years.

Thus, the moment when you have transformed your marketing and start seeing a ton of responses is a very difficult one, in a sense the defining moment of your service business. Will you be able to rise to the occasion and transform your episodic, rambling marketing into the necessary process that'll ensure your multi-million dollar standing . . . or will you collapse under the strain and prove beyond a shadow of a doubt just how amateurish and disorganized you are? That, my friend, depends in large measure on just how well you use your personal computer.

5

How To Turn Your Personal Computer Into Your Best Marketing Tool

This book is about generating the maximum number of leads as quickly as possible and closing them as quickly as possible. When you do this, you're going to get rich. When you do it right, you're going to become a millionaire.

And what's going to help you do it right? The personal computer.

In my opinion, the personal computer exists for three main reasons, to assist you:

1. generate the maximum number of leads as soon as possible;

2. close the maximum number of prospects as quickly as possible and launch profitable business relationships, and

3. work with your new clients so you both get what you want from the relationship as soon as you can.

Is your computer set up to achieve these crucial objectives? I doubt it. Over the last several years I've been doing an informal survey of businesses to see just how successfully they've integrated their computers into their marketing operations. I've been astonished by the results. Most businesses these days are computerized. But most have only the most elementary understanding about how to turn their computers into their most effective marketing tool. Modestly, this chapter should be required reading for *every* business in America . . . and not just small businesses either, since many Fortune 500 companies are equally retarded. Whether they study this chapter or not, you've got to, because effective computerization will move you a long ways towards becoming a millionaire.

A Few Words For People Who Aren't Computerized Yet

Are you crazy?

If you are one of the (thankfully) few people reading this book who remains both a computer illiterate and without benefit of computer, I am not going to suggest, rather I command you to get computerized instantly. Just how you think you're going to get to be a millionaire in the 'nineties without benefit of a computer baffles me.

I hear lots of "reasons" that the dwindling band of the uncomputerized give for their futile state. They say things like:

- I've always gotten along quite well without a computer. I don't see why I need it, or

- Computers are expensive. I can't afford one now, or

- I hate machines and they hate me. I'm sure I couldn't figure out how to run it, or

- I think computers are so impersonal. I think everyone deserves my personal attention, or

- We already have a system for all our data and records. Putting it all on computer would be very time-consuming.

Let me knock off these "reasons" as quickly as possible:

- If you're not a multi-millionaire, you *haven't* been getting along quite well without a computer. Oh, sure, you may be handling your current level of marketing in a fairly satisfactory manner, but you haven't been handling the level of marketing you need to reach the objective you've now set for yourself. If you are working without a computer now and are not a millionaire, you're not going to reach your goal. At best you'll stay at the level you're already at. Got it? Understanding the computer and integrating it fully into your marketing function is crucial to your getting to be a millionaire.

- Computers are *not* expensive. In fact, computers have never been a better bargain than they are right this minute. The prices on both computers, printers, fax machines and other office equipment have decreased; indeed, given the recession-induced price-cutting wars now on, the cost is about rock-bottom. Moreover, whatever your equipment costs, you'll more than make it back in increased productivity *so long as you follow the guidelines in this book;*

- So, you hate machines. Well, la dee dah! If you can type and can think logically, you can run a computer and ancillary equipment. When you tell me you "hate" machines what you're really telling me is that you dislike (or, more likely, fear) the logical procedures that make machines necessary. Believe me, you can't afford the luxury of this feeling if you're going to get rich.

- I've been especially perplexed by the "I like people, I hate computers because they're so impersonal" argument. It's just so stupid. If you like people and want to improve their conditions (which you purportedly do with your service), it seems to me you'd want to master everything that would make them aware of what you've got available for them and assist you in connecting with and assisting them. This is precisely what the computer does. Further, the computer itself is neither personal nor impersonal; it's just a machine. As you'll see a little later in this chapter, it's your responsibility to use the computer to make all your marketing personal. The computer can be as personal as the client-centered prose you write. And should be.

- As far as already having a system and fearing the time it will take to create a new one is concerned, I have to ask you yet again : are you already a millionaire? If you are a millionaire and you keep your prospect cards in a shoe-box, I take my hat off to you. So rare, you may end up as an exhibit in the Smithsonian Institution. The truth is it will take you time and trouble to computerize your records. It is a bore to enter all the data off file cards into the computer and enter necessary documents in your word-processing software. But the truth is: it's better to do this now, before you gear-up your marketing machine, than later, when it will be much more difficult and time-consuming to provide the system you need.

Resources

The time has long passed when any service business can afford the luxury of remaining without a computer. To get out of this benighted condition, you should connect with my friend Ted Stevens. You can either read his Special Report on the subject of how to determine the right (and least expensive) computer and printer for your business (you'll find it in my catalog in the back of this book), or you can contact him directly. Ted is a service provider who specializes in providing computers, printers, faxes and other office equipment at unbelievably low prices. Whether you're just computerizing for the first time (with the usual first-time jitters), or whether you're a battle-scarred veteran who pretty much knows what you want and is simply searching for the best price, call Ted. His company is Future Visions, P.O. Box 373, Auburn, ME 04212. (207) 786-7383.

Or read R. Wayne Parker's thorough 237 page book *The Computer Buyer's Handbook: How To Select And Buy Personal Computers For Your Home And Business*. Get a copy from Fast Forward Publishing, P.O. Box 45153, Seattle, WA 98145-0153. (206) 527-3112

So, You've Got Your Computer. Now What?

Once you've got your computer it's time to organize your software so you get the results you want. You need to organize both your data management software and your word-processing software. Since the former is done much more quickly and easily than the latter, let's get that out of the way first.

Data Management

The kind of rigorous client-centered marketing you need to do to become a multi-millionaire is going to put you in touch with large numbers of people. Information about them must be organized in such a way that you can get easy access to it and can organize and sort through it to discover groups with shared characteristics (data bases). To do this you need to think through the data fields that are important to you and create a prospect/client record that provides you with all the data you need given your objectives, to:

• make initial contact promptly;

• handle all further contacts efficiently, and

- note purchasing activity (or lack of it) for appropriate response.

The first thing you need is a good data management program. Personally, I have found dBASE IV perfectly adequate for my data management needs. Some people prefer other programs like Paradox or Q & A. I've been told they are simpler to use. The important thing, however, is that you get a program that enables you to:

- input thousands of records;

- customize the record to meet your need;

- sort for each field of data entered so that you can both preserve and use all the data you need for each prospect/ customer;

- have mail-merge capability enabling you to produce standard letters, and

- produce standard four-across cheshire mailing labels.

All the programs mentioned above can do this.

To organize your data properly, you must think through what you need and create the data record accordingly. All records, however, should have at least these fields:

LASTNAME
FIRSTNAME
TITLE
POSITION
COMPANYNAME
ADDRESS1
ADDRESS1
CITY
STATE
ZIP
PERPHONE
BUSPHONE
FAX

If you're wondering why I printed these fields in capital letters, ran words together and abbreviated personal telephone (perphone) and business telephone (busphone), it's because this is how you should create the field names for your record; certainly if you use dBASE IV you will! All service sellers need this information. However, each service seller needs additional information that's pertinent to his business. This should at least include data about:

- when the prospect inquired
- when the client bought
- what the client bought
- the amount of the client's last purchase
- the cumulative amount of the client's business.

Thus these might be your fields:

```
SER1
SER2
SER3
INQDATE
LASTPURDT
AMOUNT
CUMAMOUNT
```

With these fields you can note, store and use data about:

- when the prospect inquired ("inqdate"). This is important during your closing process. Knowing when a person comes on to your mailing list enables you to send the right materials at the right time; (you could, for instance, call up all your inquiries within the last 7 days). It also makes zapping flat worms off your list a lot easier; (delete all for inqdate <= 09/01/92).

- precisely what services the prospect is interested in. Thus, if you're running an ad about a certain service (Service 1), you could enter both the inquiry date and the service the prospect is interested in. If the prospect doesn't buy, having this information will enable you to develop the marketing communication with the right benefits and intensity given how much time has elapsed since the prospect first contacted you. For instance, if you resolve to keep all prospects on the list for 1 year, you'll easily be able to send a very focused letter to the prospect before zapping him off the list. *Note:* your data field should be arranged so that all you have to do is put a "Y" (for "Yes") after each service the prospect is interested in.

• how much the prospect has bought ("amount"), when he bought it ("lastpurdt"), and what the cumulative total ("cumamount") of his business is. Buyers demand regular cultivation. When you have this information, you can sort for everyone whose business is worth over a certain amount. They could get special offers or perhaps just a regular phone call. And certainly a personal phone call from you before being zapped off your list. The computer makes it very easy to give special people (like buyers!) special attention.

Here's what a record might look like with data in it:

SER1	Y
SER2	
SER3	
INQDATE	09/30/92
LASTPURDT	01/02/93
AMOUNT	$595
CUMAMOUNT	$595

What this record tells you is that this particular client inquired about your Service 1 on September 30, 1992. He bought Service 1 on January 2, 1993 for $595 and currently has spent $595 cumulatively with you. *Note:* I would advise deleting the inquiry date when you have data in the last purchase date field. It makes sorting your data easier. Thus, when entering purchase information, simply delete inquiry information at the same time.

You should now have a data record enabling you to do everything you need to:

• work with inquiries;

• track customers and follow-up appropriately, and

• delete flat worms who are beyond your ministrations.

Word-Processing Management

Once you've created your prospect/client record, you can get started on the more time-consuming matter of arranging the directories and files in your word-processing software.

You need to organize yourself for:

- generating the maximum number of leads as soon as possible;

- closing the maximum number of prospects as quickly as possible and launching profitable business relationships, and

- working with your new clients so you both get what you want from the relationship as soon as you can.

We need to consider all three necessary aspects of organizing your word-processing software, but first a few words about the software itself.

A Very Few Words About Word-Processing Software

Much has been written about word-processing software and which kind makes the most sense for any given business. Personally, I've been using XyWrite for years; it's software favored by many professional writers. Given the fact you'll be doing quite a lot of writing to create your marketing program, this kind of software probably makes sense for you, too.

One thing that makes XyWrite good to use is the fact that it's command-driven. That is, it operates by user commands executed on a command line instead of from help directions on every screen. Admittedly, you may find this frustrating when you're first starting out and don't yet know the commands. However, in the final analysis it's very much to your advantage to have a command-driven program; it's a lot faster to use and after you know all the basic commands, you'll find the help screen irritating.

Resources

For information on Xywrite, contact XYQUEST, 44 Manning Rd., Billerica, MA 01821. (508) 671-0888. Ask for the Marketing Dept.

The Corporate Software Guide: An Objective Guide To Personal Computer Products For The Information Center. Corporate Software, Inc., 275 Dan Rd., Canton, MA 02021-2826 (800) 677-4000. About 1400 pages, published twice yearly. Just about every conceivable software package listed. $129

Organizing To Generate The Maximum Number Of Leads As Soon As Possible

Once you've picked your software, it's time to turn to the really important matter of how to put it to use to reach your marketing objectives. This means thinking through what you're trying to accomplish at each stage of the marketing process; creating the right directories and the right files in each directory. The key is being clear about what:

- you'll be doing to generate clients;

- your prospects/clients will be doing in response;

- you've got to do as a result.

Each thing that you need or have to do must be sorted into the appropriate directory where *everything* related to it will ultimately be filed. Thus, you will probably end up creating directories for:

- information on the prospects you're targeting. You need data on who is being targeted and information on their current situations, including problems they are experiencing and benefits they want. Make sure you include complete citations about where this information came from.

- your plan. This includes your goal statement, profit objective for the next year, and a detailed breakdown of the marketing program you need to implement to reach this objective. Don't forget to include information on your expenses!

- material to be used in creating targeted marketing communications, including: envelope teasers, offers, benefits, what will happen if prospect fails to act, testimonials, post scripts, client-centered biographical details, success results, *etc.*

- examples of every marketing communication you use for contacting prospects and converting them into buyers. *Note:* some of the documents you create will have an automatic date in them and/or will be updated/edited by you regularly. In this case, keep a copy of both the original communication and the document you're working from. (While providing you with marketing communications you can mine to create new ones, this system also has the benefit of providing a complete archive of everything you've done. When reviewing it you get a very clear sense of your progress towards marketing mastery, which is no bad thing.)

Organizing To Close The Maximum Number Of Prospects As Quickly As Possible And Launch Profitable Business Relationships With Them

Think of the "prospect generating" directory discussed above as organizing everything you do to *reach out to prospects*. It includes every step you take to:

- identify prospects;

- discover what they want, and

- motivate them to take action.

Think of this directory as organizing everything so that you're ready when the prospects *respond* to you. This response directory includes:

- prospect files including name, address, telephone and fax numbers, dates contact attempted, results of contact, things you've promised prospect, dates you've done them, *etc.* You should have a file for every service you offer.

- phone pointers both for the initial prospect contact and subsequent phone contact by you. You should have the appropriate phone pointers for every service you offer;

- client-survey questionnaires and other want-assessment devices for every service you offer (getting the message?);

- notes of prospect meetings prior to engagement;

- letter of intent contractual agreement(s);

- full-scale client contract(s);

- independent contractor agreements with all independent contractors, if you are not doing the work directly.

What goes in these files is everything relating to prospects who have identified themselves and everything you need to close them, including all the contractual language you need and sample contracts.

Resource

If you are offering a consulting service, you'll find my book **THE CONSULTANT'S KIT: ESTABLISHING AND OPERATING YOUR SUCCESSFUL CONSULTING BUSINESS** helpful here. It contains a series of sample contracts and the clauses you're most likely to need both for your client relationships and those you develop with independent contractors.

Organizing To Work With Your New Clients So You Both Get What You Want From The Relationship As Soon As You Can

In this directory, create files for:

- directions on how to arrange and focus necessary client meetings. Are there particular points you need to raise at your initial meeting with a client, at subsequent meetings? They should be logged here.

- reporting progress to a client;

- reporting lack of progress (yes, you need sample language on how to put the best face on a situation where you're not going to get the client everything he wants, or which you've promised);

- summarizing a relationship;

- asking for testimonials and referrals;

- informing a client about what happened with the referral he provided;

- invoicing;

- past-due notices;

- turning over an account for collection;

- informing the client you'll be taking legal action if payment is not forthcoming;

- creating the document you need for making a complete record of client activities which you can present to a lawyer and/or court if legal action becomes necessary;

- a "no hard feelings" letter you can send to a client after you've had to sue him for payment — and won. Yes, even that should be available in a file for easy access and use!!!

Is All This Organization *Really* Necessary?

The case for being this organized is unanswerable. Doing it, as we all know, is another thing. You've gotten along so far without this degree of efficiency. You may therefore be leaning in the direction of staying relatively disorganized.

Don't do it!

Let me use just one typical marketing situation to show you how unwise it is to opt for lower efficiency.

Say you run an ad in the local newspaper to generate new prospects and clients. You have two options:

1. you can approach this exercise like you've never done it before and will never do it again, letting the chips fall where they may , or

2. you can approach this exercise as if you're going to do it over and over again and want to be as efficient, profit-making and client-centered about it as possible.

Most service sellers opt for #1. They're so busy putting out fires, they:

- throw an ad together without giving it much thought, much less the necessary client-centered application;

- rush it to the publication at the last minute;

- forget all about it until it appears;

- "wing it" when responses come in. Some prospects get called promptly; others get called late or not at all.

- enter information on the prospect erratically;

- fail to track responses, including the number of prospects generated and resulting dollars, *etc.*

In short, there is NO SYSTEM!

Yet they think they're "marketing" and wonder why things aren't going so well. Or, equally awful, can't figure out how to improve upon results which, despite their disorganization, might be promising.

Then there are those paragons who understand how the computer can help. These people identify the Profit Points, places where the computer could be used to increase effectiveness and to turn casual, episodic marketing into a really *money-making process.*

These people have an objective, figure out what they need to happen, know what's going to happen before it occurs, and fully integrate their computer to achieve the fastest, most client-centered process possible. Before their ad runs, *before a single prospect responds,* they organize:

- all previous successful ads and result tallies;

- current data about prospect desires and fears to properly refashion their new ad;

- a letter to the newspaper's ad manager with ad placement and billing information;

- phone pointers for the receptionist who talks to prospects responding to the ad;

- data records so prospect information of value to present and future contacts can be directly entered into the computer;

- a letter to prospects that accompanies marketing communications they're sending;

- additional phone pointers for the person contacting the prospect by telephone after the prospect has received client-centered marketing communications;

- a thank you letter to the prospect who buys the service;

- an upgrade letter to the new client bringing additional benefits to his attention;

- a gentle letter to the client who hasn't paid for the seller's service promptly;

- a less gentle letter to the client who still hasn't paid for the service;

- a letter to a collection agency providing details on the client with a substantially overdue invoice;

- a letter to the client who hasn't paid the invoice telling him his account has been turned over for collection;

- a letter to the client with a substantially overdue invoice telling him the seller is launching a collections suit against him;

- a letter to the prospect with whom they're been having problems connecting by phone;

- a letter to the prospect telling him they cannot provide him with benefit now . . . because others acted more quickly than he did to get it;

- a letter to the client thanking him for the opportunity to work with him and asking for a referral and a (results-oriented) testimonial, *etc.;*

- a letter to the client who provided a referral thanking him again and letting him know they got the business.

Let me tell you something: when you place a simple ad in the tiniest local newspaper you're probably going to need every single one of these responses (and maybe even more). Moreover, as the volume of your leads increases, you're going to need them *over and over again.*

Now, I ask you: how do you think the *certain* multi-millionaire is going to handle this situation? Is he going to use "catch as catch can" procedures that make everything he does erratic, unpredictable, and inefficient? Or is he going to locate every Profit Point along the way and analyze it for ways he can integrate his computer into it and make it more efficient? In short, is he going to turn muddle into relentless client-centered marketing fueled by computerized organization?

A Note About "The Human Touch"

If you're a residual humanist, you may be feeling queasy right now about the degree of focused organization I'm advocating. I've got just three words for you: GET OVER IT!!!

To use a computer in this relentless fashion is not to engage in some dehumanizing activity. Quite the reverse. If you truly care about bringing the benefits of your service to the greatest number of people, you want to do *everything* you can to bring about this result. This is the essence of real humanity. However, you can always "humanize" each step along the way by remembering that all marketing is essentially a conversation between just two people, the person wanting the benefit and the person having the ability to deliver the benefit. Thus, the way to "humanize" this process of ultra-efficiency is to remember to speak directly to your prospect in every document you turn out.

One of the things I've been experimenting with over the last few years is the degree to which machine-generated marketing communications can be turned into an even more perfect expression of my client-centered orientation. Towards this end, the marketing materials I've been writing are nowadays very direct. They are the written manifestation of an intense, personal, no-nonsense eyeball-to-eyeball conversation.

When the prospect receives this letter, his first impression may well be that it's produced by a machine (after all I produce all my correspondence on computer, have no printed stationery and print everything on plain white continuous feed computer paper). This impression lasts only until the prospect reads the first sentence which is like my hand reaching out and grabbing him by the mind, heart, throat or other bodily organs, as necessary.

Because the focus is so intensely on the prospects . . . on their pain . . . their benefits . . . their need to act . . . nothing else matters. The connection is therefore made between each individual prospect and me . . . and each takes action accordingly.

In short, the degree to which you focus on the prospect is the extent to which he'll forget that you have organized the process and approached him via machine. That no longer counts for anything. The *real* humanist, therefore, is the person who is intensely focused on the situation of the prospect and uses *every* technical advantage to motivate the prospect to take action to acquire the benefit that will improve his situation.

Thus, when people say they hate computers because they're so impersonal, I now know that they mean that they neither care to bring their benefits to the largest audiences as quickly as possible nor are they willing to put themselves in their marketing materials, to turn their marketing communications into an intense representation of themselves . . . and hence obliterate the machine that does nothing more than rationalize the production of such client-centered communication.

Helping Yourself Become Efficient

A few common-sense suggestions will help you organize your Marketing Central and make it as efficient as possible. They include:

- data-entry protocols;

- an index;

- developing your own computer guidebook, and

- setting up your computer-centered work center.

Let's look at each.

Data-Entry Protocols

A protocol is simply an organized and recognized way of doing something. All organizations have such protocols — "it's the way we do things around here" — although most never bother to record most of them. When you're dealing with the computer, however, you need to think through what you're going to do . . . then do it. The utmost forethought and organization give you the most control over your data.

One example of a protocol is the state abbreviations all of us use: MA for Massachusetts, UT for Utah. Zip codes are another protocol. These protocols have been set by the government. Others you must create for yourself. Oftentimes it doesn't matter which option you select, so long as you're consistent. Here are some of the most common items:

- capital letters. Data records should be entered in capital letters.

- titles. Will you enter MR, MS, MRS on all records? Unless the prospect has given you a title (in which case use it), don't presume to add a title. However, where the prospect has provided you with either a personal or professional designation that he uses, enter it. Thus: REV, CAPT, DEAN, DR, *etc.*

- periods after titles. In computer records, periods and other punctuation marks are generally deleted.

- position: if you are trying to solicit people in a particular position, you'll need position information. Make sure you enter the title the same way each time, thus DIR PUBLIC REL.

- company name. company names are often too long for computer entry and must be abbreviated. Thus, ENT for enterprises, AM for American, CO for company, INTL for international, *etc.*, or *whichever logical system you select.*

- delivery address. Oftentimes prospects will give you two addresses, a street address and a post office box. The address above the city, state, zip code is the delivery address. Personally, when I have two addresses like this, I make the post office box the delivery address.

- street designations. Will you spell out or abbreviate items such as street, road, boulevard, trace, crescent, *etc.?* ST , RD, BL, TR, CR will do nicely.

- suite and apartment numbers. Use the # sign instead of spelling out the word "number" or abbreviating it "no". *Note:* contemporary usage seems to be moving in the direction of just putting the suite or apartment number after the street address with no number sign. Thus, "50 FOLLEN ST 507".

- cities and towns. Long names like Rancho Palos Verdes Estates need to be abbreviated in a regular way.

Hint: think through as many of your protocols in advance as you can, but don't worry about missing a few. You will be adding new categories as you go along; that's inevitable. The important thing is that you know what you're doing and stay consistent. This means recording things as you go along and making sure you can find this information by creating an index.

The Value Of Indexing

All computers create document indexes. When you create a document, you have to give it a name, and this name is available in an index. However, as I've discovered now that I've got over 6000 documents in my directory indices, the index that the computer provides isn't all that helpful, mostly because it provides only an abbreviated version of the document name and no hints whatsoever what it' s about. This is, however, only a problem with IBM or compatible computers. The Macintosh computer is, in this particular, far more user friendly. If you are using an IBM or compatible machine, however, this problem can be very frustrating. Thus:

- create an index file for each directory;

- when you create a document, enter the full name of the document in your index, the abbreviated name you've given it, and a brief description of what it is, when you used it, even (if you're super organized) how well it worked.

You'll want an index, too, for all your data entry protocols.

Now with the push of a button and just a few seconds of your time, you can find the document you want, the name you gave it, and even what you used it for and when.

Remember: when you're in the marketing business, you're necessarily in the data discovery (research) and data arrangement/storage business. This means that you inevitably become something of a librarian and have to think and act accordingly.

Developing Your Own Computer Guidebook

I don't know how you feel, but I find most computer manuals impenetrable, perplexing and badly written. So much for user friendliness. Personally, I'm not at all technically inclined; (when I was in school I tested at 5% for mechanical aptitude, which means that 95% of the population is more mechanically adept than I am, so take heart!). I don't mind telling you I need to be walked, and very slowly, too, through all computer processes I need to know.

This is where your own Computer Guidebook comes in. It's a record, in your own language, with every step clear to you, of exactly what you need to do to achieve the results you want. Obviously, everyone's guidebook is going to be different, but here are some suggested topics of prime interest to marketers. You need guidelines on how to:

- make a new directory;
- create macro keys (that is a key which automatically inserts certain information or phrases into documents, like pressing "d" and getting today's date);
- delete bold, underlining and other embedded commands from documents;
- pull out certain records from your data base, like all inquiries above a certain date;
- mark records for deletion;
- create a new data base where you can archive old records you no longer want as part of your current records;
- delete records from your data base;
- run mail merge letters;
- run multiple copies of a document where you don't need to insert new information into each document;

- copy records on to diskette;

- delete duplicates from your list;

- print documents and records, *etc.*

You should use a three-hole binder for storing this information and, yes, at some point you may very well need an index for it, too!

Setting Up Your Computer-Centered Work Center

One of the reasons why more service businesses haven't more fully integrated the computer into their marketing is because they haven't made it central in their offices. You see this instantly. When you go into an office where the computer is stuck into a corner or difficult to reach, you know that this is an office that is engaged in the most primitive marketing. Don't let this be you!

Whenever possible, the computer should be the center of your operations. A telephone (with answering machine) and printer should be within easy reach of the data entry operator and computer. Thus when the phone rings the operator can:

- connect with the prospect quickly (I generally get most of my calls on the first ring);

- put prospect information directly into a data record without having to write it on paper;

- enter the prospect information directly into the relevant marketing documents, create the label, print the document, *etc.* — all without getting up!

When you arrange things like this, you can handle both prospects and customers quickly and efficiently. There's no question of writing information on bits of paper that can so easily get lost or having to re-enter data you've just taken moments ago. You can concentrate your attention on what's important: on the prospect or customer.

Note: this is a real blessing when you're out of your office and the data/messages build up. When the phone and computer are next to each other, you can easily enter the data right into the computer without ever having to write it down. When you get to the stage where you have information products based on your service, you can create an order form in the computer where you can enter all the information you need, including data from the answering machine, without otherwise having to write it down. This is a big time saver and helps keep you organized.

Conclusion

We're now at the end of the first part of this book. Now you're organized. Not just better organized than you've been. But really organized — and ready to go. It's now time to get started looking at all the ways that are going to produce the avalanche of leads that you need.

6

Generating Leads Through Free Media

There are many ways of generating leads for your service business, as the following chapters demonstrate. But I want to start with one of my favorites: generating leads through free media — television, radio, newspapers, magazines, newsletters.

Why do I like this?

For two reasons:

1. when you play this game right, you get a bumper harvest of leads, and
2. you get them at rock bottom cost.

Note: I say "rock bottom" and not "free" . . . because even though the media time and space are free, you incur very real costs in securing them, costs like the time it takes to do all the things I'm about to recommend, the money it takes to produce the necessary materials, and the expense of sending out materials to the people who respond to you and your media message. It costs to get free media, and it's no good pretending it doesn't. However, when you handle the media and the leads you get properly, the costs can often dwindle into insignificance.

The key word here is "properly".

These days media — electronic and print — are filled with stories about service businesses. That much is clear. Unfortunately, the vast majority of what you see and hear constitutes nothing more than ego grati-

fication for the service seller. That is, while it reads and sounds well
. . . it doesn't generate any business.

This is ridiculous!!!

To make sure this doesn't happen to you, follow these 14 steps.

Step 1: Resolve To Use The Free Media

The first thing you as a service seller must do is resolve to use the
free media as part of your marketing mix. Does this sound easy to
you? Apparently it isn't.

Despite the fact that service businesses are featured in many different
media outlets on a regular basis, the businesses that are featured
constitute a tiny minority of the service businesses that actually exist.
For a variety of reasons, the other service sellers have resolved, con-
sciously or not, to let others get *their* share of media. This astonishes
me . . . though I see evidence of it every day.

Why do these service sellers forego the benefits of media? It's most
likely because they:

1. don't feel entitled to coverage;
2. think that because others offer a similar service there's
    nothing sufficiently newsworthy about what they're doing;
3. don't know how to approach media and work with them;
4. are just plain lazy.

A few quick words about these:

1. *Entitlement.* The reason most service sellers don't get
    media is because they have an attitude problem. They
    don't expect it . . . so they don't get it. Successful service
    sellers who use the media regularly to get leads are
    different: we (for, of course, I feel this way myself) feel
    entitled to the space . . . and are prepared to do what's
    necessary to get it. Inevitably all the media people we
    deal with can hardly be expected to share the feeling we
    have of ourselves . . . but that's not discouraging. Rather,
    it's just another obstacle to overcome. If you don't feel
    you're entitled to the space and time . . . you're not going
    to get it.

2. *Similar Service.* Many service sellers feel that because there are thousands of other people doing what they do, it's either impossible for them to get media coverage or they shouldn't get it. Absurd! Why does it follow that if there are tens of thousands of caterers in the United States, your catering company shouldn't get media attention? The fact is, of course, that this deduction is entirely erroneous. The real problem is that the amount of coverage for any given service within any given market or media outlet is limited. You cannot have unending stories in the local newspaper about local caterers. Thus, you need to make the determination that *yours* will be the service that gets *disproportionate* media coverage . . . and so cuts out others from getting their "fair" share. The media game isn't about "fairness"; it's about getting a steady stream of prospect leads for the lowest possible cost in the shortest period of time.

3. *Technically Ill-equipped.* I've got news for you: nobody was born knowing how to deal with the media. For this, you need a series of skills. Every one of these skills can be mastered. Not all are easy; none is overwhelmingly difficult. The fact that you may be technically ill-equipped today to deal with the media can never constitute an acceptable reason for not proceeding. You can learn each and every thing you need to know to ensure media success. Not least by mastering this book!

4. *Laziness.* What can I say? If this is you, you richly deserve your obscurity.

Step 2: Resolve To Get The Maximum Number Of Leads From The Free Media

Once you've decided to benefit from the media, you have another crucial decision to make. Will you use media as a source of ego gratification? Or will you use it to generate leads for your business?

If you think this question is trivial, think again. The vast majority of service sellers who go to the trouble of getting media attention achieve nothing more substantial than seeing their smiling mug in the paper. Now, I warrant you, in a society where so many people suffer from low self-esteem and are generally ignored, mistreated and alienated, getting an attaboy from the media may seem like a tonic. But it isn't

. . . unless it's attached to a means of generating leads. Otherwise, it's mad self-indulgence.

Only the foolish think that they've met their objective by getting into print media or onto electronic media. The smart ones only go where they can get maximum *marketing* advantage. Now one thing's absolutely clear: you're not going to know this when you get started. You're not going to know precisely where maximum advantage is derived; you're not instantly going to master the means of generating the maximum number of leads (even with the help of resources like this). That comes with time. However, you can resolve *right now* to do everything you can to get those leads . . . and to learn the tricks of the trade as you go along. That's good enough for now.

Step 3: Understand The Media Game

To use the media effectively for your purposes, you've got to understand that your interests do not absolutely coincide with the media source's. This is not to say that you can't work together for your mutual benefit. You can. But it does mean that each of you starts off with a different objective. Thus, if you don't understand what the media source wants to accomplish, it is easy for you to come across in quite the wrong way, not only losing the benefits from this media spot . . . but all the subsequent advantages you should generate from this single source.

The media source who is open to working with service providers (as distinct from the many other people who want to use the media and who have no part of our current discussion) wants, first, to *interest* his reader/listener. To this end, he'll provide whatever fodder he thinks will keep *his* designated market happy, that is coming back for more and buying *his* product. Secondarily, but only secondarily, he wants to provide *useful* material for his market, information that will enrich their lives in any number of ways.

In no way does he see it as his job or objective to promote you and your business. Any promotional value that you receive from what he does, therefore, he regards as quite incidental and in no way a priority. He understands that you want it, that you are working with the source to get it. That, however, is irrelevant from his standpoint. He can entirely succeed in meeting his objectives without your objectives being met in any way, shape or form. You must always keep this in mind, since exceptions to this situation are infrequent . . . no matter how glad we are to have them.

By comparison, your game is quite different. While you are perfectly happy to provide a product of interest (be that print or electronic) and wish, as a civic-minded citizen, to provide information of interest and value to the media source's designated audience, you have only one major objective: to generate leads from the source, either directly or indirectly. You may also have as a secondary objective building your perceived standing in your field, developing name recognition, and showing your parents you are a success after all. These, however, are of remote significance to the only objective that truly matters: getting leads.

Unfortunately, it is very easy to forget your objective or scale it down when you come in contact with media people. Their whole focus is elsewhere. Most of the time you're on their turf; at least at the beginning, you have no independent standing to assist you. Thus, it is easy to give way and lose sight of your purpose. THIS IS FATAL!!!

While it is perfectly possible for both you and the media source to achieve your individual and distinctive objectives, in virtually all cases this will only happen because you remember what your objective is and insist, in the nicest possible way, on achieving it. It will always be *your* responsibility to ensure that you get what you came for; if any one in the media helps you, it's a gift and should be regarded as such.

Note: your vigilance on this point must never wane. While I was writing this chapter, one of my columns appeared in a magazine I regularly write for. Despite the fact that its publisher knows complete follow-up details are *always* to be run with my articles, she, who has the promotional sense of a dead horse-fly, dropped this information. I have no patience with this kind of selfish incompetence and within minutes of my noticing this crucial omission, I had called the editor (who, predictably, wasn't available) and written a stiff letter reminding her of her responsibilities to me. In the next issue, the necessary information was duly reinstated. Now, if this kind of thing is going to happen to me, who publishes hundreds of articles in any given year, and who is always ready to defend my rights (my editors can attest to this), it's definitely going to happen to you. Prepare for it. And prepare to take action in defense of your self-interest. Never expect anyone else to, ever!

Step 4: Conceive Your Client-Centered Message

Before you even *think* of approaching any media source, no matter how small, you need to think through a client-centered message that will meet the different, if compatible, needs of both the media source and yourself. This is not difficult to do if you remember the needs of the media person and his audience. Say you're running a financial planning service firm. What do you think will be more interesting: information about your firm, its officers, years in business, service line, *etc.*, or details on how the media source's listeners/readers can save money on their personal income taxes? Or make money in the current financial climate? Or reduce their estate taxes?

It's obvious, isn't it?

If you expect to get maximum media coverage, your job is plain: you've got to brainstorm not just one but a series of client-centered messages that simultaneously 1) offer an interesting program or article; 2) provide useful/valuable information to the reader/listener, and 3) get people to call you so they can get the benefits you're broadcasting/talking about. This means taking the focus off of you ("ME BAD/YOU GOOD!"), and keeping it squarely where it belongs: on the listener/reader/prospect.

The easiest way to create these client-centered messages is to take two pieces of note paper. Head one "HOW TO GET (BENEFIT YOU OFFER)"; start the other "HOW TO AVOID (PAIN/ANXIETY YOU CAN TAKE AWAY)." Now brainstorm as many client-centered messages as you can under each heading with each entry beginning "how to get" (or equivalent verb). Let me show you what I mean.

You know I offer a fund-raising service for non-profit organizations. This has gotten me, over the years, a lot of sustained media attention which has stimulated prospects to call me. There are lots of fund-raising/development consultants around the nation. I'm one of the few who gets any general media attention. I do it by using this method.

(overall heading) HOW TO GET THE MONEY YOU NEED FOR YOUR NON-PROFIT ORGANIZATION (all topics under this heading produce the benefit the client prospect/audience wants)

- How to make your direct mail more profitable . . . even in a recession;

- How to create a community Board of Directors that will work for your organization . . . and contribute to it;

- How to target the right businesses in your community for getting donations;

- How to integrate your computer into your fund-raising operation and increase your fund-raising efficiency;

- How to organize profit-making community special events;

- How to create and sell a product that brings in money for your non-profit organization;

- How to increase your United Way allocation.

You get the idea.

Now brainstorm possibilities under the general heading HOW TO AVOID DOING FUND-RAISING THAT DOESN'T MAKE ANY MONEY FOR YOUR NON-PROFIT ORGANIZATION

- How to stop sending out expensive direct mail letters that don't make money;

- How to get rid of deadwood Board members who won't help with the fund-raising and think that just going to meetings is a big enough contribution;

- How to do avoid hearing "No" over and over again when you ask local businesses to support your good work;

- How to get over your fear of the computer and ensure that it helps make your fund-raising successful;

- How to put on community special events that don't loose money;

- How to avoid the pitfalls of launching a new product for your non-profit organization;

- How to avoid getting or accepting a cut in your United Way allocation.

Now, you'll notice something important about both these lists: the same subject can be dealt with from two angles — achieving gain and avoiding pain. The fact that an idea appears on both lists isn't bad; it's good. It enables you to see which approach is stronger and makes more appealing media. *Note:* in many cases, you'll find the "avoiding pain" is stronger and makes a more compelling story . If so, use this approach.

Astonishingly, very few service sellers actually take this brainstorming approach. They come up with a single angle (usually focusing on themselves, predictably) and go with that. This makes no sense. For one thing, you've got to look for the most compelling media angle; for another, even if you don't use a particular angle now, your brainstorming will produce any number of good media possibilities for later. Store them for future use. Personally, I maintain a computer file simply called "ideas" into which I throw everything that may be useful later. On days when I need media but my brain isn't functioning up to par, I've already got a stockpile of good things to select from.

Note: you've probably noticed that each sentence begins with the words "how to". There are other openings you can use, but "how to" is the opening par excellence for a service seller. Why? Because each of us is the master of a series of steps which brings benefits to clients. These steps are best rendered in "how to" fashion.

Still if you want variations, you can try heading your brainstorming page:

- new developments in . . . ;
- problems in . . . ;
- opportunities in . . . .

Still, opening with "how to" it's almost impossible to go wrong. I know. I use it all the time.

Step 5: Do A Personal/Professional Inventory

Tip O'Neill, the former Speaker of the U.S. House of Representatives, used to say, "All politics is local." In their turn, service sellers might say, all media are local. But the key is understanding what "local" really means.

The bulk of your media will come from proving you are somehow connected to:

- a place
- a profession
- a person
- an organization, *etc.*

That is, by showing you *belong*. Where you belong is where you create the "local" angle; where you create the local angle is where you are entitled to coverage and are most likely to get it. Hence the need for a personal/professional inventory ... on yourself and all those connected with your life and organization.

The point of the personal/professional inventory is to identify information about yourself (and others) that leads naturally to future media attention. Key points in this inventory include:

- where you live;

- where your office is located;

- where you went to high school, college and graduate school;

- what organizations you belong to, including civic, social, religious, political, professional, charitable, *etc.*

Why do you want to list all this? Because each fact you list connects you to one or more media outlets. It is these media outlets that constitute your best chance for early, relatively easy and continuing promotion.

Note: once you've finished doing your own personal/professional inventory, it's time for you to create one for these people:

- your spouse;

- your children;

- your father, mother, sister(s), brother(s), uncle(s), aunt(s) and cousins reckoned by the dozens.

Just how far should you go? That depends on how much media you want. When The Patriarch of Antioch renewed in my favor my family's ancient title of Count of Raban, I sent media releases far and wide. One, published in Naperville, Illinois, got printed because I am the grand-nephew (not great nephew, as my mother pointedly told me) of a fifty-year resident of that suburban Chicago community. It was *her* deep roots rather than my exalted designation that got me the media coverage. Remember this and renew (or at least use) family ties accordingly.

Step 6: Do Your Media Research

You're eligible to get media in two different kinds of places: where you've got a natural connection and where you don't. The former are the easiest and should be used first. Thus, once you've finished your personal/professional inventory (and those of staff and family), it's time to get the additional information you need to make use of these facts. Say your father-in-law is a member of the local Kiwanis Club. What next?

- Ask him if the club publishes a newsletter. If so, ask who edits it. If he doesn't know, call yourself;

- Find out the name of the editor, the name of the publication, frequency, address and phone. Ask to be sent a sample copy;

- Log this information in your computer;

- Review the sample copy to see what departments are available; (each constitutes a separate promotional possibility). See who's responsible for that department. (It might be an individual editor or columnist);

- Decide which of your angles is suitable for this publication.

This is enough for now.

Now you know what the media source has got . . . including its individual departments (very important for sustained and continual promotion) . . . who's responsible for what, and have made a preliminary decision about which of your angles make the most sense *given the media source you're considering.*

Don't rush ahead and approach the source yet. Carry on to get all the information you need based on the logical connections of everything that emerged from your personal/professional inventory. This may lead you to several dozen or even a hundred or more very likely sources where you can get media attention. Congratulations! You now have a treasure trove of very valuable information at your finger tips.

Of course, no matter how many media possibilities you discover, what you've found so far constitutes only the tiniest fraction of media which may be appropriate for your message. How, then, do you find out about everything else?

To begin, review my book THE UNABASHED SELF-PROMOTER'S GUIDE: WHAT EVERY MAN, WOMAN, CHILD AND ORGANIZATION IN AMERICA NEEDS TO KNOW ABOUT GETTING AHEAD BY EXPLOITING THE MEDIA. My assistant Bill Reece and I went to a great deal of time and expense hunting down dozens of media directories which between them give particulars on well over 250,000 individual media resources. I've provided some of the major directories below, but if you're really serious, consult my book. Most libraries have it, but make sure you're getting the Revised Second Edition which is listed in the catalog at the end of this book.

A *Few* Key Media Resources

All-In-One Directory, Gebbie Press, Inc., Box 1000, New Palz, New York, NY 12561 (914) 255-7560. Includes basic information about daily newspapers, weekly newspapers, radio stations, television stations, general consumer magazines, professional business publications, trade magazines, *etc.*

Bacon's Publicity Checker, Bacon's Publishing Co., 332 S. Michigan Ave., Suite 900, Chicago, IL 60604 (312) 922-2400. Covers 8,000 trade and consumer magazines, 9,000 daily newspapers, and 6,300 weekly newspapers in the U.S. and Canada.

Gale Directory of Publications & Broadcast Media, 1992, Gale Research, Inc., P.O. Box 33477, Detroit, MI 48232 (313) 961-2242. Covers over 25,000 magazines and newspapers and 10,000 broadcast media listings.

Standard Periodical Directory, Oxbridge Communications, Inc., 150 Fifth Ave., Suite 302, New York, NY 10011 (212) 741-02 31. Includes information on over 70,000 magazines, journals, newsletters, directories, house organs, association publications, *etc.* Also publishes *Oxbridge Directory of Newsletters* with details on over 21,000 newsletters in the U.S. and Canada.

What To Do When You've Got Additional Media Leads

As before, you need to:

- Identify likely sources for your message (there could be hundreds, depending on the nature of your service and where you provide it);

- (With print media), ask for a sample copy so you can research the various promotional opportunities (the more you know the publication and attempt to make your message fit its existing formats, the better);

- (With electronic media), become a chronic dial switcher. Your job, again, is to familiarize yourself with what they've got;

- Log everything in your computer. You see, your objective is not merely to use this information once, but to use it over and over again. Of course, media people are notoriously mobile. That's life. The fact they are peripatetic is no excuse not to record and store everything you've taken the trouble to gather. You can update your findings as necessary and as new details come to your attention. I'm constantly doing this.

Once you've got this information, you need to evaluate it and pick your best shots. In priority order, here's what they should be:

- A media source that enables you to provide your readers/ listeners with complete follow-up details is a prime target, even if it's small. What's important is that it connects with the prospects you want to attract;

- A media source that will not allow you to provide your readers/listeners with complete follow-up details is an important target if and only if you can and will use it in your overall marketing efforts and if appearing there will raise your perceived value with your targeted markets. In short, that you can leverage this appearance either to get additional media or help induce prospects to contact you in other ways than directly from the appearance.

Thus, just what you decide to do next depends on whether the media source(s) you target will help you generate business, either directly or indirectly. Satisfying your ego must never be a consideration unless you're already a multi-millionaire with time on your hands and the need for public ego stroking.

Note: by using this process, you'll discover many more appropriate media outlets than can conveniently be used at one time. Good. You want steady, continual media attention . . . not a blast that's overwhelming but abbreviated.

Step 7: Draft The Documents You Need To Get Coverage

Part 1 . . . Short Takes

Now that you've identified several dozen or more media possibilities for your message, it's time to create the necessary documents that will enable you to work successfully with media sources. Because there are several different document formats you need to master, I've divided this step into three parts: short takes, the problem-solving process article, and several more general formats. I'll first deal with short takes.

Once you've made the decision to factor free media into your marketing mix, you need to appear in the media on a regular basis. The catch is, as you get busier from all the sources of lead generation you'll be profitably using, your time will dwindle. This is where short takes come in. They're ideal to keep your name in designated media and bring necessary information to your markets' attention. Short takes are always just a few sentences long, rarely longer than a paragraph or two. They deal with:

- personnel changes
- awards
- personal milestones like graduation, engagement, marriage, the birth of a child, *etc.*
- publications
- speeches
- involvement in professional organizations
- a new business location
- launching a new product
- sales records
- charitable involvements and donations, *etc.*

Here are a few examples from a letter I sent out a few months ago to editors publishing my Sure-Fire Business Success Column:

1. "Jeffrey Lant's Sales & Marketing SuccessDek". Do you want to reach 100,000 business decision makers for the lowest card-deck prices in America? Great! Because now

you can take advantage of Jeffrey's Sales & Marketing SuccessDek. No one offers lower card-deck prices than Jeffrey. Just $1199 for a card reaching 100,000 . . . and if you mention (name of your publication) the second color is FREE! Other card-decks charge as much as three times more than Jeffrey's price for reaching 100,000 prospects! You'd have to be daft to pay that much. Or you can take a split run, 50,000 cards, for just $650. And if you need assistance writing your card copy, Jeffrey will help — no charge! For further information and a sample call Jeffrey at (617) 547-6372 or send four 29-cent stamps to 50 Follen St., #507, Cambridge, MA 02138. 1992 mailing dates are April 1, June 30, October 1 and January 4, 1993.

2. Free year's subscription to Jeffrey's quarterly Sure-Fire Business Success Catalog. As always, your readers can get a free year's subscription to the Sure-Fire Business Success Catalog just by writing or calling Jeffrey. They'll get over 300 suggestions every 90 days on how to make more money and live better. And they'll appreciate your telling them about it!!! (company name, address and phone number follow.)

Very Special Note: Now your readers get service from a Count! In November, 1991 Dr. Jeffrey Lant received a signal honor from the Eastern Orthodox Patriarch of Antioch, Syria for services rendered to the Eastern Orthodox Jacobite Church. The Patriarch, overseer of all noble titles from the mediaeval Kingdom of Jerusalem and associated states and territories, has revived in Jeffrey's favor a title held by one of Jeffrey's ancestors who went with King Richard the Lion-Hearted of England on the Third Crusade in 1190. As a result Jeffrey is now The Right Honorable The Count of Raban. But you'll find he still answers his own telephone and will be as happy as ever to take care of your orders. Call him at (617) 547-6372.

Short Takes Tricks Of The Trade

- Whenever possible, identify your connection to the publication you're sending the item to. Thus, when I'm sending a short take to *Harvard Magazine,* I write "Jeffrey Lant, Ph.D. '75" at the top of the page. This indicates I'm an alumnus.

- Always make sure to send the short take to the appropriate editor. In the case of *Harvard Magazine,* this is the Class

Notes Editor. You need not use the person's name, although if you have it and are sure it's accurate, use it.

- If you're smart, you'll use a computer to produce short takes quickly. Store particularization information in one file (thus "Jeffrey Lant received his Ph.D. in '75") and simply copy it onto the short take you're producing. In your file, this particularization information should accompany the relevant information about the publication's editor, name of publication, and address. In an instant, you've got all the information you need on each short take and can print it accordingly.

- When you're offering free details about your service or another tangible offer, make it appear as if what you're offering is special for the readers of that particular publication: "and if you mention (name of publication)." Editors like this since it provides their readers with extra value. It also provides you with lots of leads!

- Use your automatic date key in the short take to ensure that the release always looks like it was just produced. Reason? After you've sent the bulk of your short take releases, it invariably happens that you'll find another publication where your short take should be sent (or some individual you want to have the information). With the automatic date in the document, it's always current.

- Make sure you include these words in the upper left hand corner of your release: "For further information, contact (your name, company name, address, and phone number.)" It's always possible you might get a bigger story out of this release . . . either in lieu of the short take or, better, in addition to it.

I am a short take fanatic. As my editors can attest, every 90 days I send about 200 of them a list of about a half dozen short takes they can publish. Thus, these news and feature items (many of which ask people to get in touch with me either to buy things or get free information) are popping up all the time. That's the idea. You raise your perceived value (as well as getting lots of leads) by using the media. Remember, your appearances in the media need not be lengthy. They must just be continual.

Note: before leaving this section, I must again stress that the short takes you do should not all be centered on you. Say you get an award in your field. You'll obviously want to exploit all your own media link- ages. But you'll also want the coverage that comes from being "son of Mr. and Mrs X"; "spouse of . . .", even "father of . . ." When the objective is keeping a steady stream of leads and burnishing your ego no connection is too far-fetched.

Step 7: Draft The Documents You Need To Get Coverage

Part 2 . . . The Problem-Solving Process Article

As you should now be clearly aware, when you're running a service business you're really the master of an operation that either provides your clients with a benefit . . . or eliminates the prospect of present or future pain/anxiety. You can work with the media to generate lots of qualified leads by putting what you know in Problem-Solving Process articles. These articles are composed of the following parts:

- headline that clearly addresses a benefit the prospect wants . . . or a pain/anxiety he wishes to get rid of or avoid;

- a series of client-centered paragraphs offering information that will enable the prospect to achieve what the headline promises;

- a Resource Box with complete follow-up details enabling the reader/prospect to connect with you and launch a marketer- client relationship.

Let's look at each part in turn:

— Headlines

The best headline for a service seller is the how-to headline: How to get (benefit the prospect wants), or How to avoid/eliminate (pain/ anxiety the prospect doesn't want).

You'll find these headlines by going back to your brainstorming list. Thus:

- How to make your direct mail more profitable . . . even in a recession;

- How to create a community Board of Directors that will work for your organization . . . and contribute to it;

• How to target the right businesses in your community for getting donations.

Any of these would do well, because all of these address real issues in the prospect's life . . . and all can motivate him to call and enlist you as a individual working on his behalf to get these benefits.

Negative headlines are even more powerful. Like:

• How to stop sending out expensive direct mail letters that don't make money;

• How to get rid of deadwood Board members who won't help with the fund-raising and think that just going to meetings is a big enough contribution;

• How to do avoid hearing "No!" over and over again when you ask local businesses to support your good work.

The reason negative headlines (and the articles that follow) work even better than the alternatives, is because your prospects already know they're making costly mistakes and they want to avoid them. They want to avoid them, first, by reading what you've got to say and, second, by calling and enlisting you on their behalf. Hence, the more horrendous and costly the error they're making the better . . .. so long as you show them that it can indeed be solved (if only they have the wit to call you!)

— *Client-Centered Paragraphs*

Problem-solving process articles are divided into what I call modules. Each module has a specific purpose. Thus:

Module 1: this opening paragraph speaks directly to the benefit the prospect wants to achieve and paints it in the most appealing language possible. Or, this opening paragraph speaks to the pain and anxiety the prospect/reader has and paints it as menacingly as possible. This paragraph must speak directly to the reader/prospect. You're using the benefit he wants . . . or the pain/anxiety he wishes to eliminate/avoid . . . to motivate him to pay attention to the remainder of the article.

Modules 2-9: These paragraphs tell the prospect/reader in as much detail as between 75-150 words per point will allow just how to get the benefit/avoid the pain. The paragraphs follow in logical order based on "What Next?" thinking. Using "What Next?" thinking, you posit the benefit the prospect wants . . . or pain he wishes to avoid . . . in the opening paragraph ("Most nonprofit organizations submitting grant proposals end up with nothing but frustration and depression. Certainly they don't get the money. To avoid this unnerving result, do the following 9 things: . . .") Then follow with the first thing they must do . . . then the question "What next?"; then the next module, *etc.* You can use "What Next?" thinking to write a solid, meaningful, and trust-building article with your prospect about any subject in the entire world.

Module 10: The Resource Box. Here you include complete follow-up details including the benefit you offer, your company name, address, phone number, fax, *etc.* Thus, "To get started getting more money from foundation grant proposals contact . . .." Remember, lead with benefits ("more money"); follow with features ("from foundation grant proposals").

Problem-Solving Process Article Tricks Of The Trade

- Open a computer file called "Ideas" and store possible titles for these articles.

- Outline articles as soon as you have a title. It is easy to outline a Problem-Solving Process article because each paragraph follows naturally from the one before. If you're having problems outlining an article, it means you don't really understand the subject matter . . . and need to do some more work on it.

- Keep a hard copy file of data you need for your articles. If you do discover a hole in an outline, do what's necessary (by researching, writing letters, reading books, going to the library, *etc.*) to get the data you need;

- Write both the positive and negative versions of the same article. Your objective, after all, is not to write articles; it's to get leads. Some people respond more favorably to one format, some to another. Use both.

- Store all articles for updating and continual use. I am still drawing prospects today from articles I wrote *6 or 7 years ago.* Why? Because the subjects (getting a defined benefit or eliminating/avoiding anxiety/pain) continue to be of interest to people and because I update them at regular intervals. Do editors mind printing things that are old? Yes, if they think they're old; they certainly do. But you don't have to make any confessions. Just make sure the subject is still pertinent and that you've updated all information to be *au courant* with developments in the field. Then print it again . . . and draw more leads.

- Offer your articles in hard copy and on diskette to appropriate editors. Don't expect any direct payment for them. Your payment comes from the clients you get. To launch a relationship with an editor, write with a sample or two of what you propose to run and follow up with a phone call. Indicate that he can print your articles for free so long as he runs the Resource Box. Most are happy to comply. After all, you're providing valuable information and saving them money.

At the beginning of your promotional career, you'll probably be writing all the articles yourself. Graduate from this stage as soon as possible. Keep an expert file in your computer. List the names, addresses, phone numbers and specialties of people in your field.

Once you start breaking into print, contact these experts, and ask them to write an article for your series. This article will:

- feature their problem-solving processes;
- include any number of laudatory comments about them;
- include follow-up details about their products/services as well as yours, and
- will appear under your by-line.

What??? *Yes, yours!*

Will any one write an article that appears under your name? Certainly — if you can provide a reasonable certainty the article will be printed.

Smart specialists are continually looking for coverage for their products/services and will be willing to work with you if you can help provide it. Moreover, in the article they draft they can say things about themselves they could never say if the article appeared under their own by-line. (Or, if you're a good person, you can recognize their possible embarrassment about saying such things and simply add them yourself.) In short, it's a win-win situation.

Using this system, I produce about 5-6 articles every 90 days which are made available in a complete inventory to about 200 editors/

publishers who regularly feature me and my work. About half these articles are now actually written by other people, although they follow a precise format that I provide. As a result, I get more *sustained* publicity than any other writer in the nation. Moreover, each article that's published offers readers, through the Resource Box, both the possibility of buying something direct or identifying themselves as prospects. No other service producer in the nation gets more of this kind of coverage than I do!

Note: don't overlook the possibilities of running these articles on computer bulletin boards and information services. Simply send the appropriate editor a diskette with your material. Although computer data bases are generally confusingly laid out, the cost of sending your material is minimal (diskette and postage) and the data base will not only post but archive your material indefinitely. You could, therefore, be drawing leads for years.

Resources

To get information on computer bulletin boards and information services, use *Computer-Readable Databases* and *Information Industry Directory*. Both are published by Gale Research, 835 Penobscot Building, Detroit, MI 48226 (800) 877-4253. Upgraded regularly and available in most libraries.

Step 7: Draft The Documents You Need To Get Coverage

Part 3 . . . Documents You Need To Persuade The Media To Cover You

To get continuing coverage from the media for your service business, you'll need to develop four essential documents:

- background information;
- media experience sheet;
- problem solving sheet;
- cover letter.

Please note: I am well aware that there are many other kinds of media materials you can create. But I remind you you are running a service business, that getting free media attention is only one of the marketing gambits you'll be using, and that you need to keep things as simple as possible.

1. *Background information:* This piece provides the media source with basic information about:

   • who you are;

   • what you do;

   • benefits you offer;

   • years you've been in business, *etc.*

For most service businesses, the basic brochure will suffice. This document assures the media source that you are not running some fly-by-night operation and that he can safely and with confidence bring you and your operation to the attention of his audience.

2. *Media experience sheet.* Here you list:

   • the station call letters, city and state (if not well known), name of the program you appeared on, name of the host, name of the producer and date of your appearance (if within the last year);

   • the name of the publication, subject of your article (or whether you were interviewed, with name of author), and date (if within the last year).

Now, you may wail that you've never appeared on the media in any way and you have nothing to put on such a sheet. So be it. Consider that a sad reality of your current situation and one you'll work to overcome. Everyone, after all, starts with nothing. However, understand that the more media you get, the more media you're likely to get. Work accordingly.

Point: if your media appearances are over a year old, drop the dates but use the information. Why? So you won't look old hat. My card-deck competitor Joe Doyle includes in his media packet an article he authored in 1984 when he was president of a different company . It makes him look incredibly *vieux jeu.* Too sad!

3. *Problem-solving sheet.* This is something you'll offer through your article or electronic media appearance as a freebie to lure prospects into your web. Thus, if you are a financial planner seeking new clients anxious to avoid

estate taxes, you'll offer what amounts to a self-published problem-solving process article on "The 10 Things You Can Do Right Now To Lower Your Estate Taxes!" As with the published article, this one offers a client-centered headline. Unlike the article (which may run in length between 750-3000 words), this is shorter . . . offering 9 client-centered points under the headline with minimum copy. The tenth point, of course, is the Resource Box which invites the prospect to call you to get started getting the benefit by working with you directly. These problem-solving sheets give the reader/listener/prospect a good reason to get in touch with you promptly.

4. *Cover letter*. Despite the fact that the cover letter is what the media person you're approaching will see first, you create it last. Although you may well personalize it (especially if you've worked with the media source before), this letter is still a form. It should include:

   • a clear indication of the benefit you're offering the reader/listener;

   • background information about you and why you're the right person to be featured;

   • just where you'd like to be featured (what program or in what department of the publication);

   • what you'll be doing to follow up.

You can send as enclosures the other documents you've now created.

As with all your other marketing documents, the cover letter focuses on the prospect, in this case the media person you're trying to get to feature you or run your material. Your job is to persuade him that it's in his interest — and the interest of his audience — to work with you.

Step 8: Follow-Up

Without question, one of the keys to successfully integrating free media into your marketing mix is good follow-up skills. These skills start even before you put anything into the mail or fax machine. Thus, in the appropriate computer file, log all the information you're going to need for following up. Store:

- the name of the media person you're contacting
- title
- his program/department
- address
- phone and fax
- what you've sent him, and
- when you've sent it.

If you have a networking connection (such as a person referring you), log this information, too.

Once you've sent your material, follow up five business days later if you've mailed material; within two days if you've faxed or sent your material by overnight delivery service. You want to be prompt, not over anxious.

When you follow-up either the prospect is going to be 1) unavailable, 2) negative, or 3) positive. Whatever happens, keep notes in your media prospect file. Remember: you're not just after a single media mention, but a long-standing relationship.

Step 9: When You Can't Reach The Necessary Media Person

Media people are often elusive. Moreover, unless they want you (in which case they are rudely persistent and nauseatingly insincere) , they're not known for returning phone calls or behaving in any civil manner. Expect this. Thus, when you try to connect with a media person and fail to do so . . . that's par for the course. What you do now determines whether you're going to be able to successfully use the media to generate leads . . . or whether, like most service business owners, you'll fail to make use of this promising option.

Resolve to persevere!

When you can't connect:

- Ask whoever answers the phone the best time to call back. Leave a detailed message with your program/article slant, your name and phone number. But say you'll call again at the suggested time;

- Note the time to call . . . then follow up accordingly;

- If you don't connect the second time, leave another detailed message similar to the first. Indicate that this is your second call and that you will call again. As before, if you can get some idea of the best time to call, do so;

- Call at the designated time. If your party still isn't available, and if you're talking to the same person as before, tell him you're having trouble connecting. Find out if this individual will ask your party if he's interested in what you're proposing and when you should call again. In other words, get this person to assist you. Call back accordingly.

- If you *still* can't connect with the person you're seeking, send a duplicate of your initial letter. Ask the media person simply to write on the page "Yes, I'm interested. Call at _____." Or, "No, I'm not interested." If this person has a fax machine and this is an important media source with substantial prospects for you, fax the note. Make sure you tell the media person you've called three times previously and would appreciate an answer promptly. Shame does work!

If none of this succeeds, postpone further action. Go on to other prospects. However, don't abandon this source; just recognize that for now, you're not going to get anywhere. However, the minute you secure media attention elsewhere, go back. Send a clipping. Or indicate that you've got an audio cassette available of the radio show or a video cassette of the television program you've appeared on. Keep at it.

What you've got to keep in mind is that media people are both busy and spoiled. People are always seeking them out requesting things; most have therefore become rude and ill-mannered. Still, they won't remember the fact that they've ignored you or even been rude to you. Moreover, when they've made a decision that they want you, they'll be sweet as pie. Accept this situation . . . and never give up. If you can get leads and build your perceived value from the media source you're attempting to work with, you have no choice but to keep after him. If you've taken the trouble to understand what the source wants and will be of value to his audience, the likelihood that you'll get coverage is high . . . now or later!

Step 10: When The Media Source Says No

No matter how prominent you are, no matter how good you become at the media game, sometimes you will still get turned down when you seek coverage. Expect it. But don't accept it.

Find out why you were turned down:

- was your timing wrong?

- the angle inappropriate for the source?

- were they stuffed with other material?

- had they just run or featured something similar?

- is it what you said? Or how you said it?

- did you ask the wrong person?

All of these are valid reasons for turning you down.

The key is finding out *why* you were turned down . . . and seeing what it takes to turn this no into a yes. Thus, when you hear "No!" you've got to ask "Why?" or, better, "What does it take for us to work together now?" Then you've got to *listen* to what the source has to say. For better or worse, no matter how stupid what you're hearing may be, the source must be listened to — because the source controls access to what you want: free time and space.

Thus, don't attempt to defend what you've submitted. This is fatal. Simply listen to what the source is telling you and determine what you've got to do to meet his needs. If you can refashion your approach along the lines suggested, do so. If you can't do so right now (you don't have to say why), say what you are prepared to do . . . and when. In short, after hearing the source's point, let him know what you can do to work with him. Then either do it now or confirm in writing when you can do it.

Over the years I've heard "No!" from plenty of media personnel. The word doesn't register in my brain any more. It's just another obstacle to overcome . . . a temporary set-back. What I want to know is what it's going to take to overcome that obstacle as quickly as possible. So long as the media person will talk to me, I can find out. Then it's up to me to make the decision about whether I want the media coverage sufficiently badly that I'll do what is necessary to *attempt* to get it. Note I say "attempt", because with media people there is rarely an absolute guarantee. All things in the media game are subject to change without notice. That's just the way it is. But that also works for you as well as against you.

In part this is because the person who tells you no may not be around so very long. In the 13 years since I've been seriously exploiting the media, I've lived through several generations of media people. I now know that I'll outlast virtually all of them. Thus, when I hear no, I either resolve to do what it takes to work with the media source to get the coverage I need . . . or, if things look unpromising, I decide to simply outlast the idiot who denied me and try again: "I was sorry to hear that Tom Terrific has moved to another station. I enjoyed working with him, and am looking forward to establishing a relationship with you, too." When this gambit works, how very sweet it is . . .

Note: if a source you worked with goes somewhere else where you can benefit, be sure to send a note of congratulation on the new job and follow up promptly. When the source is new and doesn't have a well-established network of contacts, you should go farther faster.

Step 11: When The Media Source Says Yes . . . Preparing To Make The Most From Your Media Engagement

Given your client-centered message and good follow-up skills, you're going to get increasingly frequent media attention. You are now in a position that would assist all service businesses . . . but which only a tiny fraction ever truly benefit from. Congratulations! Now don't blow it!!! Get prepared to make the most from your contacts with media, whether print or electronic.

- Remind yourself why you're doing all this: not for glory, but for as many leads as possible.

- If you're getting a short take in print, all you need to do is send the item. It helps if you accompany it by either a 6" x 8" or 8" x 10" glossy black and white head shot. Make sure to caption it with your name, title, company name, address and phone number. Type this caption on a sticker (I use my company mailing labels), and put it on the back of the photo. Don't write on the photo; it'll show. By the way, while you can ask for the photo back, it's unlikely you'll ever see it again.

- If you're getting a problem-solving process article in print, again all you have to do is submit the article with your photo. If you submit your article on diskette, make sure what you're submitting is compatible with the editor's system. Clearly label the diskette with your name, the title of the article and the date.

- If you're being interviewed by a print source, log the particulars of reporter name, publication, address, telephone and travel directions. Make sure you bring to the interview a complete set of all documents you've previously sent to the source. Expect the source to have nothing that you've sent. He shows up (if you're lucky); you're the one who must be prepared!

- If you're getting on a radio program, ask whether the source can tape the program and whether you need to bring your own cassette (with smaller stations you often do). Write down the particulars of when you're going to appear, with whom, who the producer is and directions to the station if you don't know where it is. Call the day before to confirm. If a major news event takes place the day of your taping/appearance, call again to make sure you haven't been preempted.

- If you're going on a television program, ask if they can run your phone number on the screen while you're on. If so, this generally has to be set up in advance. As with radio, write down the particulars of when you're going to appear, with whom, who the producer is and directions to the station. Since television stations don't usually give you video cassettes of your appearance, ask what kind you should bring to have a copy of the program made. Or use your VCR at home.

Note: for both radio and television, write your introduction yourself, provide a sample list of questions and provide the copy you want given over the air for how people should contact you and what they get when they do, thus: "To get your free tips on how to cut your estate taxes call (phone number) now!"

Another note: you'll notice the viewers/listeners are asked to call while the program is airing. This is no problem if you've taped the program. But what do you do if the program is live? If you have a receptionist, there's no problem. If you don't, get a friend to mind the phone during the program and for about an hour afterwards. (Either way make sure you get all the information you need to follow up effectively.) If you simply wait for your answering machine to take messages, your system can easily be overwhelmed, and you'll both frustrate your callers and lose some of them. However, about an hour after you're off the air, the flow of inquiries should be so spaced that your answering machine can take the messages. If you do use this machine, make sure it's got a client-centered message: "Hi, this is Cynthia Peters. I can help you save money on your estate taxes. Leave your name, address and phone number to get the free information about how you can save!"

Step 12: How To Make The Most From Media After The Fact

When you use the media you can generate leads and derive benefits both when you are on the air (or when your article appears) and from the use you make of these appearances/articles after the fact. Here's how:

- Log all appearance/publishing information and update your media records. As you now know, the more often you get media coverage, whether print or electronic, the more likely you are to get additional coverage. This is because you've already proven that you're "media worthy" . . . a distinct class of service sellers.

- Send a thank-you note to the person interviewing you or running your material. You want to develop a relationship with this person so you can get continuing media. The note you send will probably be the only one he gets . . . and you'll be remembered. Don't make this a form letter, either. Make it as personal as possible by complimenting some aspect of what has happened.

- Go back to media sources you've previously contacted (without success) or those you're currently attempting to pin down. Share copies of the article that's just been pub- lished, send a copy of your radio audio cassette or notify the source about the television program you've just appeared on (you can say a video cassette is available if he wishes to see it). The fact that you've just received media attention has raised your value in this game. Make full use of it!

- If your appearance on radio or television has been taped and will not be broadcast for a week or two (more likely with radio), send a letter to key prospects and customers to notify them to tune in. You want these people to know that you're media worthy. It doesn't matter if they tune in or not; it matters that they know you were interviewed. However, if you're talking about something of value to them, some will indeed tune in!

- Distribute your problem-solving process article in the same way. If the headline of the article is client-centered (that is, it offers a benefit or relief from pain/anxiety) and the Resource Box includes full follow-up details, you can simply mail out the article marked "FYI". However, if the headline is weak and, Heaven forbid!, the Resource Box has been gutted or deleted altogether, you'll need to add both these crucial components. You can do so by simply taping the article on your letterhead, adding a new headline and follow-up details at the bottom. You can include this article with your regular mailings and with all your outgoing mail as a package stuffer.

- Excerpt quotes from both on-air media personalities and the author of any interview with you and put them in your brochures and other marketing documents. Particularly on-air media personnel are often lavish in their superlatives. You're the beneficiary . . . but you've got to squeeze the maximum benefit from what they say.

Note: you can use past media appearances/articles for years if you're clever. Initially you should keep the date on either the tape or article. This is acceptable for up to a year. Thereafter, erase the date and use the material . . . so long as they speak to the markets you're interested in attracting and still offer relevant material. As for quotes and excerpts, you can use them indefinitely . . . again, so long as they're relevant for your audience.

Step 13: Reusing Material

This point is in the nature of a reprise. However, I want to make sure you've got it. I've advised you to create problem-solving process articles. And I've advised you to keep them updated. Now I must stress this point.

You're not only able to derive benefits from these articles by their initial publication and from subsequent use as leave behinds, package stuffers, *etc.*, but from updating. So long as your audience is interested in the subject area, so long as they want the benefit and wish to avoid or eliminate the pain and anxiety, these articles retain their value.

To be sure, certain parts of the articles will date. Technologies change. Procedures change. Ways that were once cutting edge are superior and valuable no longer. But so long as your prospects wish to achieve the benefit or avoid the pain, your article can be updated and used again.

Thus, you need a file where you can keep material for updating these articles and need to recycle them at intervals.

Say you're a planned giving consultant who has written a problem-solving promotional article on the different varieties of specialized software which assist in running a successful major gifts/planned giving program. Nothing ages so quickly as this kind of software, yet your market will always be interested in knowing what is state of the art for its uses (thereby giving you an ongoing source of promotion). Thus, you've got to store the new information on the subject as it becomes available so that at any given moment you can update the article, make it current and valuable again . . . and continue to derive promotional advantage from it.

Some of this information can be stored in an appropriate computer file (quotes, bibliographic information, details on experts and their phone numbers, companies that produce the software, *etc.*) Some, because longer and more detailed, will need a hard-copy file. Either way, these files should be established before you write the initial article and should be kept current by your adding information as soon as it becomes available.

Where most service sellers go wrong is that they don't see a problem-solving process article as something from which they can derive benefits for years; they see it as a one-shot undertaking, something from which they may (or may not) derive benefits the one and only time it's published but which, thereafter, is necessarily defunct. This is ridiculous!

My friend the well-known author Herman Holtz recently wrote an article in which he lavishly complimented me for my "increasingly ubiquitous" appearance in opportunity and other entrepreneurial publications. As a result, he said, I was now the leader in my field.

I appreciate the compliment but what's more important is the method I've used to achieve this dominance. *Everything* I write — including this book, by the way — is so constructed that it can be used and reused and reused again for the rest of my life . . . so long as the subject and its benefits remain of interest to my designated markets and so long as I take the time to update and revise as necessary. For this you need to rethink the traditional notion of what an article is and how to use it . . . and plan accordingly. Do so, and you will be put in the enviable position of deriving years of value from every problem-solving article you create.

Step 14: Thinking Like An Unabashed Self-Promoter; Making Free Media An Integral Part Of Your Marketing Strategy

Your ability to use the media successfully to generate leads and so achieve your financial objectives begins in your head. You must understand that no one is going to come into your office and say, "Behold! I've decided that you are going to get an avalanche of lead-generating media. I shall do everything for you. All you have to do is reap the benefits!"

Instead, you must say to yourself, "I've decided that I am going to get an avalanche of lead-generating media. *I* shall do everything I need to do so that I can reap the benefits!" To say this you must *think* this . . . and you must *believe* this.

Then you must *live* this, day by day.

I start every day by writing a series of marketing letters; often they are to media sources. No day of my life is complete without working with media sources, because these sources can put me in touch with tens of thousands, or even more, prospects . . . if I do what's necessary to motivate them and do the necessary work to make the contact productive.

The media sources I work with fall out along a broad spectrum of possibilities from the "No, Jeffrey, never" category . . . to those who are avid for more of my client-centered articles and broadcast programs. I accept that this is the way things will always be, with my objective being to move the prospects at the one end to a more productive relationship and to enlarge the number of prospects at the other and reap even more advantages.

I do not wait for media people to contact me (though many do); I take the initiative. So must you. I don't expect them to be willing to help me. That's my look-out, too. If I'm to get the advantage, I must do what's necessary to achieve it. In short, when working with the media, the entire responsibility is on me . . . just as it will be on you. IF YOU WISH TO ACHIEVE THE SUBSTANTIAL RESULTS MEDIA CAN OFFER.

Perhaps it is this clear sense of marketer responsibility which keeps most service sellers from benefiting from free media. Maybe, like some Hollywood starlet, they're foolishly waiting to be discovered. *Don't you wait.*

There isn't a service seller in the land who wouldn't be better off by getting free media . . . and the delightful thing, there isn't a service seller in the land who shouldn't be able to get this media. *En avant!*

7

Generating Leads Through Talk Programs

Now that you're generating leads from free media, you've got one plate in the air. But marketing is about juggling *many* marketing gambits successfully. It's therefore time to spin another plate and start getting leads through talk programs.

Before we begin, I want to make it clear that this chapter is not about how to become a successful paid speaker. I'm talking here about what you need to do to get a steady stream of prospects from talk programs, prospects you close to become paying customers of your business. If becoming a money-making talk impresario is what you want, run, don't walk, to my book **MONEY TALKS: THE COMPLETE GUIDE TO CREATING A PROFITABLE WORKSHOP OR SEMINAR IN ANY FIELD.** It's got just what you want.

The truth is, as a service seller you may or may not get paid for the programs you offer; certainly in the beginning getting paid will occur less frequently than not getting paid. This isn't a serious problem, however, SO LONG AS YOU HAVE A SYSTEM IN PLACE THAT GIVES YOU A STEADY STREAM OF LEADS AND SO LONG AS YOU WORK HARD TO CONVERT THESE LEADS AS QUICKLY AS POSSIBLE INTO PAYING CUSTOMERS. And that, gentle reader, is precisely what this chapter is all about.

A Little Background To The Talk Business

Tens of thousands of talk programs are given every single day. The vast majority of these share one important feature: they are not given

277

by celebrities with well-known names commanding substantial fees. No, the foundation of the talk business is information specialists, people who are masters of technique, process and problem-solving specifics. This is very good news for you. Why? Because you, as a service seller, are such a person.

You have at your command this exact kind of information whether it's how to get stains out of fabric or the nitty-gritty of setting up a successful home-based business. As such you are the perfect candidate not merely to give a talk program (for that is not the object of this chapter or your exertions) but to profit from the giving of such programs. That's because the people who attend such informative talk programs are the people who are most interested in achieving the results of such programs and are thus most likely to want to work with you (who knows how to deliver the benefits) to achieve them.

The question is: how do you start creating the process that puts you together in the most constructive way with these people?

Step 1: Find Out Who Sponsors The Kinds Of Programs You Should Be Giving

There are two kinds of talk programs: those you sponsor yourself and those others sponsor for you. I am a big advocate of the latter. Here's why:

- You are a *service* seller. Your job is reaching your income objective by converting as many leads as possible, as soon as possible into paying customers. The focus should not be on launching and administering talk programs, but on benefiting from them.

- Because you're not a master of the talk business, it's easy to lose money in self-sponsored programs. Certainly at the beginning of your involvement with talk programs, it makes more sense to rely on both the expertise and resources (not least, money) of program sponsors to make your program a success. Leave the management (and the headaches) to them. You'll still profit handsomely by following the details in this chapter.

- There are plenty of existing opportunities from current program sponsors and organizations you can persuade to sponsor programs. There's really no need for you to sponsor your own programs.

For these reasons, you ought to avoid sponsoring your own programs and seek to enter into mutually beneficial alliances with those already sponsoring programs. The real question is how you find these people.

Look for current program sponsors among the following:

- local non-credit continuing education facilities. Check the Yellow Pages under "schools". In the Boston-area, for instance, we have both the Boston and Cambridge Centers for Adult Education. You can also check LERN, that's the Learning Resources Network, 1554 Hayes Dr., Manhattan, KS 66502 (913) 539-LERN.

- continuing education divisions of community and four-year colleges;

- adult education programs of local high schools;

- trade and technical schools;

- professional organizations;

- civic and social organizations;

- non-profit organizations, *etc.*

You need to find out not only who is offering programs but what kinds of programs they offer. To do this, you may either call or write for their catalog or other program materials. Unless you are certain the organization has such materials (in which case you may write and ask to be put on the mailing list), I suggest you call to get your name included. This way, if you discover the organization offers no programs but reaches the kinds of people you want to reach for your business, you can later propose a mutually beneficial collaboration. *Note:* just because an organization isn't offering talk programs now doesn't mean approaching them about doing so makes no sense. The key is whether they reach the kinds of people you need to reach.

Other ways of finding out who offers programs include:

- reading program announcement columns in calendar sections of magazines, newspapers and newsletters;

- discovering which other departments of these publications announce programs (in the *Boston Globe,* for instance, careers columnist Juliet Brudney regularly features forthcoming programs about employment related issues);

- reviewing paid program ads in these publications;

- reviewing direct mail advertisements you receive, and

- (in urban areas) looking at posted bills and notices. In my neighborhood around Harvard Square, I see quite a lot of these.

By regularly reviewing such sources, you should soon have a pretty good grasp of just who's offering programs in your area . . . and should be beginning to get a sense of what they're interested in, too.

Note: to get a preliminary list of organizations in your area, check the Yellow Pages under "association". Also review the *Encyclopedia of Associations,* Gale Research, P.O. Box 33477, Detroit, MI 48232. While Gale concentrates on national organizations, these valuable directories often have state or local affiliates which offer programs. Find out!

It should go without saying that as this information starts to pour in, you should be logging it in your computer. Set up a directory called "program" and a text file called "sponsors", and log the following information:

- name of organization

- address

- telephone

- person who reviews program suggestions

- his/her title

- titles of programs similar to yours and/or an indication that the sponsor has nothing similar to what you're offering.

Also log any information they may have provided either in their written materials or by phone on what they'd like to see in a proposal.

Step 2: Brainstorm Program Possibilities

As you're waiting for all your program information to arrive, start brainstorming the kinds of programs you want to give. Luckily for you, when you were working on your problem-solving process articles you already accomplished an important part of this work: the course title and outline. That's right: your talk program should parallel the problem-solving title and format of your problem-solving article.

Thus, say you wanted to write an article called "Ten Ways To Save Big Money Remodeling Your Kitchen." This is the kind of piece a home remodeler could — and should — be thinking of.

Your course could either have this title . . . or you could expand it into as many ways to save money as the time of the program allowed, thus 10 ways for an hour speech . . . or 25 ways for a half-day workshop program. Either way you've essentially got the title and, certainly, the structure.

As with articles, however, don't stop with a single title. Brainstorm as many program titles as you can think of, thus:

- Ten Ways To Save Money Remodeling Your Bathroom;

- Ten Ways To Save Money Remodeling Your Living Room;

- Ten Ways To Save Money Adding A New Garage.

Titles like these bring together you, who have technical information, and people who need it. First, they sign up for the program; then, having learned you're good at what you're doing, they hire you to assist them achieve the objective. Very neat.

Note: you're not going to think of all possible programs at one sitting. That's fine. Just open a computer file in your program directory called "ideas" and store additional possibilities there.

As a service seller, you have a ton of problem-solving information at your finger tips. The key here is organizing what you know in such a way that it's programmatically coherent and attracts just the kind of people who want the benefit you can deliver.

Thus, remodelers should be thinking about:

- how to improve every single room of the house for the least possible money;

- where to get good supplies for the least cost;

- how to do the work yourself . . . or how to find the right remodeler (got any ideas?), *etc.*

In short, however the remodeler makes money should become the basis for a workshop (and, need I remind you?, an article, too).

Before leaving this subject, let me be very clear about something. Many people creating programs try to be clever and original; try hard to one up each other to create programs that are abstruse, difficult, narrow in their focus. This is just plain stupid. Your job is to create programs that your client prospects will come to, that deal with the things they're interested in and want to achieve. These things are often the most obvious. For instance, there probably isn't a home remodeler in creation who doesn't do kitchens and bathrooms. Why? Because that's what most people want done. That's the precise reason why your talk program should focus on this subject — not subjects of lesser interest.

Step 3: Review What Program Providers Are Offering

Before approaching any program sponsor, it's time to review what they're offering to see if:

- anyone has already preempted your spot by offering something similar;

- the sponsor does anything remotely like what you're want to do;

- there's an obvious opening for you.

To begin with, if you haven't opened that log in your computer yet where information about the sponsor and programs goes, do so now. It's all too easy to go through these program materials with paper clips and highlighting pen instead of putting the information where it really should go and where it's easiest to retrieve: your computer.

Now that your file is open, start systematically going through the program materials. Note:

- the general thrust of their program. Given what the program sponsor is doing, does it look like he's going to the same audience as you want to reach? If not, don't waste your time trying to make a connection just now. It only makes sense to approach people who are predisposed to listening to what you've got to say.

- programs like yours. Log their titles, presenters and, if the description is brief, log that, too. Get a sense of how close to what you want to present their current offering is. Is there a space for you if you rethink your program? Or is the best you can hope for just offering to take over an existing program when the current presenter decides to stop presenting the program or is unable to do so?

- the absence of programs like yours. If the audience coincides with yours, maybe this is virgin territory after all.

Having intelligently reviewed these materials, you can make equally intelligent deductions:

- If the sponsor's thrust is different from yours, if he's trying to attract different people than you are, don't waste any more time considering him. His focus may change later, but now it looks unpromising for you.

- If the sponsor's thrust is the same as yours but someone is offering a program or programs like yours, you must either 1) come up with a new program that will enable you to fit in with the mix but not threaten what is already being offered and/or 2) offer to take over for an existing instructor if he is no longer able to offer the program. Yes, you can suggest yourself as a backup.

- If the sponsor's thrust is the same as yours but he has no program like what you're suggesting, the field belongs to you, and you can proceed accordingly.

Step 4: Conceptualize Different Formats For Your Talk Program

Your first impulse might be to rush ahead and contact the program sponsor now, but you should resist this. There's more work to do to make sure you maximize that contact. Start by conceptualizing different formats for your program. Major formats include:

- *a standard 45-60 minute talk.* Here you hit the high spots. This is a perfect talk for lunch or dinner programs; also, depending on your subject area, it makes a good key-note address for conferences. This program is heavy on concepts and light on details. It should contain a motivational component and necessary steps that the audience needs to master to achieve the benefit/avoid the problem. The fact that there aren't a lot of specifics in this talk shouldn't bother you too much; if your delivery is good and your content sensible, your prospects in the audience will still want you.

- *a two-hour workshop.* This program, often offered with conventions and in continuing education programs, is an elaboration of the program above, only you get into more specifics. The outline, however, can be the same. Here you tell the audience/your prospects more of what they need to do to achieve the benefit promised by the program's title.

- *full-day (6-7 hour) workshop program.* Again, you can use the same outline as for the 45-60 minute talk, but this time you'll be providing a lot of detail. Too, whereas the shorter talk usually allows for no questions (or just a couple at the most), here there should be constant interaction with your prospects. This is good for you since you'll have a chance to discover which are serious, what level they're at and who *you'd* like to work with. Moreover, you can learn names and some details about at least some of the people in the audience. This is good for building prospect rapport.

- *two-day intensive.* This program, offered as a pre- or post-conference session, over a week-end or as part of a continuing education program, offers real hands on detail to prospects. It gives you a good chance to present your methodology, explain what the audience should be doing and why, do lots of interaction with participants, get to know most, if not all, people attending, and start good, solid professional relationships that can easily lead to future business.

What's important to point out is that all these programs are built on the same problem-solving process outline; it's just that with more time you can provide the audience with more details and build a better relationship with participants.

Why do you need to consider all these different formats? Because different sponsors want different things from you, and you've got to be ready. When someone says, "Can you do your one-day workshop in two hours?" the correct answer is, "Yes. Of course, I don't get into all the detail that the one-day program provides, but within the confines of the time available I show people as precisely as possible how to achieve (the benefit the course provides)." This is a reasonable answer.

Step 5: Develop The Right Marketing Materials For The People Who Book Programs

Years ago, I worked in continuing education finding and developing courses for Boston College. I'd regularly receive suggestions from people, often prominent in their fields, who said they wanted to teach a course. However, what they'd send as an attempt to persuade me to hire them was often laughable. At the very least they had no concept how to approach a program planner with materials that would make him want them. Don't you make this mistake. Get prepared before you approach these people. Remember, it's perfectly acceptable for them to evaluate you on the professionalism of your approach and to draw conclusions from that about your expertise in your field. Thus, create the following:

- program description;
- program objectives/outcomes;
- calendar section media release;
- general media release;
- biographical feature story/sidebar about you;
- cover letter to program planner;
- 6" x 8" black and white head shot.

Let's look at each of these.

— *Program Description*

The planner wants to know whether your program is going to draw people to it. At the very least, he wants to cover his costs; more often than not, he wants to make sure that the program returns a profit. It's your responsibility to reassure him on these points. Your program description helps.

This description need not be long. Indeed, in most cases two paragraphs will do, although obviously whenever possible your description should be the standard length used by the source you're approaching.

This description should include:

- a client-centered headline offering prospects either a believable benefit or avoidance/elimination of a problem;

- substantial benefits they'll receive by attending ("you'll learn . . ." or "you'll get . . .");

- details about what is different, better about your program. Are you offering something new? Different? More valuable? The more specific you are, the better;

- details about any handouts or materials you provide and why these are valuable to people attending.

— Program Objectives/Outcomes

The program planner wants to know precisely what attendees will come out knowing/being able to do. This overlaps with the program description and may in fact become the basis for this description.

The best way to create this form is to focus on the program outcomes. Thus, write "A person attending this program will be able to do . . .", or "A person attending this course will learn . . .", or "A person attending this program will get . . ."

List between 10-15 outcomes in priority order, the more specific the better. If you really know your material, you won't have any trouble writing specific outcomes; if you are having trouble, it's because you're uncertain about the course and uncertain about what the attendees will get out of it. Back to the drawing board!

— Calendar Section Media Release

The more work you can do for the program planner, the better. He's as lazy and overworked as anyone else, and if you make his life easier, it's to your advantage. Thus, review the kinds of program announcements that run in media calendar sections, like the Sunday newspaper and create an announcement the program planner can run for your program.

This announcement should include:

- your client-centered program title;

- your name as presenter;

- space for program sponsor's name, address, telephone, program location, date, time and price.

Everything about this release should be finished except the specific details about time, place, *etc.* Let the sponsor add these.

— *General Media Release*

Create, too, a general media release. This will be longer than a calendar announcement, although not too long; three to four paragraphs will do nicely. In other words, it should fit easily double spaced on one side of a single sheet of 8 1/2" x 11" paper.

This release should include:

- at the upper left hand corner the name, company name, address and phone number of both you and the sponsor for further information;
- the program's client-centered headline in bold or capital letters;
- an opening paragraph with who, what, where, when and why specifics about the program;
- a second paragraph with information on who should attend the program, the benefits they'll get (or outcomes) or reasons why they should attend;
- a third paragraph with details about you, the presenter. Provide information that will show why you're a specialist in this field and that proves you know what you're talking about;
- a fourth paragraph providing program price, exact location, any particulars not otherwise included as well as the contact person for registering and his phone number.

Keep this release compact and client-centered, that is focused on the people you want to attend. Again, as with the calendar announcement, you can keep the sponsor particulars blank for now.

— *Biographical Feature Story/Sidebar About You*

Here in about 250 words (one double-spaced side of an 8 1/2" x 11" paper) you get to make yourself supremely interesting and knowledgeable with the objective of 1) attracting people to your program and 2) getting them to use your service whether they attend the program or not. Here are the modules for this format:

- In the upper left hand corner, write, "For further information contact, (your name, company name, address and telephone number)";

- In capital or bold letters in the center of the page provide your name and a client-centered description, thus: "Dr. Jeffrey Lant, the man who helps thousands of nonprofit organizations raise the money they need!" *Note:* the client-centered description clearly changes depending on who you're trying to get to attend the program and, importantly, buy your service. In other words, this is a marketing piece and as such its content is focused on the buyer . . . not on you.

- The opening paragraph positions you as a knowledgeable and helpful specialist in your field who is admirably positioned to assist people through this program . . . and in person. Thus: "Hundreds of Boston-area non-profit organizations have come to know they can raise the money they need for their capital, project and operating expenses by conscientiously following the detailed fund raising steps of Cambridge consultant Dr. Jeffrey Lant." Note the words "Boston-area". These words signal that the program in question is drawing from this marketing area and shows organizations in this area that the speaker is knowledgeable about problems they face.

- Each subsequent paragraph focuses on an aspect of your life that is 1) meaningful to the person you're trying to attract and 2) only secondarily about you. Thus: "Author of **DEVELOPMENT TODAY: A FUND RAISING GUIDE FOR NONPROFIT ORGANIZATIONS,** Jeffrey has been working with local nonprofit organizations since 1979. He has represented such organizations as (list) assisting them with (outcomes desired by people attending the forthcoming programs)."

- Each subsequent paragraph should also contain a quotation from you which, while ostensibly about yourself, is actually directed to the people you're talking to, in this instance those who want to learn to more effectively master non-profit fund raising. Thus, ' "Over the course of the last 13 years, the importance of fund raising to all non-profit organizations has grown tremendously. That's obvious. What's not so obvious is how you raise the money you need in today's gloomy economic climate." Lant reeled off (ways). . . . '

- While the bulk of this document should focus on your professional achievements and methodology, you should also provide a few hints about yourself that indicate that you do have a life outside your work. People don't like workahaulics (it makes them feel inadequate). Thus, add a couple of lines in the final paragraph, like "While not helping non-profits raise the money they need, Jeffrey loves to read. 'I make it a point to read something every day that has nothing whatever to do with fund raising or non-profit organizations. It's not only good for my soul, but it reminds me there's a whole world out there that isn't concerned with the ins and outs of development." Something like that!

Why should you create such a document? Because an editor might want further details about you to complete a story (hence "sidebar"); indeed, it might motivate him to do a full scale piece on you and your important work. Anyway, this is a great opportunity for you to emerge as knowledgeable, client-centered, empathetic . . . and yet not obsessive about your work. *Note:* by the way, the more obsessive about your work you are, the more you need to come across as sane and balanced.

— 6" x 8" Black And White Head Shot

You need a standard 6" x 8" black and white head shot, though an 8" x 10" will also do. Many program planners will want one. Make sure to create a label with your name, company name, address and phone number and put it on the back. By the way, with program planners you stand a much better chance of getting these photos returned!

— Cover Letter To Program Planner

At last we come to the first thing that a program planner will see from you, the cover letter. However, write it only after you have all the other materials done.

Your cover letter should bear witness to the fact that you've now done a lot of homework and are a worthy professional ready to work with another such in pursuit of a mutually beneficial objective. Thus, this cover letter should:

- Open by indicating you have reviewed the program sponsor's materials and, as a result, wish to propose a program;

- Indicate the name of your program, the intended audience (if not obvious from the title) and when you'd like to offer it;

- If someone is already offering a program like this, indicate why yours is different. Do not attack the program already being offered; simply indicate why yours is not directly competitive;

- If someone is offering a program like yours, and you haven't been able to think of something distinctive, indicate that you are not applying to offer the program now, but when the current instructor is no longer available;

- Provide the program description (or indicate that it is available on a separate enclosed sheet);

- Also indicate that you have other materials available (those listed above). There is no reason to send these now, however. If the program sponsor is interested, he'll ask to review them when appropriate;

- Indicate how you'll follow up. Five days after sending the materials is time enough.

Step 6: Networking Your Way Into Engagements; Developing Your Networking Strategy

You might think that, having done so much work, now at last you can call the program planner and start the telephone tag game. Not yet. The world being what it is, it's going to be more to your advantage if you can network your way to the program planner's attention than if you have to call cold, even if your program is dynamite. To be sure, you're going to have to get good at making the cold calls, too, but this is a book about minimizing your work... and that means becoming increasingly adept at networking, at getting what you want by working through the already established connections of other people. Here are some suggestions for doing just that:

- Remember your personal/professional profiles. You're supposed to have gathered information from the many people with whom you are connected about organizations they belong to, *etc.* If you haven't done this yet, you can't network effectively.

- Once you've got this information, call the organization to get current program materials and/or subjects for future meetings, conventions, *etc.* You want to make sure that what you want to offer fits in with what they're doing. It's bad policy to embarrass someone you've asked to network for you by getting helped to get access to someone who can't be of assistance.

- Get the name of the program planner, title, address, phone, *etc*. Make sure to log this information. Also, get any relevant dates when this planner makes decisions. Networking is, at best, an imperfect art. However, one thing that may help motivate your contact to act on your behalf is the fact that there's a deadline pending. Make use of this!

Once you know the organization offers programs and that yours is a likely fit, draft a cover letter that can go from the person networking on your behalf to his contact. Again, the more work you're able to do, the more likely you'll get what you want. Again, this letter is a marketing document you'll use more than once. Therefore, like everything else, it needs to be available on your computer.

The networking/marketing letter from your contact to the program planner should have the following parts:

- In paragraph 1, open with a few personal comments from the person ostensibly writing this letter to the program planner. You don't need to write these comments; simply write "personal comments here."

- Paragraph 2 should provide the reason why the sender is writing: "I've got a terrific program for you and a terrific presenter: (your name, program). I'm writing because I think this would be of interest to you and valuable to the audience."

- Paragraph 3 can contain a brief description of the program and why it may be particularly timely, valuable now.

- In paragraph 4, the writer tells the planner he's suggested that you call direct and that he's looking forward to hearing what happens. (*Note:* you should always follow up this letter, but it's acceptable for the writer to include your name, address and phone number in case the planner wishes to follow up himself. Most planners are slothful, but a few will actually be as organized as you are!)

- The letter can then close with any additional personal remarks.

Note: the writer can enclose further information about you, your work, other programs you've given, *etc.,* anything to reinforce his case that you're a knowledgeable and desirable professional, one well worth speaking to.

Another Note: obviously, you'll follow up this letter promptly. However, it may well be that you'll have trouble accessing the program planner. If so, begin by leaving messages in which you stress that you're calling at the suggestion of your contact. His name and your name should be linked in the message. If this doesn't work and you still can't get through, don't hesitate to go back to the person who made the original connection for you and get him to follow up for you. That's one of the benefits of networking, and you should use it if you need to.

— *Tips For Making Networking Work Better For You*

Here are some suggestions to make networking more profitable for you:

- Both keep your ears open and ask people leading questions about organizations they belong to, so you can get networking leads. Pay particular attention to people who are already making presentations. They know people you want to know.

- Don't expect people to *offer* leads. *Ask* for them and *ask* for their assistance. Sure, from time to time people will good-naturedly offer you leads, but you'll get more if you ask. In this connection, it pays to develop a networking system. Personally, I now get a large percentage of my leads by offering people who network me into talk assignments 10% of what I get from honorarium and product sales. This can be as high as $3,000 for the networker. I've provided all details on how — and how easily — this system works in a brochure that goes out with all my books, gets handed out at talk programs, is promoted through my catalog, *etc.* Further, I provide them in my Sure-Fire Business Success Catalog. In short, it's a networking *system.*

- If a lead works out, send the person who assisted you a thank-you note; if you're paying a commission, like I do, pay it promptly and let the networker know there's plenty more where that came from — if he keeps mentioning your name to program planners. (By the way, reader, if you'd like to make some easy money, you could network *me* into some speaking engagements. Check out the catalog in the back of this book or call for further details.)

• Once you start giving programs, make sure you ask each program sponsor not just for a testimonial (which is okay) but for a referral (which is better). People who sponsor programs know . . . *people who sponsor programs.* Take full advantage of this. If the program sponsor isn't coming up with further leads for you spontaneously, ask if he knows people at places where you want to make presentations. In short, don't expect leads to fall into your lap. Push for them . . . and log everything!

Step 7: Going Direct Without A Lead

Even with the best will in the world and the best organization, you're not going to get a lead in all situations. That's life. You should always be working to augment your file of leads and use them to the max, but you shouldn't forego an approach to a program planner because you don't have a lead. Instead you should:

• Perfect the marketing materials about your program and make sure they are as compelling as possible. If the program doesn't interest you, how do you expect it to interest the program planner?

• Send your cover letter with course description and objectives/outcomes statement along with a list of other materials that are available upon request;

• Start calling for an appointment. These days I am hired sight unseen after a brief telephone conversation. This is the objective. But you're probably not going to start at the place it's taken me years to achieve. Instead, at the beginning, you're probably going to have to see some program planners personally. This means calling for an appointment.

• As with difficult-to-reach media personnel, you're not always going to connect with program planners on your first attempt, although these people are not nearly so hard to reach. Still, you need to become adept at leaving messages which stress the program you're offering and to work with secretaries and other support people to pin down a convenient time when you can talk to the planner. If you are having trouble reaching the planner, leave specific questions with the support person you're talking to: "Can you please find out if the planner is interested in my proposal and what he'd like to do? When would it be convenient for me to call you for the answer?"

• If all else fails and you absolutely cannot get through, write a brief note to the planner pointing out how many times you've attempted to get in touch, stressing the reasons why your program is particularly timely and valuable now and why you think it fits into the planner's mix, asking the planner to get in touch with you and saying that you'll try again. But don't hold your breath. Look for other engagements. As you get them, go back to this unprofessional individual (whose numbers are legion), pointing out how many people are attending your program elsewhere and that, surely, this person (insipid as he may be) won't want to miss this gravy train. In short, *don't give up* . . . and do use the planner's fear of loss as a motivater.

Step 8: Making An Agreement With the Program Sponsor

By remembering what program people want (someone knowledgeable in his field, a good presenter and easy to work with) and by persisting, you will get through and get the chance to discuss your program and how it fits in with what the sponsor wants. Given all the homework you've done, you'll find your program is regularly accepted. Now don't lose your head. Remember, the object of this exercise is *not* to do a program . . . it's to get leads for your service business.

You've got to keep this in mind in making an agreement with the interested program sponsor, because his objective is *different.* His objective will be achieved if he makes a profit and if people attending the program are happy. In other words, he can achieve his objectives quite nicely whether you achieve yours or not. You should always remember this, and remember, too, that if you are going to achieve your objective you need to start doing so as soon as the program sponsor says he wants you and your program.

Always remembering that this is not a book about making money from talk programs themselves but rather getting the maximum number of leads for your service business, here's what you want to accomplish through your agreement with the sponsor:

- the right program write-up. Program planners ought to be but usually are not marketers. They think of themselves more as educators than motivaters. This is, of course, a bad thing when you're trying to get people to your program. Thus, make sure that you have final say over your program copy. Be willing to work with the program planner to get the most client-centered copy possible and insist on reviewing this copy before it goes to print. You'll be astonished at how program planners regularly weaken copy.

- get your phone number in the program write-up. Your job, remember, is to get business from this program. To do that, you don't actually need people to attend it. Thus, try to get your business phone number in the course copy, thus: "Jeffrey will be happy to answer any questions about this program and to see whether it's right for you. Call him directly at (phone)." Ostensibly this is a service to the program planner; more subtly, it's a service to you. This way people can call you whether they come or not. These lines help transform the program planner's marketing materials into marketing materials for you and your business.

- media support. There are two kinds of media you need to consider: internal and external. If the source has a newsletter or other publication, you need to ensure that you and your program will be covered in advance, that your photograph will be run, that at least one of your problem-solving process articles will run before and/or after your talk and that your talk will be reviewed. In other words, you need to ensure not just maximum publicity for your talk (which is not your true objective) but maximum publicity for you and the service you provide. Then there's the external media to consider — radio, television, newspapers, *etc*. Does the program planner have a media representative? If so, it's crucial you know how he generally handles publicity. Make it clear that you have materials already available and would be happy to provide them. Equally, if the program planner has no media assistance, offer to help.

- list of attendees with address/phone. Oftentimes you'll find yourself giving presentations to groups that don't provide you with the names and addresses of those attending. You need this information! Either work out something with the planner for getting this information (he could provide a list for you after the fact), or arrange to pass around a sign-up sheet the day of your program. Remember, the program planner doesn't care if you get this information or not; it's only of importance to you!!!

- taping your program. Particularly at conventions and larger meetings, programs are often taped by the organization. If you are getting paid and if the tapes are sold, you should get a royalty on each sale. I suggest you ask for 50% of the net after sponsor expenses. Whether you are being paid or not, also ask for a couple copies of the tape for your own purposes. Further, make sure to include a Resource Box on each tape, thus: "You've been listening to (your name). To get (benefit you've been talking about), contact (your name) at (your company, address, phone number)." If you're offering some kind of freebie or inducement for calling, provide that on the tape. You can either word this Resource Box in the first person or in the third person so an announcer can add it at the conclusion of the tape. But make sure you include follow-up details!

Note: the program planner may well wish to send you a letter outlining your agreement. Make sure these points are added to it, since they are crucial to the achievement of your objective. Without such a letter, it's easy for the program planner to "forget" what he promised, especially since what you're asking for is not necessary for the achievement of what he wants.

One other thing: clearly, if this program works for you and the sponsor, you're both going to want to repeat it. During your conversation with the program planner you should raise the matter of what he'd like to do if the program succeeds. What is his usual policy? You should make it understood that if this program succeeds you'd like to discuss both this and other programs and would like to know how he'd like to handle that. This is enough to know right now.

Step 10: Generating Leads: Publicity Before You Speak

As I've already pointed out, you can start benefiting from a talk program before you utter a single word . . . if you handle matters properly. Let's make sure you do.

If the sponsor has internal media, make sure you get as much as it as possible:

- Arrange to get a problem-solving process article in *each* issue of the publication before you speak. Make sure that *each* article will include a complete Resource Box providing information about the benefit you provide, your company name, address and phone number. If you provide some inducement or motivation for those contacting you, do so. Make sure *each* article is accompanied by your photograph. *Note:* there's no reason why these articles cannot continue to be printed after your talk, too. In short, if this is the right audience for you to draw business from, you'll want to keep this connection.

- Try to get interviewed by the publication. The interview should be focused on the kinds of problems you solve in your business and should also provide how-to information of interest to your audience/prospects. Keep in mind that this interview is not to glorify you; it's to promote your service to more people and, whenever possible, motivate them to call you immediately.

- Make sure announcements about the talk you're giving focus on prospect benefits, not you. Thus, instead of saying "Next Thursday Cambridge consultant Dr. Jeffrey Lant will be speaking on fund raising . . .", say instead "Come Thursday and learn how *you* can raise the money you need for your capital, project and operating expenses. Our speaker, Dr. Jeffrey Lant, will show *you* how you can (achieve benefit audience/prospect wants)." Keep the focus on the prospect . . . never on yourself!

Likewise, get as much external media as possible:

- Achieving this objective is often difficult if you must work through a public relations representative or someone who regularly handles (or mishandles) publicity for the sponsor. He'll have his own ways of doing things and will probably never have met a person as focused as you are. Thus, make it clear you want to augment not usurp his functions. Begin by finding out precisely what he intends to do. Make your own publicity materials available and check in regularly to see how things are coming along. Promoting programs is often low priority work for these people and can easily get set aside.

- Whether there's a public relations person available or not, resolve to handle at least some of the publicity yourself. Identify media places that would do you good . . . a columnist or morning television or week-end radio show. Handle these important assignments yourself. If anyone questions this, simply say that you want to do your bit to make the program as successful as possible. You need never say you have a different, more important agenda.

- Contact the media you've selected as I've previously outlined in Chapter 6. Make it clear in your letters and other materials that you're working with the sponsoring organization and that a deadline is fast approaching. This should give you credibility and motivate faster action.

Note: whether you get print or electronic media, you clearly want to do two things — mention the forthcoming program and your own service business. If you handle this properly, you should have qualified leads for your business before you give your presentation and from people who won't even be attending it. Hurrah!

Step 11: Generating Leads The Day You Speak

The day you make your presentation is an important one for generating leads. Thus:

- Draw up a client-survey questionnaire asking participants to tell you what they're interested in. You need questions like these: "are you considering remodeling any room in your house in the next 12 months? If so, which ones (list) . . ."; "are you interested in helping do some of the work yourself and saving money? □ Yes □ No."; "What kinds of work do you want done? (Be as specific as possible.)"; "How much money have you budgeted for what you want done?," *etc.* The answers people give you are precisely what you need to know to make the right kind of follow-up approach.

- Whenever possible, arrive at your presentation at least 45 minutes early. Greet *everyone.* Hand *everyone* one of your questionnaires and ask them to return it to you at the conclusion of the program. *Note:* it's a good idea to arrange with someone attending to take over for you about 10 minutes before your program starts and keep handing out these questionnaires; (you'll be too busy). Equally, arrange for someone to stand at the door when the program is over to collect the completed forms. The key to this process is to get your audience/prospects to fill these forms out *on the spot*. Most people will. Others won't finish. Take what they've got done now and give them another form to take home. Remember, you can always work with them on the phone if you find out they're interested in your service.

- Make sure you get a list of all those attending with names, business names, addresses, and telephone numbers. Be sure to clarify in advance how you'll get this information.

- Make sure everyone present gets at least one piece of your client-centered marketing literature. If people at the meeting will be getting a folder or registration materials from the sponsor, arrange to have your materials in it. If participants get nothing from the sponsor, plan on handing your materials to everyone present. If you're giving a presentation accompanying food, arrange to have your materials on the plates before the meal starts. People have nothing better to do then; why not let them concentrate on your message!

- At the conclusion of your talk, invite people interested in getting the benefit you deliver to speak with you on the spot. Make the invitation warm and friendly. Because these are good prospects, ask for their cards and mark them with an "X" for immediate follow-up. Staple this to their client-survey questionnaire when you're back in the office.

You've now got lots of prospects to follow up!

Note: if the organization isn't taping your talk, tape it yourself — for two reasons. 1) Even if you're an experienced speaker, you should be listening to your presentation from time to time to see how it sounds after the fact. Where can you make improvements? 2) If you've given a good talk, packed with interesting material and benefits for the listener/prospect, you can use this as an offer in your other marketing (and provide it to media people and other program planners who need to hear what you sound like). Cassettes are inexpensive to reproduce and can either be sold for their informational content and/or used as freebie motivaters to get people to respond to your other marketing. Either way, make sure you give the tape a client-centered name. Also put a "C" (for copyright") on the tape and the year. This protects you and gives the tape greater perceived value. Don't forget to include your name, company name, address and phone number on the tape label, too. Yes, even this label is a marketing document!

Resource

For reproducing your tapes, I recommend contacting Larry Adams at Dove Enterprises, 907 Portage Trail, Cuyahoga Falls, OH 44221; (800-233-DOVE). His very reasonable prices include duplication, label printing, and see-through package.

Step 12: Generating Leads After You Speak

In addition to making an audio tape which can help generate additional leads after you speak, there are other things you can do to get maximum benefit from a single speaking engagement, even if it's no longer than 45 minutes. Try these:

- If the person handling the organization's publication is attending your presentation, make sure to see him. At that time, make sure everything's in order for both reporting this presentation and publishing future articles. If no one present is going to do a report on your talk, then give a copy of the cassette of your presentation to this person so someone can still do it afterwards. Too, nail down the details on future problem-solving process articles. If the person handling the organization's publication is not attending your presentation, call immediately afterwards to arrange these matters.

- Ask the program sponsor for two things: a testimonial and a referral. The testimonial should include information about the number of people attending, value of your information, how well you made your presentation, how interested and enthusiastic your audience was, whether they'd have you back and the writer's overall impression of what you did. The referral should be to another person known to the referrer who can sponsor your presentation. If you cannot get to the program sponsor the day of your presentation, contact him by letter the same day with a thank-you note for his assistance and a request for these two items.

- Once you have any combination of testimonial, referral, audio cassette of your presentation, and media about your presentation, start leveraging them to get further presentation dates and additional media. Send the appropriate material to both media personnel or program planners you have previously contacted unsuccessfully or those you have not yet contacted. Do this as soon as you have these materials. The fact that what you've got is fresh is very much in your favor and will help you get both media and more presentation dates . . . and, of course, additional leads.

- Take the best of the media you've received (whether a problem-solving process article, article about you and/or article about your presentation), and reprint on your letterhead. Again, if these materials suffer from weak headlines or incomplete follow-up details, add your own. Send these along with a note to client prospects or those with whom you want to bolster your relationship. With client prospects call within five business days and attempt to close the deal based on your new standing and reinforced contact.

- if the presentation you've made is to an eminent or prestigious organization, send a short take announcement about it to the publications of organizations you belong to, including civic, social, alumni, religious, professional, *etc*. Include your name, name of the presentation, name of the organization, date the presentation was made, place, number of people attending and other important details. Also include a line about your general business, service you provide and your company name, address and phone number. Just the fact that you've spoken somewhere can be turned into additional media . . . and the opportunity to generate additional publicity and leads for your company.

Step 13: Closing Business After Your Presentation

As I have continually stressed, the purpose of your presentation is not to make a presentation. It's to close business. It's easy to forget this in the heady excitement of giving a presentation and getting all the applause and personal satisfaction that come from this job well done. But you can't afford to forget this — like most service-selling speakers do.

Just recently, for example, I attended a full-day seminar on better communications that was given as part of a convention I was addressing. The speaker is a consultant who used her own (absurdly inadequate) marketing materials as the basis for the presentation. She kept talking about how she got business . . . but never understood that the session she was giving was also the basis for business generation. Neither before, during or after the program did she grasp that what she was doing could and should generate new contracts for her service business. Yet the woman claims to be a master communicator! Amazing!!! Don't you make this mistake. Understand that your real work begins when your presentation ends; for the usual speaker it is otherwise. When the applause starts, he's truly finished. Here, however, is what you have to do:

- Once back in your office, send an immediate thank-you note to the program planner and others who were helpful. Of course you want your referral and testimonial, but you also need to acknowledge their assistance, not least because you'll want their help again later.

- Then prioritize your leads. From the client-survey question-naires, comments, cards, *etc.* you've collected at the meeting, you'll have a sense of who the best prospects are. These get *immediate* telephone follow-up. When you call say simply, "From your questionnaire (or comments), it seems you want (benefit you deliver). I'd like to help you get it." Then assess the prospect's seriousness: what does he want, how badly does he want it, when does he want it, *etc.* From what you've learned at the meeting and what he tells you now, you should have a pretty good idea just how strong a prospect he is and be able to act accordingly.

- Other prospects, who do not seem to have the same degree of urgency or seriousness, you can follow up by letter. This letter should be developed *before* your talk so you can follow up even these less strong prospects fast. The letter should reinforce the benefit you provide/problem you solve, indicate you are available to work with the prospect, invite the prospect to call you to get started, and tell him when you'll call to follow up. You should be able to get this letter out immediately by creating a prospect data base when you get back to your office and importing the names into your letter. As necessary, you can add a few personal comments in a post script. The important thing, however, is that you indicate your control of the situation and the degree of your client-centeredness by following up as soon as possible both in this letter and, later, by phone.

Note: when you handle the generation of leads properly, you get a lot of leads quickly. The key is prioritizing those that you get and focusing on the best ones first. Don't make the mistake of treating all leads the same. Do stay focused on the people who have told you, in one way or another, that they've got the problem you can solve and want to solve it. Don't be afraid, as soon as you connect with them, to find out just how serious they are. Many service sellers make the mistake of treating all leads the same and of failing to discover just how serious a lead is about getting a solution. Ask and find out! If you discover that, just now, the lead isn't serious about going ahead — either because he doesn't have the interest or the resources — don't hesitate about lowering his priority and getting on to greener pastures. But make sure you log all the information about this prospect for future reference. Stay focused!

Step 14: Generate More Speaking Engagements

One of the benefits you get by delivering a good presentation is . . . more presentations. You've already got a good sense of how to get more engagements, but it's worth drawing your particular attention to this before closing this chapter. Here are the things you should be doing:

- If your presentation was the success it should have been (and by this I don't just mean you were good at the podium but that you got lots of good quality leads), contact the program planner right away and find out when you can come back. With each organization you speak to, you should be trying to discover how frequently it makes sense for you to speak and when to begin the process for returning.

- If your presentation was a success, you should talk to the program planner about doing other, related talks. If you've discovered that the sponsor reaches the kinds of people you want to reach and that this is a source of profitable business for you, go back to your brainstorming list and review your other program topics. Which ones are appropriate for this group? Let the program planner know you'd like to do other talks and plan accordingly.

- At the same time as you're solidifying and broadening your relationship with the first program planner, approach others in a logical way. Say you've made a presentation at the state chapter of a certain organization. If you draw clients from other states and from the nation at large, you need to discover the relevant information about whether this organization has other state chapters and a national organization.

If so, it's time to get networked into other engagements where you'll find the same kind of audience (and the same kinds of prospects).

- By the same token, once you've made a successful presentation at a particular kind of organization, you should be attempting presentations at related organizations. If, for instance, like one dietitian I recently counseled, you offer programs on diseases in meat, you should identify all the different kinds of meat and both the organizations (and companies) that deal with them. Moving laterally like this opens up many new markets where your current success gives you credibility.

- Equally, go back to program planners you previously had trouble contacting. You now have enhanced desirability; you've just offered a successful program. You are, therefore, not the person you were at the place you were and are more likely to get the connection you need. This is the time when you can turn indifference into an engagement . . . or at the very last make progress.

What you are seeing here is additional evidence that generating the leads you need is not the result of a series of isolated events but rather of operating and developing a carefully considered *process* from which each subsequent productive step naturally develops. Thus, while other speakers are bowing and basking in the (all too brief) afterglow of their success, convinced of what superior persons they are, you understand that what you have just accomplished constitutes a crucial *beginning* from which many additional advantages may be derived — *if you understand the system and take appropriate action.* This important insight constitutes one of the essential pillars of your success.

Last Words: A Few Tips About Speaking Style And Audience Rapport

Although this isn't a book about how to give the perfect presentation, I would like to leave this chapter with a few thoughts about how you can give the kind of presentation that will assist you in getting the leads you need. Sadly, public speaking constantly pops up on lists of what most people fear. This is unfortunate and unnecessary for everyone, but it's fatal for you. This kind of fear is a luxury you cannot afford; happily, it's also something you can do a lot about. Here's how:

- Before giving a presentation to any group, review about a year's worth of their publications. You're particularly looking for worthy articles relating to your presentation subject and to the names of prominent members of the organization. The way to get the attention of your group is to start your presentation by broadcasting as much praise as possible (in about 5 minutes) about these people. Don't forget to include the program planner, publications editor and others who have assisted you. These people are often the unsung heroes of events and rarely get the praise they're entitled to. Personally, when I became The Count of Raban, I instituted a special award called Companion of Raban. Here's what it looks like:

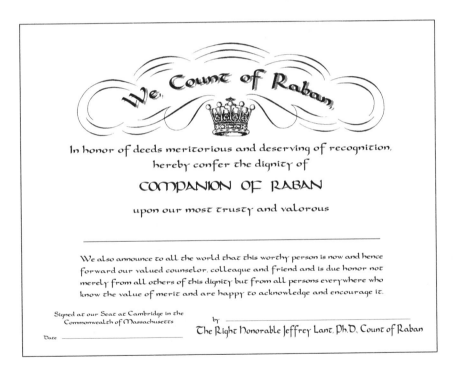

We, Count of Raban

In honor of deeds meritorious and deserving of recognition, hereby confer the dignity of

COMPANION OF RABAN

upon our most trusty and valorous

_____

We also announce to all the world that this worthy person is now and hence forward our valued counselor, colleague and friend and is due honor not merely from all others of this dignity but from all persons everywhere who know the value of merit and are happy to acknowledge and encourage it.

Signed at our Seat at Cambridge in the
Commonwealth of Massachusetts   by _____
                                        The Right Honorable Jeffrey Lant, Ph.D., Count of Raban
Date _____

I present this from the podium to people who have worked hard to make my presentation a success. Not only does it give me the opportunity to express my thanks . . . but it also constitutes a superb photo opportunity for both the honored one and myself. While you may not be able to put a count's coronet on your certificate, you should think about doing something similar.

- In your presentation, talk directly to people. Always say "you" . . . and look at people. You want each person in your audience to think you're talking to him and make each of them feel that you were there especially for him;

- Start your talk by reviewing the benefit the audience wants to achieve . . . or the problem they have and/or want to avoid. Talk to them as directly and candidly to them about these as you can;

- Then present your steps for what they have to do to get what they want. This is where "What Next?" thinking comes into play. As a service provider, you know that your prospects have to do certain things to get the results they want. Just tell them what these steps are in as much detail as time allows. By all means include telling anecdotes and interesting stories to make your points more compelling;

- If there are people in your audience who have made contributions in the area you're discussing, acknowledge them. I like to call on these people, entirely without warning, and have them get up and receive a round of applause. It staggers them . . . and they're blushingly grateful.

- At the end of your talk, invite people to come up to discuss their problems. Remind them that you solve these problems/deliver these benefits for a living, and you'd like to help them. Also, ask them to return the questionnaires they were given (hold up a copy) and indicate where they do so.

When you focus your presentation so squarely on your audience and what it wants and fears, lots of the usual issues discussed in speech books become insignificant:

- Should you write your talk or not? Since you know your subject well, an outline with your major points should suffice. Indeed these days I give 7-8 hour talks from an outline usually found on the back of an envelope in my jacket pocket. It's enough. This outline keeps me on track and enables me to focus my attention where it must go: on the prospects in the audience.

- What happens if you make a grammatical or diction mistake? Don't worry. When you focus on the audience, they're not hearing your mistakes; they're thinking about how what you're saying relates to them. In my early days on the speaking circuit, I was vividly aware as only a very sensitive young man can be about all the mistakes I was making as the result of a very enthusiastic delivery. I don't make so many of these errors today, but I still make my share. I get so caught up in helping the people in the audience that my language is less than the standard of the *Oxford English Dictionary*. You know something? No one has ever commented on this. Instead, they comment on the warmth of the presentation, the empathy, the amount of useful information imparted . . . in short on the things that relate to *them*. Learn from this.

• What happens if you can't give all the information you thought you'd be able to do? Say nothing. Just give as much as you can and never mention that you'd wanted to do more. If you've focused the presentation on the audience, they'll remember all they got . . . not what you left out. Especially if you don't remind them!

Talk presentations are a superb way of generating leads, often lots and lots of leads, quickly. What's more, they're a way of generating these leads while simultaneously bolstering your self esteem and professional standing. Now what could be better than that?

8

Generating Leads Through Direct Response Marketing

Look at the mail you received today. If you're like me, you got a pile of solicitations several inches deep from people using the mail to get leads and sell their products and services.

The net result of this daily avalanche of mail combined with all the other advertising and marketing solicitations we're subjected to is that more and more people have become skeptical about the entire marketing process and are regularly tuning out what they see and hear. This, I suspect, is a growing problem, and it's one that necessarily affects all of us whose income depends to a considerable extent on the success of our marketing. In the face of this threat, we service marketers need to be cleverer and more focused than ever so we can get what we want. This means being more knowledgeable about when and how to use direct response marketing.

Direct Response Marketing: A Definition

Direct response marketing is the process by which a marketer sends a designated prospect a client-centered marketing communication, ordinarily by mail. The prospect is supposed to be motivated through this communication either to immediately purchase the product or service through one of several means provided or to contact the marketer for further information, thereby continuing the sales process.

The Risks Of Direct Response Marketing

Few forms of marketing are as facile as direct response marketing. In that lies its charm — and the snare. To the uninitiated, direct response marketing (often called direct mail or, by the really uninitiated, "mail order") looks incredibly easy. Amateurs reckon that all they have to do is knock off a few hundred words of copy, have a marketing communication created, select some names to contact, pay the postage bill . . . and voilà, they'll be rich as Croesus. What's more, given the large number of people who provide ancillary services in this industry, they may not actually have to do anything to make this happen:

- a copywriter can craft the copy just so;
- a desk-top publisher will gladly handle the graphics and creation of the marketing piece;
- a list broker will select the names and have them delivered . . . directly to the mailing house if necessary, and
- a mailing house will affix the mailing labels, properly bundle the mailing pieces for lowest postage costs and take everything to the post office for delivery.

So clean! So easy! So dangerous!!! Dangerous? Yes, for several reasons:

- you can use all the processes of direct response marketing without understanding anything about how they work;
- the people you hire to provide the services listed above can all make money (that is, achieve their objective) even if you lose your shirt, and
- because of the cost of direct response marketing, you can lose a lot of money very fast, thereby effectively reducing your future marketing capacity.

This is why you need to think about whether you should be using direct marketing to get leads and how to make it most effective.

Understanding The Four Different Places Where You Get Your Leads

There are essentially four places where you can generate leads for your business. You can get them from people who are:

1. current customers. These are people who are currently buying your service and benefiting from it. Depending on what your service is, a "current" customer may actually be someone who hasn't purchased something for up to a year. Dentists, for instance, may only see their current customers every six months.

2. lapsed customers. These are people who bought from you at least once but who have not bought from you sufficiently recently to be reckoned current. Even though they achieved benefits once, they need to be lured back so you can sell to them again.

3. inquiries who never purchased. These people at one time told you they were interested in one of your benefits but either they never followed through or you were never able to close them. The real question here is how far back are these inquiries still good.

4. completely unconnected to your business. These are people who never inquired and never bought from you but whom you have good reason for thinking would be interested in the benefits you have available.

When you understand that these are the *only* four categories of leads that will ever be available to you and that they are in the order you should be approaching them, it's easy to see what you should be doing. Your marketing efforts should parallel the priority of these categories.

Moreover, these efforts should be made in the following way:

1. face-to-face contact;

2. telephone contact;

3. direct response contact.

Thus, the most effective marketing is face-to-face contact with current customers. The next most effective marketing is telephone contact with current customers. The next most effective is direct response contact with current customers, *etc.*

Of course, this isn't the way most service marketers work. They don't work this way for several reasons:

-   most service sellers don't like to be put in a situation where they can be rejected. They take this rejection personally and get depressed. When you personally ask even a happy current customer if he wants an additional service, more times than not he's going to say no. Service sellers don't want to hear this and turn to easier, less threatening, but not necessarily more profitable alternatives.

- service sellers are pressed for time. Face-to-face visits and telephone calls are more time-consuming than direct mail, especially when the necessary components of direct mail can be handled by others — for a price;

- service sellers are no less lazy than anyone else. Direct mail is the slothful individual's alternative. It's no surprise to me that one of the best known books in the field is entitled *The Lazy Man's Way to Riches* by Joe Karbo. Karbo's genius lay in recognizing how all of us are always looking for the easier, less taxing route, hoping against hope that it will work for us. (By the way, I don't recommend you get this book which is very thin on informational content. The book certainly describes Karbo's personal approach to his subject!)

Well, I'm here to tell you that direct response marketing isn't always the right thing to do. It depends on:

- how many people you have to contact;

- how easy they are to get hold of;

- how much time you have to get hold of them;

- when you need to get their business to reach your objectives;

- whether direct response marketing will get enough of them to contact you for a reasonable price that this form of marketing makes economic sense;

- whether you can achieve your economic objectives if only this number contact you.

Let's go through an example.

Say you're running a landscaping service in New England. You do lawns, planting, gardens, *etc.* Your work is largely seasonal with the period between April 1 and November 1 being prime time. You need about 50 home-owner accounts to reach your income objectives and last season you had 45. You've determined that you need to start marketing the beginning of January to line up the accounts you need for this season.

Your first impulse might be simply to send a letter (that is, a piece of direct response marketing) to all your past clients, reminding them of the benefits they got from you and the services you have available and inviting them to call and schedule your first visit. You could easily write, print out and mail a letter to 45 people in the course of a single morning. The cost would be just a few dollars plus your time.

The real question, however, is whether this is the *best* marketing route to take. And this is where the snare of direct response marketing comes in.

Think what happens when the prospect gets your letter. It's a wintry New England day. The thought of the problems he's going to have months from now with his grass, trees, and garden is not uppermost on his mind. He reckons he can wait. He reckons you'll follow up again. He reckons he can keep hibernating and therefore takes no action. Thus, while your letter will certainly secure *some* response, it probably isn't going to secure all the response you need. That's why instead of starting with direct response marketing, you should *start* with a plan:

1. set your objective — 50 home-owner accounts by April 1;

2. review the four categories of prospects and determine where you'll allot your marketing time and other resources;

3. put the focus on face-to-face visits and telephone contact with satisfied clients first;

4. then allot direct response marketing a role in the remainder of your marketing.

Thus, our landscape gardener should:

1. first call all his clients, remind them spring is coming along (it's easy to forget this during the long New England winter) and ask *when* they'd like to schedule his first visit. *Note:* the marketer shouldn't ask *if* they want him but *when* they want to schedule and *what* they'd like him to start on. In other words, he should make the assumption the relationship will continue and proceed accordingly. If the client has decided otherwise, this puts the onus on him to say so. And most people don't like delivering this disappointing message.

2. confirm initial appointments in writing with those he contacts and schedules with. (Of course, the marketer should have created this form before contacting anyone and have it available in his computer. This is the way *his* winter should have been spent!)

3. follow up any past clients he wasn't able to contact in person or by phone by sending a letter asking them to call him . . . or indicating when he'll call again. This is very focused direct response marketing.

This sequence will secure our marketer a substantial number of the clients he needs to reach his objective — without his using the traditional methods of direct response marketing at all!

Using A Variation Of This Routine With Lapsed Customers

Should our marketer be using direct response marketing with lapsed customers? Probably not. Let's say that 60 home-owners have used his services over the years but didn't use them during the last season. These constitute his "lapsed customers" data base.

The slothful marketer, enamored by the ease of direct response marketing, might automatically leap to the conclusion that the best way of handling these people is to send them a client-centered marketing communication that asks them to get in touch with the service provider to schedule an initial visit, discuss their landscaping needs, *etc.*

Whoa!

You know that direct response marketing is the *third* alternative you should be considering. Instead of automatically using it, try this:

1. Go through this list person by person to see if it even makes sense to contact them at all. Some of these home-owners may have moved; other people may be in those houses, but how you contact them will be different than how you contact lapsed customers. In any event, you need to review your data base before simply sending out a general letter, no matter how client-centered.

2. Set yourself an objective. You know that you need 50 household accounts to reach your financial objective. Let's say that of the 45 families using your services last year

you set as your goal getting 35 to review. Say you set as your goal getting 10 lapsed customers to renew.

3. Decide who should get initial face-to-face and/or telephone contact. Who can you simply go over and see to renew the engagement? Who does it make sense to call to schedule the initial visit? These are the most powerful kinds of marketing; you shouldn't automatically give up their advantages because sending a piece of direct response marketing is faster and easier. As above, you can confirm your engagement with a computer-generated follow-up letter written long before the reengagement is confirmed. (Obviously, with minor adjustments you can use such a letter for years once it's available on computer.)

4. Prospects you can't get in touch with in person or by phone should get a letter indicating that you've tried to be in touch, reminding them of the benefits you deliver, of the approaching season, of their need to make a decision, and asking them to contact you. Of course, you'll follow these up by phone yet again!

Where Direct Response Marketing Does Come In

The client-centered service marketer who works in this way with current and lapsed customers is going to secure the bulk of his business from them — the bulk, but not all. To get the remainder, direct response marketing does have a role to play. The question is, who gets the marketing communication? Direct response marketing may be sent to:

- people who have bought from you before;

- lapsed customers who haven't bought lately;

- people who have inquired about your benefit but have not taken the necessary action to acquire it, and

- people who have never inquired about your benefit and may not even know that you exist (painful though that is to admit!)

As you now know, in most cases I am not keen on having you begin your approach to the first two of these categories with direct response marketing unless you have:

- more clients than you can reasonably expect to see and/or telephone;

- no pressing need for new business;

- severely inadequate time in which to make these visits and calls;

- a deadline that can only be met by sending a direct response communication.

Contacting People Who Have Inquired About Your Benefit But Have Not Taken The Necessary Steps To Acquire It

Where direct response marketing begins to come into its own is with people who have inquired about your benefit but who never took the necessary steps to acquire it . . . or whom you were not able to close, for whatever reason.

Again, I must point out that too many service marketers automatically assume that these people must be contacted through a direct response communication. I do not agree.

Take our landscape gardener. Say that using the various means presented in this book, he now has acquired a data base of 250 people who have over the last two years expressed an interest in having their grass cut, hedges trimmed, trees taken care of, *etc.* by his firm. He has acquired these people from:

- an appearance on a local radio station;

- a speech he gave at the local Kiwanis club and accompanying article;

- two problem-solving process articles in the town newspaper;

- an ad in the yellow pages, *etc.*

Many of those inquiring, however, have not yet purchased the benefits he has available. What should he do? Obviously, sending a direct response communication to them is the fastest and easiest thing to do. But it is not necessarily the most effective.

Personally, I would divide his list into two parts:

- prospects the marketers talked to personally and/or who are less than 1 year old;

- the remainder.

Then I would set an objective. He needs at least 5 of these prospects to sign up for his service and given the fact that all those who say they'll buy from him probably won't follow through, he should set as his objective getting 10 to sign up, thus providing a certain margin for himself.

Say that there are 100 leads in the first category. As before, he should attempt to either personally visit and/or telephone each of them, as above. This will enable him both to 1) sign up people immediately and follow up accordingly and 2) discover, among those not yet ready to buy, who the good prospects are and handle them in the right way, too. Only those he cannot contact in any other way . . . and those who are the older, less good prospects . . . should he handle solely through direct response marketing, through means outlined below.

The Relationship Of Direct Response Marketing To Those Who Have Never Inquired About Your Service And May Have No Idea Whatsoever About You And What You Do

This is the category where direct response marketing truly comes into its own. But remember our example of the landscape service marketer. He's already got a plan by which he can reach his objective without factoring in this category; indeed, his plan already includes a margin for error and attrition. Thus, *this* category is a true cushion.

The question is, why then would he even want to use direct response marketing?

1. as a means of absolutely ensuring that he reaches his financial objective, and

2. to start familiarizing future customers with his benefits, name, firm, services, *etc.*, in other words as part of The Rule of Seven.

Note: before approaching any prospects who have not necessarily heard of him and don't already know something about the benefits this marketer provides, he should think long and hard. Before automatically leaping to the use of direct response marketing, shouldn't he either reapproach lead-generating sources that have already proven to be successful (another problem solving article? Another speech at a local service organization with accompanying article about him, *etc.*)? I certainly would. In other words, sources which generate leads which can be turned less expensively into qualified prospects should always be reviewed and used first before more expensive direct response marketing is attempted.

Let's assume that our marketer has approached direct response marketing with the deliberation and caution it deserves. Let's suppose that he's correctly factored in current clients, lapsed clients, people who have inquired but not bought, *etc.* into his mix and that he still wants or even has to use direct response marketing to reach his objective. Fair enough. Now he must begin understanding what makes direct response marketing work.

What Makes Direct Response Marketing Profitable

Although there are many direct response marketing "doctors" around, all with their books, tapes and seminars, I treat such people with more than a grain of salt. Too many of them make direct response marketing seem like a picnic in the park, when, for many, it has proven a costly and disillusioning snare.

Direct response marketing works because these three things work:

- the client-centered copy;
- the offer;
- the list.

If any one of these three things is incorrect, your direct response marketing is very likely to fail, probably causing you to lose money, perhaps all your money.

In this connection, I think of an obstinate computer consultant I know who decided to blow her complete marketing budget producing about 1000 gorgeous brochures, each of which cost $8. While the graphics, paper, ink and general presentation were excellent, the copy was "me-centered" (the general failing of most marketing documents), there was no offer and the list was compiled, that is only made up of names taken from the telephone directory. Despite the fact that she'd spent wildly on her luxurious mailing pieces (to the benefit of all those who helped produced them), the result was disastrous: there wasn't a single response. As a result $8000 was lost. And this is by no means an extreme example either . . .

We've already spent a lot of time (and will spend more before this chapter is over) discussing the client-centered copy and the offer. Now it's time to discuss The List.

Finding The Right People To Contact Through Direct Response Marketing

There are really just three kinds of lists:

- proven buyers of either a service just like you sell . . . or a product or service that's related to what you offer;

- people who have subscribed to a publication in your field, or

- people who have been compiled from telephone books, professional directories and other data bases of names, addresses and telephone numbers.

I have put these different types of lists in priority order with the most important first. A name, you see, is not a name is not a name. The question therefore of whom you mail your offer to must engage your serious consideration.

Take our landscape service provider.

- His house list is his strongest data base of names. It consists of proven buyers of his service (and those who have inquired about it). It is strongest both because people on it have already directly benefited from what he has available and because they hear from him most often thereby increasing their familiarity and decreasing their disinterest and distrust.

- The next strongest lists will be provided by people who either have services like his or provide related products and services. Who would have such lists? In this case, green houses, garden centers, plant stores, stores selling lawn mowers and other lawn and garden equipment, new home contractors — and other lawn care service providers. Some of these are in direct competition — other lawn-care service providers — and would be unlikely to make their lists available. Others are not and may be amenable to a deal.

- The next best are lists of subscribers to publications in his field. Problem is, if he's exclusively a local service provider they may not have enough readers in the target marketing area or, because they have a minimum order, the marketer may have to acquire many more names than he actually needs.

- Finally, there are compiled lists of, say, all home owners in the community.

Looking at these four sources of names should suggest how you want to approach the entire business of the list:

- Your first priority should be developing your house list. That is, getting people to inform you that they are interested in the benefits you provide. This list is obviously of the greatest value in bringing your benefits to the attention of people who have indicated their interest and thereby enabling you to close sales. But it is also valuable as a means of swapping for the names of others. (*Note:* most service providers never develop a sufficiently large mailing list that they can draw rental income from it which is yet another benefit of a list sufficiently large.)

- While you'll be spending a lot of time developing your list, you also should be spending time finding out others who have the names of people you want to reach. First, brainstorm all the likely possibilities. Since many of these people will be small businesses like you, they are unlikely to have their lists formally on the market (you can always ask, of course). However, you should call and ask if they do, how many names they have available, the form the names are in and what the rental cost might be. What you'll find in this exercise will probably horrify you. To my astonishment, many service businesses either have no mailing list or only the most rudimentary one. Further, they will not have their names set up in a data base that is both easy to use and easy to swap. The best data bases are set up so that the names can easily be duplicated on to a diskette and printed out as labels. You should also be able to find out how old the names are (current quarter names are always the best), whether the people bought anything, and when the list was last cleaned. Sure, the local garden center may maintain a list of names, but unless you're able to get this information, even if you're able to rent the names or get them on a swap, you may be getting junk. *Note:* by the way, while you're inquiring about these various lists, make sure you get your name on them. This way you can track what these businesses send out, discern whether there is a real compatibility between their audience and yours, and see how long your name stays on without your buying anything, thus indicating that the owner doesn't clean the list very often, if at all.

Many businesses of products and services compatible with yours have never thought of renting their names. Probably no one has ever asked before. Thus, do the following:

- Try to get a name swap, name for name. Swap, say, 1000 of your latest leads and buyers for 1000 of theirs. Besides swapping names , however, swap impact. That is, tell the list owners you'll be willing to write a letter of endorsement for their product/service to your mailing list . . . if they'll do the same for yours. Each of you is thereby piggybacking on the familiarity of the other with his own list.

- If a swap isn't in order (because one party has more names than the other), try swapping service for names. I do this all the time.

- If you still can't make a deal, suggest renting the names for $50 per thousand for one time usage, a low price but one the list owner might accept, especially if you let him know this is your top offer. The list owner may reckon that getting $50 is better than getting nothing.

To my utter astonishment, service firms waste millions and millions of dollars yearly renting the wrong names and mailing the wrong mailing pieces to them. This money gets wasted because:

1. the names themselves are junk. (It's a scandal just how many list owners put names on the market that are completely worthless and yet charge anywhere between $75-$150 per thousand for them.)

2. the names are incorrect for the offer they're getting, or

3. the copy and offer are wrong.

No one, not even pros with years of experience, are immune from wasting their money in this way (sadly, I speak from experience), but such waste is killing to smaller service sellers who do not have the luxury of throwing their money away in this fashion without really feeling it. This is why, whenever possible, I try to find the lists of compatible product and service sellers, even if their lists are often not conveniently arranged for immediate use.

Renting Names From A List Broker

We have now arrived after a lengthy discussion at the place where unwary service sellers *begin*, renting names. It is now time for me to tell you something very important. As you know, I am a very heavy mailer with my catalog, card deck, *etc.* But I want you to know that by following my own advice and the steps I've given you, I didn't even spend $1 on the rental of lists in the two years. The money that was saved was:

- invested in additional marketing gambits, and
- increased my profit accordingly.

I am not saying that I will never again actually pay to rent mailing lists, but I am telling you that I will do EVERYTHING POSSIBLE to make sure that I don't spend my money on mailing lists first but only after I've exhausted all other options.

. . . Now that you know this sobering fact, we're ready to take on the general subject of the list broker and how to work with him to your advantage.

— *Before you approach a list broker*

The average service marketer goes to the yellow pages, looks under "mailing lists", calls the first broker and rents some names — which ordinarily do not produce the response he wants. The broker, of course, doesn't care; he's gotten paid. If you query him about your poor result, he's fertile in excuses citing 1) the weakness of your mailing piece; 2) the lack of a strong, pulling offer; 3) the fact that others who just used the same list did fantastically and he can't figure out why you didn't; 4) that obviously this wasn't the list for you after all (you can't always be right, after all) and you ought to try another he's prepared to recommend, 5) the economy's bad, *etc., etc.* In short, he doesn't know, doesn't care, and will say *anything* to get you off the line. Get prepared for this . . . most list brokers, even if they start reputable, end up by saying anything to shift the blame from the fact that they don't understand your business, don't really know how good the lists are they'll rent you, and haven' t got a clue how well your offer will do. However, as you must understand, they can do perfectly well in their line of work without knowing any of these things . . . indeed, without delivering a reasonable product at all. After all . . . there are lots of stupid people renting lists every day. Thus, you've got to do your homework before you ever approach the list broker.

- You need to be very clear about whom you want to reach. Take our landscaper, for instance. While all homeowners have lawns, trees , *etc.*, not all have the money to pay for landscaping assistance. It's the marketer, therefore, and not the list broker who needs to know where his likeliest clients are, the streets in his marketing territory where the wealthiest people live.

- Once you are clear about who you want to reach, you need to draft your mailing piece. For one thing the list broker will have to run this by the list owner, who has final say about who gets access to his names. For another, the list broker can make better suggestions if he knows who you're trying to reach, your offer, direction, *etc.*

— *When you talk to the list broker*

Having done your homework, then contact a list broker.

- To begin with, don't just call one list broker. Call at least three. You need to see which one is most organized and helpful. There are so many slimy people in the list brokerage field that the odds of your hitting a truly qualified professional on your first phone call are not high.

- It is to your benefit to mail or fax a description of who you're trying to reach and your mailing piece to the list broker before you get down to cases. He needs to consider it at leisure before making suggestions, and you should plan accordingly.

- Make sure the list broker has time to talk when you call. I've found list brokers notoriously distracted people with conversations constantly interrupted by incoming phone calls, being put on hold, *etc.* Novice or experienced veteran, you need the opportunity to explain what you're trying to do and the list broker needs to pay close attention.

- Don't just listen to the broker's recommendations; get them in writing. Compilers have catalogs of the lists they have available. List owners have data cards with detailed information about the number of people on the list, demographic details, who the list should be used by, *etc*. The list broker can get this information to you for your review.

- Don't be rushed. The list broker makes his money as soon as you pay for the list rental. While in practice you may get 30-day credit terms, he is still getting paid before you are, so of course he's anxious for you to go ahead, ready or not. Ask for a referral to someone who has used this list. The list broker can get this information from the list owner. This person has at least been notified about who's been using his names and may even have kept the information on file! I do.

As you consider the lists the broker has recommended, remember these points:

- Buyer lists are the most expensive of all. However, if the list is good, these should be the best names, since these people have either bought the same kind of thing you offer or something similar in a given period of time. So-called "hot line" names are ordinarily the best of all since these are buyers who have bought within the last 90 days;

- Subscription lists mean that the person hasn't bought anything except a subscription. If, however, the subscription is to a publication featuring items relating to your service, this could well prove a lucrative list;

- Compiled lists mean the person hasn't bought anything at all and is about as cold a contact as they get. Also, with compiled lists you may pay extra for an actual name; many compiled lists use a function or business title instead of a name to mail to. The name may cost more.

Also, because testing is a fundamental pillar of direct response marketing, make sure your initial order of any list is the smallest available. Unfortunately, this is probably going to mean an order of 5,000 names. This is still pretty large for most service businesses, particularly those with a limited marketing territory. That's life. List brokers run a service business, and they like this quantity since it gives them a reasonable base commission.

Finally, unless you are using a single list (which itself constitutes a code) make sure your address label is coded. The best way is opening a file in your computer and simply inputting the lists and codes you use, thus code "1A" in the upper right hand corner of your mailing label would equal the name of the list, mailing date, marketing communication used and, ultimately, the response and money generated.

Note: As you see, I'm trying to get you to be very thoughtful and deliberate about your use of direct response marketing and, in this case, your list acquisition and rental strategies. However, for the service seller there is one very bright spot in all this: the higher cost of most services *vis a vis* most products means that we can both recapture our investment dollars and start making real money faster. This is why when we service sellers create really client-centered copy, craft compelling offers and use the right prospect lists we can do so very well with even a limited amount of direct response marketing.

Resource

One of the largest catalogs of compiled lists is produced by American Business Lists, 5711 South 86th Circle, P. O. Box 27347, Omaha , NE 68127. (402) 331-7169. Also see *The National Directory of Mailing Lists.* Published by Oxbridge Communications, it lists over 20,000 mailing lists. (212) 741-0231.

Squeezing The Most From Your Direct Response Communications

I've spent a lot of time warning you about direct response marketing and suggesting the occasions when you shouldn't use it. But now it's time to turn our full attention to how you can make money from it. Here are the 8 steps:

- Have an objective;
- Set up your response system so you're ready for the people contacting you;
- Review the direct response formats you can use;
- Select the most appropriate format(s) given your budget and need to hit your prospects more than once;
- Develop the client-centered message and offer;

- Accentuate the positive;
- Remember The Rule of Seven;
- Once you've mailed, mail again.

Step 1: **Have An Objective**

As should be clear to you by now, every aspect of your marketing needs a specific objective. Thus, your direct response marketing needs one, too. Just what this objective will be is going to vary depending on the number of years you've been in business, how many current and past customers you've got, how many inquiries you've generated in the last couple of years, *etc.* If today is your very first day in business, the two most likely sources of business (current and past customers) are not available to you. You will therefore be spending much more time generating leads and will have to concentrate more on direct mail. The rest of us will be using direct response marketing to complete our client list, a situation I prefer.

Either way, you've got to set a precise objective for your direct response marketing. Write it down. Look at it. Memorize it. Work to achieve it. I am an objectives fanatic . . . and you should be, too.

Step 2: **Set Up Your Response System So You're Ready For the People Contacting You**

While writing this chapter, I was talking to one of my new clients who produces trade show banners. He told me that while his last marketing gambit made money, most of the leads he received never got anything more than a brochure thrown in an envelope; there were too many of them, and he never got around to following up . . . much less closing them. In short, he wasn't *ready* for the response.

I hear this complaint constantly, and it staggers me. That's why I've constantly advocated that you get prepared for your leads . . . before you get any responses to any of your marketing activities. This means:

- thinking through what you'll say when they call;
- getting your letters and other response materials ready *before* they contact you;
- getting your computer set up to easily enter inquiry records;

- ensuring that all your follow-up steps have been plotted and the relevant materials created, *etc.*

Client-centered direct response marketing is going to get you responses . . . lots and lots of responses. The key, however, is that when someone responds, you must be ready to qualify them immediately and take the appropriate action to begin the closing process. If there is a failure to close it must be because the prospect has no money (or cannot, for some equally valid reason, go ahead now), not because you were unprepared.

Step 3: Review The Direct Response Formats You Can Use

Once you're ready to handle the responses you generate, you need to take the steps that will ensure you get the number you need. Start by reviewing the various formats you can use to connect with the prospect and generate his action. You can use:

- glossy four-color brochures;
- brochures with color photographs;
- six-page sales letters;
- three-fold brochures;
- question-and-answer flyers;
- two-page sales letters with brochure and response card;
- post cards, *etc.*

Before you make any decisions about these items, open a "sample" folder (a cardboard box will do nicely); throw all the sales materials you get for a couple of weeks into it. In that period, you will probably see most of the available formats. You need to study these for both format and presentation styles . . . now and on a regular basis. Marketing is necessarily a copycat business. There's absolutely nothing wrong with getting inspired by both the good (and the not-so-good) things you see and acting accordingly.

As you review these materials you need to keep two things in mind: 1) what ideas can you get that will improve what you send, and 2) how can you spend the least amount of money to get materials with the greatest impact?

As for the first point, you should be looking for how marketers handle:

- the outside envelope. What envelope teasers and messages are effective both in terms of message, placement and presentation?

- offers. Where have the most effective offers been placed? How have they been written and emphasized?

- the presentation of benefits. Making sure the prospect is excited by the benefits is a crucial part of successful direct response marketing. What have the best marketers said? How have they said it? How have they stressed the benefits they've got?

- objections. There isn't a service under the sun that doesn't have objections to it that must be dealt with. The key is understanding this and seeing how other marketers handle them.

- testimonials. Who's using client-centered testimonials? What's in them . . . and how are they used?

- post scripts. It is a cliché in the business that post scripts are important. You need to review the kinds of messages that are being put in them, and evaluate how effectively they are being crafted and used.

In short, you must subject the pieces you receive to a constant scrutiny, never scrupling to use the most effective of what you see . . . and avoid the rest. Everyday's mail is for you another class in direct response marketing, and I, for one, have always been astonished at the number of otherwise intelligent people who tell me with a kind of superior sniff that they never read what comes in — but throw it all away unconsidered. This kind of breathtaking stupidity and myopia are beyond my understanding. As for me, I hope I never miss the opportunity to learn both from the good and bad of what others in this business are doing. Frankly, I consider my ability to remain open to their ideas one of my best features and the reason why my own direct response copy has sharpened over the years.

By the same token, you need to pay particular attention to those marketing formats that are both successful and inexpensive. Any nit wit, you see, can spend money to produce expensive marketing communications. There's no talent in that. Where the brains come in is seeing how *little* you can spend to generate the maximum response.

For one thing, it should be your constant objective to keep your marketing expenses to the lowest possible amount that produces the necessary quota. For another, you've got to keep in mind that you can't spend all your money on hitting your prospects just once; you need to spend the minimum so you can hit them over and over again. Remember, the computer consultant I told you about who spent $8,000 producing 1000 brochures and mailing them — once. She got NO RESPONSE. Had she listened to what I told her, she would have found the appropriate format that would have enabled her to bring a client-centered message to the attention of her prospects several times . . . compelling their response. This means keeping your budget firmly in mind and mastering such inexpensive marketing formats as:

- post cards. You can use black ink on a stock color . . . or a solid color ink screened for second color effect on white stock;

- single-page computer-generated letter printed on continuous feed paper;

- a two-page computer-generated letter with tear-off response coupon at the bottom of the second page;

- a self-mailer flyer printed on stock colored paper;

- a simple three-fold brochure placed in an envelope with unstamped response card.

At first glance, you may be inclined to sniff at these formats as so many unsophisticated marketers do. That would be a big mistake.

Service sellers who are ego-invested will be inclined to dismiss these formats as insufficiently grand for the kinds of people they are. However, making a decision based on ego instead of bedrock marketing principles is a serious error — yet one I see constantly.

Why, just as I was writing this chapter, I was hired by a New Hampshire high-tech company to review two of its marketing documents, the main one being an expensive four-color brochure on glossy stock; an expensive item indeed. Problem was, it wasn't generating any response. This hardly surprised me given the fact that it was:

- me-centered;

- had no motivating offer;

- didn't pile one tantalizing benefit on another, and

- never made it clear who it was addressing itself to.

In short, the whole thing was a colossal waste of time and money. Idiotic!

How much better would it have been for the ego-maniacs running this business to have determined their marketing budget . . . then studied the available formats and worked hard to create a client-centered message which they should then have thrust home to their prospects over and over again through a series of cost-effective, reasonably priced formats. Instead, ego, not sense, drove their feeble marketing effects . . . with predictably limp results.

Don't let this happen to you.

Remember this crucial fact: your prospects want the BENEFITS you can deliver. Your packaging and presentation should not overwhelm these benefits nor should they undercut them by being inadequate. Instead, they must be appropriate for your business and what you are trying to accomplish. In short, format and presentation, either because too little or too much, must not be where the prospect focuses his attention; that must remain focused on the benefits you offer.

Step 4: Select The Most Appropriate Format(s) Given Your Budget And Need To Hit Your Prospects More Than Once

It's now selection time . . . what *formats* will you use given these objectives:

1. generating the largest prospect response in the shortest period of time;

2. utilizing your limited marketing resources to hit your prospects the maximum number of times in order to secure your client objective;

3. keeping your presentation professional but allowing it neither to overwhelm nor undercut your client-centered message?

Thus, say you are the landscape service provider discussed above. Say he has determined that he needs 10 more homeowner accounts and has an available marketing budget of $1000 for his direct response marketing. How should he spent it for maximum effect?

- First, he must realize he should not just hit his designated prospects once, but several times. This means that one large mailing is not a good idea.

- Because he's going to hit the same people as often as possible, he must be very cautious about the names he uses. *Note:* if he can not secure names other ways and is forced to resort to a list broker with a minimum of 5,000 names, he should see if he can get the same 1000 names five times for the base price.

- Once he's determined the right mailing list, he should brainstorm ways of reaching these people. Just how many people are being contacted will significantly influence which format is selected. Thus, if the marketer is contacting 1000 people, post cards and/or self-mailer flyers make sense. *Note:* the marketer can reduce his expenses by reusing the same mailing piece to the same people. Thus, he can send Mailing Piece I to his target group the beginning of the month and the *same* mailing piece to the *same* target group three to four weeks later. So long as the client-centered benefits are strong, using the same piece is not a problem. If the marketer wishes to distinguish the second mailing piece from the first, he can change the mailing panel or even the top of the inside panel by including a new headline like DON'T DELAY. ONLY (NUMBER) SPACES LEFT. It is easy to make this change when the document is first printed and costs very little. Printing all the documents you need at the same time will result in cost savings.

- Whatever formats you select at this point are tentative. You need to get budget quotes to make sure you can afford the several prospect hits you need to generate maximum response. As you get these budget quotes, remember to ask suppliers you are working with how you can cut the cost. Is there a less expensive paper you can use? A way of cutting your color cost? Don't be afraid to ask. The printer doesn't care if you achieve your prospect objective or not. But you do . . . and that's why you need to ask.

Before making your final format selections, take a sheet of paper (or work in your computer). Head the page with the objective you're trying to achieve. List the amount of money you have to work with. Then list the format you've selected and date you intend to use it. *Remember:* if you are trying to hit your objective within a brief period (like our landscape service seller), you'll be using your formats within brief periods of time, such as every two-four weeks.

Step 5: Develop The Client-Centered Message And Offer

Once you've selected the formats that will enable you to hit your prospects the greatest number of times within your budget limitations while still making a solid professional presentation, it's time to shape the message to the format.

In beginning this topic, I want to make it perfectly clear that all marketing copy is related. That is, what goes into a glossy four-color document is generically similar to what goes into a simple 8 1/2" x 11" flyer. This is because the objectives of these documents are similar: either getting a prospect to buy immediately or getting the prospect to tell you he's interested in learning more about the service you're offering. The difference between marketing documents is mainly the space you have available to provide your motivating benefits. Remember: all marketing documents should be primarily *selling*, not just *telling*, documents.

Now, because of the work you've already done (see Chapter 3), you already have available on computer the basic elements for the documents you want to create, namely:

- benefits;
- offers;
- testimonials,

and such ancillary components as envelope teasers, post scripts, *etc.*

This is not the moment to write these components . . . it's the moment to *craft* them so that they are most compelling given the space the format affords you. To show you what I mean, say that you've determined to use the following direct response formats during a six week period to gain new clients:

- post card I;
- post card II;
- self-mailer flyer I.

How do you arrange the copy for maximum impact?

First, diagram the formats you're going to use and see where the necessary components go.

Post Card I Front (Message) Side

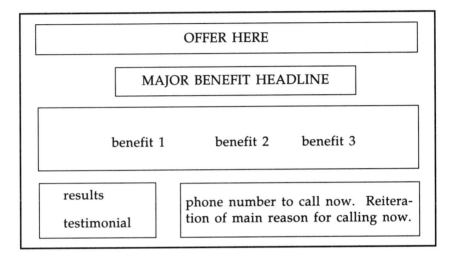

Post Card I Reverse (Address) Side

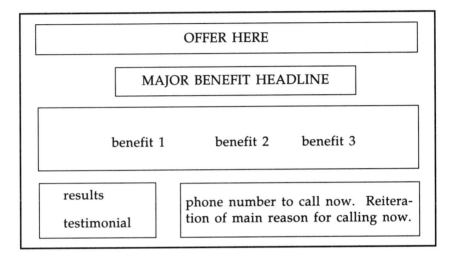

Post Card II

Follow the same format as Post Card I.

Self-Mailer Flyer I

This follows the same format, too! Here, however, you have more space for benefits . . . more space for testimonials . . . and more space for your offer. In short, Self-Mailer Flyer I and Post Cards I and II are generically the same; different only in the amount of space you have to build your case for immediate prospect response.

Let's say you decided to use *this* combination to motivate your prospects to respond immediately:

- Client-centered Letter I with three-fold brochure and response card;
- Client-centered Letter II ditto;
- Post Card I.

The first thing you've got to keep in mind is that every marketing document is a *response* document. No marketing document is simply about passively disseminating information about you and your service. While different documents may work in different ways to accentuate action, *every document is about motivating action*. Thus in Client-centered Letter I, you:

- Provide an envelope teaser of your best offer . . . that's where the prospect's eye will see it first;
- Lead off your letter with a complete rendition of this offer in the upper right-hand corner, making sure you remember to limit this offer in some way (as with a limited quantity or date when the offer expires);
- Then create a salutation that includes the benefit you have available (as "Dear neighbor who doesn't want to cut grass this summer");
- Open with the pain you take away or the gain you provide;
- Then list the major benefits you provide in priority order, most important first;
- Reinforce these benefits with client-centered testimonials from satisfied customers who have achieved substantial results;

- Then close the letter with a post script that underscores the benefit you provide and again asks for *immediate action.*

Your three-fold brochure works along with this letter. It consists of:

- an opening panel asking the prospect to call now to get the main benefit you offer;

- three inside panels (which can be designed as a single sheet instead of three panels) providing client-centered information about the benefits you offer, special aspects of your work, the best way for the client to get his money's worth from what you offer, further testimonials from satisfied clients, why yours is the best service (facts, please, not hype), and information about how long you've been in business, how many satisfied customers you've served, and anything else that makes the prospect want to do business with you now.

Your response card is simply that. It asks the prospect either to sign up now to get the benefit you deliver . . . or tell you he wants you to call and close the deal, thus:

☐ Yes, I don't want to cut my lawn this summer. I'm ready to sign up now so you can do it for me! (payment details follow), or

☐ Yes, I want to know more about having you cut my lawn this summer and spare me all that aggravation and bother. Call me now at (prospect adds his phone number here).

In other words, the prospect isn't so much telling you he wants to hire you . . . as informing you in no uncertain terms he wants the benefit you provide or wants to avoid the pain you take away.

Client-Centered Letter II

This is more of the same. Indeed, it can be the *exact* package except with a message saying something like, "I can't believe you want to cut your own grass this summer. Haven't you got something better to do with your time? Call me now so you won't have to!"

Post Card I

Here you *again* emphasize the benefits you provide and any special offer you're making . . . and you let the prospect know you only have a certain number of spaces left; that he must act now to acquire them . . . or he'll miss the benefit you have/keep the pain he doesn't want.

Note: The emphasis on these materials is generating leads, not making an immediate sale. Unless your prospects know you, they're probably not going to buy your service from a card or letter. But what they will do is tell you they want to hear from you to learn more about how they can get the benefit you offer. Further, most services are too expensive to sell directly from these communications. That's why your focus in these documents should be to get a prospect to tell you, "Yes, I want (benefit you offer)", or "Yes, I want to know how to get rid of (pain you take away)."

Obviously, as you're drafting these documents you don't need to be overcritical with yourself. You should be more worried that you're not overwhelming with copy the available space provided by the format. However, once you've finished Draft I, then you've got to go through and read with minute scrutiny:

- *each* word;
- *each* line;
- *each* paragraph;
- *each* page.

Each thing you put in a marketing communication either helps you achieve the objective of that communication . . . or it obstructs this achievement. Now read what you've produced critically:

- Is the line you're proposing to use going to get a person to take action to acquire the benefit you say you have available . . . or not?

- Is there anything in the document that slows the reader down . . . makes him pause and ponder? Remember: the objective of every document is not to get the prospect to think but to ACT! REMEMBER: THOUGHT BAD, ACTION GOOD!

This is the moment to apply such scrutiny and to be hard on yourself, because I tell you truly: the marketplace is unforgiving. If the prospect slows down, gets perplexed, doesn't see the benefit immediately, can't understand what you're driving at, or just plain has to work too hard to get to the meat in what you're offering, he'll trash your marketing communication in a flash . . . which is about as final and unforgiving as can be imagined. Think! All your hard work, your research, thoughtful reflection, drafting, consideration, and, imagine!, your money — all thrown away in an instant . . . if the prospect doesn't see the benefits you have available and doesn't know how to acquire them immediately.

It is to avoid this drastic fate that you must give earnest and sustained consideration to every crumb that goes into each of your marketing communications so that you don't endure not merely the ignominy but the destructive waste of having what you've worked so hard to produce trashed at once.

Step 6: **Accentuate The Positive**

To help achieve this objective, you've got to learn a whole new style of communication. As I've previously told you, this consists in using such devices as:

- underlining;
- bold;
- italic;
- bullets;
- indentation;
- capital letters;
- emphasized punctuation;
- ellipses, *etc., etc., etc.*

Now's the moment to use them.

With these devices you are able to create what I call the Internal Message. That is, you are able to so mark crucial words and ideas that the prospect can get the idea of the important benefits you provide without having to read every single word you've written. Take a look at the example on the following pages.

THE NEXT DECK CLOSES DECEMBER 1, 1992 AND MAILS JANUARY 3, 1993. ACT NOW.

Jeffrey Lant Associates, Inc.
50 Follen St. #507
Cambridge, MA 02138
(617) 547-6372

AS OF TODAY. . . . 11 CARDS LEFT FOR JANUARY!!

November 1, 1992

Dear Colleague Seeking The Maximum Number Of Low-Cost Leads:

My Sales & Marketing SuccessDek can make you *rich*!

But you're going to have to hustle to take advantage of what we can do for you. The closing date for my next deck is December 1 — and if you don't move fast YOU'RE GOING TO MISS THE BOAT!

We're already well along towards filling up the next issue (mailing January 3, 1993). No wonder. <u>My decks have always filled up fast.</u> Here's why:

1. My deck offers *100,000 card-deck responsive names*. Other decks offer inferior subscription or compiled names. Not me. 100% of the business decision makers we mail to have already responded to an offer in a business card deck . . . within the last 90 days! Therefore you are assured of getting to people who not only want offers that help them . . . but are willing to respond IMMEDIATELY.

2. My prices. No one in the entire industry offers you prices like mine. *We've been the lowest since our first day of business; we're the lowest now.* $650 for 50,000 cards; $1199 for 100,000 two-color cards and $1350 for 100,000 four-color cards. *No one in the industry is remotely close to us in price.* (You could pay over $3,000 more if you go with someone else.) Check STANDARD RATE & DATA for yourself. If money is important to you, we're the right place for you. We can offer you the lowest cost — and hence the *lowest per-lead cost* — in the whole card-deck industry.

   Why are our prices so low? First, we pre-pay our printing bill and pass on the savings to you. Second, we give no credit. Everyone pays for their card up front. This way, we don't have to bear the heavy cost of credit . . . and we pass all these savings on to you. Moreover, I participate in the deck myself . . . with up to 7 cards. So I make money just like you do . . . by selling my products/services.

No other publisher in the industry advertises as heavily in his own deck as I do. Other decks make their money the minute you buy their card; they are principally card-deck publishers. *We make money like you do — by selling our products and services through the deck.* I hope you understand this difference — it's crucial to why our deck works so well.

3. *Free second color.* Other decks charge you for color. I don't. If you want a second color, you get it free. And if you need help deciding where to put this color, we'll tell you.

4. *Free copy writing assistance.* If you need help with your copy, you get it — free. Other decks don't offer this service. We do. We know what's going to get you the best results, and we're happy to work with you — at no charge — so you get them. And we can do it fast, too: we can create a card right down to November 28th . . . two days before the deadline. But please don't wait this long!

5. *Free Top 20 positions.* Our policy is that if you pay for your card 60 days before publication, you get a Top 20 position (if any are left; they're obviously limited). The deadline for this for the January 3 deck is November 3!!! After that, I give preference for any top spots that are left to people who are first-time advertisers with me. Other decks generally reserve all their top spots for people who either 1) pay more for them or 2) are their best advertisers. I give the benefit of place (whenever possible) to the little guys. However, I don't hold any space at all until I've got a signed Insertion Order from you. (I've enclosed one.)

For these reasons it's no wonder *my deck fills up fast.* But there's more . . . During the last two years encompassing war & recession, the biggest decks in the industry have generally gone down in size by about 1/3; smaller decks have either gone down by 50% . . . or gone out of business altogether. DURING THIS TIME THE ONLY DECK IN THE INDUSTRY THAT'S GROWN IS MINE. That's right, at a time when ad revenues are down nationwide and projected to fall further, my deck keeps growing. Doesn't this tell you something?

So, if you'd like to get started generating leads (*the record for leads generated is about 7500 in one issue, a staggering 7.5 % return*) or making sales direct, call me now. *The January issue will be sold out soon.*

To do so, you're going to need to call me. I will try to call you, too, but if you're serious about participating in my card-deck, it'd be a smart idea to *call me today.* Unlike other card deck companies, we don't badger people to come into my deck. For one thing, we don't have to; for another, I hate being badgered, and I don't like to keep calling prospects over and over again either. We figure if you're smart, you'll realize this is a good deal and act accordingly. And if you're not so smart ... why maybe you should pay more with our competitors!

I'll be happy to answer any and all questions for you . . . and to get you started making real money with card-deck advertising. Call me now. *Let's get started!*

Sincerely yours,

Jeffrey Lant, Ph.D.
President

Note: even with this minimum amount of accenting (which you can easily add with your computer), the prospect can get the message quite nicely . . . the message that there are benefits to be had from you if only he acts immediately. Don't make the mistake of so many service sellers: don't force your prospect to read every word. Accentuate the positive and motivate him to contact you FAST. When you're talking to him, you can make sure he understands what needs to happen for him to get the benefits he's now told you he wants.

Step 7: Remember The Rule of Seven

All too often service sellers act as if their prospects were prisoners in a completely empty room, a room without doors or windows, with nothing to take their time and attention. Such people, of course, would pour over even the most jejune marketing communication *faux de mieux*. But, of course, that's not how the people receiving *your* marketing communication are living. They have lots of options . . . far more options, in fact, than they could possibly follow up. That's why you can never afford to forget the Rule of Seven . . . and implement your marketing program accordingly. Your prospects must be hit and hit and hit yet again . . . each time with the same focused client-centered message.

Now is when your marketing plan comes into play. This is the moment you want things to come together so that your designated prospects receive your client-centered message not just in a single marketing communication but through a sustained campaign that brings your focused benefits to their attention in many ways.

This means doing what you can to:

- get on a local radio show;

- publish a problem-solving process article in the local newspaper;

- give a presentation at a local civic organization and reap additional advantage from such a presentation through accompanying publicity, *etc.*

Unfortunately, these marketing steps are often largely beyond your control. You can't always get this kind of marketing when you want it. And this is where direct response marketing really comes into its own, because it can largely be controlled by you. (I say "largely" because you are always subject to personnel, machines, administrative and operating difficulties at the suppliers you use, *etc.*)

With direct response marketing, however, you can hammer home a client-centered message in the way you wish . . . at the time you wish. This is invaluable . . . and you must do it.

This means adopting the right attitude so you can make The Rule of Seven work for you. Personally, I assume that my first marketing communication, no matter how client-centered, no matter how winning the offer, no matter how much the positive has been accentuated, will not achieve my overall objective. It will, I know from experience, achieve some portion of that objective, but not all of it. Because I *expect* to have to do more, I am not disappointed when I have to do more. Neither should you be. It is only the ingenue marketer who expects 100% of his marketing objective to be achieved from single approaches to his target group. Ordinarily, one must do more — much more. Plan for it.

I look upon my prospects as a great slumbering giant. The giant wants dinner. I have prepared a lavish one for him. But while I've been working, this giant has fallen into a deep sleep. To get the giant to awaken and enjoy what I've prepared, I must be prepared to do many things:

- Say, "Giant, your dinner is ready!". And when there is no response . . .

- Tickle his feet with feathers. And when there is no response . . .

- Put an ice cube down his back. And when there is no response . . .

- Jump up and down on his chest. And when there is no response . . .

- Build a fire under his huge toes. And when there is no response . . .

- Bring the Mormon Tabernacle Choir to sing "Wake up, Little Suzie" in his left ear . . .

. . . until finally the slumbering giant will twitch, turn over and sleepily say, "I'm hungry. Where's dinner?" — and ordinarily add, "Why didn't you call me earlier?"

Your public is the giant. You must be prepared to do everything to awaken him to your benefits; you must not be surprised when the first time doesn't do that. You must be prepared to use direct response marketing to continue to bring your client-centered message to his attention at concentrated intervals until he finally realizes you are there and how much you can do . . . and takes the necessary action to acquire your benefit.

Unless you are prepared to do all this . . . and to do it with a smile . . . your march to millionaire status is doomed to be long, hard, frustrating and disappointing.

Step 8: Turn Up The Pressure

The direct response marketing of most service sellers is bland and has no bite. The service seller seems to say, "Look, here I am whenever you need me. Whenever you get around to responding to what I'm sending you is fine. I don't want to come on too strong."

This is ridiculous!

Marketing is not a garden party. It's about motivating people to do what's necessary to acquire your benefits. To achieve this aim, *everything is fair.* You are not being graded on how civil and polite you are, whether you know which knife and fork to use and whether your hair is combed. You are being graded (for what else is millionaire status?) on whether you motivate enough people to take advantage of your offer to reach your objective. To do this, you've got to turn on the heat.

For most service sellers this really shouldn't be that difficult. For one thing, each of us is severely limited in how many projects/clients we can take on at any given time. Moreover, it ought to matter to both you and the prospect when he takes action; the moment he takes action can in no way be a matter of indifference to us. Thus, in each marketing communication increase the pressure to make the prospect act faster. Thus:

- In Direct Response Letter II to prospects who have used your services successfully before but have not yet responded, start by saying "I am VERY SURPRISED I haven't heard from you yet. You already have benefited from (benefits you provide). You know you don't want to have (pains you can eliminate). And you know SPACE IS SEVERELY LIMITED. I've only got (#) of openings left. SO PLEASE TAKE ACTION TODAY!"

- In Direct Response Letter III to the same prospects say, "You are about to miss the boat. You want (benefits you deliver), but if you don't take action IMMEDIATELY, you're not going to get them. Why? Because I'm just about out of space for you."

But what if the prospect hasn't benefited from what you can deliver? Try this approach:

"I am VERY SURPRISED I haven't heard from you yet. I'm sure you want (benefit you deliver); I'm sure you don't want (pain you can eliminate). DON'T HOLD BACK. Take action today to (get what the prospect wants)."

In other words, raise the stakes. Point out what the prospect is about to lose . . . point out (testimonials are helpful here) what the prospect gets by acting NOW . . . point out that IMMEDIATE ACTION is necessary. In short, don't be shy . . . and don't write prose that suggests it doesn't matter when the prospect acts. IT MATTERS VERY MUCH . . . FOR YOU . . . AND FOR THE PROSPECT. So act accordingly!

I'm going to tell you something right here I hope you'll never forget: when you start using marketing language like this, this is what happens:

1. you move faster towards achieving your objective, not least because prospects respond to urgency, and

2. some jerk somewhere will call you and say you're coming on too strong and because you're coming on too strong, he's not going to do business with you and is going to inform the White House you're a public menace.

This is what you need to remember now: Point 1 obliterates Point 2.

In the achievement of your objective in an age when more and more people are tuning out from marketing (but when the results produced by marketing are crucial for you), you may well have to raise the impact so considerably that some creatures are disturbed. Don't let this tail wag the dog, however.

If someone tells you he is disturbed by your "hard-ball" approach, you have to make a decision about what to do. For such circumstances, you can keep a stock letter available in which you point out that 1) the benefits are important; 2) people get so much mail and other marketing communications thrown on them they often overlook good things and that the approach you're using is necessary these days and that this approach works; 3) you're sorry it offends him but that he, too, should be focusing on the benefits and not the presentation, and 4) that because these benefits would be of value to the complainer, when would he like you to start delivering them?

If you decide to follow up this letter and if the prospect continues to harp on the problem (as he sees it) of your approach and won't let you talk about the benefits you deliver, cross him off your Christmas card list; he's not a prospect for what you're selling.

He's one of the armchair nit-pickers who abound these days, who feel compelled to focus on the inessentials instead of focusing on the benefits you can deliver and when you can start delivering them to him. I have no time for such people. Still, the more leads I generate, the more of them I encounter . . . and the more of them I ignore. Your job, remember, is to offer a superior service, to offer it with focused client-centered copy, and to leverage your new happy customers to get still more happy customers in the shortest possible time. You owe nothing to the nit-pickers; you owe everything to the achievement of your objective. The minute you see such people cannot assist you, get rid of them with as much ceremony as you have the time and inclination for. And never regret their absence for an instant: THEY WERE NEVER CLIENT PROSPECTS TO BEGIN WITH. JUST HUMAN DETRITUS . . . . Besides, you have a lot of other lead generating tasks to perform . . . like creating and using classified and small space ads.

9

Generating Leads Through Classified And Small Space Ads

By now, you should already have in place several mechanisms for generating leads. Indeed, you should already be generating those leads . . . and benefiting from them. But, Oliver Twist-like, I'm sure you want MORE!

That's where generating leads from ads comes in.

To be sure, I approach this chapter with a certain caution that was not present before. Why? Because with classified and small space ads, you will ordinarily have to spend money. And anything that smacks of the old hand going into the wallet is to be approached with prudence . . . and deliberation.

Which is precisely what most service sellers don't do.

Why, just as I was writing this chapter another instance of service seller stupidity fell into my lap. I was approached by a sports dietitian who started her conversation with me by lamenting the high cost of advertising in the journals of her profession. "Have you tried the many alternatives to paid advertising?", I queried. She had not . . .

. . . the idiot.

Think what was going on in this benighted woman's brain. She needed leads. She had limited resources for getting them. Her first, indeed as it proved her only thought was to spend her limited resources on expensive paid advertising. THIS IS LUNACY.

Your constant rule must be to explore alternatives to paid advertising before plunking down your limited resources there.

Why?

Because paid advertising is a snare for most people. For most service sellers . . . and certainly for the vast majority of first-time service seller advertisers . . . paid advertising is a black hole into which they pitch their money . . . never to see results.

This is because they haven't made a study of advertising. They haven't:

- explored all suitable publications;
- made sure the publication's market is their market;
- reviewed the ads that are doing well . . . and tried to determine why;
- thought through the benefits that will interest, indeed, capture this market;
- formulated an offer that will make these people jump up and take immediate action;
- considered how to reinforce their advertising message with simultaneous editorial emphasis;
- made the commitment and created the plan that will enable them to hit their prospects through paid advertising with enough client-centered messages so that even the dimmest prospect will get the message, and
- tried to get the most advertising for the least price.

Instead, most service sellers act as if paid advertising were a lottery; the ad is their ticket. They purchase one or two . . . write some uninspired copy . . . and sit back, hoping for the best. With pitiful regularity these insipid hopes are blasted. Entirely predictably.

Armed with this chapter, this will not happen to you. Because you're going to follow these steps.

Step 1: Explore All Suitable Publications

One of the problems with service sellers who use paid advertising is that they know too few advertising sources. They may know the biggest daily paper in their area and perhaps a weekly or two. That's it. But this isn't nearly enough! You must familiarize yourself with *all* the publications that reach the people who can buy from you. This is an entirely different thing from merely browsing over your newspaper at breakfast.

To give you an idea of how service sellers often confuse these things, consider the one I met while addressing a convention of monument builders (aka tombstone makers) at a convention in Las Vegas. This man was from Western Massachusetts and like many monument builders he has had to hustle more aggressively for business in recent years due to the fact that more people are being cremated and that those being cremated don't usually order monuments. A definite problem.

Questioning him, I discovered that he and the others in the audience derive most of their leads from the obituaries. They read these . . . and then approach the grieving survivors about doing something grand and commemorative for the dear departed. By the same token they put most of their ads in or near the obituary sections of (mostly weekly) newspapers. All reasonable enough.

Under the circumstances, you'd think that all the monument builders would be packed with information on exactly how many papers reached their target markets, wouldn't you? But service seller sloth prevailed over rigorous method.

The fellow I called on admitted he couldn't even *name* the weekly papers in his marketing area . . . didn't look at their obituaries . . . and didn't advertise in them, either.

But he said he got most of his current leads from newspapers, whether from following up on the obituaries or generating leads from ads placed in or near the obituary section.

So, he wanted more leads, knew where his leads were already coming from, but wasn't doing his homework about learning how to increase his take from methods he already knew were working. Pretty dumb, huh?

Thus, the first thing is to canvass your marketing territory and familiarize yourself with *all* the publications in it that reach your market. *Note:* to find out about these publications, check out the resources in Chapter 6 or review the much more extensive list found in my book **THE UNABASHED SELF-PROMOTER'S GUIDE.** Moreover, if your market is local, your library will probably carry some or all of the publications in question. Ask. But don't assume that even the library has everything. Dig for yourself.

Another Note: while this chapter focuses on paid advertising, this research will also be useful for getting editorial promotion. Review the publications and their various sections. Note the names of pertinent editors, columnists, writers, *etc.* as well as addresses and phone numbers. The research you're doing now can easily kill two birds with one stone.

And Another Note: I'll bet you've probably never thoroughly researched the publications that reach your market(s) before. However, promise yourself that you won't just do it once for all. Media change rapidly. Publications come and go and so do all media personnel . Doing this kind of media review within your marketing territory is the kind of thing you ought to do at regular intervals, say once a year. This way you'll stay alert to openings that are available to you, whether you have to pay to use them or not.

Step 2: Make Sure The Publication's Market Is *Your* Market

Once you're sure you know about all the publications that reach your target market(s), it's time to scrutinize each publication to make sure there is an overlap between who the publication is trying to reach . . . and who you want to reach. Keep in mind that *every* media source has a defined market and the publication should be able to tell you what it is. This information may include:

- percentage of men vs women;
- income statistics;
- residence or location information;
- job titles, *etc.*

This information, along with details on the cost of advertising, is available in two places: *Standard Rate & Data* (3004 Glenview Rd., Wilmette, IL 60091 (708) 256-6067; found in libraries of any consequence) and from the publication's own advertising rate card which is available upon request. Review both.

Keep in mind, however, that this information is necessarily incomplete. Now that I'm in the advertising game myself, I realize just how much of what passes for factual data in this world is nothing more than a guess, and often not a very good guess at that. Good, solid information on the demographics of a publication is frankly difficult to get and dates quickly. Still, what you discover is a start.

There's another, more impressionistic, way of getting a sense about the overlap between the publication's market and your market. That is, by reading the ads.

These days I spend a lot of time reading the ads in lots of publications; indeed, I read a lot more ad copy than articles! I'm looking for ads that promote things similar to mine. Then I want to know if these ads are repeating; unless a person is a certifiable idiot, he's not going to keep running ads for long that are losing money. Thus, your task is to review a few issues and see if the same people keep advertising. After you've looked through about a half dozen issues you get a pretty good impression of the repeaters. These are the people the publication counts on issue after issue to come back . . . and these are the people you want to know more about .

If the ad in question is not offering something directly competitive to you, by all means call the company and ask for the advertising director. Before you do, draw up a question sheet and have it available in your computer for easy use and for storing the information you get. By having these questions available when you talk to the advertising director, you'll get the information you need and make sure you don't forget anything. Include:

- name of potential advertising source
- its address
- its phone number
- its advertising director
- name of advertiser in this source
- its address
- name of person responsible for advertising
- how long he's advertised in source
- does he track leads
- what kinds of results does he get
- is his advertising in the source profitable
- what seasons/issues tend to work best for advertiser (if not obvious from nature of service)

- has he received any special discount prices
- has he had any particular problems
- would he recommend this source to you?

Before launching into these questions, make sure this is a good time for the advertiser to talk. Say you're thinking about advertising in the publication, have seen the advertiser's very attractive ads several times (yes, a little flattery oils the apparatus) and want to know how he's doing and whether this has proven to be a profitable place to advertise. Then go through your questions. Listen closely to what you're told and complete your form. Listen, too, for what the advertiser doesn't say as much as what he does say. Are you dealing with an organized professional who is tracking results and *proving* profitability? Or are you talking to someone who just doesn't know if his advertising is working or not either because he doesn't keep track or hasn't advertised long enough to know?

Many advertisers will gladly share this information with you. Others will be very guarded unless you make it very clear (as you should) that you are not competing against them. Provide a little information about your service.

Note: after you're finished with this conversation, send the person who's helped you a thank-you note and include some information on your service. This shows what a civil creature you are. You will have such a letter in your computer, of course.

This technique is all very well and good for an advertiser who isn't a direct competitor, but, frankly, you'd like to know how your competitors' ads are doing, wouldn't you?

Here I'd start with the advertising manager at the publication. Tell this person you're thinking about buying ad space but want to know how a few of their advertisers are doing. Go through a version of the questionnaire above with this person. Good advertising managers ought to know how their advertisers are doing. To be sure, they may not have all the information immediately available, but they can get it more easily than you can under the guise of managing their accounts. However, treat everything you hear from an advertising director with a grain of salt. Particularly in the kind of advertising recession we're currently experiencing, an advertising manager will say just about anything to get your business. "How many Peruvian grandmothers with a preference for green shawls do you have subscribing to your publication?", you'll ask. Hey presto, the aggressive ad manager will have a precise answer. It'll be entirely erroneous, of course, but it will sound authoritative. *Caveat emptor.*

However, if the ad manager can tell you nothing about how well his accounts are doing, that's a sign, too — and not a good one. The good ad manager asks his advertisers how they're doing and does try to work with them to improve response. If the ad manager knows little or nothing about how his advertisers are doing, it's a sure sign that you're dealing with a "we take your money and run" operation. You should redouble your prudence accordingly.

If you're having trouble getting all the information you need from the ad manager about how your competitors' ads are doing, call the advertising manager at your competitor's business and ask the questions above. Only don't tell them the name of your company or the service you provide. Just ask the questions. Most people will simply answer the questions as asked, especially when you tell them you're considering advertising in the same publication they're using and want their opinion. If you are asked information about yourself, make it believable . . . but vague.

As a result of this research, you'll have a good idea about what kinds of advertisers are doing well . . . or not. Now you need to review their ads.

Step 3: Determine Why Various Ads Do Well

Once you've discovered that an advertiser is doing well, ask one last crucial question: WHY. Why, that is, does he think his ads are pulling for him? His response may well be impressionistic, but you need to ask the question, and you need to listen closely to the response. Which of the many variables present in advertising does he think are influencing a better response? These variables may include (but are not limited to):

- position
- ad size
- color and other design elements
- offer
- special issue of publication
- ad reinforced by editorial support

- extra circulation by publication for its own promotion
- lack of competitors, and
- any combination of peculiar (not recurring) factors.

Frankly, while it is ideal to get this information from the horse's mouth, you're not always going to be able to do so. Often you can deduce these compelling factors yourself. This is why you've got to review the ad *in situ*, as it were, to try to deter mine what made it work . . . so that you can determine if you can make this situation work for you or whether what made the ad work is not likely to be available to you.

This all takes work.

You've got to force yourself to think like an ad respondent . . . not like an advertiser; much less a sanguine advertiser who is bored by the tediousness of research. This kind of research can save you a bundle and must be done.

You are, after all, not merely trying to avoid spending your limited money unwisely . . . you are looking for a place where you can invest in a *series* of advertisements and can generate for years a predictable number of qualified leads. Thus, while time-consuming, this work is crucial.

Once you've got a clear idea of what particular ads are working and why they're working, then and only then is it time to turn your hand to crafting your own winning ads.

Step 4: Craft Benefits That Will Capture Your Market

Throughout this book, I have been urging you to think through the specific benefits that will help motivate your market to take action. These benefits are the bedrock of any ad. In Chapter 3 you learned how to transform features into benefits and to store them in your computer for later use. Here's one place you want them.

Remember that all ads are based on these four words: YOU GET BENEFIT NOW! Here's where it really pays to be precise about the benefits you offer. What are the best and most believable things your prospects are going to get from you? Then start every sentence with the words YOU (the prospect) GET. And what *will* they get?

- something bigger;

- something smaller;

- something faster;

- something less expensive;

- something more convenient;

- something more luxurious;

- something more attractive, *etc.*

Note that all these benefits are *comparative*. That is, benefits offer the prospect something *better* than he has previously been able to get or that others can offer him. Benefits, you see, provide prospects with *comparative advantage* . . . and it is to secure this comparative advantage, reinforced by a client-centered offer, that the prospect acts fast.

Your job here is to:

- list *everything* the prospect gets from you;

- make it as *specific and believable* as possible;

- write it so that what you are offering is *comparatively superior* to other choices the prospect has.

Once you've brain stormed your benefits (or reviewed the list you already have available in a computer file), it's time to prioritize them for the market you are first interested in motivating. Thus, what is the #1 Benefit that *these targeted people* want from you and which will cause the largest number to respond to the ad you're about to write? What is the #2 Benefit? The #3 Benefit? *Etc.* Remember, if the prospect will not be motivated by what you have reason to think is the #1 Benefit, it's much less likely he'll be motivated by your #2 Benefit. That's why you're going to be leading with your primary benefit . . . both in your ad and in your follow-up marketing communications. All benefits are not the same given any individual market, and you must always lead with what you have reason to know is the strongest *for the people you are approaching in this ad.*

Note: when you think this way and start crafting benefits that are squarely focused on the prospect and what he'll get from you, you're already way ahead of most advertisers. One of the major reasons why most ads fail is because they are "me- (the advertiser) centered", not client-centered. They offer no major benefit for the prospect and as such the prospect sees nothing in the equation for himself . . . and fails to take action. Thinking benefits forces you to concentrate on the only person who can make you rich: the prospect. It also forces you to consider which among the many benefits you have available is most likely to be of interest to that prospect now.

Just how many of these benefits you'll use is directly related to the amount of space you have available. If you are running a 10-word classified ad, the benefit is going to be just one or two *words;* in a small space ad 1/16th of the page, you might squeeze two short benefits in. In longer space ads, as in longer marketing communications, you'll use more benefits. The key is that you will always base your client-centered ad on the client-centered benefit you've determined is most influential with the particular group you're most interested in motivating.

Step 5: Formulate An Offer That Will Make Your Prospects Jump Up And Take Immediate Action

Recently I did an informal study at a national dietitians conference I was addressing. About 100 members of the audience brought their brochures and other marketing communications with them to a session I was offering on how to write marketing communications that get people to respond faster.

Question, I began: how many of you want to get more business faster?

Every hand went up.

Question, I continued: how many of you have provided an offer in your marketing communications that would stimulate a prospect to take faster action?

No hand went up.

This is absurd!

As a service seller you have an absolute obligation to do *everything* you can to stimulate the fastest possible response from your prospect. You want him to tell you *as quickly as possible* that he's interested in the benefit you have available . . . so you can start trying to close the deal *as quickly as possible.* This is where the offer comes in.

The offer, as you should already know, is based on the proposition that merely telling people that you have benefits available isn't as motivating to them as giving them some immediate (and fast-dwindling) incentive for taking immediate action.

Note those two key words "immediate" and "fast-dwindling". The benefit you have available must be available now . . . but it must not be available forever. It must be decidedly limited in some fashion, as with quantity or time.

Because you've been following the directions in this book, I feel confident that you now have a computer file not only stuffed with offers but into which you regularly add more. One of the reasons for reading the marketing communications of your (more with-it) competitors is to see what kinds of offers they're using . . . and to file them away for your own reference, refurbishing and use. The objective here, after all, is not to be creative; creativity takes time. It's to take what works and harness it to your success chariot.

Thus, review the ads in the publications you're interested in . . . and the marketing communications both of these advertisers (you have written for their materials, I trust?) and your competitors in general. What are they doing to generate the largest response as quickly as possible? And what can you do to make a better offer that will both 1) cut their response and 2) generate more responses for yourself?

The key, you see, to offers is this:

- every ad you create — indeed every marketing communication — must have one;

- the offer you use must be better (that is, more motivating) than the offers your competitors are using;

- your offer must be prominently featured in your ad.

Personally, because of the importance of the offer, I prefer putting it in the upper right hand corner of any marketing communication; this is a power position and hence appropriate for this crucial component.

The offer should scream, "HERE'S SOMETHING REALLY IMPORTANT FOR YOU!!! . . . ACT BY (DATE) OR MISS OUT!!! . . . ONLY (NUMBER) LEFT!!! GOING FAST!!! . . . SPECIAL BENEFIT FOR FIRST (NUMBER) ONLY!!! DON'T WAIT!!!" In short, it should seem to be as important as it really is. Not surprisingly, you'll want to reinforce its importance by using the kinds of emphasizing devices I've previously mentioned: capital letters, ellipses, exclamation points, and all the rest.

Caution: if one offer is good and must be present in every ad and marketing communication, surely a bunch of offers in the same ad is even better, right? Probably not. Multiple offers can easily confuse the prospect. Moreover, in a classified or small space ad, you frankly don't have the space to add more than one really motivational offer. The key to all ads is to keep them simple, client-centered, and not to overwhelm the space you have available with too many words.

Step 6: Reinforce Your Advertising Message With Simultaneous Editorial Emphasis

Too many service seller advertisers think about promotion and paid advertising as two distinct things that must occur and be used separately. This is nonsense. The seasoned lead generator, steeped in the profundity of The Rule of Seven, understands that once you have designated the prospect you want to motivate, you must hit that person again and again and again with client-centered benefits; if this many-sided motivating process can take place simultaneously both through combined editorial and advertising means so much the better. Thus marrying unabashed self-promotion to paid advertising to motivate your prospects makes eminent good sense.

To do this, review the chapter on unabashed promotion . . . and see how you can forward your interests through the free publicity mechanisms of the publications in which you are considering buying paid ad space. Thus:

- Review all departments of the publication. Which are the most promising for your news and feature angles?

- Contact editors and gauge their receptivity to your ideas and information. *Note:* don't tell them you are considering buying paid advertising and, above all else, don't tell them your buying paid space is contingent on your getting editorial mention. Editorial personnel are almost uniformly put off by this tactic which they see as compromising their professional integrity. Instead, simply see if the possibility exists for editorially emphasizing your message. *Another note:* if you do decide to purchase the ad space and your editorial material does have the possibility to be run in the same issue, at that point it's certainly all right to inform the editor of what's happening and say that you'd like your editorial message to run simultaneously with your ad if that's at all possible.

- Send in your material and make your follow-up contacts just as you would at any other promotional source.

Once you've really understood the editorial slant of the publication and worked to shape your promotional material to its standards, you'll find your material regularly being published . . . while at the same time you derive the benefits that come from running client-centered ads. This happens to me all the time; indeed, in most of the publications where my problem-solving process articles regularly appear, you'll find not just one Jeffrey Lant lead-generating device but several. After all, my aim is to entirely dominate every publication in which my client-centered materials run. Need I say that this should be your objective, too? The objective, after all, is not to get your share, but more than your share . . . particularly if this involves depriving your competitors of the space they need to generate leads!

Step 7: Create The Plan That Enables You To Hit Your Prospect Through A Paid Advertising Campaign

Over the last several years, I've been conducting an informal survey of service sellers and their advertising. Here's what I've discovered:

- most service sellers run random ads in insufficiently considered publications;
- most of these ads do not draw any appreciable response; indeed, most lose the service seller money;
- as a result the ads are not repeated, and
- the service seller repeats the same futile process elsewhere with equally unimpressive, indeed destructive, results.

Does this just about sum up your advertising experience?

Not any more, it doesn't!!!

Repeat after me, "REPETITION MAKES ADVERTISING PROFITABLE!"

What you are looking for is this:

- the publication that connects you to the right market . . . the people who have the want you can satisfy and the means to satisfy that want;

- a client-centered, benefit-anchored ad with motivational offer, and

- a sequence of these ads, hammering home the benefits, forcing the prospect to become aware of and to take fast action to acquire your benefit.

It is because random ads do not work to deliver the necessary and continuing stream of leads you need to sustain your business and march to profit and because this result is possible only through a sequence of client-centered ads that provides the essential reason for all the work you must do to arrive at a decision about where to invest your money and place your ads. This work is crucial because, at the end of the day, you're going to be buying not one but many ads. You are looking for the place that makes the most sense to put and pay for them.

Now to a necessary corollary: if you do not intend to repeat your client-centered ad, you should not be advertising in the source at all!!! First, because random single ads rarely produce a good response and never a sustained response; second, because each ad you run should be a learning experience for you by forcing you to focus on what you did right to generate response and what you did wrong. Your job is always to study and to eliminate the unsuccessful variables until you've created a client-centered ad that you can run without variation (or with minor variations) for years to come. However, if you change the publication (a key variable) you are always setting your research course back to square one . . . and can never derive the benefits that continually running your ad in one publication and researching its results can provide if properly handled.

A personal note: I drill this message home to advertisers in my card deck in no uncertain terms . . . but with often unsatisfying results. An advertiser, for instance, will spend the money to purchase an initial card and generate immediate results. All too often, however, instead of studying how to increase these results and learn from the possibilities of the medium and its audience, he'll fly about looking for the "something better" that will provide precisely the results he *thinks* he should be getting, little understanding that these results almost never occur when a market is first approached but only after it is approached on the basis of what has been learned from a strict analysis of previous efforts and resulting refocusing of the advertising copy and presentation. It baffles me why this crucial point is so hard for most service seller advertisers to grasp, since, in the final analysis, their failure to do so dooms so much of their advertising effort and precludes the successful use of advertising as a plentiful lead-generating system.

Step 8: Get The Most Advertising Space For The Least Price

Ingenue service sellers, having determined to buy advertising space, are inclined to ask the price and plunk down their money to pay for it. This isn't very smart . . .

Like everything in man's creation, what you pay for advertising space is negotiable. There is, to be sure, a published price; there are also any number of lesser prices which depend upon circumstances. What is important to keep in mind is this: the publishers of periodicals are owners of a perishable commodity. Space in yesterday's newspaper is unsalable. Their objective, therefore, is to maximize revenue from space that will soon be without the ability to provide them with anything. As that moment of absolute worthlessness approaches, as prospects for getting the amount they want dwindle, the time of the consummate negotiator arrives. By which, of course, I mean you! Here is the sequence you must follow to benefit:

- Understand that the price for all advertising price, whatever is said to the contrary, is negotiable;

- Call the publication in which you're interested and tell them you're interested in remnant space, that is space that cannot be sold at full price, and ask them how they handle this situation;

- Create a form letter expressing your interest in remnant space and informing the advertising manager what size space you are interested in. In this letter, ask only to be *informed* when such space is available; do not commit yourself to purchasing it;

- Create your ad and camera-ready art/mechanical so that it is available to be sent as soon as you've made the decision to purchase such space. Make sure the publication's advertising manager understands you have such camera-ready art available. It lessens his anxiety and makes it more likely you can get the space at reduced cost close to press time.

By following these guidelines, you will reduce the costs of your ads. By how much depends on your negotiating skills and the publication's need for your business and desire to fill the space. Here are some negotiating guidelines to follow:

- Make it clear to the advertising manager that you are only interested in remnant space, not full-price space. If the manager knows you're going to purchase space anyway, he has less incentive to negotiate with you;

- Understand that the price the advertising manager eventually offers you for the space you want will probably not be the best price you can get. Whatever reduced price he offers you, divide by 50% and offer that. It's unlikely you'll get the space for that most attractive price, but now you know the range . . . the reduced price he's offered . . . and the floor you've set. The negotiation will now proceed within those parameters.

- You have a lot greater chance of getting the price you've offered if you pay in advance. Indeed, given the steep discount the publication is offering, they may require you to pay in advance, so you may as well turn inevitability into leverage by *offering* immediate payment.

Note: even after you've initially contacted the advertising manager and discussed your situation, don't wait for him to contact you with an offer; remember, he is not in the business of selling discounted space. Satisfying you does not have a high priority for him. Instead, find out the real (not the published) deadline for camera-ready art and call five days beforehand to check the situation.

At this point, reiterate your offer and gauge the chances of its being accepted. If it is accepted, don't expect courtly graciousness from the advertising manager; you are, after all, breaking into his usual way of doing business. Grudging acceptance is probably about the best you're going to get. Who cares? You saved a heap of money, didn't you?

Another note: expect to follow roughly the same sequence before the publication's next deadline . . . when you still want to get remnant space rates. This time the advertising manager will press you rather more strongly to pay full price and reserve your space early; this is, after all, easier for him. If your results are good and you're converting leads to sales, say that you're certainly willing to reserve the space . . . at the same rate. Say that you realize the advertising manager wants you to pay full price but that your ability to participate depends on your getting the lower rate (even if it doesn't). If he can guarantee that rate now, you'll take the space; (of course, try to get credit terms for paying for it.) He'll probably decline . . . and the game will continue as before with very probably the same ultimate result. Understand, however, that the advertising manager will be doing everything possible to fill his space with full-paying customers and will be trying to exclude you, thereby forcing you to reevaluate your approach and come in to the next issue at full price. So be it. I understand that in each negotiation there are at least two negotiators with points of view that are quite different; you should keep this in mind, too. This doesn't mean, however, that you should deviate from a strategy that works . . . even if it is somewhat inconvenient for both you and the advertising manager. Keep in mind that if the strategy works you are getting more space for less money, which translates into a lower per-lead cost, more money left for more marketing, and profit faster.

Purchasing The Ad Space . . . At Last!

Think about the last time you purchased an ad; think about that ad's results. Now look back over all the pre-purchase steps I'm recommending in this chapter. Until you are absolutely certain the publication is working for you, the business of buying even the simplest ad should be a slow, thoughtful, deliberate one. Why? Because as I hope you now understand, you are never in the business of buying a single ad; you are always in the business of seeing where you can invest your money over a sustained period of time to generate a continuing stream of superior leads. You must see the purchase of even the tiniest ad as part of this more important process.

. . . And Cobbling The Ad Together

With all the previous work you've done, putting your ad together should be relatively easy. Especially if you remember what you're trying to accomplish: getting the most qualified person to contact you as soon as possible to get the benefits you offer. To do this, you must fit your client-centered information into the structure of the successful lead-generating ad.

— The structure of the successful classified ad

As you already know, classified ads must be short. The ideal is to keep them to the precise length the publication charges as its minimum. This is usually 10 words. To achieve this objective, first recall the basic structure of your ad:

OFFER + MEANINGFUL CLIENT-CENTERED BENEFIT + NECES-SARY FOLLOW-UP DETAILS = SUCCESSFUL CLASSIFIED AD

Then, write out your ad in complete sentences. Thus, "Jeremy Evans, copywriter, will provide a free analysis of all your marketing communications to see if they can be improved to get you more business if you contact him now at (phone) or at (address)."

Once written out in full in this manner, start saving money by turning this copy into the tightest of tight classified ads, thereby reducing its cost to the minimum. Work from what absolutely must be in the ad (contact information) forward.

Let's say that Jeremy is local. All the contact information he'll need is a phone number. This leaves him with 9 words for his offer and client-centered message:

"Sell more faster! Free marketing communication analysis. Master copywriter. (phone)." 10 words

The problem becomes more difficult if Jeremy needs to include an address. Addresses usually take up 5 or 6 words; let's make this a worst case scenario and say 6. This leaves us with four words to induce immediate prospect action. Thus:

"Free marketing communication analysis. Copywriter, (address)" If you have an extra word, add "details" after "analysis."

While you're working on this ad, brainstorm a series of classified ads and store them for later reference. I am now firmly convinced that *no one* writes the best drawing ad the first time they approach a given market; you need to analyze results, test different copy and presentations and tinker until you are reasonably confident you have an ad that will draw well. But how to you know your ad is drawing well? IT MAKES MONEY! Only at such time as you are regularly making money from an ad can you be assured that you have written the right ad . . . which means everything that comes before is in the nature of an experiment.

Note: before leaving the subject of classified ads, I want to reinforce one point. You may think that trying to get a classified ad down to minimum cost to save a few bucks is not sensible. Why not just add another word or two and have done with the project? I disagree. First, the objective of all marketing is to spend the least number of dollars you can to produce the greatest number of results. Spending unnecessary dollars on your marketing, no matter how few dollars that is, is never acceptable. Second, there's a discipline involved here. True, the extra cost for a classified ad may be only a dollar or two, but if you give in here, you'll give in when the costs are much greater. What you are learning here, even with the shortest and least-expensive classified ad, is the discipline you will carry into all your marketing work. It is the discipline that will serve you well and save you a lot of money over time.

— *The structure of the successful space ad*

The underlying structure of a successful space ad is no different from that of a classified ad:

OFFER + MEANINGFUL CLIENT-CENTERED BENEFIT + NECES-SARY FOLLOW-UP DETAILS = SUCCESSFUL SPACE AD

What is different is the amount of space you have available. Thus, instead of offering just one way of following up, you can offer two (address and telephone); instead of offering just one benefit, you can offer multiple benefits, stacking one on another to build a more irresistible case. Take our copywriter Jeremy, for instance. Given the same objective on his part, his space ad could say:

Act now. Get a free marketing communication analysis until (date). Make more money from your ads, flyers, cover letters, brochures, *etc.* Call Master Copywriter at (number) or send your documents to (address)."

Notice there is precious little about the "master copywriter" in this ad, really just his address and phone number. The rest is made up of:

- an admonition to "act now". Whenever possible, it is AL-WAYS a good idea to remind the prospect about what he's supposed to do;

- an offer (the free marketing communication analysis);

- a limitation on the offer (good until a particular date);

- a major benefit. Note that the sentence leads off with the benefit (making more money) and only follows with the feature (the ads, *etc.*)

If you have less room in your ad than this copy allows, you can easily cut words from it; on the other hand, if you have more space, you can add more benefits . . . and a testimonial. But the focus will always stay the same: on what will benefit and motivate the prospect, not on you.

Note: I have said nothing about running your logo or motto or how long you've been in business, *etc.* This is all peripheral and can be dropped without penalty. What can never be dropped, however, is the strict focus on the prospect and what he'll get . . . if only he acts NOW.

Gauging The Success Of Your Ad; Deciding To Repeat, Or Drop

Personally, I always feel a let-down after I've done the research for an ad, brain stormed various alternatives, crafted what I think is superior copy and sent the ad to its fate. There is nothing more I can do just then to help this particular ad along. It's fate is now in the hands of others . . . the publication, of course, and, in the final analysis, the market. This is necessarily a tad unnerving.

Of course, *you* won't give way to this feeling; for one thing, you have a lot of work to do to get ready to handle the follow-up. (More about that later.) And to get ready to track the responses. For tracking is a necessary part of advertising, as you already know.

Before your ad runs, you should already be sure you have your tracking facilities in place. Do you have the computer files (both word processing and list management) ready where you can enter data on respondents? Are you sure you can follow any lead through from the moment the prospect contacts you to the moment he either buys . . . or it becomes clear he'll never buy and as such is unceremoniously zapped from your list? For remember, the success of this ad must be judged not by how many responses there are to it . . . but how many dollars of revenue are generated from it and whether this revenue was generated because of reasons which can be repeated or because of unusual, non-repeating circumstances.

Unfortunately, this is not how most service sellers treat their advertising. Sadly, most regard advertising simply as a matter of scribbling an ad and dumping it into a publication; having the good intention to track the response, but being too distracted to do so when those responses start arriving. As a result, there is no way they can intelligently determine if the ad worked . . . or not. Thus , put this motto over your computer: TRACKING IS A PART OF PROFITABLE ADVERTISING.

Note: if you are simply running a phone number with your ad, you can ask all your respondents where they heard about you. This will be sufficient. If you invite mail responses, you'll need to include a written code with your ad. You can do this through your address, thus "50 Follen St./a", "a" representing the particular issue of the publication in which you advertised.

Should You Repeat Your Ad?

While you can never predict how many prospects will contact you once your ad runs, one thing is certain: you'll be promptly contacted by the advertising manager of the publication where you advertised and by his colleagues at other publications. They are among the most assiduous responders. Deal with them cautiously.

Until such time as you have had the chance to assess your leads and pursue the closing process, it is premature to book further ads either in the original publication or in subsequent publications. You need to find out if the ad you've run will make you money. And, given your business, this may take some time to discover. Give it to yourself! After all, if you've been following this book assiduously you've got profit-making leads coming in from many places . . . and after you implement the next chapter, you'll have still more coming in from others.

10

Generating More Leads Through Card Decks, Electronic Moving Message Display Signs, Package Stuffer Programs . . . And More

In case you've somehow missed this point: lead generating must go on ALL THE TIME. It is not something you do when you feel like it. It is not something you do episodically. It is not something you do intermittently. It is something you do *systematically* . . . implementing and maintaining an *unrelenting process*. Then and only then can you be sure that you will have the number of leads coming in that you need to meet your financial objectives.

It is because most service sellers do not have such a system, such an unrelenting process that they 1) have to make demeaning cold calls, and 2) spend too much time with people who are not good prospects. Service sellers without system or process never achieve one of the crucial benefits of profit-making marketing: namely, having as many leads as they need to meet their financial objectives and being able to select just the people they *really* want to work with.

To achieve this objective means continually investigating every means of generating leads and implementing as many of them as you can as quickly as you can. Thus, in this chapter I want to draw your particular attention to a number of lead generators which you can use both to generate an initial lead and to generate additional leads *after* you've made a first sale. Book purists may argue that the lead-generating mechanisms presented in this chapter could have been subsets of previous chapters. I have placed them in a separate chapter, however, because I wanted to draw your particular attention to them. Sadly, most service businesses are not systematically using these means of generating leads . . . but when you know how effective they are — you will!

Special Lead-Generating Systems Primarily To Bring In New Customers

Lead generation breaks down into two major parts: generating leads from people who have not previously been customers and generating leads from those who are or have been customers. You should have in place mechanisms to generate leads from both. Here we continue our focus on generating leads from people who have not previously been customers.

Generating Leads From Card-Decks/Val-Packs

I am as you know a card-deck fanatic. Each year millions of post cards are mailed with my address and phone number on them. Each of these cards invites the recipient to get in touch with me and get some benefit. Tens of thousands of recipients do. Now I want you to think very carefully about what I'm telling you here. *One* service provider working at home with his computer, in a situation of astonishingly low overhead, is able, thanks to state-of-the-art technology and his own ability to use words that motivate, to get thousands and thousands of people nationwide to tell him that they want the benefit he is offering them and are willing to part with some of their money to get it. It is then left to that service provider to make the most mutually beneficial deal with that respondent so that the respondent receives maximum benefits as soon as possible and the service provider receives the most money possible in the circumstances. This situation takes place day after day after day . . . without the service provider making *even a single cold call.*

Now reread this paragraph telling yourself that this is what you want, too!

One of the ways this can happen to you is through a proper understanding and use of card-deck advertising.

Card-decks or card-packs are bundles of individual post cards mailed to designated recipients in either clear plastic or color packaging. All decks are theme decks with more or less rigidly focused target markets. Just what these themes are you can tell from looking through the *Business Publications Rates and Data* (part 3) published by Standard Rate and Data. Available in most public libraries, this resource tells you the name of the deck, publisher, target audience, circulation, frequency of mailings, price, *etc.* You also find out the demographics and distribution of the mailing.

Decks are either mailed to 1) subscribers of a publication (perhaps augmented with additional, similar names); 2) a targeted professional group (like veterinarians); 3) classifications of job categories and function, or 4) compiled consumer names. In the fourth category, the names are local residents who receive the offers of local product and service sellers. These decks are often called val- (for value) packs and have a different presentation format than standard post-card mailing programs. Their intent, however, is the same: the publishers mail a designated number of these packs to the people they think will respond best and sell the available space in their package to advertisers who wish to reach these people.

While the theory is very well and good, there are significant pitfalls for the unwary service seller. As both a card-deck publisher and heavy card-deck advertiser, I am ideally positioned to tell you what they are and help you avoid them.

How Money Is Made As A Card-Deck Publisher

The first problem for card-deck advertisers is that they really don't understand how money gets made by the publishers. Because of this, they approach the business of running a card unwarily.

Let's start from the beginning and take a look at the actual card-deck product. Card-decks are always composed of multiples of four or eight cards; this is because the actual cards are printed on forms containing this number of available spaces. Thus, it is not possible to add or subtract cards except in multiples of four or eight. The publisher pays a base rate for these forms; once he has purchased the form he pays as much for one card as for four or eight (depending on which variety he has ordered). This is important for you to keep in mind for later bargaining.

Due to the complexity of printing, collating, bagging and mailing card-decks, there are very few printers in the country who actually print (as opposed to publish) them. Just how many cards they can put in an individual deck varies depending on the kind of equipment they have available. The printer I use (Schmidt Printing, Inc., 1416 Valleyhigh Dr., N.W., Rochester, MN 55901) can as of this time print a deck of only 88 cards, no more. Other printers can print larger decks but at greater cost; essentially what they have to do is print one complete deck and then append to it another partial deck in order to increase the deck's overall size. This is obviously a costly procedure. Not surprisingly, printing is always the single largest expense for card-deck publishers. In diminishing order their other major expenses are postage, commissions and salary, and list rental.

These expenses can easily raise the cost of a deck of, say, 68 cards to between $55,000-$65,000. At this point the deck publisher has two objectives: diminish expenses and increase revenue. These objectives can be met by:

- prepaying the printing bill and getting a prepayment credit against the total printing cost. This is a course most card-deck publishers have been unable to take because they grant credit terms to the bulk of their advertisers and thus do not have available the necessary money to bargain with their printer for a reduced rate. For them, therefore, this is not a viable option;

- reducing the postage bill by using carrier route sorts and other savings stemming from the batching of their decks at mailing. Due to the availability of sophisticated mailing list software programs, all card-deck publishers take advantage of such savings;

- reducing their list rental costs. Card-deck publishers are regular list renters. The success of their decks rests on their advertisers getting a consistently good response; this means list owners are involved in a constant search for lists with higher return potential. Available lists, of course, break down into compiled lists, subscription lists, buyer lists and card-deck responsive lists. You're already familiar with the first three types. The fourth type is composed of people who have *responded* to a card-deck offer, either by buying something from a card or responding to a free card-deck offer. These are the most valuable lists for card-deck publishers to acquire because these people are 1) familiar with card-decks; 2) open them, and 3) respond to card-deck offers. In this category, the most valuable names are those of people who have responded to card-deck offers within the last 90 days. These names are held exclusively by people who run cards in card-decks and constitute a very valuable form of currency. One way card-deck publishers acquire these names is by running "house" cards, often of blind (that is, non-specific) offers. They then either rent these names through a list broker to generate extra income and/or swap them with other card-deck publishers and advertisers to get access to other card-deck responsive names. Too, very often a card-deck publisher will give a heavy card-deck advertiser a discounted price on his next card if he provides a certain number of names in payment. For example, for between 20,000-25,000 current quarter card-deck responsive names an advertiser could secure a free four-color card to 100,000 prospects. In this exchange, the deck publisher would save up to $2,500 in list rental charges while the advertiser would save at least as much in advertising charges. For the advertiser, the cost of these 100,000 cards would be almost nothing at this point; just the running charge for the names. For the publisher who happened to have an empty space on a four-color form, the cost would be equally nominal. In other words, once you've invested enough money to generate this number of recent leads, you can significantly reduce the cost of your advertising program . . . yet continue your supply of leads! The objective of the smart card-deck publisher is to run a sufficient number of house cards so that he always has a significant number of new card-deck responsive names coming in and to swap with other card-deck publishers and advertisers to get the remainder — in other words, to reduce his list rental charge to no more than the actual cost of running the cards of those people with whom he's made deals.

- reducing commissions. Commissions can be reduced by running a house card in each issue detailing for potential advertisers the major benefits they'd receive by running their offer in this deck. Such advertisers contact the publisher directly and purchase and pay for their card directly, thus eliminating the need to pay any commission to a card-deck broker. All card-deck publishers use this means for generating their own leads.

- selling products and services from their own house cards. Card-deck publishers have the means for acquiring a substantial number of cards at cost and using them to sell products/services at full price. This gives them a tremendous advantage over their own advertisers. Unfortunately, most card-deck publishers do not think like *marketers*; instead they think like *publishers*. What this means is that the only cards they include on their own behalf are designed to generate names and/or fill unsold slots on their last printing form. For such purposes most publishers maintain house cards which can be inserted at the last minute and maintain relationships primarily with publishers like McGraw-Hill and Dartnell Corporation which have existing selling programs and camera-ready art-work immediately available. But as I pointed out, card deck publishers think like publishers, not marketers. This means they are primarily interested in creating their deck rather than using their deck as a means of generating a steady stream of leads and sales for more profitable products than books generally are. Thus, many diminish the income prospects of their decks accordingly.

Now, all publishers make most of their money from the sale of cards to advertisers. Unfortunately, most make virtually all of their money this way which means they are primarily interested in maximizing the amount of money they can squeeze from an advertiser. This has lead to a system full of advertiser abuse by card-deck publishers. Let me show you what I mean.

I previously showed you a chart of current card-deck prices as taken from *Standard Rate & Data* (see page 162). These are the amounts the publishers hope to squeeze out of their advertisers. As many unwary advertisers have learned to their chagrin, publishers often get these highly inflated sums. They have then met their objective . . . and the buyer be damned as a direct-mail advertisement from a card-deck publisher called New Businesses Nationwide of Clearwater, Florida clearly demonstrates.

This advertisement, which I am looking at as I write, says, "WOULD YOU INVEST $2,887 TO EARN $43,750?" They say that if you take a card in each of 6 issues going to their market of 175,000 new businesses at a price of $2,887.50 and get 5250 leads per mailing, given certain conditions of your price and closure percentage, you'll make nearly $44,000 each time. Or, for an investment of $17,325, you'll gross $262,500. (By the way, their regular insertion price is $6,025 as of this writing if you only insert once; that is, about 3 times the cost of advertising in my card-deck!)

Unfortunately, the chances of this happening are, at best, negligible; this publisher is either being knowingly deceptive in his business advertising or is just plain ignorant about his work. Either way, it's disgraceful. (By the way, for some reason Clearwater, Florida has emerged as perhaps the capital of the card-deck sharpies. There, card-deck publishers pop up and disappear with astonishingly rapidity . . . just another reason why "Caveat Emptor" should be the civic motto of that breezy burg.)

What the advertiser's representative is doing is using greed to get the would-be advertiser to stop being sensible. "Hey, kid, could you use $262,500?" Well, who couldn't? The rep, having planted the greed seed, then says to the advertiser that all he has to do is plunk down a mere 17K and, *voilà*, the quarter million plus is as good as in the bank.

As every card-deck publisher knows (though they not surprisingly remain silent on the subject) . . . as every regular card-deck advertiser knows (because, with experience, comes an understanding of how many leads he is likely to get, how many will be good leads, how many not and what he has to do to close more of them sooner and so get back his investment and actually make money), the line being used by New Businesses Nationwide is rubbish. And quite possibly larcenous into the bargain. Unfortunately, the would-be advertiser/rube doesn't know this. He doesn't know how much the card is really costing the advertiser (for 175,000 cards, the actual cost is probably about $800-$1,000); doesn't know what he can really expect to get and doesn't know how to handle the leads he does get. In addition, he doesn't know that the unscrupulous and/or careless publishers are well aware that there is a large cadre of card-deck freebie-seekers. These are people who answer virtually EVERY card-deck offer . . . but never buy anything. These people swell the response . . . but because they are almost never real prospects, there is no money to be made from them, whatever benefits they're offered. However, they do respond, and therefore the publisher can point to the unwary (now burned and relatively impecunious) advertiser and say, "Well, you got the response; it's your own fault you didn't get the sales!" *Note:* in my case, as soon as I know that a person is this kind of blood-sucker, I purge him from my list. He may keep sending in cards for a while but when he sees he's getting nowhere the smarter parasites stop. Many, however, never get the point, and I just keep throwing their responses in the trash. Pitiful, what?

Through this well-oiled system the advertiser loses what, for a first-time, small card-deck advertiser, is a significant part (perhaps all) of his advertising budget; (after all if he's getting even half of the money he thinks is coming in, he can go for broke, right?) The deck publisher has, however, made at least three times his investment (and up to 6 *times* that investment if the rube pays full price on a one-time insertion with prices like New Business Nationwide) and goes merrily on his way, eager for the next issue.

Of course, he's somewhat dissatisfied if the advertiser doesn't repeat; it's always easier to put a deck together with repeating customers. For one thing, the art-work is already on file; for another, you don't have to find someone new, instruct him in the basics, and produce the card — *and* you don't have the worry about whether you'll be paid or not. Yes, it's always easier if a customer repeats. But let me be perfectly plain about this: IT'S NO DISASTER TO THE CARD-DECK PUBLISHER IF HE DOESN'T. Why? Because 1) he'll almost certainly have a group of repeating card-deck advertisers who'll renew their engagements with him because they are doing well; 2) this number will grow the longer he's in business; 3) because his own deck inquiry card will have produced hundreds of new inquiries from would-be advertisers, and 4) most importantly of all, because his space is always severely limited. Therefore there will always be more people who want and indeed need to advertise than he has places available. Thus, what is so often such an invidious and parasitic system continues to flourish.

Enter The Count of Raban, Descendant of Crusader Knights

It is not for nothing that I am the descendent of a companion of Richard of England, Coeur de Lion, stalwart crusader. Like my valiant ancestors, I wish to do well while doing good. If I can be the scourge of evil while amassing treasure, why, I say, so much the better. And so, true son of my illustrious forefathers, I (finally) took on the card-deck industry.

Finally? Yes, it took some time; (a Lancelot is not shaped in a day). For many years, I was a fairly hapless card-deck advertiser. Sometimes I secured decent results; oftentimes I didn't. But I persisted because I knew that there was a solid group of companies which advertised — and therefore must be making money — time after time.

The card-decks I advertised with were, predictably, no assistance. They didn't help with copy or design suggestions and invariably stuck my card deep in the middle of the deck, the lowest-drawing position. I was a small company; I had no clout. I was fair game for their regularly uncaring and exploitative treatment,

Then, while writing one of the books in this series, I set out to truly understand how the industry worked. In the process, I discovered how much cards really cost and why the companies I was patronizing didn't seem to care if I did well or if I ever advertised with them again or not. I discovered why if I wasn't there to be fleeced in a moment another sucker was certain to pop up.

As soon as I understood how much cards really cost, I did what you should do; I started offering a fixed 20% over their actual cost, an amount far below the published rate-card price. There was always incredulity and even outright anger when I went from sheep to protector of my interests. "This is my price," I said. "If you have an available space at the end, call me and we'll work something out. I have camera-ready art. Otherwise, don't call me." (By the way, as anyone with any experience with card-decks can affirm, card-deck sales reps are among the most obnoxiously persistent; why not, the commissions you're paying them are immense!) In virtually every case, I received an ungracious, begrudging call at the last minute saying I could bloody well have the bloody space if I got them the bloody art immediately. And so, for some time, it went. I knew I was paying some of the lowest prices in the industry; I turned my attention to writing more client-centered copy. The number of leads went up; the per lead cost, based on increased return and much lower prices, went down. Things were better . . .

Then looking at the prospect of what became the whopping and destructive postal rate increase of 1991, I realized my mailing activities would have to be significantly curtailed (as happened with many mailers) if I didn't think of another way of generating significant revenue and reducing the cost of my own list rental. I researched the card-deck industry some more along with my associate publisher Bill Reece. I discovered that unwary advertisers were continuing to be fleeced, as outlined above, and that the situation was ripe for a revolution.

I introduced that revolution, and I can proudly boast that I helped transform this industry! I:

- priced cards just as close to their actual cost as I could without losing my shirt. Whereas my competitors were charging (so their rate cards said) $3300 and more for 100,000 two-color cards, I set my rate at a mere $1199. Thus, no one could ever touch me for price.

- threw out credit. Credit costs money. I said to my advertisers: if you want lower prices, you've got to pay in advance. Why? So I can prepay my printing bill and all my other expenses and use your money to get lower supplier prices. Of course, advertisers steeped in the lax credit policies of the '80's didn't like this, and, at the beginning, I had to make frequent compromises. However, with each deck (and the insistent repetition of my rationale) the credit got less until it became virtually non-existent. New people to card-decks didn't mind this innovation; it sounded right to them. It was the lazy old dogs, forced to change their ways in the brave new world, who complained; they complained, but, bit by grudging bit, they complied — and learned that they, too, could do their bit to making their own lives better.

- instituted an aggressive card-deck list swapping and acquisition program. For my first issue, no card-deck company would let me have card-deck responsive names at any price. They knew that any card-deck company was most vulnerable at the beginning when it didn't have a vast reserve of its own card-deck responsive names. They reckoned that it would be easier to bump me off then than later, and they were right. That's when Rich Baumer, president of Venture Communications, stepped in and offered to rent me for $10,000 the names I'd needed. Baumer's a clever guy and an aggressive one. The lists he rented me through his agent were not only not card-deck responsive; they were horrible. As a result the first deck was a disaster; we nearly didn't squeak through to a second issue. Baumer will no doubt deny to his dying day that he planned his move as a pre-emptive strike; of course, I think otherwise. After all, at one point in true abusive New Yorker fashion, he got on the phone and damned my enterprise and my ideas because I was threatening the good thing that deck owners like him had set up; he actually said he'd run me out of business . . . and he almost succeeded. However, out of much agony came much valuable experience. Since that abortive first issue, my deck has consistently grown, growing more profitable by offering a fair service at a fair price. In the same time, the size of Venture decks has dipped and that inestimable company has been forced to lower its prices (though they still publish the same astronomical rates) and, no doubt, its profit. While Baumer benefited in the short term to the tune of 10,000 of my dollars, my continued, flourishing existence has cost him tens of thousands of dollars and helped lots of advertisers avoid being entirely fleeced . . . a process which is reinforced every 90 days when each of my new issues appears; each larger than any deck Venture produces! As a crusader, I take considerable comfort in this . . . (Baumer, of course, continues to be difficult. Thus, it comes as no surprise to me that at frequent intervals, I learn that his sales reps are spreading disinformation about my company to advertisers they are trying hard to pitch. These advertisers aren't stupid, however; they regularly tell me just what's being said and who's saying it. I fax off another letter mentioning the precise circumstances in which Venture is spreading this information, who's doing it, what was said, *etc.* I again notify them that legal action will be forthcoming if they continue to spread such error. It's a bore doing all this, of course, but it's nice to know the titans at Venture and elsewhere are so threatened by our existence to keep thinking up lies about what we're doing. It means that what I'm doing keeps working!)

- established a series of other companies through which I could generate additional revenues so that we wouldn't have to raise the card prices. I am the only card-deck publisher I know who doesn't just fill up extra cards with a rather anemic program marketing a few books. I sell much higher ticket consultant services and a series of high-ticket products all of which produce necessary revenue. Moreover, I set up the companies that produce these goods and services so that I could profit in fuller measure from the benefits of card-deck advertising. Thus, I'm probably the one card-deck publisher who derives the most income from advertising in his own deck and certainly the one who derives the least percentage of profit from the deck from advertising revenues, that is money put up by advertisers. The result is that more advertising dollars stay with the advertisers . . . thereby enabling them to mount a more extensive advertising program rather than merely swelling my coffers. They appreciate this . . . and give me additional patronage.

- gave advertisers free color. Other companies offer second color as an additional cost; I provide it free to all those who want it.

- gave copy writing and marketing assistance. Because the other publishers don't care as much if you repeat or not, they won't spend the necessary time helping you create the right copy and will never provide necessary technical assistance so that you're ready to handle — and close — the leads that do come in. THIS IS CRAZY! My objective is getting *100%* of the people who advertise in my card-deck to repeat *every* time. My game will then have merely two parts: getting 100,000 new deck responsive names every 90 days and managing the process of bringing in the art-work and publishing and distributing the decks. No other publisher has this explicit objective, and therefore no other company does what it takes to ensure advertiser success. Their emphasis is and always has been merely on selling cards; their sales representatives are almost all abysmally ignorant about what it takes to write and design a top-drawing card and what you must do when your leads come in to make money. This is wrong, of course, but it is typical of the way this industry handles things, and it handles things in this lax way because your success is not their objective and never has been.

Having written all this, I do not want you to draw the erroneous conclusion that you should never under any circumstances advertise in anyone else's card deck and just in mine (though obviously I want your business and feel you'd be foolish not to avail yourself of my system *if it can meet your objectives*). After all, I advertise in lots of other people's decks and maintain profitable (if constantly watched) relationships with them. What I do want you to understand is that card-decks can work for you if you think through what you are trying to do, pay the minimum price for your card, develop client-centered copy that will generate a truly qualified lead, and have in place an aggressive lead-closing program ready to swing into operation from the moment you receive the very first lead. Let's go on to these necessary components of a successful card-deck program.

Thinking Through What You Are Trying To Do

As the fallacious advertising copy of New Businesses Nationwide (quoted above) demonstrates, card-deck publishers will try to use your greed to induce you to pay inflated costs. DON'T GIVE IN! I start from the proposition that every human can be motivated by greed . . . and usually is. But if you're going to become a millionaire selling services, you've got to be more hard-headed than that. Of course, you want to make money on your investment, but you need to be realistic. Figure: if everybody could turn 17K into 262K in six issues, the nation's richest citizens and sharpest money managers would all be in card decks. But they aren't. Card-decks remain a specialized advertising medium that works well for certain service specialists and doesn't work well for others. Thus, be cautious in your objectives. Here's what card decks can do for you. Card decks can:

- get your client-centered message to a targeted group of people who can benefit from that message if they are induced to act;

- deliver this message for as low as 1.2 cents per prospect (this is my price and, as you already know, no one can beat it);

- make money for you if you project a very conservative return and have a sufficiently highly priced service so that with this return you are, with the additional work that comes in closing the prospect, assured of a profit.

Here's what I mean:

Say, like the copywriter I've told you about before, my average sale is $1000; say that $750 of this is profit with $250 going for various fixed expenses. Say that I advertise in a deck going to 100,000 business prospects, all of whom could buy what I produce, namely ads, cover letters, flyers, brochures, *etc.* Say that 500 of these answer an inquiry card (that is 1/2 of one percent, a reasonable projection. Please note that unlike New Businesses Nationwide I am projecting a conservative return of 1/2 of one percent asking for more *information*; they were projecting 1/2 of 1 per cent to *buy*, a very considerable difference.)

Say that 50% of these are flake varieties; they either are freebie seekers, don't understand the offer, don't have any money, or are just tire-kickers who waste everyone's time. This still leaves this advertiser with 250 leads to work on, of which 80% arrive within

6 weeks. Of these 250 he needs to close just 3 to be profitable. Three out of 250. Is this possible? It most certainly is. Let's say he's a relatively poor closer; say that he can only close one out of 25. This means that he'll use up 75 of his available leads to make 3 sales. But this will still leave him 175 leads. Even at his abysmal rate of closing, he should gross an additional $8,750. And this, ladies and gentlemen, is both a realistic possibility and a very good return on his investment . . . not just once, but *every time he makes it*. Now, can you begin to see why there is a significant cadre of people who are very heavy card-deck advertisers?

This is why you should be considering card-deck/val-pack advertising, too.

Let me make sure you understand what I'm really saying here. If you have the right message (which we'll deal with shortly), of the 100,000 people who get this mailing, fully 99,500 or 99 1/2% can throw it in the trash immediately — and you can still make money. Of the remaining 500 who respond either by phone or mail, fully 250 (or 50% of the respondents) can be flakes . . . and you can still make money. SO LONG AS YOU CAN CLOSE AT LEAST 12-13 OF THE REMAINING LEADS. In other words, you will be profitable if you can close and derive income from just 12 people out of 100,000. This is not only possible . . . it's virtually a lead-pipe cinch.

This is why I smile when some fatuous ass, upon discovering at a cocktail party that I publish a card-deck, tells me he always throws "those things" away and never responds . . . as if this were somehow a demonstration of his intelligence and insight instead of further proof that he's an idiot. The world is full of these morons. But even if 99,500 of them receive a deck in which a service is advertised (and chuck it with a superior smirk), you can still laugh all the way to the bank. I know. I do.

. . . And so do all the other hard-core card-deck advertisers (of which there are many hundreds) who have made the most conservative projections for what it really takes to make their card-deck advertising program profitable . . . and proceed accordingly.

Paying The Minimum Price For Your Card

As you are now well aware, pricing in the card-deck industry is a joke. Publishers advertise a high price; the uninitiated pay it . . . or, believing that they are getting a bargain "first-time advertiser" rate, get socked for some still substantial fraction of it. Not until these babes-in-the-wood sit facing a pile of unconvertible "leads" (smaller or larger depending on their card copy, the publisher's list, *etc.*) and a much smaller dollar return, do they realize they have made a very bad deal. They then sour on card-decks . . . never realizing that while the publisher has done precious little to help them (indeed the reverse), they have done precious little to help themselves. And that includes failing to negotiate for a better price where necessary.

So, what price should you offer? One way is to check with me and find out what my current rate for 100,000 cards is. So long as I'm in business (for the duration, I trust), my price will continue to be by far the lowest in the industry. At present, it's $1199 for 100,000 cards, though this will go up if postage or paper prices rise, *etc.* You may offer other publishers the same rate you'd pay in my deck. By the way, you can tell them that if you don't get it, you'll advertise with me. Other publishers know me and know this probably isn't just an idle threat. One of my advertisers laughingly told me the other day that by using this line, he'd secured identical terms with other card-deck publishers whose published rates are at least three times mine; one of them, I'm delighted to report, was Venture Communications! It will probably work for you, too. (Give R. Baumer my love!)

Another way is to take the published rate found in *Standard Rate & Data*, divide it by 3 and offer 1/3 of what they want. No more. If the sales rep is adamant about a higher price (likely), it's probably because it's early in his selling cycle, and he optimistically thinks he won't need you. If it's later in the cycle, he may well need you; while he may not want or be able to come down to your price (publishers give their sales reps leeway but generally impose a floor price), he will give you a better price. Don't accept even that unless you've figured out what a conservative projection might be for sales of your service and factored in your own ability to mount an aggressive lead-closing program. Remember, it costs money to market even to qualified prospects.

There is, of course, one other way. You could just call me and, without wasting a minute in the kind of idiocy that distinguishes negotiating for prices with other card-deck companies, you could get the lowest prices in America *immediately*. *Note:* with other card-deck companies, no matter how good a negotiator you are, you are never really certain that you've gotten the lowest price. Just recently, a friend of mine called and bragged about the superior price he'd received in another deck. Just the day before someone else I knew told me he'd paid exactly 50% of that for his card in the *same* issue. I said nothing, but it merely confirmed me in my firm belief that in another publisher's deck of 68 cards, there are probably 68 different prices individually negotiated, with many advertisers simply getting screwed. But if they're happy, what difference does it make, right? As the Candides who run the other card-deck companies muse, surely all is for the best in this best of all possible worlds.

Developing Client-Centered Copy To Get A Truly Qualified Lead

Let me be very plain with you: no one is going to buy your service from a card. At best, the prospect will tell you that 1) he wants the benefit you have available and 2) that he is either more or less qualified, that is ready to buy your benefit now . . . or absurdly far from being able to do so. Thus, your card should be designed to:

- hammer home the benefit you have available;

- induce immediate action, and

- qualify the prospect as much as possible as soon as possible.

Your copy can assist with these three objectives.

As you should now be perfectly aware, the bedrock of any card copy is BENEFITS. That is, what have you got that will improve the prospect's life? The more specific you can be about these benefits the better.

Too often card-deck advertisers, no less than other hobbled marketers, understand this matter of benefits but dimly. Take this copy from a card currently running in a competitor's deck:

"Create A Terrific First Impression With A Banner You Can Be Proud Of. The experts agree that the first impression you make on your prospects will live forever."

This is copy obviously produced by a company (Britten Banners, Sterling, VA) that produces banners. It is also copy produced by a company that has lost its way and forgotten what card-deck marketing is all about and what its prospects are looking for.

"Creating a first impression" is not a benefit . . . it's just vague words. What the prospect wants is not to make a first impression; he wants to make more sales faster, just as every thinking business does. The advertiser is promoting "first impressions"; this relates to banners, but not to the objectives of the prospect. What the banner company must remember is that no one actually needs a banner. But what prospects always want are ways to sell more, faster. If a banner can do that, why, then, by God, the prospect wants the banner. It's as simple as that.

The last lines on the card are: "We can help you make a terrific first impression by providing trade show banners and table covers that will make your neighbor's booth look sad."

Again, there isn't one word linking banners to profits . . . and bigger (presumably more expensive banners) to faster profits.

And so this card goes astray. To the detriment of the advertiser who forgot about BENEFITS . . . BENEFITS . . . BENEFITS. (*Note:* in my experience companies which produce this kind of "me-centered" copy for both their cards and other marketing communications, often run "me-centered" operations where the interests of the client are never primary, whatever shibboleths they mouth. In my experience, this is the case with Britten Banners . . . and therefore its inadequate, selfish copy comes as no surprise to me.)

Benefits, however, are never enough. There must be a motivating reason for the prospect to sit up and take ACTION NOW. In this card there is no such reason. No such offer.

Further, that offer must be prominently presented in the upper right hand corner . . . or as a banner headline across the top . . . and perhaps repeated or reemphasized across the bottom. In short, you must make the offer just as prominent and important as you've designed it to be. And you must provide a means for the customer to respond NOW, too! This means prominently displaying your phone number (even if it isn't an 800-number). You can include this in your offer . . . and you can put it next to where the stamp goes on the address portion of your card, thus: "For faster service, call (number)" . . . , or "To get (benefit offered), call (number)".

Finally, there must be qualifiers. These qualifiers range from:

- using your regular phone number instead of an 800-number; freebie seekers love 800-numbers. Better prospects won't fail to call you even if they have to spend their own money to do so.

- having the prospect put a stamp on the card instead of using a postage-paid mailing;

- adding the words "No response without phone number" in the place where you've asked the prospect to put his phone. Let me give you one reason why: no person who has failed to put his phone number on the card in my card-deck seeking prospects to advertise in the deck has ever bought a card. In other words, people who won't follow this directive are very poor prospects. (These days I alternate between throwing those cards in the trash immediately, putting the names on my mailing list so they'll further details in my catalog, and sending a short, computer-generated note that asks them to provide the necessary details. It all depends on how I feel . . .

Here are further qualifiers which you'll learn by becoming expert at analyzing the leads which are both phoned and mailed in. For phone leads, if the person:

- simply wants "information" and won't provide the details you need to determine his level of interest and ability to follow through, he's not a real lead. Give him a low priority and either send nothing, or put it aside for a less busy time, as you see fit.

- sounds too young, too old, too vague, too uncertain, ask a qualifying question like "When did you want to go ahead and get (benefit you offer)?" If you don't like what you hear, send nothing.

- is rude, vulgar, overly demanding (take note New Yorkers) or hostile in any way, send nothing. You don't need that grief!

- won't give you a phone number, send nothing.

- gives you a post office box but won't supply a street address or other good follow-up information, send nothing unless you get a good explanation.

- is not the decision maker but won't tell you who the decision maker is, his title, or follow-up information, send nothing.

- has called before and you've sent material and tried to follow up unsuccessfully, ask point blank whether the person is ready to buy now. If you get an uncertain, vague or unsettling answer, send nothing.

All this is part of your lead-qualifying process.

Do something similar with mail-in leads:

- if the person's handwriting indicates you're dealing with someone very young, very old (unless you are trying to attract the very old), or a serial killer (unless . . . but, no, I hope you aren't!), send nothing;

- if the person hasn't provided a required phone number, diminish his priority (if you think you'll later have time to send a letter) . . . or send nothing (if you have lots of other, better leads);

- if the person has written all over the card, particularly messages of a savage, religious, or sexual nature, send nothing;

- if portions of the address are missing, don't bother looking for it. Send nothing.

- if the person is a prisoner (you can tell either because of the town it comes from coupled with an identifying string of numbers which prisoners try to disguise as a code, or because the response is stamped to indicate it's coming from a convict), send nothing.

- if the person sends in response after response but never does anything, not only send nothing, but purge this person from your mailing list. He's a certifiable freebie-seeker and not worth your time. If you're feeling benevolent, write these creeps a letter (computer-generated, of course) as I sometimes do when feeling particularly virtuous telling them that they're the kind of slime who's using up the resources of the planet. Tell them either to buy something or get lost. Virtue must be stern; besides, it'll make you feel good when you flush this kind of trash.

Note: there are many among the service marketers, as elsewhere, who equal-weight all leads, treating all the same. Again, I reiterate: marketing is not democratic. It is about targeting the right people, inducing them to take the fastest action (for your lowest cost), finding out if they are indeed serious and ready to commit, and then making the deal that does in fact commit them to getting the benefit . . . and making you the profit. It is not about spending time (out of some misguided sense of "humanism" and a pervading sadness you are not Mother Theresa) with people who cannot — for whatever reason — commit.

Why do I tell you this? Because just now I'm working with a "marketing professional" (I put the phrase in quotes because it is what he uses to describe himself . . . though, at this writing, I'd certainly never call him that except with full ironic intonation) who can't seem to grasp the point that in marketing all prospects are not equal and never will be. With a song in his heart (and apparently air where the little gray cells should be), he'll spend quarter hour after quarter hour making "friends" with people who will never buy, racking up big expenses, but accomplishing nothing more than irritating me profoundly. Let me stress again: marketing is not about being in the "like" business. It's about being in the results business. Your job is to craft benefits for people and to make them as alluring and motivational as possible. But once you've discovered that the prospect is not really a prospect, your job is to sign off as quickly and civilly as possible — not to chit-chat away the day in futile amiability. Learn this or you'll never be rich!

Having In Place An Aggressive Lead-Closing Program Ready To Swing Into Operation The Moment You Receive The Very First Response.

In the next chapter, I intend to address this matter in exquisite and microscopic detail. Here let me simply say this: your card-deck advertising program can fail for any number of reasons.

- The price you've paid for your card may be too high. Therefore even though you are getting a good response, given the realities of lead conversion you may never be able to make money;

- The copy may offer too few benefits and/or make no offer motivating immediate response. As such the audience may be right, even the price may be right . . . but you haven't done enough to generate an early, enthusiastic, substantial response;

- The target market may be wrong. Everything else may well be right, but if you're going to the wrong people, the results will be unsatisfactory;

- You're simply not ready to deal with the leads when they come in.

As I have constantly urged in this book, you must be ready to handle the leads *before a single lead materializes.* You must have thought through and created:

- all the written materials you need, both letters and support documents;

- telephone scripts that take into account the various requests the respondents may make of you;

- trained staff. If the people assisting with your lead-closing program are inept, what difference does it make if you are getting qualified leads? You are running an unqualified operation;

- the precise steps you will implement from the minute you receive a mail-in response or initial phone call right through what you'll do in court if the customer fails to pay for the service he has ordered and you have provided.

In short, you must be prepared.

Now, I know that every single person reading this book will think he is prepared to a magnitude beyond all but those of celestial standing. I also know that is very likely untrue. Over and over again, I have seen people pay good money for card-deck advertising, draw a reasonable, even a superlative response, and fail miserably because of a complete lack of thoughtful preparation and detailed, focused, client-centered follow-through. Such people, almost as a matter of course, blame the card-deck publisher, the sales rep, the copywriter, the graphic artist — anyone, in fact, but the one person who should be blamed and beaten about the head with a truncheon: themselves. Don't let this happen to you.

Card-deck advertising, as I am quite willing to stand up and publicly acknowledge, can make you very rich. It can also drain your resources with astonishing rapidity and leave you frustrated, embittered and adamantly (if unreasonably) opposed to this method of generating leads and sales. While it would be nice if the vast majority of card-deck publishers, sales reps, commissioned agents and others assisted you to realize your objectives, I, for one, no longer believe this will ever happen. However, you can still use this medium to get rich: if you follow these directions. You will, won't you???

Generating Leads Through Electronic Moving Message Display Signs

While writing this chapter a woman realtor from Virginia called Bill Reece, national sales director for my moving signs company, and told him she'd been unaware of these signs until just the other day. Then, within a 7 day period she'd seen one of the signs in the window of house being sold by a competing realtor, read an article on the subject in her professional publication, and received a prospect card from us. Was this, she wondered, the beginning of a trend? I am tempted to say, "Yes, Virginia . . .", but I won't.

While large areas of America have yet to tune into this latest trend in marketing, if you walk down places from the Champs Elysée to Las Vegas . . . you can't fail to notice that there's something new to catch your eye. That something new is the electronic moving message display sign. In point of fact they've been around for years — ever been to Times Square? — but only recently has the technology advanced to the point of developing dozens of new models and to being able to produce them in sizes and at prices suitable for every service business where they make sense.

In considering whether you should put a moving sign to work for you, these are the questions you need to mull over:

- does a moving message sign make sense for my service business?

- if it does, what kind of sign should I get?

- once I've got it . . . how can I best use it to get more business, specifically to both generate more leads and sell more of my services?

Does A Moving Message Sign Make Sense For You?

I want you to take a few minutes and consider both your office location and mode of doing business. Do any of the following apply:

- do you have front windows that people/potential customers pass on a regular basis? Are you located in a mall? The ground floor of an office building or professional complex? On a busy street? Do you want to attract the notice of new potential customers by running a series of client-centered, motivational messages 24 hours a day, 365 days a year — including a lot of time when you're not physically present? Then you need a moving sign . . .

- do clients visit your premises on a regular basis? Do they wait in a waiting room before receiving your service? Do you want them to hear about the benefits you have available? The services? Special offers and prices? Something new you've just developed? Then you need a moving sign . . .

- do you exhibit at trade shows? Do you want more people to pay attention to your booth/message? Do you want to be able to get your message out even when you're busy talking to people? Do you want to get your message out even when you're not able to be at the booth (you need breaks, after all)? Do you want to customize your message to this particular trade show without necessarily printing up special materials just for it? Then you need a moving sign . . .

- do you do talk programs like workshops and seminars? Do you want to ensure that your client-centered messages keep hammering home the benefits you have available . . . even when you're otherwise engaged? Then you need a moving sign . . .

If you've answered yes to *any* of these questions but aren't using a moving message sign, you need a kick where it helps. Let me give you the prime reasons why, if these basic conditions apply, using a moving message sign makes supreme sense:

- with the best will in the world, you can't work 24 hours and day, 365 days a year. You're going to get tired, do some traveling, be ill, even take a few days off (imagine!). Your sign, however, disseminating a constant stream of motivational, client-centered messages, will keep on working for just the tiny cost of the electricity;

- if people are passing your windows/premises and you're not marketing to them, you're losing a prime opportunity to get new business. This is lunacy. When a person passes your window, a marketing opportunity presents itself. Since the cavemen marketers have known this, of course; that's why there have been stationary signs. But a moving sign is visually more interesting and thus more compelling than any stationary sign. Moreover, a moving sign doesn't commit you to a single message forever like a stationary sign which literally must be redone, repainted, *etc.* (with all the work and expense that entails) to be updated. With a moving message sign, the changing can be done in a matter of moments. Remember your job as a marketer: if a person is passing your establishment, your job is to hit him with a client-centered message and to get him inside to buy the benefit you're selling. This is difficult with a stationary sign; easy with a moving message sign that you either place outside (bigger and customized models) or inside;

- if you have the kind of service (like a veterinarian, barber shop, cleaners, travel agency, dentist, doctor, *etc.*) where your clients come in to get your service and may have to wait for it (as no doubt happens to at least some of your clients every day), then their waiting presents you with a good marketing opportunity. Through the moving sign, you can impart messages about both your basic and special services, limited time offers, specials, premiums, and reminders. Is flu season coming up, doc? Then remind people in your waiting room to either get their shot today (best) or schedule it for tomorrow (acceptable). Do you sell products, cosmetologist, that would be of value to your customers? Either way, your job is to upgrade the value of each individual customer's visit. This makes much more sense for you than merely having the customer read an out-of-date issue of some tattered 'zine while waiting for you to get around to them, not least because the moving message sign keeps repeating and repeating and repeating your client-centered message, driving home your point. Your job, marketer, is to build client value — and your receipts. A moving message sign helps you do this.

- if you go out of your office to deliver your service or do various kinds of either fully-fledged or partial marketing activities (as with trade shows or talk programs), a moving message sign is a godsend. As above, the moving sign works nonstop. Without a moving sign, if you're busy attending to Prospect A (much less answering that insistent call of nature), Prospect B is getting away from you in any number of ways. With a compelling, eye-catching and client-centered moving message display sign, you at least stand a chance of driving home your message. (By the way, did you ever stop to consider why Las Vegas, one of America's fastest-growing and most prosperous cities, has the biggest moving sign presence? Do you think there's a connection between its prosperity and its understanding of how to use these signs? Think about it . . .)

Here are some additional reasons why moving signs make sense:

- they're cheap. You can get a reasonable moving message sign these days for around what a decent stationary sign costs ($600-$1000). Think about that! With the stationary sign, you get, well, a stationary message. There it is! Not so with an easy-to-change moving message sign which can literally be altered however often you want.

- they're light-weight and easy-to-install. Take it from a guy who has a tested mechanical aptitude at the 5th percentile (which means that paraplegic house cats have more mechanical dexterity than I do). If I can pick 'em up, move 'em and put 'em in, so can you!

- they cost little to run. Moving message signs run on regular electricity; they don't need special electrical apparatus, either. You just plug them in to a socket as you would any electrical appliance.

- good ones come with a complete one-year warranty and 800-number technical support service line. Not all, I said; just better quality ones.

- unless you buy a bargain-basement "cheapie" sign, you get considerable memory for messages — which is what you want. Your job as a marketer is not to be creative; it's to discover a series of client-centered marketing messages and keep tabs on whether they work. When you've got a winner — something that brings in prospects and closes deals — you want to keep it in memory . . . so you can use it again at some point. Over time you're going to have a back-log of these successful, profit-making messages; if you've got enough memory in your machine, you can save them all and easily reuse them.

Service marketer, I hope you're looking around your premises right now and thinking about all the situations where you've been in a crowd of potential prospects but unable to get your message to all of them. Think of the people passing your premises: are you luring them in now? Think of the people who have to wait to get your service. Are you marketing to them while they're waiting. THINK! Don't you suppose a moving message sign could help you generate more prospects and close more business? Of course it could. Therefore the real question is . . .

What Kind Of Sign Should You Get?

There are essentially three different kinds of moving signs:

1. the ones that sell for around $100-$200 that you can pick up in a merchandise club or bargain store;
2. many varieties of higher-quality signs offering a wide range of features highly desirable from a marketing standpoint, and
3. customized signs like the ones in Times Square and the big ones you see in Las Vegas.

Of these three options, you're not going to want #1! And you are going to want #2! Here's why.

— Why You Want To Avoid "Cheapie" Warehouse Signs

Being a frugal type, I'm sure you want to spend the least number of dollars for your moving sign. Seems reasonable. But don't acquire a sign that can't do what you need it to do. Remember your objectives:

- getting people outside your premises inside;
- disseminating focused, client-centered messages to people inside, and
- delivering similar messages to people whenever you take your sign off premises to trade shows, *etc.*

Now, consider this. The cheap signs that you ordinarily find in warehouses:

- offer only one color. You've probably seen these signs. The color is red and it runs repeatedly . . . uninterestingly. It's dull, prosaic and . . . after a while . . . unseen: THE MARKETER'S WORST FEAR. Just as monotone is killing, so is monochrome. You need as many colors as you can possibly get. The cheap signs either can't provide them . . . or can't provide "true" colors. The colors they do offer are hard to see . . . particularly in daylight when you're certainly going to want to use them! Finally, even when you can get these fake colors, you pay more for them!!!

• run only a single line of text at a time. A single message seems to go round and round and round. I've watched a moving sign of this type at my local post office. I've watched the crowd reaction . . . or rather lack of reaction . . . to it. The message plays but the market ignores. ANOTHER MARKETING CATASTROPHE. You need a display area that will show more than one line of typed message "on the board" at the same time. You also need room (and the ability to produce) "special effects" to create an attraction for your prospects' eyes. Special effects include "scrolling", where your message rolls up (or, down) into view; "flashing", where letters pop out at you, *etc.* The Cambridge post office, of course, (which is as retarded from a marketing stand-point as it is possible to be) doesn't get this. But then no postal clerk or administrator aspires to be the millionaire you do . . . which is why you can't afford to emulate its unproductive thinking.

• don't offer easy message-editing capability. Most moving signs make it relatively easy to get your message into the sign in the first place. However, the less expensive versions often make it fiendishly difficult to change or edit it. With low-priced, particularly foreign manufactured signs, you may not get even "partial editing" capability. Thus, you're *required* to input your entire message all over again — even if you just want to change a price! And, if you're going to have to climb a ladder or crawl into a window to do this, I bet you'll be real sorry you went for the bargain-basement model . . . when the better machines are not so very much more!

• have inadequate memory capacity. I've already touched on this. Like a computer, your sign stores more information than it actually shows in its display area at any moment. Unfortunately, the cheap signs don't give you the memory capacity you need. However, to be able to put more information in your sign, to have more use of your "special effects", *etc.*, you need at least 5000 characters of memory. And just like a computer, you'll find that however much memory you have, you're going to want more. Remember:

you're going to have days when you're either too rushed to think up more messages . . . or just uninspired. This is what memory is for!

- don't have memory back-up capability. For the same reason you back-up your computer daily (you do, don't you?), you need memory back-up for your signs. The power fails . . . lines spike . . . or something interrupts your power supply. It happens. If you're not prepared, you've lost all the messages you've specially created and painstakingly typed into your signs.

- won't give you presetting message capability. Are you going to be particularly busy next week? Out of town? Coming down with the flu? Mother-in-law coming? Put your messages in now and tell your sign when to display them. With this capability, you can save yourself and your staff lots of time and hassles by putting any messages you want into "memory" and telling the sign when to change messages — all by itself!

- won't give you transferable memory either. If you have several signs and want to run the same messages on some or all of the signs, and you are not on a "network system" (see below), you have two options. 1) You can type the same messages into *each* sign (again and again) until you've put the same messages into all your signs. Or 2) you can type your messages into one sign and transfer (in effect, copy) those messages into your other signs *without* typing them over and over and over again. Which do you prefer? Unfortunately, you can't get what you want with the discount store signs. They ordinarily don't offer a "memory cartridge."

- won't provide networking capability. Just like computers, you can connect your signs on a network of sorts and control the messages of many signs from one central location. This means you can change the messages, the effects, run different messages on different signs in different parts of your business at the same time, *etc.*, all because they are "connected" on a network that allows you to have an unequaled "master control" capability via your PC. With the better moving signs, you don't even have to go out on the floor to change the messages. You can do that from a "back room" if you want. Unfortunately, you don't get this time-saving and control feature with the cheaper models . . .

Having provided all the reasons for avoiding the cheap signs, any idiots who chance to read this book will, of course, want one of them. Being smarter, however, you'll want to get the model that'll generate the most leads and make the most sales fastest, that is one of the many solid types of standard signs now readily available with all the features you want.

Before moving on, however, let me say a word about custom signs. While at some point, as your bank balance swells, you may well want to go custom (about the time you're no longer buying your clothes off the rack and when you're using a wine consultant and not gulping plonk from the local liquor store) . . . and while custom signs certainly have all the valuable features enumerated above . . . I wouldn't suggest starting with these signs. For one thing, they're costly; for another, until you learn how to use a moving message sign effectively (which means starting with a good, solid, but less expensive version), it probably doesn't make economic sense. As soon as you "get it", however, and you see just how effective these signs are, why, then, I predict (the Jean Dixon of marketing) there will be a customized moving message sign in your future. In the meantime, get one of the solid units I've recommended. Use these suggestions:

- check your local sign store. People who make stationary signs also can get you moving signs. Because stationary signs are still their bread and butter, however, they're not always up-to-date on the latest developments, or

- call Bill Reece, national sales director of my moving sign company, JLA Ventures. We sell the moving signs of many major producers; we sell them in the United States and abroad and will work with you to get you just the right moving sign for your situation. Bill will be happy to provide several free recommendations given your marketing situation and objectives; we don't represent a single line but can generate suggestions from among the moving signs produced from many companies to get you just what will work best for you. He is, in effect, America's leading moving sign broker maintaining working relationships with any number of moving sign manufacturers. Contact Bill at JLA Ventures, 50 Follen St., Suite 507, Cambridge, MA 02138 or call (617) 547-6372.

Dealer Program: By the way, we maintain an aggressive dealer program for those who want to start their own business selling moving signs (there are no inventory requirements) or add moving signs to their current line of products. This is a high-growth business and, if you have good organizational, people and professional skills, you can easily make *several thousand dollars a day* from this line of work. It's something you can easily do from your home. Call Bill for complete details.

How Can You Use Your Moving Sign To Increase Your Business?

Okay, you've got your sign. Now what? Now, you start using it to generate the greatest number of leads as soon as possible and sell as many units of your service as quickly as you can. Here's how:

- Put a moving sign in each display window. Make sure people see your messages when they walk by. Create messages with compelling inducements that get people to come into your establishment . . . NOW!

- Put signs by your cash registers. Hey, this is where people wait, right? Don't waste their time . . . or your sales opportunities. Keep your messages coming fast and furious.

- Take them with you to trade shows. Moving signs are lightweight and easily moved. As such, they're about to revolutionize the trade show business. Recently, I attended a trade show in Omaha, Nebraska and only one booth had a moving message sign; not surprisingly, he got THE MOST BOOTH TRAFFIC. People like "trade show specials". With your moving message sign, you can easily create and market them.

- Change your messages frequently. Research shows the more you vary your messages, the better. There is one fish-shop in New York City that has become famous because of the cleverness of its messages, which are changed every morning.

- Keep a record of all the messages you've used and their responses. Face it: some of your messages are going to work better (read, "make more money") than others. Just like you code your ads and track response, you need to do the same with your messages . . . and reuse all the best ones.

- Run "human interest items" about staff . . . and customers. Moving message signs have the characteristics of both print

ads, television . . . and newsletters. People love "human
interest" items . . . contest winners, birthdays, trivia, information about your staff . . . and customers. Indulge them.
This kind of stuff always works. But intersperse these
messages with client-centered specials, *etc.*

- Focus your customers on special offers, limited offers, sales,
  etc. With a moving message sign, there's always a customer-
  centered special in your future!

- Don't let your messages get stale. The key to these signs is
  to keep the messages forever changing . . . but always make
  sure that they are focused on the prospects and buyers.
  Your signs should never say "old hat" but rather HERE'S
  SOMETHING ELSE THAT'S REALLY EXCITING AND
  VALUABLE FOR YOU, BABY!

The problem with most people using moving message signs is that
they treat them like stationary signs; just because the actual sign may
not move, they forget that the message inside the framework must
always be changing. Thus, too many moving message unit owners
don't get full benefit from their investment. I'm thinking now of one
restaurant in the center of Harvard Square, a very high traffic area;
to my knowledge (I check every time I think of it), the owner has never
changed his message! This is downright stupid. You've got to make
the message fun . . . and packed with items of both interest and value
for the prospect . . . messages that will get the person to stop in his
tracks whether he's inside your establishment or out . . . and TAKE
ACTION TO ACQUIRE YOUR BENEFITS. The reason why moving
message signs are so effective is because they offer you the possibility
of changing your marketing message every day . . . twice a day
. . . three times a day . . . or more . . . so long as every message you're
using screams WE'VE GOT SOMETHING OF INCREDIBLE VALUE
FOR YOU. FIND OUT FOR YOURSELF!

A Personal Note

When I was in high school, I had a dumb minimum-wage job working
at Pacific Ocean Park on the ocean front in Santa Monica, California.
My job was to sell tourists three anchovies for a quarter so they could
feed a tankful of lazy, spoiled seals. During slow times I used to make
up games to pass the time; one of them was to see how little of an
anchovy would motivate a great big seal to move his carcass and come
and get it. A whole fish would, of course . . . but I discovered I could

lower the portion day by day and still get movement until finally, like the great Pavlov himself, just by showing up at the edge of the tank with an empty white sandwich bag all the critters would move . . . without being given anything. In those days I thought I was just passing the time; now I realize I was preparing myself to be a marketing consultant. Thus, the objective with moving signs is to see how *little* it takes to motivate the *maximum* number of people to identify themselves as leads . . . and to buy something from you. This, ladies and gentlemen, is the game. Effective use of your moving sign will enable you to win it. Report your results to Researcher Lant instantly.

Special Lead-Generating Devices Primarily To Get Existing Customers To Buy Again

Did you notice my enthusiasm about card-decks and moving message signs? I confess to being enraptured with the bold possibilities they hold for motivating truly staggering numbers of people to do what you want. That, of course, thrills me to my very soul. But I don't want you to think that I indulge in these cutting-edge marketing endeavors at the cost of all the other available ways of both getting new leads and generating additional benefits from existing customers. No! No! No! As a marketing fanatic in good standing, I want to achieve supreme results from *all* possibilities. This means doing what is necessary to generate additional business from existing customers. Thus I propose to examine:

- catalogs in back of info-products;
- package stuffer programs;
- reciprocal package stuffer programs.

Using Catalogs In The Back Of Info-Products

As you know, I make no false and unfortunate distinctions between products and services. When one is master of problem-solving information, as all service providers most assuredly are, you will, if you're smart, get to the point of producing problem-solving products like booklets, books, audio and video cassettes. Indeed, until such time as all the problem-solving information at your disposal is so packaged and generating a regular stream of income, you should feel incomplete, unfulfilled. However, you should understand that any product you produce that does not contain within it the means for generating additional income is but a futile and lackluster creation, no matter how brilliant the problem-solving details you provide.

As you know I recently spoke at a meeting of sports nutritionists and dietitians, people who profess to have useful information for the great majority of Americans who do not feel complete unless they are sweating profusely and publicly as a result of engaging in some ludicrous physical antics. Many of these dietitians have produced problem-solving products to assist these demented souls. This being the case, I took a survey at the convention. About fifty of the dietitians in attendance had produced either audio or video cassettes, booklets and books. However, *not a single one* of them had either 1) invited readers/listeners to get in touch with them through their products (except in the most general way), or 2) added a catalog of additional products and services their client/reader/listener would have found helpful.

Yet these people persist in believing themselves to be intelligent beings!

Enter the end-of-product catalog/lead generator.

When you've created the right kind of problem-solving information product — the one offering real value by understanding what the reader/listener wants to achieve and providing precise step-by-step information so he can achieve the desired result — you have established a remarkable bond with a person who is now your client. Use it. Don't leave this person hanging; provide any number of ways, both with products and services, your now trusting client can continue to benefit from what you have available.

Let's go back to the hapless dietitians. Take one who has written a book on compulsive over-eating. As it happens, this person's service business is currently just local. Still one page at the back of her book needs to be dedicated to inviting people in that area who want to have her personal assistance in achieving the desired benefits promised by the book to get in touch with her. Essentially, she needs to have a client-centered brochure/flyer bound right into the book, a marketing communication that speaks directly to the pain of the reader/client prospect and invites this person to make immediate contact with her to begin achieving the desired result.

But what about the people in other areas where she is not currently practicing? First, she needs to ask herself whether there is indeed any necessary reason why she must practice her trade exclusively locally.

What about doing workshops and talk programs elsewhere? What about doing telephone consultations? In short, aren't there ways for this service provider/helper to expand her problem-solving practice ... and use her book to generate leads? OF COURSE THERE IS! Again, there should be marketing copy in the book inviting workshop sponsors to contact her ... as well as people who desire her telephone assistance in solving their problems.

Of course, this still leaves many people who won't be able to work with this service provider any of these ways (perhaps because they have inadequate financial resources). For these she must offer a series of problem-solving *products* through a client-centered *catalog*. I am not here going to go into the entire matter of how you either create your own info-products or select those from other people, how you negotiate discount rates and build constructive relationships, *etc.* All that has been covered in exhaustive detail in my book **HOW TO MAKE A WHOLE LOT MORE THAN $1,000,000 WRITING, COMMISSIONING, PUBLISHING AND SELLING "HOW-TO" INFORMATION.** If you expect to produce profitable info-products, you'll be making a big mistake not to consult this resource. Suffice it to say, however, that you must end *every* written info-product you produce (yes, even the shortest of special reports . . . for here is where the Resource Box comes in) with language on the additional benefits you have available (whether packaged as products or services) which YOU CAN PROVIDE IF THEY CALL NOW!

And you must do the same with your audio and video products.

There are, however, these differences with audio and video. For one thing, they are far more intimate than the written word. With audio you get the human voice; with video the service provider/marketer's image and voice. These make it much easier to build a relationship with the client . . . so long as you speak directly to this person as if you were having a one-to-one conversation. This is all very much to the good. However, unlike a printed catalog which can go on for page after page, on both audio and video tape, you must be very selective about what you offer. Thus, you might:

- offer a free catalog containing all your product/service information, inviting the listener/watcher to call you immediately to get it, or

- focus on one or two of the problems the listener/watcher is most likely to have and invite him to get in touch with you immediately to start solving them, or

- offer only one or two products, the ones that most of the listeners/watchers would want . . . given the subject matter of the tape they've just heard.

However, the crucial thing is that you make an *offer* that gets the greatest number of those tuning in to take immediate action and that you make this action as simple as possible; something they can do the very minute the tape is over. Then do everything you can to encourage your listener to take this action NOW.

Just how powerful is this technique? Well, while I've been writing just this section, two people have called me because they read back-of-product catalogs from books of mine they'd taken from the library, one in California, the other in Wisconsin. Between them they ordered $232 worth of materials. It took me about 5 minutes to take their orders . . . but the best thing of all was that I made this money while I was working on my *next* money-making info-product (this book) and I MADE THIS MONEY ON A SATURDAY. Moreover, this happens all the time . . . just as it will happen to you if you work hard to establish the human connection with the reader/listener and do not merely end your products but offer additional benefits for them, in both product and service form, if only they call you NOW!!! Further, remember the library paid for the product both these people ordered from and that both will return the product to the library so that it remains ready for others to order from . . . and profit me further. What a fabulous system!

Using Package Stuffer Programs

I have decided to end this chapter on a more traditional note in case you are now suffering from marketing vertigo. Hence, "package stuffer" programs. These have been around forever . . . but because of their antediluvian antecedents, most service marketers approach them with boredom, not with an exhilaration for their manifold possibilities; perhaps that's because they think the only way they can be handled is by popping a piece of paper in a sack when the customer buys. As you won't be surprised to learn, of course, I approach the subject more expansively. However, before getting to the fun part, I want to remind you of something crucial: IF YOU'RE BORED BY YOUR MARKET-ING, HOW THE HELL DO YOU EXPECT TO EXCITE YOUR PROS-PECTS WITH THE DELIGHTS AND POSSIBILITIES OF WHAT YOU'VE GOT AVAILABLE???

Thus resolve that you will:

- upgrade every client;

- give every current client cum future prospect an offer so valuable that it forces him either to reveal himself as an immediate prospect for buying more of your services and/ or get him to buy more right from the offer;

- either hand this to all clients personally (if technically feasible) or at the very least make sure that they receive an insert letter or flyer/brochure (if you are, say, shipping an info-product);

- follow up immediately if the value of the service warrants.

In other words, vow to take the initiative yourself and not leave full responsibility for acting (or not acting) with the client prospect.

To achieve these objectives you must:

- consider each product/service you offer not merely as an isolated incident but instead as a link in a chain. When a client gets one thing, you must understand what it makes sense for him to have *next* . . . and have that "next" properly packaged as product or additional service;

- provide some kind of special offer for the proven buyer that gets him to act faster than he might otherwise do. You should be constantly testing to determine which of these offers is in fact the most client-centered and motivational;

- incorporate this offer in some kind of marketing communication (such as a letter, flyer or brochure) that you either hand to the client or include with the product/service but which, in either case, reaches the client just as he's received the initial product/service and (we hope) is satisfied with you. It is this satisfaction . . . coupled with client-centered benefits and a motivational offer . . . that get the client/ prospect to act again quickly.

To make this upgrade system work, you must:

- think of how you currently do business;

- decide you want to induce more sales faster;

- conceive a client-centered offer that will provide the current client cum future prospect something of value;

- consider the ways of bringing this offer to his attention;

- create an appropriate client-centered marketing communication;

- ensure that this communication — with its invitation to get another benefit if he acts now — is regularly and consistently brought to all your clients' attention.

Let's review each of these points in more detail.

Thinking About How You Currently Do Business

Ask a service provider, and he'll no doubt tell you he already knows that getting repeat business from customers is important; that he knows the value of asking them and that he asks them *all* the time. Then look at the way he actually does business, and you'll discover that most of what he's told you is wrong. I think, for instance, of:

- the contractor who remodeled my house. A "marketer" of mind-boggling stupidity, he made no attempt to upgrade the value of his business. All suggestions came from me!

- the tailor from whom I recently bought some trousers. I selected what I wanted, got the measurements, *etc.* At no time did the tailor attempt to increase the value of the sale by suggesting anything. I selected; I was measured; I left. The tailor did nothing beyond brandishing his tape.

- the picture framer where I've gone for many years now to have everything framed from diplomas to the covers of my books. To my certain knowledge, at no time have any of the succession of sophomoric clerks who follow each other with dreary regularity (each wearing a more outlandish ear-ring than the last) made any attempt to generate more revenue by even *inquiring* if I needed anything else, much less attempting to provide it.

Now I'll tell you something: each of these people is either running or operating a service business; each of them is purportedly in the business of making sales (to say nothing of serving customers). Yet over and over again my experience shows that service providers miss an important, indeed crucial, opportunity to build the *value* of business. What's worse, you've probably been acting just as stupidly . . . despite a professed desire to get rich.

Let's be clear about something: ONE CRUCIAL COMPONENT OF GETTING RICH IS GETTING CUSTOMERS (WHO ARE ALSO *ALWAYS* PROSPECTS FOR FUTURE BUSINESS) TO BUY SOMETHING ELSE NOW. A client is by definition a prospect until such time as you have sold him everything you've got that meets every want he has the ability to pay for. Got it?

A client whose potential for upgrade you have failed to consider, whom, indeed, you have failed to ask about upgrading, is an opportunity for your own enrichment you have let ridiculously and thoughtlessly drift away. SHAME ON YOU!

Deciding You Really Want To Induce More Sales Faster

The first thing you must do, therefore, is pledge to yourself that you really do want to make more sales faster. Thus, pledge that you will never let a client go without your having thought through what else the client may need . . . and, in any one of several ways including both oral and written marketing communications, doing everything you can to bring your considered recommendation to his attention.

Conceiving A Client-Centered Offer Providing The Current Client Cum Future Prospect Something Of Value

If you expect to get richer with the assistance of your clients, then you must understand that it is *never* enough for you merely to decide this. You must develop a plan of action ensuring that the client will do his part . . . namely acting to shortly acquire from you another unit of your valuable service (or product). One crucial part in this plan involves making a compelling offer that will go far towards motivating the prospect to take immediate action.

Here, you return to your file of offers, a file, I remind you, that is constantly being augmented and refined thanks to your own creativity and ongoing research into the offers of both competitors and other businesses. Pluck one from this file and use it as the motivational hook which will again capture the client's interest . . . and his money! This offer should be so presented that the client is clear that it's:

- available *only* to your *buyers* . . . that is, that others cannot get it. At all opportunities, let this very special person know just how special he is;

- limited in time. While the offer may be special, it must also be finite in one way or another. Just how limited will depend on what it is you're offering. A home remodeler may wish to give a prospect 30 days to make up his mind, while a service marketer offering a health or beauty treatment may provide just a 14, or even a 7, day offer. This will vary. What cannot vary, however, is the fact of making the offer limited;

- better than others get in scope. In other words, not only must it be limited to the buyer . . . but it must give him something of greater value.

There is one other thing to consider about this offer: it must augment the possibilities for your revenue, not cut them.

Here's what I mean:

Take my barber. Say that the average length of time between hair cuts is 6 weeks. (With me, it's even longer since I go as long as possible before submitting to another scissoring!) The barber has several possible offers. He can:

- cut the price of a haircut if the client comes in earlier (say in the next three weeks);

- keep the cost of the hair cut the same but provide an extra unit of value at reduced cost (say, a shave) if the hair cut takes place in 3-4 weeks, and/or

- he can provide a discount on hair and grooming supplies at the time of the *next* visit.

Note: my barber, a service provider, does none of these things; indeed, he has never attempted to increase the value of my business by doing anything more than giving me an inefficiently suppressed dirty look when I fail to tip him. Since I never tip him, I always get this smudged expression from him . . . but he still hasn't learned that his job is not to cadge tips from me but to think through what I might need and induce me to get it from him. His failure to learn this lesson, along with my own rooted frugality, has ensured he'll never get a tip from me . . . nor does he deserve one!

But which of these offers should the barber use? ALL THREE. Not, however, all at once. With the best will in the world, a service marketer doesn't know in advance just which offer will work well. With-it competitors certainly won't say, and most professional journals inexplicably don't deal with such important meat-and-potatoes subjects. Thus, trial and error is the best method. This is why it behooves you to make as many (inexpensive) offers as you can, see which ones work best, and record the results and your observations for the next time.

The important thing, however, is that you are always:

- considering new ways to increase your revenue from existing customers without cutting your revenue;

- thinking up new offers, and that

- you are always testing them and recording results . . . so you know what works for you.

The worst thing of all is to just remain passive and slothful, failing to exploit the revenue potential of all existing clients and thinking that dirty looks at the cash register constitute any kind of effective marketing program.

Bringing This Offer To Your Client's Attention

Just when and how you'll bring your offer to your client's attention is a function of how you do business. Here are some possibilities:

- if your client will pay you at the time the service is offered (like a masseur or tailor or cosmetician), then your offer should be made as soon as you're paid. This is not only good business, it is good human relations. Presenting this offer is a gracious gesture;

- if you are sending your client an invoice, then tell the client if he pays in the next thirty days (or whatever your normal deadline is) you want to make this special offer. *Note:* you don't want to extend the client further credit unless you are absolutely sure he can pay for the service you've already provided; if you're not sure, don't make an additional offer. It's perfectly all right to dispatch the offer the day payment is received;

- if your service provides immediate results (and provided client credit is not an issue), the offer should go as soon as these results are apparent;

- if your service doesn't provide results for some time, then in addition to any offer made at the time the bill is paid, you should make an offer as soon as you're sure the client has results. If you're not certain when this will be, call to find out how things are coming along. *Note:* this is also a good time to get a satisfied client testimonial and referral.

Creating The Right Client-Centered Marketing Communication

As you see I've stressed the offer to the client. That is appropriate. But don't forget the marketing communication you create should also detail the *benefits* the client gets by using this new service or product he's about to acquire. Benefits are always the bedrock of any marketing communication, and this special "buyers only" communication is no exception. The real question is what kind of marketing communication you should create. This depends to a considerable extent on the value of the upgraded product/service the client will be acquiring. Here are some suggestions:

- if the client has purchased a service for under $100 and will be paying for it either in your establishment or his home/office and as soon as you've provided it, you need not personalize your upgrade offer. Thus, a standard letter, brochure or flyer will do nicely. On the other hand, if your clients make appointments for your service and you know in advance what they are coming for, you can create an appropriate personalized letter and generate it from your computer. This is a nice touch;

- if the client has purchased a service for over $100 and will be invoiced by you and if the service you wish to upgrade the client to has a value of over $100, your marketing communication should be personalized. In this case, a personal computer-generated letter will suffice, although you may well wish to augment it with such additional materials as appropriate brochures, flyers, *etc.* that provide the client with such further information as he may need to make a decision.

Note: if your service sells for over $1000, you should take time as soon as you have delivered it to meet with the client and ascertain what else you can do. In this case, your offer should be customized to the client's precise circumstances and should be delivered by mail, fax or overnight delivery depending on the urgency of the prospect's desire and how much you wish to be identified as a completely client-centered marketer with a very special and important offer for your already-happy client.

Ensuring That Your Client-Centered Communication Is Regularly And Consistently Brought To All Your Clients' Attention

As I've already mentioned, too many service sellers are passive, slothful, unimaginative and tunnel-visioned. What you must understand is that *each* time a client buys a unit of your service (or one of your problem-solving products) a marketing opportunity is created. Service sellers too easily forget this. Again, think of my barber, whose marketing skills are so retarded. Okay, I've been going to the same barber shop now for years. I go for one reason and one reason only: it's across the street. I don't go because the hair cuts are especially good (they're probably average). I certainly don't go because it's a nice ambience (Primitive Americana about sums it up) or because I am well treated (no one has ever asked my name, introduced himself, made much of an attempt to be friendly.) In short, its the kind of Massachusetts establishment run by the kind of Massachusetts native outsiders somehow come to regard as cold and unfriendly. Imagine! But I go because I can go there and be back in my office in 25 minutes flat.

Still, it's amazingly stupid for the proprietor to be so short-sighted about his marketing. He has forgotten that each time I step across the threshold it's an opportunity for him to:

- make current income;
- cement the long-term relationship;
- upgrade the value of my current business and hence increase his current income;
- generate future revenue faster by providing me with an incentive to come again quicker.

None of this registers on this service marketer's far-from-functioning-fruitfully little gray cells.

Don't you be so stupid and myopic.

Start the day by reminding yourself that you don't just want the same results you always get from your clients. YOU WANT MORE!

See each face afresh, no matter how many times you've seen it before. Understand what each client is offering you . . . and then make sure you do your part to get it.

Do not let a single client escape without:

- knowing what offer you'll make;

- getting that offer into his hands as soon and powerfully as possible, and

- without reviewing your performance at the end of the day to see if you connected with *every* client and did *everything* you could not just to provide a superior service but to upgrade the value of the business each client did with you today . . . and will do with you tomorrow.

If this is what you're doing, you will be a millionaire. If it isn't, you'll be like the barber across the street whose prosperity seemingly rests on the trifling amounts of money he gets out of men by adopting an attitude of cringing and demeaning servility, while clearly despising the fact he has to do so.

Establishing And Running A Reciprocal Package Stuffer Program

Right this minute, there are dozens of service providers and other businesses in your marketing territory who want to get to your prospects and clients; by the same token, you want to get to the prospects and clients of dozens of service providers and other businesses in their marketing territories. Why? Because the people they market to are the people you either are or should be marketing to. This is the entire rationale for reciprocal package stuffer programs.

The consummate service seller cannot rest easy when he knows just how many of his designated client prospects are going without benefit of knowing who he is and what value/benefits he has for them. This upsets him . . . as well it should! To solve this problem, do the following:

- Open a computer file called "swaps".

- Start thinking through all the various ways you have available to help promote other people's products/services.

Consider: your newsletter, workshops, catalog, outgoing mail and packages, special reports, moving signs, *etc.* How can you use these devices to leverage swaps with others?

- Enter into this file *all* the businesses in your marketing territory that reach the kinds of people you want to reach . . . and who, in your estimation, want to reach the markets you regularly reach. Over time, you may enter hundreds of organizations into this file.

- Now start accumulating the marketing materials of these organizations. This enables you to determine if they really do have items your clients would be interested in as well as marketing materials you could easily distribute.

- As soon as you find an organization that reaches your market with simple marketing materials you could distribute (like flyers or brochures or a one-page letter), then call and get the name of either the president and/or director of marketing, his address and phone number.

Then do the following:

- Write a letter indicating that you could be of assistance to this organization with its marketing;

- Indicate that you get to the kind of people *they're* trying to attract and sell to;

- Suggest you will be happy to bring their offer to the attention of your market . . .

- . . . if they will only bring your offer to the attention of theirs.

Then say how you see things being arranged:

- What kind of marketing communication do you want to exchange;

- How would you like your marketing communication to be distributed;

- How do you propose to distribute theirs;

- When would you like to start?

Send this letter to the president of the company that doesn't have a director of marketing; otherwise, address the director of marketing. Follow up in five business days, as usual.

If you're dealing with a marketing oriented person like me, he'll be delighted to hear from you; (by and large owners of businesses are more likely to be these people than lower-level employees). Such people are always looking for cost-effective means of increasing the number of potential prospects they can hit with their client-centered offers. You can provide that! Say you're proposing to distribute as few as 1000 flyers; the incremental printing cost of these flyers is minimal compared to sending them directly to prospects. Thus, you should be welcomed with open arms.

Unfortunately in my experience far too many "marketing" directors have far too little ingenuity and receptivity. Too many of these people suffer from hardening of the marketing arteries. For them, if it isn't routine, it isn't a possibility. To any real marketer, of course, such an unhelpful, stupid attitude is absurd. Nonetheless, you're sure to encounter it.

If you do encounter such a person, simply reiterate the benefits of your proposal both orally and in a follow-up note to any meeting. In my experience, if you keep reinforcing the benefits over and over again very often even the stupidest of "marketers" finally tunes into the fact that you have . . . a benefit for him and his company! So, if you can't make a deal with him now, don't worry. Simply go on to your next possibility.

The truth is, every service business can only handle a limited number of reciprocal package stuffer relationships at any one time. For instance, if you'll be distributing other people's marketing communications along with your own, I'd say limit yourself to about 6 relationships. This'll be quite enough; besides, you don't want to overwhelm your own message!

Thus:

- set a reasonable objective for your reciprocal package stuffer program concerning the number of other organizations you want to work with, what you want them to do and what you'll do for them;

- get cracking to establish the number of relationships you desire;

- once they are established, do your part to distribute the marketing communications you said you'd distribute . . . doing your part expeditiously is one sure way of helping this program prosper;

- then make sure the other people do their part. If the marketing communications are not going out all at once, call occasionally or drop in to see how things are going. Whenever I go to places that are distributing my literature, I tidy the materials, throw away any that may be dog-eared and dirty and generally get things organized. It would be nice if everyone were as compulsive about these things as I am, but I've (almost) accepted the fact that they never will be;

- once you've distributed what you promised to get out, tell the other party you're finished. If he's finished, too, work on your next distribution scheme. If he's not, then tell him to contact you as soon as he is, so you can arrange to help each other some more. In short, do what you can both to meet your commitment and spur the other person to achieve his . . . as well as consider the next thing that's going to help you both.

Reciprocal package stuffer relationships will probably never prove your major source of leads, but handled properly they will always generate a steady stream of prospects for a trifling amount of time and money. Why, then, do so few service sellers have such a program in place?

Consider the last time you went into any service seller's business. After he sold you *his* units of value did you get any marketing communication from him that may have included something from *another* service seller who wanted to get access to a person like you? Probably not!

We talk a lot these days about ecology and the need to be more sensible about the earth's resources. There is also a marketing ecology that blends into this discussion. Your job is to do everything you can to generate the maximum number of leads from all the various sources you have available. This includes using all these sources to make deals with others who want to get access to your market and to whose market you, in turn, want access.

Thus:

- if you are sending out a first-class envelope without filling it with as many marketing communications as you can get for the price (5 sheets of 8 1/2" by 11" paper), you're missing yet another important opportunity to generate the leads you need.

- if you are going to workshops where you hand out your materials, what about taking advantage of the opportunity to distribute the materials of others . . . who can distribute your materials to their clients?

- if you are running your client-centered messages on your moving sign, why not add those of other people . . . who can be induced to put your message on the signs they're using, *etc., etc., etc.*

Get this message!

Your job as a soon-to-be-millionaire service seller is to do EVERY-THING you can to generate leads, including assessing all the marketing means you have and then generating reciprocal deals with others who also possess the markets and the means of reaching them which will benefit you. In this way, you'll keep on generating all the leads you need to ensure your millionaire status.

Your lead sources thereby being secured, now you must learn to do everything you can to close the greatest number of the leads you get as quickly as possible.

11

How To Handle The Leads You Get So You Make The Most Sales Quickest

Due to our discussion in the previous chapters, you now have the structure to generate a continuing stream of leads. I trust you have begun to implement these ideas. There is no need for you to finish this book to begin to profit from it. Since the design and implementation of your lead-generating structure will take time, while you are learning what to do when your leads start coming in, you should be doing what it takes to generate them. ARE YOU CLEAR ABOUT THIS?

As you more fully understand and perfect your lead-generating system, your leads will come in every day . . . all the time. I know: hundreds of leads come into my life daily. And, I remind you, I'm just one guy working alone with my faithful companion . . . the computer.

If your leads still are not coming in this way, something is wrong with what you're doing. I therefore advise you to go back to the preceding chapters and really *study* them. All too often certain readers of my books call to seek my help improving their situations; upon questioning them about what's happening, I generally discover that they want a quick "fix" and haven't bothered to do their homework by reading the detailed information I've provided, much less troubling themselves to follow the directions. Such people receive short shrift here, believe me, so please don't make this mistake!

However, if you did carefully read the preceding chapters and have begun to implement its suggestions, you should notice an immediate up-tick in the number of leads you receive; moreover, this number of leads should steadily rise as you implement more and more of the suggestions. The question then becomes: how can you close more of these leads quicker?

This crucial question is as important as the one that precedes it, namely "What do I have to do to generate the greatest number of leads as quickly and inexpensively as possible?" Unfortunately, while the lead-closing question is important, it doesn't begin to get the kind of sustained attention and careful consideration of the first question. Which is entirely wrong.

For reasons which remain obscure to me, marketers seem to think they've done the job for themselves and their company if they merely generate leads. Too many care too little about whether these leads are converted into sales. Yet let's be clear about this. A lead that is not converted into a sale (whether now or later) represents a drain on the capital of your company and a drain on your ability to become a millionaire. However many financial and other resources you put into the generation of a lead that fails to become a sale are resources which you have lost and which cannot be used to help you obtain millionaire status.

Therefore at least as much sustained attention must be given to how to convert as to generate leads.

Sadly, however, I can provide story after recent story about marketers who have taken great and creative delight in finding ever more cost effective ways of GENERATING leads yet who have failed to devote any attention to CLOSING them. Some of their astonishingly inept tales pepper this book. Now that I'm managing a card-deck, where large numbers of leads are generated with astonishing ease and rapidity, my repertoire of such stories has greatly multiplied. There is, for instance, the fellow who recently went away for a week's cruise just as his leads for a certain product began to come in. He returned to find several hundred inquiries needing his attention. Instead of approaching them with any rational system, he gave way to a kind of organizational paralysis which resulted in him color-coding his files instead of contacting even the best prospects in his crammed cornucopia. Madness!

Or what about that sad, sad copywriter I told you about who, in the face of a daily mounting stack of leads, virtually locked himself in his office basement, watching the leads proliferate, overcome by a growing sense of dread and dismay. Instead of trying to realize the considerable potential in the leads he had, he froze and did nothing, ultimately losing the investment he'd made to attract all these people.

You may tell me this could never happen to you; that you handle all your leads promptly; that you follow up expeditiously; that you always are on track and have everything organized. Allow me to doubt this.

For years, I have been doing an informal survey of the means utilized by both product and service sellers for sorting, organizing, following up and tracking their leads. It is my sad duty to tell you that most of these people have "systems" which are rudimentary and embarrassingly inadequate.

That's why you must promise yourself not merely to read but to study this chapter until its message has permeated your bones and altered your behavior.

Understanding The Spectrum Of Responses

When a person responds to one of your many lead-generating mechanisms, he automatically falls somewhere along The Spectrum of Responses. As you will see in a moment, wherever he falls can be determined in advance . . . and, importantly, you can therefore be ready with the proper, prompt response.

Here is what the Spectrum of Responses looks like:

- at one end, some fraction of the leads you get will be from people who will never buy anything from you, whatever their reason;

- some fraction of the leads will be from people who will not buy from you immediately but will buy after you apply some degree of cultivation ranging from a simple nudge to a long and detailed series of contacts initiated by you;

- some fraction of the leads will be from people who will buy from you once but never again;

- at the other end of the spectrum, some fraction of the leads will be from people who will buy from you every time you contact them.

First, you must understand this spectrum. Then you must be organized yourself to find out in which category each individual lead falls . . . so you can handle the situation properly.

Failure to understand the spectrum of responses leads services marketers to make several critical errors:

- they act as if all leads will buy. Anyone, however, who generates large numbers of leads knows that there will always be more people who will not buy than those who do buy. This is only disturbing if the number of people who do buy is insufficient to boost one to millionaire status in the desired period of time. Otherwise, it is merely a fact of doing business.

- they therefore spend precious time and resources supposedly cultivating people who are not worth cultivating. The objective of the certain-to-be-a-millionaire service seller is to spend time and other resources *only* with those people who have the highest likelihood of buying his service (whether now or later is another aspect of the matter); all others must be ruthlessly and promptly flushed away.

- because they are certain all leads are likely future buyers, they don't want to take the initiative or responsibility to get rid of a failed prospect, despite that prospect's having given them every indication that he is not a prospect at all, merely a waste of time.

Let me be very clear with you about one thing: thanks to the detailed lead-generating techniques imparted in the previous chapters, you now have at your finger tips the means of generating for your service business more leads than you have ever had before. As you implement this methodology, you'll be well on your way to achieving a crucial component of millionaire status. However, as your system is more fully implemented and your leads mount, you will move to a dangerous place. You see, if you don't learn the secrets for properly sorting, organizing and closing your leads you could actually be significantly worse off by generating large numbers of leads than you were before. This is because it not only costs time and money to generate these leads. It costs time and money to service them. And to service large numbers of leads without generating large numbers of dollars from the process is both breathtakingly stupid and destructive of your interests. That's why you need to master these key steps:

- be clear about what you're doing: qualifying prospects and closing deals;

- walk through all the ways you respond to leads to make sure you can meet the objectives;

- review alternatives to strengthen how you can achieve the objectives;

- develop appropriate marketing communications and procedures;

- incorporate these into a client-centered lead-closing memorandum;

- train the necessary people to implement your procedures;

- oversee the implementation process, and

- refine the process so you achieve your objectives faster and more efficiently.

Let's look at these points in detail.

Step 1: Being Clear About What You're Doing: Qualifying Prospects And Closing Deals

The purpose of generating leads is to make sales. Although many service sellers seem to forget this — you cannot! As you approach the business of developing a lead-closing system, you must continue to ask yourself two very simple questions:

- Is what I'm doing helping to qualify prospects? That is, because of what I'm doing can I determine whether the lead I've received is in fact a *real* prospect worthy of further cultivation . . . or is he merely a time-waster who needs to be disposed of as quickly as possible?

- Is what I'm doing helping to move the prospect to a faster purchase decision . . . or retarding this movement, thereby sabotaging both my interests and the interests of the prospect who needs the benefit I have available for him?

No other questions are meaningful.

Further, the only actions that are meaningful are those that help to qualify the prospect and advance the prospect to buy. All other actions are irrelevant.

Step 2: Walking Through All The Ways You Respond To Leads To Make Sure You Can Meet The Objectives

Once you are clear about your two objectives and have committed yourself to doing everything you can to achieve them, it's time to review your current operations to see if they are designed to assist you in achieving the objectives or whether they need substantial improvement. (Can you guess which I think likely?)

This review of procedures must consider how you deal with prospects who:

- walk in to your business;
- telephone your business, and
- contact your business by mail (or mail equivalent like fax).

Here's what you need to find out:

— *when the prospect walks in to your business*

- Who is responsible for taking care of this person?
- Has he been given any instructions and training on what to do?
- How long does it take for the person responsible for the prospect to get around to dealing with the prospect?
- How does your representative open the conversation with the prospect?
- How does the representative attempt to discover both what the prospect wants and the prospect's means of acquiring it?
- How should prospect questions be asked?
- How do you evaluate what you're told?
- What do you do with what you're told?
- What do you or your representative do as soon as the meeting is over to organize the client information for future use?
- How do you or your representative follow up this meeting?

— *when the prospect telephones your business*

- Who is responsible for answering the telephone?

- Has he been given any instructions and training on what to do?

- How long does it take for your representative to answer the phone?

- What does this person say upon doing so?

- How does he open the conversation with the prospect?

- Does he attempt to find out how the prospect heard about your business?

- How is he organized to take down any information either the prospect provides or which he is asked to provide?

- How does he attempt to discover what benefit the prospect wants?

- How does he respond if the prospect merely asks for "information"?

- How does he attempt to discover when the prospect wants to go ahead and his ability to do so?

- What does he do if the prospect will not provide the information you need to assist in the qualifying and closing process?

- How does the representative advise the prospect about what will happen next . . . so that the prospect is prepared for the next stage in the closing process?

- What does the representative do when the conversation with the prospect is over?

— *when the prospect contacts your business by mail*

- Who is responsible for sorting the mail?

- What means are used to determine the importance and value of the lead?

- What is done with leads designated highest priority and when is this done?

- What is done with leads given lesser priority?

- What is done with leads that are reckoned to be without value?

- What happens to all the prospect information gathered?

- Who is responsible for following up the leads?

As you walk through your existing lead-closing process, you'll probably discover that the "system" you're using is neither comprehensive nor rational. Instead, like Topsy, it probably just grew helter skelter. What you do to close leads, therefore, is less the result of careful, client-centered consideration than for the ease and comfort of employees, some of whom may not even work with you anymore! Why are things done the way they are? If the answer is anything remotely resembling "Because we've always done things that way," you aren't running a focused lead-closing process. You're running a social club for the benefit of your employees!

Warning: all people and every organization work hard to create a universe in which they're comfortable. It is always easier to let in-efficient practices remain than to do the necessary work that forces you to review what you're doing and institute a more focused lead-closing system. The sad fact is that only the tiniest percentage of service sellers review their operations on a regular basis to see what they're doing and whether there is more they can do to 1) generate leads and 2) close leads faster. Yet this kind of scrutiny is one of the most important things you can do for your business.

Step 3: Brainstorming And Reviewing Alternatives To Strengthen How You Can Achieve the Necessary Objectives

Scrutiny of your lead-closing process, as I'm sure you'll agree, is necessary. The question is, how often should you do it? That depends on how quickly you want to become a millionaire and how tolerant you are of practices that undermine your ability to become one. Therefore I shall give you several answers.

- If your service business is under a year old, you are in one of the several dangerous periods of your enterprise. The failure rate of business new-borns is still alarmingly high. That's why you need to review your lead-closing procedures *monthly*. The objective of every new business, after all, is to "float the boat", to bring in as much business/money as possible as quickly as possible and so give yourself both the encouragement and the time you need to sort out the kinds of problems that attend the launching of any new service enterprise.

- If your service business is over a year old but not achieving your sales objectives, monthly oversight is still recommended. The mere fact that you've limped through the first year doesn't give you the right to be lax about your lead-closing procedures. Your rule of thumb should be that you need to review these procedures whenever you are failing to achieve your sales objectives and hence whenever you are falling behind in your sprint to millionaire status.

- If your sales are stuck at a certain level, if you are no longer making regular sales progress, chances are that both your lead-generating and lead-closing procedures are stuck, too. It's time to review them with a view to seeing what can be done to improve matters and get things rolling again.

- If you are regularly meeting and exceeding your sales quotas, don't sit on your laurels. Review your lead-closing procedures thoroughly once a year; there isn't a business in the world which couldn't be more efficient and productive about closing leads, no matter how well it's doing.

At this point it's time to brainstorm and review alternatives to close more leads. Here are some guidelines to help you:

- Appoint a person to review what you do now. Make this person's charge as direct and simple as possible: "What are we doing now that isn't helping us qualify leads and close sales and what can we do now to qualify more leads and close more sales faster?"

- Don't attempt to do everything at once. Overall change can be confusing and produce anxiety. Resolve, by all means, to improve your entire lead-generating and lead-closing process, but review just one part at a time, for example improving the way you handle call-in leads;

- Open a lead-closing file in your computer;

- File all observations and suggestions about what can be done to improve matters in this file. Initially don't evaluate these suggestions; just collect them. Rule nothing out. The principle of brainstorming is to get people to open up, not

to shut them off by prematurely evaluating their ideas.
Note: make sure ideas are entered into this file whenever
you have them. Just because you're not doing a formal
review doesn't mean you won't have good ideas;

- Sift through all the ideas and evaluate which are most likely
  to achieve the objectives. Again, don't implement too many.
  Lead-generating and lead-closing will always be two crucial
  activities in your business. So don't worry if you can't
  implement everything you want to do all at once. Just make
  progress!

- Don't just adopt ideas . . . implement them. This means
  taking the time to explain to those who must use them, why
  you want things done in a certain way and what you want
  the person to do. Further, don't just tell the affected individual what needs to be done; explain the process, demonstrate it, and train the person to do it. One of the reasons
  why new lead-closing ideas don't succeed is because employees are merely commanded to do things without being
  told why . . . and trained how. This is wrong.

- Reward good ideas. I am a firm believer that those who
  assist you in achieving your objectives should be regularly
  rewarded. Make the reward commensurate with the benefits
  the company is receiving from the implementation of the
  idea.

If You Run A One-Person Shop . . .

Many readers of this book will be running smaller one-person service
businesses. Nothing wrong with that. I do it myself. But this doesn't
mean that you're absolved from the responsibility of improving your
lead-closing performance. Quite the contrary. Running a smaller service
business just to escape from the responsibility of success is ignoble.
There are many advantages to running a small service business and
such a business, properly conceived and implemented, will still make
you a millionaire. By the same token, there are real pitfalls. With no
one looking over your shoulder to see if you're doing a good job or
not and with the almost limitless human ability to provide excuses
in case things don't go well ready to undermine your efforts, it's easy
to slip into bad habits. DON'T! Resolve to review your lead-closing
activities regularly along the lines mentioned above. Further, since
intra-office brainstorming is out:

- Ask other professionals in your field how they handle standard lead-closing situations;

- Review professional newsletters and other materials for ideas;

- Force yourself to come up with new ideas on how to improve matters. All too often working alone without regular stimulus from others causes our inventive powers to atrophy; force yourself to come up with new ways of meeting your objectives so this doesn't happen to you;

- Force yourself, too, to implement new ideas and see how they work. Remember, old ways are only good ways if they help you consistently meet the quota you've set for yourself to become a millionaire.

- Reward yourself for results. It staggers me just how unselfproviding many service sellers are. I say this to you: if you've been responsible for improving the quality of your lead-closing system and making more sales, you deserve a reward as much as anyone. So give it to yourself — and make it proportional to the success you've achieved.

Step 4: Developing Client-Centered Marketing Communications And Procedures

Each step in the profitable lead-closing process involves either the development of a client-centered marketing communication and/or a client-centered procedure that will assist you in evaluating the value of the lead and enabling you to close this lead and generate income faster. It is your responsibility to ensure that you have both the marketing communications and procedures you need.

— *What You Need To Do When The Lead Walks In*

- Who is responsible for taking care of this person?

Procedure: Unlike the lax and deplorable situation which currently exists on the premises of most service sellers, you will prosper by creating a system for effectively dealing with prospects as they present themselves. While most service sellers (or their scandalously ill-prepared employees) act as if the prospect were a nuisance, you must act otherwise. This can only be done by *anticipating* that prospects will present themselves . . . and being prepared to act appropriately when they do.

This begins by designating a person who is responsible for seeing to it that everyone who walks in is taken care of immediately. You should also determine this individual's back-up, or what should be done if there is only one person to attend to walk-in prospects and this person is busy when the client prospect appears. *Note:* in this case, your representative should excuse himself for just a moment from the customer he's currently serving, greet the prospect, tell him how long it will be until he can be accommodated, ask what the prospect wants, present the necessary client-centered materials, seat the prospect comfortably (if appropriate) and invite the prospect to enjoy any amenities (such as coffee) that may be available. This can all be done in two or three minutes! It should go without saying (but these days most certainly does not) that your representative should be advised that handling personal calls, reading, gossiping with other employees, chewing gum, eating, *etc.* are all inappropriate and must never be put before the interests of the prospect. I find it absolutely astonishing that such a note has to be included in a book of this kind, but so far have standards deteriorated that I cannot assume all service providers and marketers understand this!

- Has he been given any instructions and training on what to do?

Procedure/Marketing Communication: It is your responsibility to ensure that your representative knows precisely what to do when the prospect appears. No longer can we rely on homes (which are hotbeds of bad manners) or schools (which are worse) to impart client-centered behaviors. This is one of the flagrant failings of our culture and its instructing institutions. For centuries, people realized that manners were an essential element of civilized life. To this end, they instituted many different kinds of organized training programs so that those for whom manners were a cornerstone of successful life received the instruction they needed. These days we don't do this and the results are predictable: people who ought to know what to do, don't. Those who ought to be treated well, aren't. And everyone emerges from the process bruised, alienated and unhappy. This is ridiculous!

Thus, you must do what is necessary to train both yourself and your representatives in the art of client-centered behavior. You must recognize that the people you are hiring probably know little about this and that the younger they are the less they know. You must assume the responsibility for imparting this essential information and for supervising the learning process. Moreover, you must be willing to create a memorandum of this client-centered behavior both for the use of present and future employees.

Step 5: Incorporating Your Client-Centered Procedures In A Staff Memorandum

To this end, open a computer file called "manners". Start by drafting your recommendations for all the situations that regularly occur in your business. Update this file as situations occur and as your understanding deepens about how necessary such a memorandum is and just what should be put in it. Head this memorandum with these words:

We are a client-centered business. The prosperity of everyone who works in this establishment rests on the willingness of the people who walk in, call and write to us to buy our services. We are committed to doing *everything* to get them to buy these services and to make the process through which they acquire them a pleasant and comfortable one. By working here, you promise that you share this commitment to our customers and are willing to do *whatever is necessary* to assist them. What follows are both the general operating principles and specific guidelines we use to create the right kind of client-centered environment and employee behaviors. If a situation arises that does not fall within these guidelines, do what is in the best interests of the client prospect or customer; if you are not sure what that is, ask your supervisor for assistance.

Think how much better service would be in this nation if every service business, indeed if every business altogether, had this kind of goal and followed it with specific client-centered recommendations and specific training for assisting the prospect and bringing its benefits to his attention. It is a mark how far we have fallen as a civilization and culture that so few people not only have such a means of working with their prospects but have never considered such a policy even necessary.

Note: once the memo has been drafted, circulate it to all those who will deal with the prospect in any capacity. Ask for their comments and further recommendations. Adopt those you can and then provide two copies to everyone. Have each representative sign and date a copy for your files; leave the second copy with the representative and urge him to post it where he can regularly see it and so remind himself of the importance of this client-centered behavior to his own prosperity.

- How long does it take for the person responsible for the prospect to get around to dealing with the prospect?

Procedure: You know it and I know it: when you're a prospect you're acutely aware of how long it takes to get waited on. Your prospects feel this way, too — and if they have to wait an unreasonable amount of time they take it out on you by being more difficult to work with when they finally do get waited on, by buying less, by recommending you less to their friends, and complaining about you more.

Again, someone must be designated at your business to take care of this problem. It must be someone's explicit responsibility to understand that prospects don't like to wait, that what happens later in a client relationship can often be seriously affected by what happens at the beginning, that the prospect has a right to be greeted professionally and efficiently, and that it is never the prospect's responsibility — but always yours — to make sure this happens.

Personally, it doesn't matter what I'm doing, when I receive a walk-in prospect (which happens with frequency despite the fact that I do not run a conventional business and in fact work from home in the midst of an urban residential neighborhood), I ALWAYS set aside whatever I'm doing (yea, even if I'm in the middle of a perplexing paragraph in one of my books), greet the person affably, make sure I have the person's name, and find out what he has come about. Because I personally hate to be rushed when I make decisions, I tell the prospect right away that he doesn't need to feel rushed in any way; then I provide the client-centered materials that will assist his decision-making process, position him in a comfortable place and leave him for a few minutes. When I return, he has the basic information he needs and our conversation can get focused quickly. This system works because it is concentrated on the prospect; I make it a point to let him know that his interests and comfort (a significant point) are always paramount. On this basis, I do not think there has been a person who has just walked in over the last several years who hasn't left without buying something . . . and many times they make profitable referrals, too!

- How does your representative open the conversation with the prospect?

Procedure/Marketing Communication: Many books on closing the sale act as if there's some mystery to opening a conversation with a prospect, as if the words must be incantatory and the prospect thrown into a trance. I most assuredly do not agree. Let me tell you where I'm coming from.

I believe that the "magic" for beginning a conversation with the prospect starts from *within* the marketer. The marketer must be committed to assisting the prospect; the marketer must approach the prospect with frankness, civility, good manners and a willingness to both work with and accommodate the prospect. This attitude informs the marketer's behavior and is immediately apparent — just as the lack of this attitude is also instantly clear. The right opening for a client-centered conversation is not, therefore, so much a product of words as it is the product of an essential kind of behavior; the words that are used constitute proof that the right attitude exists. Thus a simple, "How can I help you?" can be perfectly effective. This is improved by adding the marketer's name, thus: "I'm Jeffrey, how can I help you?" Note I do not say "I'm Dr. Lant..." Starting that way establishes a formality and barrier which have no place in a client-centered relationship. If you want a little more formality, add your surname. Invariably people who introduce themselves as "Mr. Smith" are of lower social status and are trying to make up for it by using a spurious title ("Mr."), or they are pompous (as in "I'm Dr. Jones . . .") If you wish to indicate that you have a title, say "I'm Dr. Charles Clark."

Next, ask for the prospect's name. It is astonishing to me just how many business conversations take place without the parties knowing each other's names. This is ridiculous! The relationship between a service seller and prospect always holds out the prospect of something long-term and amicable; the possibility for that relationship should be fostered from your very first encounter with the prospect. Thus, ask for the prospect's name.

Now, help the words along by adopting the right body language.

- Turn so you are facing the prospect directly;

- Look directly at the prospect;

- Lean into the prospect slightly so that the prospect feels you are paying full attention to him.

What the prospect wants at this point is your full attention and interest. He wants to know that you are *focused on him*. This focus is a necessary part of a successful lead-closing program whether you accomplish it in person, by phone, or by mail.

Note: this opening can be altered as necessary. Say, for instance, that you are having a limited-time-only sale on one of your services. Your opening with all prospects should incorporate this information even though not all are coming for this purpose. Thus: "I hope you're coming in to get (the benefit you're providing). We're having a special sale on it right now!" The people who are coming for this sale won't mind being reminded about it; those who aren't, who didn't know about it or weren't thinking about participating, will always tell you what they were coming in for . . . but many will now also ask for details about the other matter. Thus, you increase the likelihood of augmenting the sale.

Whatever opening you use (and as you see, the opening need not stay the same but can mirror offerings you have available), write it down in a memorandum to be circulated to the people who will deal with your prospects. Make sure this memorandum is not just limited to the words your marketers will use . . . but also their presentation mode, body language, *etc.* These are as much a part of the successful client-centered opening as the words themselves.

- How does the representative attempt to discover both what the prospect wants and the prospect's means of acquiring it?

Procedure/Marketing Communication: The prospect has come to you for a reason. He has not made the resolution to call on you, gotten in his car or hazarded public transportation, and overcome the shyness that many people feel in meeting any new person for nothing. He wants you to help him! Don't let him down!!!

It is your responsibility to find out precisely what the prospect thinks he wants to achieve . . . precisely when he wants to achieve it . . . and precisely what means he has available for achieving it. Getting this information is not invasive (as one stupid service seller complained to me the other day); it's essential for both you and the prospect. It enables you to give the prospect what he wants . . . and it enables you to end the conversation as quickly as possible if you find the prospect is not ready or able to acquire the benefit you have available.

To make this encounter between prospect and marketer as productive as possible, the marketer needs to be prepared for dealing with it. This means thinking through in advance what he will need to make this meeting work. Thus, he should have available a prospect sheet. This sheet should contain questions which he needs answered so he can formulate the correct proposal for the prospect. This sheet can either be available in the computer (if the marketer has a work-station) or on simple photo-copied pages. The questions will include:

- the prospect's name
- address

- telephone number

- fax

- objective (what the prospect is trying to achieve)

- date the prospect wishes to achieve this objective/have this benefit

- budget

- whether the prospect is the decision maker

- the decision-making process the prospect must go through, *etc.*

The service you're selling will determine which questions you need to have. What is important, however, is that you think through in advance of any prospect meeting just what you need to know to be able to make the right proposal and evaluate the prospect's seriousness of intent.

- How the prospect questions should be asked.

Take a look at the questions above. Do you think they are all equally important? That is, is the prospect's address as significant as the objective the prospect is attempting to achieve and the date when he wishes to achieve this objective or have the benefit you offer? Of course not! That's why you need to consider not only what questions you'll ask but the order in which you'll ask them.

Say you're selling a financial planning service. The average marketer asks the name, address, phone questions first. The smarter marketer wants to know as soon as possible just what the prospect is trying to accomplish and when he wants to accomplish this. These questions are far more important than the others and should be asked first. Thus the conversation should go like this:

- Prospect (by name), what are you trying to accomplish? (Pause, listen and take appropriate notes.)

- When did you see yourself getting started to accomplish the achievement of this objective?

- What were you thinking of in terms of budget?

In other words, once you've greeted the prospect, found out his name, seated him comfortably, *etc.*, it's time to start the qualifying process . . . even before you have all the details about address, phone, *etc.*

These qualifying questions are of the utmost significance, for their answers enable you to determine what kind of a prospect you are dealing with. You need to ask them as straightforwardly as possible . . . and you need to pay very close attention both to what you are told . . . and the way you are told the answers.

• *How to evaluate what you're told.*

Procedure: Remember what you're trying to accomplish at this point. You want to discover if the person you are talking to is *really* a prospect . . . and, if so, what magnitude of prospect. Where most service sellers make a crucial mistake is going into the ins and outs of what they're selling without knowing whether the person they're talking to is a buyer. This is a very common problem and one you must learn to solve. Why, just last night a fellow called me and said he'd received information about advertising in my card-deck. He told me he'd thrown away the deck he'd originally received and now wanted another one. My first question was, "Are you thinking of advertising in our next issue of (date)." He said he wasn't. Was that decision firm, I said. It was, he replied. I then told him that he'd receive the next deck in the mail and that there was no need for him to receive anything else now. Essentially he then responded, "Well, send it to me because I want it now and since I'm the customer you have to do what I say you have to do."

This is a very tricky moment for the service seller. Despite the fact that this marketer has been explicitly told the prospect isn't going to buy his offer, and though he has made a perfectly reasonable suggestion about how the prospect will receive the information in plenty of time for him to make a decision by his (the client's) deadline, he may be tempted to knuckle under and do the "prospect's" bidding, just because the prospect demands it. Don't. This is where the entire matter of evaluation comes in, of paying the utmost attention to what the prospect says, how he says it, and to doing what is both reasonable for his interests and not unreasonable for yours. To arrive at this point, you must become expert at reading prospect signs, a subject you can never know too much about. Here are some clues to help you:

- Does the prospect look you in the eye and engage you directly when talking? Everyone in sales knows that "buyers are liars" . . . but fortunately most of the "liars" still feel uncomfortable fibbing to you. They'll give you sign after sign that shows you what they really mean. Lack of direct eye contact is certainly one;

- Has the prospect thought about his situation and what he wants to accomplish? People who know what they want and are ready to take action are engaged in the process of securing benefits. They have done (at least some) homework; they have an idea what they want . . . and they may have shopped around to compare alternatives for getting it. Real prospects want to share this information and often ask probing questions. The more vague the prospect the less he's likely to be real;

- Real prospects don't mind you asking questions. They know you need to get certain information from them, and they are happy to provide it. People who are not prospects will show you in many ways that they resent being asked questions, or they'll just evade you with one feeble excuse after another;

- Real prospects are realistic about money. They are not trying to secure a million dollar's worth of benefits for a dollar. They generally have a good grasp of the value of money, want to secure value for their money, but are willing to pay to get what they want. Further, real prospects can tell you where the money is coming from and when the money will be available to begin the project;

- The real prospect is clear about when he wants to get started, can give you a reasonable answer why he cannot get started now, and can provide a substantive response indicating why later will be better for him;

- The real prospect wants to get started. He wants results and knows that the sooner he can make up his mind the quicker he can get them.

The net result of these observations is that the real prospect is always easier to deal with than the unreal prospect. His expectations are generally reasonable. He is willing to listen to what you have to say and evaluate it; he wants you to listen to what he has to say and treat him professionally, too. Unreal prospects try to confuse you with any number of extraneous considerations, including:

- bragging about who they are, what they have;

- disguising their lack of power;

- failing to behave in a civil and professional way (a dead give-away that you're not dealing with a good prospect);

- trying to get you to alter your carefully considered operating procedures just because they want you to.

Your job, however, is clear: you've got to find out if this is a real prospect, a person who will buy, and you've got to find out when this person will buy. What you do next depends on what you find out here first.

Thus your job is to:

- Evaluate *each* thing the prospect says so you have a better understanding of his intentions and ability to take prompt action;

- Evaluate the prospect's body language to see if there is a dysfunction between what he's telling you . . . and what he himself knows to be true;

- Focus the prospect on the questions you must have answered either until you get the information you need . . . or until it becomes obvious the prospect won't answer them.

Far, far too many service sellers can't do this. Instead, they make the mistake of trying to sell their service before they know the prospect can buy; they make the mistake of defending themselves before it has been established that this prospect is even entitled to make objections. (Only real prospects have that "right").

As you implement the lead-generating strategies of this resource, you will find yourself with more and more leads to evaluate. You must, therefore, become expert at what it takes to determine if this person is indeed a real prospect, or a time-consuming resource-waster.

You already know that you must ask, directly and straightforwardly, of the prospect, "What do you want?"; "When do you want it?," and "How much do you want to pay for it?" What if the prospect comes back and says, "I'm not sure"; "I don't know"; "I can't say." Is it then your responsibility to carry on as if this were a real prospect? MOST ASSUREDLY NOT.

First try again to get the information you need. "I really need to know what you want, so I can help you. If you can't tell me what you want, I won't be able to help you. So, let's try again: What do you want?" Then wait, pause, and scrutinize both what is said and what you see.

If the prospect cannot answer these questions, answers vaguely, or unconvincingly, he is not a prospect and this meeting should be ended as quickly and civilly as possible.

The inexperienced or overly optimistic service seller won't like hearing this. Those of us who are experienced know that you will always attract more prospects than buyers and that the success of your business rests to a considerable extent on your ability to sort out which is which . . . and to do it as quickly as possible.

• *What to do with what you're told*

Procedure: Whatever the prospect tells you, your job is to be civil. It is also to move expeditiously towards the action indicated by what the prospect has told you.

Here's what to do:

- If the prospect is altogether vague and the answers are unsatisfying, you *still* say you want to help but indicate that the best thing to do at this point is to have the prospect carefully consider your marketing communications and respond as soon as he's ready to go ahead. Before the prospect leaves ask for the prospect's card or enter the prospect's follow-up information in your computer. If you feel there is any hope and if you have regular mailings to your prospects, by all means send your material to him; if you feel there is no hope, then delete the follow-up information the minute the prospect is out of the room. Remember, you have absolutely no obligation to send your information and waste your money on people who cannot return a profit to your business. Moreover, putting a name on a mailing list or otherwise indicating that you will be spending future money on a futile prospect is not a mark of client-centered behavior; it is confirmation of your stupidity and soft-headedness.

- If the prospect has indicated he wants to go ahead at some time in the future and has provided some indication about what he wants but cannot give you a time when he wishes to have the benefit or take action, you can add this person to your low-priority follow-up list. *Note:* in this case, you should try very hard to pin the prospect down on a date when he wants to take action.

- If the prospect has indicated when he wants to go ahead, schedule an appropriate follow-up with him and make it clear you will be following up as scheduled. Your follow-up then comes with the prospect's permission.

- If the prospect asks for some additional time to think about what you've told him, do everything you can to make explicit any potential objections . . . and do everything you can to respond to them. Schedule with the prospect an exact time for following up.

- If the prospect is ready to buy today, sell him what he wants . . . but only after you tell him what you have that is better. In other words, attempt to increase the value of his business!

• *What does your representative do as soon as the meeting is over?*

Procedure/Marketing Communication: Throughout the meeting with the prospect, your marketer should be recording information. What happens to this information is determined by what level of prospect he's determined the visitor to be:

- If future follow up has been promised, the marketer should send a confirmation of this the same day as the prospect meeting has been held. This should be no difficulty since the letter should be in your computer! This letter, however, should go beyond just indicating when the marketer will follow up; it should reiterate the benefits the prospects wants and stress the advantages for going ahead NOW! If minutes of this meeting have been deposited in the computer (which is recommended if at all possible), they are already stored; if the minutes are in hard-copy, the marketer should place them where he can easily locate them. Tickler details, however, should be stored in the computer in a follow-up file;

- If the prospect needs to think things over, send a letter stressing the benefits and, again, indicating when you'll follow up;

- If the prospect has bought your service, send a letter confirming the wisdom of the client's decision, reminding him of the benefits he'll get and what you are now doing on his behalf. One of the big mistakes service sellers make is that, in their happiness at having made the sale, they fail to confirm to the seller the wisdom of what he's done and what the seller is now doing to get the buyer the benefits he wants.

Finally, if you have determined that the person you've just talked to will never be a prospect and that there is no point in future contact, discard the name without a pang. Investing money where there is no prospect of reasonable return is the mark of a fool. Personally, I get a sort of thrill of pleasure out of trashing the names of people whom I've reasonably determined will never buy and consigning them to the scrap heap of history.

• *How does your representative follow up?*

Procedure/Marketing Communication. Unrelenting follow-up skills are an essential component of what will make you a millionaire. I can now tell the level of professionalism and client-centered concern of a service seller by how he follows up. The minute I discover that these skills are faulty, I know I'm dealing with a person who's very likely to be trouble; in my own business, I demand a high level of follow-up skills and am certain that the fact that I possess them to a notable degree has been an essential part of my own success.

Thus:

- Make it clear to all your representatives, and vow to hold such high standards yourself, that if you promise follow-up you will deliver it;

- Lay down guidelines on how follow-up is to be handled. If the prospect you've talked to is not the decision maker, find out who is, how much time they need, and just when the follow-up should be made. If the prospect is the decision maker, find out how much time he needs to make a decision and follow-up accordingly. If the prospect is unclear about how much time he needs but is local, call within three days of any meeting. If you have sent materials, call the day after you think they'll arrive to see if they've arrived . . . and to advance matters towards the closing.

Your written follow-up guidelines must include directions for what happens when the prospect is not available. Remember, the priority rating you have given the prospect determines how many times you will attempt to be in touch. Equally remember, the fact that a "prospect" fails to return your call or answer your letter is a clear indication of how he regards himself as a prospect . . . and of how, therefore, you should treat him. *Note:* if, for whatever reason, you have rated the prospect highly, have interacted with him professionally, and tried to be of service to him, but you find this person doesn't answer your written communications, respond to your phone calls, *etc.,* before you write him off as a lost cause send a very direct communication telling him:

- you have real benefits for him (enumerate some);

- you've tried to bring these to his attention on innumerable occasions, and

- that you thought he was a professional who would work in a decent, civil fashion.

Then say you'd like to hear from him whatever his decision and that you'd appreciate a response. The good people (of whom there still are many) will respond, thus giving you the chance to salvage this situation; the bad ones are flat worms who are beyond help. Treat them accordingly.

Your guidelines should be embodied in a memorandum (which like all other documents should be drafted and edited on computer). Since follow-up is so important, it is crucial that you lay down your expectations about what needs to happen and when it needs to happen. No one likes to be rejected, and follow-up necessarily invites the possibility of rejection. The closer you get to the moment when the prospect is out of evasive options brings the moment closer of possible rejection to the marketer. Believe me, you want this rejection as quickly as possible . . . if you are going to get it in any event. Unrelenting follow-up ensures that you waste the least amount of time with your prospects and that you also let them know just how ready, willing and able you are to bring them the benefit they say they want — if only they take the necessary actions to acquire it.

• *What you need to do when the lead calls you.*

You should now be clear on the essential structure of successful lead-closing, namely that:

- it is always your responsibility to remember the point of what you're doing. "Working" is not what you're trying to do. Instead, you're trying to accomplish your objectives by doing everything you can to discern the possibilities of the prospect you're contacting;

- you must assume a large percentage of the leads you receive are not real prospects and that you must divide as quickly as possible the good from the bad, the bad from the impossible, and that

- lead-differentiation and lead-closing is a subject you can never know too much about.

This is as true when you take your leads by phone as in person.

• *Who is responsible for answering the telephone?*

Procedure: I called an insurance company the other day for some information. I asked the person answering the telephone for someone specific. The voice on the other end didn't just say that the person I wanted was unavailable and take down the necessary information so the call could be returned. Instead, she felt compelled to tell me that she, the answerer, didn't usually answer the phone, wasn't at her own desk and didn't have a pen near at hand to take a message. Could I call back? Now, I ask you: IS THIS PERSON AN EMPLOYEE WANTING TO HELP THE COMPANY DO BUSINESS, OR IS SHE A SABOTEUR HIRED BY THE COMPANY'S COMPETITORS TO UNDERMINE THE INTERESTS AND WELL-BEING OF THIS ORGA-NIZATION? If the judgment must be made on the basis of what occurred, I'd have to say the latter.

To start from the beginning, you must assume that prospects will call your place of business. Logically, either the right person will be available to answer the phone, that is the person who can provide the proper information and begin the qualifying process . . . or this person won't be available, thus meaning that a back-up person will take the call. And what, pray, is the correct definition of a "back-up" person: someone who is trained to do what is necessary to either collect and/or give the proper information that will promote the qualifying process. Please note, by this I do not mean that the back-up person must do what the primary marketer should do; in the case of the insurance company, for instance, the most elementary thing that would have promoted the qualifying process was for the answerer simply to collect certain information from me which would enable the marketer to call back promptly and advance matters. The information imparted to me by the answerer about her state of disorganization did not promote this matter and should, therefore, have been suppressed.

As you are well aware, most service businesses are not set up with this degree of client-centered efficiency. Thus:

- Designate the person who is the primary phone contact;

- Train this person in what to do to qualify leads and advance the sales process;

- Indicate who is responsible for answering the phone should this person not be available;

- Be clear about what this person is to say. Thus, "I don't know where it is. I don't know what she does. I don't know when she'll call," is never a proper response. If the secondary phone answerer doesn't have the necessary information to handle the incoming call, he should simply say, "Mary Jane isn't available to assist you right now. But if you give me your name and phone number I'll have her call you this afternoon. What time would be good for you?" There is never the need for this answerer to supply unnecessary biographical details or other extraneous material.

Step 6: Training The Necessary People To Implement Your Client-Centered Procedures

• *Has he been given any instructions and training on what to do?*

Procedure/Marketing Communication: I am willing to bet that most of the people answering the telephones right this minute in most service businesses haven't had even one hour of training for their jobs. Indeed, I go farther: I don't believe that most even know what their job is. Rather, they probably think that *answering* the phone is what they're supposed to do. This is entirely wrong, dangerously, stupidly wrong. Any machine can *answer* a phone; what we need instead is a person who understands that his job is to assist in the qualifying process of the individual calling in and to help determine what the next lead-closing step should be. In short, from human beings we expect not just the robotic act of answering but thought and discerning action! To achieve these takes training.

Never again place on the telephone in your business a person who has had no experience on the phone. Never again place a person on the telephone in your business who is not clear about his job and your expectations. If you do, you are courting disaster.

Instead, take the guidelines in this chapter and turn them into an in-house training program. And have this training program even if you are the only person who answers the phone. Just because you've been doing it for forty years doesn't mean you're doing it right.

Then write down precisely what your expectations are and give precise guidelines about what the person answering the phone is expected to do. As above, check what this person does. If most service sellers acted like prospects and called their own companies, they'd be appalled at how a crucial component of their success is being (mis)handled.

Note: here is a growing problem that may well need your attention. Generally the people who answer the phones are those who are entry-level or part-time or are paid the least. Because the phone is not thought of as an opportunity to qualify but only as a means of disseminating basic information, service sellers, like other businesses, are careless about whom they put on the phones. In practice, many non-English speakers are put on the phones these days for businesses where the majority of the callers are English speakers. Since no one at the business seems to be able to deduce the obvious (namely that it is the job of the telephone answerer to make himself clearly understood) and to take the obvious steps for improving the matter (namely insisting on the development of clear communications skills on the part of all people answering the phone), the net result has become a travesty of marketing.

Time after time, I have called businesses expecting to receive service, information, *etc.*, and have found instead that I have to act as a translator and general puzzle solver. This is both frustrating and ridiculous. The renowned historian Arthur Schlesinger, Jr. has written in his monograph on multiculturalism that at some point multiculturalism threatens the viability of the nation; I wish to carry this point into marketing. It is neither a favor to the customer nor indeed to the person answering the phone to have a prospect call a business and have to fight to be understood. It is also humiliating for the answerer who is thereby subjected to much unnecessary frustration and who cannot perform his job with maximum efficiency. I remind you: the business of business is to make sales. The business of the person answering the phone is to assist this process. If this demands, as it usually does in this country, fluency in English, then the person who answers the phone must have it. Any other point of view is both naive and self-defeating.

• *How long does it take for your representative to answer the phone?*

Procedure: Calls from leads (and, it follows, from clients) must be answered promptly. Personally, I have my office configured so that if I'm at my computer (where I'm usually to be found), I can pick up the phone *on the first ring.* Invariably, the person at the other end is astonished by this degree of client-centered focus.

You may tell me that because of the nature of your business, you are not equipped to answer your calls this quickly. That, of course, is rubbish. Get a cordless phone and carry it with you like a wrist-watch or wallet.

These days there is no excuse for not being able to answer the phone promptly and so indicate to the people calling, in this case your leads, that you are glad they did and are ready to attend to them. First, however, make this a priority; the reason this kind of behavior doesn't take place in most service businesses is because those businesses do not regard prompt answering — and the prompt attention that should necessarily follow — as a priority.

• *What does this person say upon answering the phone?*

Procedure/Marketing Communication: All kisses, as those familiar with the form can attest, are not the same. Some are more communicative than others. This is true, too, of the way you answer the phone. Consider your beginning like a kiss and proceed accordingly.

These first words, like the openings to all things that are significant, cannot be left to chance. Marketers understand that good results stand a better chance of emerging from good beginnings. Here, again, however, there are many faulty ideas in circulation about what a good beginning entails.

As with the way you greet a person arriving at your business, it isn't just the words you say that make the opening successful . . . it is the way they're presented; your entire mode of dealing with the prospect.

The correct way should:

  • indicate the name of your business or who is talking;

- wait a moment for the person at the other end to indicate who he is and/or what he wants, and

- indicate that the answerer can help.

Thus . . .

 . . . one ring . . .

"Jeffrey Lant speaking."

"Oh, I didn't expect to get you on the phone."

"What's your name?"

"Pete Peterson."

"Well, Pete, how can I help you right now."

"I'm calling for some information on your copy writing service."

"Pete, I can help you. Tell me what you've got in mind."

Let's look at what's going on here.

1. I open with my name. Since I run a service business and am a primary service provider within it, this is absolutely appropriate. The prospect knows he's reached the right place.

2. "I didn't expect to get you on the phone" (a line, by the way, which I hear several times every day) These words indicate that the prospect holds me in some kind of esteem, in short that my marketing is working and that this person already thinks I can be of assistance, hence the reason for the call. Imagine how much easier this situation is to control than one where you are forced to explain who you are!

3. "What's your name?" Immediately move to establish even the thinnest sliver of personal rapport. I want the person at the other end to know that we're establishing a relationship and that as part of this relationship we'll be doing some business together.

4. "Pete Peterson". The prospect tells me how he wants to be called. I now know what to call him ("Pete"), and he's given me permission to do so.

5. "I can help you right now." Whoever answers the phone, whatever their designated job/job description, what they can do *right now* is help the prospect. Perhaps they are not the right person to answer all the prospect's questions or to provide the service, but they are the person who can help — whoever they are. Understand this. It's crucial to your success.

6. "information on". Prospects think they want information. They don't. They want the solution to the problem. The inept telephone receptionist is willing merely to send "information"; he thinks he's done his job just by getting the basic prospect details and spending your money sending stuff. No with-it marketer ever makes this mistake. You've got to bridge from what the prospect thinks he wants and which commits him to nothing (namely requesting and receiving "information") to what he really wants . . . which you can help with.

7. "I can help you." Note, not "I'll be happy to send you information." Saying you can help is affirmative; you're not saying the prospect won't get what he says he wants. You're saying you're there to help . . . and it's this help, not information, which he really wants.

8. "Tell me what you've got in mind." The prospect may *think* he's calling for information. If that's all he wants, he's a very low grade, probably a no grade prospect. Instead, he's probably calling for some other reason . . . namely to solve a problem. You've got to know what that problem is (and at some point when he wants to solve it, how much money he's got to solve it) before you can do anything. Opening with this non-threatening line allows the prospect to start telling you 1) if he really is a prospect (prospects, remember, have real things in mind, not just collecting marketing communications) and 2) how substantive that thing is.

• *How does the receptionist analyze what he's heard?*

Procedure: I reiterate — the job of the telephone receptionist/answerer is to be more than brain-dead. This person has a crucial job to perform in beginning the qualifying and sorting process that is a vital part of successful lead-closing. No one should consider this person's job done who merely:

- greets a lead;
- gets the lead's follow-up particulars, and
- some general indication of what the lead wants.

If this is all that's accomplished you are poisoning your lead-closing system.

Let's carry on with the example above so you see what I mean.

"Pete, I can help you. Tell me what you've got in mind."

"I saw your ad and was thinking about redoing our brochure. Can you send me some information about what you do?

"Certainly. First, can you tell me where you saw our ad. It might have been in (name of newspaper)."

"No, I saw it in (name of publication)."

"Okay. So, you're interested in a new brochure. I'll be happy to send you our marketing materials, but can you give me a little bit of information that'll make it easier for me to help you?"

"Sure."

"What kind of brochure are you using now?"

"I've been using the same brochure for a couple of years now. It's the kind that goes in a business envelope."

"How's it been working for you?"

"Well, at the beginning okay, but we don't seem to be closing as many prospects now with it as we used to."

"Do you use a sales letter with the brochure or does the brochure stand alone."

"We use both."

Whoa, you're saying to me. This is *supposed* to be a receptionist taking this call. Our receptionist could never ask all these questions . . . for one thing, he's too busy; too many calls come in. There's just no time to do all this.

Point 1: If this is true, you must decide how much time the receptionist can spend with the lead . . . and shape your system accordingly.

Say that you've decided the receptionist can spend just three minutes with a call. In this case the job of the receptionist is to:

- go through the initial questions listed above;
- let the prospect know that he can get help from your company (this is mandatory), and
- find out if the designated marketer in your company who is supposed to get the call can take it now.

The prospect wants to feel that he's come to the right place, that he is being treated in a responsible, even dignified way, and that he's not just another name or number. In short, that he can get what he came for. The receptionist, in three minutes, can make this happen . . .

. . . even if the designated marketer is not available right then. The correct way of handling this common situation is to:

- tell the prospect he will get the help he requires;
- say the person who provides this assistance is otherwise engaged just now;
- request the prospect to provide complete follow up details and some indication of why he's calling, and
- say the follow-up call will be promptly made (scheduling it if at all possible).

Even this short sequence can provide helpful information. Suppose the prospect won't say why he's calling; suppose he won't provide full follow-up information. Suppose, in short, that the "prospect" doesn't act like a *prospect*, merely like a time waster. What then? The receptionist can downgrade the value of this lead accordingly — and should be trained to do so.

Further, please note that to this point, the receptionist has said nothing about sending out "information." Instead, essentially what he's said is, "We can help you. Please provide the information I need so you get the help you want. Then we'll take care of it professionally and promptly here." This is the correct thing to do.

Thus, until either the receptionist sufficiently qualifies this person . . . or a designated marketer has done so *no information gets sent out!*

Again I remind you: your job is to qualify, to see if the prospect really is a prospect, not to send information. Merely doing what is necessary to send information is not marketing; it's idiocy.

Point 2: Now back to the better situation where the receptionist (who must, please be clear, be regarded as a marketer, too) gathers the information that is necessary to assign this lead the proper standing and proceed accordingly.

Towards this end, your receptionist should be trained to do as much qualification as possible. Only when the receptionist can neither qualify further nor is capable of answering detailed service delivery questions is it appropriate to remove this person from the qualifying/marketing process.

Take Pete the Prospect's second batch of questions above. Not one *technical* question has been asked; thus, any receptionist should be capable of being trained to ask such questions — and to record the answers.

Obviously, if you are working in a one-person shop where you handle the marketing and provide the service, *you* are the receptionist and qualifier and *you* will function in this role. But even in larger businesses too little use is made of receptionists to ask necessary questions and gather valuable information. Both as a marketer and as a humanist, this disgusts me. Too many jobs in this nation are jobs for the brain-dead; most receptionist jobs qualify. Yet reducing the receptionist to the level of a vegetable should not be a necessary part of such jobs. Instead, the receptionist/answerer should be regarded as a necessary and important — if necessarily limited — member of the marketing team and treated accordingly.

• *Does he attempt to find out how the prospect heard about your business?*

Procedure: As you'll notice from my illustration above, the receptionist asks early in the conversation how the prospect may have heard about the business or offer. This is important marketing research to determine what is working and what isn't to generate leads. *Note:* I have found that prospects don't mind supplying this information at all. Further, it only takes a couple of seconds to find out what you need. The important thing is that the receptionist appropriately log this information so it's available when it's needed.

• *How is he organized to record any information either the prospect provides or which he is asked to provide?*

Procedure: This recording of vital information is crucial. The prospect will provide two kinds: answers to questions he is asked and information he volunteers. What's important is that 1) the receptionist be equipped to ask questions; 2) he understands how to hear important information, and 3) he knows how to record what he both hears and deduces from his interaction with the prospect. The sad truth is, I almost never see a receptionist who is equipped to do this. Neither, moreover, are most so-called service marketers.

Let me tell you something important: right from the minute the prospect rings your office and someone at your end picks up the phone, the prospect is giving you valuable information. He tells you in many different ways if he's a real prospect, what he wants, when he wants it, why he wants it, whether he can pay for it, *etc.* Don't expect this information to be presented in perfect sentences; it won't be. But it will be presented, one way and another. Now, whoever is interacting with this prospect, be that person "receptionist" or "marketer", is responsible for gathering vital clues and other information about this prospect.

What's dumb is that most of this information is never perceived, much less recorded. If superior prospect qualifying is to occur, it can only do so if you make superior prospect qualifying a priority and prepare for it. This means helping the people who will do the qualifying to understand their importance in the process and giving them the tools they need. Here a Prospect Assessment Sheet is vital. Depending on how your office is configured, it can either be available to the marketer on computer or on photocopied sheets; either way, you must have it.

You already know the types of data this assessment must seek to gather:

- name
- company name
- address
- phone
- fax

- how did you hear about company/offer
- what are you trying to accomplish
- when do you want to do this
- what is your budget, *etc.*

Whoever is qualifying prospects for you must ask these questions. And they must write down not only what the prospect says but their impressions of what the prospect meant, as well as other information that will enable a correct determination to be made of this prospect's interest and ability to buy.

Now, I warrant you this means becoming a lot more alert than most people in most service businesses are these days. But I'll tell you something: the more prospects you deal with, the more you should be able to deduce what the prospect really means *whatever the prospect is saying*. Developing this skill is one of the most important things that can happen to a marketer; it allows him to determine which strategy is going to work best with this prospect *once you determine he really is a prospect*. You see, it is the observations of the marketer as much as mere data which enable you to determine this prospect's value and priority.

A form, for instance, will provide an indication of what the prospect says he wants. But it is the marketer who must record the further information that it took several attempts to gather even this simple data; that the prospect was unclear about his objectives, unclear on the date he wanted to achieve them, *etc.* This information is of the utmost importance, and it is continually thrown away by unthinking "marketers" who either for reasons of their own ease, their own stupidity, or their own lack of preparation and training think that throwing a few prospect facts on a page is sufficient. It isn't. Constant discernment and the ability to evaluate data and adapt your behavior accordingly is a necessary element of what makes a marketer success- ful. But if the information you've gathered is not written down, it is doubtful it can be handled properly.

• *How does he attempt to discover what benefit the prospect wants?*

Procedure: If you understand nothing else from this book but what I am again emphasizing here, you have gotten more than your money's worth. PROSPECTS SEEK BENEFITS FOR THEMSELVES. They al- ways have. They always will. Whatever else they want is secondary.

Benefits are always of principal importance. Thus, the marketer must move as quickly as possible to find out what the prospect is seeking.

Last night, for instance, as I was about to leave my office, I received a call from a man in California who called to "get some information about your card deck." As soon as I knew his name (a necessary start), I demanded to know: WHAT ARE YOU TRYING TO ACHIEVE?

It turns out that he didn't want information. He wanted to build his MLM down line. He was having problems getting leads for the people in his organization. He wanted to increase the number and quality of his leads as soon as possible. Now, let me tell you something: THIS IS A PROBLEM I CAN EASILY SOLVE. Once I understood what he wanted I told him exactly how I could help.

I talked to the fellow for about 10 minutes. At the end of this time, he had all the information he needed (I asked). THEN HE SIGNED ON . . . to the tune of $1199 for 100,000 cards.

Of course, I could have behaved in the more standard fashion. I could have said, I'm tired; it's been a long day. The prospect wants "information", so I'll send him "information". I'll call him back next week. He'll be unavailable the first three times I call; maybe he'll get around to calling me back. Probably he won't. I'll probably have to hunt him down. Meanwhile my deadline will pass. But what difference does it make: I've sent him the information he asked for!

I could have done this . . .

. . . but I don't think this way. I know when people call me they want a *benefit*. They have a problem they want to solve. They want to achieve some advantage. Either way, for whatever reason, they come to me seeking assistance. I get inside their heads to find out what they want . . . and then I start telling them what they have to do to get these benefits . . . and what I'm going to do to assist them.

Then I ask for their address, phone number, fax, *etc.* Because *then* this information is important!

• How does he attempt to discover when the prospect wants to go ahead and his ability to do so?

Procedure: The mere fact the prospect tells you what he wants does not close the deal. He must tell you *when* he wants to go ahead and *whether he has the means* of doing so.

For reasons which remain puzzling to me, many service sellers find it difficult to ask these questions. They find them invasive, as if they were trespassing into the prospect's life. I find such sentiments preposterous and futile. When you have implemented the lead-generating strategies of the previous chapters, the number of leads you get will rise, often dramatically. You cannot afford to lavish equal attention on them all; thus, you must have a means for determining just who does get some measure of your very limited time and resources. This is why asking these questions and getting answers is so very important.

So, *ask them!*

Just say: "When did you want to achieve (benefit you offer)?" Or, "when did you want to get rid of (pain the prospect has)?"

Then, *listen*. The prospect's answer provides crucial information that enables you to determine, with often minute precision, precisely how much time and attention you should be giving him *now*. Answers will range along a predictable continuum of prospect response, ranging from "IMMEDIATELY" . . .. to . . .. "NEVER, I'M JUST CALLING TO SEE HOW MUCH OF YOUR TIME AND MONEY YOU'LL LET ME WASTE."

Many, many service sellers don't like being this direct. It makes them queasy. I know why. I hear over and over again from "prospects" that they think I'm too focused; too pointed; too clipped. I now find such criticisms extravagantly beside the point. I have set financial objectives for myself. I have instituted unrelenting lead-generating systems. And I close the necessary proportion of these leads every single day so that my financial objectives are consistently met. I can no longer worry about the fact that some limited number of selfish, disorganized, vacillating, procrastinating, passive, and directionless people are irritated when they present themselves for "service." How can such people be served? Reader, take note: THEY CANNOT.

To be sure, at the very beginning of your service business, when you have too many bills and too much time, you may well make compromises with such people; you may well find yourself going too far, doing too much in your attempt to generate business. But I beg of you: do what is necessary to move beyond this situation as fast as possible. Institute as quickly as you can the mandatory asking of these probing questions and the close scrutiny of their answers:

- "When do you want to have what you say you want?"
- "What is your budget for achieving it?"

Yes, the B-question.

As I walked through Harvard Square this morning on my way back from the bank (a trip I happily make every single business day), and again saw the growing numbers of the dispossessed, the drifters, vagabonds, societal drop-outs, misfits and merely the aimless ambling, I thought again how we have arrived at a period of history where vast numbers of people count for virtually nothing from a marketing standpoint. They do not have the means of acquiring the world's products and services except at the most minimal of levels. To the extent that they do not possess this ability, they count for nothing.

Humanists, of course, will be appalled at this statement; they will try to advance some counter-argument about the essential worthiness of all people, the sacred brotherhood of peoples, *etc.* While this may well be true in some moral or religious sense, in marketing such statements are entirely irrelevant. Yet people use them to make purely business decisions.

Not you! Not now! Instead, you will, with the utmost civility and professionalism, ask the necessary budget question. And you will evaluate this "prospect" according to what you hear. Without feeling that the question is either improper or intrusive; without feeling guilty about what you must do as a result of what you hear. Such guilt, with which so many service sellers muddle their marketing, has no role in it at all.

Marketing, you see, is really a very simple thing:

- You do everything you can to generate the maximum number of leads;
- You qualify these leads as quickly as you can;
- You close deals with the people who can both profit from your service and have the means for acquiring it.

Do this, and you must be rich.

- What does he do if the prospect will not provide the information you need to assist in the qualifying and closing process or provides information which is vague?

Procedure: Some "prospects" will bridle when asked the kinds of direct questions you must ask them. This is predictable. But the ones that bridle will not be the real prospects . . . so long as you are clear about why you must get the information you're requesting.

The right to privacy has become a key issue of our times. It is so important because our privacy has never been so assaulted by so many forces. Many people, therefore, good prospects and bad, will feel uncomfortable when you start asking questions. You must be prepared for this . . . and you must have ready your polished explanation about why such questions are necessary. Be prepared for this! If you feel the slightest hesitation on the prospect's part, explain why you need this information.

The real prospect will accept your explanation. Real prospects, as I have previously explained, understand that to do your job you will need a certain level of cooperation from them; this includes answering questions which in any other circumstances might well be construed as invasive, inappropriate. Time-wasters, instead of accepting your reasonable explanation, will continue to huff and puff, getting you off the track, pushing back the moment when any real business can be transacted. They do this deliberately . . . because they are unable to transact business and want to put the burden of failing to do so on you. WHERE IT WILL MOST ASSUREDLY BELONG IF YOU FALL FOR THESE SHENANIGANS.

The same is true if the prospect provides only vague answers. If the prospect cannot tell you what he wants, when he wants it and how much he's prepared to pay, whatever else he tells you is largely irrelevant. Such "prospects" must be immediately demoted . . . or even, depending on how little they tell you and how unbelievable it is, just tossed out.

I beg you: do not confuse humanism and marketing. By down-grading this lead, or getting rid of it altogether, you are not passing a comment on the humanity of the person you're dealing with. Please remember I have consistently stressed that all the prospects you see or who call in to your office, should receive a modicum of respect and civility . . . even when they are no longer regarded as prospects. It doesn't hurt you to spend the extra minute it takes to end such conversations on an upbeat note ("We'll be happy to help you when you're ready to go ahead!").

Yet this is precisely what many service sellers fail to do. Stock brokers and insurance sales people are among the worst. I get calls from them regularly. Often, when they find I'm not a prospect for what they're selling, they merely hang up, letting me know precisely how ill-bred and rapacious they are. This is not at all what I'm talking about.

By all means, unqualified leads must be rigorously discarded as quickly as possible . . . but not rudely. And not without planting at least the seed of a future relationship ("We'll be glad to help you when you're ready!"). But what we are looking for is a means of generating maximum numbers of leads quickly, qualifying these leads quickly and establishing relationships of mutual trust with those people who are truly ready to purchase your benefit. Those who will not provide you with the information you require are not candidates for such a relationship and must be down-graded or dismissed accordingly.

• *How does the representative advise the prospect about what will happen next . . . so that the prospect is prepared for the next stage in the closing process?*

Procedure/Marketing Communication: Between the last point and this one, something very significant has occurred. Either the prospect has in fact been confirmed as a prospect, or he has been revealed as something less, and therefore less valuable or even worthless. If the latter, your representative must, as you now see, wrap up the conversation briskly and civilly. As Winston Churchill once said, when you hang a man you can afford the white gloves. Perfect civility constitutes the white gloves in the conversation in which you're downgrading or dismissing the creature who is a prospect no longer. Whether you put such people in a dim, distant tickler file, put them on your mailing list (if you think they may well respond to future prodding) or throw such leads away altogether, you can, for now, dismiss them from your mind. Moreover, if you are discarding the lead altogether, you can dismiss them from your mind forever, unashamedly. A person who is not a prospect for your benefit is someone you need never concern yourself with, whatever that "prospect" may say or think, then or later.

To the real prospect, however, something entirely different is due. When you have found out what this person wishes to achieve, when he wishes to achieve it, and that he has at hand the means for achieving it, it's time to say what you'll do to give him what he wants. Now, what you'll do entirely depends on precisely what he's told you. Thus:

- If he says he wants to go ahead now and you can make the sale now, do so. Then confirm the wisdom of the client's action by letter or immediate fax, indicating therein not only that this step makes sense, but what the client will achieve, and what you are doing to get the ball rolling. Immediate confirmation and indication of action are crucial here;

- If he says he wants time to think about what he's heard and if this request seems reasonable, tell the prospect when and how you'll be back in touch and confirm this in a letter or fax depending on the value of the contract. Provide any marketing communications the prospect needs to see to make a decision;

- If the prospect will not make up his mind for some time, again indicate how and when you'll be in touch. Send any appropriate marketing communications. During the intervening time, if you have a means of communicating with your prospects (such as a catalog, newsletter or regular mailings) indicate that this prospect will be receiving these. If at all possible, arrange a definite time (even if far in the future) to recontact the prospect. Be clear that you'll be contacting the prospect at that time and when you do get in touch, make sure you mention that this is the time agreed to by the prospect.

In all these cases, it is your responsibility to take charge of this interaction with the prospect, do the task which will result in the fastest sale and proceed accordingly, confirming everything in writing and fully informing the prospect along the way. It is important to point out that this degree of organization is itself a valuable motivater for the prospect, since he reasons that if you're so well organized about all this, you will be organized about providing what he wants, too.

• What does the representative do when the conversation with the prospect is over?

Procedure/Marketing Communication: When the prospect rings off, the meeting is not yet over . . . for the marketer. There is still very important work to do, including:

- completing notes of the meeting;

- taking care of all matters promised, and

- logging the information so that the next follow-up takes place as promised and as necessary.

Becoming a service seller millionaire is not a matter of chance; it is a matter of *system.* This is an important component in that system, yet it is all too often neglected. But not by you! You will:

- Complete the prospect assessment document. Hopefully, you've got the form on computer. It makes working on this document much easier. Make sure you've got all the factual information in a form that can easily be used. Then, add things you've learned about the prospect from your conversation. What kind of personal information did he tell you? What kind of business information? Nothing a prospect says can be eliminated at this point as being unimportant. As my hero Sherlock Holmes constantly proved, even the smallest fact may well have significant value and implications. I've never forgotten this and have, as a result, written down any number of things about my prospects realizing that each could provide yet another means of giving insight into what the prospect wants and how I should handle him. You do the same.

- Further, make an informed judgment about whether you now think this prospect will buy. And if so, when. In short, test yourself. Master marketers are always assessing themselves in an attempt to improve their game. Successful marketing is an exercise of intellectual and analytical agility, far more challenging (and much more profitable) than any academic research. It will never be something you can merely do by rote, brainlessly. It involves both grand strategy and tactical dexterity. And it provides a means through which you can constantly test yourself . . . and, by reviewing what happens, stretch and improve. This is why you must record what you think will happen and when. No ex post facto revisions, either. The only person you'll be cheating, after all, is yourself.

- Do what you said you were going to do . . . and do it when you said you were going to do it. I am a follow-up fanatic. You should be, too. For one thing, it's the right way to behave; for another, as I've stated, these good habits clearly identify you as a person the prospect can at least begin to trust. Good follow-up assists a prospect make up his mind to retain you. That's why you should do as much as you can as soon as you're off the phone, ensuring that things you said would be sent promptly go out THAT DAY whenever possible. I have found over the years that my own ability to follow through in this rigorous way has served me well over and over again. Not least, it also gives me the moral right to demand similar responsible habits from the people I'm dealing with . . . whether they like it or not!

- Log the information. Too many service sellers think they're going to remember what to do, and as a result eschew logging the information. This is ridiculous. Personally, I have a very good memory, and yet I wouldn't trust it beyond an afternoon. If it's important, it must be written down and logged in a way that is easy to find and easy to use. Not least this gives you a considerable advantage when working with prospects, because it's virtually certain they will not be as organized as you about your past dealings, what they said, what they wanted, *etc*. Organization provides control and prospects often buy because of the degree of control you bring to a situation.

— *By Mail*

We now arrive at the third and final means prospects will use to connect with you. It's the least personal, and therefore the one many prospects use. It commits them the least, and gives them the most distance from the marketer. Many prospects like this. How many? Well, we now know from the card-deck that in a situation where an advertiser includes both an 800-number for response and an option where the prospect has to put his own stamp on the card to respond, fully 80% of the "prospects" will use their own stamp to respond to the offer rather than take advantage of the free 800-number. You might think the numbers would be reversed, but this figure remains steady over many decks and different offers. The reason for this is that prospects often prefer the anonymity of impersonal mail. It commits them to nothing and gives them maximum control. This is why mail leads can prove such a costly snare for the unwary service marketer, and why you need to take especial care in evaluating them and responding.

• *Who is responsible for getting the mail-in leads?*

Procedure: Analyzing the quality of leads is an art. Therefore you should designate a particular individual to handle all the leads, keeping abreast of everything that comes in. This person will necessarily develop an expertise in determining which leads look like the best bets for what you're selling.

- What standards do you have for determining what is a high priority lead, a lower priority lead or a name which, for whatever reason, is not reckoned a lead at all?

Procedure/Marketing Communication: Those who are inexperienced in scrutinizing mail-in leads generally think that whatever they receive in the mail constitutes a real lead. This is not true, although it is easy to see how such a belief is born. The marketer may think: I've placed an ad; I've been very clear about the benefits I have available. The person who responds to this ad is clearly a prospect for what I've got available. This mail-order syllogism, however, fails to consider the following factors:

- While there are many people in the world who say they detest so-called "junk mail" and who instantly throw it away, there is another and arguably larger group of people who respond to virtually everything they receive — whether they need it or not;

- Many people use the receipt of mail (even unimportant mail) as proof of their importance. They therefore do everything they can to generate such responses;

- Many people are impulse responders. Abiding by the insistence of advertising that tells them they're "worth it," they respond to anything that takes their fancy for even an instant. They are information, freebie-seeking junkies, who get hepped up by offers they cannot afford;

- Many people think they owe it to themselves to see an offer . . . whether they're really interested in it or not; they think they're educating themselves, instead of wasting the resources of large numbers of other people.

As every marketer can tell you these people exist in large numbers, and they make the work of the marketer significantly more difficult than it needs to be. That's why you need to be very clear about your qualifying procedures for people who mail in responses to your marketing — particularly when you are providing them with premiums and other freebie benefits.

I've already detailed the kinds of people you should be wary of. These include people who:

- fail to provide telephone numbers (make sure you always insist that they do);

- have originally returned a response without the required postage. You'll know because the post office will note that the respondent didn't affix proper postage and that it was returned to sender;

- didn't include the amount of money you requested for your information. (I've discovered with the card-deck that about 20% of the people responding to a card which requests anywhere from $3-5 for the information won't provide it, often offering "reasons" why they don't want to include it. I used to send these people a note pointing out that they'd "forgotten" to send the money and reminding them to do so. Only a few people answered this, and now I just throw away all the responses where the "prospect" hasn't followed the directions.)

- send hard-luck stories about how they want you to help them . . . but want you to do it for free;

- give indications that they're not real prospects, that is retirees (if you're not seeking them), children, prisoners, *etc.;*

- tell you they don't want any follow-up calls;

- indicate they don't want to be put on any mailing list, *etc.*

I remind you: over and over again people who are not good prospects tell you in one way or another that they're not. For whatever reason, they want your information; they do not wish, however, to pay for your benefit or develop a working relationship with you. *You owe these people nothing. Note:* when you get to the point where you're doing large numbers of mailings, you'll be getting more and more of these people on your mailing list, particularly if others sort the mail for you. In this case, as you become aware of the freebie seekers and other blood-suckers, develop a special data base with their names and addresses. You can then use this list to purge these names from your mailings. This is a very responsible thing to do and will save some of your resources and keep offers out of the hands of people who shouldn't be getting them.

Over and over again, however, I learn from service sellers that they are spending precious time and resources trying to follow up people who are not real prospects. If they've asked for phone numbers and the "prospect" hasn't supplied one, they spend their time — and money — trying to get it. Don't. In this case, if it is convenient for you — and you need the lead — send this person back a computer-generated note — along with the uncompleted response vehicle they sent in — and kindly ask him to complete and return it so you can get started helping him get the benefit you provide. Or, if you don't need the lead, simply discard it. This "prospect" didn't have the brains, common courtesy, or decency to treat you in a professional way. Therefore, you owe him nothing.

Let me be very clear with you about this. Instead of wasting your time and money attempting to work with people who are not real leads, you should be investing in perfecting your lead-generating process so that have more leads to work with and the likelihood of more leads coming in. Service sellers regularly spend too much time with low-quality leads because these are the only leads they have . . . and they wrongly reckon that the person who has sent something in by mail *must* be a potential lead.

DON'T BELIEVE THIS! If you have given people the choice between calling you and sending in a mail-in lead (as you should), the people who contact you by mail start by being a less good lead. Then, if they don't provide you with the information you need or provide it in a way which makes difficulties for you, the value of this lead drops accordingly until, at last, and without a pang, it's simply more valuable to drop the "lead" in the trash than waste any time even beginning to pursue it.

You can do this without any regret if you have an unrelenting lead-generating system in place because you know, in just a few hours, or even a few minutes, another lead will arrive which may well be worth your attention. This is why such a system is so important; it saves you from investing in the wrong people, people who are not and never will be prospects for your benefits.

• *How will you handle the high priority leads?*

Procedure/Marketing Communication: As a result of your qualification process, some leads will emerge as high priority leads, people who should be followed up immediately. The question is, what will you do with them?

You will remember my story about the professional copywriter who essentially boarded himself in his basement as day by day the number of his leads grew without his being able to deal effectively with them. This man had no way of determining the high priority leads and hadn't thought through what he'd do when these leads — inevitably — emerged from the piles of other leads. This was a critical error.

Here are some options about how you can handle these leads:

- If you've identified a high-priority lead and need the work, call immediately and further the qualifying and closing process. Personally, I make the call the minute I've determined the importance of the lead and my desire to close the deal;

- If you've identified a high-priority lead but cannot handle the assignment just now, develop a client-centered letter you can send out *that day* indicating how you intend to handle this matter. Perhaps you'll simply want to send your marketing communication with cover letter, indicating when you will call.

- If you are generating more leads than you can handle for the foreseeable future, inform the prospect you have passed his name and situation to your back-up service provider. Provide this provider's name and follow-up details. Send a copy of this letter to your back-up provider, along with full particulars about the prospect, and ask him to follow up promptly. If this provider cannot do so immediately, there is a problem; you'll have to solve it immediately or risk destroying the value of this high-priority lead.

It should now be clear to you that all leads are not equal; those that you've judged superior must be treated in a superior fashion, which means that you must handle them promptly and unrelentingly.

- What different response will you use with those of lesser priority?

Procedure/Marketing Communication: By the same token, many leads will not be high-priority. Say you've used the system where the prospect tells you just when he wants to go ahead. Thus, "is your need □ immediate □ next two months □ next six months □ not sure. Please check." I like this system, because it's an easy way to determine just how you should treat the prospect.

Obviously, you'll contact those immediately who indicate that their need is "immediate"; when you're finished with them, call those who want the benefit in the "next two months." At the same time, develop a computer-generated letter which you can send to the third category, "next six months."

This is a less good prospect, but one who should not be ignored. Thus, include in your letter:

- a reminder that the prospect has asked you to get in touch;

- a list of the benefits you have available;

- an invitation for the prospect to call you to get started receiving these benefits, and

- notice of when you'll contact the prospect (presumably 5-6 months from the date of this letter).

Given your strong presentation of the benefits, some prospects will get in touch with you sooner — thereby raising their priority status. Others won't. As you have time, contact them — by telephone, if you have the time and opportunity. Otherwise, through your regular prospect contacts, newsletters, mailings, *etc.*

What you do next depends on how busy you are. If you are very busy and have about as much business as you need, about thirty days before the six months has elapsed, send a letter asking prospects to contact you if they are still interested. Again, stress the benefits, tell them what they get and invite them to be in touch.

On the other hand, if you need the business, get on the phone and re-qualify them. Remind the prospects who you are, that they contacted you and ask if they still want the benefit. If so, determine when they want it and their ability to purchase the benefit. Proceed accordingly.

• *How will you store the prospect information for subsequent ease of handling?*

Procedure/Marketing Communication: Obviously, once you've made the determination about the value of the lead, it's important you store the information properly. Since you've determined that the leads you've kept are important, arrange them like they are.

Just how you'll store them will depend on the means you have available for contacting and cultivating them. If you have a general mailing list which you use to send prospect mailings, catalogs, newsletters, *etc.*, obviously you'll want to add these good leads to this data base. However, you may also want to add them to a prospect text file where you can add further information as it becomes available. Personally, I prefer to work from a prospect text file into which I can add:

- information about when I called;

- how many messages I've left;

- who I talked to;

- what they said;

- what I'd promised to do;

- when I did it;

- where matters stand at any given point, and

- my assessment of the situation and the likelihood of getting business. (Such assessments, as you won't be surprised to learn, are often scatologically candid.)

As your prospect file grows, you can divide it into logical divisions, thus: current top prospects, possibles, low-priority, and defunct prospects. As you have time, you can work on the lower-grade prospects accordingly. *Note:* develop a computer-generated letter in which you inform prospects they are about to be added to the "defunct prospect" file. Indicate that you are ready to help them, again enumerate the substantial benefits you have available, and again invite them strongly to get in touch. Try to stimulate these people with an offer. If the "prospect" doesn't respond to this client-centered letter, the chances are remote you'll get any business from him. Treat him accordingly.

Crafting Proposals That Get Accepted

Before leaving this chapter, I must include details on another important aspect of your lead-closing system, namely crafting proposals that get business. This subject is both important and very often trying for service sellers who can get anxious attempting to create the right document for the person they're attempting to close. Here are some tips:

- Understand that a proposal is a client-centered marketing document and thus must be focused on the prospect's interests and be packed with benefits for the prospect;

- Develop the core of your proposal before you need it;

- Personalize your proposal either in the beginning of the document itself or in an accompanying cover letter;

- Send the proposal as soon as you can, whenever possible the day you speak to the prospect;

- Follow up the proposal promptly;

- When speaking to the prospect understand that you have submitted a *proposal* and that implicit in each proposal you send is a prospect's counter-proposal;

- Be willing to consider reasonable changes to your proposal;

- If changes are called for, redraft your proposal and resubmit promptly;

- Again follow up promptly and close the deal.

Let's look at each of these components a little more closely.

A Proposal Is A Client-Centered Marketing Document That Must Be Focused On The Prospect's Interests

Too often service marketers seem to forget that a proposal is a marketing communication. It must therefore follow the rules of all other marketing communications and be based on the four key words YOU GET BENEFIT NOW. Just what the prospect gets must be presented in the title and must be stressed throughout the proposal's text. Thus, what do you think is more client-centered:

Alternative A) A proposal from ABC Corporation for Jane and Michael Doe, or

Alternative B) How Jane & Michael Doe can add $15,000 to the resale value of their home by remodeling their kitchen and bathroom in the next 45 days.

It's obvious, isn't it?

The first proposal is generic. It looks like it was cooked up by some brain-dead "marketer" who hadn't a clue what the prospect might want. He knew he had to submit something to them . . . but what? "A proposal from ABC Corp . . ."

The second proposal is based on crucial prospect knowledge. The marketer who wrote it knows that the prospects are about to sell their house; that they want to get maximum resale value for it. He knows how much resale value the improvements will add, and he sells his service by using this value as leverage to induce the prospects to get started now. This leverage begins in the headline which clearly presents the major benefit the prospects will get.

The rest of the proposal is divided into the following parts:

1. an introduction that again presents precisely what the prospects want and when they want it. This is your chance to present in more detail the major prospect benefit.

2. the heart of the document consists of your recommended steps on how you'll work with the prospect to get what he wants. In other words, just like a problem-solving process article, you'll present what you need to do first, second, third, fourth, *etc.*, clearly outlining the necessary steps that will take the prospect from where he is now to where he wants to be using your service.

3. you'll then present the cost of your service. But do it so that the prospect has choices. Present a "bare bones" estimate of what the prospect gets for a certain basic charge. Then present one or two different, more expansive (and expensive) alternatives. Remember, there are usually several different ways of solving the prospect's problem, of getting him what he wants. Your job is to indicate two or three different ways — and then to sell the prospect one that is at least one step beyond what he originally thought he'd buy. That's real marketing!

Develop The Core Of Your Proposal Before You Need It

Most service sellers sell the same services over and over again. Thus, it shouldn't be too difficult to create the core of your proposal before you need it. There are many good reasons for doing so:

- you won't be rushed in creating it. It's a good idea to do your proposals deliberately; creating them in advance allows you to do this.

- you can refine them at your leisure, and

- you'll have them ready when you need them.

As I've said before, there are essentially two stages to marketing: the planning stage and the execution stage. In the planning stage you are right to be thoughtful and deliberate. That's what planning is all about. But in the execution stage you want to be as swift as possible. That's why your proposals should be developed in advance and stored in your computer.

Personalize Your Proposal Either In The Beginning Of The Document Itself Or In A Cover Letter

Many people think that a proposal must be distinct from a cover letter. I am not one of them. I see no necessary reason why you cannot personalize the opening of a proposal so that it focuses directly on the prospect and therefore acts as a separate cover letter would. By the same token, it's often just as easy to develop a separate cover letter to accompany your proposal. The important thing is that you not get bogged down in what is nothing more than a foolish problem.

Take the proposal for Jane and Michael Doe, for instance. Now, if you're a home remodeler, lots and lots of people are going to approach you about having their kitchens and baths redone. Your basic proposal, therefore, will indicate precisely what needs to be done to achieve the prospect's objective. Each prospect's reason for taking action and his time-table may well be different, however. You can either address his particular situation in the beginning of the proposal or in a cover letter; the important thing, however, is that it be clearly and early presented.

This portion should include:

- your understanding of what the prospect wishes to achieve;

- why the prospect wishes to achieve this (if not obvious);

- when the prospect wishes to achieve this, and

- how much the prospect wishes to pay to achieve this.

Further, you should indicate:

- what will happen if the prospect fails to act now (will the price be going up because a special offer will expire? Because costs are expected to rise? *etc.*), and

- how will you be following this up.

The best proposals, whether they include information that is usually found in a cover letter or are accompanied by a cover letter, are invariably focused on precisely what the prospect wishes to achieve and make it clear what both you and the prospect need to do so that the prospect's objective can be achieved as promptly as possible for the most reasonable price.

Send The Proposal As Soon As You Can, Whenever Possible The Day You Speak To The Prospect

One of the mistakes service sellers make is that they send their proposals tardily. This is ridiculous! I insist that the client-centered proposal be completed as soon as you understand what the prospect wants, why the prospect wants it, when the prospect wants it, and how much money he has to pay for it. In other words, once you succeed in getting this information either in person, by telephone or by letter *you must complete and dispatch the proposal*. How should you send it? That depends on how highly you've rated the prospect. Your highest-rated prospects should be contacted by fax or overnight delivery. Others you can send via UPS or mail. Personally I like fax delivery for potentially very lucrative or important clients and second-day UPS for lower-rated clients. Why second day UPS? Because the prospect has to sign for delivery, thus raising its perceived value a bit beyond regular mail but at reasonable cost.

What is inexcusable, however, is to procrastinate. There are only two reasons for procrastinating: either 1) you don't have the information you need to proceed, or 2) you don't have the right business traits.

Let's say it's the former. You're missing certain information. In this case, contact the prospect again immediately, preferably by phone. Tell the prospect you are at work on his proposal, that you want to get it out as promptly as possible and that you need additional information. If the prospect is not available to take this call and the prospect/potential contract is valuable, send a fax listing the information you need. Otherwise, leave a detailed message with the prospect's receptionist and/or send a letter.

The important thing, however, is that you take *action* and that you be seen as working on the prospect's behalf . . . just as if you'd already been hired. If the prospect doesn't get back to you promptly, try again. If the person doesn't cooperate with you, his value as a prospect necessarily drops. Before dropping such a "prospect" altogether, however, write a direct letter saying that you are trying to help but that you cannot provide the desired assistance until the prospect acts in a professional and reasonable manner. There is nothing wrong with saying this; the good people will remember their manners and behave accordingly. The flat worms won't . . . and should be dropped accordingly.

But what if it's the second point, namely that you just don't have the right business traits? You'll know, of course, because the information you need is sitting at your finger tips, and you just can't get it together to write the proposal. If this is you, shame, shame on you. You've got this far and are now in sight of closing the deal with the prospect. Don't blow it because of your own poor habits!

Follow Up The Proposal Promptly

Just when should you follow up the proposal? That depends on the potential value of the contract, the prospect's own time-table, and how much time is reasonable for the prospect to consider what you've sent. Take the remodeling situation above. Say that it takes you 30 days to remodel a kitchen and bath of the sort owned by the prospects. Say that the prospects want to put their home on the market in 60 days. In a case like this, you could give them 3 days before calling. In short, the amount of time must take into consideration the technical conditions of the job and the prospect's own schedule.

Where there are no such considerations, invent some. Provide a special offer for the prospect if he can make up his mind *now*. Take the home remodeler. Suppose he needs the business just now; suppose that the prospects were just considering the remodeling and had no necessary reason, short of their own desire, to go ahead now. In this case, he'd be advised to make an offer to induce a faster decision. Perhaps, for instance, he'd provide certain bathroom or kitchen fixtures free or a special price for the entire job, if the prospect made up his mind and started the job within two or three weeks.

Each Proposal Invites A Counter-Proposal

However client-centered you have been in your proposal (and this, of course, is the essence of the proposal), don't just expect every prospect to accept it without further comment. This is because a proposal is just that, an organized series of suggestions for the prospect's betterment. You can bet the prospect will have something he'll want to say about that, too, and you should be in no way surprised or disappointed when you hear his ideas.

Be Willing To Consider Reasonable Changes To Your Proposal

The correct way to handle the prospect's reaction is to listen to it carefully before responding. Thus, whenever possible get the prospect's response in writing; if this is not possible, write down what the prospect has to say yourself and make it clear that you want to hear everything he has to say before responding.

Then pay attention.

If upon hearing what the prospect has to say, you can accommodate him within the terms of what you've written, say so and get on to the business of closing the deal and getting started. If you need more time, take it. One of the mistakes service sellers make is that they try to respond instantly to matters which demand their consideration. They thus wing it with generally predictable and disappointing results. Don't do this!

Say that our remodeling prospect has said he needs more things done in less time for the same price than the original proposal details. The ordinary response is to defend the proposal . . . trying to convince the prospect that what you've written makes sense and is the only way to go. But the prospect doesn't want to be convinced . . . he wants what he wants, even if that is entirely unreasonable.

Before blowing this situation, retire to think. How much of what the prospect wants can you give him for the price you've quoted? What can you suggest for accommodating his other desires? Don't just blurt out your answers; withdraw and mull the situation over. Make it clear to the prospect that you want to accommodate him and indicate when you'll be back in touch. Schedule a convenient meeting time. Then go back to the drawing board and see what you can do.

This is all very well and good, you say, if the suggestions are reasonable and you can accommodate the prospect, but what if the suggestions are not reasonable . . . and you cannot accommodate the prospect. What then?

Each of us service sellers develops a sixth sense about prospects. Personally, I have come to believe that the prospect who is difficult right from the start will always be difficult; just what he'll be difficult about will change, but the fact he's difficult will not. Indeed, as you get deeper into the project his degree of difficulty will grow until it becomes intolerable.

If you are desperate for business, you will, of course, try to accommodate this person. But let me tell you something. It is for moments like this that you're establishing an unrelenting lead-generating system. Personally, years ago I made a vow to myself that I would not work with disagreeable, rude, vulgar, unreasonable or irritating people. Life's too short. By all means attempt to salvage this situation, if you feel it's salvageable. However, if you decide you just cannot deal with this prospect — for whatever reason — assign the task to someone in your organization — if you feel that it's probably a personality problem and that the situation is worth saving.

If this won't work, call in someone from your network to take over the lead and pay you a percentage of the contract. This is one reason why you should maintain a contact network. If *this* won't work and if the prospect is so difficult that you see nothing but trouble ahead, wish him well in a short, civil note and move on. If you've been following the suggestions of this book, your next good lead is already on its way!

Redraft Your Proposal And Resubmit Promptly

On the other hand, if the prospect's suggestions (and manner) are reasonable, if you can improve the prospect's situation with your service and you want to work with this person, redraft your proposal promptly and resubmit it promptly. Be clear that you:

- understand what the prospect wants (restate it);
- can provide this;
- show how you can provide it, and
- are clear about how much it will cost.

If you can meet all of what the prospect wants, say so.

If you can meet some of what the prospect wants, start by telling him this. Then explain how he can get the rest of what he wants.

If you cannot provide the prospect what he wants, say why . . . and suggest alternatives, including other service providers in your network.

Again Follow Up Promptly And Close The Deal

When following up a redrafted proposal, there is no reason to wait as long as before. The prospect already has the gist of the proposal; now you're down to a relatively few matters that need to be resolved before you can go ahead. Thus, move rapidly. You might, for instance, fax your proposal in the morning and follow up after lunch depending on the nature of what you're submitting and how much time you think is reasonable for the prospect to consider the matter.

If you have heard what the prospect's been telling you, if you've responded with client-centered care and focus, you should now be very close to a deal.

But what if you're not?

Very often at this point, when the deal seems so tantalizingly close, the prospect will balk. This is often because the deal *is* so close . . . and the prospect really isn't ready to commit. That's why this point in the negotiations can be so very tricky.

Here's what you can do to limit your risk and increase the likelihood of the deal going through:

- The first time you submit your proposal, ask the prospect if he's ready to go ahead if the proposal is to his satisfaction. In other words, if he gets what he wants is he ready to commit and to act? Listen carefully to how the prospect responds to this. You are looking for signs of hesitation that may later derail the deal.

- If the prospect makes suggestions for amending the proposal, ask whether if you and he can come to an agreement on these points, he is ready to go ahead. Again, listen carefully;

- Also ask if the prospect is negotiating with anyone else. He may, after all, be using you to secure a better deal with another person rather than attempting to do business with you.

Remember, the real prospect wants agreement. Sure, he wants to get the best possible terms for himself; sure, he may drive a very hard bargain. But he wants an agreement. The unreal prospect doesn't. This person may want out . . . but he doesn't want to say so. He wants the burden of the deal falling through to be on you. That's why you've got to make it clear that you want things to work and that you're working to make sure they do.

Does this ensure agreement will be reached? Sadly no. As you know, I make lots of deals. Each time I make one, I ask the other person if he's serious about going ahead. I've developed acute listening skills to try and determine if he's serious. Yet, even in situations where I'm confident I've tested and retested, people who make commitments back out. In each issue of my card-deck, for instance, some 4-6 of these people do so . . . despite the fact that each has made a commitment, generally signed a contract, and assured me he is going ahead. I have talked to many other people in my industry about this and they are astonished my drop-out percentage is so low, despite the fact that it continually disheartens me.

What's it all about, Alfie? In this nation a person's word is no longer his bond. What too many people say to you this minute is not what they're willing to admit and stand by the next. Sadly, there is not a lot you can do about this . . . except move on with the best grace possible. Unfortunately, whatever the benefits in the proposal you've submitted to these people, however client-centered you've been, the chances are very low that they'll come back later to do business with you. Why? Because at some level they're ashamed of the way they've treated you and instead of admitting it, they deprive themselves of the benefits and you of the business. This is dumb . . . but it happens more and more in America these days, another sign of our crumbling national integrity.

Fortunately, this is not the only thing that occurs. More often, your client-centered proposal will be accepted, even if you have to redraft it in response to the prospect's suggestions. As soon as it is, write the prospect a letter (yes, you should have it available on computer) confirming that he's made the right choice, setting forth the benefits he'll be receiving, when you'll be starting work and what he needs to do (*e.g.* signing your contract and returning it to you ASAP). Don't just send your contract. You're a marketer, remember; this means taking this opportunity to reinforce in your new client's mind the benefits he's about to get and your role in achieving them.

Note: I am not going to provide you with contractual language here. This subject lies outside the realm of this book. However, you can find a discussion of contracts and exact contractual language in my books **THE CONSULTANT'S KIT** and **HOW TO MAKE AT LEAST $100,000 EVERY YEAR AS A SUCCESSFUL CONSULTANT IN YOUR OWN FIELD.**

Step 7: Overseeing — And Refining — Your Successful Qualifying System

I am sure by now you *understand* the benefits of creating and introducing an unrelentingly lead-closing system. Now you must *implement* it. Given human sloth and disorganization, this will be more difficult. That's why you must resolve to make sure that the good habits and procedures presented in this chapter do come to benefit you. This means constant oversight and adjustment.

If you want the people you work with to achieve superior leads-closing results, in addition to training them you must oversee their daily performance. Thus:

- Have their prospect conversations taped;

- Get on an extension phone and listen to what your subordinates are saying to prospects;

- Plant prospect calls. Get people whose opinion you respect to call your business or drop in, and see what happens;

- Review the drafts of marketing communications and proposals;

- Most importantly, have regular and frequent oversight and review sessions.

These sessions are crucial for the success of your leads-closing system. Such sessions should:

- be held at the end of the day while prospect dealings are fresh in the minds of the lead-closers. If you are working in the same premises as the people closing the leads, hold a meeting (30 minutes should do) in your office. Make sure all people involved in dealing with prospects attend. This meeting is not a luxury; it is a command performance.

- ask the lead-closers to present cases from the day. These cases can be presented on tape or from notes taken at the end of an encounter with a lead.

It is your job as the person chairing this meeting to:

- Listen until all the facts about a prospect encounter have been presented;

- Ask the would-be lead-closer if he feels he did *everything* to ascertain whether the prospect was a good lead, to get the information that was necessary to determine this and to move the prospect closer to a sale;

- If others are participating in this meeting, ask them if they have any suggestions about how the prospect contact could have been improved;

- If the meeting is just between you and the lead-closer, provide your suggestions about what could have been improved. Were there things that could have been done to find out if the prospect was really serious? Find out when he wanted to acquire the benefits? Find out if he had the means to acquire the benefits? Follow up in a more focused manner so that the next contact could result in a closing?

I now beg everyone I am concerned with to have these regular meetings. I think them crucial to the success of your leads-closing operation. I don't care if the people you are dealing with are master marketers with years of experience; such people can develop slack habits just like everyone else. And if they are not master marketers, the chances are that they are not considering what they do as a process that can be perfected.

A Personal Note

I work with several very bright marketing professionals who are superior creatures. Because they are superior, I expect more of them; indeed, as they well know, I demand it. This means that even though they are successful, they get periodic, often daily, "tutoring" sessions from me in which I scrutinize their approaches to prospects, review what they said (we often tape sales calls) and the marketing communications they used, and offer often bruising evaluations of their work and suggestions for improvement. These are, if you will, master classes for master marketers. I do it because I know that even superior marketers will adopt bad habits and will often get into positions where they accept less from themselves than they ought and as a result generate less profit from leads and clients than they should. Does this happen in your organization? Or do you simply:

- put an untrained secretary on the telephone and expect him to figure things out for himself . . . or even, having provided some guidelines, fail to provide periodic, continuing improvement talks;

- allow those representing your company and selling your service to muddle through. Muddling through is not marketing. It is the antithesis of marketing, for marketing is always a focused, systematic pursuit;

- accept the prospect evaluations of people in your organization without bothering to ascertain whether they are simply covering their position or whether there could, indeed, be significant improvement?

And, perhaps, worse, have you given way to these slack habits yourself, learning to justify and accept less than acceptable results instead of understanding that you, too, can regularly improve by the imposition of discipline?

If you find yourself in the position of successfully generating large numbers of leads but closing low percentages of them, review this chapter closely. To become a multi-millionaire selling services you must generate all the leads you need . . . and you must qualify and close the number you need, too. Otherwise, you will never be in a position to work with the number of clients you need to reach your financial objective and bring them the beneficial results which themselves help generate the further business you need to be a success.

12

How To Work With Your Clients So You Get More Business

You have now reached a significant milestone in your march towards millionaire status. You are implementing a burgeoning leads-generating system; you are also mastering and refining the necessary leads-closing skills so you get more and still more business.

It is time for a moment of self-congratulation and reward. Enjoy it. In moments like this, I write a check for at least $1000 and swell one of my investment accounts. I like that feeling. And I've earned the right to it. So have you! Take it . . . and make the reward commensurate with the achievement. Don't stint yourself. That's a very bad habit for a future millionaire!

. . . But don't over indulge either. Remember, while you are winning victories, until you are a millionaire, you still haven't won the war. For this, you need to learn to work with prospects to ensure results.

Let's be clear about what it means to work successfully with clients. You can reckon your relationship with a client a success when:

- the client is happy. He came to you to get results . . . and you gave him the results he expected — or better;

- you get paid in full and promptly;

- you leverage your success to achieve additional business with others who want the benefits you've now demonstrated you can deliver.

479

Your relationship with each client has not produced what it should until each of these results has occurred. Therefore any system you implement with your clients must ensure that each does.

Unfortunately, all too many service sellers just don't understand this. Most just do their work. If they do it well, many then receive words of praise and thanks from their clients. Sometimes they get referrals and testimonials from these people; most of the time they don't. This is because their relationship with the client doesn't work as a *system*. This is, of course, madness!

Here are the three prerequisites for making the system work:

- set generating future business from each client as the objective;
- understand that a satisfied client is a necessary prerequisite for achieving this objective;
- resolve to understand and institute the system that will generate both current satisfied clients and future excellent prospects.

Your system must be divided into the following parts:

- satisfactorily working with your new client before you've done any work and accomplished any results;
- satisfactorily working with your new client and getting results, and
- satisfactorily working with your new client after you've finished the work and achieved results.

Let's consider each aspect.

Satisfactorily Working With Your New Client Before You've Done Any Work and Accomplished Any Results

You must be clear about what you expect from your relationship with every client. You want to:

- get the client's help to the extent it's needed to produce results;

- achieve results;

- use these results to generate future business.

Except with the first point (where applicable), it is not the client's responsibility to assist you achieving *your* objectives from this engagement. If they are to be achieved, it's your responsibility to achieve them.

Now, achieving these three things begins *before* you've done any work and accomplished any results. It's important to understand this and plan accordingly. Remember, if you start off badly, it's unlikely you'll benefit as substantially as possible for each of your engagements. Thus:

- If your service requires a contract, make sure that in providing it to the client you simultaneously confirm the wisdom of the client's decision, remind him of the benefits he'll be receiving, inform him when you'll begin work and when you'll end;

- Be clear about what you are providing the client . . . and what you're not;

- Be clear about when results can be expected . . . and what problems you may face;

- If the service you provide needs certain assistance from the client, be clear about what you'll need and when you'll need it;

- Make it clear how you will report progress, problems and keep in continuing communication with the client;

- Make it clear that you are not just working for payment but for the good opinion of the client and for the client's organized assistance in developing your business through testimonials and referrals.

— *If Your Service Requires A Contract, Make Sure That In Providing It To The Client You Confirm The Wisdom Of The Client's Decision*

One of the mistakes service sellers who use contracts make is that they simply send the contract to the client without a cover letter. This cover letter is not a luxury; it's a necessity. It should confirm the wisdom of the client's choice, let him know you intend to achieve specific results (to the extent you are able), indicate when you are beginning work, when you expect to end, what you'll be doing first and when you expect to see first results. In short, this is your opportunity to show what a professional you are . . . that you understand the client's anxieties (and desire for prompt results), and just what you'll be doing to accommodate him.

— Be Clear About What You're Providing The Client, And What You're Not

One of the biggest problems in the relationship between service provider and client is the misunderstanding between what the client thinks he's getting and what the marketer thinks he agreed to provide. The best way to handle this problem is before any work is done . . . so that any misunderstandings can be promptly — and relatively easily — cleared up. Thus, walk through the service-delivery process with the client being clear about *exactly* what you'll do. Remember, you may have offered this service hundreds, even thousands of times; you *know* what you're doing. But this client may never have had this service before and can in no way be reckoned as expert as you are about its components. Understand this and carry on accordingly.

For this situation, I recommend keeping a "walk through" list in your computer; it's a sort of destination map showing how you're going to get to where you and the client want to go. In this you list *each* thing you do for a project of this kind. Obviously each of the services you offer will have a different "walk through" list; equally obviously, there may be differences in what you'll do even with similar projects. Fair enough. Such changes are easy to make once you have the basic list. However, by keeping a " walk through" list, you can literally walk the client through the project from first step to 100th step. Do you both agree on the destination? Do you both agree on what you'll be doing? If not, settle the matter now and get him an amended copy. If so, then leave him this copy. Obviously keep one for yourself, of course. It constitutes a clear understanding of what you're going to do.

Note: this list may well be annotated and edited as you progress through the project and discover more information about what you're doing and what the client needs. Fair enough. As changes become necessary, you can inform the client why and, if necessary, easily generate another amended walk through list.

This list serves several purposes. It makes it very clear:

- just what you'll be doing and the order in which you'll be doing it;

- what the client is getting and approximately when and in what order he'll be getting it, and

- what the client will *not* be getting and what, in fact, he may be expected to either do himself or go without. Seeing this, the client may wish to expand your services, in which case you can raise your fee!

— Be Clear About When Results Can Be Expected . . . And What Problems You May Face

All clients want to know when they'll get the benefits they want. . . . and which you partly used to leverage their action and acquire their business. This is perfectly natural. As an expert in your field, you must have some idea about this. Thus you must be prepared to say:

- when results can be expected;

- what dimension of results can be expected;

- what obstacles either stand in the way of getting these results and how they'll be dealt with, or

- given your experience, what obstacles may well crop up in a situation such as the one you've been hired to deal with — and what you'll do if they do.

This is a moment for the utmost candor. Now, all of us want to be liked. One of the ways we get to be liked is to promise the moon. "Hush, little baby, don't say a word, papa's going to buy you a mockingbird . . ." Remember this song? The thrust is clear: Baby, I'll do anything to get you to do what I want, even lie to you. Well, service sellers do this all the time and their lullaby is just as sweet . . . and irresponsible. Don't sing it! The good clients want honesty from you, not miracles. Without such integrity you put yourself at serious risk.

— If The Service You Provide Needs Certain Assistance From The Client, Be Clear About What You'll Need And When You'll Need It

Sometimes you can do your work without the client's assistance in any (or any serious) way; sometimes you can't. If you cannot, be clear what you want the prospect to do and when you want him to do it. Write down your expectations and needs — and present this information to the client. Again, it's possible that upon seeing this list in print, the client will ask you to expand your job to assist with these matters. On the other hand, perhaps you cannot assist with these matters and must rely entirely on the client to accomplish certain things. It's necessary for him to know this, so that at the moment you require his assistance he's prepared to help. Either way, it's to everyone's advantage for all the parties to be clear about what each is supposed to do.

Note: your walk through list can help here, too. Just indicate where in the process the client is expected to do certain things and what these things might be.

— *Make It Clear How You Will Report Progress, Problems And Keep In Continuing Communication With The Client*

Unless the job you're doing for the client is short and can be completed within a day, you have a need for ongoing client communication. Sadly, most service sellers are appallingly bad communicators and haven't got a clue that keeping the client in the dark about what's going on is 1) not the best way to soothe the client's anxieties, 2) build the best possible relationship with the client, and 3) get the later referrals he needs from this job and which constitute an essential element of his compensation. You, however, will be different! You'll communicate with your client. Thus:

- Resolve to institute regular client communications.

- Identify which moments make the most sense for communicating with the clients. Depending on the service you're providing, these moments could come at the end of each business day; when significant results take place; when problems needing client input are discovered, or simply at other regular, sensible intervals.

- Determine how you'll communicate. If you are working with the client directly, schedule a regular time before you leave for the day. Otherwise, call at the end of the day. If the client needs to see something in writing, use a fax or mail service. But make sure you do something, and make sure you do it regularly!

- Make sure you schedule enough time so that your presentation to the client is clear and whenever possible allows for client response. You can bet your client will have questions; anticipate as many as possible but always allow time for the client to say whatever comes into his head. Part of your job is providing this opportunity to the client, and part is responding professionally to what he brings up.

— *Make It Clear You Are Not Just Working For Payment But For The Good Opinion Of The Client And For The Client's Assistance In Developing Your Business*

Clients are necessarily focused on achieving the results they're paying you for. They may occasionally think about why you're doing the work but only flickeringly. However, it's perfectly appropriate for you to tell them what you want from this relationship beyond payment. Thus,

- tell the client that one of the things you're expecting from this relationship is his good opinion and that you're working in part to achieve it;

- say you'll do your part to deserve this opinion, and

- make it clear you hope that if the client is satisfied with your work, he'll be willing to assist you develop your business.

Say that you'll only ask for this assistance if the work is to the client's satisfaction. The client will find this non-threatening and will no doubt agree to be of assistance *when he gets what he wants.* Just now you don't have to go into any detail about what you'll want then. However, if the client asks, you can say what you've got in mind, say you're hoping for a testimonial or referral to other potential business. This is sufficient for now. It's all too likely you don't say this to clients now at the beginning of your relationship. Perhaps you haven't understood that leveraging a satisfied client for future business can be done in an organized fashion. Perhaps you've simply waited until the job was done to broach the subject. Don't wait! Set the objective; make a pact with the client. Get him thinking about how he might help. Then set to work with a will so you have the basis to achieve what you want.

Satisfactorily Working With Your New Client And Getting Results

You have already set the foundation to achieve what you want with your client. This phase simply continues what you've already begun. Thus:

- Get started promptly. You should seize this project and get off to a good start with it. The prospect's remaining anxieties will diminish as he sees that you are serious in your approach to your work.

- Provide periodic progress reports, as outlined above.

- As expected difficulties arise, make it clear to the client that these were anticipated and that there is nothing to be worried about. Soothing a client's anxieties is always a part of your job.

- If unexpected difficulties arise, if you can solve them within the terms of your current engagement, do so. Let the client know that this is possible and then do what is necessary to solve the problem. Report progress to the client as appropriate.

- If unexpected difficulties arise which alter the terms of your engagement, before bringing the matter to the client's attention, first work through solution options in your own mind. What can you do within the terms of your engagement to solve the problem? What kinds of options can you present the client? How can you explain the fact that you were not aware these difficulties might arise, and why weren't you able to bring them to the client's attention before? Don't wing this matter. Just how you deal with what the client will undoubtedly see as the frustrating matter of unexpected (and costlier) difficulties will go far towards determining the success of your relationship.

Let's look at each of these factors in more detail.

— Get Started Promptly

How many times have you ordered or purchased a service and then . . . W A I T E D and W A I T E D and W A I T E D? Frustrating isn't it? And how do you feel about the service provider when he finally gets around to your project? Not charitably, I'll warrant.

That's why you must be different. That's why you must make it clear to the client exactly when you can get started . . . and then get started right then, as promptly as possible.

If, for instance, you are handling the service at the client's business or residence, start whenever possible bright and early. If this is impossible, make it clear to the client just when you can handle his situation. If you have to alter the time because you've been delayed with a prior client, call and let the client know when you can be expected.

I have a friend, a service provider, who's perfected the art of client communication. Even if he's going to be just five minutes late, he calls the client and lets him know. I find this so admirable as to be beyond pedestrian commendation. How different this is from situations we have all experienced where we are kept in the dark by the service provider and are forced to any degree of inconvenience merely because the idiot doesn't have the brains to inform us of the situation. There should be a special cycle of hell for these people, and I hope I get the chance to stoke the flames for them . . . without, of course, communicating my intentions in the slightest degree to those I shall so gleefully afflict.

— *Provide Periodic Progress Reports*

I have already addressed your thinking through how you can make the progress reports that are so important to both the client and your developing relationship with him and letting the client know when and how these will take place. Now, institute your system and live up to your promise.

As people know who deal with me on any basis, I am what I call an obsessive communicator. I need to have information about all pending projects on a regular basis. If I am getting a service, I want to know regularly precisely how things stand. If I am providing a service, I want regularly to provide the client with an indication of how things stand. Towards this end, I stay in my office as late as possible until I feel I 1) have learned everything I need from the people who are doing things for me and 2) have told all those depending on me what they need to feel calm and secure about the assistance I'm providing and what I'm doing to get them the results they want.

Because I think it will be helpful to you, I wish to say as straightforwardly as possible that I do not make these communications elegantly. Reports in person are direct, focused and very candid. Reports by phone and fax are equally pointed. Moreover, I frequently return my answers on the written communications I have received from the client . . . to the horror of those who feel you have to create a special communication every time you address a client. I most assuredly do not agree.

The essence of building a good relationship is giving the client the information he needs in a prompt, focused fashion, concentrating far more on the substance than the style. By the way, I wonder if you will be surprised to hear that I cannot recall ever receiving a client complaint (in a world full of masters of whining) about the way the communication has been handled. However, I have received dozens of compliments, many in writing, about the degree of focused, client-centered reporting I've used. This, I think, validates my remarks.

Here are some tips for communicating with your client while work is in progress:

- Think through what the client wants to hear and present this first. Clients don't want to know — certainly not first — just what you had to go through to either get to where you are or achieve results. They want to cut to the chase, to get the essential information first. Trained communicators understand this — and present their findings from the standpoint of the client . . . not from what I call the historical perspective, namely "And then . . . and then . . . and then . . ." I work with an otherwise competent service provider who cannot understand this point, though I have explained it to him frequently. Each conversation (no matter how many times I talk to him in a day) starts off with him asking how I am. Then he proceeds by going back to where we previously left off. Thereafter (if I let him) he tells me every last detail that occurred since we last talked . . . until, at last, he gets to the point. I have long since come to the conclusion that this man is uneducable . . . and certainly, on this point, not client-centered. Don't make this mistake. Always anticipate what the client will want to hear . . . and give him that first. Then go back, as appropriate, and fill in lesser details. Why, oh why, is this so hard for so many people to get? I'll hazard one answer: they think that if they show you how much they've *done,* you'll forgive them for how little they've *achieved.*

- Have an agenda of points the client is interested in and report on all of them. This agenda will both help you focus your communications and structure subsequent work. If certain matters have not yet been resolved, keep them on the list until they are.

- Add all matters of client concern and let the client know when and how you intend to address them.

- Finish any communications by providing a synopsis of what you and the client have agreed to. Where appropriate provide the client with a memo to this effect.

- Begin your next meeting by reporting progress. What have you managed to accomplish in the time you've had? Is this better or worse than or about what you expected? Go through each item on your agenda — including all the items the client brought up at the last meeting — and provide a situation report. The client's trust in you will increase to the extent that you are shown to be in control of this situation and responsive to his suggestions. If you cannot handle a client suggestion within the terms of your current engagement, be clear about why you cannot . . . and what needs to happen so you can.

— As Expected Difficulties Arise, Make It Clear To The Client These Were Anticipated And That There is Nothing To Worry About

When my house was being remodeled, I (all too vividly) recall wandering disconsolately around the place and wondering if, from so much chaos, anything remotely resembling my former comfortable lifestyle could be reconstructed. Now, the remodeler must have known better things were on the way and must have known when they could be expected . . . yet he made no attempt to enlighten me on a process which made me very uncomfortable and often extremely frustrated. Learn from this . . . and shape your behavior accordingly.

Depending on the nature of the service you provide, it may look as if matters are not progressing, indeed that things are steadily getting worse all the time. As the expert *you* know that the perception is deceiving BUT THE CLIENT PROBABLY DOES NOT. That's why you must take time to explain the process and reassure the client about what's really happening and why what is being done now is both sensible and necessary.

Here is where your empathetic professionalism is called for. You must put yourself in the place of the client and respond accordingly. I think, for instance, of the occasion when my mother was in the hospital with cancer, and her doctor called me to report on her situation. He *started* his conversation by saying, "Mother is very sick." I was appalled at the unbelievable stupidity of the man. I'd never met him. He didn't know me, nor I him. He was providing a crucial service, part of which was dealing with people who were understandably profoundly worried. Yet the words he used to establish rapport with them were so transparently insincere and smug that hearing them was like a slap in the face. I instantly made it very clear this was not *his* mother we were talking about nor some generic "mother", but my actual flesh and blood mother. Further, I brusquely informed him that he was to use her proper name with me and none other and that I didn't appreciate his ridiculous and patently insincere attempt to establish rapport with me on this utterly false basis. Thereafter, as you may be quite prepared to imagine, he dealt with me in a completely professional, if undeniably gingerly, fashion.

Your client doesn't want saccharine sweetness, insincerity, false friendship, false hope. He wants to be treated in a straightforward, candid and professional manner. It is your obligation not merely to do the work but to explain the work; to inform the client what is causing you concern (and why) and what constitutes needless anxiety. If you cannot do this, you have made your trek to millionaire status infinitely more difficult for yourself and needlessly tormenting to the people who have trusted to you for both service and clear explanation.

— *If Unexpected Difficulties Arise, If You Can Solve Them Within The Terms Of Your Current Engagement, Do So*

How many times have you gone to a service provider and asked for the simplest thing only to be told that the person you're addressing can't . . . or won't . . . do that. I remember one day asking a teller at my bank to give me some merchant master card/visa deposit tickets only to be told that it was 20 minutes before he could get access to the place where they were stored. The average person, of course, would take that for an answer; I, however, am different. I asked for one of the junior managers who constitute the generally undistinguished heads on the administrative hydra of my bank. When he arrived, I asked him to get me the slips. Since I was clearly not to be denied, he got me a handful. Before I left the bank, I turned to the clerk and said in a stage whisper, "This is service. You could do this. In future, do so." I have to admit that teller has always treated me rather well since that day!

Your job as a service provider is not to make a big deal out of everything, but to do what needs to be done whenever possible within the terms of your engagement. This means not charging more for it . . . just doing it!

To be sure, because there are clients in the world who are themselves less than saintly, you had better note precisely what you did, precisely when you did it and, where applicable, what it cost. If necessary, you can later bring this to the attention of the client as a bargaining chip — and you should, should the person you're dealing with prove especially prickly.

One of the reasons our civilization is at a point of great trouble is because too many people wish to be carried along without doing their bit; too many are consumed by a sense of being a victim rather than understanding that life is necessarily a struggle and that to succeed in this struggle means to do what is necessary and right when you can do it . . . even if it's not always convenient to do so . . . even if you won't always get credit for doing it.

Of course, if matters must be brought to the client's attention, do so. But try, whenever possible, to do so only after you've identified the problem and come up with ways of solving it. Bringing a problem to a client without having identified a solution is never a sensible thing to do.

— *If Unexpected Difficulties Arise Which Alter The Terms Of Your Engagement, Before Bringing The Matter To The Client's Attention Work Through Solution Options*

Sometimes, of course, the unexpected difficulties which arise cannot be easily handled within the terms of your existing engagement; sometimes, they call for a very significant adjustment. Here's how to handle this situation:

- Whenever possible fully assess the situation. Find out how bad it is and what needs to be done to correct it. Before bringing it to the client's attention, think through what needs to be done, when it needs to be done, what options you can use to solve the problem, and how much these various options cost. Do as much of this as you can before you broach the matter with the client. Admittedly, this isn't always possible.

- Think through why you didn't foresee this difficulty. Face it: the client is going to be very put out when you tell him about this problem. Most times, he'll want a scapegoat . . . and the most convenient one is you! You need to consider just why you couldn't have known about this problem; why it became apparent as you got into the work.

- Once you've thought through the two previous points, schedule your client meeting.

- Begin this meeting by empathizing with the client. Sure, you may actually emerge from this situation better off yourself (your contract may be enlarged), but you must understand that what you're saying can hardly be thought happy news from the client's standpoint — even if the enhanced service you provide is ultimately to his benefit. I remember, for instance, the sinking feeling I had when the remodeler told me that the wiring in my home (dating back 50 years) needed to be replaced and what the replacement would cost. Biting this bullet would have been a lot easier if I'd been dealing with a person of any empathy and communication skills.

- Once you've connected with the client on a human level, proceed as the in-control professional. Explain the dimensions of the problem, present your options and costs. Importantly, before the client questions you about this, explain why you couldn't have foreseen this problem. In other words, be thoroughly responsible.

- Anticipate that the client isn't going to be entirely calm and reasonable at the moment when you present these data. What you're telling him is undoubtedly shocking, particularly if your new estimate significantly increases the cost of the project. As he considers this, the client may not address you in an entirely civil, friendly way. Stay calm! Your job is to present the facts, anticipate this client response — and, when the first wave of shock, disappointment, anger and frustration has passed over the client to get down to the business of helping him decide what makes sense for him to do given his resources and priorities. This, too, is part of your job as a service provider.

Note: if you argue with the client now or get defensive or, heaven forbid!, come to this meeting without answers about what happened and why and what should happen and why, you're essentially throwing this relationship away. Clients can forgive you for not being omniscient; they can even forgive you for making mistakes. But what they are right not to forgive is your failure to act like the in- control professional and to bring to situations like these the empathy and expertise they have a right to expect from you. The future service seller millionaire understands this and acts accordingly. Lesser creatures just don't get it.

As soon as you begin to achieve results, you can start whistling a happy tune. You're moving from a sole focus on this client to a point where this client can begin to assist you get future business. Congratulations.

You've reached another crucial point on your road to millionaire status! Don't blow it. Now here's what has to happen:

- Report these results to the client. If these results are better than expected, make sure you say so. If they're not as good as expected, indicate how they can be improved. But at least indicate that things are moving towards the end wanted by the client.

- Pay close attention to how the client reacts to your report. Look either for signs of happiness (the client may smile, or relax a bit, or lean into you, or pat your shoulder) . . . or less than happiness. If the client is happy, he may say things that will later be useful to you ("Yes, these are the best results we've gotten to this point.") If he's not quite as impressed by the results as you think he should be, ask why. There may be a problem here, and you better find out. Keeping this client happy now is of the utmost importance to your plans.

- Indicate what you'll be doing to improve the results . . . and how the results could be still further improved if the client agreed to expand the project. Yes, as soon as you've got results, use the results to help you increase the value of your contract.

Satisfactorily Working With Your New Client After You've Finished The Work And Achieved Results

At some point, you'll be finished providing the client with your service. Just what you do at this point is crucial . . . not just for closing properly with this client but leveraging what you've accomplished here to get future business as soon as possible from others.

Think back for a minute to the last service you paid for as a client. In my case, it was a transportation service. Just the other day I shipped a large order of books to a Texas wholesaler. I dealt with two people . . . a dispatch agent and a driver. What happened is what always happens: the trucker was late reaching the warehouse. Despite the fact that he knew he'd be late, he didn't call; the dispatcher didn't call either. If the trucker was late, he was late . . . and heaven help anyone who dared to bring it to their attention. At last, the trucker got the books in the truck . . . and left. Nothing was said to build a relationship. Nothing came from the trucking company but the bill.

Now, I ask you to consider that the trucking industry in America is very competitive. There are several major carriers, all of which are — or ought to be — interested in building customer loyalty and building their businesses. Yet the "marketing" authorities and executives who must occasionally wrestle with these problems have apparently not bothered to tell either dispatchers or truckers about the company's objective. Hence, the people who deal with customers are about as rude and ill-informed as possible. Yes, this is my last "service" experience . . . and I'm sure you could match it word for word with a dozen of your own.

You, however, are going to be different.

- Begin by reminding yourself that the client you've been working for is a crucial link in the business that's going to make you a millionaire. He can either help you . . . or hinder you. What you do now will partly determine which.

- Resolve to end your current working relationship with this client in a way that bridges to both future business with *this* client and to future business with *others* because of this client.

- Start the bridging process by scheduling a time to review your work with the client. At this meeting remind the client of what you both set out to achieve; (it's important that you address the client as a member of the team). Then remind the client that you accomplished what you said you were going to do. If appropriate, review significant aspects of your work. Point out that the client is better for having them than for not having them.

- If results have begun, point out why . . . and indicate what further results can be expected and when. Remind the client that these were results he didn't previously have. Remember, it's easy for the client to forget where he's been and what he didn't have before you. It's your job to remind him!

Keep in mind that this first experience with the client can and should lead in two directions: 1) to subsequent business with *this* client and 2) to new business from *others* who hire you thanks to something this client does or says. You must consider and organize both alternatives.

*— Getting More Business **From** The Client*

Here's what you must do:

- Set getting additional business as one of your prime objectives from working with this client. If you have additional benefits for this client, if the client possesses the means to secure these benefits, but if you do not sell the client these benefits, now or later, this engagement can never be reckoned entirely successful.

- While working with the client on the first project, carefully listen as he talks to you. He may well volunteer what he wants to accomplish next. Otherwise, ask him what he wishes to accomplish next. Finally, observe his situation and see what makes sense for him to want next. Keep notes accordingly.

- Near the conclusion of the original project, schedule a meeting with the client to discuss additional possibilities. Find out what the client wishes to accomplish, when he wishes to accomplish this, and when he'll have the resources to begin. If the client cannot hire you now to begin getting him further benefits, log the information so you'll know when to reconnect with him. *Note:* one good way of getting a little bit of future business from the client and continuing to build your relationship is to schedule a "check-up " at some reasonable remove from the conclusion of your work. This way you can go back, review your work, make any necessary adjustments — and show the client just how valuable you are. It's perfectly appropriate at this time to again bring up the client's future wants and see how you can accommodate them. Building this "check-up" into your service makes very good sense.

- If you offer a service that needs regular follow-up, make sure you schedule the next installment before the client leaves this meeting. If the client doesn't have his appointment book, get the client's agreement on scheduling. Then call as soon as possible to actually schedule.

Note: if the client won't tell you what he wants next, won't schedule another meeting or is generally uncommunicative, there's a problem here that needs to be resolved. Take the bull by the horns and say, "It seems to me you're unhappy about something that's happened. If it involves something about my work, I want to resolve it. I told you at the beginning of this relationship that one of the things I was working for was your good opinion. If there's some reason I don't have it, let me know and give me the opportunity to change things." Then listen. If you leave this relationship with some client problem unresolved, the chances are good that the difficulty will fester, and you'll be denied any future benefits from the work you've already done.

One Last (*Important*) Thing

At the conclusion of this meeting, you should have 1) cleared the air if there were any problems, 2) scheduled another installment or booked another project, or 3) at least found out what the client wanted in the future and arranged a schedule of when you'd be checking back. This last point is particularly important if, given the service you provide, the results have not yet come in. You'll want to check in when they do to make sure things are coming along well — and to remind the client of your role in creating these results.

Are you at last done? Not quite. Before pouring yourself a long and cool one, congratulating yourself that you've done everything in this situation you could, think again. There's one more thing you need to do, something that will go far towards cementing your relationship with this person. Write him a note, thank him for his business, and especially thank him — in some detail — for selecting you and allowing you to help him achieve something of importance for himself. If there is any eloquence in you, now's the moment to squeeze it out. This note should be direct, sincere, personal. It should not be a form letter . . . but one from the heart. If your handwriting is decent, write it. Personally, since mine is terrible, I still compose on a computer. Still . . . such being the intensely personal content, nobody complains.

I have been writing letters like this for a long time. My associate Bill Reece has also become an expert in doing them. Indeed, he has been able to establish significant client relationships at least in part because of the power of a few carefully selected but sincerely meant words. Such words distinguish you not just as a superior marketer . . . but a superior human being. As you'll soon come to see, your clients will prize what you have to say . . . and will not only remember you when they want the kinds of benefits you provide . . . but be happy to give you the kind of assistance you need to bring in other business, too.

— Getting More Business **Through** *The Client*

As every ingenue entrepreneur knows, businesses flourish in large part because of word-of-mouth marketing. You know, too, that you get additional business because satisfied clients speak well of you. However, if you're like most service sellers, you haven't tried to create the *system* that ensures you'll regularly benefit from this satisfaction. Instead, you simply take whatever turns up. This is infantile. Instead, here's what you must do:

- Set as your objective getting at least one new client from every client whose work you handle to his satisfaction. This is the minimum acceptable objective.

- Understand that your client can help you in several ways, with testimonials, referrals, and recommendations. Resolve to get assistance with all three.

- Set up the system that produces the testimonials you need.

- Set up the system that produces the referrals you need.

- Set up the system that produces the recommendations you need.

Let's look at these points in more detail.

— Set As Your Objective Getting At Least One New Client From Every Client Whose Work You Handle To His Satisfaction

The key to getting additional business through clients is to produce good work for them. Once you've done this, you should be able to set up the system you need to leverage this satisfactory result and get more business. However, you must set an objective of the future business you want from each satisfied client. Make this at least one additional assignment. Do not think, however, that this objective is strenuous; it's minimal. However, you must start somewhere, and getting one additional assignment is better than entirely leaving matters to chance as you're probably doing now. Just resolve to up the ante as soon as you can.

— Understand That Your Client Can Help You In Several Ways, With Testimonials, Referrals and Recommendations

Your client can assist you in three different ways to get business from others: with testimonials, referrals and recommendations. You must understand these ways and set up the system to benefit from them.

- Testimonials. A testimonial presents in the client's own words a statement of benefits he received from your work. This statement offers an endorsement of you and your methods based on results the client has received.

- Referrals. Here the client presents you with follow-up details about people he thinks would be interested in both your service and the results you help generate.

- Recommendations. In this alternative, you ask the client to provide a statement of his satisfaction to a prospect who is thinking about engaging you and is interested in the results you provide.

— *Set Up The System That Produces The Testimonials You Need*

To get the testimonials you need, you need to know just what constitutes the proper testimonial and just how to get it.

First, let's analyze a suitable testimonial and see what makes it work:

" 'In just the last 60 days, we have generated an additional $12,000 in new sales using the brochure and cover letter produced by copywriter Alice Jones. We have had a very satisfactory return on our investment, will be using her services again, and enthusiastically recommend her to others.' J.D. Warren, Vice President of Sales & Marketing, (company name)."

Here are the key points in this testimonial:

- "just the last 60 days". The time period is impressive, desirable. Now, it may well take you much longer than 60 days to get results given your service. However, you can still use the important shortener word "just." Your prospects don't want to wait for results a moment longer than they have to; let them know you work as promptly as possible . . . so long as they'll do their bit to get things started.

- "an additional $12,000". Whenever possible, your testimonial should present specific, believable, attractive results.

- "new sales". The testimonial should make it clear the satisfied client got something he wouldn't have had and didn't have before.

- "very satisfactory return on investment." This is what it's all about: ROI. Your prospect will pay money if he can be reasonably assured he'll get a reasonable return. The testimonial helps provide the assurance he needs.

- "will be using her again." No time period needs to be specified. Just that the person writing the testimonial will retain the service provider's services again.

- "enthusiastically recommend her to others." Not just tepidly, mind, but enthusiastically.

- "J.D. Warren, title, company". This attribution is crucial. It suggests that a real person is willing to stand up for you. It further suggests that if the prospect wants to talk to this person and get further information, he can do so. An unsigned testimonial, or one just offering initials, is worthless.

Note: sometimes you offer a service where the person receiving it either will not or cannot provide a testimonial, perhaps because it's embarrassing to do so. In this case, see who else involved in the process could testify to what you've done. In other words, if you're running a funeral home, the dear departed clearly can't say much on your behalf. However, one of the survivors you worked with certainly can. The important thing is that you get the best testimonial you can given the nature of the service you provide.

Here are other things you should know about the content of testimonials:

- Always put the benefit you provided the client before information about what you actually did. In other words, lead with benefit, follow with feature — my standard marketing rule;

- Put the results in perspective. If these results are the best the client has achieved, say so. If they're particularly good given current conditions in his industry, say so. In short, provide the *context* that tells the prospect why these results are significant.

- Don't hesitate to add additional information that establishes a connection between the person making the testimonial and your prospect. In other words, if you're trying to convince a home-based business owner to retain your service, add information in the testimonial that indicates a home-based business owner provided it. This particular information, however, doesn't need to be part of the satisfied client identifier when you send the testimonial to someone who doesn't run a home-based business. Then it's superfluous.

Now that you know what a testimonial should be. Here's how you set up the system to get them.

- Open a testimonial file in your computer. Divide it into sections for all the services you provide so you remind yourself you're supposed to be gathering testimonials for *everything* you do.

- Arrange to get a testimonial every time your work produces meaningful results from a client.

- Don't expect the client to volunteer to give you a testimonial. Yes, this sometimes happens; more often than not, however, you must ask.

- If the client does volunteer something nice about you, put it into your testimonial file immediately. If this happens when the client is on the phone, open the file instantly and record what you hear. This can easily become the basis for the testimonial you want. As with all testimonials, add the client's name, address, and phone number along with his words. These are useful if a prospect later wants to talk to this person directly. Do not, however, use the client's street address and phone in the testimonials you publish.

- If the client doesn't volunteer a testimonial (sadly, all too frequent an occurrence in our selfish world), ask for one. But don't just leave it to the client's imagination about what to provide . . . or you may well be disappointed with what you get. Have the client speak to essential elements of both the service you provide, how you provided it, and the results he received. It's perfectly acceptable to provide a list of topics you'd like the prospect to address in his testimonial and to give him a sample of what you had in mind.

- Give the client a reasonable period of time — say one week — to provide the testimonial. If you don't get it, call and ask for it. Remember, getting this testimonial is one of the things you've got a right to expect from a job well done. And besides, the client told you he'd be helpful with this if you provided good work, remember?

- If the client is evasive or just doesn't get around to your request, ask again. Some people, however, are writing averse. For these, consider doing an audio testimonial. Either drop in on the client with a list of points you'd like to cover and tape his remarks . . . or send the list and the tape, and work with him on the phone. A good audio testimonial can be a real help with selected prospects. (Because of the expense I do not recommend sending them out to everyone.) *Note:* client procrastination can also be a sign that there's some hesitancy about recommending your work. If you sense this is the case, ask. Again, there may be a problem that needs attention.

- If the testimonial you get doesn't quite live up to your expectations and you feel the client might in all fairness to you have said more, bring your disappointment to the client's attention. What you may well find is that the client may be giving you what he regards as high praise but may need some help with the presentation of his sentiments. As above, however, these weak words may be a sign there's a problem with this client that needs to be addressed.

- If the testimonial is fine (that is, if you think it will prove helpful in motivating others to retain your service), thank the client warmly. He's just given you something of real value. And by all means send him a copy of any marketing materials in which you use his words.

Note: Because you've made it clear from the beginning of your relationship with this client that you wanted his good opinion and would be using his testimonial, *etc.* to get more clients, there's really no need to get any explicit permission from him to use what he's provided. This permission is implicit. If, however, you've altered what he said in any way, then you should secure his approval for what you've done, unless the changes are minor and merely about spelling, grammar, *etc.*

— *Set Up The System That Produces The Referrals You Need*

Whereas you are the primary agent for distributing testimonials about your business, a client can be much more involved in the process through which you get and benefit from referrals. This is because referring is a networking process, and as with any networking process you must understand and use The Pyramid of Contacts.

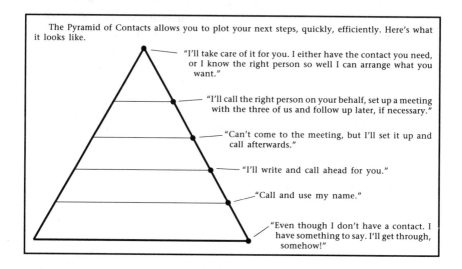

The Pyramid of Contacts allows you to plot your next steps, quickly, efficiently. Here's what it looks like.

"I'll take care of it for you. I either have the contact you need, or I know the right person so well I can arrange what you want."

"I'll call the right person on your behalf, set up a meeting with the three of us and follow up later, if necessary."

"Can't come to the meeting, but I'll set it up and call afterwards."

"I'll write and call ahead for you."

"Call and use my name."

"Even though I don't have a contact. I have something to say. I'll get through, somehow!"

Take your first look at the Pyramid. Then consider how you probably approach the matter of referrals right now. When you consider the matter (sadly infrequently), you merely ask the client if he knows anyone who might be interested in your service. The client thinks a minute, if that, and says he'll mull it over and get back to you if he has any ideas. Of course, he doesn't mull, doesn't get back to you, and promptly forgets about this entirely. You're sufficiently happy, though, just *asking* the client (you usually don't after all) and, well, if nothing results from the exchange, at least you've tried, right? IF THIS IS WHAT YOU DO (AND I BET IT IS), YOU SHOULD BE ASHAMED OF YOURSELF!

Now look at the Pyramid again.

The Pyramid of Contacts is based on the undeniable premise that people know people . . . and that properly organized and encouraged the knowers can easily connect us with people who'll be better off because of us. (We need never mention that we'll be better off because of them!)

What's key to the success of the referral process (and as you can clearly see from The Pyramid of Contacts) is that it works best when the client is most actively involved. In other words, where the client says "I'll take care of it for you" is better than where he says "Call and use my name." It is undeniably easier for the client to say the latter, however, rather than the former. But this is where the problem arises. What may be easier for the client is not at all better for you. Therefore, here's what you should do:

- Resolve to get at least one referral from *every* satisfied client. Remember, getting this referral is part of your compensation.

- Search for clues about who the client might be able to refer you to. In other words, given who the client is and what he does, who is he likely to know? Further, listen for clues. Clients talk about who they know, where they've been, what they've done, *etc.* Just by paying attention, you're very likely to pick up useful information. Log this for future reference.

- Before asking for any referral, make sure the client is happy with your work. An unhappy client will make the most tepid referral, if he makes any referral at all.

- When you're ready to discuss referrals with your client, you can, by all means, ask if the client knows anyone who might like your service. An open-ended question is not necessarily a bad thing — if it's not the only thing. Chances are, however, the client won't come up with any sugges- tions right away . . . or will ask for more time. If you accept this, the matter will probably come to nothing . . . just as most such situations do. This just won't do.

- Instead of only giving the client more time to think about (actually, forget about) this matter, prompt him. "Do you know (someone he's likely to know who is not a direct competitor)?" Or "do you have a contact in (name of related industry in your marketing territory)?" Instead of giving the client time to think, prompt his response.

- As he talks, take notes. While it is bad form to ask for too many referrals now (greed is a cardinal sin, after all), it's just plain stupid not to log whatever is said for later action.

- Once you've heard a suggestion that sounds good to you (you want to be connected to a decision maker, mind), ask the client if he'll refer you to this person.

Now the artistry really comes in.

The client may very well agree to make the referral. When he does you say, "Would you make the contact on my behalf so I can be sure to get to this decision maker?" Then pause and wait for the client's response.

Most Americans like to be liked. We hate to say no. And, after all, you've just done some very good work for this person. Besides, you did say at the beginning you'd be doing this. So, chances are you'll get what you want — to be easily connected to your next assignment — not just the chance to call the person you want to be connected to and fail to get through, get put on hold, have your letter go unanswered, try and try again unsuccessfully, the usual round-and-around scenario. No, this time you'll get someone who will pick up the phone for you . . . write to the decision maker for you . . . in short, do the thing that increases the likelihood you'll get through . . . a crucial component of getting the prospect's business.

If the client agrees to assist you, don't be afraid of asking for exactly what you want. "Could you please call your contact, and let him know I've helped you and that I'll be following up?"

In this case:

- Get an indication when your satisfied client will make the referral call on your behalf. (What's wrong with right now?)

- Arrange to recontact the referral and see what happened when he contacted the prospect. (Did the referrer get through? What did he say? What did the prospect say? What's the situation look like?)

- Then follow up appropriately.

But what if the referrer doesn't want to make such a direct contact? Say, for instance, he won't call on your behalf. What then? Why , work your way down t':e Pyramid . . . if he won't call, will he send a letter? If he won't send a letter, will he follow up your attempt if you don't succeed in getting through? You get the idea? In short, your obligation is to know what moves your client can make on your behalf and to get him to do as much as possible for you as soon as possible.

Note: if the client balks, use your charm and supple persuasiveness. Ever since I was a child, I've never hesitated to ask for things. Indeed, I've probably asked for more things in my life than 99% of the population. If I ask and I don't get, I still get discouraged sometimes. But then I ask again. If one line of reasoning doesn't succeed in getting me what I want, I try another. And, yes, another. I've become famous among my friends for my ability to just keep trying. No wonder. Out of frequent rejection has come continual success.

Thus, if the client doesn't do what you want him to do the first time and you sense that the lead he could give you would be a valuable one, do any one — or all — of the following:

- ask again;
- rework your argument;
- wheedle;
- plead;
- shame.

Remind the client about all the help you've given him.

Tell him how disappointed you'll be if this doesn't work.

Say how much you counted on this assistance.

Let him know how hard it is to get through to clients if you don't have a contact.

In short, don't give up.

And, remember, if you don't get the lead you want now . . . nothing prevents you from asking for it again tomorrow. After all, as that great marketer Scarlet O'Hara always said, "Tomorrow is another day."

Note: what happens if things get bogged down with the lead you've been given? Say the client calls on your behalf, you then follow up successfully but then . . . nothing. Or say you're only given permission to use the client's name and that that fails completely to open the door even a crack. What then? Why, go back to the would-be connector and ask for further assistance. Remember The Rule of Seven. It's as valid here as anywhere else in marketing. If you still think the client's assistance would help you get through to the prospect, don't hesitate to request it.

One Last Thing About Referring

If the referral works and you get the business, you've got another one of your famous thank-you notes to write. If the contract you get is big, you might think of sending something along with it (not in lieu of the note, please, but in addition to it). I've recognized such assistance with any number of thank-you presents, autographed books, for instance or a favorite Vouvray. The important thing is that you do something — and say something, too. These days, the people who keep the world running (and that includes people referring you to new business) get depressingly insufficient recognition. But not from you. For one thing, you know the right thing to do and will do it; for another, you have a file full of other connections this client could assist with. So it's in your interest to keep this contact green. Then when you ask for further assistance — as I'm sure now you will — you'll be far more likely to get it. Hurrah!

— Set Up The System That Produces
The Recommendations You Need

Your systems for getting additional business through the client are coming right along. It's time for the last component: getting recommendations. Here's what you need to do:

- Keep a list of all people to be asked for recommendations when the need arises. These are people who have had successful results from your service. With each, list his name, company name, address, phone, and fax. Also give an indication of the service you provided, when you provided it, and the results you achieved. *Note:* since these results may develop over time, don't hesitate to check with the client from time to time and get an update on the benefits produced by your service.

- Make sure you have people to recommend each of your services.

- Ask each person who may provide a recommendation if it is acceptable to him that you use provide prospects with his name and phone number in this way. If you're super organized, note the client's agreement in the information you have about him.

- Now match up prospects with the right recommender. Clients want to hear from people like them, people who were seeking similar results, about what you did, how you did it, the benefits achieved, *etc.*

- Don't provide the prospect with a recommendation, however, unless you need to. The names of people prepared to make recommendations on your behalf should be provided only when you feel reasonably certain that the recommendation you'll get will make the closing significantly easier. Thus, if you can close a new client without having to refer him to a past client, do so. But if you cannot, say something to the prospect like this: "It seems to me you're uncertain about whether I can provide you with the results you want." (Wait for confirmation.) "Would it help if you talked to someone I've recently worked with about the good results he achieved?" If the answer is yes, then do what's necessary to make the recommendation count.

- Tell the prospect what you did for the client and the results the client achieved. Then give the prospect the client's name and phone number. Ask him to check for himself. Schedule a time to check with the prospect to see what happened. (If the client wants more than one person to talk to, provide as many as three people, not more.)

- Then call the client yourself and advise him that he'll be getting this call. Inform the client what the prospect's reservations may be and ask him to speak to aspects of his own successful situation which would help overcome these reservations. Tell him you're relying on his help!

- Check back with the prospect and make sure he got the information from the client he needed and all the information from you that he wants, too. You should now be able to close the deal.

See how different this situation is from the usual way of handling recommendations, where you simply give the prospect a name and phone number and leave everything up to him? Because the matter of closing new business is so important, it cannot be left to such faulty, unorchestrated techniques.

Note: Because properly handling the matter of recommendations is a rather time-consuming business and undoubtedly relies on the interested cooperation of past clients, you have to be sparing about how you use people who are prepared to recommend you. That's why you cannot provide their names randomly but only in selected situations.

And, Yes, That One Last Thing

Whether you get the new business or not, thank the people recommending you. They have, after all, done their bit. Of course you can be more expansive if their assistance resulted in a fat new contract. But either way thank them. After all, you're probably going to be asking for their assistance again — soon, and with their help you are sure to get more clients.

13

Exactly What You've Got To Do
To Keep Customers

We have so far mostly concentrated on the matter of generating leads, closing leads, and working with customers. Now it's time to go on to the important matter of how to develop lucrative long-term relationships with the customers that result from these focused efforts. After all, your fortune is really based on two pillars: getting new customers . . . and keeping old ones. You must succeed at both.

Unfortunately, it took a major recession for the bulk of American businesses to figure this out. Only with the advent of the serious economic troubles inaugurating the New World Order of the 'nineties did these businesses finally discover the importance of customers. As a result, you cannot pick up a business publication these days without seeing something about working with customers.

Needless to say, I find this "our-business-is sinking, let's-rediscover-the-customer" thinking contemptible. It speaks volumes about American business values that it took a major business downturn and restructuring for our business "leaders" to discover something which any sensible student in Marketing 101 could have discerned: namely that without the generation of continuing revenue from satisfied customers businesses cannot reach their maximum profitability and that the owners of those businesses retard the development of their own personal fortunes.

It is a disgrace that this point is not an essential element in the thinking of all businesses, that so few marketers devote the sustained attention to it that the subject demands, and that the focus in most businesses remains generating new business rather than balancing this important topic with the equally important question of how to generate additional business from the customer base one has already worked so hard to acquire.

However, you won't make this mistake, will you? You'll give the question "How can I generate more business from existing customers?" the same creative attention you direct to the question "How can I get new customers?" Both are critical elements in your wealth-producing machine. You must treat them accordingly.

Key Observations On Your Relationship With Your Customers

To make sure you handle the matter of "customer development" (a phrase I prefer to "customer service" or "customer relations") properly, keep in mind these general points:

- You do not make yourself rich. You are always made rich by others.

- You have worked hard to generate the customer. You must work equally hard to keep him.

- Focusing on the customer cannot be done episodically, as seems to be the case with most businesses. There can be no "boom or bust " cycle in attending to customers. Customer development, just like the acquisition of new customers, must be a constant aspect of your business.

- You must offer either a service that the customer can use again and again . . . and/or develop complementary services that the customer can use in a sequence. In other words, customer development must have a point and that point is getting the customer to buy again. Thus, there must be something for him to buy.

- You must set as your objective having the customer buy again. And you must prominently post this objective.

- Understand that your relationship with the customer is divided into a series of parts and that there are crucial things to be done in each part that increase the likelihood of the customer buying again and thereby augmenting your prosperity and wealth.

Let's review these important general points in more detail.

- You do not make yourself rich. Others always make you rich.

Americans are fond of saying, "I'm a self-made man (or woman)." It's part of our "I-did-it-my-way" culture that you're beholden to no one; that you did it yourself, damn the torpedoes, full speed ahead. This sentiment, however, is nonsense. No one ever makes oneself rich. Others are *always* responsible for helping you. If you inherit your money, just who those people are is obvious (though those who inherit often offer ludicrously spurious explanations about why they "earned" this money). If you make your own money, however, it's easy to forget that the accumulation of wealth is based on successfully handling some finite number of exchanges of your product/service for the consideration of those benefiting from what you're selling. These people, and your own successful methods in contacting and working with them, make you rich.

When you start thinking about the production of wealth as being the result of creating a *system* where you prosper to the extent you succeed in creating benefits which more and still more people wish to acquire, you go far in the direction of actually setting up this system. At this point you realize, for instance, that you cannot do it alone, that the involvement of others, often thousands or even tens of thousands of others, is crucial and that your success is directly related to your ability to give these people something they perceive to be valuable. In short, you realize that your task is not to stand on some hillock thumping your chest and engaging in some bizarre egotistical ritual screaming about how good you are, but rather understanding that you must:

- work hard to create substantial benefits;
- identify people who want these benefits;
- create and refine the process of bringing these benefits to their attention;
- make sure they receive these benefits, and
- develop and market additional benefits to them so you can continue to generate revenue from those you've already served satisfactorily.

In short you get your fortune to the extent you get over the notion of "I did . . ." and instead focus on the benefits to others you have available: "You get . . ."

- You have worked hard to generate the customer. You must work equally hard to keep him.

As I said above, too many businesses spend a disproportionate amount of time generating customers as opposed to retaining customers.

This just doesn't make sense. Depending on the nature of your service business, some substantial fraction of your revenues will come from repeat business. This revenue is crucial in ensuring your financial prosperity and wealth. You must therefore resolve that you'll do everything you can to keep the customers you've worked so hard to get. Customers, you see, are *capital* and like all sources of capital, they must be nursed and given proper attention and oversight.

You have spent serious time and money to acquire this customer. You have spent additional time and resources to provide the benefit the customer wants. Now you must do what you can to ensure that you truly benefit from all the work you've done . . . because with minimal, sensible oversight — and making available a continuing supply of customer-focused benefits — you should be able to generate continuing revenue from this capital asset for years.

Thus, you must approach the entire business of dealing with customers with the deliberation that you approach your investment portfolio . . . because your existing customer base *is* an essential element in this portfolio.

- Focusing on the customer cannot be done episodically. There can be no "boom or bust" cycle in customers.

As the focus on "customer relations" stemming from the recession of the early 1990's has demonstrated, most businesses suffer from a "boom or bust" mentality in relation to customers. When times are good, they relegate customers to the background. When times are bad, they rediscover them. This is, of course, disgraceful business practice. It is good neither for the customer nor the business. As such, you will not make this mistake!

The importance of the customer in the development of your business and your personal wealth is a constant. Focus on the customer can not be episodic or intermittent. It cannot be done when you have nothing better to do. It cannot be allowed to become secondary or old hat. Business people who approach the customer in any of these ways — whatever they may say to the contrary — are self-centered fools.

Instead, the development of revenue from existing customers must rank as of equal importance with the generation of new business. Every day. Indeed, I go farther: in all service businesses, the focus should be *first* on generating additional revenue from existing customers and only *secondly* on generating new business. Why? Because it is always infinitely easier and more cost effective to generate additional revenues from those who start by being satisfied with your work than by persuading a person who doesn't know you and hasn't previously benefited from your service that he should try your service.

Obviously, this focus is not possible in newly established service businesses. They have no existing cadre of satisfied customers who have benefited from their services. However, by selling benefits and delivering value, they will develop this essential cadre and then must alter their initial focus to accommodate this change in their business and revenue structure. Thus, established businesses relying to a significant extent on revenues from an existing customer base will focus to a greater extent on customer development than customer acquisition — so long as this focus provides the revenue they need to meet the financial objectives of their owners.

- You must offer either a service that the customer can use again and again . . . and/or develop complementary services that the customer can use in a sequence.

Too many business people approach the matter of working with their customers in a vacuum; they have forgotten the point of the exercise. I think in some part this can be traced to the very passive nature of the usual phrases describing this work: "customer service " or "customer relations." The first of these offers a benefit to the customer ("service") but no benefit to the company; the second offers benefits to neither and is patently the least effective. Both, however, remain in constant circulation.

As I said above, I prefer the phrase "customer development" because it at least keeps before the business owner the reason he's continuing to work with the customer: the development of new sources of revenue.

In business there are really only two essential questions and both are related: how can we increase our profits . . . and how can we cut our expenses? They are two sides of the same coin. All other questions are superfluous. When a business forgets that these are the essential questions and allows distracting questions, it has essentially signed its own death warrant.

By this reckoning, the business of customer development has only one point: that is getting the customer to buy again as soon as possible. If you have a service that the customer needs at regular intervals, the job of customer development is to increase the perceived value of this service and to shorten the intervals between customer purchases. Further, it is the job of customer development to suggest and develop new sources of customer-centered value that you can bring to your customers' attention and to do what is necessary to get them to promptly acquire them.

Once you have a customer base, therefore, you must work to:

- develop new services the customer can buy;

- bring these to his attention with an offer that will motivate faster action and acquisition;

- identify how long the customer waits between purchases of your service;

- develop motivating means to get him to shorten this wait and acquire your benefit earlier;

- create additional sources of value that would benefit your regular customers and upgrade these customers so that each of their purchases is greater than they may have initially intended.

- You must set as your objective having the customer buy again. And you must prominently post this objective.

Now, I'll bet that if you asked a service businessperson if he valued his customers, the answer would be "Of course." If you asked him if he wanted them to buy again, he'd answer similarly. But if you asked him whether he started *every* day of his life *reminding* himself that he wanted these customers to buy again and that he was going to do everything he could to do get them to so, he'd tell you that, no, he didn't do this. Stupidly, he probably wouldn't see the dysfunction between what he says he wants and the way he must act to get it. This is, of course, at the root of a very serious problem.

Many service sellers spend a lifetime seeking the magic bullet that will provide them with an unbeatable competitive advantage and certain wealth. They search far and wide in hot pursuit of . . . what? They can never tell you; just that they are certain it's out there. Reader, it's not out *there*. It's in *here*: in the little gray cells of your brain and the tough fiber of your heart. Certain success lies in positing your objective and pledging yourself that you will gnaw at the problem of achieving this objective until your researches yield the wealth-producing system that will enable you to achieve it. This system begins by prominently posting the objective.

Thus, if you want to get each customer to buy from you again . . . to buy more . . . to buy sooner, POST THIS OBJECTIVE WHERE YOU CAN SEE IT EVERY DAY.

The achievement of success is not difficult, so long as you are clear what you are trying to accomplish, so long as you do everything you can to accomplish this objective and so long as you harness the vast power of your mind and heart.

I'm sure you'll agree with this. Now look around your home and office. Have you posted your objectives? And have you posted the fact that you want all customers to buy again and that you are going to do EVERYTHING you can to get them to do so? I bet you haven't. You are relying on the flickering embers of your memory to remind you; you are relying on some chance recollection instead of a very simple, powerful system. This is wrong. No, worse, IT'S STUPID!

Until you are absolutely certain your objectives have become part of the fiber of your soul, post them prominently around you.

- Understand that your relationship with the customer is divided into several important stages and that there are crucial things to be done in each stage that increase the likelihood of the customer buying again and thereby augmenting your prosperity and wealth.

Posting your objective is not, of course, sufficient. Each day you must do what is necessary to achieve this objective. I shall spend the remainder of this chapter providing means which enable you to do so. However, before getting into these means, I want to say as strongly as possible that the achievement of this objective means:

- *focusing*. Objectives are accomplished to the extent that you are willing to eschew the unessential and focus exclusively on those objectives you have determined are crucial to your success.

- *rethinking*. Sometimes what you do to achieve the objective will work. Sometimes it won't. Self-defeating behaviors must be ruthlessly abandoned. Those that work must be perfected.

- *persisting.* If you are to become a millionaire selling your service, you must resolve that defeat is the one luxury you can never afford. Very few people, if any, are going to cheer you on your way — at the beginning. Fewer will spontaneously offer up assistance — when you most desperately need it. That's why you have to do what's necessary to get yourself the tools and resources you need to win.

. . . here are some that will help.

Thinking Through Customer Development As A System

At each stage of your relationship with a customer, there are things you can do which enhance this relationship and make it more likely the customer will buy again. Before examining what these things are, let's review the important stages:

- while you're providing your service;
- as soon as you've finished providing your service:
- the period between the time you've provided the service until the customer engages you for further service;
- when you determine the customer should be buying more of your service (should be upgraded);
- when you discover the customer is either of pivotal importance to your business or can become so;
- when the customer has not bought in a while (but should have);
- when you've determined that a customer (who should be buying) seems unlikely to do so again.

Obviously, these stages are interrelated, but I want to look at each separately so you'll get an idea of what you can do to help yourself at each point.

What To Do While You're Providing Your Service

Although many service sellers forget this, one of the things you're working for with any assignment is to . . . get the next assignment! So long as you offer either a service that the customer will need again or a series of services which offer additional value to the customer, you should so shape matters that you get, in addition to your compensation, future work. To do this you must:

- Provide maximum value;

- Maintain regular client communication;

- Do what you say you're going to do;

- Ensure the quality of all work;

- Take responsibility for errors and do what is necessary to correct them without the client having to nag you to do so;

- Finish your work on schedule and with the results you set out to achieve.

As we have discussed these items in the previous chapter, I do not feel it necessary to reprise them here. However, you must understand that if you do not succeed in accomplishing these objectives you are dramatically reducing the possibility of future business from this client — not to mention the referrals to which successful service sellers are also entitled.

What To Do When You've Finished Providing Your Service

Don't just end jobs. Conclude them in such a way that you bridge either directly to the next assignment or to the period of amicable relations out of which the next assignment will come. Thus:

- If you have identified additional benefits you can bring to the client, this assignment cannot be considered over until you have said so, either attempting to begin the next job now or arranging when you can begin or when you'll again be in touch;

- If your service is one the client can use regularly, your first job is not finished until you have asked about scheduling the next installment. *Note:* it is your responsibility to know how long clients usually wait between installments of your service — and then to fashion a means of getting the client in earlier. To begin with, just try scheduling an earlier installment. If this is not sufficiently successful, make the client an offer which motivates him to acquire your benefit earlier.

- If the client is not ready to schedule another installment of your service or again hire you, end this stage of your relationship whenever possible by reminding the client what you have accomplished for him, as previously outlined. Whenever possible, emphasize the benefits you've delivered and make it clear you want this relationship to continue . . . so you can continue to deliver additional benefits. In short, let the client know it is your desire and intention to continue working with him. *Note:* if the value of the client's business is sufficiently high to warrant a personal meeting, or if you provide your service personally for the client in his home or office, you can perfectly well handle some of this in person. However, even where you are meeting with the client, do some of this by mail, namely the portion where you indicate what benefit you'd like to bring to the client next and when you'll be in touch again. It is good to bring these to the client in written form.

Note: I have consistently stressed that you make sure the client is not unhappy about your performance in any way. If he is, the chances are slim that you'll get another assignment, much less the referrals, recommendations and testimonials you should. No assignment can be considered complete if you have any suspicion the client is unhappy, much less if you have discovered such unhappiness and not corrected its source.

What To Do In The Period Between The Time You've Provided The Service Until The Customer Engages You For Further Service

Customer development, I remind you, has but a single point: getting the past customer to buy again as quickly as possible. Thus, the only customers you should deal with are those whom you have decided can buy again. If there is some reason why you have decided a customer cannot or will not buy again, he must be handled in other ways (see below). To approach people who are not likely to buy again in the same ways as you approach those who may is foolish indeed. Here then is what you need to do:

- Understand that if you have not managed to get the customer to purchase promptly at the conclusion of one engagement, you must launch another prospecting sequence. Because the prospect in this instance is a satisfied customer, your approach will be different than with a prospect who has not successfully used your services.

- Create a series of "family offers". These are offers for your various services that you make available to current and past customers only. Obviously, you've been adding offers on a regular basis to your "Offer" text file (you have, haven't you?); here's one place to use them.

- Think through the various contacts you want to make with your customers, in what frequency and in what way. This subject deserves more sustained attention.

— *Thinking through the various contacts you want to make with your customers.*

As you will not be surprised to find me saying, all too many service marketers treat the business of recontacting customers as if it were somehow an end in itself. Thus, they engage in a series of often expensive "customer relations" activities ranging from seasonal greeting cards to newsletters and social events. Too many service sellers adopt such measures because it's "the thing to do", completely missing the crucial point that the only thing to do is that which generates additional business as quickly as possible. With this in mind, I want to change the focus in the debate about customer contact. Thus:

- You should see all customer contact exclusively as a function of business development, never as an end in itself;

- You should be doing as *little* as you need to generate as much business as you need to reach your quota;

- Whatever you do should either be capable of immediately generating new business or should be followed up as promptly and efficiently as possible in order to generate new business;

- Detailed records should be maintained about the results of each customer contact activity;

- When an activity proves to be successful, consideration should be given to expanding it;

- When an activity proves to be unsuccessful, it should be dropped, no matter how enjoyable.

I want you to keep these points in mind when developing your customer development program.

1. Set a financial objective for this program. In other words, have a yard-stick with which you can measure whether it worked. The first time you set up your customer development program, you won't know what is reasonable. Do you have the kind of service where 50% of those using it ought to renew . . . or 5%? The first time you do this, you'll have to guess. That's acceptable. Nobody came into this world knowing these renewal rates. Moreover, since most service sellers keep such poor records (or no records at all) and since I personally have never seen anything written on the subject, you're probably plowing virgin territory anyway.

2. Brainstorm your options. There are lots of ways of reconnecting with customers. These include:

    • personal visits;

    • telephone contact;

    • post cards and letters;

    • newsletters;

    • seasonal greetings;

    • presents and premiums;

    • social events, *etc.*

3. Determine the best option(s) for your situation, that is the options that make the most sense given your objective, budget, personnel resources, and deadline.

4. Institute your client follow-up measures in an organized, efficient manner best designed to generate future business as quickly as possible. Here's what I mean.

Let's say you've decided you want to make an additional $30,000 this year from past customers as part of your overall financial objective. Say that you have a service your customers can use on a regular basis and that you are religious about scheduling repeat visits each time you serve them. Further say that your service sells for $60 and that a person uses it twice a year. Thus, you need at least 250 customers to schedule twice to reach your objective. Or do you?

Don't forget that it takes money to make money. The real question is, how much do you have to spend to net $30,000 from your existing customer base? The first time you do this, you just won't know. But figure an additional $5,000. You therefore need an additional 42 customers to use your service twice to pay the expenses, or 292 customers total.

Now the question becomes, how can you most wisely spend not more than $5,000 to generate an additional $30,000 from your existing customer base?

- Prioritize your options from least expensive to most expensive;

- Never select an option just because someone else is doing it;

- Institute a program using your least expensive options first;

- Focus these options so that you are offering a maximum of client-centered benefits;

- Don't take on any long-term commitments that sap your resources without offering substantial rewards;

- Keep good records of everything you do to see if it's worth repeating.

Let's go back to the example above. Say you're running a dental office where clients come twice a year and the basic visit charge is $60. The key to your customer relations is to schedule the next visit immediately upon the conclusion of the present visit. What we are talking about here, however, is what you should be doing if the client leaves your office without scheduling the next visit.

Prioritize Your Options From Least Expensive To Most Expensive

To make this point effective, you must list all client-contact options available to you and price them. Keep in mind that the goal is to generate $30,000 in additional revenue, not to spend money that doesn't generate a disproportionate return.

Say that this particular dentist has a pool of 800 clients. Of these some 400 have been clients but are not regular in their visits; certainly, they don't make the two basic visits yearly and use other services only sporadically. The initial question is what are the available options to induce these people to be better customers?

Reasonable options include:

- telephoning past clients to schedule visits;

- sending a client-centered communication first and then following up with a telephone call;

- sending a series of communications and letting the client contact you, *etc.*

Unreasonable options include:

- sending one piece of correspondence and letting the client contact you;

- buying tooth brushes and other dental products and giving them to clients as premiums;

- purchasing dental care informational materials, such as brochures, and distributing them to clients;

- distributing calendars and other products with imprinted information about the dentist and his practice;

- starting a dental practice newsletter and distributing it to clients;

- holding an annual event and inviting all clients to attend, *etc.*

Now, develop a budget for each of these activities ("reasonable" and "unreasonable"), so you know how much each will cost.

Never Select An Option Just Because Someone Else Is Doing It

All too often, service sellers approach the business of recontacting customers with a total absence of mind. Why did they order 1000 calendars? Because one of their competitors was doing this. Why did they get logo mugs? Because they looked nice . . . and thought they'd work. HOW STUPID CAN YOU GET???

Never select a means of connecting with your customers merely because others are doing it. By all means, always look at what others are doing, particularly your competitors. By all means, gather complete details and review them. But don't adopt *anything* until it passes the essential test: will this expenditure get us additional business? Or is it merely something that we think we'd like, hope will work, without having any real data about whether it will? Too many "marketers" constantly engage in wishful thinking, hoping that by doing what others are doing they can profit from their work. Unfortunately, all too frequently, the others have hoped, too, rather than investigated. The net result is an astonishing waste of money.

Institute A Program Using Your Least Expensive Options First

As I have constantly reiterated throughout this book (have you, at last, got the message?), whatever marketing activity you pursue must be effective (that is, it must get results). It should be examined with an eye towards making it as inexpensive as possible. Thus, you want to implement the least expensive options first. This is one significant factor in what makes an option "reasonable" as opposed to "unreasonable". Here are the other factors:

- You can do it easily;

- It can easily be focused on the client and on what he gets from you;

- It can produce immediate results.

Let's review some of the activities above, and I'll show you what I mean.

Again, take the dental office. I said that the best thing to do was schedule the next visit while the customer was present. But, for one reason or another, this isn't always possible. What is possible, however, is to call the client IMMEDIATELY and schedule that visit. By "immediately" I mean the same day — or, if you can't manage that, the next day. And I mean, to keep calling until the visit gets scheduled. Now, this isn't what my dentist does . . . and I doubt it's what your dentist does, much less all the other service sellers you deal with who offer services that you need regularly. Instead they either don't call at all or call once, and not achieving the objective fail to call again. THIS ISN'T MARKETING. IT'S STUPIDITY. Marketing is about setting a reasonable objective, identifying the individual who needs the benefit you can deliver, and implementing a focused client-development program that achieves your mutual objectives as soon as possible, for the least possible expense.

By contrast, take the matter of buying toothbrushes and other tooth paraphernalia. Now, every time I go to my dentist's office, he gives me a new toothbrush. That's charming. But is it sensible? His name is neither on the brush nor on the box nor does the package come with any indication of who the dentist is. (Indeed, I'm ashamed to tell you I don't even know my dentist's full name and would be hard-pressed to find him in the yellow pages. So much for my memory — and his marketing!)

Thus, the toothbrush (and all the other things he gives me) fails the results test. Sure, getting the brushes and handing them out can be done easily and, I imagine, incur minimal expense. The problem is, they just don't work. Yet while the dentist is handing me one thinking that he's a clever marketer, I have seen his office staff yabbering away about the vicissitudes of their lower middle class lives, instead of calling the customers of the professional who is paying them far too well for the little they do on his behalf. Deduction? This service seller hasn't thought about how many customers he wants to repeat, hasn't considered what means he should be using to get them to repeat faster, and has instead approached the entire matter with a breathtaking absence of mind which, if he considered it, would go far towards undermining the nauseating sense of self-satisfaction he oozes.

Shall we do another comparison? You'll have noticed that amongst the "reasonable" activities, I have placed sending a series of client-centered communications, while amongst the "unreasonable" I have planted sending one piece of correspondence and letting the client contact you.

Just as in all other areas of client prospecting, so with the prospecting you must do to get satisfied customers to buy again, you cannot simply do one thing and expect that one thing to achieve your objective. The key here then is that what you do must be client- centered and it must be offered in a sequence. Now, say that our dentist spends $750 a year on the toothbrushes he lavishly dispenses. And say that he can send 400 letters to 400 elusive clients for $300; (this is more expensive than I pay . . . but I'm being ultra-conservative here). Why, he can send two such client-centered communications and still have money left. This is all to the good because the chances of spurring business from such communications (even when they are not followed up by telephone, the preferred method) is far better than what one can expect from handing out thousands of toothbrushes. I trust you're getting the picture . . .

Focus These Options So That You Are Offering A Maximum Of Client-Centered Benefits

A key constituent of what makes a client-development activity reasonable is whether it offers client-centered benefits that get the prospect to take faster action. The standard calendar doesn't do this. A me-centered logo mug doesn't do this. A seasonal greeting card with printed signature doesn't do this. That's why these things are so wasteful and self-indulgent.

Instead, you should be:

- working hard to develop the client-centered benefits for each of your services;

- creating client-centered offers to motivate faster response;

- bringing home these important messages in ways that make it clear to the prospect you can offer him further satisfaction (remember, he's already benefited from at least one of your services) . . . if only he takes immediate action.

Unreasonable client contact activities say, in effect, "Here's something for you. It is standardized, mass-produced, certainly not focused on you and your interests. I'm doing this because I have to, because others are doing it, because it makes me feel better about myself, because, frankly, I haven't a clue what I really should be doing. Please help me out by taking some action so I can continue to delude myself that what I'm doing constitutes 'marketing', not just mindless wastefulness." Isn't this just about the size of it?

Specific Tips On Particular Client-Development Activities

Before leaving this section, I'd like to examine some of the major ways you can be in contact with clients and provide tips for determining if you should be using them . . . and how you can use them to achieve enhanced results. Let's examine:

- personal visits;

- telephone contact;

- post cards and letters;

- newsletters;
- seasonal greetings;
- presents and premiums;
- social events, *etc.*

— *Personal visits*

Personal visits — whether held at your office or the prospect's —may be an appropriate way to generate future business with a satisfied client. Here's what will determine if you should schedule such a visit:

- Ask yourself, do you really need this visit? Can you handle the matter in another way, by telephone, fax, or mail? If you don't need this visit, don't schedule it!

- Can the visit be scheduled in your office? That is, can you reduce the fuss and bother by reducing the commitment you make to the visit? Will the client agree to see you on your premises, or will he consider this an unreasonable nuisance, thereby starting the visit off on the wrong foot?

- If you must visit the client prospect, can you do so conveniently? In other words, will you have to make an unreasonable commitment of time and money to see this prospect, or can you handle the meeting with relative convenience?

- If the meeting takes place, is there a good chance the customer will place additional business with you, or are you just engaging in wishful thinking, hoping something substantial develops? What makes you think so?

- Do you have something the client will find attractive right now? How do you know?

- Is the client prospect capable of going ahead and retaining your services again in the near future? How do you know?

- If the client does want to go ahead, are you in a position to start work on the client's project immediately, thereby providing the ultimate justification for this personal visit?

What many of these questions suggest is that before you schedule any personal visit with a client prospect, you should attempt to gather as much data as possible about the prospect's situation and ability to commit. Personally, I do not believe and never indulge myself in the futile practice of merely calling on prospects just because I'm "in the neighborhood", want to get acquainted, or otherwise engage in mindless and pointless contact. Time is not only money; much more importantly, unlike money, time is irreplaceable. To sit in an office with a prospect who cannot or will not commit to an additional project, no matter how delightful the surroundings, grand the view or charming the conversation is, to me, a sin. Moreover, to engage in a meeting where *you* are ill-prepared is both disrespectful and pointless. That is why you telephone or fax a client to get such information as you need to determine if the personal visit even makes sense. You'll find in many cases it doesn't, that you can achieve your objective in other ways.

It's a pity the regional representative of a printer I use didn't know any of this before he made his initial visit. He came so ill-prepared (despite my having provided questions in advance) that it almost cost his company a million-dollar contract. What's worse, he never did understand why I was irritated that he came so ill-equipped to handle my account. Instead, he thought that offering to buy me a few "pops" when he was in town (his word by the way) constituted effective preparation and client development. Don't *you* make this costly, entirely avoidable, mistake!

— Telephone Contact

As you have perhaps noticed, I am a big believer in using the telephone, either alone or in combination with written marketing communications. Why not? Once you have delivered satisfactory results to a client and done all that I have previously recommended to nurture a strong professional relationship, there is absolutely no reason why you cannot telephone a prospect at regular intervals to bring suitable benefits to his attention: "Here's something for you. Are you interested in hearing more about it?" At that point, you can ask the necessary qualifying questions. Then you can send the necessary client-centered communications.

What staggers me is just how few service "marketers" have a calling list of various kinds of clients, including people from whom they are either getting regular business, people they are getting business from but whom they think could be upgraded, or people from whom they've gotten business but who are not currently providing business (the ones we're principally discussing in this chapter). I have, for instance, a community health client which, despite my continual nagging, absolutely refuses to put together such a list. They advance any number of "reasons" why, the list itself being sensible, they cannot make the calls. The ludicrous "dog-ate-my-homework" excuses they offer would be amusing . . . except that they are being regularly offered by supposedly intelligent people who go to imaginative extremes to sabotage the effectiveness of their own marketing. Thus:

- resolve to keep a list of clients who should be called at regular intervals to schedule new business;

- make sure you're putting the right people on this list. If the business that the client previously gave you and your projection for the business he could give you is significant in terms of your business, this person should be called;

- call at regular intervals. Just how regular? That depends on the nature of the service you're offering and what the client tells you when you talk to him. If you've just remodeled the client's kitchen and bath, you're not going to be calling about that for several years. On the other hand, perhaps while you were providing the first service you discovered he wants to add a new room. You should call to find out if he's ready to go ahead now and, if not, when. You schedule your follow-up activities accordingly;

- finally, you must log what you hear so you can follow up promptly.

As I have observed over the years, many service sellers have perfected the art of wasting time and procrastinating. Instead, you should dedicate a portion of *every* day to generating new business from past satisfied clients. Just when should you do it? Personally, I'm happy to take a break from writing a book and make a prospect call; I find the change of pace relaxing (not to mention inspirational in terms of what I may be writing!) Once you've scrutinized your day and how you spend your time, you're certain to find a vacuum which you could be better using for prospecting. God knows, the presumed "marketers" who assist in so many service businesses, the ones who find such captivating delight in the mundane details of their co-workers to the extent of gossiping the hours away, could certainly do so.

— Post cards and letters

This takes us back to pure client-centered cash copy. Whatever you send out should be relentlessly focused with YOU GET BENEFIT NOW language. But you knew this, didn't you???

— *Newsletters*

When someone (always brightly) tells me he's about to start a newsletter to be sent to clients and prospects, my heart sinks. Why?

- Most people are poor newsletter writers. Trying to emulate *The New York Times*, they forget the purpose of a newsletter is to generate additional business, not to make available all the news that's fit to print.

- Those producing the newsletter are enamored of the ease of producing it (desk-top publishing, after all, has lessened the drudgery of production considerably) . . . which means they focus more attention on the production than the content . . . much less the purpose!

- They don't understand that creating a newsletter implies a long-term commitment of time, money and personnel. Is this really the best way to use scarce resources?

This jeremiad doesn't necessarily mean you should avoid producing a newsletter. It just means you should think very seriously before launching one. Here are the things you should consider:

- Are we producing a newsletter because everyone else is doing so? Or are we doing so because we have examined all the marketing alternatives open to us and made sure that this is the one that makes the most sense to achieve our sales objectives? (If you're not sure, back to the drawing board!)

- Why do we think a newsletter is the most cost-effective marketing alternative open to us?

- Are we sure we can create client-centered cash copy articles for our newsletter, articles that motivate prospects to contact us to get started to get the benefits we bring to their attention?

- Do we really want to commit ourselves to this kind of long-term project when we have so many other client-connecting alternatives available to us?

By the time you answer these questions, the probability is strong that you'll rethink the desirability of producing a newsletter. However, if you're still determined to go ahead, prominently post these points:

- Make sure every headline screams HERE'S A(NOTHER) BENEFIT FOR YOU instead of offering some me-centered feature (which is what most futile newsletter headlines do);

- Make sure every article in your newsletter is an article that hammers home benefits to your designated audience and which gets everyone in that audience to call you and identify himself as a prospect for the service that delivers those benefits;

- Make sure that you have thought through what will happen when the prospect identifies himself and responds either by fax, phone, or mail. Have you done everything possible so that the person who gets this response is prepared to handle it expeditiously, or will he stall, as all too frequently happens, not knowing what to do to turn this prospect into your next sale?

- Have you thought through who will get this newsletter — and why — and how you'll purge people from the list of those receiving it — and when. Why, I talked to a newsletter-publishing psychologist from Pennsylvania just the other day who had NEVER PURGED A NAME FROM HIS NEWSLETTER MAILING LIST despite the fact that fully 99% of the people he was mailing to had not bought anything in the last year . . . or, in some high percentage of the cases, EVER. IS THIS MAN AN IDIOT? The objective of a newsletter, please keep in mind, is not to inflate your mailing list to enormous proportions but to generate revenue. If the people receiving it cannot be motivated to respond to the benefits you have available, PURGE THEM!

— Seasonal greetings

How many of us get deluged during the December holidays with brightly colored bits of paper offering us sugary greetings . . . these bits of paper being SIGNED BY A MACHINE? What incredible folly this is.

Now take a look at this creation.

VNA

MIDDLESEX · EAST

12 BEACON STREET, STONEHAM, MA 02180
TEL. 617-438-3770 FAX 617-438-7994

SPECIAL BULLETIN FROM S. CLAUS

It's holiday rush time
here at the Pole,
but I've got to confess,
I'm no Merry Old Soul.

True, My elves have the toys
about ready to go
And the reindeer are ready
to prance in the snow.

Yes, we've spent a long year
getting ready for you
but I'm sad to report...
Mrs. Claus has the flu.

Her dear nose is runny
And her fever is up.
Her eyes are glazed over
and she just feels punk.

With all that I'm doing
the timing's appalling
Tend to Mrs. Claus?
Leave the world's children bawling?

Lucky for me--and for them--
there's help right at hand
I've called a visiting nurse
to meet my demand!

She's here right this minute
right in the next room
tending may dear wife
not a moment too soon!

Hurray for my friends
at Middlesex-East VNA
with them on the job,
I can get on my way!

What's more to the point
I need never fret
They're here when I need them.
They're the best you can get!

With them on the job--
every day of the year--
I'll never fall behind
bringing you Christmas Cheer!

So, to one and to all,
here's my Christmas plea:
Keep their number on hand
for you & your family!

(617) 438-3770

"Whenever I feel out of sorts--or my reindeers or elves--I always
call Visiting Nurse of Middlesex-East. They work the same kind
of hours I do....365 days a year, 24 hours a day... and
Christmas!   S. Claus

VISITING NURSE ASSOCIATION OF MIDDLESEX-EAST
90 YEARS OF HOME HEALTH CARE EXPERIENCE

Someone is sure to tell me that this "poem" is not going to win a Pulitzer Prize. Another benighted creature is sure to write and tell me that such a production would hardly be the right thing for a citizen of his bloated eminence to disseminate. Egad! What fools these mortals be.

Consider the difference between the ordinary seasonal card with printed greeting and printed signature . . . ordered, addressed, sent — and promptly forgotten — by both sender and recipient, and this other effort.

- The message you see was not an isolated "hit" but part of a focused effort;

- It was designed to be different . . . and was designed with a purpose (to generate additional business during the holi-

days, a down-time for many services businesses, including
this one);

- It was not mailed . . . but personally delivered by a nurse
in a Santa hat (and, let it be noted, tingling bells) who came
not just with the message but with a small box of chocolates
and a pocket stuffed with seasonal goodies. The goodies
were dispensed to customers in physicians' waiting rooms;
the chocolate went to the physicians' staffs (who often make
crucial referral calls). In short, the seasonal message was
designed to have maximum impact (and, as you can see, a
point).

What's more, it was memorable, fun . . . and, most importantly, it didn't
just offer a homogenized, impersonal sentiment . . . but, by reinforcing
in the clients' minds that they could get the assistance they wanted,
actually succeeded in generating new business. To the extent, I should
probably tell you, of making this seasonal total the highest in the
organization's history. Ahem.

This is what I mean by thinking through the marketing activity. By
making sure you are not just doing the expected thing. The brain-dead
thing. The thing that everybody else is doing because everybody else
is doing it.

I am not against seasonable cards (Hallmark take note). I am, however,
adamantly against spending dollars on "marketing" which cannot,
due to the nature of the thing itself, do what marketing must do:
namely, generate business and renewed business.

But, you tell me, I don't have the time to spend a day visiting my
clients and dropping off personal greeting messages and packages like
this example. Moreover, my clients are spread around the world. Fair
enough. Then do the best you can . . . either drop the seasonal card
altogether in favor of some reasonable client-centered activity . . . or
create something which will hammer home, in an amusing , appropriate and client-centered way, the benefits you have available . . .
and your hope that this client, who has not used your services for
a time, will pick up the phone and use them NOW. I know you can
do this . . . and YOU MUST.

— Presents and premiums

Do you get presents at Christmas from people you've hired to provide
services? I do. Every year I get a tin of cookies with a printed note

from my printer. And endless bottles of wine (giving spirits, so popular in the 'fifties, now is *de trop*). Unfortunately, the problems that bedevil the printed cards mentioned above destroy the marketing effectiveness of such gifts. Because the recipient knows they have been ordered by machine and are accompanied with an impersonal card, they value them little (even if the wine is sparkling and the cookies delicious). What, then, is the point?

The point, my friend, is to make the customer feel special. And no manufactured greeting and impersonal present can ever do this. At this point, you might rightly conclude that such presents should be abandoned altogether and your efforts redirected into activities which can be made more telling. Fair enough. I wouldn't fight this decision. However, if you want to go ahead with a gift or premium to a customer, use these guidelines:

- Resolve to make the gift personal. That is, resolve to speak to the individual directly and humanly.

- Don't give gifts when every one else is doing it. What's the point? The value of what you send is necessarily diminished if it comes when everyone else's does. Select another season.

- Give a gift that pertains to the individual's interests. When you're talking to customers, listen for their interests. They'll be happy to tell you about the things they find enthralling. Link what you do to what they like, and your gift will be magnified in importance . . . with good results for your cause.

- Give a gift they can give to a loved one. A customer's child is devoted to dinosaurs. I found a splendid book on the subject in one of the Barnes & Nobles' catalogs (126 Fifth Ave., New York, NY 10011; (201) 767-7079), had it sent to me, suitably inscribed it (from my customer and from me) and gave it to the customer so he could present it. The present, and the happy experience it gave to the customer, were far more meaningful than some mass-produced, mass-delivered "gift". And cheaper, too, since the book was significantly marked down in price!

- Give a gift that's meaningful to you. As anyone knows who reads my books (yes, that's you!), you know I love my creations. As something meaningful to me, I am happy to give my own books as presents . . . suitably autographed, of course.

- Accompany the gift with a sincere note of appreciation. Good marketing is about establishing connections between people . . . between a person who has a benefit and a person who wants that benefit. But often the connection is as important as the benefit, and, thus , you should do everything possible to strengthen it. One of my famous notes will help. I think, for instance, of the tin of cookies my printer sends. It comes with a machine-printed card, nothing more. Yet I give that firm over $125,000 worth of business a year. I think the president of that firm could spend a few minutes telling me how grateful he was, don't you? But he thinks a printed card and some cookies (admittedly delicious) will do. I trust you do not agree. In this note, tell how glad you are for the relationship . . . and say how much you're looking forward to developing it. Mean it. The sentiment is a seed that will grow faster with your sincere enthusiasm.

- Praise people you've worked with. Put as many names as you can into your gift. The size of the gift is not so important; the fact that you have remembered all the right people is.

These suggestions will make the gift you give important and assist your relationship with the customer, whether lapsed or current. Now don't leave things alone. Follow up shortly afterwards and see how you can do further business together. Don't mention the gift, of course, beyond inquiring as to whether the customer received it; (these days you can't expect to receive a thank-you note). But do take full advantage of the amiable atmosphere your gift has helped create. All you have to say is, "I've got something to help you. Interested in hearing about it?" . . . and the remembrance of your gift will help ensure that you'll be positively received even though not a word is (or should be) said about it.

— Social events

For reasons unknown, many service marketers have the peculiar notion that if they invite a heap of people to eat their food and drink their liquor and amuse themselves a little, these people will rain business upon them. I'd say it's far more likely that, instead of business, the "marketer" would merely get a bill . . . and perhaps, from the more genteel attending, a few words of sincere appreciation.

Oh, yes, I'm a skeptic about social events . . . unless. Unless you really think them through and make sure you are not just having the social event to amuse yourself (heaven forbid!) but to generate business. Here are some helpful guidelines:

- Social events, whether they range from dinner at a nice restaurant to a cocktail party for 100, are expensive. The first thing you should ask yourself if whether this is the best use of your limited marketing dollars.

- Are you just keen on having the event, or will you use it as part of a marketing sequence? In other words, does it fit into a sequence of business development for the people invited?

- Have you selected an event which will enable you to get to know your guests/customers better . . . and so develop both your relationship and find out what they want (so you can provide it promptly)?

- Can you afford an event where you'll be free to interact with the maximum number of customer/prospects, instead of having to organize things, see to the arrangement, *etc.*?

- If you have selected a larger event (such as a cocktail party) in which other members of your organization will participate (note this verb, I do not just say "attend"), will you spend the time setting out your expectations for what they're to accomplish with those attending? All too often staff people see an event as a purely social occasion, a time for them merely to have fun. This, of course, misses the point entirely. At business development social functions, all staff attending must understand the purpose of the event and must be briefed on what they are to do, the people they are to meet, what they are to discover, *etc.* In short, they must understand they have crucial roles to play . . . not just to eat the canapés! *Note:* this means staff must be briefed (and trained if necessary) beforehand and debriefed afterwards. It astonishes me when service "marketers" spend money on such events and then don't bother to gather the crucial intelligence that always surfaces from them. WHAT ARE THEY THINKING OF! Staff must be quizzed on what happened, what guests (who are, never forget, prospects) said, what kinds of interests they have (professional and personal), what they said about the services you provide (and which services they may want next), when they may want your services, *etc.* This information must be written down and written down promptly. Just because the guests have left doesn't mean your work — or the work of your staff — is over!!!

Other tips to make these events pay off:

- It should go without saying (but, these days, most certainly does not) that everything should be done for the guests'/ prospects' comfort and convenience. This means thinking through each aspect of the affair from providing directions to the location where it's held, finding out where they'll park their cars, put their coats, freshen up, *etc.* Further, it means making sure all guests are greeted at the door, properly introduced to someone who'll look out for them, give them refreshments, introduce them to others, *etc.*

- You and your staff should make a special point of making sure there are no wall flowers, no one stands in a corner, no one is cornered by bores, shy people are given special consideration, and the inevitable "lives of the party" don't become overbearing. *Face it:* handling any kind of social event properly is an art, and if you are determined to have such a thing, you'd better do it properly, or you've wasted precious marketing dollars and perhaps even antagonized people.

- Always prepare a few well-chosen words to accompany the event. Even if your "event" is dinner for two past customers you're romancing, make sure your toast is a graceful recognition of their importance and your desire to work with them again. Yes, even a toast should be a bridge to future business dealings. The same applies to larger events. Publicly thank your guests, tell them why they're important and how happy you are to serve them. And make sure you tell them you want to serve them again and will be in touch soon to find out how you can do so!

- Make sure you bring appropriate "props" to these events, including your marketing literature. Position a table with this information near the food and other refreshments. Don't hand it out generally; that's gauche. Properly placed, you'll find people will pick it up on their own. And besides, as the conversation warrants, you may well want this information at hand to make a point or provide further details. Then it's most appropriate to make sure the guest gets it — right away!

Note: while finishing this chapter I was invited to a book function given by an increasingly well-known author who happens to live in my building. Following my own advice, I arrived with a bottle of good champagne and a winning smile. I presented the champagne . . . and then was promptly ignored. The host introduced me to no one; no one offered any amenity. It was just "sink or swim." Yet this fellow is ironically supposedly an expert on *relationships!* Sadly, my little ill-bred neighbor had no conception of what a host was to do or how to make his event successful. As a result, I left feeling not just that his manners were faulty but that he was not worth knowing. It's a pity, of course, but this kind of myopic selfishness is not just unacceptable; it's an indication of who the person perpetrating it really is.

Fortunately, you'll do better . . .

Yes, you've followed all this advice and had a fabulous affair. Everyone had a good time (some, perhaps, a tad over jolly depending on the libations you've served) and all agree they want it to be repeated. Your first impulse may well be to agree. But wait . . . Did this event help generate more revenue? Did the old customers you were trying to retrieve actually come back? Did you actually get new business from them? You see this and not a "good time was had by all" is the meaningful consideration. This means following up the guests (and those who didn't come, too, telling them how sorry you were they couldn't attend but that you've something important to share with them about benefits you have available), working to discover what they want and when they want it, finessing the necessary deals, generating the business. Only then do you know if the event worked . . . beyond giving everyone an excuse to eat your food and drink your liquor. That, you see, isn't marketing; it's madness.

What To Do When You Determine The Customer Is Capable Of Being Upgraded

All customers fall into the following categories:

- those who have bought once but are unlikely to buy again;
- those who have bought once, will buy again, but only at the same level;

- those who have bought at a particular level but can be upgraded to buy more either sooner (better) or later (less good) and so become a higher value customer;

The merest glance at these categories tells you that some of these animals, as George Orwell might have written, are more equal than others — and hence more deserving of the time and consideration of that good marketer, you!

Unfortunately, customers don't carry a sign onto your premises telling you which category they fall into. I admit this is a pity. However, because you need the information, you have to do what you can to get it.

- You must understand that all customers divide into these three categories. It is your responsibility to determine where they fall *when you are doing everything right*.

- Presently, odds are you are not doing what's necessary to get the information you need about your customers, so you know what to do with them.

- As you begin any relationship with a customer, you should be thinking about what buying action this customer is likely to take *next*. Let's explore this a little more.

Consider the case of my consulting copywriter. He sells a variety of marketing communications ranging from classified ads to full-scale marketing campaigns. His job is to find out where his relationship with each customer can go . . . so he can begin to position himself to provide additional services . . . and to see if the customer wants them now and is able to retain them.

Thus, while the copywriter is working on Project 1, his job is to assess the client's situation. Say that this initial assignment involves writing a new brochure for Client A. Clearly, this is unlikely to be the only piece of marketing communications this company uses — or needs. Thus, the copywriter should gather examples of all the other marketing communications produced by this firm, including ads, cover letters, brochures, marketing plans, media kits, *etc.* He has three jobs: to analyze these documents and see how he could improve them (and hence give the client additional benefits), to ascertain the client's ability to pay for additional services, and to find out when the client wants to begin achieving these additional benefits. Throughout the time he is working with the client, he should be working to accomplish these three tasks as well. In other words, part of Project 1 is getting to Project 2 — and beyond.

There are many ways of succeeding in these tasks, by:

- gathering examples of all other existing marketing communications and reviewing them with a view towards improving them;

- asking the customer directly about what he wants, when he wants it, and when he'll have the budget to accomplish his desires;

- following up good results and indicating to the client how much more you can accomplish for him . . . if only he is willing to work with you.

In short, you must look beyond the current project and build into it the actions which ensure you get the necessary data for going on to the next stage of your relationship with this client. Now, it is crucial to understand that what you learn will fall along a continuum ranging from "No more business" to "Immediate substantial new business." It's you who must be prepared to analyze what you hear and evaluate it properly. Thus:

- if the client won't discuss anything beyond the terms of this engagement, he gets a lower rating;

- so too if he complains about having no money and you see evidence (always too obvious) that money is indeed a problem, or

- if you can't get the client to talk about what he wants for the future and when he wants it.

If you make it a priority to discover information about your clients and their wants, you will certainly get information which will enable you to determine just where the client falls along the future business continuum.

And what should you do once you know? That depends on where the prospect falls:

- If you sell only one service and your relationship with the customer didn't prosper and you can get neither further direct nor referral business, drop the contact. The prospect is unpromising.

- If you sell only one service but things went well with this customer, cultivate to the extent necessary to get testimonials, recommendations and referrals. *Note:* it's time for you to diversify your service offerings!

- If you sell several services, but your relationship did not prosper, again drop the connection.

- If you sell several services and your initial contact went well but the customer does not want to use your service again immediately, cultivate this prospect further if you have ascertained that he can benefit from your additional services and has the means of acquiring them. Just how long you cultivate this customer depends on how valuable his business could be to you, how easily you can handle this cultivation and whether future signs from this prospect are positive or not.

Upgrading customers is a necessary part of your success. It's your responsibility to handle it so you get its benefit as quickly as possible. Thus:

- Remind yourself that it's your responsibility to look for upgrade possibilities. Yes, customers may make inquiries about other services you offer. But it is only you who can organize upgrading as a profitable *system*, not just benefit from it as an episodic occurrence.

- Try to upgrade the customer as soon as possible. Yes, there is no reason why you cannot do so while you are still working on Project 1. If the client has a want, if you can satisfy this want, and if the client can pay you to satisfy this want, then all the constituents of a successful deal are at hand.

- By the time your first engagement with a client is over, you should have determined where he falls along the continuum of future business. Based on what you've learned from the client, you should be able to make this evaluation. What you do next is a result of what you've learned from this client.

- Once you've made your decision, proceed accordingly. If you can only get a referral or testimonial or use the client for a recommendation, do that. That is, if you've determined that this is the only thing that can emerge from this relationship to further benefit you, take the necessary action so that you at least get this.

- If you've determined that the client has additional wants and will have additional resources to pay you, keep the contact green so that when you finally discover the client is ready to go ahead (yes, you must keep asking him), your relationship will be sufficiently developed that you can easily make the deal at the appropriate moment. *Note:* just in case there is any doubt on this point, I shall say again: it is always your responsibility to keep in touch with the potential client. You must never expect and rely upon the client prospect contacting you. This happens, but it happens in an unsystematic, unpredictable, and hence unsatisfactory fashion.

- Each time you connect with the prospect, start the conversation by reminding him of the benefit you know he wants. Ask him whether he still wants this benefit; (perhaps he's decided he wants something else, a very common situation). If he does, ask him whether he's ready to get started having it NOW! Then listen to what he says. Does he really want the benefit? If he says he wants it now, do the reasons he provides for not going ahead make sense . . . or do they seem like excuses to you? These moments call for the utmost coolness and scientific detachment. Do not get carried away by your hopes, but listen carefully to just what the prospect is saying and just how he's saying it. Is what he's telling you believable? Do you *believe* him, or do you simply want to believe, a very different thing? You see, until you know it's impossible to make the right decision about what to do next.

- If you've contacted the client several times (always, remember, continuing to believe he has the potential to generate further revenue for your business) and still not been able to pin the creature down, do not hesitate to say, "I really want to work with you. And you've been telling me you want the (benefit you can provide). But we seem unable to make this deal. What's the problem? When are we going to pull it together? When can you really make a decision? When can we get started?" Dear reader: there is absolutely nothing wrong with asking these questions, whenever you feel the need. One of the saddest things about the lives of too many service marketers is that they continue to delude themselves about "prospects" long after there is any basis at all for believing that these people are really prospects. The service seller goes on making contact, demeaning himself, playing an unwinnable game with the prospect, when that prospect has absolutely no intention or ability to conclude a mutually beneficial business. THIS IS ABSURD!

- If the prospect isn't closing, there is a reason and you must find out what it is. Is the prospect still interested in the benefit? (Don't assume he is. Ask!) Why can't he go ahead now? (Don't feel sheepish about this question. Ask it directly!) Is money a problem? (It often is, of course, and in recessionary days during which I'm writing the problem is seriously compounded.) Is there another problem we need to work out? Do you have some problem with the way you think I'd do the job? See what's happening? Don't *assume* the business is ready to fall into your lap. Do assume that if the prospect is not closing there is a problem which needs to be solved. Before you can do anything else, you must discover what that problem is and do what you can to solve it. *Note:* be prepared for the prospect's answer. Once you've asked the question, the prospect may be very direct in what he tells you. If you need to think about your response to this, begin by listening to everything the prospect has to say. Then tell him you've taken good notes of his point of view and would like time to consider it. Say you'll be back in touch in a day or two (schedule a time if necessary). Then consider what you've been told and craft your response. There is never a need to blurt out a response that isn't going to be helpful to you. If you need time to give the best answer — and help this relationship along — take it.

Once you've listened to what the prospect has to say, review it with two questions in mind, "Do I really think I am going to be able to upgrade this customer to get additional business? If so, am I willing to do everything that is necessary to get it?"

At this point I must remind you of the purpose of this book: to implement a *system* that produces as many leads as you want and must have to achieve millionaire status. If you have been conscientiously implementing the suggestions of past chapters, the number of your leads has been nicely, perhaps even dramatically, expanding. The question at this point is, then, whether it makes more sense to try to upgrade an existing customer or stimulate your lead-generating system and so get more qualified leads.

If you provided good service to the customer in question, if you have asked whether he wants additional benefits and he has told you he does. If he says money is not a problem (and you believe him). If you have asked him when he wants to go ahead and you've asked him directly if he is serious about this date, then by all means continue to walk through the steps of the cultivation process. If, on the other hand, you cannot pin the customer down on these points, then despite any good words he may offer, he is not a good prospect, and you should either reduce his priority standing . . . or drop him altogether depending on how much you actually believe him . . . and how the rest of your lead-generating enterprises are coming along.

Personally, I keep my lead-generating system going at a white-hot pace. I want to generate as many leads as I possibly can so that I can handle matters like the upgrading of customers in the most focused of fashions. Thus, if a customer cannot give me definite answers to the kinds of definite questions I've advised you to ask, if he cannot convince me of his sincerity and willingness to make a commitment to go ahead, if he cannot, in short, establish that he is in fact a real prospect instead of a time-waster, then I am ruthless about demoting him (if I feel there may be hope at a later date) or flushing him out altogether. Just as you should be.

What To Do With Key Customers Of Pivotal Importance To Your Business

Although this point is an elaboration of the two previous points, because of its importance I wanted to draw your particular attention to it.

In all service businesses there are two kinds of key customers:

- people who are currently buying at your highest level and can continue to do so;
- people who are not yet buying at your highest level but whom you've decided can do so.

These people provide you with a significant amount of revenue but are all too frequently taken for granted. This is hardly surprising. They:

- come in regularly without being prompted;

- pay their bills on time without becoming collections problems;

- assume full responsibility for dealing with you. They therefore allow you to be slothful and disorganized, states of the primordial beast;

- aren't any trouble, do most of what you'd like them to do, and demand nothing in return except a good service for a fair price.

Yes, such creatures are the angels of all service businesses. Problem is that like other angels in our irreligious times, these angels get regularly ignored, taken for granted, and under-valued.

This is incredibly stupid.

Because you're a smart, ambitious marketer, I'm sure you'll want to do what's necessary to treat them properly:

- Set up two computer files. Title one "Top Customers." Call the other "Future Top Customers."

- Put the key people who regularly support your business in the former. These are the people buying from you at regular intervals, continually supporting your business.

- Put customers you have determined can be upgraded into the latter. For whatever reason, you have made the determination that these people can provide your business with additional revenue.

- Into each file, add everything you know about both kinds of prospects (for that's what they are). Put in name, address, business title, kind of service purchased, regularity of purchase, amount of average purchase, personal data you know about them including birthday, spouse and children names, main interests, *etc.* In short, do a client profile.

- Now institute a client-cultivation program. This program should consist of special offers for both groups, regular cultivation and contact, regular attempts to strengthen the relationship, meaningful (that is, non-traditional) presents and premiums, in short the kinds of things discussed above. I'd like to expand upon this.

Consider your current best customers. What are you doing to keep them? Be honest. And what about the group of customers who are not yet buying at the top or at regular intervals? What are you doing — *in a systematic fashion* — for them? If you're unsure, shame on you! Yet you dare call yourself a marketer and have the audacity to aspire to millionaire status!!!

For these people, you see, you must have a systematic cultivation and upgrade program. You must determine:

- who should be contacted;

- how they should be contacted;

- when they should be contacted;

- how often they should be contacted;

- how all the details of the contact should be arranged.

Let's look at just one example.

Say you are a plumber who does regular work for several apartment buildings in your town. Because you offer a good service at a fair price and because you have worked hard to develop your client base, you now have a good solid customer roster. Is this the end to the story? Hardly. The first thing you must do is to recognize that this base, these customers, are your capital, and they must be nurtured accordingly. Something you probably don't already do . . .

Now what?

- Brainstorm different customer development techniques. Include things related to your business (how about providing your best customers with a free inspection certificate good for one complete review of the kitchen and bathroom plumbing in the next vacant apartment?) and those unrelated (send a bottle of wine with your compliments at an unexpected moment.) *Note:* personally, I like presents related to your business. Why? Because while the plumber is checking out the kitchen and bathroom plumbing in the newly vacant apartment, he's certain to find problems that need attending to . . . hence, more business.) On the other hand, sending a bottle of wine — with a charming note, of course — is also acceptable, though it will not lead to business as fast as the other alternative.

- Begin implementing this cultivation program at a time when what you do will make the biggest impact. Thus, don't send something when a customer is having his 50th wedding anniversary; everyone else he knows will do that. Go for the 49th or 51st, when you'll have the field — and all the credit — pretty much to yourself.

- Don't just do one thing. Integrate your customer development program into your overall marketing effort so that you are connecting with your best customers and those you want to upgrade on a regular basis. Once or twice, no matter how nice, is insufficient by The Rule of Seven. You want regular contact. Augment what you do by acting appropriately based on the client's personal interests and information. Thus, if the client tells you he is going to Paris for a holiday, send along a book on the wines of France to arrive a week or two before he leaves. Tell him to take it with him and to toast your happy relationship in the best wines of Burgundy. (I've already recommended the Barnes & Noble bargain books catalog for your consideration. Another you should know about is produced by Edward R. Hamilton, Falls Village, CT 06031-5000)

- When connecting with your best customers, let them know you want this relationship to go on forever. When connecting with your soon-to-be-best customers, let them know you are interested in developing the relationship and provide them with an indication of additional ways you can make their lives easier. Never expect the customer to know what you do; always assume the responsibility for making it clear about how you can help him.

The success of both your top customer and future top customer programs lies in your not taking these people for granted but in engaging with them in a positive manner focused on the mutual achievement of your joint objectives. This is not, I need hardly tell you, the way most businesses function. Consider this one illustration from among many I could provide you. For a time, I printed my books with a certain printer. The account was a substantial one. I did sizable printings, paid promptly and, in short, considered myself a model customer. Because of certain problems with this printer, however, I decided to move my account elsewhere. I never bothered to tell them I was moving; I just voted with my feet and went. Now the punchline: no one from the printing company ever called to inquire why I had left, if there was a problem that needed (or could be) resolved, or if they could get my business back. They just let an annual 6-figure account walk out the door without so much as a peep.

Personally, I'll never understand this kind of behavior. Nor would any other service-seller millionaire. If it had been my account, I would have had a regular cultivation program in place to make sure the customer was getting what he wanted . . . and ensure there were no problems. In my world, it is inconceivable that a major account would get to the point of leaving without anyone knowing why . . . much less that such an account, if it had left, would have gone uncontacted. Believe me, I would have been on the phone instantly seeking to mend that fence. But between the day I left and this, NO ONE FROM THAT PRINTING COMPANY HAS EVER CALLED ME. However, they keep sending me direct mail asking for my business *as if I had never had any dealings with them* . . . a stupid waste of their money, as each of their expensive marketing packages goes instantly in the trash. I ask you, what idiot is in charge there and why does he think what he's doing is "marketing"?

What To Do When A Customer Has Not Bought In Awhile?

Every business has lapsed customers. These are people who may have bought at some time in the increasingly distant past but not since. Like an old pair of shoes, you hate to throw them away. However, what's the point of continuing to invest in them if your prospect of future business is uncertain? What indeed!

Let me be very clear about something: the only point of continuing to contact a lapsed customer is to get him to buy again. If this person will not buy again, he's simply a drain on your resources and must be discarded accordingly. The question, then, becomes knowing into which category he goes. Here's what to do:

- Do what's necessary the first time the customer buys to determine if and when he'll buy again. As previously discussed, this means asking questions and making deductions about what he wants next, when he wants it, and whether he has the means to acquire it. If you don't gather this information, you're crippling your ability for determining what to do next and how long to work with this person.

- After gathering this information, follow up accordingly. If the customer puts you off, try to discover if he still wants to achieve the benefit he previously said he did. If he doesn't and if there is no real prospect of reviving his interest in the future, purge him now. If there is, then proceed accordingly until such time as he either takes action to acquire the benefit, or you clearly discover that he's a lost cause. (The sooner you know this the better.)

- Put together a meaningful offer to lapsed customers. Reserve one of your best and most popular offers for people who haven't bought in awhile. If they don't respond to this offer, purge them, since they are not likely to respond to anything.

- Or send them a post card asking if they want to continue to hear from you . . . to get information about the various "good-for-you" offers you have available. Do not make this a postage paid response card, either. Force them to call you so you can talk to them directly and ascertain if there is anything they want. Remember, you need data from these people to determine if you should bother to spend any more of your resources attempting to motivate them. If they don't respond, get rid of them.

- Or call to see if they continue to have the want that brought them to you in the first place and see if they're ready to schedule an appointment either to discuss purchasing additional service or buy it now.

One of the most maddening things about dealing with the sure-to-stay-poor service seller is that he retains the infuriating belief that lapsed customers will simply return of their own volition. "When they're ready," his entire mode of operation affirms, "they'll come back, wagging their tails behind them." Whatever he does, therefore, is lax, disorganized, vague, undirected, and inappropriate — like the absurd mailings I receive from the printing company mentioned above.

The thing you must discover about a lapsed customer as soon as possible is whether he remains a prospect for future business or whether he is just another one of the innumerable ways available for squandering your precious resources. To this end:

- Ask him whether he is still a customer . . . whether he still has the want . . . whether he still wants to get the benefit from you. Don't just assume that because you have someone's name, address and phone number, because you provided a benefit to him once that he remains a prospect.

Unless he's bought recently and/or has given you some indication that he remains a good customer, assume the worst — and act accordingly.

• Understand that the more time that's elapsed since the customer bought from you, the lower his standing as a "good and future" customer and the less likely he is to buy again.

• Understand, too, that an "I-won't-be-buying-from-you-again" customer doesn't feel obliged to call up and confess his intentions. Like Douglas MacArthur's old soldier, he'll just fade away. He has no obligation to tell you this decision or to do anything; you have every incentive, however, for finding out how things are . . . and attempting, if at all possible, to salvage the situation.

Have you called, tried a special offer, called again and *still* don't know what this lapsed customer is thinking? Before the last act in the drama is reached, try one of my famous notes. Send the lapsed customer this wing-ding of a message:

Dear Customer (by name),

On (date), you were good enough to retain me to provide you with (benefit you provided). As you know, the work I provided for you was successful. You achieved (result).

I want to be able to provide these — or better — results for you now. And I want to provide other benefits for you, too, like (benefits you also provide).

Unfortunately, I've tried over and over again to bring these benefits to your attention. I've sent you special offers. I've called. And called again. THERE'S BEEN NO RESPONSE FROM YOU. NOTHING AT ALL!!!

Frankly, I fear the worst. Perhaps you've died . . . gone into a coma . . . or been kidnapped by aliens.

Please take just a minute to reassure me that you're all right and that you'd like to work together again. Just a moment of your time is all I need.

But if I don't get it, I'll have to fear the worst . . . which would be too bad since we both benefited from our past relationship.

Hoping that you'll do what's necessary to get us back together,

Sincerely,

Service Provider/Marketer

P.S. I make it a point in my business to live and work by The Golden Rule. I've treated you this way, please do the same to me.

Let me tell you something, if the person has a want you can provide and if there is even the tiniest portion left of human kindness, you'll get a response . . . even if that response is "not interested, try again later." If that's all you get, at least you're talking again and can, as a result of whatever data you get, make the appropriate decision. Deduction: marketing is about motivating humans. Whatever works in motivating them is fair. This is where most "marketers" fail. They try to be "professional". Personally, I learned long ago that plenty of professionals fail; that the people who succeed are those who are willing to do *whatever it takes* to get their prospects and customers to communicate with them . . . so that they can take the appropriate action.

That's why the structure of this letter basically says, "I helped you out once and want to do so again. If you're a good and decent person, you'll communicate with me so I can help you some more. It's because you're a good and decent person that I'm writing to you now. Please don't let me down." A good and decent person, the kind of person you want to work for in any event, will respond to this letter. Any one of the innumerable varieties of flat worms who abound will not. Either way, therefore, you've had a response you can work with. Congratulate yourself that you've discovered just what you're dealing with for a single sheet of paper and a first-class postage stamp.

What To Do When You've Determined A Customer Is "Dead"

Not all customers are going to stay current. With the best will in the world, you will not derive future business from all of them — even when your system is properly established and implemented. Here, then, is what you must do:

- Before making any final determination, ask yourself: "Have I done everything I could, everything that made sense and was reasonable to retrieve this customer . . . or at least to see if future business is possible, or he is a dead loss?" If you're not sure, use a variation of the letter furnished above.

• If you have determined that future business is possible, then proceed accordingly in your usual focused manner so you get this business as quickly as you can.

• If you have determined that the customer is indeed "dead", determine what the best action is. If this is a flat worm from whom you've determined you can get nothing more, zap the name off your mailing list and dance the light fandango. Many service sellers might be depressed at this moment, but you've realized everyone isn't going to buy again, you've done what was reasonable and necessary to determine if this person would buy again, and having discovered that neither future business was likely nor any other benefit, you've taken the only action that makes sense from a business perspective — ZAPPING THE "CUS-TOMER" FROM YOUR RECORDS, thereby saving yourself from spending additional time and resources in a vain attempt to retrieve that from which no future benefit is likely. You are now functioning in a perfectly reasonable fashion and deserve to congratulate yourself. You are doing what many thousands of other "marketers" will never do, to the detriment of their wealth and business prosperity.

• If, however, you have decided that zapping the person from your list is necessary but some future benefit may accrue, take one last calculated action. Send a message like this:

Dear (person by name),

I have just zapped your name from my mailing list and records. You will not be receiving future mailings from me or indications of how I can assist you.

I am very sorry to have taken this action, but, in all seriousness, I expected better from you. In (date) I provided (benefit you provided). You were happy with what you got, and it looked like we'd be working together again. Towards that end I con-tacted you on many occasions bringing to your attention many benefits which would improve your life and business. YOU'VE RESPONDED TO NOTHING!

I don't know what happened, and I want you to know I'm disappointed in you and frustrated by your lack of communication. Frankly, I thought that we had a good strong professional and personal relationship. I don't treat people like this, and I'm chagrined to discover you do. I thought better of you.

However, I hope that whatever you're going through now is only a temporary phase and that you'll contact me some day and let me help you again. If this doesn't occur, all the best to you. I'll regret I cannot be of further assistance to you, but continue to wish you well.

Sincerely yours,

Service Marketer/Master of Motivational Guilt

What's going on here? You are being a marketing statesman. You are not merely zapping the inconsiderate pig from your records. You're letting him know that you're a superior being and that you, out of the bigness of your heart, are going to forgive him. At the very least, this enables you to close the relationship knowing that you have done everything possible — to the extent of ascending to saintliness — to preserve it. If the customer doesn't want to preserve this, why the way you've ended it will cause him to wince and grow angry . . . which always gives me a satisfactory feeling, as it should give you. Last and best, however, this shrewd letter may well motivate the person to call you and get things going again. Why not? You've just provided ample evidence of what a terrific, superior person you are — just the kind of person your smart clients really want to have on their side. And the smart ones are willing to do what's necessary to keep you. You clever, clever thing you.

Cleaning Your Slate At The End Of The Year

We have almost reached the end of this chapter on customer development. I have just one more technique to impart.

During the course of any year, there will have been customers who have treated you very well, for whom it was a joy to work and, indeed, to share your life with. By the same token, for whatever reason, you will have found that there were people you worked with who treated you badly, whom you let walk all over you and take full advantage of you. In a moment of lucidity, I trust you ended this abusive relationship (if not, do so now). Still, you may still feel angry at them for what they did to you, and this anger may be seething inside. Whichever case holds, as the year ends it is time to do what is necessary to end it properly and move on in just the right spirit to the challenges ahead.

— For the best customers

Between Christmas and New Year's Day, sit down and write a series of heart-felt notes to the people who have made this year financially profitable and helped move you towards the achievement of your objective. I am not recommending that you send a card or present (I've discussed these options before). Instead, what I'm suggesting here is that you tell each of these people in your own words just how important he is to you, how much you value the relationship and thank him for being in this world.

The best times to write this memorable greeting are Christmas Eve and New Year's Day. Not only will the rest of the world not be working, but you'll find the dates alone will put you in the right frame of mind.

In this letter, say by all means that you've enjoyed working together, that you hope your relationship will continue for a long time, but do not mention anything specific about current matters needing handling or specific future projects. Those are inappropriate in this letter.

Instead, make this a winning communication from a truly superior being to someone who has helped make you even more superior. Make it at once graceful, touching, sympathetic and sincere. After all, this person is important to you, and you just can't let him know it often enough.

Once this letter is sent, never refer to it again. Believe me, if the person you've written to is any kind of decent soul, he'll let you know, both verbally and by continuing your important relationship, that's he's heard your message — and appreciates it. Not least because your direct, sympathetic sentiments will be the only ones he'll have received from any one he works with. Everything else, you see, will be just an impersonal token.

— For the worst

Unfortunately, there will be other characters you will have encountered during the year who have treated you very differently. Assorted customers from hell, they have made your life a misery. You probably feel very angry towards them and frustrated about what you let them do. This anger, I need hardly tell you, corrodes your ability to focus on your business. It will not help you get richer. It will not help you develop your services. All it will do is dilute your limited mental and physical resources. That's why you must forgive them . . . so you can move on intact.

In the quiet of the day before Christmas or when the rest of your friends are lolling before a Bowl Game, do yourself a favor: write to the two or three people who have bedeviled your year and tell them that you forgive them for what they did, hope that they will learn that is not the way to treat people, and hope that at some point relations between you both can be different.

Again, this letter should not be an entreaty for future business; it should not be an attempt to rehash what happened. It should simply be a statement that you regret what occurred, were disappointed that your relationship was handicapped by the disagreements, and hope that things can later be better. That's enough.

As with the letter above, this one establishes you as a superior person. It gives you blessed release from the frustration, anger and pain that may have resulted from an unsatisfactory business relationship. It doesn't make sense to wait around for the sad creature who treated you so badly to recognize his sins and ask your forgiveness; this just isn't likely to happen. In the meantime, your anger may well grow. "Living well," as the Irish rightly say, "is the best revenge." And you'll live better when you're not wasting any of your resources on someone who has done you wrong. This letter is very much for you.

— The last case: customers you have wronged

With the best will in the world, during the year you may very well wrong a customer. It could be inadvertent; it might have been deliberate. Either way, it is most unfortunate, not just because you have lost this customer's business but because you have diminished yourself in your own eyes. You stand naked before yourself as less than you can or should be. This is a feeling no one likes, and it is one that you are now positioned to do something about.

If the problem that separated you can still be solved, offer a means of doing so and express your regret that the problem happened at all. Be sincere. It is unfortunate this occurred, not least because of what it has done to your self image. If the matter has been resolved previously, simply take this opportunity to say how sorry you are things worked out the way they did, say something nice about the disgruntled customer, and wish him well. This is not the time to ask for future business; it is, however, the time to renew your sense of your better self and to mend this fence.

Once you have finished these letters, mail them immediately. Then pour yourself a little seasonal grog. Lift your glass high and toast — yourself. What you've done places you in a very select band of marketers, the people who understand that success without humanity is hollow indeed. But you not only know this; you've acted on this. This is why you can hold your head high and move enthusiastically into what is certain to be the most successful year of your life, a year into which you move unimpeded by the draining baggage of thanks unrendered, rage unassuaged, or shame unconfessed. With all these well and truly taken care of, now you can concentrate indeed!

14

What To Do When You Have So Many Qualified Prospects, You Can't Handle Them All Yourself . . . Or How To Make More Money Managing Service Delivery

In the beginning of your service business, you'll very likely do everything. You'll be the person who designs the service, markets the service, delivers the service, perfects the service, augments the service and, for good measure, washes the windows and takes out the garbage. While I am not going to tell you you cannot become a millionaire this way (you can), I am going to tell you if you do things like this, it'll take you a lot longer than it should. Here's a more likely alternative:

- Start by delivering the service and marketing the service. A veritable Louis XIV, you are the company!

- Begin doing what is necessary to bring in others to deliver the service so you can concentrate more on marketing the service and administering the delivery of the service and necessary business pertaining thereunto.

- Deliver less of the service yourself, relying more on independent contractors, spend more time on marketing and administration.

- Spend virtually all your time on marketing and administering the service and, only as a mark of honor, delivering the service personally to very selected customers.

Now you know where you should be going in your service business. The question is, where are you on this continuum now and what do you have to do to move things along smartly?

Concentrate On Developing Your Lead-Generation System

The first and vital prerequisite in developing your service business as outlined above is concentrating on the development of your lead-generating system. Sadly, most service businesses do nothing more than generate the number of leads they need to maintain their current level of business. True, this may be enough to support their current lifestyle, but it doesn't help in the development of more wealth. Thus, you must look first to generating more leads . . . the entire purpose of this book. If you want to augment your wealth faster, you must do everything you can to generate more qualified leads faster, the objective being to generate many, many more than you can possibly handle yourself. Developing wealth is as simple as that.

As you develop a superfluity of leads, the following things will happen:

- You can be very selective about whom you'll work with, a real benefit.
- You won't be able personally to work with all the leads, even the well qualified ones. You'll need help!
- You'll be forced to look for additional well-qualified people to assist you deliver the benefits of your service.
- As you gather these people, you'll be forced to do what is necessary to ensure the quality of their work and hence the continuing reputation of your business.
- You will spend less and less time delivering services yourself, and become, to a greater and greater extent, the manager of a prosperity producing service delivery system that will achieve greater wealth faster.

Analyze What You Do. Can It Be Successfully Offered By Others?

But, you insist, what I do is unique. No one else can do it. I'm the only person in the entire world who can offer the service I offer. No one else can offer it or will ever be able to offer it. Hmmm . . .

Now I'm willing to believe that there are people in the world who can say this about their service, but for most of us, no matter how good we are at what we do, there are others who can do what we do (nearly) as well as we do . . . certainly well enough so that our customers are pleased with the results. The first thing you must overcome, then, is a sense of your unique indispensability. While you may be good, even very, very good, the chances are very small indeed that you are indispensable, and if you are not indispensable, you can find others to do what you do. This may not sound like a good thing, but, believe me, you'll want to get over the "uniqueness" hump so that you can begin to profit from the work of as many people as possible. Herein lies the road to real riches as a service seller.

To move towards this objective, start by analyzing just what you do. List every service you provide and list everything you do in providing this service. The goal is to determine if there really is anything you do that is unique, that others really cannot do. Thus, as a copywriter my job is to generate more leads and make more sales for businesses of every kind by improving the drawing power of all their marketing communications. To this end, I must:

- review their current marketing communications;
- analyze their results;
- transform product and service features into benefits;
- create compelling offers;
- gather and craft testimonials;
- transform "me-centered" prose into sleek, motivational client-centered prose;
- negotiate with clients to accept my point of view about how they should market their products/services;
- make corrections and changes based on our discussions;
- work with graphic designers to ensure that the final result has both visual impact and appeal;
- suggest changes in the copy and art based on the results, *etc.*

Now, I'd like to tell you that I'm the only person in the world who can do these things. I would, however, be kidding myself and lying to you. In fact, there are tens of thousands of marketing copywriters around the world. Granted the vast majority do their jobs in a pedestrian fashion. However, the point is that, with proper instruction and oversight, they could improve . . . and create marketing communications which would improve client results. As such they could be integrated into an expanded service empire. Moreover, there are many others who are very good and don't need further training. They have the skills to get people to buy from the marketing communications they produce.

Either way, there are people available who could provide my clients with a beneficial service which would produce results for them. So long as you're not the only person who can do this, your task is to find others who might be able to perform this service and begin to explore the advisability of having them do so.

Note: I am concentrating in this chapter on finding and working with other service deliverers, people who can deliver the kinds of benefits you deliver. However, after you've reviewed the steps to providing your service, you may find that an administrative assistant type could perform some of the tasks which need to be done and hence free you up to perform more crucial tasks yourself. Do this!

Bringing in an administrative assistant to perform more mundane tasks makes a lot of sense. Indeed, you'll be able to get a lot more better-paying service-delivery work done if you bite the bullet and hire such a person — as soon as your revenues warrant doing so. Which is to say as soon as you've got your lead-generating system moving along well and are closing more leads faster.

Recruiting Service Providers Into Your Network

Right from the first day running your service business, you should be considering augmenting your business by bringing in other service providers. To be sure, until such time as you have a constant flow of leads, actually bringing in these people doesn't make sense. I think, for instance, of one ill-advised computer consultant I know who actually hired another full-time computer technician (whom she expected to rent out on an hourly and project basis) her first week in business, long before she had her lead stream in place. Net result? She had to pay her would-be consultant but had no money to do so. Her slender capital resources were quickly exhausted. She became both bitter at her employee (what was he doing, she kept wondering) and frustrated about the lack of progress. In short order, she was bankrupt and on the street, in debt with a hefty bank loan to pay back. She went to daddy to bail her out. What would you do?

Who's fault is this kind of disaster? Why the business owner's, of course. She definitely put the cart (additional staff) before the horse (her lead-generating system) and, like Humpty Dumpty, she had a great fall. This, of course, will not happen to you . . .

Instead of hiring additional help before you've got the lead-generating system and business to sustain them, rather than having them drain your resources, you should:

- Identify all the places where fellow service providers are likely to be found. This includes ads in the yellow pages, professional organizations, formal networking groups, listings posted by unemployment offices, continuing education classes and, of course, referrals from people you already know in the field.

- Start looking before you need people. Go through the yellow pages and ask each related service provider to send you his information kit. Join professional organizations, review the roster of members, and follow up individuals in the same way. Go to networking events and while looking for business for yourself (always that!) find out who else offers services similar to yours. Make it a point to get acquainted with such people. Find out who handles listings for your kind of service at the unemployment office and how often new information is posted. Follow up accordingly. Review the offerings of community and four-year colleges and local continuing education programs to see who is teaching classes in your field. Almost universally these people are service providers themselves. And, of course, ask everyone you meet in your field who is good, who is looking for work, *etc.*

- It should go without saying by now that you'll open a computer file for this information. Title it "IC" for independent contractors. Compile the potential independent contractor name, company, address, phone number, fax, as well as anything you've heard about this person, who told you, whether you've requested materials from this person, who might provide a reference, *etc.* In short, start a personnel dossier. *Note:* if you've asked the potential independent contractor to send you materials about his work, note when you asked for them and when you received them. This will be an indication of how hungry the person is and how organized.

Note: as part of your client-survey questionnaire, you can add a question about whether the prospect has ever worked with any one in your field in your marketing territory. If so, find out who this person is and whether he did good work. This is another way of getting a lead to an independent contractor.

Another note: as with so many other aspects of business, service providers often wait far too long to look for people who can provide their service. Thus, when they need additional assistance, they have to take the first person they can find. This is a mistake. Start immediately! And look continually! You should provide yourself with the luxury of choice in working with independent contractors. Only by providing yourself with many leads will you be able to do so.

Ensuring Your Independent Contractor Prospects Are Suitable

One of the biggest problems you'll face if you use independent contractors is making sure they'll give your clients suitable work. The solution to this problem begins long before you enter into any relationship with an independent contractor. Thus:

- Whenever possible, start getting information about the service provider before you meet him. If someone you know has used this provider, quiz him closely about the results he obtained and the process that the provider used to obtain them. If you hear positive reports, you can move on to the next step in the process, actually meeting the provider; if you don't, that's probably not necessary.

  By the same token, whenever possible review the provider's work before meeting him. With copywriters, this is easy to do. It is less easy if you're hiring a caterer where the results are devoured. In any case, try to find out what you can from those who have used the service provider and otherwise worked with him about the quality of what he does and his professional habits.

- When you do decide a meeting is necessary, write the independent contractor prospect a letter advising him that you need additional assistance to provide service to your customers, that you wonder if the prospect would be interested in providing such assistance; if so you'd like to schedule a meeting at your office, and that in preparation for this meeting could the prospect kindly send you some samples of his work (if applicable) and/or references from satisfied clients (a must). Further, could the prospect provide you with an indication of the services he provides, his fee scale, and any special conditions that apply?

- What the prospect does now will tell you something you need to know about how he works. A prospect who is interested and client-centered (you are, after all, now a client prospect for him) will contact you immediately to let you know he's received your letter (or fax), that he is interested in seeing what you've got in mind, that he will send materials (if available) and information about those who can recommend his work, and will follow up by phone in a few days to schedule the meeting at your convenience. In short, he'll either clearly indicate to you if he wants the work and is capable of behaving in a professional fashion — or he'll show you he doesn't. Thus, note the day you sent your communication, what you asked for, the day the prospect responded, and how he handled your request. You may, at this point, learn enough so that you need not learn any more. As Ann Landers says, "The sample was ample." *Note:* before the meeting contact the references the prospect has provided. Ask tough questions like: What did the prospect do for you? What kinds of results did you get? Was the prospect easy to work with? Was he a problem solver willing to help you, or did he create problems of his own that got in the way of the work he was supposed to be doing for you? Would you hire him again? Do you have any reservations about his work or person? Again, what you discover may make you change your mind about the scheduled meeting.

- Remember, the meeting starts as soon as the prospect appears, and you can gather important information accordingly. Does he make a good appearance? Is this the kind of person you want representing you? Did he arrive on time, or was he late? If late, did he call, or just keep you waiting? Did he bring the materials you asked him to bring, or did he forget? Each of these things may be trifling individually but taken together they can well create a very clear picture about the person you're thinking of using. Make sure you don't miss their significance.

- During the formal portion of the meeting be clear with the prospect about what you're trying to do: namely expand your business by being able to offer more customers your services. Say that you are interested in adding more service providers to handle the increasing volume of your business. Give the prospect basic information about what you do; (by all means share marketing communications which elucidate your service). Then ask him about his experience not just providing a comparable service . . . but in achieving meaningful results.

- Whenever possible, review a particular case with the service provider, a case similar to one you might have him handle for you. What was the problem? What needed to be done? And, specifically, how did the service provider go about handling it?

- Listen carefully. Is this the kind of person who seems to know what he's talking about? Did his presentation of the issue make sense? Did what he do to solve it? And what about the materials he's showing you? Do they support his claim (whether explicit or not) that he did a superior, client-pleasing job? Further, did he provide a client testimonial to support his claim? (If not, by all means ask for the relevant information so you can contact the client yourself.)

I have discovered over the years, having participated in many of these kinds of interview sessions, that virtually everyone thinks the work he has done is superior. Virtually every service provider will tell you that he does good work, that the customers are happy, that all is well in this, the best of all possible worlds. However this assumption must be taken with a grain of salt. Sadly, if you are the kind of person I think you are, other service providers may not, probably will not, share your commitment to superior results. Thus, while within *their* context the results are fine, within yours they may well be mediocre. Anticipate this. Thus, ask the probing questions which will enable you to determine if you are dealing with the kind of plodding provider all too common or with someone whom you will be proud to be represented by.

It is very likely the prospect will have detailed questions for you, too. He'll most likely want to know:

- when you might have work;
- what kind of work it will be;

- what you'll want him to do:
- how much you'll pay him for this work, and
- any special conditions which apply to handling this work or working with you generally.

Answer these questions as completely and honestly as possible. This is essential if you are to have a good working relationship with this person, including being able to get any additional information you need before deciding to hire him.

Thus:

- when you might have work. Tell him this depends on your lead-generating system. I would not advise going into great detail on what you are doing (he is a potential or actual competitor, after all). But you should still be able to provide some estimate when work might become available based on what you're currently doing.

- what kind of work it will be. Here you should explain just what kind of work you do, going from the work you most often are asked to perform down to services you provide more occasionally. Unless you are altering the focus of your marketing efforts, you can fairly well predict what kind of service your clients will want you to provide. Just make sure this prospect can do it!

- what you'll want him to do. Be clear about what tasks this prospect would most likely be performing. This is especially important if he'll be working along with you or others in a team situation.

- how much you'll pay. There is no need to be sheepish about this. Either you'll be offering a fixed, flat rate of payment (which is more likely to be the case with independent contractors who offer a more technical service), or you'll need to negotiate fees based on what the independent contractor usually charges. Either way, it's a subject that interests both of you. Unless you offer fair payment, the prospect won't be much interested in working for you. And you've got to know his range so that you can factor this payment into the estimate you give to a client.

- any special conditions which apply. There might well be special circumstances pertaining to you, the independent contractor, or the job. Do you need week-end or holiday work? Is the independent contractor able to provide this? What about travel? It is most important for you to specify what you might need (or the job require) and for the independent contractor prospect to be equally forthright about his own special requirements.

As the meeting progresses and the prospect supplies information, by all means take detailed notes. Or, tape the meeting (after asking the prospect's permission). This will enable you to replay the conversation at your convenience and consider things further.

Unless you have a job that needs attending to immediately, don't feel pressed to make any decision about this prospect now. If you've followed my advice, you are holding this meeting well before you need to make a decision. Thus, it's purely exploratory. There's nothing wrong in telling the prospect this. "I want to thank you for coming. I have appreciated all that you've told me. I shall be reviewing the tape of this meeting and the written materials and samples you've provided me and will contact you again if I have further questions." In short, no commitment. Just the promise to approach this matter in the serious, conservative, thorough spirit it deserves. Remember, you are going to entrust your reputation to this person. There is, therefore, no reason to rush . . .

. . . unless you have a job that needs to be done. Being human, you may well have waited until you cannot do everything yourself. Thus, you must make a decision promptly. Even here, don't rush. Make sure you ask all the questions you need to; then take the time to review what you've learned (including the information you received from people providing recommendations for the prospect) and consider your options. Are you comfortable this prospect will do a good job for you and your client? Or are you so desperate for assistance you'll take the risk and just hope things will work out? Don't do that. Remember the importance of getting results and don't trust yourself to anyone whom you have doubts about providing them. In the final analysis, it is better to put off a client for a bit than risk your reputation by relying on a hunch that may not pan out.

Developing The Independent Contractor Services Agreement

However, once you're ready to go ahead, it's time to solidify your relationship in an Independent Contractor Services Agreement. I have discussed this matter at length in both my consulting books, **THE CONSULTANT'S KIT** and **HOW TO MAKE AT LEAST $100,000 EVERY YEAR AS A SUCCESSFUL CONSULTANT IN YOUR OWN FIELD.** I refer you to these resources for further information. Here, however, I wish to provide basic details about this agreement.

— What the Independent Contractor Services Agreement is

This agreement is a contractual understanding between yourself, the primary service provider, and those independent contractors you have retained to provide specified services to designated customers at a particular time, for a particular fee. It sets out the rights and responsibilities of both parties as the basis for your professional relationship.

— Why you want it

The reason you want such an agreement is to make the role and duties of each party perfectly clear so there is no confusion later on about who is to do what. Further, you want it explicitly understood and acknowledged that the independent contractor is *not* an employee of your firm but an independent contractor so that you are not later liable to pay anything beyond the independent contractor's agreed-upon professional stipend. This is most important.

— What should be in the Independent Contractor Services Agreement

This agreement, which should be signed by both parties before any work is undertaken by the independent contractor, should be composed of the following sections:

Section 1: List of the parties and a description of their businesses. This is a contract between ABC Corporation, Inc. of 11 Waterhouse Ave., Burlington, IA 40505, herein referred to as "ABC", a purveyor of marketing services, and Ms. Wanda Schmidt of 4906 Woodward Ave., Spirit Lake, IA 40506, marketing copywriter, herein referred to as "independent contractor", for the performance of the services described below.

Section 2: The relationship of the parties to this agreement. ABC is an Iowa corporation engaged in part in the business of providing individuals and organizations with marketing communications services. Independent contractor is a person who by education, training or experience is skilled in providing such services. The parties intend that an independent contractor-employer relationship be created by this contract. Independent contractor is not to be considered an agent or employee of ABC for any purpose.

Section 3: Duties. ABC agrees to provide contractor with the following assignment: (list of contractor responsibilities). In accepting this assignment, the independent contractor agrees to use diligence and professional skill in the completion of all tasks. Independent contractor further agrees to submit the work in question, in finished, professional quality form, to ABC on or before (date).

Section 4: Consideration. Upon timely receipt of the aforementioned material, ABC agrees to pay independent contractor the sum of (amount). The parties agree that no payment shall be made for the independent contractor's meals, travel costs, travel time, accommodations, telephone calls, stationery, supplies, *etc.*

Section 5: Cancellation. The parties agree that this contract is not subject to cancellation, except in the event that (contracting party's client) withdraws its request for the project described above. In such event, this contract will be canceled as of the date the contractor can be reasonably notified of such withdrawal. Contractor agrees to use telephone, fax or overnight delivery service, where applicable, to deliver this notification. ABC agrees to pay independent contractor for all days and fractions of days actually worked, at the rate described above, prior to such notification.

Section 6: Confidentiality. It is understood that in the performance of his/her duties, the independent contractor will obtain information about both ABC and (contracting party's client), and that such information may include financial data, client lists, methods of operation, policy statements, and other confidential data.

Independent contractor agrees to restrict his/her use of such information to the performance of duties described in this contract. Independent contractor further agrees to return to ABC and to (contracting party's client) upon the completion of his/her duties any and all documents (originals and copies) taken from either organization to facilitate the project described above.

Section 7: Bars competition. Independent contractor agrees that ABC has established the relationship with (contracting party's client) and that (contracting party's client) is to be considered a client of ABC. Independent contractor agrees not to approach this client or other clients supplied by ABC with a view towards this client/these clients directly purchasing services from independent contractor both for the duration of this contract and for a period of one year thereafter.

Section 8: Applicable law. The parties agree that this contract is to be construed as an Iowa contract.

Section 9: Assignability. Neither party can assign nor delegate its rights or duties under this contract without the express, written consent of the other party.

Section 10: Terms of contract. This contract will become effective immediately and shall remain in effect until the promises and duties described therein have been fully performed.

Section 11: Integration. This contract, executed in duplicate, sets forth the entire contract between the parties and may be canceled, modified, or amended only by a written instrument executed by each of the parties here, or as specifically provided in this contract.

Section 12: Date and signatures. Witness the signatures of the parties hereto, each duly authorized, this (date) of (month) of (year). ABC Corporation by (signature, title). Independent contractor (signature, title).

Some Commentary On Clauses Of The Independent Contractor Services Agreement

Section 3: Be very clear about what you want the independent contractor to do. Do not assume anything. If you need a task done to achieve results for the client and you are expecting the independent contractor to do it, say so here and specify what that task is. Here's where it's very important to walk through the job and be clear about how results are going to be achieved and who does what when.

Section 4: This section is written from the perspective of the hiring party, that is you! The independent contractor will very likely see things differently. In other words, the independent contractor will try to get some payment up front, or at least some payment before the work is done. When you are familiar with the independent contractor, know his work and trust his ability to deliver, this is fine. But at least the first time you do business with a new independent contractor, withhold all payment until you are sure things are going along smoothly. The independent contractor cannot be expected to like this, but if you pay money to an independent contractor who doesn't deliver what you told the client he'd deliver, the responsibility is yours. You could easily get into a situation where the independent contractor won't cooperate with you and the client rightly demands that you fulfill your engagement with him, the worst of all possible worlds. So, at least for the first time you work with the independent contractor, keep full control.

On the matter of expenses, if the client is paying for meals, travel, telephone expenses, *etc.*, then it is right the independent contractor should be reimbursed for these. What you include here, therefore, is directly related to the expenses the client is paying. Be fair to your independent contractor!

Section 7: The non-competitive component is key.

As you are very well aware, it has taken a lot of work to get this client. You've had to think through your service, learn how to deliver results, and become the master of a lead-generating and lead-closing system. It's easy for an independent contractor to forget this when he sees that you've got a client he could as easily work with directly as through you. Indeed, the short-sighted independent contractor may, in a kind of professional lust, willingly overthrow you and the possibilities of your relationship for the short -term gain of working with one or more of your clients directly. You can't let this happen!!! That's why you must include a non-competitive clause in all your engagements with independent contractors.

Smooth-talking independent contractors may well teli you they will respect your rights but, for whatever reason, won't commit themselves in writing. You are right to mistrust such people. Without this clause, you are making it far too tempting for the independent contractor to steal your client and claim, as so often happens, that it was the client's idea that you be robbed of your part in this relationship.

Section 9: It's important that the independent contractor not be allowed to sub-contract his responsibilities without your express permission. If he does, you'll have less control over the process than ever. Make sure you've imposed such language that if the independent contractor wishes to employ his own sub-contractor that he be forced to deal with you first. Then you can make the determination about whether the person he wishes to do the work is actually qualified to do so.

Working With Your Service Providers: Developing An Oversight And Reporting System

Bringing in other people to provide your service will help you become a millionaire faster. It could also give you a lot of problems that you didn't have before. Luckily, most are avoidable if you approach the business of overseeing your independent contractors in the same cautious, sensible way you handled recruiting them in the first place. Here is what you must do:

- Establish oversight and reporting procedures before you hire anyone. The solution to working with independent contractors begins before you actually start working with them. Open a computer text file called "oversight", and enter your guidelines. Include the following:

- If you need oral reports, consider how many you'll need and when you should get them. Personally, (you already know I'm an obsessive communicator) I like to get reports at the end of *each* day and also more frequently when crucial parts of a project are under consideration. As previously discussed, these reports can be as short as a few minutes so long as you get all the information you need.

- If you need written reports, provide a handy form the independent contractor can either fax or mail to you and an indication of how often you'll need them. The easier you make it for the independent contractor to give you data, the more likely you are to get them.

- Make it clear both when you interview a prospective independent contractor and when you hire one that providing you with regular reports is part of the job. It is easy for most independent contractors to forget this. They concentrate, if they're good, on doing the job right and on time; they do not see that reporting to you is an essential part of their responsibilities. Further, because they are *independent* contractors, they are probably not used to reporting to anyone; it's not part of the way they generally do business. They must, therefore, be trained to report. Further, if the independent contractor is eminent, he probably hasn't had to report to anyone besides his clients in a long time and therefore may resent doing so or seek to evade this portion of his responsibilities. Indeed, working with "eminent" independent contractors is often needlessly difficult for this very reason, since they feel they're beyond having to report to anyone . . . to the detriment of your position. Remind such people, however, that *you* are the client in this instance, and you trust you'll be treated with the same professionalism and courtesy they extend to their other clients!

- Establish good oversight and reporting procedures right from the start. If you've asked for a regular end-of-day report and the first day you don't get it, don't wait and hope that things will be better tomorrow. Ask the independent contractor to provide it *immediately*. Moreover, if you get the report and it's sketchy, press for the details you need to determine if things are actually proceeding on course. I have learned from sad experience that when everything you're hearing is vague that's a clear indication things are not getting done, whatever the independent contractor says to the contrary. Indeed, in one notable case, I took the word of a purportedly professional marketer that "everything was going along fine" and that he was "on top of the situation" for thirty days while I devoted myself to other, pressing matters only to find at the end of the month that this man had done nothing and that the project was in a terrible mess. Of course, I blame him for the deception, but I blame myself more. Had I followed my own good advice, I would have known in 24 hours, not 30 days, that I had a problem on my hand. Deduction: if you're not hearing information about specific results, chances are very good you've got a problem on your hands, and you should act accordingly.

- Make sure you take the time to review any written materials, plans, samples, *etc.* that the independent contractor may have produced. Again, never take the independent contractor's word for it that things are going well. Take time to see for yourself . Unless you have worked with the independent contractor before and really know how he functions (insight which a single job cannot provide), insist on getting all the information you need in the way you want it. Further, as the deadline for the job approaches, be willing to spend even more time ensuring that everything is going along so that the client will get what he wants . . . so that you can leverage this job to get more business for yourself — and the independent contractor who delivers!

What Happens When The Independent Contractor Doesn't Perform Up To The Client's Standards — Or Yours?

Using the techniques I've just given you should reduce your problems substantially. Still, you may well find yourself in situations where your worst fears are not just insubstantial phantoms, but unhappily real: your independent contractor is letting you down. Now what? "What" is directly related to how much time you have left before the client's project is to be satisfactorily completed. That's why staying on top of an independent contractor and his work is so important from the beginning; it gives you maximum time either to correct the problem with this independent contractor or arrange an alternative. However, if you sense or discover you have problems, do the following:

- Get an *immediate* status report from the independent contractor. You want to know *exactly* how matters stand, what the problems are, and whether the independent contractor understands and is willing to do what is necessary to correct them.

You can't do anything until you have a situation report, until you are given the facts about the matter in question and about what the independent contractor is doing to rectify things. Get this report as fully and as soon as possible.

Note: just how the independent contractor handles providing you these details will tell you a lot about how bad your problem really is. Will he schedule a meeting? Take your call? Does he answer questions directly? Is he willing to assume any responsibility for the situation? Or do you sense you're getting the run-around? In my experience, responsible people, while occasionally procrastinating, allowing themselves to fall behind, or acting erratically, act responsibly. Remind your independent contractor that you expect his responsible assistance now. If he is the responsible person you thought you hired, chances are you'll get it. If he's not, you're going to know right away. That's when you've *really* got a problem . . .

- Once you've had a status report, think. Consider your options. Do you really think this independent contractor, given what you've heard and the time remaining, can salvage this project, not just so it's completed but so that you can provide the client, the vitally important person in this whole scenario, with satisfactory results? Why do you think this? I hope you're not just relying on what an already suspect independent contractor has told you. It's easy to make promises after all . . .

- If you decide the independent contractor can salvage this situation himself, without additional direct help in providing the service, then give both him and yourself a deadline for seeing whether improvement is going to happen. Don't just rely on this independent contractor's rather flawed word; give him a deadline for improvement. How much time does he need to show the kind of improvement you need to feel that he can handle the job without bringing in the cavalry? Half a day? A day? Two days? Notice these time periods are short. Remember, you have a deadline approaching, and you can't waste one of your most valuable resources: time. Whatever you decide, you must monitor this situation closely. Get frequent reports, perhaps as often as every two or three hours. Some people work better under this kind of close scrutiny and where there's an important deadline approaching such minute oversight is clearly in your interest. At the very least, it will provide you with more conclusive data about what you should do next.

- If you decide that the independent contractor cannot handle his part in this project alone anymore, then what are your options for relieving him? The next option is seeing whether he can handle *any* part of the work he is supposed to be doing. Once you know the independent contractor cannot do that for which you retained him, very cool thinking is mandatory. Just how cool depends on the clock ticking closer to your deadline and your desire to avoid an outraged customer . . . with all the problems that entails both presently and as regards the possibility of future work and referrals.

- Once you've decided the independent contractor needs help, explore your options. Who do you have available to assist? Another independent contractor? A member of your staff? You yourself? All may be possibilities. Just what you do depends on how serious the matter is and how much help the independent contractor needs. Frankly, I'd play this very, very conservative . . . which means making extra assistance available quicker rather than threatening your client relationship. It is usually easier, after all, to find a replacement for a shoddy independent contractor than for a good client.

- If you decide to keep the independent contractor involved in the problem-solving process, determine with him exactly what he will do and exactly what others will do to expedite matters. Make sure that this division of labor is realistic. You must secure the explicit assurance of the independent contractor that he can handle this new assignment . . . and you must make the commitment to watch him carefully so that you can be assured he does. Of course, this new division of labor changes your original engagement. The independent contractor while no doubt gladly giving up the work probably won't be so happy about giving up the extra consideration. Yet this, too, is necessary. A renegotiated contract must accompany the new division of work. Again, the failure of your independent contractor to work with you to make this new contract as quickly and smoothly as possible indicates the severity of your problem with him and the fact that his further involvement in this process may be inadvisable.

- Indeed, you may have already reached this point. You may have already decided that this independent contractor is not worth the trouble he's giving you and that his inability to deliver the necessary results by the specified deadline poses a greater threat to you and your company than anything you do to sever the relationship now. As a result, it's time to take decisive action to save your relationship with your client. *Note:* many service providers have a hard time reaching this decision sufficiently quickly. As a result, they squander precious time and limit their options. Don't make this mistake! You must keep in mind that the most important person in the triangular relationship between you, your independent contractor, and your client is the *client.* Whenever possible, the client's interests must be safeguarded above all others. This means trying to solve this troublesome problem with your independent contractor without alerting the client that there's a problem, or by handling it so that the client is inconvenienced as little as possible. It is easy to forget this important fact when a harassed independent contractor is throwing all kinds of "dog-ate-my-homework" excuses at you about why he's unable to do what he's contracted to do. Don't let your sympathy for the independent contractor, who put you in this situation after all, obscure the client's interest, which is more vital.

- Once you've determined that the problem-creating independent contractor cannot be part of the solution, take instant action to solve the two problems you now have: relieving yourself of the burden of this uncooperative independent contractor and getting the job done by the alternative you've selected. As for the first, notify the independent contractor by phone and confirm by fax that his services have been terminated because of his inability to satisfy your client. Ask for the return of all papers, documents, materials, *etc.* he has which bear on the client and this case. Ask him to inform you immediately how he intends to get these materials to you. If you have an account with an overnight carrier, supply your account number to expedite shipment. Ask him to confirm immediately that he has stopped work on the project and made arrangements for you to have all the materials. You've got another problem if this doesn't happen . . . but if you have withheld at least a portion of the independent contractor's stipend, you have some leverage. If you cannot get prompt confirmation of these points, notify the independent contractor that no further payment will be made until it is resolved and that failure to provide the needed materials promptly will result in a regular diminution of what the independent prospect is due. Remember . . . you have a client to satisfy and this kind of escalation, made necessary by the independent contractor's failure to act in anything remotely resembling a professional manner, has made such tactics necessary. Many service providers forget this and because they feel guilty about using such methods, do little or nothing. This does nothing to solve their two problems!

- If the independent contractor remains recalcitrant, or becomes threatening in turn, escalate further. Make it clear that if your reasonable demands are not met, you will be forced to take prompt legal action against the independent contractor for the monetary damages resulting from his behavior. At this point, you'll have to estimate what these damages are. If you're not sure what a reasonable number is, just give them as the total value of the contract plus legal fees. Tell the independent contractor that if you do not secure satisfaction within 24 hours, you will take immediate action against him in Small Claims Court (if the amount is under the legal limit in your area) or put the matter in the hands of your attorney (if the amount exceeds the small claims limit). If you can handle the matter through a small claims suit, call the district court in your area and get the information and materials you need to file your claim and begin the legal process. File these papers promptly and send a fax or letter (return receipt requested) to the independent contractor notifying him you have filed papers against him and that you will leave the matter to the courts to determine. Say that you regret this action has been necessary, that you hope some settlement can be reached, but that if it cannot be, you'll be happy to explain the situation in court. If the independent contractor is determined to be difficult, you can do nothing more to rectify matters until the papers in your suit have been served. At that point, write once more and say that you want a settlement and outline what you want it to be. Ask for an immediate response. Proceed according to what you hear. If, before the papers have been served, you still think a settlement is possible, call and again offer to make one. Again, what you do next will be determined by the attitude and response of the independent contractor. *Note:* notifying the independent contractor that you intend to file, then notifying him that you have filed against him is an important step in inducing this creature to see reason. This kind of suit, where the burden of proof is so clearly on the independent contractor, has a marvelous ability to clear his mind . . . and so help create the climate where a meaningful settlement is possible. Just because you've filed, doesn't mean the suit will go to court. But it does mean the defendant will focus his attention on the matter and decide whether he *really* wants to be called before a judge to explain himself . . . especially when you're offering a general settlement which will solve the matter more cleanly. You must, you see, learn to use the legal system, including the courts, as a weapon . . . that's one of the things it was designed to provide. *Another note:* if the amount in question exceeds the small claims limit in your jurisdiction, get your lawyer to take prompt action against the independent contractor. The lawyer can make it clear that a suit will be filed promptly against the independent contractor and that a quick resolution is in everyone's interest. Invoking the assistance of a lawyer will signal to the independent contractor that you mean business and should help solve the problem.

- One hopes, of course, reason will otherwise prevail. Thus, if the independent contractor cooperates with you, doing what he can to facilitate the transition to the new regime, cooperate with him. Send promptly whatever he may be owed and pay whatever expenses he may be entitled to. And, for good measure, send a note saying that you hope you can work together again in the future; (it doesn't matter if you mean it). In short, unless you have reached the point of no return with this poor soul, don't burn the bridge. All religions believe in the possibility of human regeneration; so should you!

- Now, turn to the more pressing matter of getting this threatened project back on track. If you've brought another independent contractor in, I trust you've made clear what happened before and secured agreement about what needs to happen with this person, including regular progress reports, so that it does not recur. If you've had to take on the project yourself, don't feel sorry for yourself. Things could have been a lot worse . . . you might have lost not only the independent contractor but the client, too, and suffered all the indignities which come when an outraged client tears into you with righteous wroth. Yes, it could have been a lot worse . . .

Securing Good Relations With Your Independent Contractors

Fortunately, because you are going to live by the guidelines in this book, such muddled situations will not occur often; indeed, they should be as rare as the proverbial hen's tooth. Instead, you will come, as I have come, to develop solid, productive independent contractor relationships with many people. You will understand their quirks and habits, their moods and patterns of behavior (as they, bless their souls, will understand yours) so you can properly read what they're doing. Moreover, as your business matures, you'll only be adding independent contractors with studied deliberation and can therefore follow the steps above for ensuring the best results. However, with things working so well with your established independent contractors, it's easy to make another telling mistake: taking these crucial people for granted. Here's how to avoid *this* problem:

- Expand the information in your independent contractor text file. Include such information as the names of spouses, children, birthdays, anniversaries, favorite foods, interests, educational experience and graduation dates, civic and religious organizations, *etc.* These data become the basis for productive contact.

- Compliment your independent contractors often.

- Offer to provide them with testimonials they can use to build their independent businesses. You are, after all, in a position to evaluate their work and tell a prospective client (one, mind, you have not provided them) the things he needs to know to make a purchase decision.

- If an independent contractor has achieved notable results working with you, send a short media release to one of the newsletters of an organization he's connected to, be that professional or personal. This is not only a good way to secure some pleasant recognition for this person, but . . .. for yourself, too! (You will mention, won't you, that these results were secured while the independent contractor was working for you?)

- Give the unexpected gift. Follow the gift-giving suggestions I've already provided and make your independent contractor's day. And, of course, make sure it's accompanied by one of those notes for which you're now becoming famous in which you laud this important person and the relationship you've developed.

- Establish your own certificates of recognition. As you know, I make the important people in my life (both business and personal) "Companions of Raban" and have created a suitably impressive certificate which I often present at suitably impressive dinners in only the finest of restaurants. While you may not wish to go to these lengths (but why not?), the mere fact that you are running a smaller service business is no excuse for not creating a significant means of recognizing the important people who are helping you get wealthier.

For that's part of why such recognition is important. It is both right and sensible. Which is why you must provide it!

Last Words

One way and another as you generate more leads and find that the most limited resource in your life is time (one of the most infuriating aspects of human life), you'll find you either have to work with more and more independent contractors and/or take on permanent staff. While I have concentrated in this chapter on the matter of independent contractors, virtually everything I've said equally pertains to your part- and full-time staff.

The important thing is that these people be trained to provide the results you insist your clients receive and that you provide the necessary oversight so that they do. If you don't, you'll not only be generating a constant stream of qualified leads . . . but a constant stream of more or less unhappy clients who didn't get from you what they had a right to expect. What's the point of that?

Thus, you must spend the time to find the people who can provide the high caliber of benefits you demand for your clients, and you must resolve that you'll do what is necessary both to set high expectations for those who work with you and spend the time to make sure you get the results you want from them. In our corrupt times, where shoddy has become the totem of the age, you can take nothing for granted . . . whatever either your independent contractors or employees say to the contrary.

You see, the success of your business and the development of your personal prosperity is directly related to the imposition by you on all aspects of your organization of an insistent vision of excellence. Every action of every person connected with your organization either assists in the achievement of this excellence, or detracts from it. No action is or can ever be neutral; hence each action is significant and subject to your thoughtful consideration. It is the failure of too many service providers and marketers to realize this that damns their businesses to mediocrity and themselves to the perils of a diminished income.

This won't be you, however, for you now know how to generate all the leads you need and how to recruit and oversee the people to serve the prospects who just keep coming to you. Now the problem becomes developing not just direct services, which you're already doing, but the host of how-to products which will take your justly celebrated problem-solving methods nation-, if not world-, wide. This is your next great step . . .

15

Putting It All Together: Making Money From The Mobile Mini-Conglomerate

If you faithfully follow the steps I've so far laid down, you're going to be rich . . . indeed, because you've already begun to follow them, you're getting richer *right this minute*. The real question now is HOW MUCH RICHER WILL YOU GET? That entirely depends on how closely you follow these steps, how focused you are and remain and . . . how hungry you are. If you're willing to do what it takes to implement the previous chapters of this book and don't let yourself get derailed by the continuing waves of trivia that always threaten to overwhelm us, you are going to do very, very well.

But you can do even better . . .

. . . if you understand and implement the stages of the Mobile Mini-Conglomerate.

What Is The Mobile Mini-Conglomerate?

The Mobile Mini-Conglomerate is a process that enables you to take all the problem-solving information at your command and derive maximum income from it, not just now but for years to come. It has the following objectives, to:

- derive maximum income from what you know and can do by suitably packaging the skills and information at your disposal for sale to the maximum number of people both in this country and in all other places where targeted marketing groups could benefit from what you know, and

581

- assisting the maximum number of people by selling them useful information at a price which is both fair to them and to you.

A Definition Of The Mobile Mini-Conglomerate

The Mobile Mini-Conglomerate derives its name from three aspects. It's:

- *mobile* since it targets those people who can benefit from what you know and can do wherever they are located;

- *mini* because it can be run out of a small space, indeed even out of your home (as I run mine), and it's a

- *conglomerate*, because it functions just like any other multi-national corporation, being made up of a series of divisions or even separately incorporated entities, which are either wholly or in-part owned by you.

Components Of The Mobile Mini-Conglomerate

A Mobile Mini-Conglomerate is made up of the following eight parts:

1. As a service provider, you work directly with your clients/customers;
2. You hire independent contractors and/or part- or full-time employees to work with your clients/customers;
3. You publish and sell problem-solving special reports;
4. You publish and sell a money-making problem-solving newsletter;
5. You publish and sell problem-solving booklets, books;
6. You produce and sell problem-solving audio and video cassettes;
7. You provide and profit from problem-solving talk programs;
8. You publish and profit from a problem-solving catalog, which includes both your own problem-solving products/ services and the problem-solving products/services of other producers.

Please note: the MMC is *not* a sequence; it's a circuit. By that I mean, you do not have to start at Point 1 to make it work for you (although given what you are currently doing that's probably where you will start). You can break in *anywhere* and move in *any* direction, although, as you'll see, there are ways that are more logical to approach the development of your MMC.

Benefits Of The Mobile Mini-Conglomerate

There are many, many benefits of establishing your own MMC. They include:

- broadening your market. With the best will in the world, you and your service delivering employees can only deal directly with so many customers. Given your service, there will be thousands, perhaps even millions, of other people who can benefit from what you know and can do. However, for one reason or another (cost and limited time are certainly big factors), neither you nor a member of your organization will be able to directly work with them. Thanks to the conglomerate, however, you *can* work with them — through one of your problem-solving products.

- squeezing the most income from what you know. All service providers are specialists who know how to produce (at least some level of) problem-solving results. Unfortunately, both because of their limited markets and incomplete line of products and services, they do not make the maximum income from what they know and can do. With the Mobile Mini-Conglomerate this changes. You are now able to derive more income — often a very, very substantial income — thanks to the fact that you have more products/services available and increasingly broad markets.

- selling products that promote all your products and services. As you'll see, each aspect of the MMC promotes all other aspects. Thus, you find yourself in the enviable position of having your customers not only purchase problem-solving products from you, but having these promote your *other* products and services. Your customers, that is, will be *buying* your marketing materials from you . . . which is not at all what happens with other service marketers for whom marketing is an expense, not a profit center.

- creating products that create publicity for your business. The MMC enables you to derive regular publicity from products and services you're selling. Properly handled, everything you do can become the basis for the kind of publicity which will not only help develop your standing and reputation but bring in additional revenue.

- minimizing the impact of the swings that naturally occur in business. As you succeed in making each division of the MMC profitable, you will derive revenue from many sources on a regular basis, thereby making yourself increasingly immune to the ill effects of the business cycle that bedevil others. (Having just comfortably come through a major recession, I am able to testify to the importance of this point!)

- taking advantage of many marketing and promotional means not available to your competitors, including libraries, bookstores, catalogs (including end-of-product catalogs), card decks, publications, *etc.*

- spreading the cost of your office overhead and expenses among many different enterprises so that you achieve economies not available to your competitors. When you are running many different profit-making enterprises without substantially increasing your overhead, you are able to divide that overhead and so increase the profit of each undertaking.

If There Are So Many Advantages, Why Don't More Service Sellers Have A Mobile Mini-Conglomerate?

I have long wondered why, with so many advantages, more service sellers don't have even a rudimentary Mobile Mini-Conglomerate. I have arrived at the following "reasons":

- They don't understand how money is made. Most service sellers think that to make money as a service business you must provide the service yourself . . . or have an employee or independent contractor do so. This is not true. While it is certainly true that you do make money in a service business either by offering the service yourself or having your employees do so, these are by no means the only ways to make money from knowing how to deliver the results provided by your service. Personally, these days I provide very little direct service. I am far too busy creating the means and then overseeing the processes that bring the services in which I am expert to those who wish to profit from the results in one way or another. Providing these services myself would get in the way of my prosperity!

- They haven't studied and don't understand how technology has altered the way they can make money from what they know and can do. The advent of such sophisticated technology as the personal computer, fax, desk-top publishing, laser printer *etc.* has significantly altered the way a service provider can make money. Unfortunately, most service providers haven't figured this out. However, you must understand that the ever-changing technologies at your disposal are nothing more than means provided to you to reach ever expanding and more closely targeted constituencies which could, if properly motivated, provide you with escalating amounts of money. Technology, in short, is your best friend in making more and still more money. Unfortunately, most service providers simply concentrate on their labor intensive tasks (in the name of "personal service"), forgetting how mastering the available technologies will enable them to bring their problem-solving methodologies to the benefit of thousands more than they can ever deal with through the means they're currently employing.

- They haven't understood that the new world order is made up of highly specific groups of prospects and that the interests of these prospects are similar wherever they are located. Your job, therefore, is to serve these interests (and make money) wherever these prospects are to be found . . . not just the ones in your immediate neighborhood. The Great Age of Marketing, into which we are now well along, is an age of specificities. More and more the world is made up of groups which are either highly defined or highly define themselves in terms of their very specific interests, outlooks and characteristics. There is a very negative side to this intensified self- and other-identification; the race wars already under way in the former Soviet Union, in the Balkans and elsewhere are proof of that. Indeed, the remainder of our lives will be severely troubled by this kind of identification; various marketers will take full advantage of that fact. On the other hand, for our purposes this kind of highly specific identification is a good thing. It enables us to vastly expand our marketing territories (and areas of profit) from the neighborhoods which once characterized virtually all service businesses and still characterize most, to generating clients and revenue from all appropriate groups wherever they are in the world. Thus, even the smallest service business, properly focused, can have a significant national or international dimension — even if it is located in what, by previous standards, would have been a most unpromising area for establishing a service business, (a small town, isolated mountaintop, *etc.*). *Note:* You'll find useful information about how to profit from places previously thought unsuitable for business by consulting the book *Country Bound.* Written by my friends Tom & Marilyn Ross, you can get a copy from Communication Creativity, Box 1500-NLR, Buena Vista, CO 81211 (719) 395-2459.

- They haven't understood the different methods available for tapping into the expanded markets. The average service provider who either delivers his service directly or offers his service through independent contractors or employees offers a high-priced service. Because services are based on labor and because the cost of labor in this country is high, the cost of the service is necessarily high, often dwarfing the cost of whatever materials are necessary to provide the service. This high cost necessarily limits the provision of the service to those who can pay this high price. If this is all you offer, you therefore lose the benefits to be derived from those who want your service and the results it delivers . . . but cannot pay your price. The MMC solves this problem . . . if you understand the various means of both distributing products and services.

A person wishing to benefit from an MCC makes a conscious decision to truly understand how all the technical aspects of the system work. He commits himself to mastering the recruitment and overseeing of independent contractors; the production and marketing of audio and video cassettes, special reports, booklets and books; the creation and marketing of talk programs, *etc.* Each of these aspects of the MMC is based on certain technical specifications which can be mastered by any service provider . . . but usually aren't. The developer of an MMC is necessarily a continual student of both the means of production and the means of distribution. He is consistently keen to discover how to produce more products and services at less cost and how to reach and close more and more prospects at less cost . . . so that his profit is continually greater.

- They do not have and will not get the necessary technical skills. If you are going to succeed in running a money-making MMC, there are certain skills you need. Among these are writing, speaking, negotiation, organizing and other crucial product/service development and management skills. Each of these skills can be learned, yet few service providers make the commitment to do so. Is it any wonder, then, that they do not profit from what they know or can do?

- They accept the second rate and are willing to excuse the fact that they are wallowing in it. I have a college-educated, service-providing acquaintance who lives nearby in a small apartment. He sleeps on a mattress on the floor, has no possessions of any value, has a net worth of well under $5000, eats the most nondescript food and wears the most nondescript clothes. Now 35, he tells me he's ambitious, but when I quiz him about what he is doing, about why he has only written one article in his career and has nothing in the works, about why he isn't giving talk programs and lectures, he tells me that 1) there is time enough, 2) he's happy with the way things are, and 3) anyway talking to me is unsettling! He has learned, you see, to accept the second rate, to justify whatever he does, to talk about progress instead of working to achieve progress. As a result he is vulgar in the truest meaning of this word — and will likely always remain so. He, of course, considers himself well adjusted. I consider him a travesty of what a service provider should be and a disgrace to the way a successful service provider should live and behave. If you see yourself mirrored in any way in this paragraph, it is time for you to commit yourself to the revolution . . . it is time, that is, for you to commit yourself to understanding and profiting from the Mobile Mini-Conglomerate.

How You Take Your Problem-Solving Knowledge And Skills And Package Them Through The Mobile Mini-Conglomerate

Let's now look more closely at each aspect of the MMC. As we do, I'll provide some further insight into how it works by showing you how I've developed mine through one of my services, namely helping sell more client products/services faster. Thus:

- Working directly with your clients/customers. This, by now, should be fairly self-explanatory. Here you are the direct service provider. You develop your client-centered service(s) and provide them yourself. Many of the readers of this book, and certainly those just starting out in their own service business, will be at this point. Fair enough. You now know how to make this aspect of the MMC work . . . and how to grow beyond it. For myself, as a marketing consultant I work directly with targeted individuals and organizations interested in selling more of their products and services. Among the many services I offer are: researching current markets to see how to increase business, researching new markets, analyzing and improving marketing communications, training staff, providing regular situation analysis and suggesting improvements, *etc.* In short, working directly to improve bottom-line results. As already outlined, your job is to develop as many related services as you can, to be able to offer them individually or, whenever possible, as part of more lucrative packages.

- Hiring independent contractors and/or part- and full-time employees to work with your customers/clients. Whereas above you were both primary lead generator and primary service provider, here your focus changes so that you concentrate more on lead generation and on simultaneously ensuring that you have available all the qualified personnel to handle both the leads and ensuing business.

Note: many service providers arrive at this point (indeed, for most, it's as far as they ever go). However, when they do they make a major error by defining their service territories in far too limited a manner. What you should be asking yourself is: do I provide a service that could be offered in other areas through independent contractors or employees? Do I need to be physically present to oversee these contractors? If so, could I still extend my marketing territories by taking on one or a series of partners who could be responsible for organizing the delivery of services in various areas? Could I set up a leads-generating system which would produce all the leads these different divisions would require?

If you've answered yes to these questions, you should consider all the alternatives for handling this situation and not accept any artificial limits on your development. You can either work with an independent contractor, hire an employee, or set up a separate business with a managing partner. In the latter case, the managing partner could either get the leads directly (or you could have them sent to you for dissemination), could handle some or part of the work himself (or arrange with local independent contractors to handle all of it), and remit regular reports and appropriate payments to you. The key to this system is working with someone you trust . . . someone who will follow up the leads promptly, close them in a timely, professional manner, who will either do professional work or oversee the production of such work and who will handle the finances in a trustworthy manner. Personally, I have found such a person in Dan McComas, previously an independent copywriter, now Director of my National Copywriting Center.

The National Copywriting Center is a good illustration of how technology, an appropriate division of responsibilities, and some good old-fashioned personal characteristics have shaped a profitable business. I am based in Massachusetts and am in charge of generating leads from anyone who needs marketing communications; Dan is based in Maryland where he functions as managing partner of this enterprise and where he and other copywriters provide the service. This system works because of our mutual solid business skills, client-centered focus, and regular communication between us. As a result, we have taken what has generally been a fairly localized cottage industry, the production of marketing communications, and turned it into a national business. I suggest this model for your consideration (but not if you're a copywriter)!

Resources

To both sell your own services and those of your employees and independent contractors, I again advise you to use my books **THE CONSULTANT'S KIT: ESTABLISHING AND OPERATING YOUR SUCCESSFUL CONSULTING BUSINESS** and **HOW TO MAKE AT LEAST $100,000 EVERY YEAR AS A SUCCESSFUL CONSULTANT IN YOUR OWN FIELD.**

If you want to improve all your marketing communications — ads, cover letters, flyers, brochures, media kits, *etc.* — so they generate more prospects and close more business faster, contact Dan McComas at the National Copywriting Center *immediately.* (301) 946-4284

• *Publishing profit-making problem-solving special reports*

You already know about special reports. We've previously discussed them as a means of generating favorable publicity and leads for your business. Now it's time to also consider them as a profit-center in their own right.

Special Reports constitute one of the most cost-effective ways available for generating large numbers of leads from targeted constituencies, building your perceived value as an expert, getting your clients to *buy* your marketing materials, and making money directly.

As a service provider who provides marketing information, there is almost no limit to the number of special reports I could write. Take a look at the catalog in the back, and you'll see some of the ones I've already created. Please note that these special reports are:

- focused on topics of real value to my clients. The concentrated special report format works because it dispenses valuable information quickly. It shouts to the reader/customer, "HEY, BUB, HERE'S SOMETHING FOR YOU!", starting with the client-centered headline and continuing through a series of detail-rich paragraphs that speak directly to the client and let him know he can achieve the benefit of the headline . . . if only he has the brains to follow your specific directions.

- short. Busy literate people don't have a lot of time to stay current; non-readers don't have a lot of ability. Both, however, have the need for up-to-the-minute information. With the special report you can cater to this need, providing such information in a highly readable, immediately usable format.

- proportionately a lot more profitable than books. Why will people pay $6 for a special report when certain paperback novels cost about the same price? Because the special reports offer *immediate value;* the $6 is an *investment,* not just an expense. To the extent you get your readers/customers to understand this (which is a direct function of how you title your reports and what you put in them), you can raise the price higher and higher without substantial price resistance. This makes special reports a very lucrative profit center.

- capable of being refocused, depending on who you're talking to. Say I'm writing a special report on creating a brochure. Now there isn't an industry or business going that doesn't use some kind of brochure. Thus, once this special report is written, it can easily be adapted to the particular requirements (if any) of every industry. Therefore, you can use this special report — edited, if necessary — to get clients in the poultry business . . . and in the high tech business. Instead of taking the time and trouble to write two separate articles, you need only do the far easier and more sensible thing of adapting. This enables you to broaden your reach in a very time-effective way.

- easily kept up to date. The reason I call myself an info-entrepreneur and not a writer is because I do not consider what I write finished, belonging to the ages. I seize a subject that will be of interest to my prospects now and forever more and commit myself to keeping it up to date as necessary. Special reports are perfect for this. Will there be classified ads in twenty years? A hundred years? Of course! The methods of producing and benefiting them may well change . . . but the basics will not. Thus, a special report on this subject written today can easily be updated to be entirely current and valuable a century from now. This means that simply by keeping up with your field (a neces-sary prerequisite for the successful service provider in any event) and by doing what is necessary to incorporate new information into the basic format you've created, you can continue to benefit from special reports for as long as you need additional clients and further income.

- not a drain on your capital. You need never actually *produce* (that is print) a special report until you either have a media source to publish it or a client to buy it. Unlike more traditional booklets and books, you can not only create your special report on computer . . . but leave it there until you have a market to publish or buy it. Thus, you have no production expenses until you have either the prospect of publicity or the actuality of immediate money. This is a very important point, indeed!

- products you don't have to create yourself. You should continually be on the look out for specialists in your field who have knowledge your customers would profit from. You should encourage these people to write special reports themselves (following a strict format provided by you) in which they quote themselves as the expert. When finished, these reports will, of course, feature your specialist . . . but they'll both be published under your by-line and contain the crucial concluding Resource Box packed with details about how the reader/prospect can get in touch with you and buy selected of your products/services. The more experts write special reports for you, the more times you get to piggyback information about the products/services you're offering!

• *Publishing a money-making problem-solving newsletter*

We have previously discussed creating a free newsletter from which to generate new business from your existing clients and prospects. I have made it plain that such newsletters are of no value unless they focus on benefits available to your customers/prospects and seek to motivate their immediate response. In other words, the emphasis is on marketing the *benefits* of your products/services, not on providing *news*. With a paid subscription newsletter, the emphasis subtly shifts in the direction of providing more hard news. Please note I have indicated that the shift is "subtle", not absolute. In other words, whether you are providing your newsletter free or selling it, you will still be using it to generate business for the other problem-solving products and services you have available.

In a paid subscription newsletter, this means:

- including lots of involvement devices. This includes telephone numbers the readers can call for more information, free offers, specials, coupons where the reader can indicate what kinds of benefits he's interested in . . . so you can follow up accordingly, *etc.* You are not running a newspaper, mind; you are running a client-centered newsletter where having the customer read what you've provided is not the sole objective. Having him act to acquire additional benefits is.

- including "ads" focusing on your other products and services. Even if there is not another paid ad in the publication, there should always be client-centered ads for what you do;

- emphasizing information the reader cannot get anywhere else. What you provide should not only be useful and timely . . . but exclusive. You should provide tips, secrets, insider information, and client-centered procedures and techniques designed to increase the value of your publication to the reader/prospect and to strengthen the relationship between you.

What makes paid subscription newsletters work is:

- having a very clearly defined niche. The more defined the targeted population of your newsletter, the better;

- doing everything you can to enhance the feeling the reader gets of special value and useful, insider information, and

- making everything client-centered, focused on the reader's interest, not just on the material itself. Whatever you publish, you see, is of no value in itself; it is only important insofar as your readers can profit from it.

Personally, I have so far skipped this stage of the MMC. This is both a personal and a business decision. On the one hand, I already have more than enough to do; more important, I think my subject area of "marketing" per se too broad a topic to be the basis of a successful newsletter. It doesn't offer the kind of narrow definition which I think crucial in a successful newsletter. A good idea of something I am involved with that does offer this kind of focus is the subject of planned giving for charitable organizations. I have always thought (and continue to do so) that Debra Ashton's work in this area constitutes the basis of a very profitable newsletter. She is, after all, not only expert in the field but her book *The Complete Guide To Planned Giving* (which I publish) has given her national name recognition, another useful marketing point. Unfortunately, both she and I are just too busy to do it . . . Still, the point is, this kind of complex, constantly changing subject area with a highly targeted group of potential readers/subscribers is precisely what makes a newsletter viable.

Resources

If you do decide to go ahead and publish a paid-subscription newsletter, the following sources will be helpful to you:

First, the following books by newsletter authority Mark Beach

- *Editing Your Newsletter: A Guide to Writing, Design & Production.* ISC Press, Div. of Institute for Contemporary Studies, 243 Kearny St., San Francisco, CA 94108

- *Editing Your Newsletter: How to Produce an Effective Publication Using Traditional Tools & Computers.* Coast to Coast Books, 2934 N.E. 16th Ave., Portland, OR 97212

- *Papers for Printing: How to Choose the Right Paper at the Right Price for All Your Design & Printing Needs.* Coast to Coast.

Then, Howard Penn Hudson's, *Publishing Newsletters.* Scribner.

Finally, you'll find the work of desktop publishing specialist Roger Parker very helpful:

- *Looking Good in Print: Basic Design for Desktop Publishing.* Ventana Press, Box 2468, Chapel Hill, NC 27515

- (and with Howard Shenson) *Publishing the Competitive Newsletter.* Peachpit Press, 1085 Keith Ave., Berkeley, CA 94708.

• *Publishing problem-solving booklets and books*

When you undertake a subscription newsletter you have necessarily bound yourself to producing a product at regular and announced intervals. This is not the case with booklets and books which is why, perhaps, I prefer them! There are, however, other, less self-indulgent reasons, including:

- permanence. People are much less likely to throw away either a booklet or book than they are a newsletter.

- inclusion of lots of end-of-product marketing information. While most booklets and books don't take advantage of this feature, you should. Because people retain the product, they are also necessarily retaining your marketing communications.

- ability to develop rapport with prospect. A prospect who is spending time with one of your publications is, without even being aware of it, slowly developing a better relationship with you. He sees how you think, he gets impressed by what you know, he develops a comfort level, a liking, even a friendship for you. This does not happen with a brochure or paid ad. But it happens all the time in books, and to a lesser extent with booklets.

- creative distribution channels. Unless your competitors have booklets and books, they are not getting their marketing communications distributed through libraries, bookstores, catalogs and all the other marketing means through which these products are distributed. This means you have the field pretty much to yourself. For instance, I regularly get clients for our businesses because someone has gone to his local library, picked out my book on any given subject, been impressed by its message, and decided it would be a good idea to work with me. Is this happening to you?

- the money. Your booklets and books (as well as the other products in the MMC) can and should be priced according to the *value* they deliver, not according to what "regular" publishers charge for their products. Thus, most of my books sell for $35 (as of this writing), at least 10 times what they cost to produce. Not only is this a good return on investment but when you consider that these products are often the beginning of much more lucrative relationships, you can see how really profitable they can be. Furthermore, once you've established relationships with catalog companies, other distributors, wholesalers, *etc.*, the orders you receive can be considerable, thus producing the kind of "passive" revenue that minimizes cash flow crunches and makes for more immediate profit.

- celebrity. Books, and to a much lesser extent booklets, give you the kind of professional standing and recognition which is both very valuable in developing your business, enabling you to raise your prices and attract new clients and buyers, and also in satisfying your considerable ego needs. This is no bad thing . . .

• *Producing problem-solving audio and video cassettes*

Much of what I've already told you about booklets and books applies, too, to audio and video cassettes. We have previously discussed using these as premiums and to motivate a quicker response from your prospects, but here again you have a considerable profit-center . . . if you handle things right. Here's what you need to keep in mind:

- Both audio and video are intimate formats. What's crucial here is that you work to establish the closest possible rapport with your audience. What makes these media work is both the close contact you establish with your audience and the clear, step-by-step information you provide them. The combination of closeness plus problem-solving content is irresistible.

- Both audio and video can be handled in a cost-effective fashion. Remember, you are providing useful problem-solving information, not expensive special effects. Too many service providers put off creating audio and video cassettes because they think the expense will be too great. In fact, as I have discussed in my book **MONEY TALKS,** you can easily create an audio cassette, at least, at home with a simple tape recorder. You can reproduce the tapes and include a box and label all for about $1 apiece. This is not expensive. Moreover, when you consider that you can price your tapes at 15 times or more what they cost you to produce, you can easily see how profitable they can be for you.

- Both audio and video cassettes should feature various offers motivating your prospects to call you to get further benefits. Although these offers and marketing communications are necessarily shorter than you can use in booklets and books, there is no reason why any member of your audience should fail to learn about additional means you have available to help him.

Resource: For information about producing and selling special reports, booklets, books, and audio cassettes, I refer you to my volume **HOW TO MAKE A WHOLE LOT MORE THAN $1,000,000 WRITING, COMMISSIONING, PUBLISHING, AND SELLING "HOW-TO" INFORMATION.**

• *Profiting from problem-solving talk programs*

Many service providers give talk programs. They may speak to civic organizations like the Kiwanis Club or go into the schools and do a "career day" presentation. Some give talks at professional meetings and conventions; others provide adult and continuing education courses. Few, however, have turned this into a lucrative part of their business.

As you know, I like talk programs for many reasons. Properly handled they:

- produce a lot of good publicity;
- use someone else's money to attract client prospects for your business, and
- make you money both from their stipends and the products and services you sell.

Yes, I like talk programs, do a lot of them, and make often laughably great sums of money. Unfortunately, I'm the exception. Most service providers, who seem unable to think multi-dimensionally, seem to think it enough if they're invited to give a talk, the talk goes well, and they get a round of applause. If they get the chance to hand out a few business cards, they feel positively ecstatic. Why? Like every-thing else in the MMC, the talk hasn't worked unless you've both made money from it directly and properly organized it so that you make money from as many of the other aspects of your MMC as possible. Thus, for a talk to work you must:

- Bargain for a stipend. Of course, you're not always going to get it, especially when you're unknown, but you can ask, can't you? I hear from my readers over and over again that they started making more money when they gave talks because, following my advice, they simply asked to be paid. Astonishing!

- Get the organization to feature you, as previously described, in pre- and post-talk articles, both by and about you. This helps enhance your image and makes you appear to be a more valuable service provider.

- Get the organization to distribute your materials. Why should you be put in the role of huckster (unless you have to be)? Get someone from the organization to pass out your marketing communications . . . or get them put at the luncheon plates . . . or in the conference packets, *etc.* In short, think through what the sponsoring organization could do . . . then ask them to do it.

- Get everyone attending to complete a client survey ques-tionnaire . . . then follow up accordingly.

- Arrange to have your products sold at the meeting. If you're smart, make sure everyone attending gets one upon arriving. (The price can be included in the cost of the ticket.) If you can't do this, have the organization help you sell your products by setting up and manning a sales table, *etc.* You need to be a gracious dispenser of pivotal wisdom . . . not a harassed shop keeper.

Resource: To make money from your talk programs and get all the other benefits to which you're entitled as the problem-solving specialist, use my book **MONEY TALKS: THE COMPLETE GUIDE TO CREATING A PROFITABLE WORKSHOP OR SEMINAR IN ANY FIELD.**

• *Profiting from a problem-solving catalog, including both your own products and services and those of other providers*

You have spent a great deal of time developing a lead-generating system. Some of these people will buy your most lucrative services, most will not. If they don't buy the top of your line, is the prospect useless? Not if you both develop and find additional problem-solving products and services in which he's interested. Your catalog enables you to bring all these products and services to the attention of both prospects and customers on a regular basis . . . and so both promote your products and services (as is necessary with The Rule of 7) and derive regular income from them. Here's what you need to know to make this catalog work:

- As with any marketing communication, focus on the benefits, not the features. Thus, whatever you're selling, product or service, must be presented in terms of what the reader/prospect will get from it . . . not what you have, but what he gets.

- Write your catalog as if it were an extended conversation between you and the reader. Remember, you've worked hard to make all your marketing communications client-centered. This focus must now continue. The reader must feel you are talking directly to him, urging him to take action, working to make his life better.

- Stud your copy with testimonials from satisfied buyers. Your prospects want to know that you've achieved results for others. Reassure them that you have.

- Don't think for a minute that you have to include only products . . . and don't think for a second that you have to include only *your* products and services. Use your catalog to promote related products and services . . . from whose venders you can take a commission. Until such time as you can fill your catalog with only your own products and services, there is absolutely no reason why you shouldn't benefit from the complementary work of other product and service providers. Indeed, even when you can fill your own catalog with your own products and services, I'd still recommend benefiting from what others produce and do. Expand the length of your catalog!

- Fill your catalog with lots of interactive devices. A catalog is not a library book to be read and returned in perfect condition to some dusty shelf. It's a marketing communication which should be marked up, ripped apart, and used, used, used! You facilitate this process, indeed you make it inevitable, to the extent you pack your catalog with special offers, coupons, phone numbers, call outs, and other involvement devices. A catalog which is not so used by your readers, is a catalog which is insufficiently motivational and hence insufficiently profitable for you.

- Interject yourself into your catalog whenever possible. A catalog, like an article, special report, booklet, book, audio or video cassette presents a splendid opportunity to develop your name recognition, reputation and rapport with your audience. A catalog should not read as if it were produced by some disembodied intelligence, but rather as the production of a bright, vitally concerned, thoughtful, problem-solving service provider who knows what the prospects want, knows what needs to be done, and constantly offers telling insights into how to achieve the results his prospects crave. This means your prose should make use of the full gambit of human emotions, including humor, scolding, exhortation, transfiguration, affection, even anger. Your catalog must be as personal as you are, as knowledgeable, as concerned, as caring, as insistent and as indefatigable. You see, in a catalog you are not just another mundane service provider; you are the indispensable problem-solver every single one of your prospects has been long awaiting. Don't disappoint them!

Getting Started With Your MMC

You may say that all this is very well and good but . . . you've got a business to run . . . a house to clean, errands to do, kids to feed, a million and one excuses. Reader, I warn you: excuses will never make you a millionaire. The important question is not how you will juggle everything but whether you are content with the amount of money you are making/can make without implementing the various stages of the MMC. If you are, you don't need to implement these stages. But if you're not . . . if you cannot produce all the income you need simply by offering direct service and taking on employees and independent contractors, then you have no choice: you must create and run your own Mobile Mini-Conglomerate. The question then becomes, where should you begin?

What's great about the MMC is that you can implement it a little at a time, by comfortable stages, without committing large amounts of your time and significant amounts of money. Moreover, because each thing you do under the aegis of the MMC helps develop the rest of your business, you can easily justify all your work as part of the marketing for your current service line.

Here, then, are some easy ways to break into those portions of the MMC beyond direct service provision and hiring independent contractors and employees:

- Write a special report. This report should deal with a characteristic problem your customers come to you to solve. Use this report as a premium, as a means of getting publicity, and (by including an order form in your marketing communications) as a means of generating additional revenue. *Note:* once you've written one report, don't stop. Set yourself a deadline when you'd like the second one to be finished. Then write on how to solve another important problem about which your customers come to you. When you've finished with Report #2, you now have a line of reports. It's a small line, to be sure . . . but it's a start!

- Get a speaking engagement. When you do, use your special report to generate additional publicity and generate leads. Get yourself interviewed by the organization's publication editor so you further develop your perceived standing and expertise. Tape your speaking engagement, and use the audio tape you've created both as a premium . . . and, by including an order coupon with your marketing communications, as a product for sale. Don't forget to include complete follow-up details about how the listener can get in touch with you to enjoy further benefits you have available.

- Once your initial audio cassette has been done, brainstorm a series of topics for additional programs. Either get yourself booked to provide additional workshops and talks (thereby creating the opportunity for additional audio cassette programs) or expand your special reports and turn them into scripts. *Remember:* if you're smart, you'll turn every special report into a longer booklet, an audio and video cassette, and a book . . . as well as a workshop program. This is the way you get maximum mileage from your problem-solving information and develop maximum revenue possibilities!

- Publish a booklet. Booklets are merely elaborated special reports. Ten printed pages is a good minimum length for a booklet. That's surely possible for you. This constitutes both a good learning experience and, again, a good premium . . . and profit center. My friend Bob Bly, that clever fellow, has mastered the art of bookletry with his *Recession-Proof Strategies: 14 Winning Methods to Sell Any Product or Service in a Down Economy.* (16 pages long, you can get a copy for $7 by writing to Bob Bly, 22 E. Quackenbush Ave., Dumont, NJ 07628 or by calling 201-385-1220.) So has Art Sobszak, another cunning promoter. His newest is entitled *99 Ways To Sell More By Phone: What You Can Do And Say Right Now To Get More 'Yes's' By Phone.* (You can get this through my Sure-Fire Business Success Catalog.) Both these guys make some money with their booklets . . . derive a heap of publicity, and generate lucrative new clients thanks to the motivational invitations they include.

- Create a short problem-solving catalog. Identify 10-20 products and services (yours included, of course) that would help make your clients' and prospects' lives easier. Then whip up a "catalog" that need be no longer than one back-to-back 8 1/2" x 11" piece of paper. Use this as an insert piece in your mailings; as a package stuffer. This is how my own Sure-Fire Business Success Catalog got started about 10 years ago, and you can see how it's grown!

Caution: notice I do not recommend getting started right away with a major book, or a video, or anything else that's going to sap a lot of your time and money. This isn't the way I think . . . and it isn't the right thing to do. When you've made the commitment to yourself to become a millionaire and you're in for the long haul, sure and steady should be your motto. Take your time. Begin with something that you can easily handle *right now.* See how your prospects like it. See how you like it. *Remember:* with the best will in the world, the first special report you create isn't going to be your best; neither is your first audio cassette. You need to learn the tricks of the trade for developing client-centered materials, for learning what kind of information you need, finding out where to get it and how to present it. You're not going to learn these things overnight. You need to be seasoned, like a fine wine, to be able to produce info-products properly. That's why it's a mistake to rush off and create a book instantly. All too often these books are thin, shallow, unhelpful . . . and, worst of all, unsalable. Believe me, having a thousand or so information products sitting in your garage gathering dust is not the way to boost yourself to millionaire standing. That's why you should take the time you need to build your MMC.

Even at this point, however, there are things you can do to help yourself, both now and for the long term. Here they are:

- Keep an idea file. Ideas will come to you at all hours of the day or night. Obviously your idea file should be kept in your computer (where else?). But you should also keep pads of paper and pens around the house and with you at all times. Plop in every thought you may have that bears on the creation of any information-based product or service.

- Keep an expert file. The objective, remember, is for you, as consummate marketer and info-impresario, to benefit from the brains and bright ideas of all the specialists in your field, wherever they are located. This means keeping good records about these experts, their products and services, addresses and phone numbers. I warn you: if you are going to make your empire large and robust you will need more minds than your own. Start gathering this information now. *Note:* working on this expert file early is especially important when you have to work through another source to get access to the expert. For instance, it may take several letters to a specialist's publisher before someone gets around to telling you the person you want is on leave in Latvia just now. So, start your research early!

- Open your "research department." Collect articles, reports, books, tapes, newsletters, specialized publications of every kind in your field. You're looking for ideas, of course, and experts, to be sure . . . but also data you can use in the development of your own products and services. In a world where the only constant is change, you cannot succeed without becoming an info-fanatic. If you want to see what I mean, stop by and see me some day: my shelving situation is as alarming as the Library of Congress'! One of my crucial insights was just how many other people I needed to know and work with to become a millionaire, and now my life is packed with what they produce and with the means of connecting with them.

- Always be working on the development of a new product or service. There isn't a day that goes by that I don't spend a portion, sometimes just the smallest fraction, on developing the *next* product/service. Your mind and skills will develop through constant use. In 1979 when I started my business I had a net worth of about $12. I'm a millionaire now because I have forced myself to stay creative . . . which has meant constantly brainstorming new ideas and taking the best of these into development.

- Sketch out projects for the next ten years or more. Future millionaires see their productive life in the longest possible terms. They know they'll be productive today, productive tomorrow, productive years into the future. This means brainstorming projects you'd like to accomplish and putting down your ideas in as much detail as you can right now. Sure, you may falter on the road to implementing all these ideas; any number of things might happen to change your direction. But the important thing is that you have begun the crucial sorting and sifting process which will result in a steady stream of business developments. If you are going to develop new products and services, you must constantly tinker with new ideas.

- Get a brainstorming partner. I have one of the best of them: Bill Reece. I can see him right this minute. In the cool of a summer's evening, he's lounging in my living room, comfortably ensconced under my much babied hibiscus, blue bandanna on his head, a glass of my best port in his hand, talking up a storm as he usually does when he confronts his favorite subject: how we can make more money and what we need to do to make it happen. I have worked hard all day; I am, frankly, just about played out. I am older than Bill. Right now, I really don't want to stretch. It is easier — lots easier — to reminisce and celebrate old triumphs (wasn't this why port was invented in the first place?). But Bill's vitality, hunger for more success and goading insistence *make* me focus on new ideas, the next triumph, the problem that needs to be solved tomorrow so that at that day's end we're even more successful. And so, while grumbling just discernibly and pushing my tired brain and body to the only form of exercise in which I ever indulge, I amble into the spirit of yet another of our regular success brainstorming sessions, sessions which take place constantly and which, I publicly attest, have done me a world of good. Just as they will you!

- Keep records about what worked. Most people are tourists in their own lives. They don't know where they came from, how they got where they are, where they are going, or anything else of much importance about themselves. Their bodies are mysteries, their minds unexplored inner space, their dreams and aspirations as fleeting as the morning dew. Sadly, this is also the condition of most service sellers. Their objective is to get through the day as comfortably as possible, make a little money, and stay out of trouble. They do not see the connection between yesterday and today . . . between today and tomorrow. There is no attempt to winnow what worked from what didn't and to use it to build an even stronger business, make even more money as soon as possible. This absence of the historical imagination is, of course, fatal to a business; it condemns these limited creatures to keep perpetrating past errors and fail to benefit from past success. Don't let this be you. Working smart means constantly evaluating both what worked and what didn't. Each contains insight into what will make you more successful faster. But trying to remember all this is pointless; gathering data is an essential element of your success.

Getting Serious

Bit by bit, following these directions, you'll notice some very favorable straws in the wind:

- People start calling you after reading your special reports. They not only give you compliments (always welcome, of course) but suggest you handle their business;

- Others press business cards into your palm after you've made a speech and tell you they want to know more about the products and services you produce;

- A publication calls to ask for reprint rights to a special report they've just read;

- Someone else wants you to be a speaker . . . do you do that sort of thing?

- A friend has told someone he knows to call you because you've written a real good book, what's its name anyway?

And so it goes. You are becoming well-known, respected, sought after, not just a good service provider but someone people seek out and want to handle their affairs. They don't take you *faux de mieux*. Instead, they insist on having you. You, dear friend, are a personage . . . well on your way to becoming a millionaire! Congratulations. It is now time to get serious, to implement the Mobile Mini-Conglomerate in an intense, systematic, thorough-going way. Here are some suggestions about how you can move ahead further, faster:

- Start your problem-solving process book. You're competent enough now to do this; you know enough. You've mastered enough of the form. You're practiced enough in being client-centered. Don't wait. If too many service sellers rush into books too soon, there is a perhaps larger fraction who waits too long. I know such a person, and she is a pitiable being. She started her book, oh, 7 or 8 years ago . . . and it isn't finished yet! She wants every sentence to be perfect, every thought to be unique, every page to be a polished jewel of awe-inspiring prose. THIS WOMAN MUST BE INSANE! What writer ever wrote such prose . . . and in a first book at that? The first problem-solving book you write will not be your best. This does not mean you shouldn't try to make it superb: you should. But you should not die a thousand deaths because every line is not deathless. You are crippling yourself . . . and helping no prospects. Start your book . . . give yourself a deadline . . . and then flog your-self to reach it. I do . . . and I turn out another volume every year. Behold! And emulate!!!

- Mine the book for problem-solving articles and special reports. The minute you have finished a problem-solving section that is coherent and substantial in itself, turn it into a source of lead-generation for your company . . . and start selling it, too. Why wait? Do you really think the world will remember what you've said in a special report . . . that selling it now will eviscerate your sales? I can assure you, dear reader, that you are woefully deceiving yourself. In fact, special reports whet readers' appetites for more . . . as well as giving you the opportunity to promote everything else you do.

- While you're working on your first problem-solving book, outline your second and start collecting material for it. Once you've identified a market and begun satisfying its wants that market will expect, indeed demand, to hear more from you. And why not? You're just not the kind of person who's either going to let your problem-solving expertise go to waste . . . or leave your loyal customers in the lurch. But you will . . . if you don't think and plan ahead. I pity the info-specialist who has worked hard to gain all that problem-solving knowledge, who writes a single book (which is a learning experience for the author), gathers a following (however limited) . . . and then by creating nothing more, fails to capitalize on all that has gone before. What, then, was the point of all that arduous work?

• Turn the special reports into audio cassettes. Again, there is no reason to wait. You have the material. It is your obligation to use it to build your empire.

• Get focused about booking talk appearances. You already know the benefits of talk programs. Now get organized booking them. Use a commission-paying lead-generating program, like I do. Identify all the likely sources who could use you . . . and direct winning marketing communications to the program directors. In short, implement the process that gets you invited. Develop a variety of programs and brainstorm others based on the technical information at your disposal, the kinds of clients you want, and the kinds of benefits they want.

• Develop more relationships with complementary product and service suppliers. You will never command all the information and problem-solving skills there are to know in your field; you will never be able to produce all the products and services your prospects need. But you can receive your cut of all of them . . . by making mutually beneficial deals with all the suppliers of products and services which are complementary to your own. This is well within the bounds of possibility . . . if you work hard to identify what your prospects need . . . who can supply it to them . . . and to make the kinds of deals which will enable you to profit by bringing this information to their attention.

Experiencing The Delightful Caress Of The Money Stream

If you are now a full-time employee working for someone else, you get paycheck money, weekly, perhaps, or every month. If you're a service provider working for someone else, you see money only when you are paid for your work. If you're a service provider working for yourself, you see money only when the customer pays you . . . and that, during business down turns, may be a long time coming. You are making money, to be sure, but you are not experiencing the joy of the money stream.

We are, you see, surrounded by a great river of money. Unlike the usual river, the money river continues under and along the ground, in the air, even from hand to hand. From this, you are getting your diminuitive dribs and drabs. It is, it seems, enough to keep you alive; it may even be enough to nurture your dreams . . . but it is not enough to give you that feeling of constant well being and content that can only come when you are caressed by the stream many times every single day.

This, however, the MMC can do . . . as you develop it and benefit from its power.

When the MMC is working:

- Money comes in by telephone at all hours of the day or night. You are no longer just generating revenue locally; you are serving the interests of targeted markets worldwide. They make you richer while you sleep;

- Money comes in by mail. Six days a week, you derive more income. Every letter that comes, every card is either additional present income or the prospect of future income, if only you handle it correctly;

- Money comes in via fax, since, with your ability to handle credit card orders, you can accommodate any client anywhere in the world who possesses the means to make them;

- Money comes in through the overnight mail and package carriers. Each carrier has the potential, as I know so well, to rain riches on you, once in the morning, again in the afternoon, every day of the year.

- Money comes in when customers arrive on your door step and are grateful for the time you give them and delighted to have had the chance to see their honored guru. Presenting money to a guru is a habit so sanctified by time they would never think of flouting it.

- Money comes in every time you open your mouth at one of your talk programs. The people whose lives you have demonstrated a readiness and ability to improve are only too happy to thrust money at you in often staggering amounts. And, no wonder: you offer, as no one else can, the possibilities of transformation which, in so many ways, they let you know they want.

- Money is wired into your bank account from people who want your benefits — now! They cannot wait for them . . . and know that by walking to or calling up their bank and having a few digits electronically directed to your account, they can put you — you the very person they want — to work for them IMMEDIATELY!

Day in, day out these rivulets run — all of them! They are running now all around you, all around the world. But now you may not know it, may not have experienced it. I know otherwise. The money river never stops flowing. It runs night and day. It runs through telephone lines and is carried on the wheels of delivery trucks; it flies on the jet stream and moves on the heels of grumbling postal carriers. It shows itself in brightly colored bits of paper and on a series of computer screens. *It never stops.* This stream, fellow service provider, is as crucial to our well-being and development as the ancient Nile was to Pharonic Egypt. We must tend it as carefully, as worshipfully as did the priests at Luxor.

To be sure, in the beginning this river may nourish you sluggishly; sometimes it may seem to dry up altogether, forcing you to rethink your strategy and actions. Bit by bit, however, you will come to understand that this river runs deep and true and never stops, and you will learn how to harness it to your advantage. You will see that billions of people all around the world regularly add to it and that the return for those who understand how to cater to these people and their wants, who are prepared to use all available means to do so, is beyond reckoning. As this understanding ripens and your Mobile Mini-Conglomerate flourishes, you will find yourself continually blessed by effluents from the money river until you no longer have merely enough . . . but superfluity.

At such a moment, you should pause to congratulate yourself. You have reached a point which has eluded most of the people who have, for their brief moment, trod upon this planet. Most have known nothing more than the perilousness of making do. Verily, when you understand how to work the money stream you have passed into another, more interesting, beneficial and soothing stage. You have passed from the stage of working because you must and because there is no alternative, to that of working because it is only through your work that you can take control of your own life and enrich the lives of countless others. Work is your benediction to the world, and in return you are made not merely rich but continually richer.

At this point some of our less anchored colleagues give way to a kind of incessant saturnalia, wasting through puerile jollities and tawdry acquisition the fruits of their long and careful apprenticeship. But not you. You now know something of money and know that it is time to put the final component of your wealth-producing machine to work for you: investment. All the streams which now run increasingly bountifully for you are producing current income, the raw material of capital. Properly deployed these streams do more than continually improve your current circumstances; they produce the capital which ensures you will never be held hostage to them.

16

Using Your Service Business To Produce The Investment Capital And Unearned Income You Need To Maintain And Improve Your Lifestyle

As the population continues to age, anxiety about how to maintain one's lifestyle both before and after retirement continues to grow. Articles on the subject appear regularly in both financial and general interest publications . . . and much of what they contain makes for very depressing reading. Here, to give but one example, are some findings taken from a recent Gallup Poll conducted for Phoenix Mutual Life Insurance.

Item: the average person has only accumulated retirement investments of about $35,000; $25,000 in a retirement plan and $10,000 in other personal savings.

Item: about 1/4 of those surveyed have *nothing* saved.

Item: sixty percent of those polled said they would like to stop working before age 65, despite the fact that this will lower their earning and saving years and lower the amount of Social Security benefits they eventually receive.

Item: a 45 year old man earning $50,000 today who wants to retire on 70% of his income may need $77,000 a year in 20 years (adjusting for 4 percent inflation). But by age 85, he would need $168,000 a year!

Survey findings like these (and believe me, these are very typical) make for sober reading. When you add to them the information about consumer debt, the rising cost of college education, and the likelihood of future tax increases to balance the federal budget and fund overdue improvements in the nation's infrastructure, you begin to wonder if you can ever get control of your own financial life and get what most of us want: financial independence.

Most people will never figure out what they've got to do to achieve this objective. But since you're the owner of an increasingly prosperous service business, you can . . . if you follow some very simple steps.

Starting At The Beginning: Why You Want Financial Independence

You hear the phrase "financial independence" a lot, particularly if you move in entrepreneurial circles. Yet all too often it's bandied about with precious little consideration. Perhaps sharing with you a recent incident in my life will help define why financial independence will always be a crucial objective.

Most nights I stay home and read, but just the other evening I could no longer resist the seductiveness of the spring evening and went for a walk. Along the way I stopped at a Boston watering hole I used to frequent as a graduate student but hadn't visited for many years. Ever the information fanatic, I was sipping my drink and flipping through a stack of newspapers when I became aware that someone next to me was getting positioned to start talking. Ordinarily, I'm not very open to these kinds of encounters; these days they often lead to some kind of unwelcome solicitation. This time, however, I allowed the conversation to begin. Indeed, in an unwontedly festive mood, I even bought the fellow a drink.

But soon, so very soon, the familiar tale of urban woe started to unfold. An unemployed musician, he was in Boston to visit his mother in a major hospital. He'd been staying with his brother, but (predictably) the brother had just been arrested. Now the fellow had no place to stay and no money to get home to Bridgeport, where he was "temporarily" living with his cousin. Since I was clearly "rich", couldn't I assist him?

Like many well-off people leading a comfortable life, I am susceptible to these tales. I like to be able to help and, in this case, I did. I gave him money for food and a bus ticket back to Bridgeport. It would have been nice if the tale had ended there. I would have gotten the surge of satisfaction that comes when one not only can be but is helpful. But, of course, every such tale has a sting. "Couldn't you give me just a little more?," the not-so-grateful recipient of my spontaneous bounty asked. When I said I couldn't (I literally gave him all the folding money in my wallet), I could see he was *angry,* and he started to remind me that his 53 year old mother had just had a second stroke that week, that he had four illegitimate children from three mothers, had no place to live, *etc., etc., etc.*

I will not share all the emotions that surged through me, but I will tell you the result was a potent combination of gratitude that I was not in these circumstances, fear of what he was going through, irritation that I was being asked to do more, and disgust that the happiness of my perfect spring evening had been destroyed by the encounter with this person who was so obviously not in control of his destiny and who spewed a constant litany of profanity against all the unseen forces which had brought him to this pass.

I'll tell you the truth. When I arrived back home, I took a quick shower as if I could clean myself of the unsettling experience. I then went into my study and wrote a check for $1000 for one of my investment funds and, not waiting for the morning to mail it, went out immediately and did so. You see, I wanted the reassurance that comes from knowing I have control over my own destiny and would not find myself in the kind of situation which is all too frequent nowadays.

For me, then, financial independence means:

- having freedom of choice. Being able to go where I want to go, when I want to go there. Being able to select whom I want to be with and how I want to be with them, instead of being forced by my needs to make soul-destructive compromises.

- being able to enjoy better things, instead of less good things. Each situation in life offers a series of possibilities. The person with the greatest financial independence is more likely to get the best of whatever is going, wherever he is.

- enjoying the possibilities of spontaneity. When you are poor, you must be excessively deliberate; such deliberation kills the human spirit. If you have financial independence and want to do something, you do it. If that "something" doesn't work out the way you wanted, it's not a catastrophe. It's simply part of your human learning experience. If you lose some money, so be it. It doesn't cripple you. Those without such means, however, will find their options narrowing and will so come to doubt themselves that they will cease to be able to take any beneficial action that has any risk attached to it at all.

- being able to take a necessary respite. I watched the recipient of my charity closely. Although he was only 32, he looked much older; his clothes were worn, his hands shook, he had bitten his nails down to the quick. His eyes had the unnerving habit of darting this way and that, seeming to focus on nothing. Whatever extra money he had literally was going up in the smoke of the countless cigarettes he went through. Each moment to such a person is a trial, because each moment demands the utmost concentration. Any mistake could undermine an already precarious reality. It is not, of course, thus for people with financial security. We can take a respite when we need it, assess our situations, and move steadily, deliberately. Time is on our side in ways which those without financial independence can never understand or experience.

There is in certain so-called progressive circles a myth about the peculiar virtues of the poor and the almost saintly fortitude of their lives. Such people, of course, have spent no time with the people they are writing about, for there is nothing ennobling about poverty, nothing remotely attractive about the people who are consumed by it, by the people whose lives are constrained and entirely defined by it. The problems that come when one is continually the servant of financial limitations destroy youth, beauty, spirit, dreams and, at last, hope itself. That's why your first obligation must be to arrange your life so that every single day you are doing what is necessary to free yourself and your family from this terrible threat.

Committing Yourself And Your Business To Financial Independence

Look around you, and you'll find most of the people you know working. They work for any number of reasons but most are decidedly unthoughtful about the experience which takes the flower of their lives. You, however, are different. You are thoughtful about the work you do, and you know there are only two reasons for working, to:

- improve the lives of the maximum number of people who have the problem you can solve through your products and services, and

- turn your business into a money machine that provides not only the income you need to maintain your current lifestyle but the capital you need to assure this — or a better — lifestyle in the future.

In short, work is never its own reward. It is only a means to these two ends.

Throughout this book, I have urged you to commit yourself to improving the lives of the maximum number of people through your products and services. Now I ask you to commit yourself to doing what it takes not only to make a satisfactory income through your business but to learn how to turn this business and the money that comes from it into the capital you need to provide for your lifestyle.

By making this commitment to yourself you have properly defined the problem. Remember, most people who work are in debt; this means their income doesn't cover their current expenses. A smaller percentage of those who work are not in debt, but they either do not invest from their current income or do not have enough in investment income to cover their lifestyle needs should their primary income cease. The most goal-oriented of these people are working to alter this situation; they are doing what is necessary to generate the income they need to create the capital base they must have to sustain their lifestyle. The less goal-oriented are not, for whatever reason, acting as sensibly. Finally, there is the much, much smaller group of people who have so arranged their affairs that they already have in hand sufficient capital from which they can generate the income they need to sustain at least their current lifestyle. These people are at the top of the heap . . . and it is these people . . . and the methods they used to achieve this eminence . . . that you should be emulating.

But first, of course, you must make the pledge to join them and to achieve financial independence. Without this pledge to yourself, you cannot achieve this objective. So make this pledge NOW!

Reviewing Your Personal And Business Expenditures

As a service business owner, you are ideally placed to both construct your business to provide the income you need to develop a capital base . . . and to continually use and regularly reposition it to take advantage of both general market trends and changes in the law favorable to the development of your wealth. As you're starting out in business, however, these may look like advantages too far down the road to cheer you now. Perhaps . . .

However, the development of your investment habit can and should start NOW . . . even if you haven't started your own business yet or if you're in the early days of developing it. You see, the development of this habit is crucial in the building of wealth.

Consider, for instance, the story I've just told you about my bar-room encounter. The man was severely disadvantaged. He was hungry . . . yet he had money for cigarettes. The soft-headed might have given him cigarette money thinking that this was a kind gesture. I disagree; that's like handing a rope to someone inclined to suicide . . . and not just because of the health implications, either. You see, he was smoking his income. Sure it gave him momentary pleasure, but it did nothing to get him out of the mess he was in. Again, you must be different!

Once you've made a decision not just to *spend* your income but to *use* your income as a tool in the development of the capital you need to ensure your lifestyle, you must review every expenditure closely. This means doing both a personal and business expense assessment. Thus:

- Make a commitment to review *all* business and personal expenses;

- Create a text file in your computer for both business and personal expenses. (*Note:* there are also software packages available such as MoneyCounts and Quicken ready available commercially);

- List everything you spend your money on. While close scrutiny of these matters may not be so important after you have significant capital resources, it is crucial when you don't. Thus, do not lump all food items together as "groceries". Break out precisely what you spend your money on. Only when you know what you're spending your resources on can you begin to investigate and use suitable alternatives.

- Account for *every* penny. It is very easy, given your past slackness about expense accountability, to forgive yourself for not paying attention to all your expenditures. However, "watch the pennies, the pounds will take care of themselves."

- Resolve to scrutinize all your expenses not just with a view towards decreasing them but towards investing what you save. It is not the decreasing of expenses which is the most important thing; it is the investment of the difference. To decrease without investing just doesn't make sense!

Here are the criteria to use when you are reviewing all your expenses:

- Do I really need this item? That is, is this item either helping produce the objectives towards which I'm striving, or isn't it? If it doesn't, then it cannot be justified and must be removed.

- If I need this item, is there a way I can get the results it offers but pay less for it? In other words, do I have to pay as much for it as I am now?

- If I need this item but cannot find a less-expensive alternative, is there a way I can make this item last longer (perhaps by buying a higher quality version), buy less of it, buy more of it (thereby reducing the longer-term cost) *etc.*?

What's missing in the lives of most people regarding their money is intelligent deliberation. When a person says, "I just don't know what happens to my money," you know you're talking to someone who has a minimal net worth and for whom the possibility of financial independence will always prove elusive.

Hint: if this kind of expenditure-by-expenditure scrutiny over your personal and business expenses proves difficult, simply decide to cut your expenses by a fixed amount, like 10%. Then arrange both your business and professional life to live within this budget, making sure that the 10% you save is religiously invested.

Here, again, I must remind you: you are not reviewing and cutting your expenses for the sake of economizing. You are doing this for the sake of developing your capital base and moving towards financial independence. I am not one of those who thinks that economizing per se is somehow a noble thing. If you are content with your lifestyle, have decided to play Russian roulette with your own future and the future of your family, and won't use the money saved in the way outlined here, then don't go through the often frustrating business of economizing.

Setting Investment Objectives

Very well, you have now begun to scrutinize your expenditures. The question, however, is how much money you need both a) to sustain your current lifestyle and b) for the lifestyle you *really* want to have?

This means:

- reviewing your current lifestyle expenses;
- determining how much money you'll need to sustain this lifestyle in years ahead, and
- determining how much money you'd need to live the kind of lifestyle you say you really want.

Remember, investing is never an objective in itself; it is always the means to either sustaining what you have . . . or getting more of what you want.

Say for the moment you have arrived at the kind of lifestyle you wish to maintain in the years ahead. For you, it is simply a question of projecting how much money you'll need to sustain it. You must consider:

- future anticipated expenses. If your children are currently in elementary or junior high school and will be going to college, you need to determine just how much money you'll need to finance their education. This is an anticipated expense.
- future unanticipated expenses. What kinds of things may happen to you that you cannot definitely predict? These very often fall in the health category.
- inflation rate. The Gallup Poll I quoted above figured in a constant inflation rate of 4%; many, including myself, would consider that too low. I'd feel better with one of at least 6 percent. Either way, there will be inflation, and you have to factor it in.

If you haven't arrived at the kind of lifestyle you want (more likely), your "future anticipated expenses" category will look substantially different from that of people who are not considering making these kinds of major changes. Either way, however, whether you've reached a "satisfied" plateau or are still ascending, you need to develop a chart.

This chart should include the following factors:

- list of years to when you'd like to achieve your objective;
- income projected from business for each of these years;
- amount you plan to invest through your business in each of these years;
- the additional income you can expect to derive from investments made through your business in each of these years;
- amount you plan to invest personally in each of these years;
- additional income you can expect to derive from personal investments made in each of these years.

This chart has several purposes. It:

- encourages you to take both the short and the long view. By this I mean that simply by looking at the chart you'll understand that each period of time is a necessary component of your entire plan. When you have a chart you will move beyond the destructive "today is all there is" thinking that bedevils most people. You'll understand that your better tomorrow begins with better use of today . . . and tomorrow, too.

- makes you patient. You'll realize that, like Rome, your fortune cannot be built in a day. Of course, there are illustrations of business people who make substantial sums of money quickly. But these are — and always will be — the exceptions. Your motto needs to be "slow and steady wins the race." Hitting the financial jackpot is always chancy; getting rich is not — if you're willing to follow these sure and certain guidelines.

- forces you to consider various income streams. You will understand that there is money to be made both from and through your business as well as through your personal investments. Each of these streams has power; you must put them all to work for you.

- focuses you on how you'll make money in the years ahead. When you are just starting out with your service business, the bulk of your income will come as revenue from the business. However, as the chart amply demonstrates, when you use all the means of capital development at your disposal, over time the relative value of business income drops compared to the importance of investment income. This is just how it should be!

To show you what I mean, let's look at the completed chart of the person the Gallup Poll cited above says is typical, that is the 45 year old currently making $50,000 who wants to retire on 70% of his full income at age 60. Remember, he already has $25,000 invested in a pension plan and an additional $10,000 of other assets which must be figured into the computation. At age 60 he wants an inflation adjusted income equivalent to $35,000 in today's dollars. (Adjusted at six percent annual inflation, his income at age 60 would have to be nearly $84,000 to reach his objective!)

Note: for purposes of illustration I am going to suppose that all his investments increase in value 8% every year. Now we all know this isn't likely; some years, depending on what he invests in, his return might be higher, sometimes much higher; in other years, lower. However, I have chosen 8% as both a conservative and manageable return.

Additionally, I am assuming you are contributing both personal and business investments as early in the year as possible thus giving your investment maximum time to mature. The results of this chart will be different if you make your investments late in the investment cycle as opposed to early. Early investing is always better than late investing since it gives your money additional time to compound and work for you!

Further, I am assuming that you religiously make pension contributions equal to 20% of your annual income and equally religiously invest an additional 10% of your personal income each year.

Finally, I am assuming that your business grows at a gentle pace, rather than a frantic one. Indeed, I am assuming that some years your business doesn't grow at all; in other years that it grows moderately but that, over time, the overall direction is positive, as it should be if you are carefully following this book! It is unrealistic to assume that you will have gigantic leaps in business income every year.

Here, then, is the chart:

Year	Income projected from business for this year	Amount invested through business (pension plan) for year	8% return on $25,000 retirement plan plus additional business contribution	Amount invested personally this year	8% return on $10,000 personal investment capital plus additional annual personal contribution
1993	$52,000.00	$10,400.00	$52,056.00	$5,200.00	$23,112.00
1994	54,000.00	10,800.00	67,884.48	5,400.00	30,792.95
1995	60,000.00	12,000.00	86,275.24	6,000.00	39,736.40
1996	60,000.00	6,000.00	99,657.26	6,000.00	49,395.31
1997	62,000.00	12,400.00	121,021.84	6,200.00	60,042.93
1998	65,000.00	13,000.00	144,743.58	6,500.00	71,866.36
1999	70,000.00	14,000.00	171,443.06	7,000.00	85,175.67
2000	70,000.00	14,000.00	200,027.85	7,000.00	99,549.72
2001	73,000.00	14,600.00	231,798.07	7,300.00	115,397.69
2002	75,000.00	15,000.00	266,541.91	7,500.00	132,729.50
2003	80,000.00	16,000.00	305,145.26	8,000.00	151,987.86
2004	85,000.00	17,000.00	347,916.88	8,500.00	173,326.88
2005	85,000.00	17,000.00	394,110.23	8,500.00	196,373.03
2006	90,000.00	18,000.00	445,079.04	9,000.00	221,802.87
2007	100,000.00	20,000.00	502,285.36	10,000.00	250,347.09
2008	100,000.00	20,000.00	565,068.18	10,000.00	281,174.85

Our fictitious character has now completed the 15 years at the end of which he said he wanted to retire with 70% of his 1992 income. Adjusted for inflation at the annual rate of 6 percent, he'd need about $83,000 a year to do this. His combined pension and personal investment accounts have capital of $846,243.03. At an 8% annual return on investment, his income would be $67,699.44. While this is substantial "unearned" income, at this level it doesn't give him the income he needs. This being the case he would either have to:

- increase the percentage of money invested in his company pension plan from 20% to 25%, the current maximum percentage, or

- increase the business derived income earlier by expanding his service line and developing his Mobile Mini-Conglomerate, or

- earlier look for investments paying a higher rate of return, or

- earlier invest more personally, or

- work another year or two to make up the difference in capital needed, or

- (worst case) lower his sights and agree to live on less. (This, of course, is unthinkable!)

Note: this discussion has not included one very important variable: taxes. While your pension plan is tax-deferred, your personal investments are not. The taxes you have to pay on these investments obviously figure significantly into both your ability to develop capital and just when you can afford to start living on the earnings. Additionally, the discussion has not factored in potential Social Security payments you may receive, the capital you may get from selling your business, rights to any products you develop, *etc.* Obviously these will both bolster current income and capital assets.

The chart, therefore, does not take into account everything you need to consider when developing your capital. It does, however, point to many crucial things you must consider in developing your wealth. You must:

- Build your business so that it becomes the vehicle for generating the necessary income for both your business and personal investing;

- Invest regularly, religiously;

- Have a lifestyle objective and develop your investment strategy to achieve it;

- Invest early in the year;

- Reinvest all dividends and capital gains whenever possible;

- Sacrifice current (and necessarily short-term) pleasures to the achievement of long-term (and more lasting) results;

- Not expect unrealistically high returns on your investments. While you may do marginally better or worse than other investors, the odds are that you'll achieve an average, rather than the outstanding, return. It is better to plan on this conservative basis than on the basis of what you daydream about achieving.

Posting Your Investment Objectives

Like other important things in your business, your investment objectives need to be posted where you can regularly see them. You won't be surprised to learn I have a computer text file with these objectives, and that I review them regularly. If you work alone like me, there's also no reason why you shouldn't prominently post them, perhaps on the wall in front of your computer where you can see them every day. If you work with others, tape them where you alone can see them. Either way, learn to look at them regularly. *Remember:* this is a continuing objective, not a short-term one; this means you must refresh the objective often. Further, don't be afraid to change the chart as your circumstances change. Making $100,000 a year seemed like a lot of money to me back in 1979 when I launched my business; it seems pretty minuscule now. The chart I did then reflected my circumstances and aspirations *then;* it wouldn't do at all for now. This means you need to review your chart and make appropriate changes as necessary.

Posting Your Investment Reality

By the same token, create a text file that shows your current investment reality (or "portfolio" as some like to say). List the following:

- name of investment
- address of investment

- account number

- current value of investment

- maturation date and amount due at maturation (if bonds)

- purchase price (if stocks or mutual fund shares)

- designated beneficiary of investment (that is, the person you have informed the company who is to have this asset in the event of your death).

Particularly if you are purchasing bonds (which have specific maturation dates), you can arrange your investment chart by year so that you can project just how much capital you'll have in any given year. This enables you to fill in the capital amounts you'll need for generating the income you want.

Knowing Your Investment Rights

To be a wealth-builder in America in the '90's means having to familiarize yourself with applicable laws that pertain to the development of your wealth through both investments you make personally and through your business. This is not the place to go into all these laws in detail. For that you can consult my book **HOW TO MAKE AT LEAST $100,000 EVERY YEAR AS AN INDEPENDENT CONSULTANT IN YOUR OWN FIELD** and your accountant and financial adviser. I will, however, say this:

- Ask your accountant precisely how much money you can contribute into your pension account each year through your business. At this writing, contributions are generally limited to the lesser of 25 per cent of payroll or $30,000 per annum. Contribute this money as early as possible in the year. Further, if you're investing your pension money in an asset that you think will appreciate quickly, don't worry about over contributing to this fund. If the 25% overall limit for contributions to different types of plans is exceeded, the excess may be carried over. However, the combination of carryovers and regular deductions for any succeeding year may not exceed 25% of the compensation paid to participants in that year.

- Stay alert to current IRA regulations. Many workers are eligible to make tax deductible IRA contributions, particularly if they are not currently enrolled in a company pension plan or make under $25,000 yearly ($40,000 if filing jointly with your spouse). *Resource:* For more details on Individual Retirement Accounts, I recommend *IRA Investing Made Easy* by Anna Marie Hutchison. Eagle North Publications, P.O. Box 551, Oakhurst, CA 93644.

Note: it's a very good idea for you to develop a relationship with a knowledgeable certified financial planner or certified public accountant who can advise you on both how to minimize your tax obligations and take full advantage of whatever options currently exist for minimizing both your business and personal taxes and increasing the amount of money you can invest, particularly in tax deferred vehicles.

Keeping Abreast of Current Investment Vehicles

By the same token, you need the advice of investment professionals about where to invest the monies you are working so hard to save from your expenses and make through increased service sales. Here are a few ways of keeping abreast of investment developments:

- Read the business pages of your newspaper. Here you'll find regular columns and features on money management and investments which have done well. Make it a point to read these features on a regular basis.

- Clip out articles that both address specific investments and, more importantly, sources of investment information.

- Develop relationships with at least *two* investment advisers from whom you can request analyses of particular investments. I say two so that you can compare the advice they are giving.

Resources

Thousands of books have, of course, been written on how and where to invest. I am by no means opposed to them, although I think *books* should be used to provide general guidelines about how to invest and what to invest in rather than for specific recommendations. This is because the information in books, which may well be current when written, is apt to be somewhat dated by the time the book appears. That's why I prefer getting specific advice from investment services, advisers and periodicals where it's more apt to be up to date. Here are some sources which will help you:

- For mutual funds. Check your local library for the
  Morningstar Mutual Fund report (it's published every other
  week in two sections and costs $395 yearly. You can sub-
  scribe, if you want, from Morningstar, Inc., 53 West Jackson
  Blvd., Chicago, IL 60604; 800-876-5005). Morningstar covers
  about 1,200 of the larger and better-performing funds. The
  advantage of Morningstar is that it's not only full of statistics but evaluations based on longer-term performance. Also
  check out the annual mutual fund directory published by
  The Investment Company Institute, 1600 M St., NW, suite
  600, Washington, DC 20036. $5. It's a 232-page book that
  includes information on 3,400 mutual funds including each
  fund's investment objective, investment adviser, minimum
  and subsequent investments, the kinds of fees that may be
  charged (but not their specific levels) and information about
  where to buy shares. Another directory, this one published
  by Mutual Fund Educational Alliance, is limited to funds
  with either no load or a sales charge of 3.5 percent or less.
  This directory gives thumbnail figures on performance and
  more information on sales and expense charges than the
  Investment Company Institute offering, but covers only 500
  or so funds. (Mutual Fund Educational Alliance, 1900 Erie
  St., suite 120, Kansas City, MO 66116; $5). If you want to
  start with the information available from the funds themselves, here are the toll-free telephone numbers of some of
  the largest fund families: Dreyfus Corp., 800-782-6620;
  Fidelity Investments, 800-544-8888; Janus Capital Corp., 800-
  525-8983; Scudder, 800-225-2470; T. Rowe Price Associates,
  800-638-5660; Twentieth Century Mutual Funds, 800-345-
  2021; and Vanguard Group, 800-662-7447. If you want to
  talk to a real person, I recommend my friend and colleague
  Chris Lowry. Chris is the knowledgeable and friendly
  publisher of *No-Load Advisory*. This monthly publication
  ($108 yearly) focuses on commission-free investments and
  life and disability insurance. He gives you model portfolios,
  recommends funds you should own, and tells you how to
  avoid costly investment mistakes. You can contact him at
  No-Load Advisory, 23 Empire Dr., suite 209, St. Paul, MN
  55103 (612) 227-1843. If you mention my name, Chris will
  send you a free sample copy! You can also get a free "Mutual Funds Performance Guide" from Charles Schwab & Co.,
  Inc. Either contact your local Charles Schwab office or their
  headquarters at The Schwab Building, 101 Montgomery St.,
  San Francisco, CA 94104.

- For stocks. Try *Value Line Investment Survey*. This well-known publication covers about 1500 stocks and updates about 100 of them every week. You get historical information on all these companies, analysis and opinion by the Value Line research staff, and industry recommendations. Contact Value Line at 711 Third Ave., New York, NY 10017 (800) 833-0046. $525 annually. You can also get Value Line software. Call for details.

- For bonds. The most thorough information is provided by *Moody's Bond Record: Corporates, Convertibles, Governments and Municipals*. Updated monthly, $225 annually. Contact Moody's, 99 Church St., New York, NY 10007 (212) 553-0500. Like buying individual stocks, buying individual bonds can be hazardous. Thus, check the bond funds operated by the mutual fund companies mentioned above and those found in the current edition of *Business Week's Annual Guide To Mutual Funds* (McGraw-Hill, Inc.).

- For annuities. Annuities may or may not be right for you given your circumstances. As I write, lower interest rates are refocusing interest from fixed-rate annuities to variable-rate annuities. Is an annuity right for you, however? First, check with an impartial source like *Variable Annuity Performance Report*. It's published by Morningstar, Inc., 53 W. Jackson Blvd., Chicago, IL 60604 (800) 876-5005. Published monthly, $125 annually. Also check with your insurance agent. Of course, he'll have a vested interest in whatever product he represents!

Now Start Investing

If you're one of those 25% of people the Gallup Poll discovered has no assets and isn't investing, beginning to invest may seem strange or even unsettling. For one thing, the amount you initially contribute may seem — or indeed be — small. Don't worry about this. I agree with the old Chinese proverb that says the journey of a thousand miles begins with one step. The important thing is that you take that step as soon as you can . . . and start your children doing so, too. I made my first investment when I was about 12 years old and went into the Citizens National Bank of Downers Grove, IL with my father to buy a single share of Kroger stock, our local grocery store. No one at the bank either knew or told me I was underage and so couldn't legally buy the stock; my father didn't know, either. (If you're under 18, the contract isn't legally binding, you see). Thus, years ahead of my legal ability to do so, I became a capitalist. It was a very good thing, too. (Not least, because the stock made money.) At a time when other boys were catching frogs, I had a series of charts where I faithfully followed my stock picks every single day. Starting this early made investing an exciting game, not something alien.

If you've decided you must invest weekly to reach your objective, do so . . . even when the shoe pinches. It is most difficult to invest when you have little or no margin for doing so; when you have to give something up to make the investment. Then it's temptingly easy to postpone the action just until "things are a little better." Well, things will only be a "little better" because of investment . . . not because of postponing investing.

Even now, there are weeks in my life when I don't feel like investing . . . or when I've committed my funds to other projects and don't want to give anything up. The discipline, however, is the most important thing in investing. And so I'll share a little secret with you. On days when you don't have the money for the investment, send in your check anyway. Then get on the phone and start calling prospects and making deals. If you have to, make a deal that will cover the check and keep your investment program rolling, even if it's a deal you wouldn't ordinarily make. Living life this way also provides a certain competitive zest that enlivens the day.

If you're not quite so adventurous, write the investment check the day it's supposed to go in. Keep it ready to send as soon as you have the money to cover it. In other words, remind yourself that sending that investment check is as much a necessity as paying the electric bill.

Further, give yourself a day of the month . . . or a day of the week if you're a frequent investor like I am . . . when you automatically invest. These days, for example, many mutual funds will automatically deduct a certain amount of money from your checking account whenever you say so, like the 15th day of every month, without your having to do anything more than cover the charge. To make this situation work, either get religious about depositing the necessary funds to cover this charge the day before it's due or put overdraft protection on your account. Not only will you see your asset grow regularly this way, but you'll also take advantage of Dollar Cost Averaging. That is, you'll buy fund shares during both rising and falling markets and so, on average, lose the least and make the most. *Note:* make sure you keep good records about the cost of these shares. If you've been buying shares regularly, when the market drops, you should consider selling the shares you've paid top price for to reap tax advantages. The knowledgeable Chris Lowry brought this to my attention one year when I was looking for some tax savings. However, as he pointed out you've got to be clear just which shares you're selling. This means keeping good records. I suggest you keep both the hard-copy record of the transaction and a record in your computer. The latter is a lot easier to work with.

Do a reality check on your investments at regular intervals. Either check monthly or every ninety days to make sure you are on schedule for reaching your investment objective for this period . . . and for the year as a whole. As you know, I am a firm believer in Mind Channeling. Mind Channeling works very well with achieving investment objectives . . . so long as you know what you've got to do. If you find after 90 days you are not reaching your investment objective, arrange your professional and personal activities and lifestyle so you can make up the deficit. Will yourself to get the money you need . . . then do what's necessary by: 1) asking old clients to use your services again; 2) getting current clients to upgrade the value of the services you've providing, and/or 3) hammering home client-centered benefits to prospects you want to convert faster. By reviewing your investment portfolio at regular intervals, you can determine just how much you need to get back on track. You can then adjust both your business and personal activities accordingly and, by using the focused concentration of Mind Channeling, do what's necessary to achieve the objective.

Does all this take work? You bet your life it does! But here's something to keep in mind. You should regard what you must do to reach your investment objective as simply another part of the Mobile Mini-Conglomerate, that is as a necessary part of your business and personal life. For most people, investments remain terra incognita . . . to my complete astonishment. Just imagine what I'm saying. For millions of American adults, including large numbers of those running supposedly profit-oriented service businesses, one of the crucial elements of capitalism remains a black hole. Daily they contribute to the development of what remains the greatest capitalist culture in the world, daily they contribute to the financial success of other individuals who make this culture work for them . . . without themselves understanding this culture or doing what they can to benefit from it themselves. I find this absolutely mind-boggling — and abhorrent.

The minute you launch a business, you need to spend as much time understanding and researching investments as you do understanding and researching the development and marketing of your service.

Doing what is necessary to have the money to invest and to oversee the development of these investments, you see, are necessary components of the successful business.

The Next Investment Stage: Preparing For The Lifestyle You Really Want

So far we have geared our discussion to developing the capital for your *current* lifestyle. Indeed, in the Gallup Poll mentioned above, the example provided was an individual who wants to retire in 15 years with the equivalent of 70% of his current income. In other words, a person who either is satiated or who cannot envision himself leading a better lifestyle or doesn't want to do what's necessary to achieve it.

Now, if the person is genuinely satiated, I say more power to him. If he has looked deep into his heart and consulted with his soul and determined that what he has achieved is truly what he wants, then I congratulate him for the insight he has into himself and the work he has done to reach this point. Such a person must be happy, indeed.

If, on the other hand, no such process of introspection has taken place . . . and circumstances rather than yourself have shaped the decision (including, perhaps, an unhealthy dose of sloth and procrastination, fear of failure, and a disinclination for further action in life's battle), then I offer this individual nothing but contempt.

Thus, at this point, I ask you to search your heart and determine what is really important to *you;* not what others say is important . . . but what matters to you. Will you feel complete if, living in the midst of the greatest accumulation of wealth in the history of the world, you have nothing more than what you need to sustain your *current* lifestyle?

If not, then you must go to the next stage in this process: doing what is necessary to develop your business, its income flow and the capital assets that give you the life you *really* want.

Let me say a few general words about this superior life. Many people today attack this concept. They are the ones who argue that less is more; that less is moral; that we must live with limits and that we must be satisfied with them. I am not one of these irritating little creatures.

I cannot believe we were put on this earth to accept the limits others are so anxious to force us to accept. Instead, I believe we were put here to express ourselves to the furthest degree and to become everything we need to be to truly be ourselves. Thus, when you pursue financial enrichment, you are not merely involved in the mindless pursuit of wealth for the sake of wealth but of wealth so as to be able to better express all aspects of yourself.

As such, you may well decide that merely doing what you can to safeguard and ensure your current lifestyle is inadequate; that the achievement of this objective, while important in the short-term, can never be sufficient for you. If you reach this point, I congratulate you . . . and I welcome you to the elite corps of service marketers who have determined to use their technical skills, their business, their ingenuity, persistence, and determination to transform the circumstances of their current lives into the condition of events they truly desire, in the process becoming not merely richer themselves, but more complete and happy, too.

How will this happen?

You must start by being entirely honest with yourself about what you want. Frankly, so many of us in this culture have become so adept at lying about who we are and what we want (not least because chameleon-like we take on the shadings of those around us) that it may well prove difficult to achieve clarity about our own desires. So self-deceitful and accommodating for so long, you cannot expect to achieve this clarity in a single session or even in several. It will take time and patience during which you consider all the possibilities of the world . . . and rate them according to your own value system.

As you begin to achieve the necessary personal clarity that determines your future course of action, write down the results of your deliberations. You previously assessed your current lifestyle. Now it's time to assess your putative objectives. Do you *really* want them? How badly do you want them? Do you want them because *you* want them . . . or because *others* have told you you should want them? And if you indeed want them, are you willing to do what's necessary to get them?

When at last you've broken through to this kind of clarity, it's time, again, to draft a budget. How much money will you need to get what you now say you want?

As soon as you know, you draft another chart, just like the one above and begin projecting how you can raise the money to achieve what you want. In the final analysis, of course, this all translates into molding your business so it produces the income you need. This means following the guidelines presented in this book even more closely. In short, the realization of your dreams is both a process of being brutally honest with yourself about what you want . . . and mastering the necessary procedures which ensure that you get it. If this sounds simple, of course, both you and I know that it isn't. I know, however, if you will take the time to clarify your objectives and harness your heart and soul to their achievement, then the rest of what you need is right here in this book . . . and eminently achievable!

An Investment Potpourri

To help you along the way, I want to provide some more snippets of investment advice. They are "tricks of the trade" for getting you started faster and helping you achieve your objective earlier, with less frustration, uncertainly and anxiety.

- Don't invest alone. If you're married with a family, make investment a game. Get your spouse to invest and your children. Each member of the family should have his or her own bank account and should be encouraged to contribute to the joint effort of making your family wealthier. I do not approve of the notion that only "daddy" should be investing. I think *every* woman and *every* child out of the cradle should look out for constructive ways of saving money and investing money. Nor do I think that the efforts they put in should go unrewarded. Obviously, the major reward will always be the return on investment and consequent improvement in the family's lifestyle. However, along the way there should be a lot of camaraderie and prizes, too. I fail to understand why the hoopla that goes along with the American sports culture shouldn't be transferred, in part, to the far more important business of developing wealth. Thus, if your children recommend ways that help cut your expenses . . . and find ways of developing new income sources for themselves (and for you?), reward them. The same goes with your spouse. If you are not married or cannot get your family involved, either join an investment club (contact the American Association of Individual Investors, 625 N. Michigan Ave., Chicago, IL 60611. 312-280-0170), or get an investment crony, like I have. A little healthy competition and some old fashion bragging is no bad thing once in a while. Indulge yourself!

- Make your first investments very, very conservative. You will read article after article about "risk tolerance", which is the threshold beyond which you do not feel comfortable investing. Personally, my risk tolerance level is very low. That's why I put my first million into U.S. Treasury bonds. True, at the time I was doing this, other people were sinking their money in heavily leveraged real estate that returned them substantial paper profits in very short times. True, I was not always inwardly content when I heard about their hefty annual returns against my more plodding rates. He who laughs last, however . . . I've had an ex-real estate millionaire work for me for $8 an hour, while many others have complained to me about how their real estate portfolios crashed. But when interest rates dropped substantially, the bonds I had that were paying 12-15% annually appreciated substantially. Moreover, through it all I never had to worry about anything more substantial than the United States, Inc. going out of business. These days, of course, U.S. Treasury bond rates are far lower. What's the conservative equivalent now? Investing in a solid, no-load, growth and income mutual fund. All the companies whose 800-numbers I've provided above have them. After you've got a million tucked away in this kind of investment, then you can fly a little higher.

- Pay off your home mortgage early. A lot of your investment capital is being eaten away by your mortgage interest payments. When interest rates started dropping and the return on other investments dropped, too, many programs popped up showing how much you could save in mortgage interest payments by making twice monthly mortgage payments. You don't pay any more this way, but you do save tens of thousands in interest payments. I'm in favor of this. I am also in favor of making regular principal reduction payments (weekly if possible). I've been doing this myself for some time now and by Christmas, 1993 at age 46, I will no longer have any mortgage payments to make. Sure, I will have lost this interest as a deduction from my personal income taxes . . . but I will have gained a very significant source of investment capital, too. *Note:* some mortgages still retain a penalty for paying off your mortgage early, but they are in the minority. Check with the customer service department of your bank or mortgage company, however, before doing anything! And if you refinance your mortgage, make sure there is no prepayment penalty in your new mortgage. *Resource:* you can get further details on how to reduce your mortgage in the booklet *How To Cut Your Mortgage In Half!: A Step-By-Step Guide To Saving Thousands Of Dollars On Your Home Mortgage* by R. David Cartwright. It's published by Data Communications Group, P.O. Box 1087, Montpelier, VT 05601. They'll also do a personalized computerized printout for you based on your situation and the amount of prepayments you wish to make.

• Delay payments to others so you can invest. Cash management means getting your money early . . . and delaying payments to others to the very last minute. There are many reasons for wanting to get your payments in in a timely fashion; one of them is so you can invest earlier. My policy on this matter is clear: if the amount in question is significant (by which I mean anything over $100), check with the people who owe you the money a week before it's due and ensure they have all the paperwork they need to get you your money promptly. If the money is really significant (over $500), open a Federal Express or other overnight carrier account. If you have the slightest doubt the money will be late, provide the debtor with this carrier number and urge him to use it. If the money is even one day late, call and find out where it is. This can be done in the very nicest way . . . but always pointedly. Through the often nerve-wracking period of the Gulf War and the extended recession that inaugurated the 'nineties, I have become an expert in collections. As a good Calvinist, I come from a legacy of mistrusting people anyhow; as a businessman in good standing, I know just how often people will lie about when and how they intend to pay you. It is only the ingenuous and the stupid (often it's hard to tell them apart) who don't spend time perfecting their accounts receivable techniques. By the same token, you must master the art of slow payment so you get the extra time to pay your bills. I would, for instance, rather pay a bill on a credit card (so long as I didn't pay this bill late and so incur finance charges) than pay with a company check. This way I'd both get frequent flyer mileage (make sure you use a card with this advantage) *and* several extra weeks before I had to pay the bill. Then I'd take the money I had in my account for paying the bill . . . and invest it instead, thereafter getting on the phone immediately with prospects, clients, *etc.* to drum up additional business. Is this what you're doing?

- Set an investment objective that is beyond your current reach. If you're finding it easy to reach your investment objectives, you're investing too little. Investing should always be a stretch, a challenge, just like exercise . . . or building your overall business for that matter. If you're feeling no pain investing $250 a week, raise the amount $100. This will be good for the development of your capital assets . . . and for the development of your business, too, since that's where you'll have to search for the extra money to cover your enhanced investment program.

- Balance your portfolio. Charles Clough, chief investment strategist for Merrill Lynch, recommends that if you have at least five years to go before retirement, 2/3's of your assets should be in stocks and the other 1/3 in bonds. (By the way, he suggests the exact opposite for retirees.) Gordon Snyder, in charge of retirement products for Twentieth Century Investors, suggests investors subtract their age from 100 to give a baseline percentage: someone age 40, say, should put at least 60 percent of his money earmarked for retirement in stocks. When you're a service business entrepreneur your balanced portfolio will include the usual stocks and bonds, real estate (principally your home) . . . and, don't forget, your business — and its various divisions. Growing a business also means growing a capital asset. *Resource:* you'll want to know how to get the most money from this capital asset when it comes time to sell. In this regard, see David P. Francis' book *How To Sell Your Business Without A Broker & Save Big Commission Dollars.* (John Wiley & Sons, Inc.)

- Look for long-term gains, instead of precise market timing. I remember a rather pathetic story some time back in the *Boston Globe* about the retirement of the manager of Harvard University's large investment portfolio. After many years of doing well, he'd missed a major turn in the stock market, keeping Harvard uninvested at a time when other institutional funds were making sizable gains. A short time later, despite a previously substantial career, he retired in disgrace. The solution to this problem is to put time to work for you . . . and not worry about precise market timing. When even the big guys with access to the best information cannot figure out precisely when and where to put their money, you should not only not be trying to do this, you should try a different course altogether. When, for instance, the Dow average dropped over 500 points in October, 1987, after I got over my initial shock (like everybody else in the market I'd taken a pounding that day) I started the next day *buying*. The shares I bought that day have been some of my highest appreciating assets since that time. Time and its ally compounding interest are where it's at for most of us and when they're further allied with tax-deferred gain, we're sure to do well.

- Avoid investing in individual stocks. Everybody I know has a story about some guy who made a fortune in an individual stock. It is the lure of this big hit that keeps people sinking sizable amounts of money in this kind of investment. However, I urge you to take another course of action. Unless you are prepared to spend some serious research time hunting down individual stock investments and monitoring them closely, you can lesson your risk (and still take advantage of equity appreciation) by investing in mutual fund shares. These need less oversight. Instead of having to worry about the rise and fall in individual share prices, put your time into the development of your own business where, thanks to the fact that you are an expert and know your market, you can ensure greater returns than what usually happens to stock market ingenues. *Note:* if you do still want to invest in individual stocks, read *Value Line* as recommended above and take the advice about having at least two investment advisers you can consult for information . . . both about when to get in and when to sell.

- Review your investment chart frequently. Developing money is like developing a well-tended garden. Day by day you can see the results of your work. Approaching investing in the deliberate, conservative, even plodding fashion I've recommended here may never produce truly spectacular results, but it will produce meaningful results. When you look at your chart you can see them for yourself and take the kind of quiet pleasure you ought from what you've done.

- Make a small investment rather than make no investment at all. As I have regularly stressed in this chapter, you must develop the investment *habit*. If you can only to invest the price of a pack of cigarettes a day, do so. Make the trek to the bank and deposit it; (don't just keep it in a sock drawer). Yes, the amount is small, but it is still an investment and as such will still return income. Give the small amount you have to invest the same deliberate consideration as a big amount. Go through the same steps to make the investment. Even at this level, you're a player . . . and as such you should be proud of yourself.

- Reward yourself. Of course, you are going to have the money from your investments, the security and peace of mind they bring, the joy of achieving such solid results. But while you're still working on the foundation of your wealth, take time to reward yourself along the way. Just because your Treasury bill isn't going to mature for 23 years, doesn't mean you shouldn't reward yourself *now* for making the investment. After all, think of all you went through to get to the point where you're able to make it. You had to think up the service you offer, refine and develop it, identify prospects, market it, close the deal, deliver the service (with all the work that entailed), collect the money, set an investment objective, find the right investment vehicle . . . and actually invest the money. Yes, I'd say that for all that you are certainly entitled to a reward *right this minute*. Give it to yourself! You deserve it! Personally, when you come and visit me you'll find that I've surrounded myself not only with evidence of my achievement but with the rewards I've given myself as congratulation for working so hard to achieve. Each old master painting; each silken Persian rug; the lead crystal; the fine china . . . most of it represents a reward for a demanding task well done . . . or an action — like an investment — that took time and trouble to accomplish. These rewards are a crucial part of my life, and they should be a crucial part of yours, too. No one is waiting to reward you; most of what you do, in fact, will secure no recognition whatsoever from others, even if they benefit. But there is one person who should never overlook what you've done . . . and never be too busy, too committed, too broke or too rushed to recognize it . . . and that person is YOU. Here is one of the places rewarding yourself is most necessary and desirable.

Conclusion

The End Of The Beginning

You and I are old friends now. We've come a long way together. I must say I've enjoyed this opportunity to provide the guidelines you'll use to become a multi-millionaire selling your service.

Now it's time for you to really get down to business!

You've learned all the mistakes that can derail your enterprise . . . and pledged yourself not to make them.

You've learned how to craft the multi-million dollar plan, how to create the cash copy that'll get your client prospects to sit up, pay attention to the benefits you've got for them . . . and take immediate action to get those benefits.

You've learned how to craft the kinds of marketing communications that focus on your prospects and customers . . . and produce them quickly, easily, and economically.

You've learned how to turn your computer into a client-centered marketing department of truly awesome power.

You've learned the secrets of generating all the leads you need . . . from free media, talk programs, direct response marketing, classified and space ads, and through such specialized lead generators as card decks, electronic moving message display signs, and package stuffer programs.

You've also learned how to set up a lead-closing program that's as aggressive and successful as the lead-generating program that necessarily precedes it.

You've learned how to work with your clients to get more business faster . . . and how to work with clients and customers so you keep and profit from them longer. You've learned how to expand your business both through independent contractors and employees and through all the components of the wealth-producing Mobile Mini-Conglomerate. Finally, you've learned how to take the increasing profit you're producing and turn it into capital, the bedrock of both financial independence and the lifestyle you've always wanted for yourself and your family.

Yes, we have come a long way together!

. . . But our journey together doesn't stop now. It just changes.

As you know, unlike other authorities I haven't just packaged this information to create a book . . . but to launch a relationship. As you set out to implement these techniques and achieve your greater fortune, I want to know how you're doing. Thousands of people around the world regularly share their odyssey with me. They tell me what's working, what's not, how they've perfected the techniques they got from me, and what kind of additional information they require to reach their objectives. I confess that dealing with so many success seekers so continually can be draining. More importantly, these vital stories keep me in touch with the reality of achieving success in the '90's in a way matched by very few others. *They* orate, pontificate, design paradigms, and launch buzz words. *I* keep looking at people like you . . . because that's where the action really is.

As such I invite you to keep in touch and keep me informed about your progress. Moreover, I invite you to keep me as your secret success weapon. I know, you see, that success is not achieved by some effortless two-stepping. It's not inevitable as the poor Victorians used to imagine. It's the result of continual deliberation and constant refinement. It's the product of thoughtfulness, persistence, unrelenting focus, and, yes, great humility and an ability to remain open to beneficial change when those around you succumb to the numbing banality of the "tried and true".

There will be days, even many days, as you implement and develop your success system that you will encounter the fate of all those who strive to make the world a better place using the engine of business.

People whose lives you can transform and improve will ignore you, hang up on you, throw your marketing communications away without reading them, even ridicule you. All this, however, you must take in stride. You are, you see, a necessary and superior person, the kind of person who must succeed, or put our civilization at further hazard. Having conceived the kind of service that improves the lives of your clients and customers, you must not let *anything* stand in the way of your integrating it into their lives. If you do, you fail them and leave them with relatively disadvantaged lives; you fail yourself, and you fail all the rest of us who are in league with you to make the world a better place. Were you to fail you would leave us all a little weaker, a little more hopeless, a little less likely to transform the world.

So you see, a lot rests on your succeeding . . . which means a lot rests on your successfully implementing the beneficial guidelines of this book.

When those days come, however, when things are not going your way, when you feel the world is too much with you, take this resource down and study it some more. Too, use the catalog that follows. Familiarize yourself with the many other tools I've fashioned over the years and the ones I've also found and recommend to help you. Finally, keep my telephone number close at hand. It helps to know you have a friend, supporter, and fellow service tactician just this close ready to listen to you, push, empathize, or exult as the case may be.

You see, we're all in this together. And if I can help you achieve the promise of this book's title, I will. Just remember to share the joy of your achievement with me. After all, I know how very hard you've worked to earn it!

About The Author

Surrounded by a mountain of paper, an underused exercise machine and the incessant hum of his computer, Dr. Jeffrey Lant confronts each day with one insistent question: "How can I help even more people develop their businesss by helping them raise the money they need, by helping them sell more of their products and services?"

He's answered — and continues to answer — this question in a variety of ways. Over the last 13 years, he's created the 8 volume "Get Ahead" Series that presents the exact steps people need to sell any product or service. In addition, he's written the standard book on how non-profit organizations can raise the money they need from corporations, foundations, and individuals. His other books include a volume he edited on Harvard College and a rollicking history of Queen Victoria's Court that was presented to Queen Elizabeth II on a blue silk pillow.

Jeffrey also created and regularly writes the Sure-Fire Business Success Column now reaching over 1.5 million people monthly in about 200 print and electronic information sources in many countries... puts out the quarterly Sure-Fire Business Success Catalog... his quarterly Sales & Marketing Success card-deck... and is president of JLA Ventures, which develops and markets many different products and services. Further, he is a well-known speaker on many business development and fund raising topics, offering programs around America and in other countries.

Holder of four earned university degrees, including a Ph.D. from Harvard, Jeffrey and his work have been honored by many institutions, both public and private. In 1991, he was raised to the dignity of The Rt. Hon. The Count of Raban by His Beatitude Alexander II, Patriarch of Antioch, Syria. This title was originally held by one of Jeffrey's ancestors who traveled with King Richard I of England to the Third Crusade, 800 years ago. Through his mother, a peeress in her own right, he is also heir to both the Barony of Barlais and the Barony of Kezoun, Crusader titles 8 centuries old.

At some point, like millions of people around the world who first connected with Jeffrey through a workshop, media program, audio or video cassette, article or book, you'll want to be in closer touch with this man to see how he can help you better. No problem! Whenever you're ready, simply call (617) 547-6372 or write 50 Follen St., Suite 507, Cambridge, MA 02138 to request your free year's subscription to his quarterly catalog (a copy of which concludes this book). He's ready for you *now!*

645

THE UNABASHED SELF-PROMOTER'S GUIDE

What Every Man, Woman, Child And Organization In America Needs To Know About Getting Ahead by Exploiting The Media

Thousands and thousands of people around the world are already profiting from this book. They range from people running small businesses to two sitting members of the United States Senate, from people with the most idealistic motives to those who have no other motive than simply wanting to get filthy rich. Members of state legislatures and celebrities with well-known names are using this book to build their stature and promote their interests... entrepreneurs swear by it because it promotes their products and services to targeted markets.

> *"Your knowledge of the subject of marketing is mind-boggling!"*
>
> Richard Lawrence, Lowell, MA

You need this book if you're:

- running *any* kind of business entity;
- selling *any* product or service;
- running *any* charitable or nonprofit organization;
- a professional who's tired of laboring in obscurity!

> *"THE UNABASHED SELF-PROMOTER'S GUIDE is for everybody. I don't care what you're doing!"*
>
> KIEV Radio, Los Angeles

You get 364 of Jeffrey's characteristically information-dense pages. Learn how to:

- create Quintessential American Success Images... and avoid Failure Images;
- produce the documents you need to deal with the media. It's all here from media advisory, standard media release, biographical documents, fact sheets, chronology, position papers, prepared statements, media schedule, clip sheet, announcements, etc. *Every* form you'll ever use when dealing with the media is already done... and immediately available for you;
- create and maintain a media Self-Promotion Network;
- produce all the print articles you'll ever need... you get exact formats the print media use every day and how and when to use them;
- handle every kind of media interview... including hostile ones;
- get just the right photographs... and how to use them;
- constantly appear on radio and television programs... and know what to do to promote your products/ services when you get there;
- get "waves" of media... not just isolated, single-shot appearances;
- create and promote books through free media... yes, there isn't an author or publisher in the world who should be without this book!
- use negative media... to enhance your image.

And much, much more.

Over 20,000 copies in print!

Item #B2

365 pages. $39.50 postpaid!

649

651

#B7
HOW TO MAKE A WHOLE LOT MORE THAN $1,000,000 WRITING, COMMISSIONING, PUBLISHING AND SELLING "HOW-TO" INFORMATION

> *"I love HOW TO MAKE A WHOLE LOT MORE THAN $1,000,000... TREMENDOUSLY! Thanks for writing it."*
> Don Floyd, Gainesville, FL

Stop trying to make your million dollars selling yourself by the hour. That's stupid. Learn what it takes to find problem-solving information and turn it into a multi-million dollar information empire.

This is the most detailed resource ever created — all 552 pages of it — providing you with *precisely* what you need to make real money from how-to information.

You get exactly what you need to:

- create the information products people want to buy;
- produce products you can profit from for a lifetime... not just a season;
- produce your products fast, accurately and for the least money;
- make tens of thousands of extra dollars from end-of-product catalogs;
- save money — and avoid problems — by following Jeffrey's product production guidelines. You also get the names, addresses and phone numbers of reputable production people who won't rip you off;
- turn your personal computer into the most effective customer service center imaginable;
- get other people to produce money-making products for you so you can

make your million-dollar fortune faster;
- get all the free publicity you can handle for your products from radio, television, newspapers, magazines... in this country and abroad;
- master the essentials of direct response marketing so you bring your message to just the right people — and get them to buy your products fast;
- make big money through talk programs, bookstores, libraries, overseas rights, exhibits... and more.

This book is packed with the names, addresses and phone numbers of dozens of people who can help you sell more products fast. As with all Jeffrey's books, he doesn't just provide the step-by-step details you need... he directs you to the specific people you need to make money fast.
552 pages. $39.50

HEY, BARGAIN HUNTERS... HERE ARE FOUR PACKAGES THAT'LL SAVE YOU MONEY AND GIVE YOU MORE DE-TAILED, PROFIT-MAKING INFORMATION THAN YOU'VE PROBABLY EVER SEEN IN ONE PLACE IN YOUR LIFE.

#C4
Combined offer for the future information millionaire...

Four fast-paced, densely detailed books by Jeffrey give you a fast start towards becoming a million dollar+ producer & seller of books, booklets, audio cassettes and Special Reports. Whatever your field! Get **HOW TO MAKE A WHOLE LOT MORE THAN $1,000,000 WRITING, COMMISSIONING, PUBLISHING AND SELLING "HOW-TO" INFOR-MATION; CASH COPY; THE UNABASHED SELF-PROMOTER'S GUIDE** and **MONEY TALKS.** Just $115. You save over $35!

#C6
Combined offer for the people who want to sell more of their products and services faster...

Now benefit from Jeffrey's step-by-step marketing advice and learn how to sell more of your products and services for the least possible cost. Get a deal on **THE UNABASHED SELF-PROMOTER'S GUIDE, MONEY MAKING MARKETING** and **CASH COPY**. $80 for all three. You save $23.45.

#C7
... when you want to master all the master's profit-making techniques.

Get all eight books in Jeffrey's "Get Ahead" Series, including **CASH COPY, THE CONSULTANT'S KIT, THE UNABASHED SELF-PROMOTER'S GUIDE, MONEY TALKS, HOW TO MAKE AT LEAST $100,000 EVERY YEAR AS A SUCCESSFUL CONSULTANT IN YOUR OWN FIELD, MONEY MAKING MARKETING, HOW TO MAKE A WHOLE LOT MORE THAN $1,000,000 WRITING, COMMISSIONING, PUBLISHING AND SELLING "HOW-TO" INFOR-MATION and NO MORE COLD CALLS!** Well over 3,000 pages of detailed step-by-step guidelines on achieving success by creating and selling products and services. No other specialist — anywhere — has ever written such complete instructions on what it takes to make money — lots of money. We'll be flabbergasted if you don't make back the cost of this package many hundreds of time. Get all eight for just $240. Save nearly $60! You automatically qualify for a free 60-minute cassette with this order!!!

#C9
Combined offer for service sellers who won't rest content until they're millionaires...

Now get a deal on the four essential resources that'll turn your service business into a cash-generating process that'll make you a millionaire. Package includes **NO MORE COLD CALLS!; CASH COPY; MONEY MAKING MARKETING,** and **THE UNABASHED SELF-PROMOTER'S GUIDE**. Just $110. You save $47!

652

YOUR NONPROFIT OR CHARITABLE ORGANIZA- TION IS LOOKING FOR MONEY. HERE'S WHAT YOU NEED TO GET IT...

#B8 New Edition! Just Published!
DEVELOPMENT TODAY: A FUND RAISING GUIDE FOR NONPROFIT ORGANIZATIONS

"DEVELOPMENT TODAY isn't for the faint of heart or those with a penchant for pondering. Lant orders you into the heat of the battle and barks "Fight!" His is a refreshing approach, one especially suited for those unafraid of braving the fund raising trenches. We recommend it!"

Contributions

Tens of thousands of nonprofit organizations around America have made this book by Jeffrey the premier fundraising resource of its kind. Why? Because by following its detailed step-by-step guidelines, you raise the money you need for your capital, program and operating needs... even when money is tight.
You'll learn how to:
- determine how much money you can realistically raise;
- create the plan that'll get it for you;
- get even recalcitrant Board members to assist;
- pick just the right corporations and foundations to solicit;
- write fund raising proposals that get results and...
- ... follow up proposals that get rejected... so you can turn a no into a yes;
- raise money from community residents and businesses;
- use direct mail effectively and raise more money faster;

- mount profit-making special events... year after year;
- do your own capital campaign needs assessment and save tens of thousands of dollars;
- find volunteers... and get them to do what needs to be done...
and much, much more — including one of Jeffrey's characteristically packed Samples Sections containing ready-to-use documents, letters, log forms, etc. 282 pages. $29.95

PG#2
THE COMPLETE GUIDE TO PLANNED GIVING: EVERYTHING YOU NEED TO KNOW TO COMPETE SUCCESSFULLY FOR MAJOR GIFTS.

Look who's recommending Debra Ashton's definitive planned giving book these days:
American Association of Museums
American Lung Association
CASE
Christian Management Association
National Catholic Stewardship Council
National Hospice Organization
National Easter Seals
National Society of Fund Raising Executives
Planned Parenthood
Public Broadcasting System
Society for Nonprofit Organizations
and many, many more.
Why? Because if you expect to raise money from major gifts, the experts agree you must have this book.

"This is the most complete, practical guide ever written on planned giving!"

Frank Minton, President, National Committee on Planned Giving

Awesomely detailed information on how to:
- start a pooled income fund and gift annuity program
- use life insurance to facilitate major gifts
- conduct screening sessions to identify prospects capable of making major gifts
- find & use planned giving software & consultants;
- build board support for planned giving;
- use planned gifts to solve major donor problems
- develop a 12-month plan ensuring success for your program!
Based on current tax laws, this is a book you cannot afford to be without. 400 pages. $54.

BOTH THESE BOOKS ARE RECOMMENDED BY THE AMERICAN LIBRARY ASSOCIATION. IF YOUR CASH IS TIGHT, YOUR LOCAL LIBRARY WILL EITHER HAVE THEM... OR GET THEM FOR YOU! ASK!!!

"I'm midway through HOW TO MAKE A WHOLE LOT MORE THAN $1,000,000... and had to stop to order additional books from you. I've read such junk published by hucksters, I wanted to let you know how grateful I am for your book. Besides being incredibly informative, it's downright funny! Thanks."

Frances O'Brien, Westport, CT

Special Reports

We've already sold tens of thousands of these quick and dirty profit-making reports (#R1 – #R88). They're densely written five-page, single-spaced computer print-outs personalized with your name so you know you're supposed to follow the good-for-you directions. Don't expect fancy packaging. Just solid, up-to-date information you can use right now. Each report is packed with use-it-now details so you can achieve what the title promises. No one else in the country offers this kind of instantly available, eminently practical information in this form or gets them to you this fast. Stock up on 'em. **Just 6 bucks each, 3 for $14.**

#R1

THE SECRET TO BECOMING A MILLIONAIRE SELLING "HOW-TO" INFORMATION: 10 STEPS FOR CREATING, COMMISSION-ING, PUBLISHING AND SELLING PROBLEM-SOLVING BOOKS, BOOKLETS, SPECIAL REPORTS AND AUDIO CASSETTES. In honor of his new book **HOW TO MAKE A WHOLE LOT MORE THAN $1,000,000 WRITING, COMMIS-SIONING, PUBLISHING AND SELLING "HOW-TO" INFORMA-TION,** Jeffrey lays down the rules for profitably selling problem-solving information. $6

#R2

SIX STEPS TO MORE SUCCESS-FUL NEWSLETTERS. If you're putting any money into producing either a free or subscription newsletter... or even thinking about it... don't do anything until you get Roger Parker's steps for designing the product so it accomplishes your objectives. Roger's one smart cookie, and he knows what it takes to get people to pay attention to your newsletter. Here he shares this vital information with you. $6

#R3

WHICH 2% WILL YOUR AUDI-ENCE SIT STILL FOR? In honor of the publication of her new book, Jeffrey interviews author Marian Woodall on how to find the focus that is appropriate for each audience. Too many speakers try to cram everything they know into their talk... and end up alienating their audience. Not you. Here you learn exactly what you've got to do to give the right talk to the people you're speaking to. $6

#R4

HOW TO ELIMINATE JOB STRESS AND INCREASE PROF-ITS AND PRODUCTIVITY THROUGH STRESS MANAGE-MENT. Jeffrey interviews author Dr. Andrew Goliszek about what you can do to cut stress in the office. Stress doesn't just debilitate and even kill you... it cuts your profits! Here's what you can do to help yourself and break your stress habit. $6

#R5

MEGATRAITS: 12 TRAITS OF SUCCESSFUL PEOPLE. Jeffrey interviews Doris Lee McCoy, author of a new book based on interviews with several hundred successful people, and identifies the crucial traits, the "megatraits", they possess in common that helped get them where they are. $6

#R6

HOW TO MAKE YOUR PR MAKE MONEY. For most businesses, public relations is a useless activity that is not tied to the profit picture. Now Jeffrey tells you how to turn your expensive public relations into a money-making activity that will sell your products and services faster. $6

#R8

OVERWORKED ENTREPRE-NEURS' GUIDE TO LUXURIOUS CRUISE DISCOUNTS. Jeffrey interviews Captain Bill Miller, author of the superb new book Insider's Guide To Cruise Discounts, and provides you with specific information on how you can take some of the world's best and most luxurious cruises for ridiculously low rates. $6

#R9

WHAT EVERY INVENTOR ABSO-LUTELY MUST DO BEFORE CONTACTING ANY MANUFAC-TURER. Jeffrey interviews consultant Arnold Winkelman, author of the new book The Inventor's Guide To Market-ing, about precisely what you've got to do before you show any manufacturer your creation so that your rights are fully protected. Must reading if you're an inventor! $6

#R10

EIGHT SELF-DEFEATING BE-HAVIORS PREVENTING YOU FROM BECOMING THE MILLION-AIRE YOU *SAY* YOU WANT TO BE... AND WHAT TO DO ABOUT THEM! Here Jeffrey lays out eight significant behaviors making it difficult, if not impossible, for people to become millionaires and tells them just what to do to overcome them. If you keep talking about wanting to be a millionaire but just can't seem to get started... or keep failing along the way... these behaviors are probably bedevilling you. Learn what they are... and how to get rid of them. $6

#R11

EVERYTHING YOU NEED TO KNOW TO PREPARE YOUR OWN WILL — WITHOUT THE EXPENSE OF A LAWYER! Eight out of ten people in America die without a will, throwing their accumulated posses-sions and savings into the hands of the court system which then allocates what's available. To stop this idiocy, Jeffrey interviews Attorney Daniel Sitarz, author of the new book Prepare Your Own Will And Testament — Without A Lawyer. Here's exactly what you need to do to prepare your own legal will without a lawyer, securing your estate and saving the lawyer's fees. $6

654

#R12

WHY MOST CONSULTANTS CAN NEVER MAKE AT LEAST $100,000 A YEAR... AND WHAT TO DO SO YOU WILL. Jeffrey shows you why most consultants fail to make at least $100,000 a year... and provides specific steps to follow so you will. $6

#R13

HOW TO GET FREE AND LOW-COST SOFTWARE FOR YOUR IBM AND IBM-COMPATIBLE COMPUTER. Jeffrey interviews John Gliedman, author of the new book Tips And Techniques for Using Low-Cost And Public Domain Software, on how to get your hands on some of the stupendous amount of free and low-cost software currently available for IBM and IBM-compatible personal computers. Gliedman provides the names, addresses and phone numbers of just where to go to save big money on your software and techniques on how to use it effectively. $6

#R14

HOW TO CREATE CLASSIFIED AND SMALL SPACE ADS THAT GET YOUR PROSPECTS TO RESPOND... AND WHAT TO DO WHEN THEY DO! Jeffrey gives you the low-down on how to create classified and small space ads that get people to respond... and how to create an effective, profit-making program so you can turn your new prospects into buyers... fast! $6

#R15

SETTING AND GETTING YOUR FEE. Jeffrey interviews author Kate Kelly upon the occasion of a new edition being published of her well-known book How To Set Your Fees And Get Them. People selling a service either run the risk of pricing themselves too low (and working for too little) or too high... and losing the business. Kate tells you just what you need to do so you price your services just right... for fast sale and maximum return. $6

#R16

HOW TO MAKE MONEY BUYING PRE-FORECLOSURE PROPER-TIES BEFORE THEY HIT THE COURTHOUSE STEPS. Jeffrey interviews property investment advisor Tom Lucier, author of the new book How To Make Money Buying Pre-Foreclosure Properties Before They Hit The Courthouse Steps, on just what it takes to make big money in pre-foreclosure properties. New workshops have sprung up recently charging as much as $6000 for a weekend providing this kind of advice. Why pay 6G's when specialist Tom Lucier provides the detailed steps right here? $6

#R17

HOW TO DEVELOP AND USE A CLIENT-CENTERED QUESTION-NAIRE THAT GETS YOUR PROS-PECTS TO TELL YOU WHAT THEY WANT... SO YOU CAN SELL IT TO THEM. In this report, Jeffrey helps people who hate making cold calls... and can't figure out how to get their prospects to tell them what they want. If you can solve this problem, you can sell any product or service. Here are the guidelines you need to create this unique client-centered prospecting questionnaire... and how to use it. When you do, your prospects start telling you precisely what they want... all you have to do is give it to them. $6

#R18

HOW TO DO "HOW-TO" (BOOK-LETS AND BOOKS, THAT IS). Here Jeffrey tells you exactly how to produce a how-to booklet or book that really tells your readers how to do what your title promises. Most how-to products are dismal failures, because they don't provide the details your readers need to achieve what they want. Don't let this happen to you. Learn how to create a truly useful how-to. $6

#R19

HOW TO MAKE OVER $100,000 *EVERY* YEAR WITH YOUR OWN CATALOG SELLING PROBLEM-SOLVING INFORMATION PROD-UCTS. Most people in mail order try to make a big kill from a single problem-solving information product... or just a few. Here Jeffrey shows you why that's futile... and how to go about establishing a client-centered catalog selling how-to information products that will make you at least $100,000 every year... and maybe a whole lot more. $6

#R20

HOW TO USE JOB ADS TO LAND THE JOB YOU *REALLY* WANT. If you've ever tried to get a job using classified job ads you know how time consuming and frustrating it is. Here Jeffrey interviews jobs-finding special-ist Kenton Elderkin, author of the new book How To Get Interviews From Job Ads: Where To Look, What To Select, Who To Write, What To Say, When To Follow-Up, How To Save Time. With these techniques answering job ads can lead to the interviews you need... and the good job you want. $6

#R21

YOUR WORST FEARS REALIZED, OR WHAT TO DO WHEN THE CORPORATION OR FOUNDA-TION DECLINES YOUR PRO-POSAL. The competition for corporate and foundation dollars for non-profit organizations has never been greater... and will get worse. You can count on getting turned down, often. What you do next determines whether your organization will ever get the money it needs from these sources. Here are Jeffrey's guidelines for turning a no into a yes, for doing what it takes to build a lucrative relationship with a funding source that has just turned you down. Since this will happen to you (if it isn't happening already), prepare for it now. $6

655

Ordering multiple products? If what you're ordering comes from different producers, it will not be delivered at the same time. So, if you've only received a partial order, don't worry. THE REST IS ON ITS WAY!

#R22

IT ISN'T JUST SAYING THE RIGHT THING THAT MAKES A SUCCESSFUL PRESENTATION... OR WHAT YOU'VE REALLY GOT TO DO TO CONNECT WITH YOUR AUDIENCE AND PERSUADE THEM TO LISTEN TO YOU. This isn't a report about speech content... it's a report about how to deal with your audience so they like you and want to listen to what you have to say. Verbal presentations aren't just about imparting information; they're about persuading people to do things. Here's what you've got to do to achieve this crucial objective. $6

#R23

HOW TO CREATE A BROCHURE AND COVER LETTER YOUR PROSPECTS WILL RESPOND TO... NOW! In honor of the new second printing of his book CASH COPY: HOW TO OFFER YOUR PRODUCTS AND SERVICES SO YOUR PROSPECTS BUY THEM... NOW!, Jeffrey tells you how to solve one of the most basic marketing problems of any business: what it takes to create a brochure and cover letter that gets people to respond, instead of being tossed. $6

#R24

HOW TO RAISE MONEY FOR YOUR NON-PROFIT ORGANIZA-TION WITH AN ANNUAL PHON-A-THON. Jeffrey tells you what you've got to do to use telemarketing to raise money for your non-profit organiza-tion... when you've got to work with community volunteers and can't afford professional help. $6

#R25

HOW TO BRING ORDER TO DESK CHAOS, OR ESSENTIALS OF ORGANIZING YOURSELF. Jeffrey talks to organizational specialist Kate Kelly, author (along with Ronni Eisenberg) of the best-selling book ORGANIZE YOURSELF!, about what you've got to do to control clutter and get all those papers in your business life under control. $6

#R26

HOW TO AVOID DESKTOP DIS-APPOINTMENT, OR WHAT YOU'VE *REALLY* GOT TO KNOW TO MAKE DESKTOP PUBLISH-ING WORK FOR YOU. Jeffrey interviews desktop design specialist Roger Parker, author of Looking Good In Print, on what to do to avoid the pitfalls of desktop publishing and use design to create compelling marketing communications. $6

#R28

HOW TO CREATE A MARKETING PLAN THAT SELLS YOUR SER-VICE... WITHOUT COSTING YOU ALL YOUR MONEY. Most people selling a service are "winging it" with predictable results: their marketing is episodic, spasmodic... unproductive. Jeffrey tells you how to create a market-ing plan that will sell a service for the least possible cost and greatest results. $6

#R29

TELESELLING: HOW TO GET THROUGH THE SCREEN THAT'S KEEPING YOU FROM YOUR PROSPECT. Jeffrey talks to Art Sobczak, editor of Telephone Selling Report, on what you've got to do to get through your prospect's screens... switchboard operators, secretaries... anybody who stands between you and your next sale. $6

#R30

HOW TO OPEN A TELEPHONE SALES CALL WITH EITHER A PROSPECT OR A CUSTOMER... SO YOU GET THE BUSINESS. Jeffrey again talks to Art Sobczak, editor of Telephone Selling Report, on what to say during those crucial opening moments with a telephone prospect... and how to build profitable relationships by phone with existing customers. $6

#R31

HOW TO CREATE A PROPOSAL THAT A CORPORATION OR FOUNDATION WILL FUND. Jeffrey tells you and your non-profit organiza-tion what it takes to create a proposal that a corporate or foundation funding source will give money to support. $6

#R32

WHAT YOU HAVE TO DO TO SELL YOUR PRODUCTS AND SERVICES THROUGH A FREE CLIENT NEWSLETTER. Jeffrey tells you how to produce free client newsletters that get your prospects to buy your products and services. $6

#R33

HOW TO CREATE INEXPENSIVE, EFFECTIVE AUDIO CASSETTES TO GET MORE OF YOUR PROS-PECTS TO RESPOND FASTER... AND MAKE EXTRA MONEY, TOO. Jeffrey tells you how to create inexpen-sive 60-minute audio cassettes in your home or office that you can use to induce more and faster sales... and sell profitably, too. $6

#R34

HOW TO PROFIT BY INVESTING IN USED AND BRUISED HOUSES. Jeffrey gets step-by-step advice from Florida author and investor Thomas Lucier on how to make money in real estate through affordable used and bruised houses, one of today's smart investments for people with a moder-ate amount to spend. $6

Jeffrey's Summer Vacation

People are always telling me I work too hard... and it's true you'll usually find me at the phone talking to customers. But this summer I allowed myself to be persuaded to go to London... and spend some of the ample amounts of money my good customers send my way. I'm happy to report I acquired an excellent 18th century English portrait of the Rev. John Upton by the eminent portrait painter George Knapton, Keeper of the King's Pictures. Painted and signed in 1740, it's a superb edition to my burgeoning collection of fine, fine art. If you visit me (like so many people do nowadays), I'll happily show it to you... And remember, when you buy something, the money goes into my next acquisition fund!

#R35
HOW TO USE WORKSHOPS AND OTHER TALK PROGRAMS TO GET CLIENTS. In honor of the publication of the new Second Edition of his well-known book MONEY TALKS: HOW TO CREATE A PROFITABLE WORKSHOP OR SEMINAR IN ANY FIELD, Jeffrey tells you how to use lectures and talk programs to get clients. $6

#R36
THINKING ON YOUR FEET, ANSWERING QUESTIONS WELL WHETHER YOU KNOW THE ANSWER — OR NOT. People who can't deal effectively with questions present a poor self-image and can harm a company. Here Jeffrey interviews Marian Woodall, author of a popular book on the subject, about how people can master the crucial "thinking on your feet" strategies. $6

#R38
WHY YOU NEED SPECIAL REPORTS: HOW TO WRITE THEM, USE THEM TO GET PEOPLE TO BUY WHAT YOU'RE SELLING NOW, TO PUBLICIZE YOUR BUSINESS, AND MAKE MONEY! The secret to successful marketing is making people take action NOW to get what you're selling. Jeffrey shows you how to create inexpensive but powerful Special Reports and how to turn them into compelling marketing tools that get your prospects to respond NOW, and that you can also sell profitably. $6

#R39
COPY FLAWS THAT DOOM YOUR EXPENSIVE MARKETING DOCUMENTS TO LINE BIRDCAGES IN SAINT LOUIS. Jeffrey tells you just what you need to know to write marketing copy that gets people to buy. Key rules of profit-making copy. $6

#R40
YOUR GRAND OPENING: HOW TO START YOUR MARKETING DOCUMENTS SO PEOPLE *BUY* WHAT YOU'RE SELLING. If your marketing documents don't draw people in immediately, you — and your next sale — are lost. Jeffrey tells you precisely what to do to begin documents so your prospects read what you have to say — and buy what you have to sell. $6

#R41
COMPUTER-ASSISTED MARKETING: HOW TO INCREASE YOUR PRODUCTIVITY AND MAKE EVERY PROSPECT AND CUSTOMER FEEL YOU'RE DELIVERING *EXACTLY* WHAT HE WANTS. People have computers but aren't using them effectively. Now learn to turn the computer into your best marketing tool. You'll read things here you've never seen before and increase your marketing productivity astonishingly. $6

#R42
MONEY MAKING MAIL, OR HOW TO AVOID THE TEN BIGGEST MAIL ORDER MISTAKES. Every day I get deluged with mail order offers that make me weep for the trees that have died. What rubbish! There are rules to succeed in mail order. Here's what you should avoid — and what you should do. $6

#R43
HOW TO CREATE AND USE OFFERS YOUR PROSPECTS FIND IRRESISTIBLE. The trick to marketing is to create and sell offers — not products and services. Here's what you need to know about offers, how to create them and use them so that your prospects will buy. $6

#R44
KNOWING WHAT TO DO WHEN PEOPLE OWE YOU MONEY, OR HOW TO GET PAYMENT IN FULL. Don't give way to the rage and frustration of being owed money by deadbeats. Get what you're owed. Here's what you need to do in practical detail. $6

#R45
HOW AUTHORS AND THEIR PUBLISHERS MUST WORK TOGETHER TO SELL MORE BOOKS. Follow these precise steps to construct a profitable author-publisher partnership, so each of you makes money from the book. $6

#R46

YOUR IRA: WHY YOU *STILL* NEED IT, WHAT YOU NEED TO KNOW ABOUT INVESTING IT. If you've lost interest in the IRA, think again. Tax-free compounding of earning's no joke, and millions can still take their contribution off their taxes. Here's the low-down. (By the way, last year IRA contributions were substantially up. This report no doubt helped!) $6

#R47

TELESMARTS: EFFECTIVELY USING TELEMARKETING TO SELL YOUR PRODUCTS AND SERVICES. Most people are hideously ill-equipped to use the phone to sell anything. Here are the basics (and some advanced tips, too) on how you can turn the phone into a profitable business tool. Have I reached out and touched you? $6

#R48

HOW TO OVERCOME SALES OBJECTIONS, INCLUDING THE BIGGEST ONE OF ALL: "YOUR PRICE IS TOO HIGH!" If you're in sales (and if you're reading this, you are), you've got to learn how to deal with objections. Here's what you need to know so that you can. $6

#R49

HOW TO STOP BEING THE LOWLY ORDER-TAKER, BECOME THE CONSUMMATE MARKETER, AND GET MORE SALES FROM NEW BUYERS. The dumb marketer simply sells a prospect what that prospect wants to buy. The expert marketer learns the prospect's problem and persuades him to take an upgraded solution. Here's how to do that. $6

#R50

TESTIMONIALS FOR YOUR PRODUCT OR SERVICE: WHY YOU NEED THEM, HOW TO GET THEM, HOW TO USE THEM. If you aren't using testimonials now, you are missing a prime marketing device. If you are, make sure you're doing it right! $6

#R51

UNDERSTANDING AND PROFITING FROM THE RULE OF SEVEN: CONNECTING WITH YOUR BUYERS AND CONNECTING WITH THEM AGAIN UNTIL THEY BUY WHAT YOU'RE SELLING. Most marketing gambits don't work. In part this is because you don't hit your prospects sufficiently often to interest them in what you're selling. Now learn how you can. The Rule of Seven is the prime rule of marketing. $6

#R52

MARKETING YOUR BOOK BEFORE IT'S PUBLISHED. Stupid authors and publishers wait to begin marketing and making money from their books until they are physically available. Don't you be one of them. Follow the detailed guidelines in this report and make money long before your book is even printed. $6

#R53

WHAT TO DO WHEN YOUR PROSPECT SAYS NO. We all get turned down. Now what? Tears? Rage? No! Use Jeffrey's step-by-step guidelines to get the sale after all — or do what it takes to get the next one! $6

#R54

ESSENTIALS OF MONEY MAKING MARKETING. Successful marketing is the key to business success. Now learn precisely what you have to do to improve your marketing. Follow these steps; sell more. $6

#R55

WHY YOU NEED A BUSINESS PLAN, WHY YOU RESIST CREATING ONE. Makes a clear case for why you must have a business plan to succeed, how to overcome your resistance to creating one, and what should go in it. A must, particularly for new and struggling entrepreneurs. $6

#R56

HOW TO GET THE LOWEST CARD-DECK ADVERTISING PRICES AND MAKE THE MOST MONEY FROM CARD-DECK ADVERTISING. Card-decks can get you maximum response for the least price. Now in honor of Jeffrey's Sales & Marketing SuccessDek, you can learn the secrets of how to get the lowest prices and biggest response. $6

#R57

TEN THINGS YOU CAN DO RIGHT NOW TO GET MORE MONEY FROM YOUR NEXT FUND RAISING LETTER. If you're running a non-profit organization and expect to raise money using fund-raising letters, read this report first. Jeffrey's been writing profit-making fund-raising letters for non-profits for over a decade. Here's what he's learned to make you more money. $6

#R58

HOW TO GET THE MOST BENEFIT WHEN WORKING WITH CONSULTANTS: THE 10 BIGGEST MISTAKES YOU'RE NOT GOING TO MAKE. All too often organizations hiring consultants don't get their money's worth. This won't happen to you if you follow the guidelines in this sensible report. $6

#R59

WHAT YOU THINK MAY BE A COPY PROBLEM MAY REALLY BE A STRATEGIC MARKETING PROBLEM ... HERE'S WHAT YOU CAN DO TO SOLVE IT. All too often what people think is a copy problem is actually a strategic marketing problem. Your marketing strategy has got to be right before you can create the most effective copy. For just $6 you learn how to create the strategy that gets people to buy what you're selling. (Then you can use CASH COPY to create the copy itself!)

#R60

HOW TO HAVE AN EFFECTIVE MEETING, OR WHAT YOU'VE REALLY GOT TO DO TO STOP WASTING YOUR TIME AT NONPRODUCTIVE BUSINESS GETTOGETHERS. Before you waste another senseless minute in a pointless meeting (or, God forbid, chair such a meeting) get this report and learn how to structure meetings so you get what you want — the only reason for having a meeting in the first place. $6

#R61

HOW TO TURN YOUR (PREVIOUSLY UNREAD) ANNUAL REPORT INTO AN ACTION ORIENTED MARKETING DOCUMENT THAT GETS PEOPLE TO DO WHAT YOU WANT THEM TO DO! For most organizations — profit and not-for-profit — annual reports are a complete waste of time and money. Who reads them? But properly created annual reports can become powerful marketing documents that get you new business. Here's what you need to know about creating them. $6

#R62

HOW TO GET YOUR CLIENTS TO GET BUSINESS FOR YOU. There are tricks for getting your existing (and past) customers to get new business for you. Here they are. When you have a customer you get not only current income but future business ... if you use these techniques. $6

#R63

HOW TO SET UP AN INDEPENDENT AGENT REFERRAL SYSTEM AND GET HUNDREDS OF PEOPLE TO REFER YOU TO ORGANIZATIONS NEEDING PAID SPEAKERS. Talk programs remain a superb way to make money — often astonishingly large amounts of money. Problem is: booking agents don't want you until you're a celebrity and cold calling is an agony. The solution? Set up your own Independent Agent Referral System to generate a constant stream of program leads. Here Jeffrey — one of America's best-known speakers — explains just how to do it! $6

#R64

HOW YOU CAN MANAGE YOUR BUSINESS' CASH FLOW EFFECTIVELY. Prosperity in the 'nineties means getting your hands on money earlier and managing that money more effectively. Here Jeffrey gets tips from Les Masonson, author of a new book intriguingly titled *Cash, Cash, Cash,* about the secrets of better cash management. Details about how to work with your bank you've never seen before. $6

#R66

HOW TO WRITE A BUSINESS PROPOSAL THAT GETS YOU THE BUSINESS. If you have to write proposals to get contracts, learn Jeffrey's secrets for creating proposals that get you the business — instead of wasting your time and money. $6

#R68

MARKETING IN THE BAD TIMES: HOW TO SELL MORE OF YOUR PRODUCTS AND SERVICES EVEN IN A RECESSION! If you didn't read this in my syndicated column and are still in a part of the country (as I am) where the recession isn't over, here are detailed suggestions to keep selling your product/ service — yes *more* of your product/ service! — even when times are bad. $6

#R69

WHAT YOU'VE GOT TO DO BEFORE YOU WRITE ANY MARKETING COMMUNICATION — FLYER, PROPOSAL, AD, COVER LETTER, ETC., OR DOING THE HOMEWORK THAT PRODUCES THE MARKETING COMMUNICATION THAT GETS YOUR PROSPECT TO BUY WHAT YOU'RE SELLING In honor of the publication of the new Revised Second Edition of his well-known book MONEY MAKING MARKETING: FINDING THE PEOPLE WHO NEED WHAT YOU'RE SELLING AND MAKING SURE THEY BUY IT, Jeffrey tackles one of the most important marketing problems: showing how lack of client-centered preparation makes it impossible to produce marketing communications that get people to respond. Here are the steps you need to take so you'll regularly produce profit-making marketing documents. $6

#R70

FIVE CRUCIAL THINGS YOU NEED TO KNOW TO MAKE REAL MONEY IN YOUR HOME-BASED BUSINESS. Up to 22,000,000 Americans derive some or all of their income working from home. Yet the vast majority gross only about $15,000 yearly — peanuts! Here Jeffrey, who's run a home-based business for over 12 years and became a millionaire in the process, provides crucial information on how to create a business at home that will produce $100,000 a year — or more. $6

The list of Special Reports continues on page 662. First look at the Special Offers on pages 660 & 661!

Jeffrey Lant's
Sales & Marketing
Successdek

Are you selling nationwide? Are you offering a product/service that will increase another business' profitability? How about a health, travel or investment service? Or a business opportunity? Do you offer business equipment or products? Or have you got a way of making a business more efficient? Are you interested in getting thousands of qualified leads for the least possible cost and so making money faster? If you've answered yes to any of these questions, and you're not already in my card deck, ARE YOU CRAZY?

"We received over 2,100 leads on our first insertion alone," says multi-time card-deck advertiser Robert Blackman of Diversified Enterprises. "We'll be advertising with you every time! Thanks for all your advice, too. You've been a big help in showing us how to make more money!!!"

Every 90 days I send out 100,000 of these decks for advertisers who want more high quality leads fast. These advertisers have made mine one of America's two largest card decks... for very good reasons:

- **price** — my prices are by far the lowest in the industry. I charge just $1199 for 100,000 two-color cards; just $650 for 50,000 two-color cards and $1350 for 100,000 four-color cards. Other decks charge up to $3000 more for the same thing. If you get a discount from them, you have to negotiate for it. With me, you get the rock-bottom lowest cost offered by any deck in America — and you get it immediately.
- **free color**. Other decks charge you for a second color. You get it free from me.
- **free copywriting assistance**. If you don't have a winning card already, I'll help you create it — free. No other deck does this.
- **guaranteed top 20 position**. If you pay for your card 60 days prior to publication, you get a guaranteed spot in the top 20 cards (our decks average 88 cards). Other decks give the best positions to the big guys or to those who pay more; we give them to whoever pays first, not extra.
- **free closing assistance**. Getting leads is no good if you can't close them; that's

why I provide tips on how to generate maximum sales from the leads you get.
- **100% deck-responsive names**. Other decks use inferior subscription or compiled lists. Not me. The people who get my deck have all responded to a deck offer in the last 90 days. You go to people who want deck offers, who respond to deck offers, and who buy deck offers. And every 90 days the list is different! That's why advertisers stay in every issue and why we have so few spaces available. (By the way, our current response record is 7,500 responses — a whopping 7.5% — to a card in a recent issue!)
- **on time mailing**. Our decks go out when we say they'll go out. Recently, other major decks in the industry have been as much as *three months' late*. Not us. We flog you to get your art in on time... so the deck can go out on time. So you get your leads on time.

Yes! We can provide your camera-ready art; (there is a charge).

Mailings take place every 90 days, in January, April, June and October. Call for complete details.

Card deck advertising can make you rich. If you want either large numbers of qualified leads fast or to sell to a national audience fast, call Jeffrey at (617) 547-6372. If you're simply interested in receiving the deck, you may also request a copy.

If any of these conditions apply to you... you need an electronic moving message display unit NOW!

* you've got cash registers;
* you've got a waiting room where your customers wait to see you;
* sidewalk traffic passes your establishment;
* you've got a streetside location;
* you go to trade shows
* you need to communicate messages to your employees (like safety messages to assembly line personnel);
* you've got windows potential customers see...

> *Moving signs have been the rage for years in Europe and Japan... and they're increasingly popular here. Been to Las Vegas lately? You know what I mean!!!*

These are the kinds of places electronic moving message display units make sense.

You've already seen them... in airports, banks, malls, airports, in schools, industrial settings... why the restaurant down the street from me has been pulling in customers with its moving sign for years.

Now it's time for you to start benefiting from them.

* They're easy to set up and move.
* They're easy to use.
* You can change your messages promptly and easily.
* You get true colors, lots of dazzling special effects, both text and animation features.

With your moving sign, you can:
* announce specials, mark-downs and sales;
* run contests, news items and trivia;
* talk directly to your customers;
* build the value of all your sales (when you've got a potential customer waiting... use your sign to sell him something else!).

Warning: maybe you've been thinking about getting a moving sign and have been checking out the cheapie models in discount stores and merchandise clubs. Don't even think of getting your sign there. You want extra colors, at least 5000 characters of memory, special effects, the ability to run multiple lines of text simultaneously, easy message-editing capability... and all the other features you need to give your sign the most impact and have the greatest effect on your customers. Cheap signs just don't have what you need. For just a few more dollars, you can get all the special effects and features you need. Don't short-change yourself on this valuable marketing tool!

For assistance in getting you the right moving sign at the right price, call Bill Reece, Nat'l Sales Manager, at (617) 278-4344 or by fax at (617) 547-0061. He'll help you find the sign that's just right for you... including making recommendations on a custom sign .

Once you've got your moving sign, get Jeffrey's special report on how to use them most effectively to make money faster.

#R83

661

The Special Reports
listing continues here...

#R71
HOW YOU CAN OVERCOME WRITER'S ANXIETY AND PRODUCE EFFECTIVE LETTERS, MEMOS, REPORTS, PROPOSALS, ETC. Virtually everyone in American business is called upon to write something for the job. Yet the vast majority of people hate to write — and do it badly. Here Jeffrey interviews New York writing coach Jim Evers, author of *The Hate To Write But Have To Writer's Guide*, to get specific suggestions on how you can overcome your writer's anxiety and produce effective business writing. $6

#R72
HOW TO TALK SO MEN WILL LISTEN. Women regularly report that talking to men (bosses, colleagues, Significant Others) is like talking to a brick wall. They talk, but does anyone really *hear* them? Now Oregon specialist Marian Woodall tackles one of civilization's oldest problems and, as usual, offers detailed suggestions on what women can do to get their points across — and what men should do to hear women. A perfect report for women who want to communicate more effectively with men... and men who really care about women! $6

#R73
HOW TO DETERMINE THE RIGHT COMPUTER OR PRINTER FOR YOUR BUSINESS AND WHERE TO BUY THEM FOR THE BEST PRICES. This report is for people who may be selecting their first computer and printer, or for seasoned veterans who want to make sure they get just the right kinds of machines for their needs — and don't overpay for them. Jeffrey interviews Maine computer expert Ted Stevens on how to determine how to get the right computer and printer for your situation and where to get the best prices for them. $6
Want to get started getting the lowest computer and fax prices? Call Ted direct at (207) 783-1136.

#R74
HOW TO MAKE MONEY WITH REAL ESTATE OPTIONS. Here Jeffrey interviews real estate expert Tom Lucier, author of the new book *How To Make Money With Real Estate Options*. Tom provides step-by-step details about how investors with limited funds can profit from real estate — without *owning* any real estate... thanks to real estate options. Shows you how to get the right properties, pay the lowest option fees, and create the right kind of option to purchase agreements. Crucial information so you can make money in real estate despite the current real estate market "melt-down." $6

#R75
THE TOP FIVE SALES-KILLING MISTAKES YOU'RE MAKING IN TELESALES... AND HOW TO AVOID THEM! Jeffrey interviews Art Sobczak, the super-smart publisher of *Telephone Selling Report* newsletter, about the five biggest mistakes telephone sales people make that kill sales — and how to avoid them. Must reading if you're trying to sell a product/sell by phone. $6

#R76
HOW TO LOWER YOUR PROPERTY TAXES THIS YEAR — AND KEEP THEM DOWN YEAR AFTER YEAR! Jeffrey interviews Gary Whalen, author of the new book *Digging For Gold In Your Own Back Yard: The Complete Homeowners Guide To Lowering Your Real Estate Taxes*. Million of Americans are paying too much property tax. This could be you. Here Jeffrey draws on Gary Whalen's experience to show you how to pay the lowest legal real estate tax. $6

#R77
CONSULTANTS: EIGHT CRUCIAL THINGS YOU MUST DO TO MAKE AT LEAST $100,000 EVERY YEAR. Smart consultants now have mid-six figure and even 7-figure incomes. But most consultants earn a tiny fraction of these high flyers. Why? Here Jeffrey lays out the reasons most consultants consistently fail to reach their income objectives and lays down specific rules you can follow so you'll make at least $100,000 every year from your practice. $6

#R78
THE TEN THINGS YOU MUST DO TO BECOME A MILLIONAIRE SELLING SERVICES. Millions of Americans sell services but most of them aren't anywhere close to being millionaires. This is because they don't understand how to use their service business as a lever to make themselves really rich. Here Jeffrey shows exactly what service sellers must do to become millionaires. Clear, easy-to-follow steps that could make you really rich, even in the deflationary 'nineties! $6

#R79
HOW TO GET RICH USING CARD-DECK ADVERTISING. Many more people than currently advertise in card-decks should be in them, Jeffrey asserts. They're a superb and cost effective way for generating a large volume of fast leads and making sales; a crucial part of a sensible marketing program. Here Jeffrey points out just what businesses must do to use card-decks effectively so they get the most leads and make the most sales from them. Getting rich from card-decks is possible for many businesses. Jeffrey's suggestions show you how to do it. $6

#R80
HOW TO CREATE AND MAKE MONEY FROM AN INFORMATION PRODUCT... FOR LIFE! Tens of thousands of 'how-to' booklets, books, audio & video cassettes and Special Reports are produced annually — but most of their creators don't make much money, much less turn their creation into a life-time income. Here Jeffrey, the doyen of America's info-producers, lays out the necessary

662

steps that ensure that *each* information product produces maximum income for life. $6

#R81

THE 10 THINGS YOUR (NON-PROFIT) MARKETING SHOULD NEVER BE! Are you working for a nonprofit organization? Then chances are your marketing is rudimentary and inefficient. Here is Jeffrey's hard-hitting look at the mistakes nonprofits make and precisely what to do to correct them. With virtually all nonprofit organizations facing tough budget times, it is immoral to fail to learn exactly how to use the limited dollars you've got for marketing more productively. Here's what you need! $6

#R82

MAXIMIZING MEMORY POWER: MAKING SURE YOU NEVER FORGET GOOD OL' WHAT'S HIS NAME. Jeffrey interviews Bob Burg, creator of the six-cassette tape album "On Your Way To Remembering Names & Faces", about how to solve the important business problem of remembering names and crucial information about the people you meet... people you want to remember and do business with. The perceptive Burg offers an easy-to-follow six-step method that gives you just what you need so you never forget crucial information about the people you're meeting. $6

#R83

HOW TO MOVE A WHOLE LOT MORE OF YOUR PRODUCTS AND SERVICES.... THANKS TO MOVING MESSAGE SIGNS! Jeffrey interviews moving message sign king Bill Reece about how to use these signs to move more products and services faster. These signs have been popping up everywhere... in airports, banks, school cafeterias, at trade shows... everywhere! Now learn how to select the right sign for your business and how to turn it into a fascinating client-centered marketing tool that gets your message out 24 hours a day for just the cost of the electricity. Whatever you're selling, Reece clearly shows why there's a moving message sign in your future. $6

Note: You can profit from moving signs in two ways: use them to attract business and

move merchandise faster or sell them to make money. Either way, call Bill Reece direct at (617) 278-4344 or by fax at (617) 547-0061. He has dozens of different moving sign varieties available from smaller ones that will fit nicely into your store window... right up to the big monster in Times Square. He can do it all. Just tell him what you want!

New! #R84

HOW TO MAKE $100,000 EVERY YEAR FOR YOUR MLM OPPORTUNITY USING CARD-DECK ADVERTISING
Most people in MLM make pitiable amounts of money. The disaffected drop out of one program, latch on to another, hopeful all over again, only to find they're not making money in that either. Here, however, Jeffrey shows you how to use card-deck advertising to generate thousands of leads quickly at minimum cost and build a 6-figure MLM income. Up till now card-decks have been too expensive for most MLM people, many of whom run small organizations. Not any more! Indeed, Jeffrey even shows you how to get 100,000 cards for no direct cost... $6

New! #R85

THE INGENUE MARKETER'S GUIDE TO CERTAIN FAILURE... OR, IT WOULD BE A LOT FASTER AND EASIER SIMPLY TO THROW YOUR MONEY OUT THE WINDOW
This article is principally for non-profit organizations but the lessons are relevant to all ingenue marketers who need to be aware of the mistakes they're making so they can correct them and start running a marketing program that achieves substantial results. If that's your objective, you'll be certain to want to read this step-by-step report. $6

New! #R86

WHEN YOU CAN'T WRITE THE MARKETING COPY YOURSELF, OR HOW TO GET THE BEST RESULTS FROM YOUR COPY WRITER

Most business people are terrible writers, and as a result they produce terrible marketing communications which don't get them the clients they need. Here Jeffrey interviews nationally known copywriter Dan McComas, director of the National Copywriting Center, on how to find the right copywriter and how to work with him/her to get the results you want. $6

Note: ■■■■■■■■

Want to get started producing superior copy faster?

Call Dan McComas directly at

(301) 946-4284!

Order from this catalog by January 1, 1994 and you get these special free premiums:

1) Order anything, and keep getting this catalog. Don't miss out on Jeffrey's latest recommendations for improving your business.

2) Order at least $150 and get — *absolutely free* — your choice of any one of Jeffrey's three 60-minute audio cassettes (#T1,2,3). A $16 value, practical information you can put to work immediately.

3) Order at least $275 and get any one of Jeffrey's "Get Ahead" Books absolutely free... up to a $39.50 value. Select any title from #B1, B2, B3, B4, B5, B6, B7, B8 or B9 AND GET THE 60-MINUTE AUDIO CASSETTE OF YOUR CHOICE, TOO!!!

663

New! #R87

HOW TO GENERATE FAR MORE LEADS FOR SELLING YOUR PRODUCT AND SERVICE AND HOW TO DETERMINE WHICH OF THEM ARE WORTH YOUR TIME AND MONEY

Most business people get too few leads, too few good leads, and thus spend far too much time with both too few people and the kinds of people they shouldn't be trying to work with at all. Here Jeffrey, one of America's most aggressive lead generators, shows you how to generate all the leads you want... and how to decide which of them you should be spending your time with. $6

New! #R88

DO YOU *REALLY* WANT TO BE RICH? TAKE THIS REVEALING QUIZ AND FIND OUT...

I've often wondered how many of those people talking about wanting to be rich actually will do what it takes to become rich. If you're wondering about yourself, take my handy quiz and find out if you *really* have what it takes to get rich. $6

... *HERE'S WHAT YOU NEED IF YOU'VE GOT LESS THAN AN HOUR TO GET SMARTER...*

Right between Special Reports (Jeffrey's unique contribution to get-ahead literature) and full-scale books, are Crisp publications. You've probably seen them. Thousands and thousands of businesses and professionals have made them best sellers. What's different about them is that they take less than one hour to read (Mike Crisp bills them as the 50-minute publications), have sensible, easy-to-follow information you can put to work immediately... and are good value. I've listed below as many as I could pack into just two pages. With Crisp, the title says it all... you don't need a lengthy description. (All Crisp item numbers begin with CR. Please make sure to include complete number on the order form on page 32.)

#CR1

LEADERSHIP SKILLS FOR WOMEN by Marilyn Manning, Ph.D. Provides details on the essential factors that help women become business leaders. 88 pages. $10.95

#CR2

DELEGATING FOR RESULTS by Robert Maddux. If you're overwhelmed, you need to delegate. Here are the key elements of successful delegation. 80 pages. $10.95

#CR3

INCREASING EMPLOYEE PRODUCTIVITY. Of course you want to get more benefit out of your employees. Lynn Tylczak shows you how. 100 pages. $10.95

#CR4

AN HONEST DAY'S WORK: MOTIVATING EMPLOYEES TO GIVE THEIR BEST. My friend Twyla Dell knows that if your employees aren't motivated, they can't produce. She shows you how to motivate your employees to increase their productivity. 80 pages. $10.95

#CR5

MANAGING FOR COMMITMENT: BUILDING LOYALTY WITHIN AN ORGANIZATION. This practical book by Dr. Carol Goman shows you how to build a level of commitment and loyalty with today's new, more independent workforce. 96 pages. $10.95.

#CR6

TRAINING METHODS THAT WORK by Dr. Lois Hart. Want to sharpen your training skills? In just 96 pages you'll learn how. $10.95.

#CR7

RECRUITING VOLUNTEERS: A GUIDE FOR NONPROFITS. Carl Liljenstolpe knows that your nonprofit needs extra volunteer help. Here's how you get it. 100 pages. $10.95

#CR8

STEPPING UP TO SUPERVISOR. Revised edition by Marion Haynes. If you want to become a supervisor or have just become one, here's what you need to make a success of your position. 280 pages. $17.95

#CR9

NO MORE MISTAKES. Twenty four techniques for doing things right the first time. 48 pages. $5.95 (I'm applying for a govt. grant to give every congressperson a copy!)

#CR10

PLAN YOUR WORK — WORK YOUR PLAN. James Sherman shows you how to plan and get what you want. 96 pages. $10.95

#CR11

DEVELOPING POSITIVE ASSERTIVENESS by Sam Lloyd. If you're the mouse who can't roar (or know one of these poor creatures), learn how to develop the positive assertiveness you need to get ahead on the job or in life. 80 pages. $10.95

#CR12

MANAGING ANGER by Dr. Rebecca Luhn. Here you get the methods you need to manage your emotions in a positive manner. 90 pages. $10.95

#CR13

GUIDE TO AFFIRMATIVE ACTION. Pamela Conrad gives you guidelines supported by case studies to ensure that managers make correct decisions on affirmative action, equal employment opportunity, age and sex discrimination and sexual harassment. 96 pages. $10.95

#CR14

YOUR FIRST THIRTY DAYS: BUILDING A PROFESSIONAL IMAGE IN A NEW JOB. Elwood Chapman shows you how to adjust with greater confidence. If you're new, get off to the right start. 96 pages. $10.95

#CR15

QUALITY INTERVIEWING. Robert Maddux' best-selling book helps you master interviewing skills that will lead to sound hiring decisions. 72 pages $10.95

#CR16

PROFESSIONAL EXCELLENCE FOR SECRETARIES. Marilyn Manning provides the information a professional secretary needs so office work gets done promptly and right. 80 pages. $10.95

#CR17

GIVING AND RECEIVING CRITICISM by Patti Hathaway. There are right ways and wrong ways to give it… and to take it. Here they are. 96 pages $10.95

#CR18

WELLNESS IN THE WORKPLACE: HOW TO DEVELOP A COMPANY WELLNESS PROGRAM. Merlene Sherman provides the components of an effective health program with case studies, resources, diagrams, inventories, examples and strategies. 100 pages. $10.95

#CR19

BALANCING HOME AND CAREER: SKILLS FOR SUCCESSFUL LIFE MANAGEMENT. Pamela Conrad's revised edition is for busy people who have to juggle. Includes chapters on home, business, travel and relocation. Shows you how to put quality time where you want it. 80 pages. $10.95

#CR20

OVERCOMING ANXIETY by Lynn Fossum. Anxiety is one of the most common problems medical doctors encounter. Learn what anxiety is and is not and how to overcome it. 96 pages. $10.95

#CR21

PREVENTING JOB BURNOUT by Dr. Beverly Potter. Burnout is a terrifically common problem in all businesses these days. Here are 8 proven strategies to beat job burnout and help you deal with the pressures of your job. 80 pages. $10.95

#CR22

FIRST AID ESSENTIALS. Written by the National Safety Council, you get the latest information on how to deal with a wide variety of injuries and emergency situations. Quick emergency index so you'll know what to do when problems arise. Should be in every business — and home. 222 pages. $11.95

#CR23

MAKING HUMOR WORK. Dr. Terry Paulson shows you how to use humor in the workplace with problem-solving, defusing resistance to change, disarming anger, and improving memory. 108 pages. $10.95

#CR24

FORMATTING LETTERS AND MEMOS ON THE COMPUTER. Dr. Eleanor Davidson has written this for computer beginners. Offers tips and exercises for designing letters, reports and memos on the computer. 90 pages. $10.95

#CR25

BUSINESS REPORT WRITING by Susan Brock. A super quick guide for writing business reports and proposals. Teaches how to organize, research, develop and edit winning documents. 90 pages. $10.95

#CR26

SPEEDREADING IN BUSINESS by Joyce Turley. Of course, you have more to read. So, you either skip it (and stay uninformed)… or learn speedreading HERE! 96 pages $10.95

#CR27

EXHIBITING AT TRADESHOWS. Susan Friedman shows you how to gain a competitive edge at a tradeshow in a cost-effective manner. 90 pages. $10.95

#CR28

CALMING UPSET CUSTOMERS by Rebecca Morgan. You're going to have them, so let author Morgan show you how to deal with both a disturbed and an upset customer. (No, they're not the same!) 74 pages. $10.95

#CR29

STARTING YOUR NEW BUSINESS by Charles Martin. If you're just getting your toe in the water, get this. In addition to a thorough discussion of the basics, includes superb annotated bibliography pointing you to lots of other helpful materials. 110 pages. $10.95

#CR30

EFFECTIVE NETWORKING by Venda Raye-Johnson. Shows you how to use networking to share information, resources and support to build and maintain effective career and personal relationships. 96 pages. $10.95

60 Money-Making Minutes with Jeffrey (on tape)

#T3

HOW TO GET FREE TIME ON RADIO AND T.V. AND USE IT TO GET YOUR PROSPECTS TO BUY WHAT YOU'RE SELLING. Listen as Jeffrey gives you the secrets of getting valuable free time on radio and television so you can sell your products and services without spending any of your money. Getting on *just one* program could return your investment dozens of times! $16

#T4

HOW TO CREATE MARKETING DOCUMENTS THAT GET YOUR PROSPECTS TO BUY WHAT YOU'RE SELLING … NOW! Since you spend thousands of dollars on your marketing documents, don't you think you should know what will get people to respond to them faster … to buy what you're selling **NOW**? Here's just what you need to know. $16

#T5

ESSENTIALS OF MONEY MAKING MARKETING: WHAT YOU'VE REALLY GOT TO DO TO SELL YOUR PRODUCTS AND SERVICES, EVERY DAY! Jeffrey shares his secrets of successful marketing, what you've got to do, when and how you've got to do it to sell your products and services. $16

#C3

ALL THREE OF JEFFREY'S 60 MINUTE AUDIO CASSETTES (T3, T4, T5). Just $38. You save $10!

666

Got three bucks?

Then take advantage of these deals:

#F2

MAIL PROFITS. If you expect to succeed in mail-order, you need this publication. Now you can get two free issues of America's premier mail-order publication. Each issue packed with details on what it really takes to make money by mail. $3

#F3

TELEPHONE SELLING REPORT. If you sell by phone, you can profit from Art Sobczak's infinitely intelligent publication. Each monthly 8 page report gives ideas you will use to close more sales and set more appointments by phone. $3 gets you three issues ($25 value)

#F4

99 WAYS TO SELL MORE BY PHONE: WHAT YOU CAN DO AND SAY RIGHT NOW TO GET MORE 'YES'S' BY PHONE. This just-published 40 page booklet by Art Sobczak lists 99 proven techniques (with exactly what to say and how to say it) for closing telephone sales. These techniques have already closed millions of dollars worth of business. Unbelievable! Just $3.

Special: if you'd like to hear some free tele-tips from the tele-master himself, call Art Sobczak's tips line: (402) 896-TIPS (8477).

#F6

RADIO & TV INTERVIEW REPORT package. Send $3 and get complete details on how to get interviewed — for free — on thousands of radio and television stations. You can do the radio interviews from your home or office! Perfect if you're an author or publisher or represent a cause that people are interested in or should know about.

#F7

JEFFREY GOES MLM. I'm an MLM sceptic... or was, until I started getting monthly checks (my first one was 9

cents!) from an old line company that sells thousands of products all of us use every day: household products, hair, skin & health care, nutritional products, food, water filters, home care, gifts and even gourmet products. Now you can join my fast-growing organization and start making money, too. Send $3 for complete details.

#F9

IDEA DIGEST. Considering starting a low-capital, home-based business? Then send me $3 bucks and get three free issues of Gary Davis' well-known IDEA DIGEST publication. Packed with articles and information sources to get your home-based business off to a fast start.

> *"I have already purchased six of your special reports. They were all excellent, and I am certainly satisfied with the quality of your products."*
> Timothy Turner, Raleigh, NC

FREE INFORMATION!

#F1

JOIN THE HUNDREDS OF PEOPLE WORLDWIDE WHO ARE SELLING JEFFREY'S BOOKS AND PRODUCTS AND MAKING MONEY NOW! Do you offer workshops and talk programs? Publish any kind of publication? Do you have a catalog or regular mailing program? Then you should be selling Jeffrey's books, tapes and special reports and making easy extra income.

Write "F1" on page 32, and you'll get complete free details about how you can profit from America's most relentlessly focused and detailed money-making products. Jeffrey is recognized world-wide by people who know that his name on the product means it works. This means easy sales for you!

Dealer already? Call and get Jeffrey's newest dealer catalogs. It's time to upgrade to your new catalog!

MLM $! Join These 7 Network Marketing Programs... Make Money Now!!! Call for complete details...

1

JOIN NUTRITION EXPRESS! Make Money from over 200 quality nutritious foods, weight control, personal care, homeopathic, herbal and household products! *You'll be glad you joined Nutrition Express* because of the most *generous and profitable* pay plan in the industry... because the product line is of exemplary quality which creates enthusiasm and product loyalty in your group... people reorder the consumable products constantly MAKING YOU MONEY EVERY TIME. **Call now and get your free Starter Pak**, a proven 'no selling' mail program, free booklet and learn how to make money with NUTRITION EXPRESS fast! No meetings! No selling! A complete system! Contact Richard Brooks at 318-992-5790 or write: Cypress Support Services, P.O. Box 1201, Rhinehart, LA 71363.

2

JOIN ADNET! Profit with both LEADS AND INCOME from the program for MLM professionals. ADNET helps you be successful in any Network Marketing program. ADNET sends you 30-40 highly qualified MLM leads every month! And make your business more profitable by adding an additional profit center. ADNET advertises for you in USA Today and Entrepreneur magazine. **You'll also get free advertising!** Fast start bonus! Profitable with only three people in your group! Call Peter Regan **now** at 413-445-5357 to join ADNET or write: 7 Onota Lane, Pittsfield, MA 01202

3

JOIN UNITED DENTAL PLAN OF AMERICA! *Exceptional income possible* marketing this incredible new dental service! Everybody needs quality dental care — You can earn top income by selling this to both companies and individuals! Virtually no competition! Unbeatable values! This is NOT insurance. Complete Family Plans just $150 per year! Individual Plans only $85 per year! All oral exams and x-rays... No Charge! Cleanings just $20.00! 25-60% Discount off **all** other dental procedures. No Waiting! ... Even on orthodontia, cosmetics and implants! 33% Commission plus same on renewals! Multiple sales to companies are LUCRATIVE! **Call** Bill Crocker NOW at 617-547-8340 for **FREE** details or write Bill at: UDPA, 2592 Mass. Ave., Cambridge, MA 02140.

4

JOIN JEWELWAY INTERNATIONAL! This is one of the *most lucrative* programs available to join today! The FINE JEWELRY mega-industry has a huge market niche for high quality 14K Gold FINE JEWELRY at substantial savings! People buy FINE JEWELRY in a recession *where value is offered... we have it!* GROUND FLOOR! LUCRATIVE! No inventory—catalog sales. No quotas. Call to get your 100 page color catalog with 1000s of high quality FINE JEWELRY. Pays $1000s infinitely deep WEEKLY! **Upline forced to help you!** Call Kathy Byrnes at 313-772-8968 or write: JEWELWAY INTERNATIONAL, 22439 Doremus, St. Clair Shores, MI 48080.

5

JOIN INFINET TRAVEL CLUB! Go anywhere in the world and never pay full price to get there... *ever again!* PLUS, earn FREE vacations and cash... quickly and easily just by recommending INFINET to anyone you know. Members get:

- FULL SERVICE Travel Agency
- **SAVE 5 – 60% off everything you book!**
- GUARANTEED lowest available airfare
- 50% Hotel Discount Program
- Up to 60% off last-minute travel
- PROVEN Referral System! Spreading the word is easy!
- **ENORMOUS earnings potential — Everyone loves to travel**
- ABSOLUTELY no selling or travel experience required for success!!!

Save money on every vacation! Call NOW: 800-966-CLUB for free info. Tell them Jeffrey Lant sent you and save $30 off your membership. (Reg. $79, yours now for $49)

6

JOIN MARKET AMERICA! Make money with us when you join with your *many* (not just one) distinctive product lines to represent. You'll profit when you and your group sells complete product lines including diet/nutritional products, jewelry, personal care products and more! Benefit from a very motivating, powerful pay plan! This translates into HIGH PROFITS! And high sponsoring closing ratios! **You'll be glad you joined MARKET AMERICA** when your four figure *weekly checks* come rolling in! You'll collect on unlimited levels... your upline rejoins in your downline *to help you make money faster!* Get qualified leads from company run infomercials! Call John Jette today at 508-937-2910 or write: MARKET AMERICA, 26 Varney Street, Lowell, MA 01854.

7

JOIN CONSUMERS' BUYLINE! 'CBI' is "The Original" and Best American Discounting Service! *You'll be glad you joined* CBI with its GUARANTEED low prices on over 600,000 products and services or DOUBLE the DIFFERENCE BACK! *You* have the right to earn steady monthly income in the process! SEE PAGE 292 FOR COMPLETE DETAILS. Then call Greig Hollister at (404) 768-0838.

HERE ARE THE WAYS TO BUILD YOUR MLM ORGANIZATION FASTER... AND START MAKING YOUR ANNUAL 6-FIGURE MLM INCOME

Most people in MLM piddle along, making pitiable amounts of money. They jump from "opportunity" to "opportunity", always hopeful, never making enough money to pay for all the stuff they're forced to buy.

If this is you, take heart. I've now got these 4 ways to help you build a big organization fast.

1) **For the littlest guys**. If you're someone who just wants to get a toe in the water, doesn't want to spend too much money but wants to generate new leads, you want a place on the MLM card Gery Carson runs in my card-deck and other decks. For just a few dollars, you can run a line (about 10-12 words) on your opportunity. All the leads go back to Gery who sorts them out and ships them to you. You'll be the only representative of your opportunity, and you'll get leads for a very reasonable price. Contact Gery Carson, Carson Services, Inc., P.O. Box 4785, Lincoln, NE 68504, (402) 467-4230, Fax (402) 467-4292. Also get Gery's fine publication MAIL PROFITS. See #F2

2) Want **more leads faster**? Join Jeffrey's TNT Team. Here you and your opportunity join 4-5 others on a bingo card that runs in Jeffrey's card-deck. What's different about both this program and #3 below is that Jeffrey will join your organization and help you generate leads. All leads go to Jeffrey for processing. He'll send them to you weekly. Note: people who start in this program usually decide to go on to #3 option below (as you can see from page 24)! You probably will, too... This option was created to get you a substantial number of leads for a reasonable price... and to develop your organization so you can process and close these leads promptly. Second note: you can co-op your participation so that you get your leads free. Ask for details.

3) Want **even MORE leads**? Great! Join Jeffrey's TNT team, take a full run in the card-deck (100,000 cards) and get a free listing in this catalog... just like the people on page 24. You'll get at least 750 leads... and possibly 2,000 or more! All the leads will go to you directly. Note: you can also take a split run (50,000 cards) in Jeffrey's deck as an intermediate step. But if you do this, you do not get the free listing in this catalog! You can also co-op this option!

For complete details on items 2-4 on this page, contact Jeffrey directly at (617) 547-6372 or Fax (617) 547-0061.

4) If these three options don't satisfy you, but you still want to generate hundreds of new leads to build your MLM organization, no problem. Just buy a card in my card deck at the regular price ($1199 for 100,000 two color cards; $650 for 50,000 cards). All leads go to you, and you have no involvement with our MLM team. Note: as always, if you pay for your card (full run) 60 days prior to publication, you get a Top 20 position... if any are available!

Special note: Don't forget. Generating leads is only half the battle. Closing them is the rest. For aggressive, client-centered response packages, call Dan McComas at the National Copywriting Center, (301) 946-4284.

670

I'M CONSTANTLY ON THE LOOK-OUT FOR SUPERB BOOKLETS, BOOKS AND AUDIO AND VIDEO CASSETTES THAT WILL HELP YOU IMPROVE YOUR BUSINESS PROFITABILITY AND LIFE. IF YOU'RE A PUBLISHER WITH SUCH MATERIALS, GET IN TOUCH ASAP. WE PAY CASH WITH OUR ORDERS, NO CREDIT AND ARE ALWAYS HAPPY TO BRING GOOD THINGS TO OUR READERS.

READERS: HERE'S THE BEST OF WHAT I'M CURRENTLY RECOMMENDING FROM OTHER PUBLISHERS. BUY THEM AND SUPPORT THIS FINE WORK!

Get the Lowest Air Fares

New! #B106
FLY THERE FOR LESS: HOW TO SLASH THE COST OF AIR TRAVEL WORLDWIDE. The title says it all on this new, much-needed 312 page book by travel whiz-author Bob Martin. You find out precisely what you need to know to get the lowest air fares all the time. Martin provides insider knowledge on flexibility, off-peak flights, flying weekdays and week-ends, travel seasons, promotional fares, how to work with travel agents, air taxis, charters, consolidators, coupon brokers, ticket auctions and hundreds of other ways to save money now. If you fly and want to cut your costs, you need this book. It's as simple as that. $20.45

Select The Best Computers For Home & Office

New! #B107
THE COMPUTER BUYER'S HANDBOOK: HOW TO SELECT AND BUY PERSONAL COMPUTERS FOR YOUR HOME OR BUSINESS. If you're in the market for a computer, better shop with R. Wayne Parker first. In 237 information-dense pages, he tells you exactly what you should know about computers, how to define your needs, the best home computers (pay attention parents!); business computers; standards and

compatibility issues; where to buy the most computer for the least cost; the software you need... and how to get up and running fast. You get helpful lists of mailorder computer dealers, a glossary of computer terms and the publications you should be reading to keep abreast of developments. Whether you're buying your first or thirteenth machine, this'll be real helpful. $19.95

Making At Least $100,000 A Year In MLM

New! B155
HOW TO EARN AT LEAST $100,000 A YEAR IN NETWORK MARKETING. If you expect to make **real** money in MLM, connect with this six-tape audio training series by authority Randy Gage. You'll discover the entire system from prospecting a potential distributor to securing a line for walk-away income 50, 60 and 70 levels deep! How to build a line once and get paid for decades. How to reduce drop-outs by 80 to 90 percent; how to effectively sponsor; why you never lead with the products; the science of building a large group; building security with out of town groups; how to turn yourself into a key player... and much, much more. Thousands take Randy's national workshops on this subject. Now you can get his precise, money-making information and start profiting fast. Just $63.95.

Finding Facts Fast

#B29
All of us are dependent on information, knowing where to find it and where to find it fast is important. That's why you need **FINDING FACTS FAST**, the best little book ever written on quick, economical information gathering. $7.45

Finding A Job

#B83
HOW TO GET INTERVIEWS FROM JOB ADS. If you're unemployed and looking for work, or know someone who is, get this comprehensive book by my friend Ken Elderkin. It tells you where to look, what to

select, who to write, what to say, when to follow up, how to save time and a whole lot more. The best jobs go to people who know the system and use it to their advantage. Be one of them. 249 pages. $19.95

Launching Your New Product

New! #B111
HOW TO BRING A PRODUCT TO MARKET FOR LESS THAN $5,000. Author Don Debelak tells you in 298 pages how to test your product idea, market your product and keep costs low, prepare a business plan and get financing. As Debelak points out, each year over 250,000 inventors and entrepreneurs spend as much as $50,000 on their dream product — without a single customer ever hearing about it! Now you don't have to be one of them... for just a few bucks find out if your product idea will work; when to get a patent and when not to; how to minimize all your costs throughout the whole process; how to predetermine manufacturing costs; how to conduct an evaluation after initial sales... and much, much more. $20.95

Mail-Order Money

New! #B139
THE COMPLETE MAIL ORDER SOURCE BOOK. This new 288-page book by John Kremer is a must if you want to make money in mail order. I've been an unabashed admirer of John's books for many years. He produces the kind of nitty-gritty, focused, unrelentingly detailed books I like... and this one is no exception. You get everything you need to start a direct marketing campaign right away and detailed check-lists on what you've got to do and when you've got to do it. If you're not familiar with Kremer's painstaking work, you should be. $24.95

Prestigious... At Last!

New! #B114
STATUS FOR SALE: THE COMPLETE GUIDE TO INSTANT PRESTIGE. The human animal, as author Wayne de Montford-Yeager

knows, is a status seeker and always has been. In this, one of the most clever books I've seen lately, he tells you how to elevate yourself by providing page after page of ingenious suggestions. You learn where to get the best quality real and reproduction antiques; portraits of yourself and your animals; how to change your name to something grander and who provides the speech course you need to sound better. You find out how to get an honorary doctorate, a diplomatic passport, a foreign title, how to get in reference books and prestigious clubs, how to get a coat of arms, and much, much more. You may have seen articles about Wayne and his book lately; he's been getting a lot of press. But then... he's been using the guidelines in THE UNABASHED SELF-PROMOTER'S GUIDE, which is what any prestigious person would do! And all for just $11.

Since you can't take it with you...

New! #B115

THE COMPLETE PROBATE KIT: STEP-BY-STEP COVERAGE OF EVERYTHING YOU NEED TO KNOW ABOUT PROBATE. Authors Jens Appel III and Bruce Gentry have provided not only a 196 page book but pages of forms you need to handle probate. You get the basics of probate planning, how to settle your estate, real and personal property issues, state by state requirements, and more. Over 5,000 estates enter the probate process every day. Make sure if you're involved in the process, you use this book so you and your beneficiaries can gain greater control of the financial fate of your estate. $25.95

Before You Fire Him/Her...

New! #B117

PROBLEM EMPLOYEES: HOW TO IMPROVE THEIR PERFOR-MANCE. Are you a boss? Have you got a problem employee? If you're not ready to fire the offending creature just yet, use this 260-page step-by-step approach by Dr. Peter Wylie & Dr. Mardy Grothe. Learn what won't

work... and what will; how to analyze your employee's performance, how to handle employee meetings, how to begin the interview, how to get your employee to talk, how to get your employee to do a "self analysis," how to get your message across, and how to present your analysis of your employee... and negotiate a performance agreement. Finding a new employee is time consuming and expensive. Use these techniques to see if you can salvage the present situation. Just $25.95

Winning Your Small Claims Case

New! #B119

SMALL CLAIMS COURT WITH-OUT A LAWYER. Attorney W. Kelsea Wilber has written the book you need if you're going to small claims court and want to win without a lawyer. In 211 pages, you get the details you need about: deciding if you have a case, when, where and how to file a lawsuit, how to prepare for your day in court, easy ways to serve a summons, and collecting your money after the judgment. You get sample letters and forms and a complete listing of individual state-by-state information. $22.45

Incorporating Your Business

New! #B124

HOW TO INCORPORATE: A HANDBOOK FOR ENTREPRE-NEURS AND PROFESSIONALS. This 235-page paperback by Diamond and Williams tell you how to select the right form, what to do before you incorporate, how to handle the financial structure, dividends, the articles of incorporation, bylaws, corporate operations, taxes, and more. $25.95

Getting Rich with TV Ads

New! #B126

HOW TO MAKE YOUR SALES EXPLODE WITH TELEVISION ADVERTISING. Lots of particularly small business people think they're too

little to benefit from tv advertising. Author D.B. Carson shows otherwise. This very helpful step-by-step book tells why you should be advertising on television, shows you how to understand your market, budget, plan your television creative strategy, develop the right message, write the script, select a production company (and not overpay), find the talent you need, shoot and edit your spot, develop a media plan... and much, much more. This book is long overdue and is perfect for breaking you into television advertising. Just $38

Making Money in Mutual Funds

New! #B153

BUSINESS WEEK'S ANNUAL GUIDE TO MUTUAL FUNDS. If you're investing in mutual funds like I am, you need this 154-page guide to finding the best funds for you, complete data on over 1100 funds, how funds invest your money, and a whole lot more. Individual stock picking is too risky for most investors... but you still want to get the advantages of the stock market. Therefore mutual funds make sense... and this book makes sense of mutual funds. $29.95

Getting Listened To... At Last!

#B84

HOW TO TALK SO MEN WILL LISTEN. Marian Woodall, whose books I've recommended for years, has done it again. This is for you, ladies. If you've wondered why so many men really don't get it when you talk, get this book and follow its 108 pages of sensible suggestions. It'll help you with bosses, committees, adult children, even spouses and boyfriends. Marian shows that the genders communicate differently and offers detailed guidelines on how you can finally get your message across. Look, these methods must work, right? Marian constantly persuades me to put her books in my catalog... and she's never even taken me out to lunch! $10.00

Getting The Money You're Owed

#B46

You've got uncollected and uncollectible invoices sitting in your drawer right now. Makes you sick, right? Well, if you used th e techniques in **PAYMENT IN FULL: A GUIDE TO SUCCESSFUL BILL COLLECTING**, some of them wouldn't be there. If you'd use it now, you can still collect on some of them. $27.95 is also a pretty fair price to pay to cut the anger you feel about the deadbeats who're ripping you off.

What You Need To Know To Launch Your Invention

#B40

FROM CONCEPT TO MARKET. Gary Lynn's 243-page book tells you how to protect your idea without submitting a patent, how to license a new idea, market your innovation, start your own company, raise money, build a prototype, write a business plan and produce your product. Developing a product is one of the best ways to get really rich. Making a small investment in Lynn's extensive research tells you how to devleop it right and launch it fast. $22.95

New #B149

MARKETING YOUR INVENTION. Once you've got your idea, you've got to market it. Start off right with Gary Lynn. Then move on to this new 240-page resource by Thomas E. Mosley, Jr. Find out whether you should manufacture your invention or license it to an outside company; why most inventors should not become entrepreneurs, and everything you need to know about the business of *inventing*. If you expect to make money from your invention, you need these two resources. This one is just $24.95.

Selling More

New #B150

THE COMPLETE SELLING SYSTEM: SALES MANAGEMENT TECHNIQUES THAT CAN HELP ANYONE SUCCEED. Author Pete

Frye's new 192 page book is for you if you haven't yet figured out that to make money in sales means developing a *sales system* and following it religiously. Here you get both the structures and strategies you need to succeed in sales. Sensible answers to key questions like: "I can't get my sales people to do what I want them to do;" "We get a lot of people through the store every day, but not enough of them buy," "Whenever I question a salesperson's performance, I get an argument," and "I sell through independent reps — it's impossible to manage the process." This is a no-nonsense book designed to do one thing: SELL MORE. When that's what you want, send me $26.95 .

All The Accounting Information You'll Need

New! #B151

SMALL TIME OPERATOR. If you've never heard of this book, you must have your head in the sand. Author "Bear" Kamaroff's become famous for the kind of practical advice he dishes out on starting your own business, keeping your own books, paying your taxes and staying out of trouble! 190 fact-filled, easy-to read pages provide complete information for sole proprietors, partnerships, corporations, independent contractors, freelancers, employers, home businesses, consultants and all other self-employed individuals. If that's you, rush me $18.95 and keep this essential resource close at hand!

Key Information on Patents, Copyrights & Trademarks

#B66

PATENTS, COPYRIGHTS & TRADEMARKS. If you're going to use any of these three things, you need this useful 236-page paperback by Foster & Shook. Crammed with useful information about what's patentable, how to conduct a patent search, apple for a patent; what's copyrightable, your copyright rights; how to register your work; how to protect your trademark; frequently asked questions and their answers; myths, etc. Save yourself a bundle by sending me $24.95 for this exhaustive resource.

Speakers' Resource

New! #B55

SPEAKER'S & TOASTMASTER'S HANDBOOK. If you speak... if you introduce speakers... you need Herbert Prochnow's pile of 500 humorous stories, 500 epigrams & quips, 100 stories and comments, 292 humorous definitions, 190 statements on important subjects by great thinkers, 209 wise & witty proverbs, 160 unusual quotations from world leaders, etc. You'll be a lot smarter (and get better speaking reviews) if you send me $22.95 for this book.

Continue on...
there's more to come!

Building a Lucrative Catalog Sales Business

#B68

STARTING & BUILDING YOUR CATALOG SALES BUSINESS. This is Herman Holtz' latest volume, and you'd better get it if you're not already making millions in the catalog sales game — but want to. 271 pages tell you what types of merchandise sell well by catalog; how to write catalog copy that sells; necessary elements in any catalog mailing; what you need to know about mailing lists; pricing details and much more. You can lose a bundle fast with a money-losing catalog. Use Herman's latest to make sure *you* profit. A steal at $33.

Staying Covered for Less

#B85

INSURANCE SMART: HOW TO BUY THE RIGHT INSURANCE AT THE RIGHT PRICE. Jeff O'Donnell's new 236 page book covers EVERY type of insurance — including homeowners, car, health, business, life, farm & ranch, and medicare supplement. There isn't a single reader of this catalog who wouldn't be better off using what he says to get the best coverage at the lowest cost. Also explains forms & terminology, tells you how to file a claim, provides consumer protection information & more. $17.95

Creating A Business Plan

#B154

You know you need a written business plan, and you know you don't have one. That's why you need **THE BUSINESS PLANNING GUIDE.** It's not just a book. It's your basic business tool and roadmap. Packed with forms, checklists and immediately usable examples, this will give you exactly what you need: a specific, written business plan. In about 130 pages, you'll get your MBA in small business management. Over 250,000 businesses are already profiting from this book. You should, too! $23.45

When You Need Someone To Spend Your Money On...

New! #B90

HOW TO BE OUTRAGEOUSLY SUCCESSFUL WITH THE OPPO-SITE SEX: HOW TO SOLVE EV-ERY PROBLEM YOU'VE EVER HAD... MEETING, DATING, OR MARRYING THE MAN OR WOMAN OF YOUR DREAMS. Why is this book here? If you're alone... or looking... I really don't need to tell you, you know. Besides, it's written by my shrewd, yea brilliant colleague Paul Hartunian who's parlayed his own encyclopedic knowledge on the subject into appearances in a string of nat'l tv shows. 141 pages. And a lot cheaper than calling those 900 numbers! P.S. If you order before 01/01/93, Paul will include a FREE copy of his Special Report "The 5 Things You Have To Do To Impress That Special Someone." $22.95

Getting Organized... At Last!

#B102

ORGANIZED TO BE THE BEST! Subtitled "New Timesaving Ways to Simplify and Improve How You Work", this 434-page book has been selected by NINE major book clubs as a special pick. No wonder. It's awesomely detailed! Author Susan Silver takes on the gigantic task of organizing America — and you! And succeeds! Details about organizing your desk and its paper jungle; getting files up-to-date; organizing IBM personal computer & Macintosh files; work and project management shortcuts; special tips for collectors who "can't" throw anything away... and much, much more including tip after tip for organizing your work environment. People just love this book. If organization isn't your strong suit, get this crucial resource. $15.95

Getting Merchant Charge Card Status

#B10

STRATEGIES FOR GETTING CHARGE CARD MERCHANT STATUS AT YOUR BANK (EVEN IF YOU'RE A MAIL ORDER DEALER). This 49-page booklet by my friend John Cali tells you how and where to get a Merchant MC/VISA account and how to handle your credit card orders. Particularly mail order merchants (who know just how difficult it is to get MC/VISA status these days) will want to get this very useful resource which is always kept updated by its author. I referred one friend to it who had had incredible difficulty in getting such an account. By following the steps here he had one in just five days. Cheap at $21.95.

Free Help From Uncle Sam

New! #B152

FREE HELP FROM UNCLE SAM TO START YOUR OWN BUSINESS OR EXPAND THE ONE YOU HAVE. If you're interested in getting money from the govt. for your business, you need this "must own" 304-page resource by William Alarid and Dr. Gustav Berle. Contains over 100 government programs for small businesses plus dozens of examples of how people have taken advantage of this help. 22 loan programs; 10 loan guarantees; 5 direct payments; 109 grant programs; 26 information services; 11 counseling services. And much, MUCH more! Just $17.95.

Running An Effective Partnership

New! #B129

THE PARTNERSHIP BOOK. If you're going to have a partner, you need this 221-page resource by Clifford & Warner. It's subtitled " How to Write Your Own Small Business Partnership Agreement." For years, it's been the most thorough guide to how to set up a partnership — and make it prosper. All aspects covered, including choosing a legal form, getting your business started, the partners and their relationship, terms, no-no's, partnership decision making, financial considerations, changes, growth & new partners, and much, much more. If you want your partnership to work, you want this book. It's as simple as that! $27.95

Do-It-Yourself Marketing Research

#B121

DO IT YOURSELF MARKETING RESEARCH. Too many businesses simply "market" without researching or planning. Their poor results should cure them of this folly, but too often do not. However, if you want better results, use this detailed 251-page resource by Breen & Blankenship. It's got just the information you need to handle your own marketing research... and improve your results. Includes information on collecting the information, conducting a focus group interview, making sure you question the right people, how to develop a good questionnaire, summarizing the results of your study... and much more. $49.95

Publishing Your Newsletter

#B19

Howard Penn Hudson is America's newsletter guru. If there's something to be known about newsletters, he knows it. That's why you should use **PUBLISHING NEWSLETTERS: A COMPLETE GUIDE TO MAR-KETS, EDITORIAL CONTENT, DESIGN, PRINTING, SUBSCRIP-TIONS, AND MANAGEMENT**. Take my word for it: this is the best book on newsletters ever written. $16.95

#B108

NEWSLETTERS FROM THE DESKTOP: DESIGNING EFFEC-TIVE PUBLICATIONS WITH YOUR COMPUTER. If you're even thinking about producing a newsletter and using your computer, get this detailed 306-page book by Roger Parker right away. I've often recommended Roger's books; they are always good value. Here he gives you the details you need to plan your newsletter, select a grid, create a nameplate, work with body copy, add reader cues, place and manipulate visuals, add graphic accents, and a whole lot more. You're going to spend a lot of money producing your newsletter. Let Roger help you do it right! $28.95

Order Form on page 676.

675

Order Form

Complete 30-Day Money-Back Guarantee!

Photocopy or return this page to: Dr. Jeffrey Lant, Jeffrey Lant Associates
50 Follen St., #507, Cambridge, MA 02138

Special Edition for No More Cold Calls

CLEARLY write down the item number(s) of what you order here. Each number is composed of a letter and a number. Please make sure to give both!

___, ___, ___, ___, ___, ___, ___, ___, ___, ___, ___, ___, ___, ___, ___, ___, ___, ___, ___, ___,

Remember, if you're ordering my Special Reports (#R1 – #R88), you get **any three for $14**. Individual Reports are $6 each.

Total your order here $ _____. Are you a Massachusetts resident? ❑ Yes ❑ No
If so, add 5% sales tax here $ _____.   Total enclosed $ _____.

Your Day Telephone

(   )_____

Shipping. If you are ordering books, tapes and Special Reports by Dr. Jeffrey Lant, they are sent the day you order (unless you are using a post office box address that is not guaranteed by a MC/VISA/AMEX). Other books are sent to you direct from their publishers by fourth class/book rate shipping. Allow four-six weeks. If you want them faster, add $3 per item for first class or UPS shipping. Remember: to ship UPS, I must have a street address!

Canada and overseas. If you want your items shipped to Canada, add $1 for *each* item ordered and $1 to the total for our bank's fees, even if you pay in U.S. dollars. If you want shipment to any other country, you must pay by credit card. I'll charge your account surface or air shipping, as you like. Check ❑ surface ❑ air.

Premiums. If your order totals at least $150, you can select any one of my three 60 minute audio cassettes as my gift to you. The three titles are listed on page 665. Write down the one you want here # _____. If your order totals over $275, you get your free audio cassette and any one of my eight "Get Ahead" books (#B1 – #B7 & # B9) or **Development Today** (#B8). List the item number of the one you want here _____. Remember to get these free premiums, you must order from this catalog by 01/01/94.

Payment & Billing. Unless you are a government agency, college, library or other official public organization (in which case, include your Purchase Order # here _____), COMPLETE PAYMENT MUST ACCOMPANY YOUR ORDER. I cannot invoice individuals and private businesses. If paying by check, make it payable to Jeffrey Lant Associates, Inc. If you are using a post office box number for shipment, I require a Master Card/VISA/AMEX number and expiration date to guarantee your check, or else I wait for the check to clear. Sadly, several rip-off artists use post office boxes to defraud reputable merchants like me, so I have to inconvenience good people like you. You can also Fax your order to me at 617-547-0061.

If paying by credit card (or using a post office box for shipment):

✓   ❑ MasterCard   ❑ VISA   ❑ AMEX   #_____

Expiration date_____   Signature_____

For faster service, place your order by telephone twenty-four hours a day at (617) 547-6372. (Yes, I really do answer my own phone.) Before calling make sure your credit card is handy. The order tape doesn't last forever! **Speak clearly!**

Your books and materials will be sent to the address on the shipping label below, unless you indicate otherwise. Please be clear about where you want your items sent.

Send materials to:

Name _____

Organization _____

Street Address _____

City _____ State _____ Zip _____

Telephone (_____) _____

Order Form

Complete 30-Day Money-Back Guarantee!

Photocopy or return this page to: Dr. Jeffrey Lant, Jeffrey Lant Associates
50 Follen St., #507, Cambridge, MA 02138

*Special
Edition for
No More
Cold Calls*

CLEARLY write down the item number(s) of what you order here. Each number is composed of a letter and a number. Please make sure to give both!

___, ___, ___, ___, ___, ___, ___, ___, ___, ___, ___, ___, ___, ___, ___, ___, ___, ___, ___, ___,

Remember, if you're ordering my Special Reports (#R1 – #R88), you get **any three for $14**. Individual Reports are $6 each.

Total your order here $ _____. Are you a Massachusetts resident? ❏ Yes ❏ No
If so, add 5% sales tax here $ _____.   Total enclosed $ _____.

Your Day Telephone
( )_____

Shipping. If you are ordering books, tapes and Special Reports by Dr. Jeffrey Lant, they are sent the day you order (unless you are using a post office box address that is not guaranteed by a MC/VISA/AMEX). Other books are sent to you direct from their publishers by fourth class/book rate shipping. Allow four-six weeks. If you want them faster, add $3 per item for first class or UPS shipping. Remember: to ship UPS, I must have a street address!

Canada and overseas. If you want your items shipped to Canada, add $1 for *each* item ordered and $1 to the total for our bank's fees, even if you pay in U.S. dollars. If you want shipment to any other country, you must pay by credit card. I'll charge your account surface or air shipping, as you like. Check ❏ surface ❏ air.

Premiums. If your order totals at least $150, you can select any one of my three 60 minute audio cassettes as my gift to you. The three titles are listed on page 665. Write down the one you want here # _____. If your order totals over $275, you get your free audio cassette and any one of my eight "Get Ahead" books (#B1 – #B7 & # B9) or **Development Today** (#B8). List the item number of the one you want here _____. Remember to get these free premiums, you must order from this catalog by 01/01/94.

Payment & Billing. Unless you are a government agency, college, library or other official public organization (in which case, include your Purchase Order # here _____), COMPLETE PAYMENT MUST ACCOMPANY YOUR ORDER. I cannot invoice individuals and private businesses. If paying by check, make it payable to Jeffrey Lant Associates, Inc. If you are using a post office box number for shipment, I require a Master Card/VISA/AMEX number and expiration date to guarantee your check, or else I wait for the check to clear. Sadly, several rip-off artists use post office boxes to defraud reputable merchants like me, so I have to inconvenience good people like you. You can also Fax your order to me at 617-547-0061.

If paying by credit card (or using a post office box for shipment):

✓ ❏ MasterCard   ❏ VISA   ❏ AMEX   #_____

     Expiration date_____   Signature_____

For faster service, place your order by telephone twenty-four hours a day at (617) 547-6372. (Yes, I really do answer my own phone.) Before calling make sure your credit card is handy. The order tape doesn't last forever! **Speak clearly!**

Your books and materials will be sent to the address on the shipping label below, unless you indicate otherwise. Please be clear about where you want your items sent.

Send materials to:

Name _____

Organization _____

Street Address _____

City _____ State _____ Zip _____

Telephone (   ) _____

Order Form

Complete 30-Day Money-Back Guarantee!

Photocopy or return this page to: Dr. Jeffrey Lant, Jeffrey Lant Associates
50 Follen St., #507, Cambridge, MA 02138

CLEARLY write down the item number(s) of what you order here. Each number is composed of a letter and a number. Please make sure to give both!

——, ——, ——, ——, ——, ——, ——, ——, ——, ——, ——, ——, ——, ——, ——, ——, ——, ——, ——, ——,

Remember, if you're ordering my Special Reports (#R1 – #R88), you get **any three for $14**. Individual Reports are $6 each.

Total your order here $ _____. Are you a Massachusetts resident? ❏ Yes ❏ No
If so, add 5% sales tax here $ _____.   Total enclosed $ _____.

Your Day Telephone
( )_____

Shipping. If you are ordering books, tapes and Special Reports by Dr. Jeffrey Lant, they are sent the day you order (unless you are using a post office box address that is not guaranteed by a MC/VISA/AMEX). Other books are sent to you direct from their publishers by fourth class/book rate shipping. Allow four-six weeks. If you want them faster, add $3 per item for first class or UPS shipping. Remember: to ship UPS, I must have a street address!

Canada and overseas. If you want your items shipped to Canada, add $1 for *each* item ordered and $1 to the total for our bank's fees, even if you pay in U.S. dollars. If you want shipment to any other country, you must pay by credit card. I'll charge your account surface or air shipping, as you like. Check ❏ surface ❏ air.

Premiums. If your order totals at least $150, you can select any one of my three 60 minute audio cassettes as my gift to you. The three titles are listed on page 665. Write down the one you want here # _____. If your order totals over $275, you get your free audio cassette and any one of my eight "Get Ahead" books (#B1 – #B7 & # B9) or **Development Today** (#B8). List the item number of the one you want here _____. Remember to get these free premiums, you must order from this catalog by 01/01/94.

Payment & Billing. Unless you are a government agency, college, library or other official public organization (in which case, include your Purchase Order # here _____), COMPLETE PAYMENT MUST ACCOMPANY YOUR ORDER. I cannot invoice individuals and private businesses. If paying by check, make it payable to Jeffrey Lant Associates, Inc. If you are using a post office box number for shipment, I require a Master Card/VISA/AMEX number and expiration date to guarantee your check, or else I wait for the check to clear. Sadly, several rip-off artists use post office boxes to defraud reputable merchants like me, so I have to inconvenience good people like you. You can also Fax your order to me at 617-547-0061.

If paying by credit card (or using a post office box for shipment):

✓ ❏ MasterCard   ❏ VISA   ❏ AMEX   #_____

Expiration date_____   Signature_____

For faster service, place your order by telephone twenty-four hours a day at (617) 547-6372. (Yes, I really do answer my own phone.) Before calling make sure your credit card is handy. The order tape doesn't last forever! **Speak clearly!**

Your books and materials will be sent to the address on the shipping label below, unless you indicate otherwise. Please be clear about where you want your items sent.

Send materials to:

Name _____

Organization _____

Street Address _____

City _____ State _____ Zip _____

Telephone (_____) _____